Mental Retardation

A Community Integration Approach

LYNDA CRANE

College of Mount Saint Joseph

WADSWORTH
—✦—™
THOMSON LEARNING

Australia • Canada • Mexico • Singapore • Spain
United Kingdom • United States

WADSWORTH

★ ™

THOMSON LEARNING

Education Editor: Dan Alpert
Development Editor: Tangelique Williams
Editorial Assistant: Alex Orr
Marketing Manager: Becky Tollerson
Marketing Assistant: Adam Hofmann
Project Manager, Editorial Production: Trudy Brown
Print/Media Buyer: Robert King
Permissions Editor: Joohee Lee

Production Service: Penmarin Books
Copy Editor: Steven Summerlight
Illustrator: Elizabeth Morales
Cover Designer: Sandra Kelch
Photo Researcher: Connie Hathaway
Compositor: ColorType, San Diego
Text and Cover Printer: R. R. Donnelley,
    Crawfordsville

For permission to use material from this text, contact us:
Web: www.thomsonrights.com
Fax: 1-800-730-2215
Phone: 1-800-730-2214

Wadsworth/Thomson Learning
10 Davis Drive
Belmont, CA 94002-3098
USA

For more information about our products, contact us:
Thomson Learning Academic Resource Center
1-800-423-0563
http://www.wadsworth.com

International Headquarters
Thomson Learning
International Division
290 Harbor Drive, 2nd Floor
Stamford, CT 06902-7477
USA

UK/Europe/Middle East/South Africa
Thomson Learning
Berkshire House
168-173 High Holborn
London WC1V 7AA
United Kingdom

Asia
Thomson Learning
60 Albert Street, #15-01
Albert Complex
Singapore 189969

Canada
Nelson Thomson Learning
1120 Birchmount Road
Toronto, Ontario M1K 5G4
Canada

Library of Congress Cataloging-in-Publication Data

Crane, Lynda L.
    Mental retardation : a community integration
approach / Lynda L. Crane.—1st ed.
        p. cm.
    Includes bibliographical references and index.
    ISBN 0-534-33923-9
    1. Mental retardation. 2. Social integration. I. Title.
HV3004.C73 2001
362.3'8—dc21   2001026940

For Donald, Marvetta, Danielle,
*and all those others who have touched me
with their plight and inspired me
with their promise.*

Contents

12   Educational Issues   291

Preface

Mental Retardation: A Community Integration Approach offers an introduction to the field of mental retardation that is designed for undergraduate or beginning graduate students, and where the goal of community integration provides a coherent, unifying conceptual focus. The majority of students who take a course in mental retardation either expect to work with people who have intellectual disabilities or are already employed in that capacity. And virtually every current educational and service program aims to help people with MR achieve fully functioning roles within their families and communities. As a consequence, focusing on community integration provides students with a meaningful vision for study. It furnishes a context for learning—a goal or end point toward which study is aimed so that students can better understand why the information and techniques they are learning are important and useful. They will thus have the means to understand the material as part of an ongoing process, one directed toward ultimate ideals and goals.

Consistent with the focus on community integration, I have based this text on three guiding principles:

1. People with mental retardation are a *legitimate part of their communities*.

2. Effective service delivery—whether educational, medical, psychological, or related to supported employment and living—depends upon interdisciplinary *collaboration*.

3. A clear understanding of mental retardation and its implications depends on a *systems perspective*.

These three themes are threaded throughout the text, and as theoretical points of view and research findings are presented, they are related to these principles.

The interdisciplinary nature of this text makes it appropriate for students who hope to work in any field related to retardation, including special education, regular education, physical therapy, psychology, recreational therapy, and pre-med. Regardless of a student's major or particular discipline, the interdisciplinary nature of both the field and successful practice requires that students have a basic familiarity with the functions of other related disciplines—information that is provided in this text.

This text, then, takes an applied approach both to concepts and research results. Rather than a review of the MR literature, the reader will find a selection of scholarship and practice presented in a style that is accessible, functional, and applied. Such an approach capitalizes on the practical hope of students who wish to learn material they can use in professional life. In fact, the concepts in mental retardation are so closely tied with practice that an applied approach is integral to the meaningful nature of such a course.

From a pedagogical standpoint, too, I am committed to the notion that learning should be meaningful rather than rote. Students find any subject more interesting if they can personally relate to it, identify with it, or imagine themselves *purposefully* involved in it. As a result of that empathy with the material, I believe that they remember more and are better able to generalize from what they learn. Providing information within such a meaningful context facilitates deep rather than shallow processing, and encourages critical analysis and application.

To further that aim, my writing style is discursive and accessible. My aim has not been to talk down to students, but rather to speak directly and conversationally (much as I would in class) and to engage them through the use of examples and anecdotes. I ask them to think critically about the material and to relate both personally and professionally to the concepts and ideas.

To facilitate the goals of meaning and critical study, I have:

- included with each chapter discussion questions that require students to put themselves in the position of a practitioner, a researcher, a family member, a friend, or an individual with retardation. These questions obligate students to consider (with the instructor's guidance) the implications of what they are learning rather than simply repeat what they have been told.

- included numerous quotes from original authors so that students can gain firsthand insights *as* scholars rather than simply receive the information as filtered through the textbook author.

- provided an opportunity for students to envision themselves in future professional roles by allowing them (intellectually and emotionally) to share in the process of the development of intervention plans and ideas—with all of the conflict and compromise that is involved. In addition, there are several interviews with working professionals who are asked to give students their best advice.

- asked students to develop a mental relationship with the people presented in the case stories so they can understand the complexity of the lives of people with mental disabilities and the complications inherent in providing effective services, as well as to illustrate above all the similarity between the lives of people with mental retardation and their own.

It has been said that problems in special education and other service delivery systems revolve around, if not reduce to, relationship problems. Although we do not have the technology or clinical skill to make everyone learn equally well, we can aspire to help people interact more successfully and thus improve their chances to become fulfilled and productive both at school and within the larger community.

From this, I conclude that the education of future professionals must *feature* the development of relationships with others in the field and with people who have MR, as opposed to including such issues as extras or elements of human interest. I hope that students will be able to identify with and relate to people with mental retardation and their families, relevant methods of research and practice, their own future professional roles, and the fallibility of professional judgment. To this end, the material in this text is designed to appeal not simply to students' intellect, but also to their emotional and relational experience.

An essential component in both comprehending and relating to textual material is enough depth and detail on a particular topic to allow the reader to grasp the concept in its full importance. Yet many texts present material in list or note-card fashion, with topics addressed in only one or two sentences. In this text, I have attempted to discuss the ideas presented in enough depth to show their interest and relevance.

As another example of relevance, complex ethical and social implications that are involved in prevention and treatment are discussed throughout. The text provides a forum to consider these matters, and students are invited to discuss and analyze both implemented and proposed solutions that concern many of the major problems surrounding the causal influences on and intervention with mental retardation.

Finally, the text provides coverage of applied behavioral and cognitive principles and techniques. For those with MR, behavior is the primary predictor of successful adjustment in school, employment, and community living. Behavior is a better predictor of adjustment outcome, in fact, than IQ or vocational preparation. Anyone who works with individuals who have intellectual disability—whether in schools, homes, families, or job sites—faces behavioral and emotional issues for which these principles are essential to problem solving. For these reasons, I contend that an introduction to the field should include an introduction to behavioral and cognitive principles.

Although "characteristics" of mental retardation are covered in Chapter 6, I have not focused the study of MR on categorizing milder and more severe traits. Although I agree that there are general differences in characteristics that often differentiate between milder and more severe conditions, I believe that the variability in characteristics within individuals is substantial enough that it is better to focus on the characteristics of the individual rather than on the characteristics of a category. Here my concern is not simply related to the wish to avoid stereotyping—this is a practical matter as well. My experience in psychological assessment has taught me that skills and abilities often vary widely among people with MR, and that categorization often leads to more confusion than it resolves. I have many times had the experience of a student coming to me in frustration and asking why a particular client is not doing better with a particular task: for example, "She is categorized as 'mild.' She should be able to read this." But a closer look at the client's assessment will show that although her skills are "mild" overall, one or more of those important to reading are markedly lower. In other cases, the client may be categorized as lower in ability overall, with some skills markedly better. To the extent that categorization stands in the way of a closer and more detailed look, I believe it to be counterproductive in both research and practice.

As those of us in the field are keenly aware, the study of mental retardation is rewarding *and* challenging. It is my hope that the students and instructors who use this text will find that it contributes to the effective experience of both.

ACKNOWLEDGMENTS

To all those who shared their knowledge and experiences with me, it is essentially you who form the foundation of this text. To these many parents and professionals who have spoken of their challenges and satisfactions, and who have contributed both heart and substance to this endeavor, I am deeply grateful. I am also appreciative of my students, Vicki Lauer and Chris Ward, who spent countless hours finding articles and books, and of Erin Mantell, who helped with the glossary. Charlotte Postel printed copy after copy of the manuscript, and without the help of Sue Bross I would not have found several key references. My sincere thanks for all these efforts.

Over the several years of this book's development there have been numerous changes in the editorial staff associated with it, and all those involved were supportive and helpful. Particular thanks are especially due my original editor, Vicki Knight, who believed in this project and without whom it would never have been launched. My current editor, Dan Alpert, has also provided continued encouragement, and Trudy Brown has been thoroughly professional in directing the project at Wadsworth. I am especially indebted to Connie Hathaway for her heroic work in obtaining the photos that illustrate so many of this book's ideas so well. Hal Lockwood at Penmarin Books has been tireless in coordinating the publishing process and in keeping track of the thousands of details that have been necessary to make this book a reality.

I appreciate too the many reviewers who have taken the time and interest to provide substantial suggestions, many of which are incorporated here: Mary Lynne Calhoun, University of North Carolina at Charlotte; Joanne M. Curran, State University of New York College at Oneonta; Barbara C. Gartin, University of Arkansas; Annie Hawkins, University of Cincinnati; Edith Lombardo, Marshall University Graduate College; Gabriel A. Nardi, West Virginia University; Ernest L. Pancsofar, Central Connecticut State University; Adrian Sorrell, Prairie View A&M University; John S. Trach, University of Illinois at Urbana-Champaign; Jane M. Williams, Arizona State University west; Eleanor B. Wright, University of North Carolina at Wilmington.

But most of all, I am grateful to my husband, Dr. David Blythe, who has believed unfailingly in this effort, and who has read every word of the manuscript several times. It is his editing and insights that have made this text more interesting, and so much more readable, than otherwise it might have been; for in matters of style, he has been my partner in composition.

Lynda Crane
Cincinnati, Ohio

About the Author

Lynda Crane earned her Ph.D. in Psychology from the University of Maryland, and completed a postdoctoral Fellowship in Pediatrics at the John F. Kennedy Institute for Handicapped Children. While an Associate Professor in Psychology at Grand Valley State University (near Grand Rapids, Michigan), she taught courses in Mental Retardation and the Exceptional Child. Dr. Crane is presently Chair of the Behavioral Sciences Department at the College of Mount St. Joseph, in Cincinnati, Ohio.

Part I

Understanding Mental Retardation

1

Building a Framework: Community Integration and Interdisciplinary Systems

A task without a vision is drudgery; a vision without a task, is but a dream; only a task with a vision is victory.
—Anonymous

COMMUNITY INTEGRATION

The study of mental retardation (MR) is the study of a community of people: people with retardation, their families and friends, and those who work in their service. It is also the study of others who make up the community where people with retardation live, study, work, and enjoy their families and leisure time. Any meaningful understanding of mental retardation must develop, therefore, from first seeing the wide community context in which mental retardation occurs.

FOR DISCUSSION   *What other groups might be involved in welcoming or providing services for people with retardation?*

As we will see in Chapter 3, people with mental retardation have not always been accepted as part of the larger community. Today, however, there is a growing recognition that people with retardation are entitled to community membership as well as a growing awareness that they can contribute to the community to which they rightfully belong. Because this text presents knowledge about retardation as it is applied to professional concerns, the ultimate goal of genuine community integration provides a meaningful direction for study.

Who Provides Services to Clients with MR?

Examples of community agencies that typically provide services to people with mental retardation include:

- departments of human services,
- state and local educational agencies,
- the United Way,
- Easter Seals,
- the Arc,
- law enforcement agencies, and
- agencies specifically designed to provide housing, work opportunities, and other services for those with mental retardation.

Other community groups that often provide services or opportunities for those with MR include:

- churches,
- chambers of commerce,
- individual businesses, and
- individuals such as foster grandparents, student "buddies," and neighbors.

A community consists of all its
members—with disabilities and without.

Above: © D. Young-Wolff/PhotoEdit; right: © Don
Smetzer/Stone

Social Role Valorization

The current trend toward greater community acceptance and integration of those
with MR relates to (and to a large extent has grown from) a philosophical position termed the principle of **normalization.** The 1970s saw a growing interest
in normalization among parents and professionals, an interest based on ideas originating in Scandinavia as a response to demands of the Scandinavian parent movement (Nirje, 1976). In its basic form, normalization asserts the right of all people
to a lifestyle that includes the privileges and opportunities typically afforded in the
culture, including privacy, mutual responsibilities, leisure time, school, work, and

A Community Program for Everyone

Sister Barbara Cline lives with 13 other women from the Franciscan order on a farm in Lowell, Michigan. For more than 20 years, these self-supporting women, who grow and raise all of their own food, have worked to provide a place for children, adults, and the elderly to learn and play together. Many community-oriented activities—both outdoors and in a beautiful facility adjacent to their home—illustrate the spirit of integration, sharing, and cooperation. Among the many opportunities available are nature, art, and music education; preschool and counseling programs; respite day programs for aging adults; adolescent retreats; classes in daily living skills; and occupational therapy. Individuals can learn to grow and can vegetables, bake bread, decorate cakes, and construct aerodynamic kites, or they can simply pet the baby animals. At the center, thousands of people from the surrounding communities (with and without disabilities) participate together over the course of each year, not only to enjoy the opportunities to learn and grow, but also to contribute to them and thus enhance the development of everyone involved.

Sister Barbara with her baby lambs.

Lynda Crane

friends (Nirje, 1976). Normalization also assumes that these rights can only be enjoyed if people remain a part of their communities and are not segregated for purposes of living, working, and learning.

Wolfensberger (1975) described the connections among lifestyle, place of residence, and social role and insisted (with Nirje) that one cannot live a "normal" life while living in completely atypical circumstances. Furthermore, Wolfensberger argued that because people with retardation have typically been devalued by society, they have been excluded routinely from mainstream privileges. The challenge for normalization—Wolfensberger (1995) now prefers the term **social role valorization**—is to increase the likelihood that an individual can experience the opportunities ordinarily available in life. Theoretically, this is accomplished by working with individuals to improve their own competency *and* by working to enhance their social image and related acceptability. Table 1.1 describes these goals.

Although the basic goals of normalization were almost universally accepted by professionals a decade ago (Menolascino & Stark, 1990), there has been disagreement about implementation. In particular, some professionals have been concerned that normalization policies may completely eliminate alternative institutional settings (Heal, 1990) or special classes for children (Gottlieb, 1990). More especially, greater significance may be placed on *where* services are provided rather than on *how* they are provided (Zigler, Hodapp, & Edison, 1990). These issues

Table 1.1 Goals of Normalization

LEVELS OF ACTION	TWO MAJOR GOALS	
	Personal Competencies	**Social Image**
The Individual	Direct interactions to enhance skills and abilities	Promoting perceived similarities with valued persons: e.g., dress, activities, labels
Social Systems (Family, School, Work, Neighborhood, Etc.)	Promoting change that will enhance the individual's skills and abilities	Promoting perceived similarities with valued social systems
Societal Systems (Health and Human Services, Educational Systems, Laws, Government)	Promoting change that will enhance the individual's skills and abilities	Working to create a climate of acceptance of diversity

SOURCE: Adapted from Wolfensberger (1985).

remain of particular concern in light of evidence indicating that simply remaining in the community (in and of itself) does not ensure good living conditions for those with retardation anymore than for others, and that some "community-living facilities" are virtually small institutions in which people with retardation actually remain segregated (Smith, 1995).

FOR DISCUSSION *In our society, to what extent does* normal *mean that everyone should look or act in a prescribed way? In what ways do these prescriptions limit or enhance our lives?*

These are critical concerns, and as we work to integrate people with disabilities into mainstream life, we must remember that as long as those with MR are subjected to prejudice and intolerance, they are likely to remain segregated, even within their own communities. Although some of the methods of normalization remain to be worked out, the vision that people with mental retardation really can live as valued and functioning members of their communities provides the guiding energy for most families and professionals.

CONCEPTUAL FRAMEWORK
FOR THIS TEXT

Our framework, then, for the study of retardation holds this vision of increasingly interdependent functioning for people with MR, as they take their place—more and more rightfully—as members of the larger communities of family, neighborhood, city, nation, and the world. This framework is enhanced in detail by a viewpoint that recognizes living, working, and social aspects of any community as interacting systems that make up the total ecology for someone's life. These "systems," of course, are themselves composed of individual people with their own goals, talents, and emotions—as well as the rules and procedures they create—so that successful and effective system functioning depends on the cooperation and collaboration of all those involved (Briggs, 1997). Three major themes therefore run throughout this text to provide a context for the study of mental retardation:

1. The primary goal of service delivery and educational intervention is to promote the successful functioning of individuals within the communities in which they live—**community integration.**

2. Successful interventions to promote enhanced functioning are more likely when they are developed from a **systems perspective.**

3. Because mental retardation occurs within interacting systems, successful intervention depends on **interdisciplinary collaboration.**

This text will help you understand mental retardation *within* those systems that make up the larger community. It also stresses the *application* of research findings to professional service delivery and intervention—with the goal of full community participation always in mind. After all, the purpose of research and study in MR is to enhance the ultimate outcome. Medical, psychological, and educational research in mental retardation, therefore, is applied—by its essential nature—and cannot be meaningfully divorced from its relevance and usefulness to intervention.

As we proceed through this text, you will be able to identify and better understand some of the relevant and important social, political, biological, and individual influences on the development and outcome of mental retardation. You will also learn about current trends toward interdisciplinary collaboration in service delivery. As you gain more general information about mental retardation, you will also become familiar with much of the knowledge—and many of the skills—that are necessary for contributing to the integrated betterment of those with intellectual disabilities and their families.

In this chapter (as, indeed, throughout the text), you will be introduced to professionals who are currently working in their communities to provide opportunities for people with retardation to live the same safe, healthy, and challenging lives that all people want. These professionals share many of the challenges and fulfillments of their work, and they offer helpful advice about career preparation. You will also meet people with retardation who share insight into their lives and demonstrate their common humanity and their unique challenges.

All professionals and family members share a common goal: the welfare of people with mental retardation. To reach that end, it has been necessary to make several assumptions about those circumstances that are considered "best." Two of the assumptions integral to the goals of community integration are:

1. It is better to be able to function more independently or interdependently (rather than less), and

2. It is better to be included in the regular community than to be excluded from it.

Practical Advice for New Professionals in Mental Retardation

Michael Wrench, former director of case management for the Hamilton County Board of Mental Retardation, in Cincinnati, Ohio, coordinates program and residential placement services and crisis intervention for people with retardation. From the vantage point of experience, he discusses an example of collaboration among agencies and describes some of the practical and educational experiences that will best serve new professionals in the field:

A couple of years ago, we started talking about beginning a cooperative venture between major agencies. I got part-release time to work on this. These agencies work with each other so that they know who is doing what for a particular client. They developed a common form for deriving information from the client, so that he or she only has to fill that out once, and all of the agencies have access to the same information. One of my major concerns was that some people were being overserved. They were getting services that they didn't need, or there was duplication of services. Then, too, some other people were underserved. I felt that if we could eliminate overserving, then those resources could be used to provide services for those people who were underserved.

For us, our success has partly been the luck of the draw. The directors of the major agencies involved liked each other. They were able to see a common issue and put aside issues of turf and control, to focus on how to best provide services for the client. Now that this is underway, those agencies who were not initially part of it want to get involved. It's in their best interests now not to be left out.

To me, what students need is to get some good solid experience in the reality of the way things get done in our society. They need to get some perspective on the different viewpoints and agendas of people from different agencies as soon as possible. I don't mean the formal government and business structure, but in the reality of the way things actually work. I don't know if that can be done in a university setting. Young professionals need to understand the extent to which compromise surrounding different agen-

Michael Wrench, former case management director.

Lynda Crane

das is necessary. I don't want them to lose their idealism; that is really important. But they have to have a sense of realism as well. They have to understand that compromise and cooperation are the way things get done. I can't just look after my own goals. I have to take into consideration what the other person is trying to accomplish as well.

And students need to learn about the dynamic systems in which the client is involved—for example, family dynamics. They need to realize that families (and other groups of persons) function with particular expectations, and if you go in and mess that up (even though you maybe want to mess that up) you had better know what you are doing. We need more people coming out of school who have some understanding of that.

Community Integration of Agency Services

As people with disabilities become more and more integrated into the larger society, service agencies must view themselves as part of the larger community as well. With the goal of full participation in mind, organizations designed to provide services particularly for MR might ask themselves the following:

1. If this person were "normal," where would she get this service?

2. Why do we have to provide this service if it is already available in the community?

3. What does the individual and her family want?

4. Are we meeting the individual's needs or the agency's?

SOURCE: Adapted from L. Rucker (1987), "A difference you can see." In S. Taylor, D. Biklen, & J. Knoll (Eds.), *Community integration for people with severe disabilities* (pp. 109–128). New York: Teachers College Press.

This text has two additional assumptions about how the previous goals can be best met:

1. Professionals within and between service agencies must work collaboratively among themselves and with families and individuals.

2. Mental retardation is best viewed from a "systems" perspective.

A SYSTEMS PERSPECTIVE

It is one thing to formulate desirable goals but quite another to develop technologically sound educational, behavioral, and medical interventions to meet those goals. And it is still another to implement these plans successfully in the real world (rather than simply within the confines of a research lab or college classroom) (Bronfenbrenner, 1995). A major element in successful service delivery is understanding the context in which any intervention takes place. Consideration of the necessary interrelationships among the personal, social, and cultural elements of life is crucial to effective service delivery, and the systems approach to intervention has much to teach in this regard.

The systems perspective is a *way of thinking* about service delivery and intervention that acknowledges the multiple influences on service delivery agencies, families, and individuals. It also underscores the importance of understanding interventions in the context of their occurrence (Austin, 1993). Social, political, cultural, and economic influences, for example, are as important to the success of intervention as the technical effectiveness of the methods used (Briggs, 1997). Medical care provides a good illustration. Medical researchers develop technologically sound medical procedures, and physicians develop the skills to carry them out. Whether the procedures are ultimately effective in improving the health of individuals, however, depends as much on their accessibility, cost, and cultural acceptance as on their specific ability to alleviate a disease or medical condition.

> **FOR DISCUSSION**   *Can you think of other technologies where successful imple-*
> *mentation depends on cultural, political, or economic influences?*

Individuals can be viewed as a system, as can families, organizations, and nations, and all of these systems seek to maintain a balance or equilibrium. For an individual, this balance may be at the biochemical level (homeostasis) or at the social level, where one may attempt to maintain a comfortable balance between personal solitude and social activity (Powers, 1991). For the family, equilibrium may involve the predictability of the roles of individual family members—for example, who cleans and when, who cooks, who can be counted on in a crisis, and who causes problems. With organizations, balanced comfort comes from a clear view of goals and functions; for staff members, this includes their perceptions of what is expected of them, as well as what they are accustomed to doing to meet those expectations.

A basic concept in the systems perspective is that a change in any part of the system affects the entire system (Powers, 1991). For example, a formerly passive child who begins to assert herself may pose increased challenges for teachers and family. Or another child who learns to take care of most of her own daily living needs will free her parents for other activities. Such a change may affect parents positively: They now have time to pursue their own development in new ways; it also can produce stress when parents need time to adjust to lost roles (Brotherson et al., 1996).

> **FOR DISCUSSION**   *Thinking of your own family, workplace, or school as a sys-*
> *tem, can you think of changes that were intended to affect one person or area but*
> *which had (perhaps unimagined) effects on the rest of the system?*

Because change affects the whole system, the person with retardation cannot be the sole consideration when designing intervention plans—though she must be the central focus. And, though change is inevitable (and often desirable), the disruption created in the existing balance can result in some disorientation and discomfort. As a result, there is a natural tendency to resist change, and often individuals attempt to restore balance by getting back to where they were—unless a clear and acceptable vision exists of how an even more satisfying balance can be achieved. Essential in the systems perspective is that this vision must be based on already existing *strengths* (Cobb & Gunn, 1994; Garanzini, 1995). For both individuals and groups (such as families or organizations), strengths already in place enable growth and change.

> **FOR DISCUSSION**   *Assuming that virtually every person or group has some exist-*
> *ing strengths, how might you start to identify them?*

As an example, let's look at a community-based group home for three women with mental retardation. The live-in staff members have become accustomed to roles in which they ensure that the residents are well fed and clean and do not hurt themselves or each other; beyond these functions, they do not interfere in their activities. Typically, one young woman spends most of her time at home rocking in a rocking chair and staring into space, while the other two women watch TV. Everyone is comfortable, seemingly happy, and no one sees any reason to change. They have their "system," and it works for them.

Then the system is threatened when an outside consultant who has been hired by the operating service agency comes to evaluate the programming in existing homes and make recommendations for modifications where needed. For several good reasons (including those of physical health and personal development), this consultant believes that the residents should use their time differently and that the house staff should implement a behavioral plan to encourage them to do so.

> **FOR DISCUSSION**   *Besides the technical soundness of the behavioral plan, what factors in this situation are likely to influence the success of the proposed intervention?*

From a systems perspective, clearly a system is already in place, so one must seek to understand the needs currently met as well as the goals of the resident staff. For example, it might be discovered that staff members believe the residents should have the right to spend their leisure time as they choose. Furthermore, the workers themselves spend every evening watching television, and they consider it enjoyable and appropriate behavior. Any true change from a behavioral plan, therefore, will depend on the future development of shared goals among the staff, the consultant, and the residents about the need and desirability for spending at least some leisure time in other activities. At the same time, the existing strengths of mutual respect and genuine concern that are apparent in the household offer an excellent basis for making this change. The systems perspective helps service providers remember that individuals, families, and other groups have multiple needs, goals, and material realities that must be considered when developing realistic strategies for change—whether that change involves improved behavior, increased learning, or better health (Powers, 1991).

Interagency and Interdisciplinary Collaboration

System interactions similar to those examined above exist among agencies that provide services within the community. If successful coordination of service programs is to occur, there must be cooperation among the providing agencies. This is especially important, because the absence of coordination too often results in duplication of services, gaps in crucial services, and conflicting goals for or among family members or the individuals with MR—problems that undermine program goals.

The recent trend toward deinstitutionalization provides real incentive for collaboration in community services. Before the early 1970s, most people with MR were provided services in segregated facilities, primarily large residential institu-

---

Suggestions for Successful Collaborative Problem Solving

1. Present your position clearly and logically, but listen to others' reactions and consider them carefully before you press your point.
2. Support only those solutions with which you have some agreement and that have objective and logically sound foundations.
3. Avoid conflict-reducing procedures (for example, majority voting and tossing a coin) that are not based on working through the problem.
4. Seek out differences of opinion and try to involve everyone in the decision process. Ultimately, disagreements can result in more adequate solutions.

5. Do not assume that someone must win and someone must lose. Instead, look for the most acceptable alternative for all members.
6. Discuss underlying assumptions, listen carefully to one another, and jointly define conflicts.
7. Communicate positions and feelings, communicate cooperative intentions, and imagine an opponent's perspective.

SOURCE: Adapted from D. W. Johnson & D. P. Johnson (1987), *Joining together: Group theory and group skills* (2nd ed.), as presented in B. Rainforth, J. York, & C. Macdonald (1992), *Collaborative teams for students with severe disabilities: Integrating therapy and education services.* Baltimore, MD: Paul H. Brookes.

---

tions. With the acceptance of normalization goals, many of these people have been returned to their communities with the expectation that services will be locally provided (Noonan & McCormick, 1993). Some funds that were previously targeted for large residential settings are now available to community agencies to provide services at the local level. Community service provision requires collaboration of all involved agencies and depends on the interest and participation of the community at large.

As more people with mental retardation remain in or are returned to their communities, they must turn to existing providers to meet many of their needs. Although community agencies that are newly designed specifically for those with MR can help provide many of these services, a large number must or should be provided by previously existing agencies and professionals who themselves must have the knowledge and skills to provide appropriate assistance. For example, medical and mental health care are typically provided by practitioners within the community—many of them with little experience with mental retardation.

Most professionals are willing to learn about and accept people with MR. For example, most physicians agree they are responsible for treating patients regardless of intellectual ability, yet they believe they are hindered by inadequate medical information about conditions related to retardation (Minihan, Dean, & Lyons, 1993). As another example, more children with intellectual disabilities are currently included in regular classrooms, yet it is still the case that many regular teachers have had no coursework in MR. If professionals are to join meaningfully to provide services collaboratively, then they need information about mental retardation; and if people with MR are to become fully integrated members of community life, then all professionals will need to be educated about and accepting of intellectual differences.

Some colleges and universities are joining in the effort to promote integrated (often called *inclusive*) communities by providing educational and informational support for localities that want their assistance. Many of these programs seek to help community leaders and professionals establish ongoing collaborative processes to determine their own needs and priorities and to find means to reach their goals for community inclusion (Sheriff, 1995).

Collaboration is crucial not only between community organizations, but also among disciplines within organizations. Within schools, for example, interdisciplinary cooperation (often called teaming) is the **best practice.** Members of different disciplines (often including teachers, occupational therapists, and speech therapists) form a team with family members to plan intervention for a particular student (Frey & Lane, 1995). For students with MR between ages 6 and 21, team planning is mandated by federal law. Legislation that mandates services for preschoolers with disabilities and encourages intervention for infants and toddlers also requires interdisciplinary collaboration, and the resulting programs have provided models for intervention with older children, adolescents, and adults. (A thorough discussion of these coordinated early intervention services is presented in Chapter 10.) Among the many advantages of interdisciplinary team planning and problem solving are the greater diversity of knowledge, perspectives, and expertise that are made available for creating new ideas and identifying and eliminating potential difficulties (Rainforth, York, & Macdonald, 1992).

> **FOR DISCUSSION** *Think about group problem-solving ventures in which you have participated. What advantages and difficulties did this method offer?*

This interdisciplinary focus has recently extended to activities that are actually **transdisciplinary,** with professionals sharing techniques and crossing traditional disciplinary boundaries in their practice (Carpenter, King-Sears, & Keys, 1998). An occupational therapist working to make writing easier by helping a child with hand positioning, for instance, would no longer remove the child from the classroom, but would work with her there, allowing the teacher to see and receive coaching in the new techniques. In this way, the teacher has new tools with which to help the child, and the child gets the benefit of practice throughout the school day, rather than only at "therapy time." It is important that the teacher and occupational therapist remain in communication and work together to modify the techniques as needed, and they can develop new ones as the child progresses.

Successful interdisciplinary and transdisciplinary collaboration requires substantial changes in the thinking and approach of professionals toward their roles and responsibilities; collaboration also requires substantial change in organizational structures from what has been typical in specialized, disciplinary settings. Primary among these are a cooperative, interdependent attitude that replaces the all-too-common competitive and individualistic focus of the past. Such changes usually encounter difficulty and some resistance. It helps if team members are clear about and comfortable with their roles but still flexible enough to try new things. An understanding of systems operation can help in clarifying roles, negotiating collaborative agreements, and setting boundaries (Rainforth, York, & Macdonald, 1992). A systems perspective encourages team members to identify and vocalize their differences of opinion. Not everyone needs to conceptualize a situation the same way or use identical intervention approaches; through discussion, however, mutual long-term goals can be formulated so that efforts become complementary rather than redundant or at counterpurposes.

Always remember that the individual who is receiving the service is central to team functioning. This means that the team is not simply making intervention and support plans *for* that individual but is formulating plans *with* him (Pfeifer, 1998). His ideas, responses, goals, and reactions are as important as those of any other team member—and are, in fact, crucial to the success of any intervention. In reality, his feedback determines the success or failure of a plan and provides the information on which future plans must be based. Because the effects of mental retardation are usually lifelong, intervention and support services must be seen in terms of an ongoing process that supports an individual in managing his own life with as much autonomy and self-direction as possible (Sloman & Konstantareas, 1990)

Individual Efforts: Friends, Neighbors, and Peers

Throughout this chapter, we have referred to the goal of success in service delivery, but how do we define *success*? From what standards are the criteria derived? A common gauge of failure has been the return of an individual to institutionalization, but that is an inadequate measure because simply remaining in the community does not guarantee success. What if, for example, an individual is completely successful by service standards—living independently, working steadily, managing her own money—and yet miserable by her own account. Alternatively, if another

---

Principles of Advocacy

The following "learning messages" are among those disseminated worldwide to United Nations organizations and other international nongovernmental organizations by the International League of Societies for Persons with Mental Handicap (ILSMH):

1. We are all likely to experience disability at some time in our lives either personally or through members of our family and community.
2. Society can add to or lessen the effects of a disability.
3. People with mental retardation have abilities. They can and do contribute to society, but their ability to do so is often underestimated.
4. People with a disability have a right to be consulted, to make informed choices, and to exercise control in planning their own lives.

SOURCE: Adapted with permission from H. Mittler (1995), *Families speak out: International perspectives on families' experiences of disability.* Cambridge, MA: Brookline Books.

Community Responses to Neighbor Children with Mental Retardation

Here families from around the world talk about social support and the encouragement they have felt or the pain they have endured.

Our home is situated in the company flats. There is a total of 12 families living there. All the elders, children, and their relatives know her almost from her birth. So she has been simply accepted. They treat her normally. The children try to play with her; the elders encourage her by listening to her, wondering at her achievements.

FAMILY MURTHY, INDIA

The neighbors and other people around us not only didn't accept him but attacked us.

FAMILY EED, JORDAN

When Khalid was young, [the neighbors] would look out for him and took really good care of him.

FAMILY JARER, JORDAN

The majority of neighbors and local people see the whole issue as a curse from God.

FAMILY MARANDU, TANZANIA

Sometimes Mrs. Ng recalled incidents when they went out; people might just stare at them and nudge their friends to take a look at Leslie, as he has difficulty in talking and uses gestures to communicate with his parents.

FAMILY NG, SINGAPORE

Our relationship with neighbors and the local community is very good. We have very caring, warm, and supportive neighbors and friends. . . . Ghinwa goes out to visit neighbors, relatives, and friends.

The support we received from the neighbors and local services was overwhelming. They did not turn their back on us but welcomed Ghinwa with open arms and love.

FAMILY GHAREB, LEBANON

SOURCE: Mittler, H. (1995). *Families speak out: Integrational perspectives on families' experiences of disability.* Cambridge, MA: Brookline. Reprinted with permission by Brookline Books.

---

individual is living an unorthodox existence, defying traditional mores, and facing constant flux and instability and yet is satisfied with his existence, is he a failure? Even the very meaning of *success* varies, and any fair determination must take into account the judgment of professionals, family, and the individual.

By any definition, however, successful community outcomes for those with mental retardation depend not only on interdisciplinary or transdisciplinary efforts, but also on community-wide understanding, acceptance, and effort. After all, almost everyone is touched by retardation, either by someone in their own family or by someone in the families of friends or neighbors, so the quality of life for those with MR is a common personal concern. Fortunately, many individuals within communities work informally to support better living for people with retardation.

Studies show that every family depends heavily on social support, including expressions of friendliness and respect, agreement, and assistance (Pfeifer, 1998). These attitudes and responses are particularly meaningful among extended family, friends, and colleagues, but they are especially important during the course of

---

A Foster Grandparents Program

Brigette Baker, occupational therapist at Fairfax School in Cincinnati, Ohio, talks about the foster grandparents program at the school:

We have a program called foster grandparents, where low-income elderly persons adopt a class. They ride the buses to the school, and spend time in the classroom where they help out as aides. It's a neat program, and I wish we had more, because they tend to be really patient with the kids and some of the kids really get attached to them. Some of our students are in wheelchairs, and when there is a lot of activity in the room and the teacher's attention is elsewhere, that child might be left sitting. But the foster grandparents often bring a little tape recorder and play music with them, or work with them on something one-to-one.

---

service provision as well—for example, between parents and their children's teachers and when medical help is sought in illness. In the case of families of people with MR, social support is particularly significant—and the major factor in enabling many of them to maintain satisfying family lives (Mittler, 1995).

FOR DISCUSSION *What part has the support or lack of it of friends, relatives, and co-workers played in your own life and that of your family?*

At one level, all of the challenges of successful service delivery and intervention involve developing cooperative relationships—among professionals, families, people with MR, their peers, and their employers. As you proceed through the text, you will discover many examples of interdisciplinary and transdisciplinary collaborative efforts—and for all of these efforts, the participation of families and people with mental retardation (as well as that of professionals) is essential.

LOOKING AHEAD

This chapter has set the stage by introducing community integration goals, offering a systems perspective, and stressing the importance of interdisciplinary collaboration. The remaining chapters will fill in knowledge and techniques that will help you understand what mental retardation is and how it develops, how it can be assessed, and how people with MR can be helped to learn and live so that they make the best of their considerable abilities. While you learn facts about and intervention techniques for people with MR, keep in mind that these are always intended as useful generalizations. At the same time, each individual, family, and organization is in some ways unique, and a large part of the art—as well as the challenge—of professional service is the ability to remain open to new insights.

INFOTRAC COLLEGE EDITION

A systems approach to community service provision should be at the center of any plan to make full community integration a reality for people with mental retardation. Using *InfoTrac College Edition,* type *community systems* as the keyword, and find an article that discusses a community-based service provision system. Describe some of the advantages and challenges presented in the article.

REFERENCES

Austin, C. D. (1993). Case management: A systems perspective. *Families in Society, 74*(8), 451–458.

Briggs, M. H. (1997). A systems model for early intervention teams. *Infants and Young Children, 9*(3), 69–77.

Bronfenbrenner, U. (1995). The bioecological model from a life course perspective: Reflections of a participant observer. In P. Moen, G. H. Edler, Jr., & K. Luscher (Eds.), *Examining lives in context: Perspectives on the ecology of human development* (pp. 599–618). Washington, DC: American Psychological Association.

Brotherson, M. J., Cook, C. C., & Parette, H. P., Jr. (1996). A home-centered approach to assistive technology provision for young children with disabilities. *Focus on Autism and Other Developmental Disabilities, 11*(2), 86–95.

Carpenter, S. L., King-Sears, M. E., Keys, S. G. (1998). Counselors + educators + families as a transdisciplinary team = more effective inclusion for students with disabilities. *Professional School Counseling, 2*(1), 1–9.

Cobb, H. C., & Gunn, W. (1994). Family interventions. In D. C. Strohmer & H. T. Prout (Eds.), *Counseling and psychotherapy with persons with mental retardation and borderline intelligence* (pp. 235–255). Brandon, VT: Clinical Psychology Publishing.

Frey, L. & Lane, C. (1995). *The bridges program: Promoting home school inclusion through a continuum of services.* Paper presented at the 73rd Annual International Convention of the Council for Exceptional Children, Indianapolis, IN.

Garanzini, M. J. (1995). *Child-centered, family-sensitive schools: An educator's guide to family dynamics.* Washington, DC: National Catholic Educational Association.

Gottlieb, J. (1990). Mainstreaming and quality education. *American Journal on Mental Retardation, 5*(1), 16–17.

Heal, L. W. (1990). Bold relief or bold re-leaf? *American Journal on Mental Retardation, 95*(1), 17–19.

Johnson, D. W., & Johnson, D. P. (1987). *Joining together: Group theory and group skills* (2nd ed.). Englewood Cliffs, NJ: Prentice-Hall.

Menolascino, F. J., & Stark, J. A. (1990). Research versus advocacy in the allocation of resources: Problems, causes, solutions. *American Journal on Mental Retardation, 95*(1), 21–25.

Minihan, P. M., Dean, D. H., & Lyons, C. M. (1993). Managing the care of patients with mental retardation: A survey of physicians. *Mental Retardation, 31*(4), 239–246.

Mittler, H. (1995). *Families speak out: International perspectives on families' experiences of disability.* Cambridge, MA: Brookline Books.

Nirje, B. (1976). The normalization principle and its human management implications. Reprinted in M. Rosen, G. R. Clark, & M. S. Kivitz (Eds.), *The history of mental retardation: Collected papers* (vol. 2, pp. 363–376). Baltimore, MD: University Park Press.

Noonan, M. J., & McCormick, L. (1993). *Early intervention in natural environments: Methods and procedures.* Pacific Grove, CA: Brooks/Cole.

Pfeifer, T. (1998). Collaboration: The use of the construct of agency in fostering change. *Infant–Toddler Intervention: The Transdisciplinary Journal, 8*(4), 333–343.

Powers, M. D. (1991). Intervening with families of young children with severe handicaps: Contributions of a family systems approach. *School Psychology Quarterly, 6*(2), 131–146.

Rainforth, B., York, J., & Macdonald, C. (1992). *Collaborative teams for students with severe disabilities: Integrating therapy and education services.* Baltimore, MD: Paul H. Brookes.

Rucker, L. (1987). A difference you can see: One example of services to persons with severe mental retardation in the community. In S. Taylor, D. Biklen, & J. Knoll (Eds.), *Community integration for people with severe disabilities* (pp. 109–128). New York: Teachers College Press.

Sheriff, G. (1995). *Welcome everywhere: Inclusive communities for young children with disabilities and their families.* Paper presented at the 73rd Annual International Convention of the Council for Exceptional Children, Indianapolis, IN.

Sloman, L., & Konstantareas, M. M. (1990). Why families of children with biological deficits require a system approach. *Family Process, 29,* 417–429.

Smith, J. D. (1995). *Pieces of purgatory: Mental retardation in and out of institutions.* Pacific Grove, CA: Brooks/Cole.

Wolfensberger, W. (1975). *The origin and nature of our institutional models.* Syracuse, NY: Human Policy Press.

———. (1995). An overview of social role valorization and some reflections on elderly mentally retarded persons. In M. P. Janicki & H. M. Wisniewski (Eds.), *Aging and developmental disabilities: Issues and approaches.* Baltimore, MD: Paul H. Brooks.

———. (2000). A brief overview of social role valorization. *Mental Retardation, 33*(3), 163–169.

Zigler, E., Hodapp, R. M., & Edison, M. R. (1990). From theory to practice in the care and education of mentally retarded individuals. *American Journal on Mental Retardation, 95*(1), 1–12.

2

Theoretical Influences on Understanding Mental Retardation

This chapter was written by Dr. Jim Bodle of the College of Mt. Saint Joseph.

Psychological theorists have influenced professionals as well as the general public and have enhanced our understanding of mental retardation. Theories have focused on (among other things) processes of maturation and learning, how these processes interact with each other, and the influence of culture upon them. This chapter briefly reviews some of the core concepts of several theories that have particular relevance to understanding and working with people with MR.

THEORIES OF GENETIC MATURATION: DEVELOPMENTAL MILESTONES

G. Stanley Hall (1844–1924) is often considered the founder of the scientific study of child development (Dixon & Lerner, 1999), and both Hall and his student **Arnold Gesell** (1880–1961) adopted ideas from **Charles Darwin's** (1809–1882) theory of evolution: They believed that maturational development is determined almost entirely by genetics, and that every child develops in a predictable manner, regardless of environment (Gesell, 1952; Hall, 1907). On that basis, they reasoned that if they could document what most children do at a particular age, then that information could be used to identify children who were not developing normally.

As a physician at the Yale Child Study Center, Gesell had an opportunity to see many children from different environmental backgrounds. He made detailed notes on their development; from these and other data he attempted to describe *developmental norms:* precise descriptions of the behaviors that could be expected at particular ages for all children regardless of culture or social class. From these norms, he created schedules (or measures) of infant development that are used today in revised form.

In spite of his belief in the predominance of genetics, Gesell was interested in educational efforts for children with retardation, believed they could learn, and published materials on individual instruction designed for teachers (Gesell, 1925; 1932). Although most professionals today believe that development is the result of both genetics and environment, scales of infant development are still widely used to determine whether children are developing as expected, and they often play a part in identifying very young children with mental retardation. Normed rating scales are discussed in greater detail in Chapter 5.

The relationship between Gesell and Hall illustrates an interesting and important aspect of scientific work in general: Newer ideas and methods are almost always built from previous ones. Gesell took important ideas from Hall, and both learned from Darwin. Gesell's child-rearing advice was derived from both his understanding of genetics, and from **Jean-Jacques Rousseau's** (1712–1778) notions of permissive parenting. Similarly, later professionals have created measures of infant development based on Gesell's methods (see Table 2.1). As students and professionals, we develop our ideas and theories about atypical development and about the appropriate techniques for intervention from each other and from our predecessors in much the same way.

G. Stanley Hall believed that genetics determine maturational development.

Courtesy of Clark University, Worcester, Mass.

Table 2.1 Some Language Milestones

Age (months)	Behavior
2	Social smile
3	Cooing
4	Laughs aloud
6	Babbling
9	Waves goodbye or plays patty-cake
11	One word (other than *Mama* or *Dada*)

SOURCE: Adapted from CLAMS language scale in A. J. Capute & P. J. Accardo (1991). Language assessment in A. J. Capute, P. J. Accardo, et al. (Eds.), *Developmental disabilities in infancy and childhood* (pp. 165–179). Baltimore, MD: Paul H. Brookes.

LEARNING THEORIES

You have seen that maturational theories assume that genetics control development. At the opposite extreme, **learning theories** take the view that development is a product of experience. And just as maturational theories are related to Rousseau's ideas that healthy development unfolds naturally and that children should be little interfered with, learning theories follow the philosophy of **John Locke** (1632–1704) that children are "blank slates" and shaped entirely by the events of their lives.

Operant Conditioning

In his theory of **operant learning, B. F. Skinner** (1904–1990) described how development proceeds as a series of behavioral and environmental events. According to Skinner, in the normal course of life, we all perform actions that act as a stimulus for some response that occurs in the world. This response that follows a behavior is treated by the individual as a consequence of the behavior, and if it has reinforcing or punishing properties, the original behavior will occur more or less frequently, respectively.

As an example, Skinner describes sitting in a chair, holding his infant daughter on his lap. Next to them was a lamp. She happened to raise her arm, and it occurred to Skinner that he could treat her action (arm lifting) as a stimulus to operating the lamp (response). Quickly, Skinner turned the lamp on and off. The baby waved her arm again, and Skinner turned the lamp on and off again. Soon she was waving her arm in a wide arc to "turn the lamp on and off" (Skinner, 1969). With this illustration, Skinner describes the process by which his daughter learned that the lamp was to be operated by waving her arm. Of course, when the baby tries this again and Skinner is not there to assist, she will see soon enough that it does not work and will drop this strategy. This process of "unlearning" Skinner calls **extinction.**

Skinner's story has several important implications for our study of mental retardation. Perhaps most important, these "psychological laws" of learning can be used to teach specific behaviors. This is sometimes called **behavior modification,** and it provides the basis for the more complex techniques of applied behavior analysis used in designing most educational and behavioral programs that teach academic, daily living, and social skills to people with MR.

> **FOR DISCUSSION** *What are some of the ethical implications of modifying someone else's behavior? Would their knowing cooperation affect your view?*

As the anecdote about Skinner's daughter shows, one can also learn incorrect behaviors. We can associate two things in our minds, believing that they are connected when, in fact, they are not. Behavior analysis is also concerned with creating circumstances in which people "unlearn" inappropriate associations.

Finally, it is possible to use the ideas from operant conditioning to understand and modify our own behavior. We can identify those situations and events that we find rewarding, set desirable goals, and reward ourselves for reaching them. We can also better understand and perhaps eliminate some of our unreasonable fears and reactions. Chapter 11 describes several applied behavior analysis techniques.

Imitation and Modeling

Skinner believed that all learning occurs through overt reinforcement, so that only behaviors that were specifically reinforced would be repeated. **Albert Bandura** thought that learning could occur (and the likelihood of a particular behavior would increase) simply as a result of watching someone else—even in the absence of an overt reward (Bandura, 1977). He set up a now well-known event to test this idea. He allowed children to watch an adult playing with toys in a playroom. Among those toys was an inflated plastic clown named BoBo that was weighted on the bottom so that it bounced back whenever it was pushed over. Some children watched an adult play in a calm and "normal" manner with the doll, pushing it over and watching it return to an upright position. Other children saw an adult who grabbed BoBo by the neck, wrestled him to the ground, punched him in the face, and pummeled him to pieces. Now the question was, what did the children do when they were allowed to play in the playroom? Exactly! The children who watched the calmly playing adult usually played calmly themselves, while the children who had seen BoBo beaten up were far more likely to do the same.

Bandura later emphasized the importance of four qualities for observational learning to be successful (Bandura, 1986):

First, the demonstration or model must catch the child's *attention*.

Second, the child must *retain a memory* of the model.

Third, the model must be sufficiently desirable to *motivate* the child.

Fourth and finally, the child must be able to *produce* a copy of the model.

Exciting models are likely to be copied because they catch the child's attention, heighten her retention, and strengthen her motivation. On the other hand, highly complex models are not likely to be fully copied because the complexity minimizes the child's ability to produce a copy. Still, children who are sufficiently motivated will persist in trying to produce a copy of the model, and they will continuously compare their performance with their memory of the original model.

The implications of Bandura's ideas in regard to development are enormous. For one thing, the effect of modeling explains why the admonition "Do what I say and not what I do" is so often doomed to failure. Children learn from what they see in others. Furthermore, if the individual who models the behavior is liked or admired, children are even more likely to imitate him or her (Bandura, 1977). Notice that whether the model intends to have an influence on onlookers makes absolutely no difference. A physical therapist, teacher, parent, rock star, or cartoon character is just as likely (and conceivably more likely) to influence children when they have no intentions of doing so as when they do. Even such implicit characteristics as character and personality, then, are inherently influential. Although the effect of modeling was first systematically demonstrated by Bandura, it is not a modern notion. In 1690, John Locke wrote about the enormous influence of modeling (Locke, 1963).

Because **imitation** is so important to learning, children who do not naturally do so are at a distinct disadvantage. Children with autism, for example, tend not to notice or copy the behavior of people around them, so teaching them to pay attention and imitate others becomes a major focus of intervention. (We will have more on autism in Chapter 9.) Both behavioral interventions and educational methods rely heavily on the principles of modeling and imitation.

> **FOR DISCUSSION**   *Comment on the implications of modeling for learning from everyday experience. Give examples of the kinds of events you suspect would have a particularly strong effect, and describe what you believe a child would learn from these events.*

Theory of Multiple Intelligences

Whereas learning theories emphasize the importance of environment in a child's development, other theorists emphasize the child's inherent abilities or intelligence. Although intelligence tests were originally thought to identify a single trait, newer conceptions of intelligence remind us that it entails a range of abilities. **Howard Gardner** (1993) suggested that people may possess intelligence in a wide variety of domains, many of which are not now measured on intelligence tests. In particular, Gardner postulated the following seven types of intelligence:

1. **Logical-mathematical intelligence** involves the ability to use numbers and reason.
2. **Linguistic intelligence** is found in people who communicate well, either orally or in writing.
3. **Spatial intelligence** is the ability to think about objects in space, and it is shown in such abilities as reading and using a map.
4. **Bodily-kinesthetic intelligence** is the ability to think about moving oneself in space, and it is seen in such abilities as dancing and playing sports.
5. **Musical intelligence** is the obvious domain of musicians, singers, and composers.
6. **Interpersonal intelligence** is the ability to relate well to other people, to motivate them, and to negotiate solutions to others' problems.
7. Finally, one's self-knowledge is a part of **intrapersonal intelligence,** as is the ability to motivate oneself and manage one's own emotions.

More recently, in examining the completeness of this model, Gardner (1999) has added an additional type. Those who are interested in plants and animals, and who readily learn and use plant and animal classifications excel in what Gardner now calls **naturalist intelligence.**

Gardner's ideas are useful for working with people who have mental retardation, because they suggest the need to look at each person's strengths and weaknesses. In addition, the theory of multiple intelligences reminds us that any one person's abilities may vary widely, so that some people may have strengths focused in one area, while other people may have strengths in a wide variety of areas. This can be especially true for those with MR. Finally, we need to remember that most people are able to excel at some task, but finding that task involves examining one's individual strengths and understanding which abilities are involved (Torff & Gardner, 1999).

Howard Gardner describes several different types of intelligence.

© Jerry Bauer, 1994

STAGE THEORIES

Maturational theories such as Gesell's regard development as primarily genetic. Learning theories such as Skinner's and Bandura's regard it almost entirely as the result of experience. And Gardner's theory of multiple intelligences focuses on strengths and weaknesses. **Stage theories,** however, consider development the product of an interaction between genetics and innate physiological functioning on the one hand and one's experience in the world on the other. Thus, stage theorists are often called **interactionists.** Their theories tend to focus either on **emotional development** (the manner in which people adjust to their world); or on **cognitive** or **intellectual development** (the ways in which people think and learn).

All stage theories have the three necessary characteristics or assumptions listed in Figure 2.1. It is these assumptions that make a particular theory a stage theory.

The first assumption dictates that the stages always occur in the same order for everyone, regardless of the circumstances of their lives: Stage 1 comes first, then Stage 2, and so on for every person. Remember that even though stages are often associated with particular ages, it is the order and not the age that is important. The age at which a person reaches a particular stage can vary, but the sequence of that stage does not.

For people with MR, not every stage may be reached, but the sequence of development is assumed to be the same. According to a stage theory, then, the cognitive and emotional development of a person with mental retardation is the same as for someone without this disability, though development may take place

1. Stages occur in an invariant order.
2. Each stage is qualitatively different.
3. Each stage has a particular domain of accomplishment.

FIGURE 2.1 Three characteristics of stage theories

more slowly and not proceed as far. This assumption has important implications for intervention, because it suggests that if someone with mental retardation is functioning as would a child of a particular age, then it is appropriate to design intervention programs for that level of development (while still providing age-appropriate materials and activities). This idea sounds simple and straightforward but it is fraught with complications when applied to a particular individual. For one thing, just as Gardner's theory suggests, any given individual may be functioning at several different levels in different areas of development. For example, one may not be as advanced in problem solving as in social development. We will return to this important idea many times.

The second characteristic is that each stage is qualitatively different from the next—different in kind, rather than in amount. Accordingly, when a child moves from one stage to another, she is emotionally or cognitively as different from the previous stage as a butterfly is different from a caterpillar and a tadpole from a frog. She is not just taller or smarter or braver; she has a completely new quality or ability.

FOR DISCUSSION *Assuming the stage position to be true, what would happen if one attempted to interact at the "wrong" developmental level? For example, what if a person approached a toddler with material that is more appropriate for a grade school child?*

The third characteristic is that each stage involves a particular developmental goal that must be accomplished (at least to some extent) before the individual can go on to successfully accomplish the next stage. Erikson's theory (described below) provides an example whereby an individual can go through life and fail to resolve the issues at each stage and then return much later in life to work them out. Erikson writes a fascinating analysis of Ingmar Bergman's film *Wild Strawberries* to illustrate this possibility (Erikson, Erikson, & Kivnick, 1986). His analysis clearly describes the invariable order of stages and the unpredictability of the age at which each stage is reached.

Emotional Development

Erik Erikson (1902–1993) was an American follower of Austrian psychotherapist **Sigmund Freud** (1856–1939). Although he believed that Freud's **psychoanalytic theory** was particularly useful in describing the development of emotional adjustment, Erikson added new ideas to expand upon Freud's theory.

Table 2.2 Erikson's Psychosocial Stages

Psychosocial Stage	Typical Period of Development	Domain of Accomplishment
Basic trust versus mistrust	Birth–1 year	Infants gain a sense of trust or confidence that the world is good.
Autonomy versus shame and doubt	1–3 years	Using new mental and motor skills, children learn to choose and decide for themselves.
Initiative versus guilt	3–6 years	Children develop a sense of initiative and responsibility.
Industry versus inferiority	6–11 years	Children develop the capacity to work and cooperate with others.
Identity versus identity diffusion	Adolescence	Adolescents find their own values and vocational goals. They answer the question, "Who am I?"
Intimacy versus isolation	Young adult	Young adults learn to establish intimate ties.
Generativity versus stagnation	Middle adulthood	Adults find ways to create meaning for the next generation.
Ego integrity versus despair	Old age	Individuals reflect on their life and accomplishments. Integrity results from the sense that one's life has been worthwhile.

Whereas Freud concentrated primarily on the *psychosexual development* of the individual, Erikson expanded that focus to include other aspects of social experience and called his theory one of **psychosocial development** (Erikson, 1950).

Table 2.2 may convince you that Erikson addresses some of the most important and profound matters in all of our lives. The ability to trust others and the world we live in, autonomy and confidence in our own skills, the discipline to apply ourselves to work and the ability to succeed in it, the insight to know ourselves and the relational skills to share our lives with another, and the maturity to live in such a way as to feel that our lives are or have been worthwhile—all of these are issues central to our very existence.

One of the most compelling of Freud's lessons is that the hallmark or the proof of healthy emotional adjustment is the ability to *love* and to *work*. Erikson describes the developmental path to working and loving in some detail, and his theory proclaims these landmarks of health and adjustment equally important for all of us with and without MR. Thus, Erikson's ideas have been of interest to those who are concerned about people with mental retardation, and they are central to the assumptions of community integration: that people with disabilities have the same needs and rights as others. It will be helpful to remember Erikson's stages while studying Chapters 13, 14, and 15 as we explore the roles of family, social relationships, and work for those with mental retardation.

Cognitive Development

Whereas Erikson focused his stage theory primarily on emotional development, **Jean Piaget** (1896–1980) was concerned with cognitive development. Piaget was a Swiss **epistomologist**—that is, he studied the development of knowledge. He

Table 2.3 Piaget's Stages of Cognitive Development

Stage	Typical Period of Development	Domain of Accomplishment
Sensorimotor	Birth–2 years	Child experiences the world through senses and actions.
Preoperational	2–7 years	Child mentally represents the world through symbols and images.
Concrete operational	7–12 years	Child can apply logical rules to concrete situations.
Formal operational	12 or 13–adult	Child can apply logic to abstract and hypothetical situations.

was interested in children, because he believed that he could come to understand how one acquires knowledge by studying those in whom it was first developing. Piaget got many of his ideas from observing his own children and those who participated in his research in Geneva. Though he did not work with children who had mental retardation, his theories have since been applied to special education because of his stage theory approach, which implies that intellectual development proceeds in the same manner for all children, however slowly.

Piaget described four stages of cognitive growth. As shown in Table 2.3 (Piaget, 1952), children begin in the **sensorimotor stage,** where their mental lives are limited to what they perceive through their senses and experience through their actions. An important accomplishment during the sensorimotor stage is learning to coordinate their sense information and active behavior such that they can, for example, reach for and obtain what they see or locate the direction of a sound. In the **preoperational stage,** children gain the capacity to use symbolism (such as language) to represent objects. They also use mental images in make-believe play. The child in this stage may present his bare hand and request that his mother taste the "cookie," an act that demonstrates his mental representations for both the verbal label and his mental image of the object. It is in the preoperational stage— many theorists believe—that children first develop true thought. In the **concrete operational stage,** children first learn that things are not always as they appear, and they come to rely on logical rules of problem solving—in addition to information from their own physical senses—to make decisions and solve problems. Piaget illustrated this new ability by demonstrating young children's response to a numbers (or volume) problem.

Finally, the **formal operational stage** announces the capacity to apply these logical rules to completely new problems and situations, for which the child has no previous experience. Piaget describes formal thinking as the basis of truly creative thought.

For Piaget, development proceeded from immediate, simple, and concrete forms of thought to increasingly logical, complex, and abstract forms. Remember, though, that the child's thought in each stage is qualitatively different. She uses completely different ways of thinking and problem solving at each stage, and she has gained entirely new cognitive abilities.

> **FOR DISCUSSION**   *What are some implications for teaching and learning from the idea that each stage has its own cognitive skills? For example, could even an extremely bright child learn to read while in the sensorimotor stage?*

As new skills and thought patterns are developed, old assumptions usually must be abandoned. This process naturally involves some temporary confusion and discomfort, and it can be likened to the sense of "losing one's balance." Piaget called this period of discomfort **disequilibrium,** and he believes that it signals cognitive growth and development.

Typically, disequilibrium is brought on by a beginning and nagging suspicion that our old accepted ideas are not actually consistent with our experience or adequate to solve a particular problem. The increasing awareness of the inadequacy of present strategies or ideas causes discomfort and pushes us to find a more appropriate solution so that our balance and comfort are restored; that is to say, we seek to regain our equilibrium. Thus, to learn, one must first recognize the inadequacy of a current way of thinking. The resulting mental adjustment is called **accommodation.**

> **FOR DISCUSSION**   *Can you describe examples from your own experience in which you became uncomfortable about previously accepted ideas that seemed no longer to "fit"? Did you adjust or change them as a result?*

Although Piaget believed that intellectual growth came both through maturation *and* the presence of the appropriate experience, he was clear that it is natural maturation that brings an individual to the cognitive stage where he is capable of benefiting from that experience. The notion of "readiness" (as in "reading readiness") comes from this idea.

Piaget's ideas have been criticized, and recent research suggests that thought processes and problem-solving strategies are probably more variable (Case, 1999) and more dependent upon the child's prior knowledge and fact learning than Piaget thought (Keating & Crane, 1990). Nevertheless, people who work in the field of mental retardation often find it useful to think in terms of an individual's cognitive stage of development rather than his age when designing intervention plans and strategies.

DELAY AND DIFFERENCE THEORIES

The theories of Erikson and Piaget stress the extent to which all children develop alike, and both suggest that the emotions and thoughts of children with mental retardation differ only in that development is *delayed*. This viewpoint is called the **developmental position** on mental retardation (Hodapp & Zigler, 1999). The **difference position,** on the other hand, suggests that children with developmental disabilities have *different* rather than simply delayed development (Brooks & McCauley, 1984). These distinct viewpoints imply unique approaches to intervention. If children with MR simply develop more slowly, then intervention methods need only be geared toward the developmental level of the individual. If the cognitive functioning of people with mental retardation is actually different than for others, however, then methods also will probably need to be different.

As you might suspect, the resolution of this issue is far from simple. To begin with, all children develop more similarly in some areas than in others. For example, language acquisition tends to occur in a predictable sequence for all children. They start with cooing, then babbling, go on to first words, then two-word sentences, and so forth. But in areas of language pragmatics—as in the ability to guide and follow a conversation, for example—development is far more variable (Hodapp & Zigler, 1999). Furthermore, two children, both with retardation, may develop quite differently in the same skill area, and this can sometimes be related to the cause of retardation. The language development of a child with Down syndrome, for example, is likely to vary from that of a child with Fragile X, and both will develop language somewhat differently from children without these disabilities—*but only in some ways*. No wonder professionals in the field of retardation so often speak strongly about the need to focus on the individual child!

The challenge for the professional, however, is even more difficult. One must know the individual child, certainly, but one must also understand (1) those areas in which the child is most likely to develop similarly to all children, (2) those areas in which he will probably develop individually, and (3) the specific path this individual difference is inclined to take—and all without losing sight of the unique individual, who is bound to be full of surprises.

For this reason, understanding the characteristics of mental retardation is challenging, and the assessment of the characteristics of a child who has MR must of necessity reflect this complexity of his characteristics. These issues are discussed in further detail in Chapters 4 and 6, which cover issues of assessment and characteristics of people with mental retardation.

DIALECTICAL LEARNING

Whereas the preceding theories examine the role that a child plays in his or her own development, **dialectical theories** examine development within the child's environment or context for learning. **L. S. Vygotsky** noted that development is a process of socialization into the mental lives of those around us (Vygotsky, 1994). Barbara Rogoff (1997) likens this theory to an apprenticeship, whereby the child is gradually led to acquire more adultlike concepts by interacting with adults, older siblings, and even "more sophisticated" peers. As did Piaget, Vygotsky noted that children must be ready to learn any particular skill or concept, and he referred to the range of material that a child is ready to learn as the **zone of proximal development** (Vygotsky, 1978). This zone is bounded at the lower end by the most complex concept that a child has mastered alone, which is called the *current* *level.* At the upper end, the zone is bounded by the most complex concept a child can master with some assistance, which is referred to as the *potential level.* Take, for example, a child who has mastered single-digit division on her own but needs several prompts to complete long division: This child would be said to have a current level of single-digit division and a potential level of multiple-digit long division. The zone of proximal development is the range of skills or concepts that lie between these two levels, a dynamic measure that is different for each skill or domain of knowledge and constantly changes within a skill as the child's learning or mastery shifts (Vygotsky, 1978). Unlike the stage assumptions of other theories, the zone of proximal development allows for the widely varying abilities that are common across domains, as is often the case with children with mental retardation.

According to Vygotsky, learning takes place in social situations, and for learning to take place, both partners must achieve a common understanding of the activity and the goals for that activity. Often this means that the partners must agree on common terms or labels for various aspects of the task, and they must agree on the task itself and how it will be achieved. This necessary shared understanding is known as **intersubjectivity** (Wertsch, 2000). Wertsch points out that intersubjectivity is also a dynamic understanding and that these common goals and terms will change within any one task. The concept of intersubjectivity illustrates an important point about Vygotsky's partnership model for development: Learning is reciprocal. It is through the shared dialectical influence of the social interaction that learning occurs. Both the child and the adult learn something new, even if it is merely learning that they don't agree on the task. The adult may look at a puzzle as a task for making a big picture, for example, while the child may look at it as an opportunity to talk about shapes and colors. For this situation to work, the partners must recognize that they do not initially share goals for the task, and they must negotiate a common understanding for the interaction to continue.

> **FOR DISCUSSION** *Can you think of a situation in which you worked on a project with someone else but did not agree on a common goal? Was your work difficult? How were you able to make progress on the task?*

ECOLOGICAL SYSTEMS THEORY

Certainly learning theories and dialectical theories (and, to some extent, stage theories) focus on environmental influence. But environment is usually conceptualized as relatively straightforward stimulus—that is, as events that occur directly to the individual or between two individuals. **Urie Bronfenbrenner,** an American psychologist at Cornell University, takes a much more complex and far-reaching view of environmental influence (Bronfenbrenner, 1995). Environment, he says, affects the individual at many levels, all of them working in a system to influence

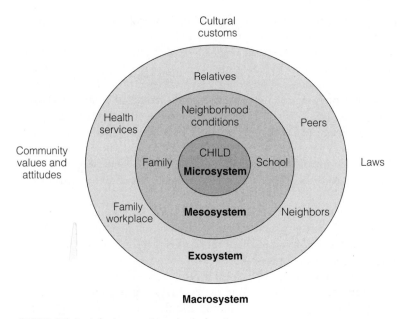

FIGURE 2.2 Bronfenbrenner's ecological system

and affect one another. Thus, the name *ecological systems* suggests a complex interdependence among many components. Figure 2.2 illustrates this system.

The child is at the center of the environmental system, where she not only is influenced by all that happens but also affects what happens around her. Influence at the **microsystem** level is bidirectional and reciprocal. A child's parents, for example, sway the child's development, but the child also directs the parents' lives, which in turn influences the child. To illustrate: A child who is highly active, sleeps little, and has poor attention may control the parents' ability to get enough rest. They, in turn, may become impatient. Or a child may resist cuddling and affection, making the parents less likely to bestow such attention.

The **mesosystem** level also comprises situations in which the child is directly active, but it includes only conditions that indirectly affect him. For example, a child is influenced not only by direct classroom instruction but also by the amount of support his teacher receives from the principal or the general safety of the surrounding neighborhood.

The **exosystem** describes circumstances that do not directly involve but nonetheless affect the child. Examples are the home life and living conditions of her neighbors and peers, available health insurance or nursing services, and the satisfaction and economic benefit her parents derive from their workplaces.

The **macrosystem** involves wider community and cultural conditions, including the prevailing attitudes and values of the historical time and particular community in which the child lives. In Chapter 3, we will see the profound effects these circumstances can have on individual lives.

Bronfenbrenner's ecological theory is extraordinarily useful in understanding mental retardation and community responses to it. With current federal legislation—in particular Part C to PL 105–17 (IDEA) (see Chapter 10)—there is new emphasis on services that recognize the complex environmental system in which the child and family live. Current planning involves interdisciplinary focus on effective coordination among services, including accurate and useful assessment, physical or occupational therapy (and sometimes both), obstetrical and other medical care, social work services, and early educational intervention, to name only a few. Many professionals believe that improvements in programs for those with mental retardation depend upon the success of these interdisciplinary efforts, which recognize the complex community system within which the child lives. Toward that goal, perhaps the most important task for a student undertaking the study of mental retardation is understanding the multiple interrelated influences upon it and recognizing the effect these influences can have on the lives of people with disabilities.

LOOKING AHEAD

This chapter has presented a few important concepts of some of the theories that inform research and practice in mental retardation. These theories provide a basis for attempting to understand the development of intellectual abilities, as well as other important aspects of human functioning. They also allow us to identify integral ingredients in our common development—whether or not mental retardation is present. In the next chapter, however, it will become clear that individuals with mental retardation have been too often viewed as completely different from others. Those with MR have been singled out, separated from their rightful communities, and misunderstood and treated unjustly. Fortunately, there have been recent changes in those views, and Chapter 3 tells that story as well.

INFOTRAC COLLEGE EDITION

Chapter 2 describes theories of interest to students who want to understand mental retardation. Choose one theorist who especially interests you, and in a paragraph or two describe why you chose that theorist. Then, using *InfoTrac College Edition,* enter the theorist's first and last name in the keyword search, and choose a related article. In what specific way did the information in that article add to your understanding of the theorist's ideas?

REFERENCES

Bandura, A. (1977). *Social learning theory.* Englewood Cliffs, NJ: Prentice-Hall.

———. (1986). *Social foundations of thought and action: A social cognitive theory.* Englewood Cliffs, NJ: Prentice-Hall.

Bronfenbrenner, U. (1995). The bioecological model from a life course perspective: Reflections of a participant observer. In P. Moen, G. H. Edler, Jr., & K. Luscher (Eds.), *Examining lives in context: Perspectives on the ecology of human development* (pp. 599–618). Washington, DC: American Psychological Association.

Brooks, P. H., & McCauley, C. (1984). Cognitive research in mental retardation. *American Journal of Mental Deficiency, 88*(5), 479–486.

Capute, A. J., & Accardo, P. J. (1991). Language assessment. In A. J. Capute, P. J. Accardo, et al. (Eds.) *Developmental disabilities in infancy and childhood* (pp. 165–179). Baltimore, MD: Paul H. Brookes.

Case, R. (1999). Conceptual development in the child and in the field: A personal view of the Piagetian legacy. In E. K. Scholnick, K. Nelson, et al. (Eds.), *Conceptual development: Piaget's legacy* (pp. 23–51). Mahwah, NJ: Erlbaum.

Dixon, R. A., & Lerner, R. M. (1999). History and systems in developmental psychology. In M. H. Bornstein & M. E. Lamb (Eds.), *Developmental psychology: An advanced textbook* (4th ed., pp. 3–46). Hillsdale, NJ: Erlbaum.

Erikson, E. H. (1950). *Childhood and society.* New York: W. W. Norton.

———, Erikson, J. M., & Kivnick, H. Q. (1986). *Vital involvement in old age.* New York: W. W. Norton.

Gardner, H. (1993). *Multiple intelligences: The theory in practice.* New York: Basic Books.

———. (1999). *Intelligence reframed: Multiple intelligences for the 21st century.* New York: Basic Books.

Gesell, A. (1925). *The retarded child: How to help him.* Bloomington, IL: Public School Publishing Co.

———. (1932). *Individual instruction of subnormal children in the rural schools of Connecticut.* Hartford, CT: State Board of Education.

———. (1952). The diagnosis of infant development. *International Record of Medicine, 165,* 149–153.

Globerson, T. (1989). What is the relationship between cognitive style and cognitive development? In T. Globerson, T. Zelniker, et al. (Eds.), *Cognitive style and cognitive development* (pp. 71–85). Norwood, NJ: Ablex.

Hall, G. S. (1907). *Aspects of child life and education.* London: Routledge/Thoemmes.

Hodapp, R. M., & Zigler, E. (1999). Intellectual development and mental retardation: Some continuing controversies. In M. Anderson (Ed.), *The development of intelligence* (pp. 295–308). Hove, England: Psychology Press.

Keating, D. P., & Crane, L. L. (1990). Domain-general and domain-specific processes in proportional reasoning. *Merrill-Palmer Quarterly, 36*(3), 411–424.

Locke, J. (1963). Some thoughts concerning education. Reprinted in *The works of John Locke Vol. IX.* Germany: Scientia Verlag Aalen. (Originally published, London, 1823.)

Piaget, J. (1952). *The origins of intelligence in children.* New York: International Universities Press. (Original work published 1936.)

Rogoff, B. (1997). Evaluating development in the process of participation: Theory, methods and practice building on each other. In E. Amsel, A. K. Renninger, et al. (Eds.), *Change and development: Issues of theory, method, and application* (pp. 265–285). Mahwah, NJ: Erlbaum.

Skinner, B. F. (1969). *Contingencies of reinforcement: A theoretical analysis.* New York: Appleton-Century-Crofts.

Torff, B., & Gardner, H. (1999). The vertical mind: The case for multiple intelligences. In M. Anderson et al. (Eds.), *The development of intelligence* (pp. 139–159). Hove, England: Psychology Press/Taylor & Francis.

Vygotsky, L. S. (1978). *Mind in society: The development of higher psychological processes* (M. Cole, V. John-Steiner, S. Scribner, & E. Souberman, Eds.). Cambridge, MA: Harvard University Press.

————. (1994). *Thought and language* (A. Kozulin, Ed.). Cambridge, MA: MIT Press.

Wertsch, J. V. (2000). *Intersubjectivity and alterity in human communication*. In N. Budwig, J. C. Uzziris, & J. V. Wertsch (Eds.), *Communication: An area of development* (pp. 17–31). Hamford, CT: Ablex.

3

Origins:
Historical and Cultural

Mental retardation is an idea, rather than a specific thing: a concept in people's minds. Ideas about mental retardation have varied over time. Often, too, there have been contrary but simultaneous answers to the question "What is mental retardation?" In a very real way, mental retardation itself has changed along with the perceptions about it. This change is only possible because MR is not a specific entity, but rather a constellation of characteristics that are related to intellectual abilities and that vary in all of us. To develop an understanding of mental retardation, we first must see how it has changed throughout history.

This chapter offers examples of historical and cultural ideas and events that have profoundly influenced the lives of people with mental retardation from ancient times through the last decades of the 20th century.

MENTAL RETARDATION:
A CULTURAL INVENTION

Mental retardation is a historical and cultural invention (Singh, Oswald, & Ellis, 1998). It is not in itself a disease or an illness, but a group of recognized characteristics. People throughout history have noticed that some individuals did not appear to learn, solve problems, develop language, and otherwise behave at the level or in the manner that was expected at the time. Many societies decided that these "different-from-average" characteristics were worthy of notice. They developed various ideas about why these characteristics occurred and about the nature and worth of people who had them. Still, in some earlier times, when almost no one could read or write, many people who would be considered retarded today would not have been thought of as different. Thus, those people who have been identified with *retardation* have changed with the times—although the term itself is fairly recent. We have decided to call our modern selection of unusual intellectual and behavioral characteristics *mental retardation*. The word *decided* is important, because it reaffirms that our idea of mental retardation is both arbitrary and subjective, and that mental retardation is literally made in our minds: We have invented it. It is a social and cultural construct.

We are all theorists in an informal but still important way. We all hold theories about why things happen and the way things work, and these determine our attitudes and often our behavior. Ideas about mental retardation have been quite different at various times in history. Historically, ideas about the causes of mental retardation and about the nature of people with it have been largely responsible for attitudes toward those with MR. In the past, much like today, attitudes influenced the treatment people received and the social goals and expectations that were prescribed for them (Rees, Spreen, & Harnadek, 1991).

Among the major and influential historical perceptions and beliefs about people with MR have been that they are or were: (1) sick or diseased, (2) subhuman or inhuman (possessed by the devil), (3) menaces to society, (4) objects of pity,

(5) burdens of charity, (6) holy innocents or gifts of God, and (7) developing individuals (Scheerenberger, 1982; Wolfensberger, 1975). Life for people with MR has changed profoundly over time, along with the prevailing perception about their disability. Although several of these ideas have sometimes been present together, often one or the other has predominated or been particularly influential at a given time.

> **FOR DISCUSSION** *Which of these historical notions have you heard even today? As this chapter continues, watch for other ideas that continue even in the present.*

HISTORICAL AND CULTURAL INFLUENCES

Ancient Ideas

Various disabilities were noticed in earliest recorded history, and even then there were social attitudes toward those who were affected. **Infanticide** (killing an infant) was one frequent response to the birth of a child with disabilities. Sometimes this was even an accepted practice, as among the Spartans of ancient Greece. Newborns were brought before a state council of inspectors, who ordered them thrown from the cliffs of Mt. Taygetus if a disability were found or suspected (Scheerenberger, 1982). At other times and places—such as in 17th- and 18th-century Europe—infanticide was common, although not officially sanctioned (Berk, 2000).

Often, attitudes toward those with disabilities were influenced by religious beliefs. There is evidence that as early as 7000 B.C. some people believed that mental retardation, mental illness, and epilepsy were caused by evil spirits or demons (Scheerenberger, 1982). From ancient Palestine, the Torah (450 B.C.) attributes mental retardation (and deformities in general) to a punishment from God for sin; this idea was continued in the Old Testament, and in the New Testament Jesus "drives out the devil" from those afflicted with disabilities. Martin Luther, a leader of the Christian Reformation, believed that people with mental retardation had no souls, but were possessed of the Devil, who had stolen them. He recommended that such people be drowned (Wolfensberger, 1975).

The New Testament, however, also teaches love and compassion toward those who are afflicted and exhorts Christian followers to "comfort the feebleminded" (1 Thessalonians 5:14). Likewise, founders of Buddhism, Confucianism, and Islam all taught love and generosity toward those with disabilities (Scheerenberger, 1982). And in that light, people with mental retardation have been sometimes considered holy innocents, and have been viewed as special gifts from God. This was true also in some American Indian cultures as well as in medieval France (Wolfensberger, 1975). Religious teachings also have inspired humane treatment and acceptance, as when people with MR have been protected and cared for in monasteries (Beirne-Smith, Patton, & Ittenbach, 1999).

Too often, however, treatment of those with physical and mental differences has been callous or punitive. Pope Leo X kept dwarves with mental retardation that he and his guests played tricks on and ridiculed to amuse and entertain themselves (Hibbert, 1975). Perhaps the most infamous and notorious example of bad treatment toward those with mental deviations occurred at the Hospital of St. Mary of Bethlehem in London (established in 1247), which was popularly known as "Bedlam." Here people with mental retardation and mental illness were chained, whipped, frozen, and starved in the belief that such treatment would punish the lurking demons into submission. Bedlam was typical of the institutions of the day and the belief that people with mental abnormalities were incapable of suffering from heat, cold, or hunger (Wolfensberger, 1975).

In secular societies, as well as in religious settings, treatment has been inconsistent. Some 2nd-century Roman citizens advocated and practiced humane treatment toward people with mental afflictions, while others bought and sold people with mental retardation and other disabilities or kept them as sources of amusement. Yet, impressively, in Gheel, Belgium, beginning in the 1200s, a program incorporated people with retardation into family settings. They were provided privacy, companionship, and a legitimate part to play in the community. And, even in earliest recorded history, there is evidence that people with disabilities were accepted by and played integral roles within certain societies (Scheerenberger, 1982).

You see, then, that attitudes and treatment toward those with MR have been mixed throughout human history. Although there were constant and continual examples of atrocious and cruel treatment—and these seem to have been more typical—there have also been examples of compassionate and humane responses. It is notable that many of the fears and attitudes that formed the basis of these behaviors persist today.

More Recent Influences

Two philosophers and writers of the 17th and 18th centuries whose ideas were to have a decisive influence on the treatment of mental retardation were John Locke (1632–1704) and Jean-Jacques Rousseau (1712–1778) (see Chapter 2). Locke believed development primarily results from *nurture,* or a child's experiences in life. He described the newborn as a *blank slate* upon which the world wrote the adult that was to be (Locke, 1963). As we have seen, Locke's ideas were the forerunners of behaviorism, which stressed the importance of guiding and molding young children. Although Rousseau agreed that children could be affected by the world, he thought such influence was usually for the worst. He believed children were born good, and he described them as *noble savages.* He thought they should be allowed to grow naturally—blooming like flowers—with little outside interference (Rousseau, 1955). These ideas provided the basis for later permissive practices of child development. Although Locke and Rousseau disagreed about appropriate child-rearing practices, they agreed that children's development was importantly influenced by the world in which they lived, and both writers advocated kind and humane treatment of children. The increasingly widespread acceptance of these ideas fostered a humanitarian awareness that prompted more socially benevolent treatment of those with mental retardation and other disabilities.

FIRST EDUCATIONAL EFFORTS

You have greatly ventured, but all must do so, who would greatly win.
—Byron

Jean-Marc-Gaspard Itard (1774–1838) was one who believed that people with mental retardation have the ability to learn. He has been called the father of special education (McNeil, Polloway, & Smith, 1984), because he was the first to attempt educational efforts with a child who appeared to have mental disabilities. A physician, Itard accepted the challenge of educating such a boy, whom he named Victor. Around the close of 1798, Victor was captured in the woods of southern France (close to Aveyron) by three sportsmen who found him living wild and alone. He was taken to Paris, where he was examined by **Philipe Pinel** (1745–1826), the superintendent of an asylum. Pinel is well regarded and remembered for his reforms, which included the elimination of abuse and chains, and the provision of kindly treatment for inmates. Based on his work with "idiocy" (the term then used for mental retardation), Pinel believed that Victor suffered from that condition. As had all those before him, Pinel thought that MR was most likely incurable (Itard, 1972). Victor, however, was admitted not to an asylum, but to the National Institute for Deaf-Mutes, where Itard was assigned to try to teach him (McNeil, Polloway, & Smith, 1984; Scheerenberger, 1982).

Having been influenced by Locke, Itard believed deeply that the intellectual and moral development of humans is determined by their experience. Here, in his own strong words, are Itard's views on development:

> Cast on this globe, without physical powers, and without innate idea; unable by himself to obey the constitutional laws of his organization, which call him to the first rank in the system of being; MAN can find only in the bosom of society the eminent station that was destined for him in nature, and would be, without the aid of civilization, one of the most feeble and least intelligent of animals. (Itard, 1972, p. 91)

Itard's goal with Victor was to "determine . . . the degree of understanding, and the nature of the ideas of a youth, who, deprived, from his infancy, of all education, should have lived entirely separated from individuals of his species" (p. 93). Itard vowed to use all of his knowledge of teaching and learning to educate Victor and thus show the "knowledge and . . . ideas for which man is indebted to his education" (Itard, 1972, p. 93).

Under this tutelage, Victor made substantial progress. From Itard's description, he went from a "disgusting, slovenly boy" (Itard, 1972, p. 96), who showed virtually no interest in anyone or anything but food, and who tore small dead animals apart with his hands, to someone attentive to instruction, sensitive to his

Itard was only partly successful in teaching Victor, the Wild Boy.

National Library of Medicine

failures in academic work, and excited by his successes. Academically, he learned numbers, colors, and shapes, and he also learned to comprehend the speech of others. He could read and understand a few common French nouns, including some object names and simple verbs. He did not, however, learn meaningful speech, and Itard, who was strongly in favor of a strict oral approach in teaching language to the deaf, did not try to teach him gestural language. After several years, Itard became discouraged and gave up teaching Victor to speak.

While many people believe Itard considered his work with Victor a failure, Itard's own account suggests otherwise. In his progress report to the French minister of the interior, Itard wrote:

> . . . whether one sees it as the methodical education of a wild man, or whether one restricts oneself to considering it as the physical and moral treatment of one of those creatures born ill-favored, rejected by society and abandoned by medicine, the care that has been lavished on him, the care that is still his due, the changes that have taken place, those one hopes are still to come, the voice of humanity, the interest aroused by so cruel a desertion and so strange a fate, all these things combine to commend this extraordinary young man to the attention of scholars, the solicitude of our administrators and the protection of the government. (Itard, 1972, p. 179)

As a result of Itard's work and writings, other people were inspired and encouraged in the effort to educate those with mental retardation.

Edouard Seguin (1812–1880) was one of those who eagerly carried on such efforts. Also a physician, Seguin studied with Itard and eventually opened a private school for people with mental retardation in France. Seguin is especially remembered for his educational methods: He developed elaborate systems of education and training for people with severe and milder forms of retardation, and he was among the first to use formal strategies of modeling and reinforcement (Scheerenberger, 1982). His book *Idiocy and Its Treatment by Physiological Methods* was an important teaching resource for the remainder of the 19th century, and some of his techniques provide the basis for efforts in special education today (Beirne-Smith, Patton, & Ittenbach, 1999).

One of Seguin's most important beliefs was that the motor functioning of affected children was related to their intellectual functioning, and as a result he concentrated on methods of physical training and therapy, as well as on educational efforts. These methods were designed to help children improve their coordination and physical agility (Seguin, 1866).

After moving to the United States, Seguin worked with others, including **Samuel Gridley Howe** (1801–1876), to open several institutions and finally a day training center in New York City (Scheerenberger, 1982). Like Howe, Seguin believed that residential institutions should be primarily educational facilities. He thought that children should go home on vacation, and he expected that they would stay in the facility only during their school years. Still, it soon became apparent that not all children could become self-sufficient, and some had no place to go after leaving the institution (Switzky, Dudzinski, Van Acker, & Gambro, 1988). As we will see, the circumstance of long-term care set important, though almost certainly unintended, precedents for future institutional development in the United States (Gardner, 1993; Switzky et al., 1988).

INSTITUTIONALIZATION IN
THE UNITED STATES: THE BEGINNINGS

Until the middle of the 19th century, there were no schools, programs, or residential facilities specifically for people with developmental disabilities. Those with mental retardation were often confined in prisons or almshouses, where serious mistreatment was common and people were frequently kept and sometimes chained in small, cold, airless, and filthy cells. **Dorothea Dix** (1802–1887) was concerned both for those with mental retardation and mental illness. She visited public institutions of the day and documented the abuses she found. In presenting her findings to the Massachusetts legislature in January 1843, Dix said:

> I come to present the strong claims of suffering humanity. I come to place before the Legislature of Massachusetts the condition of the miserable, the desolate, the outcast. I come as the advocate of helpless, forgotten, insane, and idiotic men and women; of beings sunk to a condition from which the most unconcerned would start with real horror; of beings wretched in our prisons, and more wretched in our almshouses. (Dix, 1976, p. 5)

It was clear to the legislature and others who were concerned about mental re-tardation that something needed to be done.

The first residences in the United States designed specifically to train and educate people with mental retardation were established by **Hervey B. Wilbur** (1820–1883) and Samuel Gridley Howe. In 1848, Wilbur opened the first private residence, the Barre School, while Howe founded the Massachusetts School for Idiotic and Feeble Minded Youth (public residence) in 1850 (Gardner, 1993). These schools were designed for small numbers of students who were expected to become self-sufficient and return to their communities (Switzky et al., 1988).

Both Wilbur and Howe planned to admit only those who were young and able enough to benefit substantially from educational efforts, but several circum-stances worked against them. Almost immediately, Howe in particular began to have doubts about what was being accomplished (Gardner, 1993). For one thing, assessment and diagnostic procedures were even less precise than today. Nearly anyone who appeared unable to learn in the regular schools, regardless of how old or how severe their disability, was eligible for admission (Scheerenberger, 1982). Ironically, Howe's social welfare motives also worked against him (Gardner, 1993). Because he was saddened and appalled by the living conditions and cruel treat-ment endured by many potential students and the "dreadful degradation in which they now grovel" (Howe, 1848, p. xi.), he admitted numerous residents from alms-houses, impoverished families, and prisons. Some did improve substantially and returned to the community (Wolfensberger, 1975), but many did not quickly gain self-sufficiency. Within a few years, academic training was abandoned in favor of training for simple labor (Gardner, 1993). Even so, it soon became clear that many students would be returned only to the abusive conditions from which they came—a situation deemed unethical (Wolfensberger, 1975).

Howe and Wilbur both came to see the necessity of continuing care arrange-ments for some students, but they disagreed about the most desirable plan. Wilbur believed permanent residential institutions on farms afforded the best solution, whereas Howe, influenced by the family-type arrangements of the Gheel system, believed that community living plans were more likely to succeed. According to Wolfensberger, Howe was "probably the most significant and foresighted figure in American history of special education" (1975, p. 17), and indeed his vision sounds astonishingly modern. Howe believed that homeless people with mental disabil-ity should be housed in the community in what are now called foster homes. Speaking of the importance of community acceptance, he said: "The idiot child needs more than any other to preserve that kind of sympathy, and feeling of in-terest arising from the ties of neighborhood" (Howe, 1969). Thus, he advised against long-term removal from the community:

> If he is absent temporarily, and goes back every year, he is still considered as belonging to the place; he considers it as his home, so his neighbors recog-nize him as belonging among them. But if he is sent away for five or six years, the tie is broken and people do not recognize in the grown up idiotic man or woman, the child whom they once regarded with sympathy and pity. (Howe, 1969)

Howe's ideas found no acceptance. Indeed, it was to be more than 100 years before the idea of community integration was taken seriously. Wilbur's notion of farm living, on the other hand, gained advocates. The remote, segregated, and increasingly large farm institution, where people with retardation were expected to be self-supporting through manual labor, became the institutional model for several decades (Wolfensberger, 1975).

Impact of Causal Theories

During this early period of institutionalization, professionals were struggling to understand the causes of mental retardation. In a paper titled *The Causes of Idiocy,* Howe (1848) describes the thinking of the times. Much of what he wrote indicates an initial understanding of the causal factors that are considered valid today. There is discussion, for example, of multiple causation (that is, retardation has many causes). There is also a recognition that heredity could play a part and yet might not be a sufficient cause in itself:

> The wife's family was tainted with idiocy, her aunt having an idiotic child. We find, therefore, both intermarriage and idiotism in the family; but still this was not cause sufficient, because the parents of this boy had seven other children, all of tolerably good parts. (Howe, 1848, p. 24)

Howe also believed that alcohol consumption could affect the unborn child adversely, an idea confirmed by modern research. But several 19th-century notions of causation will seem shockingly vague and presumptuous to the modern reader. For example, parents of children born with disabilities supposedly could be identified by their "scrofulous temperament and poor flabby organization" (Howe, 1848, p. 25). Though Howe admitted that *scrofulous* was hard to define, he claimed that one could identify people "inferior to others" and "unfit to breed," just as a farmer could identify unfit animals: by looking at them (p. 25). The characteristics of scrofulous included poor posture, red and sore eyelids, spongy gums, swollen glands, and skin eruptions: conditions that are present in an overwhelming percentage of the population. Furthermore, there was the underlying belief that such individuals were to blame for their own condition:

> By temperance, cleanliness, and careful observance of all the natural laws, they might have corrected the vicious humours of their bodies, lived pleasant lives, and been blessed with children to comfort their old age; but they chose to outrage nature in every way, and she sent them their punishment in the shape of those idiotic children. (Howe, 1848, p. 27)

It is true that parental drug use, poor nutrition, and ill health may contribute to the birth of a child with disabilities, but the idea that people who are likely to produce children with mental retardation are easily identifiable by looking at them set dangerous precedents (discussed further below). Furthermore, the tone of recrimination coupled with the incredibly mistaken idea that most parents of children with retardation were undesirable and degenerate was unlikely to promote a cooperative, mutually understanding relationship between parents and professionals.

One more "habit" to which Howe attributed the outcome of mental retardation was "self-abuse"—a term then used for masturbation. Parents were admonished, in the strongest terms, to keep their children from this practice. Describing the dangers, Howe wrote:

> There are among those enumerated in this report some who not long ago were considered young gentlemen and ladies, but who are now moping idiots, idiots of the lowest kind; lost to all reason, to all moral sense, to all shame—idiots who have but one thought, one wish, one passion—and that is, the further indulgence in the habit. (Howe, 1848, p. 30)

From today's perspective, such assertions were not only astonishing hyperbole, but also absolutely incorrect—yet they were presented with total assurance.

It is a sobering exercise to read, in their own words, of the deeds, attitudes, and beliefs of our predecessors in this field: to see, as one can perhaps see only in hindsight, both the courage and innovation of their work, and the extent to which they were influenced and even blinded by the values and expectations of their times. It can serve as both inspiration and warning: an inspiration to be unafraid to try new methods and ideas, and to risk in the service of an ideal; and as a warning against assuming either complacency or absolute certainty in the infallibility of our own ideas.

Increasing Segregation

Beginning in the mid-1880s and continuing until the mid-1920s, people with retardation were viewed more and more as a social menace (Wolfensberger, 1975). It was increasingly thought that people with low intelligence were inevitably immoral: practicing thieves and prostitutes, or, at the very least, sexually unrestrained and promiscuous people. As a result, they were seen as a blight on the community. Earlier notions of multiple causation also were replaced by the idea that virtually all cases of retardation were exclusively hereditary. Institutions were expected to serve a dual purpose: keep people with disabilities from creating trouble in the community and prevent them from reproducing. In this way, it was thought that mental retardation could be eliminated. There was little interest in educating people with retardation, because it was considered useless. Instead, emphasis was placed on both training for manual labor and confinement.

FOR DISCUSSION *Disregarding for a moment the ethical implications, why was this institutional plan doomed to failure? Why could it not eliminate retardation?*

The thinking of this period was influenced by the works of **Gregor Mendel** (1822–1884) and **Charles Darwin** (1809–1882). As a botanist, Mendel demonstrated the inheritance of physical characteristics in plants, while Darwin described the evolution of species, including humans. **Sir Francis Galton** (1822–1911)—Darwin's cousin—applied both Mendel's and Darwin's ideas to human intelligence and developed a theory of the heritability of genius (Galton, 1869). Galton also coined the term *eugenics,* which he defined as the scientific study of hereditary influences that might improve the human race (Smith, 1985).

The Story of Deborah Kallikak

Henry Herbert Goddard (1866–1957) provides one outstanding example of the influence of inheritance theories on institutional policies and attitudes. Goddard was research director at the Training School for Feeble-Minded Girls and Boys in Vineland, New Jersey. Hired to study the causes of mental retardation, he became interested in the family background of a training school resident named **Deborah Kallikak** (not her real name) and set out to discover her pedigree. Pedigree studies involved outlining a family tree, identifying those members with mental retardation, and demonstrating any consistency with Mendel's laws of hereditary transmission. Though common at the time, by modern standards of research, such studies can only show that mental retardation occurs frequently in a particular family, not whether it is caused by heredity or environment.

Goddard traced Deborah's family back five generations to Martin Kallikak, Sr. According to Goddard, Martin came from a good family, one with no "taint" of retardation. While away from home, however, Martin took up with a tavern waitress, who bore him an illegitimate child. Afterward, Martin repented and went home to marry a "respectable" woman, with whom he also had a family. These events allowed Goddard to trace the distinct, diverging family lines. The resulting study showed that the "good" side of the family was composed ever after of upstanding citizens, while the "poor" side—"contaminated" by the tavern waitress— was replete with "morons," criminals, and ne'er-do-wells.

Goddard offered this study as proof that heredity is the overwhelming cause of mental retardation. In his words:

> We find on the good side of the family prominent people in all walks of life and nearly all of the 496 descendants owners of land or proprietors. On the bad side we find paupers, criminals, prostitutes, drunkards, and examples of all forms of social pest with which modern society is burdened. . . . (Goddard, 1931, p. 116)

> They were feeble-minded, and no amount of education or good environment can change a feeble-minded individual into a normal one, any more than it can change a red-haired stock into a black-haired stock. . . . (p. 53)

> Feeble-mindedness is hereditary and transmitted as surely as any other character. We cannot successfully cope with these conditions until we recognize feeble-mindedness and its hereditary nature, recognize it early, and take care of it.

> In considering the question of care, segregation through colonization seems in the present state of our knowledge to be the ideal and perfectly satisfactory method. (Goddard, 1931, pp. 116–117)

"Colonization" (by which Goddard meant permanent institutionalization) was the "solution" in which Deborah found herself. Yet Deborah was far from helpless.

Today, Deborah Kallikak would live in her community.

From Henry Herbert Goddard (1913), *The Kallikak Family: A Study in the Heredity of Feeble-Mindedness.*

A look at some of her "handiwork" accomplished at Vineland school is impressive evidence of her abilities. She is also described as beautiful, charming, and with that "extra spark of personality which makes one stand out in a crowd" (from Smith, 1985, p. 27). She did have trouble with academic skills: She read and wrote at beginning levels and could perform only simple arithmetic, but these were difficulties that would probably now be considered learning disabilities (Smith, 1985).

In fairness, Goddard and others at Vineland seem to have been as interested in protecting Deborah from society as they were in protecting society from her. Goddard described Deborah's chances outside the institution this way: "Today if this young woman were to leave the Institution, she would at once become a prey to the designs of evil men or evil women and would lead a life that would be vicious, immoral and criminal, though because of her mentality she herself would not be responsible" (Goddard, 1931, p. 12). True, Deborah did appear to have been well cared for at Vineland and was apparently quite fond of Goddard, saying that though she didn't care for the feebleminded part, Goddard was the one who made her famous (Smith, 1985). Yet, as a result of this "benevolence" and paternalism, Deborah lived her entire 81 years of life in an institution.

In *Minds Made Feeble* (1985), J. David Smith powerfully and persuasively recounts the story of the Kallikak family. Smith detected the identity of the actual family and retraced its family tree. In doing so, he found that neither the "bad" side of the family was so uniformly bad nor the good side so entirely good as Goddard had believed. In addition, he discovered that some of the photographs in Goddard's book had been deliberately retouched with the result that certain faces seem evil and distorted. Today, the scientific implications of Goddard's work (though not necessarily the sincerity of his intentions) have been recast. Smith's work, however, came more than 70 years after the study of the Kallikaks was published, while Goddard's remained influential and essentially unquestioned for several decades.

INVOLUNTARY STERILIZATION

By 1920, both the heredity hypothesis of causation and the belief that retardation was related to practically all social ills were firmly established. Institutions were no longer residential schools that students would eventually leave; now they served the dual purpose of removing the "menace" of retardation from society and ensuring that those who were removed did not reproduce. By the late 1800s, there were laws against marrying or having "carnal knowledge" of those with epilepsy or feeblemindedness, but it soon became evident that such laws could not be enforced (Barr, 1973; Wolfensberger, 1975). As an additional safeguard against reproduction, powerful voices advocated involuntary sterilization.

Involuntary sterilization seemed a sure answer. Martin W. Barr, a respected professional of the time, spoke effectively on the topic:

> It is impossible to legislate for conscience at the best, and in dealing with the low and the bestial, with the ignorant and the weak, the silly and the irresponsible with utter incapacity to comprehend any law but that of self-will, there is nothing to convert or to convince, for the moral sense is not there to appeal to.
>
> For these, and against these—festering sores in the life of society—the only protection is that which the surgeon gives. . . . (Barr, 1973, p. 190)

Barr believed that sterilization would provide the most effective solution if it were applied universally and early against all those who were suspected of having any sort of deviance:

> Let asexualization be once legalized, not as penalty for crime but a remedial measure preventing crime and tending to the future comfort and happiness of the defective; let the practice once become common for young children immediately upon being adjudged defective by competent authorities properly appointed, and the public mind will accept it as a matter of course in dealing with defectives. . . . (Barr, 1973, p. 191)

In 1907, Indiana passed the first compulsory sterilization law (Smith, 1985). In 1924, the Virginia legislature voted to allow involuntary sterilization for those with feeblemindedness, insanity, alcoholism, epilepsy, or any of several other conditions

(Smith & Polloway, 1993). **Carrie Buck,** a young woman who had an illegitimate child and was thereafter committed to the Virginia Colony for Feebleminded and Epileptics, became the test case for sterilization laws, her own case was eventually presented to the United States Supreme Court. Justice Oliver Wendell Holmes, influenced by testimony that Carrie's mother was feebleminded and that her young child was now showing signs of delay, summarized the favorable opinion of the majority toward the sterilization law in this now-cited line: "Three generations of imbeciles are enough" (*Buck* v. *Bell,* 1927, p. 50).

Between 1927 and the early 1970s, tens of thousands of people—mostly women—were involuntarily sterilized in U.S. institutions (Scheerenberger, 1982). Many were neither told the purpose of the operation nor given appropriate medical or psychological assistance (Smith & Nelson, 1989). Some discovered what had happened only after leaving the institution, marrying, and trying unsuccessfully to become pregnant (Herr, 1983). The sterilization laws originating in the 1920s were not repealed for a long time. It was 1968 before the Nebraska legislature repealed a law that mandated sterilization for women before they were discharged from state institutions (Perske, 1981), and it was 1972 before the last operation was performed at the Central Virginia Training Center (renamed after Carrie Buck had been a resident) (Smith, 1985).

A recent study of the records of the Central Virginia Training Center indicate that at least 15.8 percent of those residents who were sterilized and discharged did not have mental retardation by modern assessment standards, and many were classified as "not retarded" even at the time of their operations. As it turned out, Carrie's illegitimate daughter became an honor student, and more than likely Carrie herself had no serious mental disability (Smith & Nelson, 1989).

MENTAL TESTING

Complicating the dilemmas of institutionalization and sterilization, of course, was the imprecise nature of assessment. Until the beginning of the 20th century, assessment of MR had been almost entirely subjective and based on informal observations of abilities. There had been some use of sensory reaction measures (Galton, 1883), but there was no test of actual thought processes. In 1905, **Alfred Binet** (1857–1911), along with Theodore Simon, designed a test that required the use of memory, abstract thinking, and "common sense." Although these mental processes certainly could not be measured directly, their functioning was inferred by performance on items that were thought to depend upon these abilities, items that could be quantitatively measured. Binet's test, however, was like any other: It could only measure performance at the time it was taken and could not provide evidence for what performance might have been earlier or could be later. Binet's goal was simply to provide an objective means of identifying children for special education classes. He was concerned, in fact, that his test might be inappropriately viewed as a direct measure of innate potential (Gould, 1981). In point of fact, Binet was interested not only in measuring intellectual ability at a given time, but also in demonstrating improvement in those abilities as a result of instruction, as he clearly states:

> Some recent philosophers appear to have given their moral support to the deplorable verdict that the intelligence of an individual is a fixed quantity, a quantity which cannot be augmented. We must protest and act against this brutal pessimism. We shall endeavor to show that it has no foundation whatsoever. (Binet, 1911, p. 141, taken from Skeels & Dye, 1939)

Binet's test, however, was soon adopted as a means of diagnosing permanent mental incapacity. For example, Goddard used the Binet test to determine Deborah Kallikak's mental age at 9 years and decided that she was permanently unfit to live outside an institution. In fact, Goddard initially believed that any older person who tested at 12 years or younger was mentally retarded and therefore incapable of handling her own affairs, a position he later reversed when he stated that even the 8-year level might not indicate "true" feeblemindedness (Scheerenberger, 1982). Notice, though, there remains the assumption that if one *were* truly feebleminded, then one could not learn.

Reliance on mental testing quickly became widespread. The government began to use the Binet test to identify mental retardation in immigrants. People were often chosen for testing from crowds of immigrants based only on their physical appearance. On the basis of these tests, published results asserted that more than 50 percent of those Jews, Hungarians, Italians, and Russians who entered the country between 1913 and 1917 were probably mentally defective (Goddard, 1914). Such data were used to provide evidence for more restrictive immigration laws, in spite of the fact that testing was often not in the newcomer's native language (Patton, Payne, & Beirne-Smith, 1990).

The military, too, became involved in mental testing when it developed the alpha–beta tests of intelligence to measure the intelligence quotients (IQs) of enlisted men. These tests were group-administered, rather than carried out individually, so that many people could be tested at once—a technique now considered inadequate for assessing mental retardation. From these results, it was assumed that mild mental retardation was widespread in the military, thereby fueling fears of the "growing menace" of retardation.

SOCIAL CONTROL AND "CLEANSING"

You have seen that many institutionalized people did not actually have retardation, even according to the assessment procedures of their own eras. Institutionalization and sterilization began to be applied as a more general means of social control, because retardation was thought to be characteristic of all those who seemed socially undesirable—the poor, homeless, and unemployed, the psychiatrically ill and the alcoholic. The reality of this disturbing trend is reflected in a 1921 paper delivered to an annual audience of the American Association for the Study of the Feeble-Minded by a psychologist at Pennsylvania Village for Feeble-Minded Women. The lecture detailed typical problems with "girls" in the institution:

> Another type of the adult defective that presents a problem is the woman who has been out in the industrial world. As we look over our records and talk with the girls we learn that the majority of them have held varieties of jobs. As a result when they reach us they are veritable Jills of all trades and mistresses of none. Because of the fact that they have been wholly or partially self-supporting they are restless and dissatisfied since they are under the restraint of an institution and no longer receive remuneration for their work. As a consequence they foment disturbance among the other girls. (Vanuxem, 1921–22)

We can easily imagine that women proven capable of employment might feel frustrated and resentful when confined to an institution. But the implications of eugenics policies—compulsory institutionalization and sterilization—went well beyond such frustration. Mandatory sterilization laws in Nazi Germany (first passed in 1935) were based on the U.S. model and were applauded by many in this country (Smith, 1985). Policies in Germany quickly moved from sterilization to "mercy killings" carried out on anyone who was handicapped or sick or who otherwise presented problems for the establishment. Perhaps it can help us remain skeptical of our own theories and assumptions to understand that the elimination of people with disabilities from society was not an idea original to the Nazi plan: It had its roots in the eugenics movement that came out of Western science (Wolfensberger, 1987).

Humanitarian Reforms

> We are all travelers in the wilderness of this world, and the best that we find in our travels is an honest friend.
> —Robert Louis Stevenson

At the same time that the eugenics movement was finding advocates and gaining influence, others worked for more supportive solutions to society's problems. Among them, **Jane Addams** (1860–1935) recognized the serious social problems of poverty, ignorance, disease, and crime and opposed institutionalization and removing people from communities. Addams herself moved to a poor immigrant neighborhood in Chicago and opened Hull House, which provided services for area residents that would help them find a legitimate role in the community (Addams, 1911). Addams believed that we are all interdependent and what affects one of us ultimately affects all of us. She was sure that *every* person has something unique and worthwhile to offer, and that society also suffers when *any* person is deprived of an education (Addams, 1964). For these reasons, it seemed clear to her that community members have mutual responsibility for each other, and that the health of the community depends upon the contribution of *every* member. Hull House was to be a community resource—not an institution. For Addams, positive change could come only from individuals working together (Addams, 1964).

Addams was one of a group of reformists who had similar ideas and who were widely influential at the time. Others included **John Dewey,** perhaps the foremost writer in his day on education, and **William James,** who is sometimes known as "the father of psychology." In Italy, **Maria Montessori** (1870–1952) was advocating the right of those with MR to the same care and educational opportunities enjoyed by others. Her work in early education was with exceptional children, and with them she developed concepts for educational methods that have been adopted internationally (Eichstaedt & Lavay, 1992). In the United States, too, there were those who continued to promote education for children with disabilities, and special education was becoming more available. There was also research that demonstrated its effectiveness. For example, **Elizabeth Farrell,** founder of the Council for Exceptional Children (1922), published follow-up studies that indicated the success in work and community life of special class students (Farrell, 1915). Other studies were carried out by the federal Children's Bureau (at one time directed by Julia Lathrop, a friend and co-worker of Jane Addams) (Channing, 1932).

Research on people with mild retardation indicated that the vast majority of them were successfully employed and that instances of crime and delinquency were rare. When job problems were present, they were related to social and behavioral, rather than to intellectual, issues. In fact, such studies concluded that the work problems of those with mild retardation were much the same as for the general population (Ingram, 1935).

By the end of the 1920s, professionals in the field, including Herbert Goddard, had completely reversed their position on the possible life outcomes for those with mental retardation (Scheerenberger, 1982). In 1935, the U.S. Office of Education called a conference to consider the curricular needs of children with retardation. Among the conference's conclusions were that "each child shall be educated in keeping with his capacities, limitations, and interests, looking toward the happiest adjustment he can make in life and the most constructive contribution he can bring to society" (Ingram, 1935, p. ix). Widespread reform, however, was not immediate. For one thing, special education classes were available only in a few larger communities. In most places, children with mental retardation were either excluded from class or allowed to attend regular classes without special help (Ingram, 1935). Furthermore, special education classes admitted only students who were mildly affected, and it was still assumed that those who did not become capable of self-support would be placed in institutions (Ingram, 1935).

Self-Determination: A Beginning

Probably the most persuasive force for change was families. In 1933, the first parent group was formed in Cuyahoga County, Ohio (Wallin, 1962), and it was soon followed by numerous others. By 1950, there were parent organizations in 19 states, in addition to the newly formed National Association for Retarded Children (NARC), more recently named the Arc. The new association produced an education bill of rights that claimed the entitlement of every child with MR to a "program of education and training suited to his particular needs" (Zigler, Hodapp,

& Edison, 1990, p. 4.)—a virtual restatement of the 1935 position (see Ingram, above). At this time, however, real changes were made: NARC members were effective lobbyists, and the political climate was correct for educational reform. In fact, parental advocacy was occurring worldwide (McCleary, Hardman, & Thomas, 1990), and since that time the International League of Societies for Persons with Mental Handicap has provided the impetus for volunteer organizations around the world (Rosen, Clark, & Kivitz, 1976).

Coinciding with the parent movement—and largely as its result—was a strong trend toward deinstitutionalization. In 1966, *Look* magazine published an excerpt from a book titled *Christmas in Purgatory,* showing pictures of severely abused people in institutions (Blatt & Kaplan, 1967). Blatt reported that the conditions for some residents were identical to those found by Dorothea Dix more than 100 years before. He wrote of people kept for days in solitary confinement, naked, sometimes tied, and often in their own filth (Blatt, 1976). Much of the general public was outraged. Legislation was passed that mandated improved institutional conditions, and President Richard Nixon declared a national goal to reduce institutional residency by 30 percent before the turn of the century. Between 1970 and 1979, the number of people living in state institutions decreased by more than 50,000 people (Scheerenberger, 1982).

POLITICAL AND ECONOMIC INFLUENCES

Because mental retardation is, in many ways, a cultural and social construct, and the forces that drive our society are importantly political and economic, political power and money often serve to define MR itself. Furthermore, the attitudes of philosophers, psychological theorists, and the general public interact with political and economic influences to substantially affect the lives of those with mental retardation and their families.

Private and Political Influence: The Kennedy Family

Often the effect of politics on personal lives occurs directly in the form of laws. Other times, it is more subtle—but equally powerful—and affects attitudes. In the United States, perhaps the most notable example of the latter is the influence of the Kennedy family. John Kennedy (president of the United States from 1961 until he was assassinated in November 1963) came from a wealthy family that had long been politically active and influential in the country. John Kennedy's sister Rosemary had mental retardation, so Kennedy was especially committed to the issue. He had the money, power, and prestige to make his influence felt, and he did so. His family had already created the Joseph P. Kennedy, Jr. Foundation (in 1946), an organization that continues to provide funds exclusively for programs related to MR. As president, Kennedy established the President's Panel on Mental Retardation, which established recommendations in the areas of research, education, prevention, civil rights, community facilities, and public awareness that influence policy to this day (Mayo, 1962).

Given earlier attitudes about the causes of mental retardation and the immoral characteristics believed to be associated with it, it is understandable why (in spite of growing parent advocacy) many families were reluctant to talk openly about the difficulties of caring for someone with MR. However, the Kennedy family had been open about their experience since the 1940s, and with the Kennedy presidency, the family's advocacy became much better publicized. When this family—obviously influential in the country and revered by many—spoke openly in support of people with developmental disabilities, it encouraged a climate far more receptive to social programs designed for those with MR than previously existed. In addition, people began to understand that such challenges occur even in the "best families," and so the stage was set for a greater acceptance of those with mental retardation in the community.

Since John Kennedy's death, the family has continued its advocacy role. Robert Kennedy was among the first to visit residential institutions and speak out against the abuses he found, thereby encouraging others to work for change (see Blatt, 1976, p. 23) In addition, Eunice Kennedy Shriver established the Special Olympics in 1968 to provide opportunities for people with MR to enter the world of athletic competition.

Legislative Milestones

Important legislative events at the federal level also advanced the cause of people with MR. For example, in 1957 the **Social Security Act** was amended to cover payments to adults with developmental disabilities. In 1973, the **Vocational Rehabilitation Act** (PL 93-112)★ was amended to include civil rights statements that those with disabilities should have access to education and jobs and should not be denied the rights of other citizens (LaVor, 1977). Then, in 1975, the Education for All Handicapped Children Act (**PL 94-142**) revolutionized educational opportunities for children with disabilities. Among its provisions was that *every* child with a disability between ages 3 and 21 was entitled to free, appropriate public education in the least restrictive environment. This law provided a mandate to every school district in the nation to offer programs for children with mental retardation regardless of their degree of disability; as a result, educational opportunities were made available to thousands of children who had not previously been served. In addition, it required that every child have an **individualized education plan (IEP)** that would design specific educational goals and objectives for that child and provide a timetable for meeting those goals. In 1983, **PL 99-457** (an amendment to PL 94-142) mandated services for children ages 3 to 5 and provided financial incentives for the development of early intervention programs for infants and toddlers.

★PL stands for *public law.*

In 1990, PL 94-142 was renamed the **Individuals with Disabilities Education Act (IDEA)** partly to reflect the understanding that disabilities need not be handicaps. In addition, autism and traumatic brain injury were added to those categories of people who must be served, and it was then required that a **transitional IEP (ITP)** be provided for all students by age 16. The ITP describes the plan by which the child is to move from the more protected school environment to the world of work and community living. In its most recent authorization in 1997, IDEA became PL 105-17 and extended services to children who show developmental delays through age 9, thereby promoting early intervention and prevention.

In addition, the **Americans with Disabilities Act** of 1990 (PL 101-336) (ADA) is a tremendously important piece of recent legislation that affects those with MR. This law extends civil rights protection to those who have disabilities not only in employment but also in public accommodations, transportation, and telecommunications. Even more important, PL 101-336 makes discrimination in these areas illegal, unlike the Vocational Rehabilitation Act, which simply states that it "should not" happen. Further, the ADA states that discrimination includes inaccessibility, and it provides deadlines by which many major public and transportation services must be made accessible to those with disabilities. Although the ADA has done much to promote greater integration for people with disabilities, much remains to be accomplished both in regard to access and attitudes (Reno, 2000).

Political Influences on Funding

When we talk about the influence of politics and economics, we are talking about power and money (Castellani, 1987). People with power and wealth are in a position to make changes that affect the lives of those who have neither. Power, politics, and economics are inextricably intertwined—they go together and cannot be separated—and together they affect, change, and sometimes control the lives of those who have developmental disabilities (Braddock, Hemp, & Fujiura, 1987).

Budgets are political documents, and some say the most important policy statements (Dye, 1977). The majority of funding for programs related to mental retardation comes from government, not from the private sector. And where government funding was once primarily at the state and local levels, a far larger share now comes from the federal government. Government programs to which people with MR may be entitled include Supplemental Security Income, Social Security Disability Insurance, and Medicaid (Castellani, 1987). Current implementation practices for these and other programs provide both opportunities and disincentives for those with MR and will be discussed in more detail in Chapter 14, "Adult Living and Work."

LOBBYING AND VOTER SUPPORT

There is a constant, ongoing struggle among powerful, competing forces for government money. Successful lobbying is an important factor in determining which programs are funded and to what extent. We have seen, for example, that parent groups became a powerful lobbying force. In fact, it was largely because of the effectiveness of parent lobbying efforts that community residential alternatives for people with MR were created (Switzky et al., 1988). Although there are many other ways to advocate for those with MR, lobbying remains crucial.

Voter support is as essential as lobbying. Although public endorsement of MR programs is influenced by many factors, including general economic conditions, the absolutely necessary elements are a positive attitude toward those with MR and a sense of optimism about the effectiveness of existing programs. Those professionals who are also advocates are keenly aware of these factors and are working to enhance the public image of people with MR as well as the programs that serve them.

CYCLICAL CHANGE

History repeats itself; that is one of the problems with history.
—Clarence Darrow

We can conclude from our study so far that some ideas disappear, only to reappear; conditions for those with retardation have sometimes improved only to worsen again. Still, there has been a general trend toward greater acceptance of those with retardation, especially over the last several decades. Research confirms that college students showed more favorable attitudes toward people with MR in 1988, even compared with those in 1975, which suggests that these changes may be related to community integration and awareness (Rees, Spreen, & Harnadek, 1991).

> **FOR DISCUSSION**   *What ideas or conditions were eliminated, only to reappear, perhaps in a slightly different form?*

Public attitudes and political climate tend to change, and this change does not usually result in straightforward progress on an issue. As we saw from our look at history, some ideas prove better than others, and when social and educational programs appear to be ineffective, public support often vanishes. In addition, issues that have nothing directly to do with mental retardation can affect the amount of interest in MR. For example, a political or economic crisis such as a war or depression can make people less positive toward social programs in general. And even though we have seen that public interest is often strongly influenced by a single powerful person, when such an advocate is not currently in the limelight, support can fall off or even be influenced negatively. Attitudes and corresponding policy relating to people with MR are complex. Many plans or philosophies compete at a given time, and policies and programs often change as particular ideas gain acceptance and popularity. Change sometimes tends to be cyclical, so that older notions are dropped but later reemerge. If we, as professionals, are to learn from our mistakes and improve our understanding of and practices in mental retardation, both an awareness of the past and an openness to new ideas are essential.

▌▌ LOOKING AHEAD ▰▰▰▰▶

This chapter has described many of the important historical and cultural circumstances and events that have influenced the lives of those with mental retardation. We also have seen that MR has been understood differently during different historical times. But what is mental retardation, really? How do we define mental retardation today, and how do we know if someone has it? Some answers to these questions are offered in Chapter 4.

INFOTRAC COLLEGE EDITION

History is clear in showing that even the most knowledgeable and capable people of any era make mistakes. Enter *mistake* as the keyword in *InfoTrac College Edition,* and choose two articles that discuss mistakes with serious consequences. What conclusions can you draw from these about the nature of mistakes? (For example, are they inevitable?) What means can possibly be taken to avoid them?

REFERENCES

Addams, J. (1911). *Democracy and social ethics.* New York: Macmillan.

———. (1964). Democracy and social ethics. Reprinted in A. F. Scott (Ed.), *Democracy and social ethics.* Cambridge, MA: Harvard University Press. (Original work published 1907.)

Barr, M. W. (1973). Mental defectives. Reprinted in *Mental illness and social policy: The American experience.* New York: Arno. (Original work published 1904.)

Beirne-Smith, M., Patton, N. R., & Ittenbach, R. (1999). *Mental retardation* (5th ed.). New York: Merrill.

Berk, L. E. (2000). *Child development* (5th ed.). Needham Heights, MA: Allyn & Bacon.

Binet, A. (1911). *Les idées moderne sur les enfants.* Paris: Flammarion.

Blatt, B. (1976). Purgatory. Reprinted in M. Rosen, G. R. Clark, & M. S. Kivitz (Eds.), *The history of mental retardation: Collected papers* (Vol. 2, pp. 347–360). Baltimore, MD: University Park Press.

Blatt, B., & Kaplan, F. (1967). *Christmas in purgatory: A photographic essay on mental retardation.* Boston: Allyn & Bacon.

Braddock, D., Hemp, R., & Fujiura, G. (1987). National study of public spending for mental retardation and developmental disabilities. *American Journal of Mental Deficiency, 92,* 121–133.

Buck v. Bell (1927). 274 U.S. 200.

Castellani, P. J. (1987). *The political economy of developmental disabilities.* Baltimore, MD: Paul H. Brookes.

Channing, A. (1932). *Employment of mentally deficient boys and girls.* Children's Bureau Publication No. 210. Washington, DC: Superintendent of Documents.

Dix, D. (1976). Memorial to the legislature of Massachusetts, 1843. Reprinted in M. Rosen, G. R. Clark, & M. S. Kivitz (Eds.), *The history of mental retardation: Collected papers* (Vol. 1, pp. 3–30). Baltimore, MD: University Park Press.

Dye, T. (1977). *Politics in states and communities.* Englewood Cliffs, NJ: Prentice-Hall.

Eichstaedt, C., & Lavay, B. (1992). *Physical activity for individuals with mental retardation.* Champaign, IL: Human Kinetics Books.

Farrell, E. E. (1915). A preliminary report on the careers of three hundred fifty children who have left ungraded classes. *Journal of Psycho-Asthenics, 20*(1), 20–26.

Galton, F. (1883). *Inquiries into human faculty and its development.* London: Macmillan.

———. (1869). *Hereditary genius.* London: Macmillan.

Gardner, J. F. (1993). The era of optimism, 1850–1870: A preliminary reappraisal. *Mental Retardation, 31*(2), 89–95.

Goddard, H. H. (1931). *The Kallikak family: A study in the heredity of feeble-mindedness.* New York: Macmillan. (Original work published 1912.)

Goddard, H. H. (1914). *Feeblemindedness, its causes and consequences.* New York: Macmillan.

Gould, S. J. (1981). *The mismeasure of man.* New York: W. W. Norton.

Herr, S. (1983). *Rights and advocacy for retarded people.* Lexington, MA: Lexington Books.

Hibbert, C. (1975). *The house of Medici: Its rise and fall.* New York: William Morrow & Co.

Howe, (1969). The causes of idiocy. In J. F. Gardner (1993). The era of optimism, 1850–1870: A preliminary appraisal. *Mental Retardation, 31*(2), 89–95.

Howe, S. G. (1848). On the causes of idiocy. Reprinted (1972) in *Medicine & Society in America.* New York: Arno.

Ingram, C. P. (1935). *Education of the slow-learning child.* New York: World Book.

Itard, J. M. G. (1972). *The wild boy of Aveyron.* New York: Monthly Review Press. (Original work published as *Les enfants sauvages,* 1801.)

LaVor, M. L. (1977). Federal legislation for exceptional children: Implications and a view of the field. In R. D. Kneedler & S. G. Tarver (Eds.), *Changing perspectives in special education.* New York: Merrill/Macmillan.

Locke, John (1963). Some thoughts concerning education. Reprinted in *The works of John Locke Vol. IX.* Germany: Scientia Verlag Aalen. (Originally published, London, 1823.)

Mayo, L. W. (1962). *A proposed program for national action to combat mental retardation.* Report to the President's Committee on Mental Retardation. Washington, DC: U.S. Government Printing Office.

McCleary, I. D., Hardman, M. L., & Thomas, D. (1990). International special education. In T. Husen & T. N. Postlewaire (Eds.), *International encyclopedia of education: Research and studies* (pp. 608–615). New York: Pergamon.

McNeil, M. C., Polloway, E. A., & Smith, J. D. (1984). Feral and isolated children: Historical review and analysis. *Education & Training of the Mentally Retarded, 19,* 70–79.

Patton, J. R., Payne, J. S., & Beirne-Smith, M. (1990). *Mental retardation.* Columbus, OH: Merrill.

Perske, R. (1981). *Hope for the families: New directions for parents of persons with retardation and other disabilities.* Nashville, TN: Abingdon.

Rees, L. M., Spreen, O., & Harnadek, M. (1991). Do attitudes towards persons with handicaps really shift over time? Comparison between 1975 and 1988. *Mental Retardation, 29*(2), 81–86.

Reno, J. (2000). *A message from the Attorney General.* Department of Justice ADA Web page.

Rosen, M., Clark, G. R., & Kivitz, M. S. (1976). *The history of mental retardation: Collected papers.* Baltimore, MD: University Park Press.

Rousseau, J. J. (1955). *Emile.* New York: Dutton. (Original work published 1702.)

Scheerenberger, R. C. (1982). Treatment from ancient times to the present. In P. T. Cegelka & H. J. Prehm, *Mental retardation: From categories to people* (pp. 44–75). Columbus, OH: Merrill.

Seguin, E. (1866). *Idiocy and its treatment by the physiological method*. New York: W. Wood. (Reprinted 1976.)

Singh, N. N., Oswald, D. P., & Ellis, C. R. (1998). Mental retardation. In T. H. Ollendick & M. Hersen (Eds.), *Handbook of child psychopathology* (3rd ed., pp. 91–116). New York: Plenum.

Skeels, H. M., & Dye, H. B. (1976). A study of the effects of differential stimulation on mentally retarded children. Reprinted in M. Rosen, G. R. Clark, & M. S. Kivitz (Eds.), *The history of mental retardation: Collected papers* (Vol. 2, pp. 241–266). Baltimore, MD: University Park Press. (Original work published 1939.)

Smith, J. D. (1985). *Minds made feeble: The myth and legacy of the Kallikaks*. Rockville, MD: Aspen.

———, & Nelson, K. R. (1989). *The sterilization of Carrie Buck*. New York: New Horizons Press.

———, & Polloway, E. A. (1993). Institutionalization, involuntary sterilization and mental retardation: Profiles from the history of the practice. *Mental Retardation, 31*(4), 208–214.

Switzky, H. N., Dudzinski, M., Van Acker, R., & Gambro, J. (1988). Historical foundations of out-of-home residential alternatives for mentally retarded persons. In L. W. Heal, J. I. Haney, & A. R. N. Amado (Eds.), *Integration of developmentally disabled individuals into the community* (2nd ed.). Baltimore, MD: Paul H. Brookes.

Vanuxem, M. (1921–22). Self government as applied to feeble-minded women. *Journal of Psycho-asthenics: Devoted to the care, training and treatment of the feebleminded and of the epileptic, 27,* 18–26.

Wallin, W. (1962). New frontiers in the social perspective of the mentally retarded. *Training School Bulletin, 59,* 89–104.

Wolfensberger, W. (1987). *The new genocide of handicapped and afflicted people*. Syracuse, NY: Wolfensberger.

———. (1975). *The origin and nature of our institutional models*. Syracuse, NY: Human Policy Press.

Zigler, E., Hodapp, R. M., & Edison, M. R. (1990). From theory to practice in the care and education of mentally retarded individuals. *American Journal on Mental Retardation, 95*(1), 1–12.

4

Definition, Classification, and Prevalence

Introducing Joyce, Susan, and Jason
Joyce Elger
Susan Polaski
Jason Cunningham

Labeling
The Label Chase
Alternatives to Labeling

Incidence and Prevalence

Definitional Issues

Early Definitions and Changes

Newer Definitions
Definition of Developmental Disabilities
The 1992 AAMR Definition

Understanding the 1992 Definition

The Debate Over Adaptive Behavior

Classification and Levels of Functioning
IQ- and Ability-Based Systems
The 1992 Classification System
Rationale for Change
Debate Over Classification
Different Goals and Purposes

Applying the Definition to Joyce, Susan, and Jason

Looking Ahead

InfoTrac College Edition

References

This chapter discusses the use of the term *mental retardation* and it describes both past and present definitions. Further, it describes systems for classifying the severity and nature of particular instances of MR and offers information about the rate at which mental retardation occurs within the general population.

Before these issues are addressed, however, we introduce three individuals who have intellectual disabilities. In many of the upcoming chapters, Joyce, Susan, and Jason will reappear, and they will provide "living" examples of the concepts and ideas presented.

INTRODUCING JOYCE, SUSAN, AND JASON

Joyce, Susan, and Jason are children who have intellectual disabilities, and such children have much to teach about what mental retardation really is and what life is like for those who have it. The events, challenges, and rewards of their lives illustrate many of the ideas that will be covered in this text. As you study mental retardation, you will share in their life experiences. Time will pass for them, and their stories will provide the opportunity to see how they are handling some of the challenges and how they are affected by some of the issues discussed in this text.

Mental retardation occurs in all racial groups and all social classes, and Joyce, Susan, and Jason come from diverse racial, economic, and family backgrounds. Joyce is being reared by an extended family, while Jason's parent is an adoptive single mother. Susan's family is the more traditional mother, father, and siblings composition and, unlike the other two, economically advantaged. These personal and family characteristics are not intended to be typical of people with mental retardation, but rather that there is no typical person or family living with MR. They also indicate how particular family and economic circumstances help shape the challenges faced and the supports that are (or are not) available. In addition, these three young people portray some of the complicating conditions that can coexist with mental retardation. For example, Susan has physical challenges in addition to MR, and Jason has complicating health conditions. Joyce has been diagnosed with learning disabilities, but her ability to function intellectually indicates that she does have pervasive deficits that would probably be more accurately diagnosed as MR. However, like others whose diagnoses have been "missed," she is not eligible for many of the services offered to those with the diagnosis of mental retardation.

Joyce Elger

Joyce is a stunningly pretty 14-year-old African-American girl in an eighth-grade learning disabilities classroom. Her school records show a full-scale IQ of 68, but her adaptive behavior—based on a survey-type rating scale not typical of the current best practice in the field—was measured at a level close to that of her peers. As a result of her adaptive behavior score, she was given a learning disabilities rather than a mental retardation designation. The diagnostic designation of students such as Joyce who have what was once termed "borderline" IQ scores varies not only from state to state, but also often from district to district. It is these children who are most likely to be inappropriately diagnosed and placed—as it appears that Joyce may have been—or overlooked entirely.

Joyce lives at home with her mother, her 22-year-old sister, her 2-year-old nephew, her grandmother, and her 8-year-old tabby cat. Her father died when she was a baby, and her grandfather passed away two years ago. Joyce took her grandfather's death hard. Her mother works full-time, and her sister has a part-time job and the major responsibility for her young son. Her grandmother stays at home and does most of the cooking and housework. She has always relied heavily on Joyce's help with these duties. The members of Joyce's family are all close, but she is especially fond of her grandmother.

Joyce is extremely unhappy at school. She is struggling to read at the fourth-grade level, and she feels stupid and discouraged. Even worse, she does not feel part of the social life and activities of students in regular classrooms. She believes that the school exists for them, and that the students with disabilities do not really belong. All three of the older women at home tell her how important it is to stay in school, but Joyce has secretly resolved to drop out when she reaches 16. She does not believe that school will be of any real use to her.

Joyce has recently become close friends with three girls in her neighborhood who are part of a "fast" crowd. For the first time in her life, she is starting to feel accepted by her peers. To Joyce, her new friends seem to live appealing lives. There are always parties and excitement, and the "regular" kids that Joyce has always wanted to hang around with are starting to notice her and talk about her "wild" behavior. Although their attention is somewhat negative, Joyce is enjoying it. She is experimenting with alcohol and marijuana, and an attractive boy has been hanging around both at school and when she is with her girlfriends. He has made it plain that he thinks she is "hot," and Joyce likes to think of him as her boyfriend. Because of Joyce's new friends, her grandmother has become concerned about her, especially after catching Joyce lying about her activities twice in the last month.

Joyce seems reluctant to talk about her future. When pressed, though, she says she wants to "get married and have a place of her own."

Susan Polaski

At Susan's last birthday, she had a party with 50 people, a clown, pony rides, and a three-tiered cake; she was 10 years old. Susan is in a regular fifth-grade classroom at a private parochial school. She uses a motorized wheelchair, because she has no mobility from her waist down. She is unable to use her left arm and has limited use of her right; she also has poor neck control. Susan's measured IQ is 60, but because of her limited manual abilities and the fact that she is nonverbal, testing is difficult and may not truly reflect her actual intelligence. Based on her school performance (discussed in Chapter 5), this IQ score seems to underestimate her ability. She is labeled with mild retardation and severe cerebral palsy (CP). Her adaptive skills are limited, but this is more strongly related to the motor problems caused by her CP than to her intellectual disabilities.

Susan lives with her mother, father, two older brothers, and a live-in nanny named Jolene. She also has two large Dalmatians. She is of Polish ancestry; her family is wealthy and lives in a prosperous section of a large Eastern city. Her father is a major executive at a large corporation; her mother is active in politics. One of her brothers is a student at a well-known university; the other is still in high school.

Susan's wheelchair is custom-designed to provide a posture she can sustain for long periods and to allow her the greatest movement. She controls it herself with a device like a joystick. The wheelchair also has a removable tray on which a computer is mounted and used by Susan to communicate. When asked, she says that her school is "Okay"; that most of the kids are "all right," but one or two are a "real pain"; and that she has two good friends who come to her house to play. Jolene also often takes Susan to visit those friends in a specially adapted van. Susan has many educational computer games, and she is most interested in and successful with those that are designed at a second- or beginning third-grade level. When she grows up, Susan wants to design "pretty clothes" and be a "mom."

Jason Cunningham

Jason is 2 years old. He is the adopted son of a single mother, Cathy, who has two other adopted children with disabilities: Justin (age 7) and Ricky (age 4). Cathy owns and operates a preschool and day care facility, and the family lives in a medium-sized, Midwestern city. Justin has Down syndrome, and Ricky has fetal alcohol syndrome, but both children are easy-going, and Cathy enjoyed the joys and challenges of their early years.

Jason's condition is thought to result from a postnatal brain injury. He was born five weeks prematurely to a 14-year-old Vietnamese girl who was pregnant as a result of rape. When he was three days old, he suffered an intracranial hemorrhage that resulted in brain damage.

Cathy traveled to Vietnam to adopt Jason when he was 6 months old, and although she was informed he had disabilities, the severity could not be predicted. At 2 years of age, Jason is just now starting to pull himself up. He can sit alone, but his motor coordination, both in sitting and standing, is "wobbly." He does not yet talk, but he does babble. At this time, his developmental delay is thought to be severe. In addition to motor and cognitive delays, Jason has developed asthma and has been hospitalized three times in the last year.

Both Justin and Ricky are healthy, though Justin does have minor heart damage. Jason's delay and health pose by far the most serious problems. He is regularly seen by a pediatrician, a physician who specializes in respiratory disorders, a physical therapist, and an occupational therapist. Cathy feels overwhelmed by all of the necessary appointments.

When he is feeling well, Jason is a happy and responsive child. He smiles and laughs often, is affectionate, and likes to be cuddled. Cathy says that his sunny personality during those times is what keeps her going. But when he is ill (which is frequently) he cries for hours at a time, and Cathy cannot console him.

All three children attend activities at church, and the older boys are involved in school-related activities as well. Cathy comes from a large family: She has three sisters and two brothers, and all but the youngest boy and girl, who are still at home, are married. Cathy and her entire family live in the same town, and her parents live only a few blocks away. All of Cathy's family, especially her parents and one of her married sisters, take an interest in Cathy's children and help out when they can.

We will return to the stories of Joyce, Susan, and Jason later in the chapter and start to understand their disabilities in terms of the currently used definition and classification system. First, however, we turn to some descriptions of terms.

LABELING

Disability and *handicap* are terms or labels that are related to mental retardation, and they are sometimes used synonymously. There is an important distinction between them, however: A disability does not have to be a handicap. **Disability** refers to the condition itself, while **handicap** refers to a restriction or inability to carry out important or essential activities (Hardman, Drew, & Egan, 1996). As an example, because Susan is not able to use her legs for mobility and must get around in a wheelchair, she has a disability. This only becomes a handicap, however, if she wants to go to places that are not accessible to wheelchairs. One goal for professionals in the field of mental retardation is to create situations where disabilities do not become handicaps.

> **FOR DISCUSSION** *What conditions in your community create handicaps?*

The term *mental retardation* is a label, as are *autism* (see Chapter 9) and *gifted*. The very act of defining a particular condition requires that the condition have a name or label, though people usually do not want to be characterized by just this one aspect of their lives. Even when the label implies positive attributes, such as intelligence and creativity (as with *gifted*), people often experience difficulty with the assumptions that are carried with the label. The problem, then, is less that conditions have names than that people can become overly associated with the conditions. When this happens, others may not notice individuality and may see only those attributes thought to define the condition. The more socially negative those perceived attributes, the more stigmatizing a label can be.

> **FOR DISCUSSION** *What assumptions are often made about people with mental retardation other than the associated problems with learning?*

Research on the stigmatizing effect of labels, however, has produced mixed and controversial findings (Hastings, 1994). Early studies found that the labels *mentally retarded* and *learning disabled* do indeed influence the expectations and attitudes of others, sometimes in ways that are inconsistent with the child's actual behavior (Aloia & MacMillan, 1983; Jacobs, 1978; Ysseldyke & Foster, 1978). When labeled children succeed, they may be given less credit for it; and when they fail, they may get less blame than unlabeled children get (Severance & Gasstrom, 1977).

Still, teachers, parents, and others often hold conflicting views about the meaning of a given label and therefore hold differing expectations as well (Bromfield, Weisz, & Messer, 1986; Smith, Osborne, Crim, & Rhu, 1986). Also, as a result of labels, children sometimes get even more positive interaction from teachers than do nonlabeled children. In addition, labeled children can benefit from services that would otherwise be unavailable to them, often including financial aid and educational help (Hastings, 1994). You can see, then, that the effects of labeling are complex and involve factors other than the label itself.

In a now classic study, Rosenthal and Jacobson (1966; 1968) studied the effects of teacher expectations on children in their classrooms and found that labeling results in *self-fulfilling prophecy:* Teachers' expectations led children to behave consistently with them. If Joyce's teacher expects her to fail, for example, then she may fail simply because it is expected of her. Almost immediately, however, there was criticism of Rosenthal's methodology—criticism that cast doubt on his findings (Thorndike, 1968). Furthermore, several investigators were unable to replicate Rosenthal's results (Dusek & O'Connell, 1973; Mendels & Flanders, 1973). It is likely, then, that children's behavior is more strongly determined by other factors than individual teacher expectations, though these probably play some part (Rosenthal, 1987). But notice that this research has measured the influence of only one person's attitude. It certainly does not describe the effects of pervasive pessimism, such as when children are reared with negative expectations from family, school, *and* society. Such effects are almost certainly far greater.

Both formal and informal labels are associated with many conditions—some disabling and others not. **Formal labels** are those officially sanctioned by professionals for identification or diagnosis. **Informal labels** are names other than the official ones; these are used by peers and others, usually to taunt or insult. For example, *gifted* is a formal label, and *nerd* is informal.

The research involving responses to labeling refers only to official labels. Although those results suggest that formal labels are not always harmful, negative informal labeling is cruel, abusive, and certainly challenges the self-esteem of those on the receiving end.

The Label Chase

What's in a name? That which we call a rose
By any other name would smell as sweet.
—William Shakespeare

Usually, formal labels become informal ones. Older official categories, such as *idiot* and *imbecile,* soon provided fuel for name-calling and became pejoratives. Because formal terms become associated in this way with unpleasant feelings and images, professionals often suggest new ones to replace the older derogatory labels in an effort to reduce stigma.

The newer term *retard,* for example, comes from Latin and means to make slow or delay, so *mental retardation* literally means mentally late or slow. This term was thought far more neutral than *idiot* or *moron* and was adopted as a descriptive and less insulting label. Now, however, the word *retarded* has taken on many of the negative connotations once associated with *idiot*. Children can be heard calling each other "retards" as put-downs, for example, and in that way the once relatively neutral and formal label has now become an offensive and informal one.

At the most basic level, words are simply sounds. We decide that certain combinations of sound will stand for an object or idea, but the sounds themselves have no intrinsic good or bad meaning. It is our associations and feelings with the named idea that determine whether it is an insult or a compliment. In an important way, then, the stigma associated with labeling is an attitude problem rather than a word problem. As long as we, as a society, have trouble dealing with diversity, and so long as we respond to our own fears of physical and mental challenge by attempting to distance ourselves, then we are likely to associate bad feeling with labels for such conditions. Until we change, whatever name is chosen will soon become stigmatizing.

Understanding this, some stigmatized groups have decided to try to change negative associations rather than find new names. During the civil rights era of the 1960s and 1970s, for example, the word *black* (which had previously been used as an insult) became a source of pride for African-Americans. In like manner, some people with physical disabilities refer to themselves as *crips*. In this same way, Susan might decide to use the term *cripple* in a manner of pride so that some of her confidence and good feeling will be noticed and absorbed by others. Whether this strategy succeeds in changing public attitudes or not, Susan's own attitude makes her less vulnerable to insult: Names will no longer hurt her.

> **FOR DISCUSSION** *What other stigmatized groups have adopted an informal label and presented it as a positive trait? In your opinion, what has been the result?*

Recently, many people with mental retardation and their families have taken a different approach. They have preferred to educate the public to the truth that someone *has* a disability; they are not the disability itself. As an example, the self-advocacy group People First adopted its name to indicate that its members are first and foremost human beings with many personal characteristics, only one of which is mental retardation (Castles, 1996). Other advocates stress that labels are nouns for particular conditions and do not refer to people; furthermore, labels are never adjectives. One should say, "Jason *has* mental retardation," or "Jason is a person *with* MR," but never "Jason *is* a retarded person" or "Susan *is* a paraplegic."

> **FOR DISCUSSION** *What other groups have insisted that language toward them should change? What has been the result?*

Making this language adjustment can be troublesome, and the result may seem trivial in comparison to the effort required. But advocates point out that each time it is necessary to correct our speech or recompose a sentence, the act itself causes us to stop and remember the humanity of others. From this may come a greater awareness, one that becomes embedded in our language and signifies much more than current political correctness. These are worthwhile goals, and you will notice that official terms and labels in this text are used only to describe conditions—never people.

Alternatives to Labeling

At one level, the impossibility of talking about something without using terms is clear. Conditions must have names. At another level, however, such names become officially associated with individuals so that educational, medical, and other social services can be provided. It is here that concern arises. Some educational labels may be viewed as more stigmatizing than others. For example, there is an apparent but not well documented belief that *mental retardation* is a more stigmatizing category than *learning disabilities* (Frankenberger & Fronzaglio, 1991). This belief is thought to be part of the reason that approximately 3 percent fewer children are identified with mental retardation each year, while the learning disabilities category is increasing by 2 percent to 3 percent (Gresham, MacMillan, .& Bocian, 1998; U.S. Department of Education, 1990). Some parents and professionals are reluctant to assign the *mental retardation* label, particularly for those with mild disabilities; they instead opt for the *learning disabilities* category (Frankenberger & Fronzaglio, 1991).

As a response to concern about stigma, some writers have questioned the necessity of a specific label for educational purposes (Somogyi, 1995). They argue that children should be viewed individually in order to facilitate the most useful curriculum development and identify the most appropriate teaching methods. Categorization, they argue, stands in the way of individualized assessment, and it is often misleading rather than accurately descriptive of a particular child. Ironically, even when a label does convey information about the nature of a child's condition, it too seldom influences the instructional approach. More important, children could still be classified as eligible for services based on more general criteria without specifying an exact diagnostic category.

> **FOR DISCUSSION** *If you were working with a child with disabilities, would you want or need information about her particular classification? Why or why not?*

INCIDENCE AND PREVALENCE

Incidence and prevalence are statistical measures of the number of people with a particular condition. The **incidence** of mental retardation refers to the number of *new* cases that occur within a particular period. **Prevalence** is the *total* number of people with MR at a given time; the number is often expressed as a percentage. Experts generally agree that people with mental retardation make up approximately 2.5 percent to 3 percent of the total population (Fryers, 1993). Government data, however, indicate wide variability in prevalence among the states, with rates ranging from .003 percent for Alaska to more than 3 percent in West Virginia (U.S. Department of Health & Human Services, 1996).

Children with mental retardation, learning disabilities or without disabilities have many of the same needs, while those within a category may be quite different from each other.

© Elizabeth Crews

The 3 percent figure also varies according to age and the definition used for identification. Some people are included within the MR definition only during their school years, for example; they later become self-sufficient adults. When anyone who has ever been identified with MR at *some* time during their lives is counted, the figure is close to 3 percent. This figure is probably also valid when IQ alone is used as the criteria. But the population identified with mental retardation at any given time is probably closer to 1.5 percent when both IQ and adaptive behavior are considered (Forness, 1994).

Problems in identification make completely accurate counts of incidence and prevalence impossible. In regard to incidence, more than 70 percent of those who are born with mental retardation cannot be diagnosed at birth. Usually, unless there are obvious physical characteristics that are typically associated with retardation (as with Down syndrome or fetal alcohol syndrome), even those with severe retardation may not be identified for several months and even years. Furthermore, many babies with congenitally caused disorders die before or shortly after birth (Rowitz, 1991). For all of these reasons, children are missed in the incidence count, even though they have MR. Because of the uncertainty involved with incidence statistics, prevalence rates are seen as a more reliable index of the relative frequency of mental retardation (Kiely & Lubin, 1991). However, prevalence rates also provide only an estimate. Many people with milder forms of retardation may never be officially identified, or they may be inaccurately identified as learning disabled, making prevalence figures also inaccurate.

By far, most people with mental retardation are mildly affected, and therefore most of the diagnostic decisions about whether retardation is present take place with this group (MacMillan, Siperstein, & Gresham, 1996). But accurate identification with this population is extremely problematic. When someone is more severely affected, there is little disagreement about whether mental retardation exists. With mildly affected people, however, conflicting diagnoses are much more likely.

Boys are more likely to be identified with MR than are girls partly because X chromosome–related conditions that lead to mental retardation are far more likely in boys and partly because of circumstantial reasons. In general, boys tend to be more active and aggressive than girls, and children with these characteristics are more likely to be noticed and referred for assessment.

The impossibility of directly counting everyone who is diagnosed with retardation compounds the problem. There are several methods of estimating this number; all of them rely on taking counts or samples from some specific population and then generalizing those results to the population as a whole. For example, samples of the number of people with retardation may be taken from small communities, where it is possible to count and where people do not move in or out frequently. These percentages are then used as estimates for the larger population. But rural communities tend to have a smaller percentage of residents with retardation than are found in large urban areas. Also, these techniques are expensive and require extensive training of personnel (Rowitz, 1991).

Another method involves obtaining figures for all people with MR who are served by agencies or schools within a region and then applying these figures to the nation. Here, though, people who do not come into contact with agencies are missed. School districts also use widely differing criteria to identify mental retardation (Frankenberger & Fronzaglio, 1991) because policy makers in each state have developed their own eligibility criteria and, ultimately, school districts must conform to state guidelines if they are to receive funds for special education services.

Although the trend has been toward greater uniformity, eligibility for special education in one community does not ensure eligibility if a child moves somewhere else (Frankenberger & Fronzaglio, 1991). And many children, such as Joyce, who have academic skills in the retarded range, are categorized instead with learning disabilities. Furthermore, definitional differences are not limited to the school system. For example, vocational rehabilitation agency policies vary by state as well (Dowdy, Smith, & Nowell, 1992), as do criteria for all other programs related to MR.

Unfortunately, then, for all of these reasons, our estimates of those with retardation are only that—estimates. Still, these figures must serve as the basis for many funding decisions and for much program planning.

> **FOR DISCUSSION**   *What are some practical uses for incidence and prevalence information? Who needs to know this and why?*

DEFINITIONAL ISSUES

Mental retardation is not a disease, and no medical test or technology can determine its presence. Mental retardation is, however, sometimes associated with conditions that can be medically determined. For example, **Fragile X syndrome** is a genetically identifiable condition that usually results in mental retardation. Serious brain injuries also can often be seen with a CAT scan, and such damage many times results in mental retardation. But mental retardation itself cannot be seen directly, and because it can be inferred only from performance, some agreement must be reached on exactly what performance will indicate retardation and how that will be measured.

On the surface, the definition of mental retardation is determined by professionals in the field. The particular individuals who write a definition are, however, responsive to existing research, practice, and the knowledge and opinions of many others. Those who develop definitions also must do so in such a way that state policy makers are likely to adopt them—and practitioners will apply them. In actuality, then, building a definition is a political process (Rowitz, 1991), one that ultimately determines whether someone will be labeled with retardation and thereby become eligible for services. Understanding this helps clarify the idea of social construction that opened Chapter 3. Whether one is officially included within the category of retardation is ultimately determined by those who create and implement the definition. And, as a result, an individual's view of herself (as well as the official and unofficial view of others toward her) is also importantly determined by that socially constructed definition.

EARLY DEFINITIONS AND CHANGES

Before the 1900s, definitions were vague and general, and they concentrated on an individual's lack of understanding as demonstrated by failure to develop expected intellectual skills and communication (Guttmacher & Weihofen, 1952). By the beginning of this century, however, definitions focused more formally on the individual's ability to get along in the world—that is, on his adaptive behavior (Doll, 1941; Tredgold, 1937). All of these early definitions assumed that mental retardation was incurable.

During the 20th century, the most widely used and accepted definitions have come from the **American Association on Mental Retardation (AAMR)**, formerly called the American Association on Mental Deficiency (AAMD) and originally the American Association for the Study of the Feebleminded. These definitions, from the first, included both the concepts of measured intelligence (based on an IQ test) and social and personal competence (adaptive behavior).

FOR DISCUSSION *What do you think the AAMR name changes indicate? In your opinion, what, if anything, did these changes accomplish?*

> 1959 and 1961 (Heber): Mental retardation refers to subaverage general intellectual functioning that originates during the developmental period and is associated with impairment in adaptive behavior.
>
> 1973 (Grossman): Mental retardation refers to *significantly* subaverage general intellectual functioning *existing concurrently* with deficits in adaptive behavior and *manifested* during the developmental period.
>
> 1983 (Grossman): Mental retardation refers to significantly subaverage general intellectual functioning *resulting in* or *associated with* concurrent impairments in adaptive behavior and manifested during the developmental period.

FIGURE 4.1 AAMR definitions

Figure 4.1 presents the AAMR definitions since 1959 and illustrates some of the important changes.

> **FOR DISCUSSION**   *If you were reading these definitions for the first time, what else would you need to know in order to use them to determine if someone has retardation?*

With the advent of IQ tests, there was a seemingly objective way to measure intelligence. The IQ test was given to vast numbers of people, and the scores from those tests were used to provide a benchmark for individual scores. Figure 4.2 shows the distribution of IQ scores so that all the scores from those tested fall under the line on the graph. It can be seen that most people receive a score of 100; as scores become higher and lower, fewer people are represented.

For the 1961 definition, **subaverage** meant one standard deviation below the average score on an IQ test (Heber, 1961). The most widely used tests have a mean score of 100 and a standard deviation of 15. **Standard deviation** indicates the average number of points within which most scores vary from the mean. Looking at Figure 4.2, you can see that the overwhelming majority of people score within 15 points on either side of the mean, so 15 points represents one standard deviation. By looking at the 1961 definition, then, it follows that all those who scored 85 or below on an IQ test fell into the range of retardation. Officially, deficits in adaptive behavior were also required for diagnosis, but in actual practice they were seldom taken into consideration, largely because of problems with fair and accurate measurement.

In 1961, the developmental period was defined as the years from birth through age 16. This part of the definition described the time period during which the characteristics of mental retardation *must* appear initially. If the same characteristics (low IQ and deficits in adaptive behavior) were to appear later, they would not constitute mental retardation. For example, if someone had developed a brain infection at 5 years of age that left him with IQ test scores below 85 and low adaptive skills, then his condition would have been described as mental retarda-

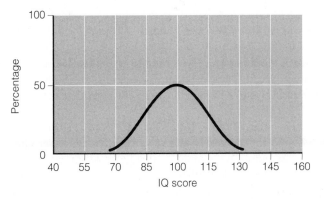

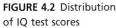

FIGURE 4.2 Distribution of IQ test scores

tion. If, however, the same thing happened at 25, then the person would not have been diagnosed with MR but with brain injury.

> **FOR DISCUSSION** *Why should the same condition be labeled* mental retardation *when it occurs at an early age but not when it occurs in older people? What does this suggest about the purpose of the definition?*

There were several objections to the 1961 definition. For one, a substantial percentage of the population had scores between 70 and 85 (Zigler, Balla, & Hodapp, 1984). If one thinks of retardation as involving intellectual abilities that are decidedly different from the norm, then this level of performance would not qualify because such scores are, in fact, common. Also, minority groups were highly overrepresented in those who scored between 70 and 85 (Franks, 1971). Some advocates argued that minority children are reared in different cultures with different experiences than those from the cultural mainstream who devised the tests (see more on problems with IQ tests in Chapter 5). They insisted that lower performance resulted from a lack of task familiarity and relevant practice (as a result of different cultural experiences) rather than actual retardation. These differences in experience, it was argued, resulted from influences of the wider society that disallowed the opportunities that would promote the development of the abilities required for higher test scores (Ogbu, 1995; Dunn, 1968; Mercer, 1973).

In addition, critics pointed out that many of those people who scored below 85 functioned perfectly well within their homes and communities; it was only at school that they performed within the retarded range. Recognition of this circumstance—which came to be called **six-hour retardation**—prompted increased awareness of the essential role of adaptive behavior in determining MR, because it was the overemphasis on IQ test scores and the failure to adequately consider adaptive behavior that resulted in young people being diagnosed with MR when their only intellectual problems were school-related (President's Committee on Mental Retardation, 1970).

At the same time, there were corresponding legislative pressures for change. In California in *Larry P.* v. *Wilson Riles* (1979), a federal appellate court ruled that

California school districts could no longer use IQ tests (as typically administered) to determine the placement of African-American children in classes for those with mild retardation. Attorneys for plaintiff "Larry P." argued successfully that he (and the six other children represented) functioned well outside of school and that traditional IQ tests were biased against black children. This and other court cases warned school districts throughout the nation that assessment and placement procedures were likely to be legally questioned.

Finally, providing special services for such large numbers was expensive. Obviously, if the IQ score required for the retardation label were lower, fewer children would qualify for services and money would be freed to offer more services to those with more severe disabilities or for other purposes.

In 1973, the AAMR definition was revised, and adaptive behavior was formally defined as follows:

> The effectiveness or degree with which the individual meets the standards of personal independence and social responsibilities expected of his age and cultural group. (Grossman, 1973)

Emphasis was placed on *both* low IQ and deficits in adaptive behavior as necessary elements for determining mental retardation. Also, the cutoff for those identified within the MR category was lowered to two standard deviations below the mean. As a result, one would now be diagnosed with mental retardation only if his IQ was 70 or below, although some flexibility (within a few points) was allowed for clinical judgment. In addition, the 1973 definition extended the developmental period from birth to age 18 (rather than 16), thus providing increased eligibility for some people. But because of the lower IQ requirement, the final effect was that more than 80 percent of those who were previously eligible were now excluded. Children who had mental retardation one day literally did not have it the next (Zetlin & Murtaugh, 1990). Because the 1973 definition was adopted by PL 94-142, these changes had important implications for educational interventions (see Chapter 3).

Although children with IQs between 70 and 85 have now escaped any stigma associated with the MR label, they are also ineligible for services. Many neither qualify with specific learning disabilities nor meet the criteria for any other eligible category; and although they may continue to experience school difficulty they are no longer entitled to special education help. It has become easier to think of these children as simply "slow," without envisioning specific means to help them improve, especially because they are not automatically entitled to any official program. Sometimes help is available through Title I (which provides federal funds for compensatory education for children from families with low incomes), but this is by no means guaranteed (Beach, 1996). Although the appropriate designation for these children may not be mental retardation, many still need additional intervention if they are to succeed in school.

FOR DISCUSSION   *If you were teaching in general education, what help would you want for a child who seemed "slow?" Do such children require special help?*

As a result of the 1973 changes, the number of students eligible for services declined dramatically and the composition of classes for students with mild retardation was altered somewhat. Students in these classes do tend to have lower IQ scores than did previous students, although the percentage of children with behavioral problems remains unchanged and the overrepresentation of minorities unfortunately remains an issue (Polloway, Smith, Patton, & Smith, 1996).

In 1977, there were no changes to the definition itself, although the role of clinical judgment was highlighted, and allowance was made for the inclusion of children with IQs up to 10 points above the 70 cutoff—*if* they also showed serious deficits in adaptive behavior (Grossman, 1977). However, adequate assessment of adaptive behavior continued to be overlooked, and many states did not actually include it in their identification process (Frankenberger & Harper, 1988).

Changes in the 1983 definition included expanding the developmental period from conception (rather than birth) to age 18, which then made eligible those people with conditions stemming from the prenatal period. Practitioners also were cautioned against a strict reliance on the standard deviation, because scores from any test are likely to vary because of random error (chance) alone. For the most widely used IQ tests, the random error is approximately three points. Emphasis was again placed on the separate and specific measurement of adaptive behavior. Although the committee acknowledged that some of the same abilities underlie both adaptive behavior and IQ performance, it did not believe that adaptive behavior could be adequately measured by IQ, and it described adaptive behavior as follows:

> Adaptive behavior refers to the quality of everyday performance in coping with environmental demands. The quality of general adaptation is mediated by level of intelligence; thus, the two concepts overlap in meaning. It is evident, however, from consideration of the definition of adaptive behavior, with its stress on everyday coping, that adaptive behavior refers to what people do to take care of themselves and to relate to others in daily living rather than the abstract potential implied by intelligence. (Grossman, 1983, p. 42)

With the 1983 definition, official acceptance of AAMR guidelines became more widespread. The new definition was more compatible with both the World Health Organization's International Statistical Classification of Diseases system (ICD-9) and the American Psychiatric Association's 1980 *Diagnostic and Statistical Manual of Mental Disorders* (DSM-III). By 1990, 30 states cited the AAMR definition in their eligibility requirements, and 44 included both adaptive behavior and IQ—the two major components of the AAMR definition (Frankenberger & Fronzaglio, 1991). The actual measurement of adaptive behavior continued to lag behind, however. In 1990, none of the states used the same method for measurement, and existing adaptive behavior scales continued to be criticized for limitations in both validity and reliability (Reschly, 1990). These problems play a prominent role in the controversy surrounding the adaptive behavior component of the 1992 AAMR definition.

NEWER DEFINITIONS

Definition of Developmental Disabilities

People with mental retardation also fall within the definition of developmental disabilities (DD), although this larger classification includes many other disabilities. Developmental disabilities are defined by the **Developmental Disabilities Act** (PL 95-602), which was newly amended under the Developmental Disabilities Assistance and Bill of Rights Act (1996). This act provides funding for planning activities, program services, program demonstrations, and research projects in addition to university-affiliated programs for comprehensive training and service.

The 1996 legislation states that a developmental disability must be chronic, severe, and conform to all of the following:

- [be] attributable to a mental or physical impairment or a combination of mental or physical impairments
- [be] manifested before the person reaches age 22
- [be] likely to continue indefinitely
- [result] in substantial functional limitations in three or more of the following areas of life activity: a) self-care, b) receptive and expressive language, c) learning, d) mobility, e) self-direction, f) capacity for independent living, and g) economic self-sufficiency
- [reflect] the person's need for a combination and sequence of special, interdisciplinary, or generic care, treatment, or other services which are of lifelong or extended duration and are individually planned and coordinated, except that such term, when applied to infants and young children means individuals from birth to age 5, inclusive, who have substantial developmental delay or specific congenital or acquired conditions with a high probability of resulting in developmental disabilities if services are not provided. (PL 104-183, 1996)

As with other definitions, however, actual identification practices are often inconsistent. Although some states have adopted the developmental disabilities definition for determining eligibility for state funded services, including programs for those with MR (Wrench, 1994), developmental service programs in many states (and even some federal programs) use other criteria for eligibility (Jacobson, 1991).

> **FOR DISCUSSION** *Should all states use the same criteria for eligibility? How would this be accomplished? What would be some of the advantages and disadvantages?*

The 1992 AAMR Definition

Nothing will ever be attempted if all possible objections must be first overcome.
—Samuel Johnson

1. Valid assessment considers cultural and linguistic diversity as well as differences in communication and behavioral factors.
2. The existence of limitations in adaptive skills occurs within the context of community environments that are typical of the individual's age peers and is indexed to the person's individualized needs for supports.
3. Specific adaptive limitations often coexist with strengths in other adaptive skills or other personal capabilities.
4. With appropriate supports over a sustained period, the life functioning of the person with mental retardation will generally improve.

SOURCE: Adapted from Luckasson et al., 1992, p. 1.

FIGURE 4.3 Four assumptions for assessing mental retardation

In 1992, the Ad Hoc Committee on Terminology and Classification of the AAMR published the revised definition and instructions for its application in *Mental Retardation: Definition, Classification, and Systems of Supports* (9th ed.). This most recent definition includes major changes that have profound implications for professional practice and research. Differences in wording with previous definitions are extensive and reflect substantive conceptual changes. The highlighted phrases indicate these important new ideas:

> Mental Retardation refers to substantial *limitations in present functioning.* It is characterized by significantly subaverage intellectual functioning, existing concurrently *with related limitations in two or more of the following applicable adaptive skill areas: communication, self-care, home living, social skills, community use, self-direction, health and safety, functional academics, leisure, and work.* Mental retardation *manifests before age 18.* (Luckasson et al., 1992, p. 1)

In addition to the definition itself, the four assumptions in Figure 4.3 are essential to a diagnosis of mental retardation.

UNDERSTANDING THE 1992 DEFINITION

The 1992 definition provides a *functional* view of mental retardation: It determines mental retardation by how well someone actually functions in her daily life as a result of her "conceptual, practical and social intelligence" (Luckasson et al., 1992, p. 5). The definition focuses on the relationship among "*capabilities* (cognition, learning, and adaptive skills), *environments* (the characteristics and expectations of one's living situation), and *functioning* (a result of the 'fit' between capabilities and environments)" (Luckasson et al., 1992, pp. 9–10). It defines mental retardation as the outcome of disabling circumstances involving these three aspects. According to the authors, this conception reflects a paradigm shift: MR is no longer seen as simply the trait of an individual but as the result of an interaction between the individual and the characteristics and expectations of his environment.

The change in wording to *limitations in present functioning* indicates that mental retardation is a state rather than a trait. A **state** is a circumstance in which an individual currently finds herself, but one that will not necessarily always exist. For example, someone may be depressed or have little money at one time of life, yet experience markedly different conditions at another. On the other hand, a **trait** is an enduring characteristic such as eye color. This change in emphasis indicates that someone can have mental retardation at one time of life and not at another. Perhaps more important, though, it underscores the fact—included in AAMR definitions from the first—that mental retardation can improve.

> **FOR DISCUSSION**   *Can you think of more examples of states or traits? Explain why they are one or the other.*

Next, significantly subaverage intellectual functioning is defined as an IQ standard score of approximately 70–75 or below. Where diagnosis is uncertain, the committee has declared that consideration of adaptive skills should take precedence over rigid reliance on IQ (Schalock et al., 1994). Although the cutoff score in 1983 was officially 70, scores of 75 or even 80 could qualify, with allowances for random error and clinical judgment (Reiss, 1994). There have been concerns that, in actual practice, the new phrasing may result in more identified cases (MacMillan, Gresham, & Siperstein, 1993), but that remains an empirical question (Reiss, 1994).

The **adaptive skill areas** are completely new in the 1992 definition. Where adaptive behavior was previously seen as a *general* ability to manage life circumstances (refer back to the earlier definition of adaptive behavior), *specific* skill areas are now identified. For the previous definition, then, some measure of general adaptive behavior and an IQ test score were required. Now, in addition to IQ, adaptive behavior must be identified in at least two of the specifically named domains. The new guidelines for adaptive behavior have generated considerable controversy, as we will see.

THE DEBATE OVER ADAPTIVE BEHAVIOR

One objection to the new requirements for adaptive behavior is that they are not empirically based. They are derived from theoretical ideas rather than from research findings, so critics question the basis on which these particular 10 skill areas were chosen rather than others. Do deficits in these areas really mean that one has retardation? Or could such deficits be as easily related to something else such as motivation or mental illness (Greenspan & Granfield, 1992)? And how has it been determined that the areas are equally important? Are deficits in self-direction and leisure as central in importance as self-care and functional academics, for example? And why has it been decided that work skills or leisure skills are as important as communication skills (or vice versa)?

> **FOR DISCUSSION**   *Do you know anyone who has poor adaptive skills in two or more of the named areas but does not seem to have retardation? Do you know anyone with significantly low IQ who does not belong in the retardation category? How do you explain these differences?*

Although there has been progress (Salvia & Ysseldyke, 1995), some authors continue to question whether instruments to measure adaptive behavior have sufficient validity and reliability. Critics contend that when unreliable measures are used, the chance of mistaken diagnosis is unacceptably high (MacMillan, Gresham, & Siperstein, 1993). Again, such problems are likely to occur primarily with those who would traditionally have been classified with mild retardation.

> **FOR DISCUSSION**   *Imagine you are in the home of a person with mental retardation to observe some of his adaptive skills. How will you decide whether these skills are adequate?*

As we have seen, criticism of adaptive behavior measurement has been long-standing (Zigler, Balla, & Hodapp, 1984). An additional important concern is that adaptive behaviors are at least as culturally prescribed as traditional IQ tasks, and fair assessment may therefore be even more difficult. This is a problem for which those who develop adaptive behavior measures (and those who use them) must remain vigilant. There are, however, important challenges to the validity of the IQ test as well (Ceci & Williams, 1997; Ogbu, 1997). In spite of these difficulties, professionals must continue to find better and more reliable measurement methods, because both IQ and adaptive behavior are essential characteristics of intellectual functioning. In addition, functional community-based adaptive abilities are crucial to the life outcomes for those with retardation.

> **FOR DISCUSSION**   *Are adaptive abilities adequately measured by IQ tests? What evidence is there that they are or are not?*

The AAMR committee's intention, in fact, is to move away from the strict use of psychometric measures and to rely more strongly on clinical judgments and home and community observations. The committee argued that it is precisely because IQ has had questionable validity in determining MR for those in the 60-to-80 range that assessment of adaptive behavior is needed. Although they encourage the development of quantitative adaptive skill instruments, they believe that measurement can and should depend on other methods such as functional structured interviews (which are, in fact, preferred in psychiatric journals) (Reiss, 1994). At a basic level, the controversy over adaptive behavior involves whether assessment decisions about performance are likely to be more accurate and fair if based on individual clinical judgment or standardized quantitative measures.

In service delivery, there is a trend toward using more clinically and community-based assessment measures. The new AAMR definition includes criteria similar to that in the definition for developmental disabilities (see p. 78), and several of the AAMR adaptive skill domains are consistent with the mandated transitional areas in IDEA. The committee sees intervention planning as a "primary purpose of diagnosis," and it has designed the definition to provide information that will facilitate programming (Schalock et al., 1994, p. 183).

Critics have charged, though, that the new description of adaptive skills does not sufficiently consider developmental concerns. The individual categories are relevant mostly for older children or adolescents, yet mental retardation is a developmental disability that most often occurs in the first stages of life. How helpful is the 1992 definition, then, for early diagnosis and intervention (MacMillan, Gresham, & Siperstein, 1993)?

Another concern involves the distinction between the adaptive skills usually assessed by existing measures of adaptive behavior and the social incompetence often demonstrated by people with milder forms of retardation. It is with these people that diagnosis is often in question, so the distinction is particularly important. Many such people have perfectly adequate skills in most of the areas related to the 10 named skill areas, but they have serious problems in making social judgments about appropriate behavior or carrying on suitable conversations—problems that have serious implications for their successful functioning (Greenspan & Granfield, 1992). These are people who would probably not fit the new definition but who would still need help and support, a description that best defines Joyce's situation (from our case stories). This concern, however, actually underscores the importance of adaptive behavior to the definition, and it suggests that the adaptive skills be expanded rather than reduced.

The AAMR definition by no means presents the only criteria for identifying mental retardation. The newest American Psychiatric Association diagnostic manual, the DSM-IV, has its own definition, one that incorporates much of the 1992 AAMR definition (including the adaptive skill areas) but retains the IQ-based levels of severity rather than the new classification system described below. The American Psychological Association's own Division on Mental Retardation has also developed its own definition (Jacobson & Mulick, 1996). This definition is similar to the 1983 AAMR version (relying on general adaptive behavior rather than separate skill areas), except that it defines the developmental period to age 22, which is in line with the Developmental Disabilities Act. Young people between ages 18 and 22 make up the population most often affected by traumatic brain injury from traffic accidents. Raising the eligibility level to 22 makes this group eligible for MR services.

The Mental Retardation and Developmental Disabilities Division of the Council for Exceptional Children has also expressed reservations about the 1992 definition. Although the division acknowledges the AAMR committee's innovation and applauds the open vigorous discussion generated by the new definition, it questions the effect of the changes on teacher training programs and funding, and it asks that the committee study these and several of the other issues expressed above (Smith, 1994).

CLASSIFICATION AND LEVELS OF FUNCTIONING

The most radical departure from previous definitions in the 1992 revision involves the system of classification. Until now, AAMR definitions have included classification systems based on IQ scores, as do the American Psychiatric Association and the World Health Organization.

IQ- and Ability-Based Systems

The earliest IQ-based classification system, suggested by the American Association for the Study of the Feebleminded, used the terms *moron* (IQ 75–50), *imbecile* (IQ 50–25), and *idiot* (IQ less than 25). In 1961, these terms were replaced by AAMR-suggested classifications: *mild, moderate, severe,* and *profound.* Table 4.1 shows the IQ guidelines used for three IQ-based systems. Table 4.2 describes functional outcomes for each level of severity.

The IQ classification requires that an individuals' IQ test score be matched to a severity level: Assumptions have been made about expected outcomes, and

Table 4.1 IQ-Based Systems of Classification

	AAMR (before 1992)	APA (DSM-IV)	Educational Expectations*
Mild	50–70	50–55 to 70	Educable 55–75
Moderate	35–50	35–40 to 50–55	Trainable 20–55
Severe	20–35	20–25 to 35–40	Custodial <20
Profound	<20	<20 or 25	

*Now rarely used

Table 4.2 Expected Outcomes at the Severity Levels

	Academic	Daily Living	Work
Mild	Second- to fifth-grade achievement	High degree of independence	Totally or partially self-supporting
Moderate	Functional word recognition and math skills	Capable of most self-care and community mobility with some supervision	Community employment with some support
Severe	Preschool or kindergarten skills (counting and color recognition)	Highly supervised	Supervised community or workshop
Profound	Requires care for all basic needs		

Intermittent	Supports on an "as-needed" basis, usually in life transition or crisis
Limited	Consistent but often time-limited support
Extensive	Daily support of a long-term nature
Pervasive	Constant, high-intensity, life-sustaining supports across environments
Four dimensions	Dimension I: Intellectual functioning and adaptive skills
	Dimension II: Psychological and emotional considerations
	Dimension III: Physical health and etiology considerations
	Dimension IV: Environmental considerations

SOURCE: Adapted from Luckasson et al., 1992.

FIGURE 4.4 Levels of support intensity

intervention plans were to be based on this information. In reality, however, this IQ-based classification system provided little information for intervention, and it was often actually misleading (see Chapter 5, "Assessment of Mental Retardation").

The 1992 Classification System

The 1992 revision uses neither IQ scores to classify the severity of mental retardation nor direct measures of functional abilities. Instead, it bases level of severity on the intensity of needed supports in four dimensions as illustrated in Figure 4.4.

As you can see, this method replaces a simple system of classifying by IQ score with a complex analysis of the individual's functioning and her needs for support in several important life areas. The new definition requires clinical analysis of adaptive skills and abilities in far more detail than has previously been the case. First, the level of functioning and needed supports must be determined for each skill area within the four dimensions in Figure 4.4. Dimension I, for example, Intellectual Functioning and Adaptive Skills, involves assessment in 11 areas—IQ and each of the 10 adaptive skills.

Dimension I requires assessment of cognitive and adaptive skills according to developmental level. Dimension II considers the psychological and emotional functioning of the individual according to DSM-IV, while Dimension III considers the physical and health needs of the individual including those related to the cause of any existing retardation. Finally, Dimension IV requires an ecological analysis of the family, home, neighborhood, larger community, and other environments in which the individual lives (Luckasson et al., 1992).

Rationale for Change

Unfortunately or not, human beings do not classify easily. Thus, with the IQ-based systems, one can readily determine that an overall test score qualifies for a particular level of severity, but an individual's actual skills and abilities are usually far more variable than this system implies (Baumeister, 1987). If, for example, someone has communication abilities in the profound range and visual–spatial problem-solving abilities in the mild range (which is not uncommon for people with autism), where should he be classified? Less extreme but no less real variability in individual skills is common in many people with MR, but variability cannot be detected from an overall IQ score. (This important matter is discussed in Chapter 5, "Assessment of Mental Retardation.")

The new classification system is designed to focus on the actual functioning of people with retardation in specific environments. Where the previous system "averaged over" and often obscured various skills and abilities in order to determine a single classification level, the new version relies on multiple levels. The committee hopes to promote interdisciplinary coordination of services by requiring relevant assessment across several disciplines and orienting the system toward and making it consistent with service delivery. It is important to note that the 1992 definition is designed to provide the most useful information to guide intervention and public policy. To that end, it is responsive to the opinions of those with mental retardation and their families by facilitating the development of inclusionary services. In this context, Reiss (1994) has observed that "consumers do not want to be tested, they want to be included" (p. 6).

Debate Over Classification

According to some professionals, however, the new classification scheme is overly cumbersome. Even the older IQ-based scheme has been plagued with inconsistencies in application (Taylor & Kaufmann, 1991), and some critics believe that disparities are infinitely more likely under the new scheme. Further, researchers especially are concerned about adopting a system that bears no relationship to the previous one, on which 30 years of research has been based.

The validity of research outcomes, however, is integrally tied to the validity of initial data. When research subjects are grouped by perceived similarities, validity demands that people within the groups must indeed be similar. There has long been evidence, though, that the categories of mild, moderate, severe, and profound do not consist of homogenous groups but contain considerable variability (Berkson, 1966; Baumeister, 1987). Although there is some similarity in that MR at the moderate, severe, and profound levels is more likely to be organic in origin than at the mild levels, these organic conditions are numerous and present varying intellectual and behavioral characteristics. For example, the cognitive abilities and behavioral characteristics typically manifested by people with Fragile X are decidedly different from those ordinarily associated with Down syndrome. If we study a group of individuals who are thought to have moderate retardation and expect them to be similar when they are, in fact, enormously different, it does not matter whether the classification system was easy to use. Information from such a system is worse than useless: It is misleading. To make matters worse, there is evidence that the *inter-rater reliability* for diagnosis of severity levels is low (Macmann & Barnett, 1993). This means that many times those who are doing the assessment disagree about which classification someone should receive in the first place.

Still, the new classification does not clarify the genuine differences between most people who are now classified with mild retardation and those who have more severe conditions (MacMillan, Gresham, & Siperstein, 1993). These differences are thought to include causation, typical abilities, effective intervention, and likely outcome. As mentioned above, the causes of mild retardation are less likely to be known than are those for more severe conditions.

People with mild retardation of unknown etiology have been described as **familial** or **cultural–familial** (Zigler & Hodapp, 1986), terms that refer to retardation having no known cause but appearing most frequently in people living in poverty. This large number of people makes up the vast majority of those with the mild classification, and most people with retardation are classified at the mild level. Some researchers have assumed that retardation for this group is the result of normal genetic variability in intelligence (Zigler, Balla, & Hodapp, 1984), although it is certain that people growing up in poverty are at risk for many reasons. Intervention for this population is likely to be unique in many ways, and such people are more likely to move out of the retarded range of functioning.

The previous mild retardation classification did not distinguish between cultural-familial and organic retardation—it confused them (MacMillan, Gresham, & Siperstein, 1993). Mild retardation is not necessarily synonymous with inorganic causation, because people with mild retardation sometimes have clearly organic conditions (in Down syndrome, for example.) And people who grow up in impoverished circumstances can still have retardation for related but organic reasons such as lead poisoning. In fact, for many people with milder forms of retardation, there are several possible causal factors that can be cumulative or interactive in their effects. The assumption that the mild category includes a homogenous group almost certainly creates research difficulties in itself. Some theorists have proposed that people with mild retardation of unknown origin and relatively good adaptive behavior should be classified in a group separate from the retardation category, one that might be titled "generalized learning disability" (MacMillan, Siperstein, & Gresham, 1996).

Some researchers are also concerned because a system based on supports describes not only personal characteristics, but also aspects of the environment. In a highly nurturing environment, let us say, someone might function more independently and therefore need fewer supports than in a stressful environment. In this case, the intensity of supports needed tells us less about the person than about the environment in which she is living.

> **FOR DISCUSSION**   *For what reasons would distinguishing between personal characteristics and environmental aspects of MR be important?*

The 1992 AAMR manual, in fact, stresses the integral nature of the person–environment interaction. But for many researchers, it has been important to distinguish the characteristics of the individual from those of the environment. IQ scores do often provide a relatively stable indication of intellectual functioning, whereas support designations are expected to fluctuate with environmental circumstances.

If, however, MR is not simply an individual characteristic but really does result from an interaction between personal attributes and environmental characteristics (an idea supported in this text), it *must* be studied in the context of environment. You may remember that theorists such as Bronfenbrenner describe the futility of understanding *any* developmental phenomenon outside of its environmental and cultural context (see Chapter 2). Beyond that, culturally fair assessment demands that we consider environmental factors (Schalock et al., 1994).

FOR DISCUSSION *Is mental retardation entirely a personal characteristic or is it also a social and cultural one? On what evidence do you base your position?*

Different Goals and Purposes

Developing a simple, straightforward, easy-to-apply, and yet useful and accurately descriptive definition and classification system is no small challenge. Much work remains in this area. One element that adds to controversy over any definition of retardation is the differing goals and purposes of those who use the definition. Parents of children with intellectual challenges may want identification so that they can receive helpful services, while state and federal programs need to accurately identify eligible people. Service providers and teachers want meaningful information about their clients and their students that will contribute to the development of effective intervention plans, and researchers want to understand the causes of retardation and evaluate interventions.

The definitional issues relevant for those with widely pervasive conditions may not be consistent with those for people with milder and subtler deficits (MacMillan, Siperstein, & Gresham, 1996). The answer to the question "What is mental retardation?" may not necessarily be the same as the answer to "How should we define retardation for service eligibility?" or "How should we define retardation for instructional purposes?" (Dever, 1990). Still, everyone involved has a common goal: to contribute in some way to the welfare of those with mental retardation and their families. To that end, one definition may not meet every purpose. Given that natural limitation, the major test of the new AAMR definition will be whether it is actually adopted and applied more successfully than previous definitions have been.

APPLYING THE DEFINITION
TO JOYCE, SUSAN, AND JASON

Now that we have seen the 1992 AAMR definition and have discussed important concerns related to it, how might it be applied to Joyce, Susan, and Jason? All three are currently identified under older existing definitions.

Joyce

As we have seen, Joyce has a learning disabilities label. She was not labeled with MR, because it was decided that her adaptive behavior (her ability to take care of herself and interact with her friends) is similar to her peers. Although her IQ is low and she is having severe academic problems, she does not really fit the typical profile of students with learning disabilities either, because she has no relative academic strengths. Many students with characteristics similar to Joyce's would have no particular designation at all—they are simply overlooked by the special education system. Although Joyce's intellectual problems seem to be confined to academic learning, there are indications that she has subtle but significant difficulty in making decisions and problem solving in her personal life. These problems did not show up on traditional survey-type rating scales of adaptive behavior, but they are real nevertheless. Better measures of adaptive ability would help in more accurately defining her problems. Joyce's difficulties are having serious effects in other areas of her life, despite the help she is currently receiving in her learning disabilities (LD) classroom. Still, as defined by the new AAMR definition, her category probably would not change.

Susan

For the new AAMR definition, it will be important to know how Susan would function adaptively if not for her physical limitations. In other words, would she have adaptive behavior deficits that are related to her *intellectual* functioning? As a practical matter, however, the 1992 manual states that if any doubt exists, decisions should be made in terms of need for services (p. 14). Under the new AAMR definition, Susan's mild classification will be dropped, and she will be classified according to the supports she needs. In Dimension I, Susan will receive extensive supports; and in Dimensions II, III and IV, supports will be intermittent.

Jason

Jason is currently receiving services under the developmental disabilities definition. Whether he qualifies for the AAMR definition must wait for a measure of IQ and some assessment of his adaptive skills. As far as supports are concerned, he is currently receiving limited supports in Dimensions I and III.

▋▋ LOOKING AHEAD ▶

This chapter described several definitions that are importantly related to mental retardation (development disabilities, disability, handicap), discussed sometimes conflicting goals and concepts that affect the creation of definitions, and reviewed the history of AAMR definitions to the present. It also introduced the case stories of three individuals who have intellectual disabilities—stories that will illustrate some of the concerns and challenges faced by actual young people.

The next chapter will build on this definitional information to show how assessments are conducted to determine whether and how an individual fits these definitions. In addition, Chapter 5 will take a detailed look at assessment measures and methods for Susan and Joyce, and it will study several of the specific problems with existing assessment techniques. A complete assessment for Jason is included in Chapter 10, "Early Intervention."

INFOTRAC COLLEGE EDITION

Although the diagnosis of mental retardation results in benefits in the form of services, there is a stigma attached. Enter *stigma* as the keyword in *InfoTrac College Edition,* and find an article that discusses stigma and mental health or disability. How might the author's suggestions for reducing or coping with stigma increase acceptance for those with mental retardation?

REFERENCES

Aloia, G. F., & MacMillan, D. L. (1983). Influence of the EMR label on initial expectations of regular-classroom teachers. *American Journal of Mental Deficiency, 88*(3), 255–262.

American Association on Mental Retardation (AAMR). (1992). *Mental retardation: Definition, classification, and systems of supports* (9th ed.). Washington, DC: Author.

Baumeister, A. A. (1987). Mental retardation: Some conceptions and dilemmas. *American Psychologist, 42*(8), 796–800.

Beach, M. (1996). Meeting high standards: The challenge of ensuring that homeless children are part of it all. *Journal of Education for Students Placed at Risk, 1*(4), 295–297.

Berkson, G. (1966). When exceptions obscure the role. *Mental Retardation, 4,* 24–27.

Bromfield, R., Weisz, J. R., & Messer, T. (1986). Children's judgments and attributions in response to the "mentally retarded" label: A developmental approach. *Journal of Abnormal Psychology, 95,* 81–87.

Castles, E. E. (1996). *We're people first: The social and emotional lives of individuals with mental retardation.* Westport, CT: Praeger.

Ceci, S. N., & Williams, W. (1997). Schooling, intelligence, and income. *American Psychologist, 52*(10), 1051–1058.

Dever, R. B. (1990). Defining mental retardation from an instructional perspective. *Mental Retardation, 28*(3), 147–153.

Doll, E. A. (1941). The essentials of an inclusive concept of mental deficiency. *American Journal of Mental Deficiency, 46,* 214–229.

Dowdy, C. A., Smith, T. E., & Nowell, C. H. (1992). Learning disabilities and vocational rehabilitation. *Journal of Learning Disabilities, 25*(7), 442–447.

Dunn, L. M. (1968). Special education for the mildly retarded: Is much of it justifiable? *Exceptional Children, 35,* 5–22.

Dusek, J. B., & O'Connell, E. J. (1973). Teacher expectancy effects on the achievement test performance of elementary school children. *Journal of Educational Psychology, 65,* 371–377.

Forness, S. (1994). *Syndromes on the margins of mental retardation.* Keynote address to the Fourth International Conference on Mental Retardation and Developmental Disabilities, Arlington, Heights, IL.

Frankenberger, W., & Fronzaglio, K. (1991). States' definitions and procedures for identifying children with mental retardation: Comparison over nine years. *Mental Retardation, 29*(6), 315–321.

Frankenberger, W., & Harper, J. (1988). States' definitions and procedures for identifying children with mental retardation: Comparison of 1981–1982 and 1985–1986 guidelines. *Mental Retardation, 26*(3), 133–136.

Franks, D. J. (1971). Ethnic and social characteristics of children in EMR and LD classes. *Exceptional Children, 37,* 537–538.

Fryers, T. (1993). Epidemiological thinking in mental retardation: Issues in taxonomy and population frequency. In N. W. Bray, *International review of research in mental retardation,* Vol. 19. Novato, CA: Academic Therapy Publications.

Greenspan, S., & Granfield, J. (1992). Reconsidering the construct of mental retardation: Implications of a model of social competence. *American Journal on Mental Retardation, 96*(4), 442–453.

Gresham, F. M., MacMillan, D. L., & Bocian, K. M. (1998). Agreement between school study team decisions and authoritative definitions in classification of students at-risk for mild disabilities. *School Psychology Quarterly, 13*(3), 181–191.

Grossman, H. J. (Ed.). (1973). *Manual on terminology and classification in mental retardation.* Washington, DC: American Association on Mental Deficiency.

———. (1977). *Manual on terminology and classification in mental retardation.* Washington, DC: American Association on Mental Deficiency.

———. (1983). *Classification in mental retardation.* Washington, DC: American Association on Mental Deficiency.

Guttmacher, M., & Weihofen, H. (1952). *Psychiatry and the law.* New York: W. W. Norton.

Hardman, M. L., Drew, C. J., & Egan, M. W. (1996). *Human exceptionality.* Boston: Allyn & Bacon.

Hastings, R. P. (1994). On "good" terms: Labeling people with mental retardation. *Mental Retardation, 32*(5), 363–365.

Heber, R. (1959). *A manual on terminology and classification in mental retardation. American Journal of Mental Deficiency* monograph supplement, 62.

———. (1961). *A manual on terminology and classification in mental retardation* (2nd ed.). *American Journal of Mental Deficiency* monograph supplement, 64.

Jacobs, W. (1978). The effect of the learning disability label on classroom teachers' ability objectively to observe and interpret child behaviors. *Learning Disability Quarterly, 1,* 50–55.

Jacobson, J. W. (1991). Administrative and policy dimensions of developmental disabilities services. In J. L. Matson & J. A. Mulick (Eds.), *Handbook of mental retardation* (2nd ed.). Elmsford, NY: Pergamon.

————, & Mulick, J. A. (1996). *Manual of diagnosis and professional practice in mental retardation.* Washington, DC: American Psychological Association.

Kiely, M., & Lubin, R. A. (1991). Epidemiological methods. In J. L. Matson & J. A. Mulick (Eds.), *Handbook of mental retardation* (2nd ed.). Elmsford, NY: Pergamon.

Larry P. v. *Wilson Riles* (1979). 495 F. Supp. 96 (N.D. Cal. 1979) Aff'd (9th Cir. 1984).

Luckasson, R., Coulter, D. L., Polloway, E. A., Reiss, S., Schalock, R. L., Snell, M. E., Spitalnik, D. M., & Stark, J. A. (1992). *Mental retardation: Definition, classification, and systems of supports.* Washington, DC: American Association on Mental Retardation.

Macmann, G. M., & Barnett, D. W. (1993). Reliability of psychiatric and psychological diagnoses of mental retardation severity: Judgments under naturally occurring conditions. *American Journal on Mental Retardation, 97*(5), 559–567.

MacMillan, D. L., Gresham, F. M., & Siperstein, D. L. (1993). Conceptual and psychometric concerns about the 1992 AAMR definition of mental retardation. *American Journal on Mental Retardation, 98*(3), 325–335.

MacMillan, D. L., Siperstein, G. N., & Gresham, F. M. (1996). A challenge to the viability of mild mental retardation as a diagnostic category. *Exceptional Children, 62*(4), 356–380.

Mendels, G. E., & Flanders, J. P. (1973). Teacher expectations and pupil performance. *American Educational Research Journal, 10,* 203–212.

Mercer, J. R. (1973). *Labeling the mentally retarded.* Berkeley: University of California Press.

Ogbu, J. U. (1995) Origins of human competence: A cultural-ecological perspective. In N. R. Goldberger & J. Veroff (Eds.), *The culture and psychology reader* (pp. 245–275). New York: University Press.

————. (1997). Understanding the school performance of urban blacks: Some essential background knowledge. In H. J. Walber, O. Reyes, & R. P. Weissberg (Eds.), *Children and youth: Interdisciplinary perspectives* (pp. 190–222). Thousand Oaks, CA: Sage.

Polloway, E. A., Smith, J. D., Patton, J. R., & Smith, T. E. C. (1996). Historic changes in mental retardation and developmental disabilities. *Education and Training in Mental Retardation and Developmental Disabilities, 31,* 3–12.

President's Committee on Mental Retardation. (1970). *The six-hour retarded child.* Washington, DC: U.S. Government Printing Office.

Reiss, S. (1994). Issues in defining mental retardation. *American Journal on Mental Retardation, 99*(1), 1–7.

Reschly, D. J. (1990). Adaptive behavior. In A. Thomas & J. Grimes (Eds.), *Best practices in school psychology* (2nd ed., pp. 29–42). Washington, DC: National Association of School Psychologists.

Rosenthal, R. (1987). Pygmalion effects: Existence, magnitude, and social importance. *Educational Researcher, 16*(9), 37–41.

————, & Jacobson, L. (1966). Teacher expectancies: Determinants of pupils' IQ gains. *Psychological Reports, 19,* 115–118.

————, & Jacobson, L. (1968). *Pygmalion in the classroom.* New York: Holt, Rinehart & Winston.

Rowitz, L. (1991). Social and environmental factors and developmental handicaps in children. In J. L. Matson & J. A. Mulick (Eds.), *Handbook of mental retardation* (2nd ed.). Elmsford, NY: Pergamon.

Salvia, J., & Ysseldyke, J. E. (1995). *Assessment* (6th ed.). Boston: Houghton Mifflin.

Schalock, R. L., Stark, J. A., Snell, M. E., Coulter, D. L., Polloway, E. A., Luckasson, R., Reiss, S., & Spitalnik, D. M. (1994). The changing conception of mental retardation: Implications for the field. *Mental Retardation, 32*(3), 181–193.

Severance, L., & Gasstrom, L. (1977). Effects of the label "mentally retarded" on causal explanations of success and failure outcomes. *American Journal of Mental Deficiency, 81,* 547–555.

Smith, J. D. (1994, September). The revised AAMR definition of mental retardation: The MRDD position. *Education and Training in Mental Retardation and Developmental Disabilities,* 179–183.

Smith, R. W., Osborne, L. T., Crim, D., & Rhu, A. H. (1986). Labeling theory as applied to learning disabilities. *Journal of Learning Disabilities, 19*(4), 195–202.

Somogyi, K. M. (1995). On "good" terms: Labeling people with mental retardation. Response. *Mental Retardation, 33*(1), 63.

Taylor, R. L., & Kaufmann, S. (1991). Trends in classification usage in the mental retardation literature. *Mental Retardation, 29*(6), 367–371.

Thorndike, R. L. (1968). Review of *Pygmalion in the classroom* by R. Rosenthal and L. Jacobson. *American Educational Research Journal, 5,* 708–711.

Tredgold, A. F. (1937). *A textbook of mental deficiency.* Baltimore, MD: Wood.

U.S. Department of Education (1990). *To assure the free appropriate public education of all handicapped children: Eleventh annual report to Congress on the implementation of the Education of the Handicapped Act.* Washington, DC: Author.

U.S. Department of Health and Human Services (1996). State-specific rates of mental retardation—United States, 1993. *Morbidity and Mortality Weekly Report, 45*(3), 61–67.

Wrench, M. (1994). Personal communication.

Ysseldyke, J. E., & Foster, G. G. (1978). Bias in teachers' observations of emotionally disturbed and learning disabled children. *Exceptional Children, 44*(8), 613–615.

Zetlin, A., & Murtaugh, M. (1990). Whatever happened to those with borderline IQs? *American Journal of Mental Retardation, 94*(5), 463–469.

Zigler, E., Balla, D. & Hodapp, R. (1984). On the definition and classification of mental retardation. *American Journal of Mental Deficiency, 89*(3), 215–230.

Zigler, E., & Hodapp, R. M. (1986). *Understanding mental retardation.* New York: Cambridge University Press

5

Assessment of Mental Retardation

INTERDISCIPLINARY APPROACH

What is the purpose of assessment? The answer to that question guides and determines who is assessed, how they are assessed, what skills and abilities are assessed, and by whom. If the purpose is diagnosis and the requirement is simply to provide a "yes" or "no," then the assessment will be quite different from one that seeks rich and context-specific details. The 1992 AAMR definition clearly intended to encourage assessment practices that would compile detailed information not only for diagnosis but also for developing effective service delivery. Whereas this chapter focuses on IQ tests and measures of adaptive behavior, Chapters 10 ("Early Intervention"), 11 ("Behavioral and Cognitive Interventions"), and 12 ("Educational Issues") describe procedures and applications of assessment principles.

Intervention-oriented assessment must be interdisciplinary, because no single discipline offers the knowledge and expertise to understand every need or measure skills and abilities that best predict success in every endeavor. No one professional can keep up with new developments in several, let alone all, disciplines. The task of understanding individual functioning and support requirements in academics, daily living, communication, social relationships, emotional adjustment, health, and work is of necessity a team effort. Relevant disciplines may include audiology, neurology, occupational therapy, pediatrics, physical therapy, psychiatry, psychology, social work, speech and language pathology, and special education.

The effective interdisciplinary approach requires that professionals put aside turf concerns in favor of mutual cooperation. One could argue that mental retardation is primarily medical in origin, or behavioral, or intellectual, or cultural— but no single conceptualization provides a truly adequate description. Practitioners must have the breadth of vision to recognize that mental retardation is not simply a medical or an educational problem, but also one that affects behavior, relationships, motivation, and emotional adjustment.

In interdisciplinary assessment, teams composed of professionals from various disciplines work together to understand the functioning and needs of someone with mental retardation. Sometimes these teams are **fixed,** with the same individuals working together for every assessment; at other times they may be **flexible,** with different team members participating in different assessments (Wodrich & Joy, 1986). University-affiliated facilities for people with developmental disabilities usually have fixed teams. Most individuals selected for assessment, however, are first referred to one professional, often a psychologist or pediatrician, who is responsible for making any further referrals.

The multidisciplinary team approach depends upon each professional's general familiarity with the domain, training, and assessment procedures in other disciplines. To make an appropriate referral, the initiating parent or professional must first recognize the probable nature of a problem. If the first referral is to a physician or psychologist rather than to a fixed team, then that practitioner must be able to identify any other needs requiring further consultation. Not everyone requires every available service, so it is important to recognize not only which referrals are not needed but also those that are essential. Issues of expense and time must be balanced with adequate comprehensiveness to avoid redundancy. Table 5.1 describes some of the signs that indicate particular referrals.

Table 5.1 Indicators and Rationale for Appropriate Referrals

	Indication	Rationale
Referral to Psychologist	*Obviously* delayed development in child 6 weeks to 2 years	Referral may not be appropriate for subtle conditions, because cognitive measures can confirm only severe delays
	Suspected delayed development in child older than 2 years	IQ measures after 2 years of age offer better prediction of risk
	Academic problems unresponsive to informal intervention	Intellectual testing can provide information for intervention and help determine eligibility for special services
Referral to Special Educator	School-age children initially assessed outside of school	Educational observation and data are essential for intervention
	School-age children in need of remedial instruction	
Referral to Audiologist	Frequent ear infections or	High incidence of associated hearing loss
	family history of sensorineural hearing loss with	Loss may be hereditary
	complaints of hearing difficulty or observation of possible hearing loss	Examination can produce conclusive findings. All people are testable
Referral to Speech-Language Pathologist	Preschoolers with one or more years' delay in vocabulary, grammar, or articulation	There may be an identifiable and treatable language problem
	School-age children with verbal IQ 15 points less than performance IQ	
	Stuttering or dysfluency *after* age 4 or 5	Earlier diagnosis and treatment is not advisable; the problem may be transient
Referral to Occupational Therapist	Child who requires detailed assessment or planning of activities of daily living	Early assessment and intervention prevents learning of inappropriate motor habits
	Child with physical disabilities involving severe motor problems	Specialized expertise facilitates intervention plans
Referral to Physical Therapist	Individual with severe motor problems	Proper positioning and appropriate exercise may be required
Referral to Developmental Pediatrician	Child with history of severe birth trauma or prematurity	May be at high risk for learning and behavior problems
	Child with unusual physical appearance *and* delayed development	Physical appearance may be relevant in identifying cause of mental retardation
	Child with school difficulty *and* complex or chronic medical disorders	Appropriate intervention must incorporate management of medical issues
Referral to Child Psychiatrist	Child with suspected attention deficit (may refer to pediatrician instead)	Medication may be required
	Child with delay and evidence of family or parental dysfunction (may refer instead to psychologist or social worker)	Family or parent treatment could be important to intervention for child
	Unusual combination of symptoms or behaviors across many areas	May have additional psychiatric diagnosis

(continued)

Table 5.1 *(continued)*

	Indication	Rationale
Referral to Neurologist	Neurological indications on psychological testing	Specific diagnosis requires consultation
	Developmental plateau, regression, or impairment that seems to "come and go"	Possible degenerative disorder or seizure activity
	Significant central nervous system trauma	May assist in establishing prognosis and in shaping intervention

SOURCE: Adapted from D. L. Wodrich & J. E. Joy (1986), Practical issues and illustrative cases. In D. L. Wodrich & J. E. Joy (Eds.), *Multidisciplinary assessment of children with learning disabilities and mental retardation* (pp. 281–308). Baltimore, MD: Paul H. Brookes.

Although various disciplines usually take responsibility for their particular assessment areas in an interdisciplinary manner, functions can sometimes become transdisciplinary. Educators, for example, often perform behavioral as well as educational and curriculum assessments, whereas psychologists sometimes test not only intellectual abilities, behavior, and personality, but also academic skills. The following sections describe several important assessment areas in more detail.

MEDICAL ASSESSMENT

A child's physician is often the first professional to suspect a developmental disability. He or she may be an obstetrician, a pediatrician, or a family practitioner. These licensed medical doctors rely on several methods to assist in the diagnosis, including consultation with one another and referrals to other professionals who are members of either fixed or flexible teams.

Motor and Sensory Development

Abnormal motor and muscle conditions, most notably in cerebral palsy, are often associated with mental retardation. To spot possible atypical **motor development,** physicians are especially alert to infants' and children's muscle tone, posture, and reflex activity. Development in relation to motor milestones is an important indicator as well. Assessment of **sensory development** includes tests of tactile sensitivity, vision, taste, and hearing.

Language Milestones

Language development is an important predictor of later IQ for infants and young children (Capute & Accardo, 1991). Although early motor development (such as crawling and walking) has little relation to intellectual precocity, early language development often predicts later exceptional intellectual performance. Likewise, delayed language can foreshadow problems in later intellectual development. This relationship is not perfect, and extensively delayed language development can indicate deafness (or other conditions) rather than mental retardation. Still, physicians are generally alert to language growth as an important indicator of more general development. The CLAMS test (see Table 2.1 in Chapter 2) is an example of a language-milestone scale used by physicians.

Behavior

Sometimes behavior is the best cue to abnormal development. A child's interest in others, his reaction to toys, and his tendency to imitate or engage in gesture games such as "patty-cake" or "peekaboo" provide important indications of his developmental progress and functioning. Physicians often purposefully interact with and observe children to understand their social and behavioral development.

Physiological Testing

Physiological testing can sometimes help determine the cause of mental retardation, as well as identify medical problems associated with it. **Computerized axial tomography** (CAT) scans can locate structural brain abnormalities, **positron emission tomography** (PET) scans measure metabolic brain activity, and **electroencephalograms** (EEGs) measure electrical activity in the brain. In addition, chemical testing often reveals conditions associated with abnormal brain chemistry such as phenylketonuria (PKU) that can result in mental retardation. The presence of other toxins—such as the all-too-common case of lead—also can be detected.

INTELLECTUAL ASSESSMENT

Intellectual functioning has historically been assessed through the IQ test, and such testing can provide important information. IQ testing has been strongly debated over the last three decades, however. Before we go into detail about the methods of intellectual assessment, we must consider some of the conceptual issues and problems that are associated with IQ testing (problems with IQ tests are also discussed in Chapters 3 and 4).

In Chapter 3, we discussed the development of the first IQ test by Binet and Simon and its subsequent wide acceptance for diagnosing mental retardation. Remember that Binet's intention was to measure abilities in order to identify those who could profit from special education. He did not consider his test a measure of innate potential, yet for most of the 20th century, IQ was mistakenly considered an innate characteristic.

Reifying the Concept

Subsequent research has discovered that IQ scores remain quite stable over time, especially after 5 or 6 years of age. As a result, the intelligence quotient has gradually become confused with a personal trait or individual attribute, and it is often considered as invariable and unchangeable as adult height. The IQ, however, is not a tangible part of an individual's makeup. One does not have an IQ as one has hands or a nervous system; rather, IQ names a test upon which someone can have a score. Although a test score is necessarily related to individual characteristics (such as brain functioning or motivation), it is not one of those characteristics itself. When a concept or idea that has no physical reality begins to be treated as if it did, then that concept is said to be **reified.** Reification clouds thinking, because it confuses intangible notions with physical reality.

Further, that something *usually* does not change (IQ scores are quite stable) is not to say that it never does. IQ can and does vary, although the lower someone's IQ test performance the less *likely* it is to change (Crnic, 1988; Keogh, Bernheimer, & Guthrie, 1997). This is because quite low scores (below approximately 50) usually do reflect organic brain damage, and where brain damage exists, dramatic improvements in the abilities tapped by IQ tests are unlikely.

Data regarding IQ stability are based on averages for groups of people and help us understand the usual or typical course of events for most people. Such information, however, cannot be applied with certainty to an individual, for what *usually* happens is not what *always* happens. Put another way, even though IQ scores usually remain the same, scores for particular individuals do sometimes improve (see the results of early intervention research in Chapter 10). Therefore, it is important to retain an open mind about the specific outcome for a particular person, while retaining a realistic outlook about the probabilities. For those who work in intervention, this requires a delicate yet crucial balance: One must maintain a positive outlook about growth potential while not pressuring someone to perform the impossible.

> **FOR DISCUSSION**   *Do you agree that it can be difficult to hold high expectations for a child with MR and still not expect too much? How can a teacher or other professional know if she is expecting too little or too much?*

Nature–Nurture

The so-called nature–nurture debate refers to the ageless (and seemingly endless) arguments over whether intelligence is more strongly affected by nature (genetics) or by nurture (environment)—an issue obviously central to assumptions about the meaning of IQ scores. Certainly every scientific question or hypothesis has political implications, but those surrounding the question "How much is IQ determined by heredity and how much can it be influenced by environment?" are particularly obvious. If it is assumed that intelligence is primarily a birthright, then public attitudes toward programs to improve intellectual deficits are likely to be markedly different than if intelligence is thought to be principally shaped by environment. Proponents of either side cite the political implications.

A psychometrician who considers genetic influence overwhelmingly important wrote in *The Atlantic Monthly:* "If people differ genetically in their capacities for school and work, then at least some of society's inequalities cannot be wiped out by merely equalizing opportunity" (Hernstein, 1982, p. 74). In the same article, an adherent of the environmental view is quoted as accusing the "hereditarians" of perpetuating a "counsel of despair" (Hernstein, 1982, p. 73). You may recall in Chapter 3 that we considered the historical affect of genetic and environmental theories on public and professional policy; they are no less influential today.

> **FOR DISCUSSION** *Discuss some of the political assumptions and policy implications surrounding the nature–nurture debate.*

The nature–nurture question has generated some of the most emotional and heated debates in all of psychology, and it has sometimes thrown up battle lines involving not only the issue of theoretical dominance but also funding for intervention services and genetic research. It has generated scandal, as in the matter of Cyril Burt, who falsified data about the IQ similarity in identical twins (Hawkes, 1979), and suspicions surrounding the well-known Milwaukee Project, which claimed to raise participating preschoolers' IQs by 30 points. Out of this turmoil, however, has come the gradual realization that we have been asking the wrong question.

Intelligence obviously depends on normal brain functioning, which in turn depends on healthy genes. The normal development of genetic material, however, can only occur within the context of a receptive environment. Both nature and nurture, then, are absolutely indispensable. Furthermore, they are not independent and cannot be studied independently. Environmental events such as auto accidents, toxic poisoning, and early abuse and deprivation clearly affect brain development, while atypical genetic changes such as those occurring with Fragile X and Down syndrome often have important effects on one's ability to relate to the environment. For several decades, researchers have suggested that the pertinent question is not "How *much?*" but rather "*How* do heredity and environment work together in development?" (Berk, 2000; Wingerson, 1998). For those of us interested in helping people with mental retardation, the latter question certainly guides the more relevant exploration.

Some Widely Used IQ Tests

Because the IQ previously was the basis of diagnosis and because it is still used so widely, it is important to understand how the IQ test is administered and be familiar with the skills and abilities the test is designed to measure. Whereas the famous Stanford-Binet test (derived from the original Binet IQ test) set the example of content and method for all others, the Wechsler tests are now used more often, although the Kaufman Assessment Battery for Children (K-ABC) has also gained popularity. All of these tests are individually administered—that is, one-on-one between clinician and test taker; this is essential for genuine diagnosis of intellectual disabilities. Group tests may be less expensive and less time-consuming to administer, but they do not provide adequate information for individual diagnosis.

Wechsler Tests The three Wechsler tests in current use offer the advantage of specificity for particular age groups (Wechsler, 1981; 1989; 1991). For people with more severe mental retardation, however, tests often must be chosen according to

One-on-one assessment is essential for accurate diagnosis of intellectual abilities

© Laura Dwight/Corbis

mental rather than chronological age. The Wechsler tests are listed in Table 5.2 according to the age group for which each is intended.

Table 5.3 lists the Wechsler Intelligence Scale for Children–Third Edition (WISC-III) subtests. Like the Wechsler Adult Intelligence Scale–Revised (WAIS-R) and WPPSI-R, the WISC-III provides three composite scores. There is an overall IQ for the entire battery, as well as composite scores for both major subdivisions: the *verbal* portion (for verbal thinking skills) and the *performance* section (for visual–spatial reasoning). Each verbal and performance scale is divided further into five subtests, with one optional subtest for the verbal scale and two optional subtests for performance. The specific subtests for the WAIS-R and especially for the WPPSI-R vary slightly, but all three assess similar reasoning skills. From Table 5.3, you can see examples of the cognitive abilities required for each WISC-III subtest, and Figure 5.1 shows examples of terms similar to those found in the subtests.

The reasoning skills in Table 5.3 are examples of those thought most important for each WISC-III subtest, although there is considerable overlap. For instance, short-term memory and attention affect performance on every subtest, but strengths in those areas are particularly likely to influence performance on arithmetic and coding. Receptive and expressive language abilities also facilitate performance on all subtests, but good expressive language skills are likely to increase scores on the verbal scale more than on the performance.

Receptive language refers to the ability to understand what others say; **expressive language** describes the ability to express one's own thoughts to others.

Table 5.2 Wechsler Tests

Scale	Appropriate Testing Age
Wechsler Adult Intelligence Scale–Revised (WAIS-R)	16 years and older
Wechsler Intelligence Scale for Children–Third Edition (WISC-III)	6 years through 16 years, 11 months
Wechsler Preschool and Primary Scale of Intelligence–Revised (WPPSI-R)	3 years through 7 years, 3 months

Table 5.3 Wechsler Intelligence Scale for Children (WISC-III) Subtests and Necessary Reasoning Skills

	Subtest	Reasoning Skills
Verbal Tests	Information	Verbal long-term memory, knowledge of facts, learning experiences
	Similarities	Verbal abstract reasoning
	Arithmetic	Auditory short-term memory or attention, conceptual numerical reasoning
	Vocabulary	Verbal long-term memory, expressive language, learning experiences
	Comprehension	Practical judgment, common sense, and expressive language
	Digit span (optional)	Verbal attention or short-term memory
Performance Tests	Picture completion	Visual attention, visual long-term memory
	Coding	Visual short-term memory or attention, visual tracking
	Picture arrangement	Visual sequential reasoning
	Block design	Visual abstract reasoning
	Object assembly	Visual reasoning and manipulation, visual *gestalt* (see text discussion of the K-ABC)
	Symbol search (optional)	Visual tracking, visual attention
	Mazes (optional)	Visual tracking and planning

People can have strengths or weakness in either area, and it is important that assessment distinguishes between them. Similarly, there is a distinction between visual and auditory attention. People with strengths in one modality may or may not be strong in the other.

FOR DISCUSSION *If you were working with someone who had relatively strong abilities in auditory attention and short-term memory but weaker abilities in visual attention, how might you interact with her differently than if her abilities were equally good in both?*

Information (30 questions)

How many legs do you have?
What must you do to make water freeze?
Who discovered the North Pole?
What is the capital of France?

Similarities (17 questions)

In what way are pencil and crayon alike?
In what way are tea and coffee alike?
In what way are inch and mile alike?
In what way are binoculars and microscope alike?

Arithmetic (18 questions)

If I have one piece of candy and get another one, how
  many pieces will I have?
At 12 cents each, how much will 4 bars of soap cost?
If a suit sells for 1/2 of the ticket price, what is the cost of
  a $120 suit?

Vocabulary (32 words)

ball   poem
summer   obstreperous

Comprehension (17 questions)

Why do we wear shoes?
What is the thing to do if you see someone dropping his
  packages?
In what two ways is a lamp better than a candle?
Why are we tried by a jury of our peers?

Digit Span

Digits Forward contains seven series of digits, 3 to 9
  digits in length (Example: 1-8-9).
Digits Backward contains seven series of digits, 2 to 8
  digits in length (Example: 5-8-1-9).

Picture Completion (26 items)

The task is to identify the essential missing part of the
picture.
A picture of a car without a wheel.
A picture of a dog without a leg.
A picture of a telephone without numbers on the dial.
An example of a Picture Completion task is shown below.

Picture Arrangement (12 items)

The task is to arrange a series of pictures into a meaningful sequence.

Block Design (11 items)

The task is to reproduce stimulus designs using four or
nine blocks. An example of a Block Design item is shown
below.

Object Assembly (4 items)

The task is to arrange pieces into a meaningful object. An
example of an Object Assembly item is shown below.

Coding

The task is to copy symbols from a key (see below).

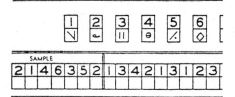

Mazes

The task is to complete a series of mazes.

Note. The questions resemble those that appear on the WISC-R
but are not actually from the test. Chapter 7 describes each subtest in more detail.

FIGURE 5.1 Some examples of items typical of the WISC-III verbal and performance scales

Because all of the performance subtests are timed, and higher scores are earned for faster performance, it is essential to separate intellectual ability from motor performance. The intellectual component of performance tests involves the ability to see and understand spatial relationships, and we assume that faster performance depends on faster reasoning. However, visual–spatial reasoning may be excellent, even though motor problems may impair the ability to carry out physical manipulations. Implications of this distinction are discussed below under "Physical and Sensory Disabilities."

> **FOR DISCUSSION** *In your opinion, to what extent is mental speed a critical component of intelligence? Please explain your reasoning.*

The popularity of the Wechsler tests is based on widely tested psychometric properties and useful conceptual design. For people with exceptionally low abilities, however, the Wechsler tests are too difficult, as are all of the other school-age and preschool-age standardized tests. For such people, assessment must rely primarily on adaptive behavior (see the discussion below) and developmental milestones.

Stanford-Binet The Stanford-Binet test had changed so little since its introduction early in the 20th century that by the 1980s some professionals were recommending that it be discontinued (Reynolds, 1987a). In 1985, however, a major revision was published (SB-IV) (Thorndike, Hagen, & Sattler, 1985), although the new version has met with criticism. Several states have recommended against its use for determining special education placement, and there is some evidence that it presents problems for assessment with preschoolers (Glutting & Kaplan, 1990; Walker, 1987a). Other studies indicate, however, that the 1985 Stanford-Binet has adequate reliability and validity for testing students with mild intellectual disabilities (Dacey, Nelson, & Stoeckel, 1999).

Even so, the design of the SB-IV has several advantages, including applicability for ages 2 through adulthood and flexibility in allowing the examiner to choose from among the 15 subtests rather than run the entire battery. These theoretical advantages, however, contribute to the practical difficulties. Even though the SB-IV is intended for preschoolers, several of the subtests are inappropriate for such young people, and its test–retest reliability is extremely low for people younger than 5 (Kamphaus, Kaufman, & Harrison, 1990; Singh, Oswald, & Ellis, 1998).

What is more, the sample used to standardize the SB-IV is not representative of the U.S. population. It includes significantly fewer people from lower socioeconomic backgrounds and substantially more with college degrees (Reynolds, 1987b; Walker, 1987b). Although standardization data were weighted in an effort to counter this known bias, statistical error is necessarily introduced as a result (Reynolds, 1987b). When standardization data do not adequately reflect the performance of a particular population, then the relative meaning of scores for those people is obscure. Probably because of these problems, the SB-IV is used less widely than the Wechsler tests. Finally, there is evidence that both the SB-IV and the older Form L-M are inappropriate for assessing younger children with mild retardation and anyone thought to have more severe mental retardation (Wilson, 1992). Recent studies show, however, that prediction for preschoolers is better when two or three rather than all four factors are considered (Kaplan & Alfonso, 1997).

Kaufman Assessment Battery for Children   The K–ABC is appropriate for children between the ages of 2½ and 12½ years (Kaufman & Kaufman, 1983). Like the SB–IV, the K–ABC has a flexible design, but it also has good test–retest reliability for preschoolers and uses an adequate population for standardization (Anastasi, 1988; Kamphaus, Kaufman, & Harrison, 1990). The K–ABC also has the advantage of providing teaching and modeling items for each subtest; these clarify instructions and guide children who may be unfamiliar with similar tasks.

Whereas the Wechsler tests divide subtests to reflect verbal and visual–spatial reasoning, the K–ABC includes scales designed to reflect the mental processes of simultaneous and sequential reasoning. **Simultaneous reasoning** describes the ability to process several pieces of information at one time in a holistic or **gestalt** manner; **sequential reasoning** is the ability to order pieces of information reasonably (step-by-step) and logically (one after the other). Still, there has been some question whether the simultaneous and sequential processing scales really reflect these mental processes or whether they might actually demonstrate other memory and nonverbal reasoning skills (Keith & Dunbar, 1984).

The K–ABC also includes a nonverbal scale that relies exclusively on gestures for administration and response, and it can be used to test children with hearing and language problems. In addition, an achievement scale focuses on academic skills.

The K–ABC has been used to illustrate varying patterns of strengths and weaknesses among groups of people with milder forms of mental retardation (Hodapp et al., 1992), but because the lowest possible standard score is 55, it is not appropriate for measuring the abilities of people with more severe disorders.

Infant and Toddler Assessment

Assessing infants and toddlers poses unique challenges. IQ scores for babies and the youngest children are not good predictors of later functioning, except for those who have substantial and clear delays in language and motor functioning. In fact, one of the best predictors of mental retardation is delayed language development, though delays can occur for other reasons such as deafness or specific language impairment.

Bayley Scales   The Bayley Scales of Infant Development, designed for ages 2 months to 2½ years, is the most widely used psychometric measure for determining mental retardation in infants (Bayley, 1993). The Bayley scales include a psychomotor development index, an infant behavior record rating scale, and the mental scale for cognitive skills. Although correlations are low between Bayley scores at early and later ages, as are those between Bayley scores and IQ scores for older children, long-term prediction is better for extremely low-scoring babies,

The Bayley Scales assess intellectual skills in babies and toddlers.

© Laura Dwight/PhotoEdit

and the Bayley test therefore can be useful as a screening device to identify babies who may profit from early intervention (Kopp, 1994).

Habituation There is evidence that tests of infant recognition memory (**habituation**) are better predictors of later IQ than are more traditional tests of cognitive skills, and these measures can test even the youngest infants (Rose, Feldman, & Wallace, 1992). The Fagan Test of Infant Intelligence has been highly effective in identifying babies who (without intervention) will eventually manifest serious cognitive delays (Fagan & Detterman, 1992). In fact, some studies show that habituation is just as accurate in predicting mental retardation as **socioeconomic status (SES)** (Fagan, Shepherd, & Knevel, 1991). Living in poverty remains the strongest indicator of risk for MR, but habituation may provide a means of identifying those low SES babies who are especially likely to manifest cognitive problems. It can also aid in identifying at-risk infants from more advantaged backgrounds.

Biases and Limitations of IQ Tests

By now, almost everyone has heard the criticism that IQ testing is "biased." This charge, however, may refer to the test itself or to the examiner. In either case, language and other cultural differences are involved. As we saw in Chapter 4, mistakes in diagnosis and biases in assessment are most relevant for those who test at the upper end of the definitional cutoff.

Language Bias Certainly, if language differences are not taken into consideration, test results can be misleading. In *Diana* v. *California State Board of Education* (1970), a state court ruled that all intelligence testing in California must be carried out in a child's native language. In addition, the Individuals with Disabilities Education Act (IDEA) requires that testing occur in the language used in the home. In actual implementation, however, native language is more often defined as the one the child normally uses in school (Fradd, Figueroa, & Correa, 1989). Problems can then occur because a child may have sufficient skill to get by in school but not the language expertise to do well on an intelligence test. Further complicating matters, a bilingual child might have a real language impairment masked by her poor English so that native language testing is the more important.

Sometimes, English speakers have regional or dialect differences that interfere with testing, and these can involve vocabulary, grammar, and syntax, as well as accent. Such differences can interfere with comprehension of test directions and affect knowledge of content. By the same token, an examiner who is unfamiliar with the rules governing a particular dialect can misinterpret or devalue responses. Responsible IQ testing requires familiarity with and understanding of cultural dialect differences. As a practical matter, however, IQ tests do not translate easily in some languages, and they may not be available in the native language.

Cultural Experiences As you recall, in *Larry P.* v. *Wilson Riles* (1972), a federal court ruled that IQ tests could not be used to place children in special education classes in California, because the tests are biased against minority children. In this sense, *bias* means that tests cover content that minority children are so completely unfamiliar with that they should not be judged by the same standards as children who have grown up in the mainstream culture. In this argument, we see once again, elements of the nature–nurture debate. The viewpoint of the California state court (and of some minority leaders) is that the tests actually judge a child's experience rather than his native intelligence. In fact, the IQ test measures both. If a child's lack of experience results in a low score, then it is neither accurate nor just to treat that failure of experience as if it were a limitation in native intelligence.

Many special educators, however, believe this argument misses the point that children with academic difficulties and low IQ should be entitled to special help, regardless of whether poor performance results from experience or organic causes (Polloway & Rucker, 1997). Some minority families do not want this help, however, because they believe that it is stigmatizing and results in little or no practical benefit. Further, not everyone values the abstract reasoning abilities measured by IQ tests as much as the mainstream culture does, and some people resent having intelligence defined by someone else's rules (Ogbu, 1997).

This debate continues because a disproportionate number of African-American children are still diagnosed with mild MR and placed in special education classes. A high percentage of those students also drop out of school (Oswald et al., 1999). Two crucial questions are implicit in these figures: (1) Are minority children diagnosed with MR truly similar in intellectual functioning to those in the majority population? (2) Is special education less effective for minority children? Unfortunately, these questions remain unanswered.

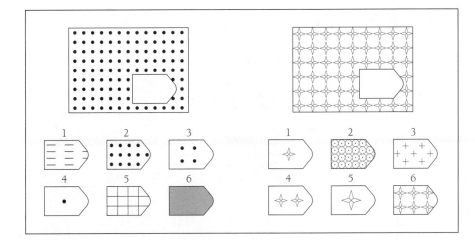

FIGURE 5.2 Items from Raven's Progressive Matrices

SOURCE: © John C. Raven 1938, 1958; © J. C. Raven 1976.

FOR DISCUSSION *Should every child be expected to strive toward the same academic and intellectual goals, like it or not? Please explain.*

Some intelligence tests are considered relatively "culture-free"—including Raven's Standard Progressive Matrices (Raven, 1938) (see Figure 5.2) and the Matrix Analogies Test (Naglieri, 1985). These tests rely primarily on nonverbal content and avoid factual knowledge. The K–ABC also reduces culture bias, because it includes items that are designed to teach desired skills during testing. Cultural experience, however, is by no means limited to verbal content, and learning a new skill during testing does not give the advantage of many years of practice. Because cultural experience necessarily affects performance on any skill, there can be no such thing as a completely culture-free test.

This dilemma underscores the extent to which measuring intelligence relies on clinical judgment as well as scores. It also indicates why assessment of adaptive behavior is so important, and why it is currently receiving increased emphasis. A clinician must use every available tool, including personal observation and interviews, to get the clearest possible view of an individual's abilities. She must learn as much as possible about differing cultural expectations and should consider this information in interpreting performance.

Physical and Sensory Disabilities Intelligence testing also can be problematic for people with physical disabilities. Because visual, auditory, and motor deficits can interfere with the expression of intellectual abilities, valid assessment demands alertness to physical problems and requires methods that can reveal hidden abilities. However, most standardized assessment measures are typically normed on people without disabilities so that scores for those with physical disabilities cannot be

Ruth's Story

Ruth Sienkiewicz-Mercer is a remarkable woman. She has extraordinary persistence, unusual optimism, and profoundly serious physical disabilities. Because of cerebral palsy, she is unable to walk, sit unsupported, speak, or feed herself. She spent 16 years of her life in a state institution for people with mental retardation; for much of that time, she was classified as an "imbecile."

In her biography, *I Raise My Eyes to Say Yes* (Sienkiewicz-Mercer & Kaplan, 1989), Ruth relates the profound personal tragedy that can result from inadequate assessment. The overworked physician who diagnosed Ruth an "imbecile" took only minutes to make his decision. It was several years before anyone noticed that her eyes were alert and that she was responsive to her environment. It was 10 years before her diagnosis was officially changed. During most of that time, she was treated as if she had no ability to understand.

Measuring the intelligence of someone with severe physical disabilities is extremely difficult. Clues to responsiveness and thought patterns are subtle, and their perception requires time, patience, and insight. Adequate assessment cannot be conducted in a few minutes or even in a few hours; it requires repeated sessions over weeks or months, and it must be based primarily on observation of behavior.

Today, Ruth lives in the community with her husband. She is better able now to convey her thoughts and demonstrate her intellectual ability through the use of communication boards. These boards provide more than 1,800 words and phrases from which Ruth can choose to express herself by moving her eyes. In this manner, she told her life story. Even so, many of her more

Ruth Sienkiewicz-Mercer's story illustrates the importance of accurate assessment.

complicated thoughts and feelings remain imperfectly expressed, which is a source of real frustration for her.

For Ruth, it was the people who took time to really look at her and attempt to understand her who made such a positive difference in her life. Those who were patient and seemed to care about her were more successful in understanding her, and they inspired the hope that made her life in the institution more bearable. In telling her story, Ruth provides a living, powerful, and humbling reminder of the crucial human element in our professional responsibilities.

compared with published performance levels. Most standardized tests rely heavily on verbal instructions, and many (notably the Wechsler tests) require high levels of motor skill so that modifications must be made for those with language and motor problems.

Some instruments, however, were developed specifically for people with physical disabilities. The Hiskey–Nebraska Test of Learning Aptitude, for example, tests people with deafness by providing all instructions in pantomime. It does not require that an individual comprehend oral language (Anastasi, 1988).

Testing people with language problems necessarily should concentrate on nonverbal abilities, but assessment for those with motor problems must necessarily focus on verbal abilities—even though severe motor problems also can preclude speech. In such cases, assessment is particularly challenging, and the clinician must be especially perceptive to subtle clues that indicate understanding. The Columbia Mental Maturity Test is designed specifically for those with cerebral palsy and requires only that the child point or nod in response to questions. Please note that the tests just discussed are simply examples. Many others are available, and all of them have both disadvantages and strengths.

Elements of a Useful Intellectual Assessment

Mental retardation's central characteristic is low intellectual functioning, and one important measure of that functioning (though certainly not the only one) continues to be IQ. For this reason, the results of IQ testing are of interest not only to every professional who works in mental retardation, but also to the families of those involved. As a result, anyone studying mental retardation must be able to distinguish the elements of a quality IQ assessment. If any of these elements are missing, then it is entirely appropriate to request them.

Families and professionals need—and should expect—much more from IQ testing than simply a score or set of scores. They need specific information about the meaning of the child's performance with reference to:

1. individual subtest scores,
2. actual skills and mental processes (shown in Table 5.3 for the WISC-III),
3. an explanation of what these scores suggest about the child's strengths and problem areas,
4. **qualitative impressions** that are interpretative and enlightening, and
5. recommendations and suggestions for intervention.

Regardless of which IQ test is used, each element should be present in the final written evaluation that is presented to clients, families, and other practitioners.

Individual Subtest Scores The assessment should include all of the individual subtest scores, not simply the overall composite. Each score should be accompanied by an IQ equivalent (IQE) or be interpreted in a way that the reader can understand each subtest's level of performance. By itself, an overall composite score gives little information—and can even be misleading—because it is derived from several different skills and abilities that often vary widely, especially in people with MR (Kaufman, 1994; Lezak, 1983). This is one reason why the use of overall IQ-score classification levels (*mild, moderate,* etc.) are problematic (see Chapter 4). Because the composite test score is essentially an average, an individual's overall score can represent a level that describes none of her actual abilities.

For example, the child who receives a WISC-III verbal score of 70 and a performance score of 130 is assigned an overall IQ of approximately 100 (average IQ), just as is the child with a performance score of 70 and a verbal score of 130. Yet these children demonstrate vastly different skills and abilities, and neither is "average" in any sense. Although scores so widely disparate as these are rare, they do occur and variability among scores is common. In like manner, the subtests can indicate relatively strong or weak skills in different abilities within the verbal and performance domains. To understand the performance of individual children, we must look at the level of separate skills while often disregarding the composite score.

FOR DISCUSSION *Do you know anyone who seems to be able to figure out how almost any device works just by looking at it? Are these "mechanically inclined" people equally good at understanding and describing complicated verbal ideas? Please be detailed in your examples.*

Because of the way many tests are scored, people with low intellectual abilities sometimes may have scaled subtest scores that all fall at the lowest level, even though there is variability in their performance. There are methods for re-standardizing such scores so that existing variability can be determined; you may want to ask the examiner about this possibility (Burns, 1990).

Skills and Mental Processes The reports also should include a clear description of the skills and mental processes revealed by the subtest scores. Table 5.3 shows some of the skills and abilities reflected by the various subtests for the WISC-III. As examples, receptive or expressive language, abstract verbal reasoning, visual or auditory memory and attention, visual–spatial comprehension and reasoning, and verbal problem-solving abilities are related to the performance on specific subtests (Sattler, 1990). To facilitate understanding, these descriptions should be accompanied by an example of the behavior actually required to complete the task. A child's score of 47 on the block design subtest means little to us, for example, if we do not know what abilities are required to perform the task or what types of real-world tasks may be affected by those abilities.

Strengths and Weaker Areas The IQ test may be the pivotal part of intellectual assessment, but it is not the only measure in a quality assessment. It should serve instead as the basis for the psychologist's hypotheses about individual strengths and weaknesses. Supplemental tasks that test the same or related skills should follow to confirm these hypotheses (Anastasi, 1988; Morison, 1996; Sattler, 1990). If someone appears to have difficulty paying attention to oral language during the IQ test, for example, then she may be given additional tests that require auditory attention to see if she also has trouble with those.

While this hypothesis-testing approach is crucial for a true understanding of strengths and weaknesses, it depends on the clinician's skills and experienced judgment. There have been empirical attempts to determine various patterns of subtest performance that could indicate particular diagnoses, but there is little evidence for the validity of these formula-based interpretations, especially for individual diagnosis, because the same subtest pattern may have different implications for different people (Anastasi, 1988).

Giving too many tests is also possible, leading to the occurrence of chance effects (O'Neill, 1993). The purpose is neither to give as many tests as possible nor to give every available test but to choose one or two relevant supplemental tasks to see if performance is steady. We do not look for a single confirming instance in regard to a hypothesis or referral question but rather for consistent evidence.

Checking the consistency of performance is especially important when we make assumptions about poor task achievement. Confirmation of suspected disabilities too often rests on syllogistic reasoning, as noted in the following example:

1. People with cerebral lesions have difficulty copying designs on the Bender Gestalt (a test of design copying);

2. Rasheed has difficulty copying designs from the Bender Gestalt,

3. therefore Rasheed has cerebral lesions (O'Neill, 1993, p. 69).

The first premise may be correct: Some people with cerebral lesions do have difficulty copying designs. The second observation also may be correct. The assumption stated in number three, however, does not necessarily follow because there may be other reasons for poor performance. In sum: Almost no sign or symptom *always* signifies a particular disorder.

A professor from my graduate training, quoting a professor of his, stressed one of the most important points in testing: "There are many ways to fail a test, but only one way to pass it" (Malone, 1986). For our purposes, this means that people can do poorly on a test for dozens of reasons besides poor ability, and we may never be absolutely sure why they failed. But when someone does well on a test, or even on some items from a test, it is absolutely certain that she has the ability to do that much. For that reason, tests tell us far more about what someone *can* do than what she cannot. Unfortunately, the analysis of test results for people with mental retardation usually focuses on measuring their disabilities, while the more certain and important information—especially for intervention—is the demonstration of their abilities.

Qualitative Impressions of Behavior The importance of qualitative behavioral explanations for understanding intellectual performance has long been recognized but often ignored (Cronbach, 1970; Sattler, 1974). More recently, authorities on testing have emphasized even more strongly the mistakes that can result when IQ scores are isolated from qualitative, observational data (Anastasi, 1988; Sattler, 1990). Reports should include descriptions of the child's approach to tasks and her behavior during the testing, as well as an interpretation of the meaning of that behavior. Was the child equally attentive to both visual and auditory stimuli? Did she make comments that indicated nervousness, aversion, fear, or enthusiasm, or did she otherwise express herself in a way that provided insight?

For people with physical disabilities such as Susan (from our case studies), it can be particularly difficult to obtain meaningful quantitative information, and for them there must be even greater reliance on qualitative indicators. The report also should describe the safeguards taken to ensure that such people's test scores were not unfairly affected by problems of mobility, coordination, vision, or hearing. There also should be a detailed account of their interactions with the tasks (Aiken, 1991).

Specific Recommendations The report should provide specific recommendations for additional referrals and support needs or follow-up testing as appropriate. In particular, the recommendations should respond to the initial reasons for referral, and they should be based on implications of the test results. Readers should not be required to figure out the implications and conclusions for themselves. Recommendations (as well as the whole report) should be clear and nontechnical, and they should suggest a logical next step for families and other professionals to consider.

ASSESSMENT OF ADAPTIVE BEHAVIOR

Adaptive behavior assessment differs markedly from IQ testing because it focuses on an individual's actual performance instead of his capabilities. For purposes of understanding adaptive behavior, the point is to discover whether someone *does* use a skill, rather than whether he *could* use it (Demchak & Drinkwater, 1998).

Remember that measurement of adaptive behavior (AB) is specified by all of the major definitions of mental retardation. The 1997 legislation, PL 105-17 (IDEA), increased the emphasis on assessing adaptive behavior for identification and classification. Many people with more severe forms of mental retardation are not testable with standardized intelligence tests, simply because they are unable to perform the required tasks, yet they are often able to function in numerous other settings and activities. Whereas adaptive behavior assessment is essential at all levels of functioning, it may provide the *only* means for understanding the abilities and needs of people with more severe disabilities.

Adaptive behavior is the best predictor of success in inclusive education and community living for those with mental retardation. It is true that IQ may predict achievement in school, but school accomplishment does not predict later job performance or success as well as do adaptive behavior and the absence of problem behaviors (Nutall & Fozard, 1970). For this reason, and because problem behaviors may preclude the development of more adaptive ones (Demchak & Drinkwater, 1998), behavioral assessment should include determining the presence of problem behaviors (such as excessive rocking and twirling) or self-injurious behaviors (such as head banging) as well as adaptive behavior.

Determining behavioral functioning is crucial to understanding an individual's current performance level, developing programs and strategies to improve that performance, and identifying those people who are most likely to benefit from a particular strategy. Those most often engaged in extensive adaptive behavior assessment include occupational therapists, psychologists, social workers, and special educators.

Interviews

Traditionally, the primary technique for measuring adaptive behavior has been the self-report of a third person (usually a parent or teacher) as recorded on a ranking-scale instrument. Although the *Handbook of Mental Deficiency* (Ellis, 1979) mentions 110 such inventories, three common ones are the Vineland Adaptive Behavior Scale (VABS) (Sparrow, Balla, & Cicchetti, 1984), the AAMR Adaptive Behavior Scale (ABS) (Ellis, 1979; Matson, 1988; Nihira et al., 1974), and the Scales of Independent Behavior (SIB) (Bruininks, Woodcock, Weatherman, & Hill, 1984). All three measures have acceptable validity and reliability, although the ABS has been validated only for people older than 18 (Demchak & Drinkwater, 1998). All AB interview scales focus on information about what the individual "can do" in such areas as sensory-motor, self-help, practical academic skills, and interpersonal functioning. These scales also identify problem behaviors.

Interview ratings can be limited because they rely on the informant's judgment about the *capabilities* of the individual—that is, they ask what someone "can" do rather than record what they actually do. Furthermore, interviews rely on the memory and perception of the parent or teacher for this judgment, and they concentrate entirely on the individual's behavior. The adaptive behavior concept, however, implies an exchange between individual and environment. Someone may respond adaptively only to certain people in the environment, or at particular times of day, or when not hungry, or if he thinks he will get something he wants, or in relation to many other circumstances. Therefore, information about actual performance must rely on behavioral observation. The Adaptive Behavior Scale–School: 2 (ABS–S:2, 1993) measures behavior in relation to particular environmental demands, but unfortunately even though the ABS–S:2 was developed by AAMR, the domains measured do not match the 1992 AAMR definitions, thereby making it less useful for diagnosis (Stinnett, 1997).

Behavioral Observation

Behavioral observation is a critical component of adaptive behavior assessment. With behavioral observation, fewer behaviors can be assessed than with interviews, but they can be described in greater detail. Observations are usually conducted in the individual's natural surroundings and involve specific recording of events, information about the frequency of behaviors and their duration, and such environmental variables as times, places, and circumstances surrounding specific behaviors. Objectives of behavioral assessment often include the development of an intervention plan and an evaluation of the effects of intervention, as well as diagnosis and classification. Because behavioral assessment is rich in detail, it provides useful information for intervention, and when it is central to initial diagnostic assessment, this early information becomes far more useful to families and professionals in working toward effective intervention plans. Behavioral observation typically focuses on behaviors that relate to instructional goals, and such observations should take place in several settings—home, school, work, and other relevant community settings. (See Chapter 11 for techniques of behavioral observation and assessment.)

Functional Assessment

The current direction in adaptive behavior assessment for identification of mental retardation includes elements of both the interview and observational methods.

Table 5.4 An Ecological Inventory for a Community
Setting (Domain) and a Fast Food Restaurant (Environment)

Subenvironment	Activity	Skills
Counter area	Ordering	Go to the counter
		Stand in line
		Move forward with line
		Place order when asked
		Pay for order when asked
		Pick up tray or bag and leave counter
Eating area	Eating meal	Go to eating area
		Scan for empty table
		Go to empty table and sit down
		Eat meal
		Collect trash on tray or in bag
Trash area	Throwing away trash	Go to trash area
		Throw trash in receptacle
		Place tray on top of receptacle

SOURCE: Adapted with permission from M. Demchak & S. Drinkwater (1998). Assessing adaptive behavior. In H. B. Vance (Ed.), *Psychological assessment of children: Best practices for school and clinical settings.* New York: John Wiley.

One approach includes both in a *functional* (or *ecological*) assessment that is designed to gather information about behavior and its environmental context. This information is then used to understand current abilities and plan intervention (Lennox & Miltenberger, 1989). Observations occur in multiple natural settings, and interviews may involve grandparents, siblings, the person himself, parents and teachers, and others who are important in his life. Motivational characteristics are also considered, because they play a crucial part in the performance of people with mental retardation (Merighi, Edison, & Zigler, 1990).

Functional assessment is consistent with both the goals of IDEA (PL 105-17) and the 1992 AAMR definition, and it focuses on highly specific behaviors that are required to perform a particular task. The assessment identifies those aspects of a task in which an individual is competent, as well as those that must be acquired for the person to be most successful. Table 5.4 presents an example of an ecological inventory that might be used to assess skills related to eating in a fast food restaurant (the environment).

Functional assessment is time consuming and involves the participation of highly trained individuals, but if we are to really understand an individual's abilities and gain information useful for intervention, then expensive and time-consuming multiple measures are required. Yet we live with practical and financial realities that limit available resources. For this reason, the interdisciplinary approach can be es-

Table 5.5 Comparison of Traditional and Intervention-Based Assessment

	Traditional Evaluation	Problem-Solving Assessment
Underlying Assumptions	Individual characteristics are the problem. The individual must adapt to fit the situation.	Problem is situation-centered, a mismatch between expectations and individual performance. Situation must adapt to support individual needs.
Purpose	Determine eligibility for special education or other services by documenting student deficiencies.	Identify the supports or accommodations needed for an individual to be successful.
Role of "Assessors" and Information Gathered	Predetermined by eligibility criteria. Generally involves standardized tests.	Will vary according to what information is needed to resolve the concern. Design supports and monitor progress.
Focus	Focus is on the individual, documenting that he or she possesses characteristics that constitute a disability.	Focus is on variables that, when modified, can result in a better match between the individual and the environment.
Setting	Data is primarily gathered in an isolated setting that is conducive to individualized testing.	Data is primarily gathered in the setting of most concern.

SOURCE: Adapted from Forcade, 1993.

pecially valuable. Cooperative efforts that pool information and eliminate duplication of effort can help reduce costs and save time while increasing the quantity and validity of findings.

Today's assessment practices are increasingly driven by an intervention-based, problem-solving approach. Such an approach requires a substantial shift in thinking on the part of those who are involved in gathering information. Table 5.5 compares some of the assumptions of traditional assessment with those of more intervention-oriented methods.

A comprehensive assessment of adaptive behavior will include standardized instruments, informal interviews with others who are significant in the person's life, and direct observation in multiple environments. Such an assessment is a crucial part of initial diagnosis and classification, and it forms the heart of assessment for intervention purposes in school, home, and work settings.

Quality-of-Life Assessment

An increasingly common focus for assessment of adaptive behavior is **quality of life** (QOL), a subtype of functional assessment. The QOL approach relies primarily on clinical judgment to look at individual behaviors according to how they relate to the person's participation in a full and satisfying lifestyle. QOL assessment is especially relevant from a community-integration point of view, because

1. New skills
2. Reduction of side effects from negative intervention
3. Reduction of medical and management crises
4. Increase in community integration
5. Increase in individual choice and satisfaction
6. Improved perceptions of others
7. Expanded social and support relationships

FIGURE 5.3 Areas of focus for quality-of-life assessment

Adapted from C. A. Macfarlane (1998), Assessment: The key to appropriate curriculum and instruction. In A. Hilton & R. Ringlaben (Eds.), *Best and promising practices in developmental disabilities.* Austin, TX: Pro-Ed.

it focuses on personal competence and successful community adjustment (Singh, Oswald, & Ellis, 1998).

QOL measurement may be carried out either *objectively* by looking at actual specific behaviors or *subjectively* by recording the individual's perceptions about life satisfaction (Simeonsson & Short, 1996). Whether objective or subjective, the QOL approach aims to measure the fit between one's needs and the extent to which those needs are being met. For that reason, QOL measures are particularly suited to evaluating service provision (Heal, Borthwick-Duffy, & Saunders, 1996).

Because the focus in QOL assessment is on the fit between the individual and the environment, ecological inventories that gather detailed information about the demands of the environment are essential. With this information, intervention plans can be better tailored to individual needs. Figure 5.3 shows areas that are of particular interest in relation to quality of life.

EDUCATIONAL ASSESSMENT

Typically, someone who is skilled in educational assessment is part of the interdisciplinary team. Because an educational assessment usually occurs after diagnosis, it concentrates more specifically on information related to remediation rather than on issues of identification (Hannafin, 1986). Information from educational assessment comes from both standardized, or *norm-referenced,* and curriculum-based methods. Behavioral observations in both the classroom and community are often included.

Norm-Referenced Tests

Most educational achievement instruments are norm-based (as are IQ tests) and subject to the same psychometric issues of standardization, validity, and reliability. They differ only in testing specific academic skills rather than assessing reasoning and problem-solving abilities related to more general intellectual achievement. Educational achievement tests are most useful for making identification and placement decisions and for identifying general strengths and weaknesses in academic

Table 5.6 Specific Skill Objectives

Who	What	To What Degree
Susan	Will select the correctly spelled *sh* word from among 5 choices	With at least 80% accuracy
Susan	Will compute the products for 3 × 0 through 3 × 10	At least 19 out of 20 times within 5 minutes
Susan	Will insert the correct article (*a* or *an*) into an incomplete sentence	A minimum of 80% of the time

SOURCE: Adapted with permission from M. J. Hannafin (1986). Special education assessment. In D. L. Wodrich & J. E. Joy (Eds.), *Multidisciplinary assessment of children with learning disabilities and mental retardation* (pp. 77–108). Baltimore, MD: Paul H. Brookes.

functioning. Norm–referenced testing compares individual performance with a group standard and determines the child's actual level of accomplishment relative to where she "should be" based on chronological age and typical development.

You have probably taken norm–referenced tests yourself. In most school districts, they are given periodically to test performance in comparison with national or state norms. Well-known examples include the California Achievement Test (CAT), Iowa Tests of Basic Skills, and the Metropolitan Achievement Tests (MAT), although these are not given as part of an assessment for MR.

Other tests are more specific in diagnosing particular academic strengths and weaknesses. These include the Metropolitan Instructional Tests, the Gates-MacGinitie Reading Test, the Woodcock Reading Mastery Test, and the Key Math Diagnostic Arithmetic Test. Testing for people with mental retardation often measures beginning math, reading, and knowledge skills, too, on tests such as the Wide Range Achievement Test–Revised, the Minimum Essentials Test, and the Adult Basic Learning Examination.

Curriculum-Based Assessment

Curriculum-based assessment is a general term that includes many different but always highly specific measurement strategies. All curriculum-based methods differ from norm-based achievement tests by measuring individual progress toward a goal rather than relative standing in comparison with peers. Curriculum-based measurement increasingly takes advantage of computer technology, but the long-term goals of detailed skill measurement over time remain unaltered (Allinder, Fuchs, & Fuchs, 1998).

Criterion–Referenced Tests   Criterion-referenced tests (one kind of curriculum-based method) measure specific skills that constitute a more general ability. For example, choosing the main idea from a passage is a specific skill involved in reading comprehension. Table 5.6 illustrates the highly specific skill objectives that could be used to develop a criterion-referenced test.

One advantage of criterion-referenced testing is that progress toward objectives can be measured frequently, sometimes daily, and at least several times each week.

These results are then graphed and analyzed in terms of the specified goals. Tests that are labeled as *proficiency, precision teaching, master, objective-referenced, competency,* and *basic skills* all use criterion referencing (Fuchs & Fuchs, 1990).

Curriculum-Based Measurement Curriculum-based *measurement* is a specific type of curriculum-based assessment designed to measure performance on long-term goals rather than on specific subskills. As with criterion-referenced tests, measurement occurs frequently, progress is graphed, performance is analyzed, and instructional modifications are made if progress is insufficient.

As an example, Susan's long-term goal may be to improve her reading comprehension to the fourth-grade level by year's end. Reading comprehension is then measured directly (rather than determined through subgoals), perhaps by answering questions about a passage, by retelling or rewriting the passage, or by filling in missing words. Many computer programs also are now available to test, score, graph performance, and make suggestions for instructional change (Fuchs, Fuchs, & Hamlett, 1992).

SPEECH AND LANGUAGE ASSESSMENT

Early intervention (and therefore assessment) for children with speech and language delay is especially important. Because speech and language problems can be related to deficits in cognition, hearing, or motor skills, as well as to emotional or environmental factors, assessment must differentiate among related conditions, in addition to identifying existing language problems.

Speech and language therapists usually have Master's degrees and are certified or licensed, depending on state requirements. Because many states have few regulations that govern practice, however, consumers will want to check the qualifications of those who offer speech and language therapy.

Speech and language pathologists respond to an extensive array of problems, including disorders in comprehension, expression, auditory processing, articulation, tone of voice, and fluency. Assessment techniques involve both standardized tests and behavioral observations, and they require highly specialized clinical judgments.

Commonly used standardized tests include the Peabody Picture Vocabulary Test–Revised (for receptive word recognition), the Expressive One-Word Picture Vocabulary Test, and the Boston Naming Test (for vocabulary expression). Important to the assessment are behavioral observations that result in **detailed recordings** of the frequency and duration of problem occurrences (for example, stuttering) and **rating scales** that compare behavioral aspects of speech and language with normally expected patterns.

Because difficulty with and delay in language can be symptoms of cognitive deficits, they are common in people with mental retardation, and language problems become more likely as the severity of mental retardation increases. Table 5.7

Table 5.7 Continuum from Normal Functioning to
Severe Retardation in Language Pattern Recognition

	Normal Functioning	Mental Retardation
Discourse and Pragmatics	Applies social setting rules from previous knowledge to new situations.	May function only in familiar contexts.
Syntax–Morphology	Application of general rules.	Reliance on stereotypical expressions.
Receptive Vocabulary	Memory load reduced through general rules.	Increased memory demand because patterns are not recognized.
Phonology	Production handled by rule: *dig, dog, dip.*	Sounds depend on the word they are in.

describes the relationship between the cognitive skills of pattern-and-rule recognition and language development in people with MR.

OCCUPATIONAL THERAPY ASSESSMENT

Occupational therapists help others achieve personal, physical, social, and emotional productivity. The term *occupation* thus refers to a wider sense of purpose and worth rather than the more limited sense of job or profession. Occupational therapy (OT) is relevant for people of all ages and can occur in hospitals, sheltered workshops, neonatal intensive care units, and school systems, among other places. Occupational therapists receive specialized training at the Associate's, Bachelor's, or Master's levels, and they are certified and licensed. As with special education, occupational therapy continues over long periods of time, so assessment is an ongoing process.

OT assessment may initially involve screening to determine whether further treatment is required. The MAP test and the Denver Developmental Screening Test (DDST) are common examples.

Most directly related to OT methods of intervention are Activities of Daily Living (ADL) assessments (Short-DeGraff, 1986). Relevant domains include self-care, home-care, and communication-related behaviors. Unlike standardized testing, ADL assessment tries to elicit best performance by making context changes that can involve altering position, using adaptive equipment, modeling desired behavior, or making changes in time of day or place. Special attention is paid to possible perceptual or motor problems that interfere with performance. Timing of movement, joint limitation, weakness or fatigue, and posture are often recorded in detail. OT assessment may also involve oral–motor function, range of motion, muscle strength and grasp, and pincer strength. Assessment data can be used to design individualized adaptive equipment as well as identify domains and methods for training.

Individualized Education Plan for Susan May Polaski

Date Established: 9/27/00   Teacher: Sarah Carron

Next Review: Monday, Jan. 29, 2001, 7:00pm

Long-Range Objective for Reading Comprehension:
By **5/27/01:** Susan will read at the 4th grade level with 90% comprehension accuracy.

Skill Steps:
1. Accurately define five new vocabulary words each week.
2. Choose main idea from passages with 80% accuracy.

FIGURE 5.4 One section of Susan's IEP

DEVELOPING THE INDIVIDUALIZED EDUCATION PROGRAM

Information from both norm-referenced and curriculum-based assessment, along with essential information from interviews and observations of adaptive behavior, is crucial for developing an individualized education program (IEP). Usually the IEP includes both the short-term goals (measured with criterion referencing) and longer-term achievement goals (measured by curriculum-based measurement). Progress also is referenced in relation to norms, usually according to grade level. Figure 5.4 is a portion of Susan's IEP.

At the scheduled IEP meeting, team members (including Susan's general education teacher, occupational therapist, speech and language pathologist, and parents) will look over the assessment graphs, discuss her progress, and make plans for the second half of the school year.

ASSESSMENT FOR JOYCE, SUSAN, AND JASON

Joyce

Interdisciplinary Team
Special Education Teacher, School Psychologist, Grandmother, Joyce

Although her IEP has been reviewed regularly, Joyce had not been tested on an IQ or adaptive behavior test for three years. This year's review, however, requires planning for the important transition to high school, a rite of passage for every student and a landmark change that includes both risk and promise. To help smooth the transition and prepare Joyce for a productive future, her assessment included (1) retesting for IQ and adaptive behavior, (2) several interviews, (3) behavioral observations, and (4) a thorough analysis of her current academic skills.

Test Results

Testing on the WISC-III showed little change. Joyce's overall score was 67, with scores on verbal tasks generally higher than on performance. Joyce was stronger in areas that required knowledge of facts and weaker in tasks of abstract reasoning. Her adaptive behavior was consistent with expectations for her age, except in functional academics.

Standardized testing placed Joyce's academic achievement at the upper third-grade or beginning fourth-grade level for reading and at the beginning of third grade for math. Joyce enjoys reading when the vocabulary is not demanding, but she dreads and resists math instruction. Curriculum-based testing indicated slow but steady progress through the year and a high percentage of material forgotten at later retesting.

Behavioral Observations

At school, Joyce is friendly and outgoing with her particular group of friends but self-conscious and cautious in larger groups. Except for math, she seems motivated to do well with her work, and she presents no behavior problems. At home, she is helpful and responsible, handling personal care, housework, and child care with skill. She loves to sew, and her efforts result in simple and attractive clothing.

Interview Findings

Joyce's grandmother, mother, and sister are concerned that Joyce seems "headed for trouble," but they admit that their fears are vague and based mostly on a new "secretiveness" about her. They suggested that "Aunt" Olive (a longtime family friend to whom Joyce is close) might provide more help. Although Olive would not betray Joyce's confidence, she did say that Joyce had told her things that confirmed her family's worries.

There was general agreement that Joyce has developed some good practical skills but that these required much practice and repetition in instruction. Once Joyce learns something, she does it the same way every time. She knows that her socks always go in her upper-left dresser drawer, for example, so that when she received several new pairs, she simply stuffed them all in, leaving the drawer open because it was too full to be closed. According to the family, Joyce does not reason well on her own and is easily influenced by others.

Team Decisions

The team agreed that its first priority is helping Joyce gain constructive direction and vision for her future. While she continues to work on improving her math and reading, it is crucial that she gain work experience that could lead to an interesting future occupation. It was determined that Joyce would be enrolled in the high school work-study program when something suitable could be found. Joyce is to be heavily involved in planning for this. Lisa Bryant, a regular education

(continued)

student in the peer tutoring program, was identified to work with Joyce and include her in activities outside of school. Privately, Joyce's grandmother agreed to find more activities for Joyce at home and to allow her less unsupervised time away.

Susan

Interdisciplinary Team
General Education Teacher, Speech and Language Pathologist, Occupational Therapist, School Psychologist, Mom, Dad, Susan

Because of Susan's physical disabilities, she is unable to complete standardized norm-referenced IQ tests (Spitz, 1986). Thus, none of the psychometric data on validity, reliability, and standardization discussed in Chapter 4 pertain to her scores. If we were to adhere strictly to the appropriate administration of these instruments, Susan would be untestable. Clinical judgment must guide the choice of tasks that will result in information about her skills, because testing must be custom-designed. The information from standardized tests is of limited use for intervention with Susan, though previous testing did determine that she has good attention in both the auditory and verbal modes, and that she is more comfortable and skilled on verbal than visual–spatial tasks.

For the above reasons, the team saw no reason to repeat standardized testing. It chose instead to concentrate on intervention-based measures, including (1) curriculum-based testing, (2) behavioral observations at home and in school, and (3) interviews with Susan's parents and Jolene (Susan's live-in caregiver).

Curriculum-Based Testing
Curriculum-based testing showed that although Susan is working approximately two years behind her grade level, she makes steady progress toward her goals and retains what she learns. Susan's teacher presented future curriculum goals at the meeting, and these were accepted by the team.

Behavioral Observations, Interviews, and Team Decisions
Susan's teacher, occupational therapist, and speech and language pathologist work together closely. They see each other frequently and stay current on Susan's performance and progress. Susan is highly motivated and usually cooperative, though she sometimes has "down" days when she expresses more frustration than usual. Following a suggestion from the school psychologist, Susan is given more time to herself on days such as these and then gently encouraged to resume her activities with reminders of her typical success. Susan seems to appreciate this approach and does not take advantage of it.

There was agreement that the major goal currently is to help provide more and better ways for Susan to express her thoughts and emotions and experience the world. The speech pathologist and occupational therapist together developed suggestions for new computer adaptations and software that could contribute to that goal. These are described in Chapter 9.

Jason

(More on assessment and an IEP for Jason are found in Chapter 10, "Early Intervention.")

Interdisciplinary Team
Psychologist, Physician, Occupational Therapist, Local Education Agency Representative, and Cathy, Jason's mother

This is Jason's first team assessment. He was referred by his pediatrician to early intervention, and the coordinator in his district arranged the team. Three assessments were done: (1) psychological testing on the Bayley; (2) behavioral observations at home, at the preschool, and during occupational therapy; and (3) personal interviews with Cathy and Jason's preschool teacher. Cathy's mother and sister were interviewed by phone. Reports were received from Jason's physical therapist and respiratory physician.

Test Results
On the Bayley, Jason's developmental quotient (DQ) was 8 to 12 months. His language skills were weaker (6 to 8 months) than his visual problem-solving skills (14 months). When Jason was held in an appropriate position, he was relatively skillful in manipulating objects, and his fine motor skills were better than his gross motor or balance abilities, especially in his right hand. Further, Jason's gesture language was consistent with his visual problem solving rather than his verbal skills; this indicates that his poorer verbal abilities are probably related to specific speech and language difficulties rather than more general communication problems.

Behavioral Observations and Interviews
The major behavioral finding was the dramatic contrast between Jason's performance when he was ill and when he was well. The time that Jason spends ill seems literally lost in terms of his development. What is more, Cathy reported that she sometimes finds it difficult to keep her patience with him. Although her other children have disabilities, she said that she had not expected the stress she is experiencing with Jason's health and that her parenting with the older two children is suffering as a result.

Team Decisions
The team developed an individualized family service plan (IFSP) for Jason and his family (see more on this in Chapter 10). The first (and related) priorities are to keep Jason well and reduce stress in the home so that Cathy and her family can enjoy each other more. Cathy was put in touch with respite services and encouraged to take some time for herself. Cathy's mother said that she will watch the children for a few hours each week but that she is afraid of mishandling Jason's asthma attacks if they occur. She expressed the desire to learn more about Jason's respiratory problems and assist Cathy at his next attack. Both Cathy and Jason's physician are pleased with his response to new medication and hope that the attacks will be less severe.

(continued)

A report from the physical therapist indicated that Cathy can be trained to carry out Jason's exercises, thus eliminating any immediate need for a physical therapy (PT) appointment. Occupational therapy visits were arranged at the pre-school. It was decided that consultation with a speech and language pathologist would be helpful, and the occupational therapist will incorporate those suggestions so that additional appointments will not be required. With these changes—and because visits to the pediatrician will be less frequent with Jason's advancing age—the regular appointments with the respiratory specialist seem much more manageable to Cathy.

LOOKING AHEAD

Chapter 5 has presented information about the varied professionals that must take part in a complete assessment, as well as some of the methods and instruments they use to assess mental retardation. In addition, it has covered many of the strengths and problems with this existing technology and made you aware of some of the challenges yet to be met in accurate and useful assessment. Chapter 6 discusses the characteristics found to varying degrees in individuals who have mental retardation and illustrates many of the new directions that assessment and classification of mental retardation are taking to better understand and assist those people served by professionals in the field.

INFOTRAC COLLEGE EDITION

Ideally, assessment of skills and abilities for those with mental retardation is interdisciplinary. Good interdisciplinary practice depends upon every professional's familiarity with other disciplines. Choose one discipline about which you know little, and enter it as the keyword in *InfoTrac College Edition*. Try entering your terms by discipline (for example, *occupational therapy*) and by profession (*occupational therapist*). What did you learn about that discipline or practice relevant to assessment of mental retardation?

REFERENCES

Aiken, L. R. (1991). *Psychological testing and assessment* (7th ed.). Boston: Allyn & Bacon.

Allinder, R. M., Fuchs, L. S., & Fuchs, D. (1998). Curriculum board measurement. In H. B. Vance (Ed.), *Psychological assessment of children: Best practices for school and clinical settings* (2nd ed., pp. 106–132). New York: Wiley.

Anastasi, A. (1988). *Psychological testing* (6th ed.). New York: Macmillan.

Bayley, N. (1993). *Bayley scales of infant development*. New York: Psychological Corporation.

Berk, L. E. (2000). *Child development* (5th ed.) Boston: Allyn & Bacon.

Bruininks, R. H., Woodcock, R. W., Weatherman, R. F., & Hill, B. K. (1984). *Interviewer's manual: Scales on Independent Behavior.* Allen, TX: DLM Teaching Resources.

Burns, C. W. (1990). Assessing the psychological and educational needs of the moderately and severely mentally retarded. In Reynolds, C. R., & Kamphaus, R. W. (Eds.), *Handbook of psychological and educational assessment of children: Intelligence and achievement* (pp. 789–802). New York: Guilford.

Capute, A. J., & Accardo, P. J. (1991). Language assessment. In A. J. Capute & P. J. Accardo (Eds.), *Developmental disabilities in infancy and childhood* (pp. 165–179). Baltimore, MD: Paul H. Brookes.

Crnic, K. A. (1988). Mental retardation. In E. J. Mash & L. G. Terdal (Eds.), *Behavioral assessment of childhood disorders* (2nd ed., pp. 265–302). New York: Guilford.

Cronbach, L. J. (1970). *Essentials of psychological testing* (3rd ed.). New York: Harper & Row.

Dacey, C. M., Nelson, W. M. III, & Stoeckel, J. (1999). Reliability, criterion-related validity and qualitative comments of the fourth edition of the Stanford-Binet Intelligence Scale with a young adult population with intellectual disability. *Journal of Intellectual Disability Research, 43*(3), 179–184.

Demchak, M., & Drinkwater, S. (1998). Assessing adaptive behavior. In H. B. Vance (Ed.), *Psychological assessment of children: Best practices for school and clinical settings.* New York: John Wiley.

Diana v. State Board of Education. (1970, 1973). C-70, 37 RFP (N.D. Cal., 1970, 1973).

Ellis, N. R. (Ed.). (1979). *Handbook of mental deficiency.* New York: John Wiley & Sons.

Fagan, J. F., III, & Detterman, D. K. (1992). The Fagan Test of Infant Intelligence: A technical summary. *Journal of Applied Developmental Psychology, 13,* 173–193.

Fagan, J. F., III, Shepherd, P. A., & Knevel, C. R. (1991). *Predictive validity of the Fagan Test of Infant Intelligence.* Paper presented at the biennial meeting of the Society for Research in Child Development, Seattle, WA.

Fradd, S. H., Figueroa, R. A., & Correa, V. I. (1989). Meeting the multicultural needs of Hispanic students in special education. *Exceptional Children, 56,* 105–110.

Fuchs, L. S., & Fuchs, D. (1990). *Curriculum-based assessment.* In C. R. Reynolds & R. W. Kamphaus (Eds.), *Handbook of psychological and educational assessment of children: Intelligence and achievement* (pp. 435–455). New York: Guilford.

————, & Hamlett, C. L. (1992). Computer applications to facilitate curriculum-based measurement. *Teaching Exceptional Children* (Summer), 58–60.

Glutting, J. J., & Kaplan, D. (1990). Stanford-Binet Intelligence Scale, Fourth Edition: Making the case for reasonable interpretations. In C. R. Reynolds & R. W. Kamphaus (Eds.), *Handbook of psychological and educational assessment of children: Intelligence and achievement* (pp. 277–296). New York: Guilford.

Hannafin, M. J. (1986). Special education assessment. In D. L. Wodrich & J. E. Joy (Eds.), *Multidisciplinary assessment of children with learning disabilities and mental retardation* (pp. 77–108). Baltimore, MD: Paul H. Brookes.

Hawkes, N. (1979). Tracing Burt's descent to scientific fraud. *Science, 205,* 673–675.

Heal, L. W., Borthwick-Duffy, S. A., & Saunders, R. R. (1996). Assessment of quality of life. In J. W. Jacobson & J. A. Mulick (Eds.), *Manual of diagnosis and professional practice in mental retardation* (pp. 199–212). Washington, DC: American Psychological Association.

Hernstein, R. J. (1982). IQ testing and the media. *The Atlantic Monthly* (August), 73–74.

Hodapp, R. M., Leckman, J. F., Dykens, E. M., Sparrow, S. S. Zelinski, D. G., & Ort, S. I. (1992). K-ABC profiles in children with Fragile X Syndrome, Down Syndrome, and nonspecific mental retardation. *American Journal on Mental Retardation, 97*(1), 39–46.

Kamphaus, R. W., Kaufman, A. S., & Harrison, P. L. (1990). Clinical assessment practice with the Kaufman Assessment Battery for Children (K-ABC). In C. R. Reynolds & R. W. Kamphaus (Eds.) *Handbook of psychological and educational assessment of children: Intelligence and achievement* (pp. 259–276). New York: Guilford.

Kaplan, S. L., Alfonso, V. C. (1997). Confirmatory factor analysis of the Stanford-Binet Intelligence Scale: Fourth edition with preschoolers with developmental delays. *Journal of Psychoeducational Assessment, 15*(3), 226–236.

Kaufman, A. S. (1994). *Intelligent testing with the WISC-R.* New York: John Wiley & Sons.

————, & Kaufman, N. L. (1983). *Kaufman Assessment Battery for Children (K-ABC).* Circle Pines, MN: American Guidance Service.

Keith, T. Z., & Dunbar, S. B. (1984). Hierarchical factor analysis of the K-ABC: Testing alternate models. *Journal of Special Education, 18*(3), 367–375.

Keogh, B. K., Bernheimer, L. P., & Guthrie, D. (1997). Stability and change over time in cognitive level of children with delays. *American Journal on Mental Retardation, 101*(4), 365–373.

Kopp, C. B. (1994). Infant assessment. In C. B. Fisher & R. M. Lerner (Eds.), *Applied developmental psychology* (pp. 265–293). New York: McGraw-Hill.

Larry P. v. Wilson Riles (1972). Federal District Court Sitting in California, C-71-2270 (RFP, District Court for Northern California).

Lennox, D. B., & Miltenberger, R. G. (1989). Conducting a functional assessment of problem behavior in applied settings. *Journal of the Association for Persons with Severe Handicaps, 14,* 304–311.

Lezak, M. S. (1983). *Neuropsychological assessment* (2nd ed.). New York: Oxford University Press.

Malone, D. (1986). Personal communication.

Matson, J. L. (1988). Mental retardation in adults. In V. B. Vanhasselt, P. S. Strain, & M. Hersen (Eds.), *Handbook of developmental and physical disabilities* (pp. 353–369). New York: Pergamon.

Merighi, J., Edison, M., & Zigler, E. (1990). The role of motivational factors in the functioning of mentally retarded individuals. In R. M. Hodapp, J. A. Burack, & E. Zigler (Eds.), *Issues in the developmental approach to mental retardation* (pp. 114–134). Cambridge, England: Cambridge University Press.

Morison, P. (Ed.). (1996). *The use of IQ tests in special education decision making and planning. Summary of two workshops.* Washington, DC: National Research Council.

Naglieri, J. A. (1985). *Matrix Analogies Test: Expanded form.* San Antonio, TX: Psychological Corporation.

Nihira, K., Foster, R., Schellhass, H., & Leland, H. (1974). *AAMR Adaptive Behavior Scale, manual.* Austin, TX: Pro-Ed.

Nutall, R. L., & Fozard, T. L. (1970). Age, socioeconomic status and human abilities. *Aging and Human development, 1,* 161–169.

Ogbu, J. U. (1997). Understanding the school performance of urban blacks: Some essential background knowledge. In H. J. Walber, O. Reyes, & R. P. Weissberg (Eds.), *Children and youth: Interdisciplinary perspectives* (pp. 190–222). Thousand Oaks, CA: Sage.

O'Neill, A. (1993). *Clinical inference: How to draw meaningful conclusions from psychological tests.* Brandon, VT: Clinical Psychology Publishing.

Oswald, D. P., Coutinho, M. J., Best, A. M., & Singh, N. (1999). Ethnic representation in special education: The influence of school-related economic and demographic variables. *Journal of Special Education, 32*(4), 194–206.

Polloway, E. A., & Rucker, H. (1997). Etiology: Biological and environmental considerations. In T. E. C. Smith, C. A. Dowdy, E. A. Polloway, & G. E. Blalock (Eds.), *Children and adults with learning disabilities* (pp. 160–187). Boston: Allyn & Bacon.

Raven, J. C. (1938). *Standard progressive matrices.* London: Lewis.

Reynolds, C. R. (1987a). Playing IQ roulette with the Stanford-Binet, 4th edition. *Measurement and Evaluation in Counseling and Development, 20,* 139–141.

———. (1987b). Sympathy not sense: The appeal of the Stanford-Binet fourth edition. *Measurement and Evaluation in Counseling and Development, 21,* 45.

Rose, S. A., Feldman, J. F., & Wallace, I. F. (1992). Infant information processing in relation to six-year cognitive outcome. *Child Development, 63,* 1126–1141.

Sattler, J. M. (1974). *Assessment of children's intelligence.* Philadelphia: W. B. Saunders.

Sattler, J. W. (1990). *Assessment of children* (3rd ed.) San Diego: J. M. Sattler.

Short-DeGraff, M. A. (1986). Occupational therapy assessment. In D. L. Wodrich & J. E. Joy (Eds.), *Multidisciplinary assessment of children with learning disabilities and mental retardation* (pp. 161–193). Baltimore, MD: Paul H. Brookes.

Sienkiewicz-Mercer, R., & Kaplan, S. B. (1989). *I raise my eyes to say yes.* Boston: Houghton Mifflin.

Simeonsson, R. J., & Short, R. J. (1996). Adaptive development, survival roles, and quality of life. In J. W. Jacobson & J. A. Mulick (Eds.), *Manual of diagnosis and professional practice in mental retardation* (pp. 137–146). Washington, DC: American Psychological Association.

Singh, N. N., Oswald, D. P., & Ellis, C. R. (1998). Mental retardation. In T. H. Ollendick & M. Hersen (Eds.), *Handbook of child psychopathology* (3rd ed., pp. 91–116). New York: Plenum.

Sparrow, S., Balla, D., & Cicchetti, D. (1984). *Vineland Adaptive Behavior Scales.* Circle Pines, MN: American Guidance Service.

Spitz, H. H. (1986). Disparities in mentally retarded persons' IQs derived from different intelligence tests. *American Journal of Mental Deficiency, 90*(5), 588–591.

Stinnett, T. A. (1997). AAMR Adaptive Behavior Scale-School: Test review. *Journal of Psychoeducational Assessment, 15*(4), 361–372.

Thorndike, R. L., Hagen, E., & Sattler, J. (1985). *Stanford-Binet Intelligence Scale* (4th ed.). Chicago: Riverside.

Walker, N. W. (1987a). The Stanford-Binet, 4th Edition: Haste does seem to make waste. *Measurement and Evaluation in Counseling and Development, 20,* 135–138.

———. (1987b). Response to Hopkins: Emotional loyalty does not a good rejoinder make. *Measurement and Evaluation in Counseling and Development, 21,* 43–44.

Wechsler, D. (1981). *Wechsler Adult Intelligence Scale—Revised.* San Antonio, TX: Psychological Corporation.

———. (1989). *Wechsler Preschool and Primary Scale of Intelligence—Revised.* San Antonio, TX: Psychological Corporation.

———. (1991). *Wechsler Intelligence Scale for Children* (3rd ed.). San Antonio, TX: Psychological Corporation.

Wilson, W. M. (1992). The Stanford-Binet: Fourth edition and Form L-M in assessment of young children with mental retardation. *Mental Retardation, 30*(2), 81–84.

Wingerson, L. (1998). *Unnatural selection.* New York: Bantam.

Wodrich, D. L., & Joy, J. E. (1986). Practical issues and illustrative cases. In D. L. Wodrich & J. E. Joy (Eds.), *Multidisciplinary assessment of children with learning disabilities and mental retardation* (pp. 281–308). Baltimore, MD: Paul H. Brookes.

6

Characteristics of Mental Retardation

BASIC ISSUES IN
UNDERSTANDING CHARACTERISTICS

The integral characteristics of mental retardation are described in its definition: (1) low IQ and (2) deficits in adaptive behavior (see Chapter 4). The IQ measurement, however, reflects skills and abilities that include attention, comprehension and memory, language abilities, spatial cognition, learning and generalization, and problem solving. In addition, when mental retardation results from brain damage, that damage may also cause motor problems. Personality and motivational characteristics also play an important role in performance. Depending on the existence and severity of these characteristics and deficits, various adaptive behavior problems result. Many of the adaptive behaviors of particular relevance to the lives of those with mental retardation are included in the 1992 AAMR definition: communication, self-care, home living, social skills, community use, self-direction, health and safety, functional academics, and leisure and work (Luckasson, 1992).

The characteristics of mental retardation typically have been taught by relating characteristics of interest to the level of severity represented by the traditional classification system—*mild, moderate, severe,* and *profound.* As discussed in Chapter 4, however, this categorization system has serious limitations, and its strict usage actually promotes confusion and misunderstanding. As you will recall, these problems stem from the fact that category membership is based on IQ, and a large number of skills and abilities make up the IQ score, which is a kind of average of these skills. If all of the skills that make up the IQ fall at the same level, then there is no problem. But for many people, there are important variations in those skills so that one or more may fall within the mild category, and others may be moderate or severe to profound. Such individuals obviously cannot be accurately described by characteristics that are consistent with the behavior and abilities of those typical of the general score.

Largely because of the confusion caused by the existence of variability among skills, practitioners often experience practical problems in applying their knowledge of characteristics as it is tied to classification categories. For example, one of the author's students expressed considerable frustration with helping "her" student learn functional reading skills: "She *should* be able to do this. She falls in the mild category." A closer look at the young person in question, however, soon revealed that although her skills were consistent with the mild classification in several areas, they were much lower in one or two areas that are often important for reading— including visual memory for abstract stimuli.

Another and just as important reason to avoid categorical thinking is that the characteristics and challenges are quite similar for individuals whether they have milder or more severe conditions. It is generally agreed that most educational programs still vary according to "degree" of retardation rather than in response to some other characteristic (Hallahan & Kauffman, 1997), but some researchers have long maintained that the primary differences among people with MR are not between those with milder or more severe retardation but between the individuals and what they aim to achieve (Grey, 1981). It is generally true, of course, that as

IQ decreases (especially at the lowest levels) the intensity and duration of needed supports increases; however, the areas of concern typically remain the same. It is more helpful, therefore, to think about the characteristic deficits for those with retardation as occurring on an individual continuum, as well as to think in terms of what will help the particular student or client lessen the gap between current reality and promise for each characteristic.

Because of these important practical difficulties (and the confusion that is likely to result), this text approaches characteristics by describing those that often exist for people with mental retardation in general without regard to categories. It also describes the adaptive challenges that individuals are likely to have when these *specific* characteristics are milder rather than more severe. However, because the instructional needs and supports for those with generally milder conditions are sometimes different from those required for more severe disabilities, those few differences in approach are covered.

This text highlights the necessity of assessing, understanding, and developing teaching and intervention approaches that relate to the particular characteristics of an individual rather than relying on a general categorization. The principle in this approach goes well beyond any general reluctance to "pigeonhole" individuals or place them in "slots": It addresses the practical and integral matters of adequate assessment and effective practice.

PHYSICAL AND MENTAL HEALTH

The number and intensity of needed supports frequently result from physical and mental health challenges rather than any level of intellectual deficit. For those individuals with genetic and chromosomal disorders, associated physical disabilities are often present. As Jason's case story has shown, health problems may create the greatest stress for the family, and these can further delay or even preclude growth and development.

Psychiatric disorders are also common in people who have retardation, affecting as many as 20 percent to 35 percent of that population (Fletcher, 2000). In addition, there is some suggestion that people with particular MR-related syndromes may be more likely to evidence psychopathology (Dykens, 1996).

Besides psychiatric conditions, people with MR may have a higher incidence of behavior problems, including aggression, withdrawal, and other inappropriate behaviors (Dudley, Ahlgrim-Delzell & Calhoun, 1999). Because of the frequency of health and psychiatric problems, the determination of needed supports involves careful assessment of these factors for each person.

MOTIVATIONAL CHARACTERISTICS

People with mental retardation sometimes have certain motivational and personality characteristics that affect both their behavior and intellectual achievement. For example, those with MR may have little desire to influence their environment or try new or difficult tasks (Bennet-Gates & Zigler, 1999a). In part, this passive tendency may be related to **learned helplessness.** Individuals with learned helplessness believe they cannot be successful—even in situations where they are perfectly capable of success. Because of these mistaken beliefs, they refuse to try because they do not want to risk failing (Elliot & Dweck, 1988). Such children have no faith in the power of practice or effort to improve their performance, and when they do experience success, they attribute it to luck. Learned helplessness is usually the result of early failures combined with repeated criticism and low expectations on the part of parents, teachers, or other caregivers, and it can develop even in the brightest children.

Children with learned helplessness can gain more confidence in their abilities and the power of effort, however, if adults point out their successes and explicitly show the obvious connection between good performance and ability. Peter, for example, displays learned helplessness and typically explains any success he experiences as the result of luck; he believes his failures are caused by his own lack of ability. As a result, he usually will not attempt any task that he is not absolutely sure he can accomplish, and so his thinking stands in the way of successes that are perfectly possible for him.

Peter can learn to recognize and believe in the effects of his own effort if others consistently point out the valid results of his ability. In other words, if his teachers, caregivers, and others give him the opportunity to succeed, point out the obvious ability implied by that success ("See, you can _____"), and encourage him to make greater efforts, his motivation will increase. It will first be necessary to offer external reinforcement for persistence, but as statements that highlight the role of effort ("See what your hard work has done!") are paired with external reinforcements, Peter will gradually internalize those statements and begin to believe in the power of his own application. And as Peter learns to believe in his own abilities, he will become that much better able to determine and control his own life.

It is also important to help children learn to accept failures as inevitable experiences that happen to everyone, not as indications of the uselessness of trying. Because "retraining" children's beliefs about their chances to succeed with effort is best accomplished before their attitudes become deeply entrenched, it is especially important to begin when children are young (Eccles, Wigfield, & Schiefele, 1998).

Individuals with MR may also look to adults to see what to do, even in situations where they know the correct behavior. This **outerdirectedness** is more common in people who have little opportunity to make their own choices or try things on their own (Bybee & Zigler, 1999). Furthermore, those with MR may be especially eager to gain the approval of those who are familiar and supportive, while they often are wary of and avoid interacting with people they don't know— although these tendencies, too, are related to lack of experience and opportunity for social interaction (Bennet-Gates & Zigler, 1999b).

Understanding the role of motivational factors for people with MR is important because such characteristics not only can influence the willingness to try, but also reduce the efficiency of cognitive processes themselves such as attention and memory (Utley, Hoehn, Soraci, & Baumeister, 1993). Furthermore, motivational

Individuals with MR sometimes rely on cues from others, even for tasks they can carry out perfectly well on their own.

© Peeter Vilms/Jeroboam

aspects of temperament are influenced by many other factors, including the etiology of the retardation, living conditions, and age (Bybee & Zigler, 1999). IQ and achievement, then, are not simply the result of intellectual ability but are affected by complex interactions among individual characteristics. Singular focus on level of IQ can obscure these differences and lead us to miss those characteristics that can be changed to improve performance. Such focus often brings a kind of circular reasoning by which one attempts to explain problems on an IQ test by attributing them to some amount of IQ deficit without referring to the possible brain damage, motivation, attention, strategy use, and other factors that are actually involved. Though referring to category of impairment may be more parsimonious, it neither is more accurate nor promotes the best interests of either research or practice.

LEARNING AND GENERALIZATION

Mental retardation always implies difficulties in learning. Learning, however, is not itself a single skill but an intricate intellectual process that involves attention, memory, and comprehension. One way to illustrate how these processes interact is through a model of information processing (see Figure 6.1).

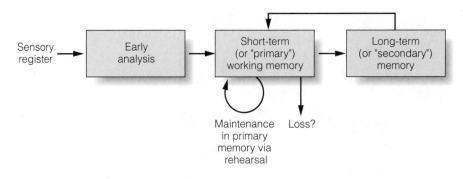

FIGURE 6.1 An information processing view of memory

As Figure 6.1 shows, information processing involves several subprocesses, beginning with the **sensory register.** The register represents one or more sense functions—vision, audition, taste, smell, and touch—that first pick up a stimulus. Attention to this stimulus is required, however, if one is to be aware of it. So the sensory register picks up the "signal," but attention brings it to consciousness—or to working memory (or short-term memory). Once a stimulus is held in working memory, it can be retained for a time, mentally altered, or connected to another idea or memory. It is in working memory that conscious thinking takes place. From working memory, a stimulus idea also can be transferred to **long-term memory** (or storage.) While working memory can hold only a discrete amount of information, the normal capacity of long-term memory is virtually limitless. Once information is placed in long-term memory, getting it back (or thinking of it again) is called **retrieval.**

Several important things should be noticed about this system. First, the components work together and depend on one another. In other words, long-term memory (or learning) depends on the effective functioning of all of these processes: sensory functioning, attention, working memory, long-term storage, and effective retrieval. Second, the most effective functioning of these processes does not happen automatically but involves the use of information-processing strategies that enhance the functioning of the system. In fact, with normal development the efficiency of the learning system improves in two ways: (1) the capacity of the working memory increases, and (2) the individual learns to use more effective strategies (Guttenberg, 1997).

Comprehension is also integral to learning, of course, and all of the information-processing systems work together toward that end. Understanding, though, comes from experience. For someone to increase her level of understanding of the world and the things in it, rich experiences and the opportunity to ask questions and receive clarification are required. For those with MR, such experiences are often severely (and unnecessarily) limited. The first step, then, in improving comprehension for those with MR is environmental enrichment in the form of many community experiences and the help and friendship of patient people who are willing to converse and explain. Although people with MR may not initially know that they do not understand or may be reluctant to ask for clarification, they can often learn to monitor their own comprehension and ask for additional information (Ezell & Goldstein, 1991; Fujiki & Brinton, 1993).

Usually we hope that once a learner has learned a task, she will apply her knowledge to other similar tasks or to the same task at other times or in other circumstances. This ability is known as **generalization.** People with MR, however, often have difficulty taking what they learn and generalizing it to new contexts or tasks. Certain teaching methods, however, such as community-based instruction (see Chapters 12 and 14), can promote generalization (Langone, 1990).

ATTENTION

Several aspects of attention may be used less effectively by those with retardation, including **selective attention** (focusing on a particular object, task, or idea) and **sustained attention** (maintaining focused attention while blocking out competing stimuli).

As previously noted, problems with attention also can affect other processes. For example, selective attention affects the efficiency of the sensory register, and lack of focus during tasks has a major effect on encoding and storage in long-term memory (Tomporowski & Tinsley, 1997). Problems with selective and sustained attention often play an especially large role in learning difficulties, because learners with MR often pay less attention to learning tasks, whereas the encoding process may require even more focus for them than for typical learners (Merrill, 1992).

In addition to problems with focus, individuals with mental retardation often have difficulty in shifting attention from one task to another (Bergen & Mosley, 1994). Poor attention also makes comprehension less likely, whether that involves understanding instructions or learning from a model. Fortunately, attentional abilities can improve with practice, and even for those with the lowest levels of intellectual functioning, stimulating environments increase alertness and improve the ability to relate to surroundings (Belfior, Browder, & Mace, 1993).

MEMORY

People with mental retardation have more trouble with at least two memory processes: *procedural* (learning a step-by-step process) and *declarative* (remembering new words or facts) (Vakil, Shelef-Reshef, & Levy-Shiff, 1997). Furthermore, people with retardation typically have more trouble retaining what they do learn. Still, there are individual differences in these abilities. People with such identified etiologies as Down syndrome, Fragile X syndrome, and Williams syndrome often have distinct memory strengths and weaknesses, and knowledge of those general patterns can help inform teaching methods and techniques (Bebko & Luhaorg, 1998; Hodapp & Fidler, 1999).

Remember, though, that the efficiency of memory largely depends on effective strategy use, and those with MR usually do not use memory strategies spontaneously. When they are taught specific strategy use, however, their memory performance does improve—although it is generally agreed that a maturational age of 5 years or so is required for individuals to use **metacognitive** strategies (or those that involve thinking about and analyzing strategy use). Most people with MR can perform better when they are prompted or helped to use such strategies (Turner, 1998).

LANGUAGE ABILITIES

People with mental retardation have widely varying language abilities. With the most severe instances of retardation, speech may not develop at all and communication may be limited to external devices or nonverbal gestures. Absence of speech, however, is not necessarily an indication of extremely low IQ, as can be seen in the case story for Susan. And even within particular syndromes such as Down syndrome, there is considerable variability in language strengths and weaknesses (Smith & Phillips, 1992). Research has shown, however, that there is often more consistency within syndromes related to retardation than within IQ category levels (Tager-Flusberg, 1999). A major challenge in IQ assessment is disentangling the effects of cognition and language (Warren & Yoder, 1997).

Language itself is made up of several subcomponents, including **articulation,** speech production, **semantics,** and **pragmatics.** Individuals with mental retardation often have trouble with all of these language aspects to varying degrees.

Articulation consists of the production of phonetic speech sounds such as *puh, buh,* and *grrr. Semantics* refers to understanding the meaning of words, and *pragmatics* involves conventions of language such as the length of the pause between words and the timing of turn taking in conversations.

Individuals with mental retardation can improve in language skills—just as they can grow in any other area. Formal language-intervention programs should be based on a clear understanding of the typical developmental order of language skills and should highlight the individual components of language (Rondal & Edwards, 1997). Teaching strategies also can facilitate language skill, just as they can with memory and problem solving. As an example, because people with mental retardation may focus on the sound of the words and their order rather than on meaning and concepts, practice on the semantic aspects of language can improve performance (Abbeduto & Nuccio, 1991).

Living circumstances and experiences, though, are especially important to language acquisition and usage (Hatton, 1998), as they are to all other aspects of functioning for people with retardation. The more enriched and varied the environment and the more opportunity there is to interact with supportive people, the better one's chances of developing good language skills.

Children with mental
retardation usually
need help with
language learning.

© Laura Dwight/Corbis

DISTINCTION BETWEEN OVERALL
MILD AND SEVERE CHARACTERISTICS

The majority of individuals who are diagnosed with mental retardation have characteristics that are relatively mild (MacMillan, Siperstein, & Gresham, 1996). Although the educational and other service-related interventions that are appropriate for the needs of this group may be different from those for individuals with more severe characteristics, the nature of the deficits involved are primarily the same—that is, typically individuals with mild retardation have difficulties in the same areas of learning, comprehension, memory, attention, language, problem solving, and motivation as described above. Still, focus may be placed on different curricular issues, and many supports that are often needed for those with more severe conditions may not be appropriate whereas others may be required.

Self-help and academics are the two areas where differences for those with milder and more severe conditions are most pronounced. Those with more severe retardation are often unable to learn to dress and feed themselves and take care of everyday domestic and transportation needs without explicit training, but those with milder conditions usually manage these needs independently and do so more or less within developmentally expected time periods. Similarly, many people with milder conditions are able to learn **functional literacy** skills that those with more severe symptoms are unlikely to master. Educational interventions reflect these differences.

Even though people with mild retardation usually have less trouble with self-help and academic tasks, they often face challenges in adult living that those with more severe retardation do not. Simply because they do function more independently, they may be subject to peer influences and adult challenges that they cannot manage effectively because they lack the cognitive reasoning skills. Joyce, from our case stories, provides an example.

Joyce

Joyce's Future Adulthood: Living and Work

Of the three young people we have followed in this text, Joyce has the least severe disabilities in terms of definitional assessment. In terms of successful adjustment to adult life, however, Joyce may not experience fewer problems simply because she is "higher functioning" than Susan or Jason. Someone functioning at a higher level might have even more difficulty in adulthood for several reasons.

To begin with, there is the danger that Joyce may have the confidence and pride to assert her independence from her family without the good judgment to make wise and effective decisions. She also may be unduly influenced by others to gain acceptance and have people "like" her. Furthermore, Joyce may have the daily living skills to care for herself in most everyday situations but lack the employment skills that would enable her to earn the money necessary to maintain financial independence—and judgment problems can, of course, make living on a tight budget even more difficult. Often adults who have characteristics similar to Joyce's maintain a fair level of independence but experience frequent crises while doing so.

Actually, a fair number of adults even without diagnosed learning problems live only semiindependently while experiencing more or less constant crises. But this does not mean that Joyce is absolutely destined to do so, because there are options that can minimize the challenges she faces. For one, few people live completely by themselves, and if Joyce finds a compatible housemate whose skills and abilities complement hers, then fewer problems may arise. Joyce is well organized and able to adhere to a strict routine. She is an excellent seamstress, and she is friendly and personable. If she has a living partner who can provide a tempering influence and encourage Joyce to "check things out" and think them through—sometimes with the advice of others—then Joyce may avoid many problems that she would otherwise face. And she may, in turn, be able to offer her strengths to her housemate's benefit.

For those with a diagnosis of mental retardation, many residential service agencies would help in finding an appropriate living situation (and provide supported living). Joyce, however, will not be eligible for those services. Her family may be invaluable in providing the additional support Joyce needs (with budgeting and keeping her checkbook, for example)—if she can feel secure and independent enough to allow them to help. For all too many people in Joyce's situation, however, there is no close and capable family to provide help and guidance.

As to her work life, Joyce has done well at the fabric store, but she may want to test her abilities and grow into new skills by trying other options. Many students who have no official label but nonetheless have mild learning problems or other social impediments need career guidance and work experience beyond what they can get on their own or what their families can provide for them—and beyond the traditionally provided school counseling (Zetlin & Murtaugh, 1990). If transitional programs were available to all students, then they could sometimes make the difference between wasted lives and directed futures. This is all the more reason to move toward integrated career growth programs that are designed to help all students prepare for adult work life through individualized planning.

Individuals who are now included in classrooms for children with mild mental retardation have more serious deficits than those who were diagnosed several decades ago (Polloway, Smith, Patton, & Smith, 1996). Children like Joyce who have characteristics that are synonymous with those of the previous group are now frequently classified as *learning disabled,* yet their problems and abilities reflect general intellectual challenges rather than the wide disparity among skills that formally defines the LD category. It is these individuals—along with a segment of those highly functioning people who do have the MR diagnosis—whose needs differ most from the group with more severe disabilities. Yet such people do have special needs and can profit from educational, transitional, and adult support services that are typically available to those with MR, although with a modified focus. Because of these differences, some authors have suggested forming a new diagnostic category to describe people who have problems primarily with academic functioning, interpersonal skills, and problem solving, but not with self-care (MacMillan, Siperstein, & Gresham, 1996).

From a community-integration perspective, however, it is most productive to maintain focus on individuals and their strengths and weaknesses. Most educational and support services for people with mental retardation are individually designed for this reason. Classifying people into categories of mild and severe has historically been seen as useful in terms of school programming. Increasingly, however, there is an emphasis on providing all students with the widest range of experiences possible and integrating children with disabilities into school activities with typical peers. Chapter 12 highlights several reasons why integrated education, whenever possible, is beneficial for all students.

▌▌ LOOKING AHEAD ▶

In this chapter, many of the characteristics of mental retardation have been discussed, and reasons for focusing on the individual variability of these characteristics have been explained. Chapter 7 covers many of the genetic influences on the development of mental retardation that result in these and other characteristics, most of which provide challenges for those with MR and require support if people are to gain their full potential.

INFOTRAC COLLEGE EDITION

You have been tutoring Kevin, a 14-year-old boy with mental retardation, for six months, and you are convinced that he is capable of much better performance than he usually demonstrates. In fact, Kevin seems afraid to try even tasks with which he has sometimes had success. Kevin's mother, Mrs. Zimmer, also has noticed this behavior and wants your help in understanding it. In *InfoTrac College Edition,* enter *learned helplessness* as the keyword. Choose one article to share with Mrs. Zimmer to help her understand what learned helplessness is and how it might explain Kevin's behavior. Describe the aspects of the article that influenced your choice. These could include specific information, the manner of description, the nature of the application, and the style of writing.

REFERENCES

Abbeduto, L., & Nuccio, J. B. (1991). Relation between receptive language and cognitive maturity in persons with mental retardation. *American Journal on Mental Retardation, 96*(2), 143–149.

Bebko, J. M., & Luhaorg, H. (1998). The development of strategy use and metacognitive processing in mental retardation: Some sources of difficulty. In J. A. Burack & R. M. Hodapp (Eds.), *Handbook of mental retardation and development* (pp. 382–407). New York: Cambridge University Press.

Belfior, P. J., Browder, D. M., & Mace, F. C. (1993). Effects of community and center-based settings on the alertness of persons with profound mental retardation. *Journal of Applied Behavior Analysis, 26*(3), 401–402.

Bennet-Gates, D., & Zigler, E. (1999a). Effectance motivation and the performance of individuals with mental retardation. In E. Zigler & D. Bennett-Gates (Eds.), *Personality development in individuals with mental retardation* (pp. 145–164). New York: Cambridge University Press.

———. (1999b). Motivation for social reinforcement: Positive- and negative-reaction tendencies. In E. Zigler & D. Bennett-Gates (Eds.), *Personality development in individuals with mental retardation* (pp. 107–129). New York: Cambridge University Press.

Bergen, A., & Mosley, J. L. (1994). Attention and attentional shift efficiency in individuals with and without mental retardation. *American Journal on Mental Retardation, 98*(6), 732–743.

Bybee, J., & Zigler, E. (1999). Outerdirectedness in individuals with and without mental retardation: A review. In E. Zigler & D. Bennett-Gates (Eds.), *Personality development in individuals with mental retardation* (pp. 165–205). New York: Cambridge University Press.

Dudley, J. R., Ahlgrim-Delzell, L., & Calhoun, M. L. (1999). Diverse diagnostic and behavioral patterns amongst people with a dual diagnosis. *Journal of Intellectual Disability Research, 43*(2), 70–79.

Dykens, E. M. (1996). DNA meets DSM: The growing importance of genetic syndromes in dual diagnosis. *Mental Retardation, 34*(2), 125–127.

Eccles, J. S., Wigfield, A., & Schiefele, U. (1998). Motivation to succeed. In N. Eisenberg (Ed.), *Handbook of child psychology: Vol. 3. Social, emotional, and personality development* (5th ed., pp. 1017–1095). New York: Wiley.

Elliot, E. S., & Dweck, C. S. (1988). Goals: An approach to motivation and achievement. *Journal of Personality and Social Psychology, 54,* 5–12.

Ezell, H. K., & Goldstein, H. (1991). Observational learning of comprehension monitoring skills in children who exhibit mental retardation. *Journal of Speech & Hearing Research, 34*(1), 141–154.

Fletcher, R. (2000). *Information on mental health aspects of mental retardation and dual diagnosis.* National Association on Dual Diagnosis (NADD) Web page: www.thenadd.org/cgi=bin/router.pl?session=1781538168Location=/pages/dual/serv.htm.

Fujiki, M., & Brinton, B. (1993). Comprehension monitoring skills of adults with mental retardation. *Research in Developmental Disabilities, 14*(5), 409–421.

Grey, R. A. (1981). Services for the LD adult: A working paper. *Learning Disability Quarterly, 4,* 426–434.

Hallahan, D. P., & Kauffman, J. M. (1997). *Exceptional children: Introduction to special education* (7th ed.). Boston: Allyn & Bacon.

Hatton, C. (1998). Pragmatic language skills in people with intellectual disabilities: A review. *Journal of Intellectual & Developmental Disability, 23*(1), 79–100.

Hodapp, R. M., & Fidler, D. J. (1999). Special education and genetics: Connections for the 21st century. *Journal of Special Education, 33*(3), 130–151.

Langone, J. (1990). *Teaching students with mild and moderate learning problems.* Boston: Allyn & Bacon.

Luckasson, R. (Ed.). (1992). *Mental retardation: Definition, classification and systems of support.* Washington, DC: American Association on Mental Retardation.

MacMillan, D. L., Siperstein, G. N., & Gresham, F. M. (1996). A challenge to the viability of mild mental retardation as a diagnostic category. *Exceptional Children, 62*(4), 356–380.

Polloway, E. A., Smith, J. D., Patton, J. R., & Smith, T. E. C. (1996). Historical changes in mental retardation and developmental disabilities. *Education and Training in Mental Retardation and Developmental Disabilities, 31,* 3–12.

Merrill, E. C. (1992). Attentional resource demands of stimulus encoding for persons with and without mental retardation. *American Journal on Mental Retardation, 97*(1), 87–98.

Rondal, J. A., & Edwards, S. (1997). *Language in mental retardation.* London: Whurr Publishers.

Smith, B., & Phillips, C. J. (1992). Attainments of severely mentally retarded adolescents by aetiology. *Journal of Child Psychology & Psychiatry & Allied Disciplines, 33*(6), 1039–1058.

Tager-Flusberg, H. (1999). Language development in atypical children. In M. Barrett (Ed.), *The development of language* (pp. 311–348). Philadelphia: Psychology Press/Taylor & Francis.

Tomporowski, P. D., & Tinsley, V. (1997). Attention in mentally retarded persons. In W. E. MacLean, Jr. (Ed.), *Ellis' handbook of mental deficiency, psychological theory and research* (3rd ed., pp. 219–244). Mahwah, NJ: Lawrence Erlbaum.

Turner, L. A. (1998). Relation of attributional beliefs to memory strategy use in children and adolescents with mental retardation. *American Journal on Mental Retardation, 102*(2), 162–172.

Utley, C. A., Hoehn, T. P., Soraci, S. A., & Baumeister, A. A. (1993). Motivational orientation and span of apprehension in children with mental retardation. *Journal of Genetic Psychology, 154*(3), 289–295.

Vakil, E., Shelef-Reshef, E., & Levy-Shiff, R. (1997). Procedural and declarative memory processes: Individuals with and without mental retardation. *American Journal on Mental Retardation, 102*(2), 147–160.

Warren, S. F., & Yoder, P. J. (1997). Communication, language, and mental retardation. In W. E. MacLean, Jr. (Ed.), *Ellis' handbook of mental deficiency, psychological theory and research* (3rd ed., pp. 379–403). Mahwah, NJ: Lawrence Erlbaum.

Zetlin, A., & Murtaugh, M. (1990). Whatever happened to those with borderline IQs? *American Journal of Mental Retardation, 94*(5), 463–469.

Part II

Etiology and Prevention:
The Community Challenge

7

Genetic and Infectious Influences and Prevention

This chapter presents many of the genetic and chromosomal conditions that may be involved with mental retardation. It also explains how these conditions can be identified and sometimes prevented.

Anyone interested in mental retardation wonders about its cause. For families, there is often a period during which the question "Why did this happen?" occupies much of their thinking. Gaining some understanding of how and why any misfortune occurs can often be important to adjusting to change and moving on with our lives. In the case of disabilities, it is natural to want to learn all one can about the condition if it can be identified with certainty, or, if it cannot, to search for possible or likely causes. For many people, this question can never be answered, because in most instances, the cause or causes of retardation cannot be identified. Still, the desire for answers often remains.

The question "Why?" is also important in its relationship to prevention. When the cause of mental retardation is known, something might be done to avoid or even cure it. Whether a developmental disability results from a genetic or chromosomal abnormality, an infectious disease, exposure to environmental hazards, or child abuse and deprivation, prevention often closely follows from understanding the cause.

In addition, when a condition can be identified, it is often possible to learn something about a "typical" course of events in terms of expected behavioral and

---

Looking for an Answer to "Why?"

Elizabeth, who has an 18-month-old baby with severe disabilities involving mental retardation, talks about her search to understand what went wrong for Danielle:

One of two things were possible. One was called **craniostosis,** where the plates of the head (pieces of the skull) fuse too early, and it doesn't allow the brain to grow. We were hoping for that. It would have meant going in and cutting her skull open and putting spacers in, but we were hoping for that, because the alternative was **microcephaly,** which meant, for some other unknown reason, her brain just wasn't developing. And that's what it turned out to be. It was a rough time then. Things were just unfolding so quickly. I'd had two years of nursing and I've always read about babies and their development, so I could read between the lines. And what little bit of information I could get my hands on to read about microcephaly, all of that was pretty bad. It said "severe motor development retardation" and "severe mental retardation," and the prognosis always said "poor." We went to get a second opinion, because we wanted confirmation, and because we still didn't really know what

Elizabeth and her family.

Courtesy of Lynda Crane

happened. We were still searching for a cause, a reason, for everything that had happened to us.

intellectual characteristics, and this information may turn out to be more useful to intervention than was once believed (Hodapp & Fidler, 1999). We can be forewarned about possible behavioral problems or associated health or psychological difficulties and can learn about those techniques and services that have been helpful for others. But there is tremendous variability among people, and such information only offers guideposts. It does not provide a roadmap.

Even the severity of the disability often does not predict eventual functioning or life satisfaction. Those conditions caused by genetic abnormalities usually are more severe with regard to related health and physical problems and decreased intellectual abilities. Frequently, however, such people lead satisfying and productive lives in spite of these disabilities. On the other hand, people with milder forms of retardation (for which the cause is often unknown) may function poorly and lead troubled and difficult lives. Because environmental factors such as community and educational supports, and personal factors such as motivation and persistence, are so important to life functioning, those with milder forms do not necessarily function more effectively in their lives than those with more severe forms.

Genetic influences—the subject of this chapter—are complicated and often interact with environmental factors. Still, many are relatively well understood. In fact, over the last two decades, there has been an enormous expansion in the number of identified genetic conditions that result in mental retardation—as many as two or three new discoveries every week—so that genetic conditions are now known to account for approximately one-third of all cases of MR (Matalainen, Airaksinen, Mononen, Launiala, & Kaariainen, 1995).

GENETIC TRANSMISSION

Genes provide the instructions for our physical development and are the biological basis for appearance, health, psychology, and emotions. Genes are passed from parents to children at the time of conception.

Individual genes are made of **deoxyribonucleic acid (DNA),** a series of nucleotides that consist of four nitrogen-based substances: *adenine, cytosine, guanine,* and *thymine.* These nucleotides form a code that contains the molecular message of heredity—the literal instructions for our physical makeup. The specific and individual genetic code for each living being is determined by the particular structure or order of the nucleotides. Figure 7.1 gives an example of a normal code sequence and then possible changes (**mutations**) that could occur. By definition, such mutations are genetic abnormalities.

Genes are arranged on chromosomes; each chromosome consists of approximately 1,000 to 2,000 genes. Every cell in the body (except the reproductive cells) contains 46 chromosomes arranged in 23 pairs. Twenty-two of these are matching pairs called **autosomes** and are not sex-linked, but the 23rd pair (called **allosomes**) contains the XX (female) or XY (male) sex chromosomes. The reproductive cells in women (the ova) and men (the spermatozoa) contain only 23 single chromosomes (no pairs). Genes are passed through the reproductive cells.

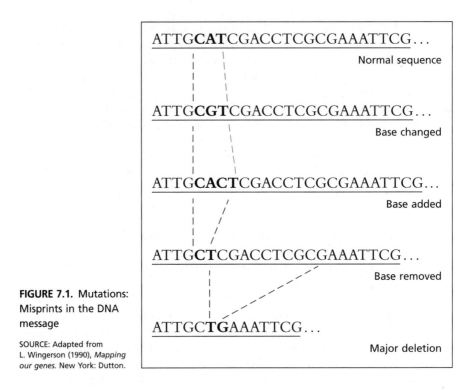

ATTG**CAT**CGACCTCGCGAAATTCG...
Normal sequence

ATTG**CGT**CGACCTCGCGAAATTCG...
Base changed

ATTG**CACT**CGACCTCGCGAAATTCG...
Base added

ATTG**CT**CGACCTCGCGAAATTCG...
Base removed

ATTG**CTG**AAATTCG...
Major deletion

FIGURE 7.1. Mutations: Misprints in the DNA message

SOURCE: Adapted from L. Wingerson (1990), *Mapping our genes.* New York: Dutton.

These cells combine and then undergo the cell division processes of **meiosis** and **mitosis** to produce a single cell with 23 paired chromosomes that becomes the embryo. At conception, then, the developing potential embryo receives one set of genetic material from each parent.

Genetic problems can be carried on either the autosomes or the allosomes and then passed directly from the parents. They can also occur after conception because of gene mutations or disjunction problems during cell division. Disjunction errors result in altered chromosome structures.

Gene Type and Appearance

The structural DNA composition of a gene is called its **genotype,** while the expression of that gene in some physical or psychological characteristic is called its **phenotype.** For example, those genes that determine eye color have a particular and specific DNA structure (genotype) that manifests itself in a corresponding eye color (phenotype). This distinction is important, because not every gene carried will express itself phenotypically; and whether it does is determined by many factors. It is therefore possible for someone to carry a gene for a disabling condition without that condition actually manifesting itself. Some of the reasons for this are described in the following sections, where we look at each of several types of hereditary transmission of genetic disorders. These types are classified in Figure 7.2.

I.   Single gene
    A. Autosomal dominant
    B. Autosomal recessive
    C. X-linked
II. Multifactorial
III. Chromosomal

FIGURE 7.2 Classes of Genetic Disorders

SOURCE: From D. Abuelo (1991), Genetic disorders. In J. L. Matson & J. A. Mulik (Eds.), *Handbook of mental retardation.* New York: Pergamon.

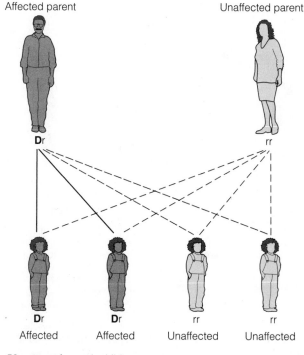

Affected parent

Unaffected parent

Dr

rr

Dr
Affected

Dr
Affected

rr
Unaffected

rr
Unaffected

Risk factor: 50 percent for each child.

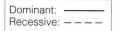

Dominant: ——————
Recessive: — — — —

The faulty gene (bold) dominates over its normal recessive counterpart.

FIGURE 7.3 Autosomal dominant inheritance

Autosomal Dominant Inheritance

Disorders that are transmitted through autosomal dominant inheritance are carried on a single gene, as illustrated in Figure 7.3. Often the members of a gene pair are not exact duplicates of each other and carry genotypes that potentially express opposing phenotypes. When a gene pair differs genotypically, it is sometimes the case that one **dominant** gene will express itself over the other. Those genes that will *not* manifest themselves phenotypically in the presence of a dominant gene

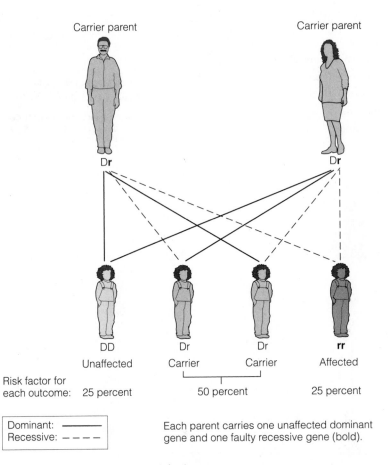

Carrier parent   Carrier parent

Dr   Dr

DD   Dr   Dr   **rr**
Unaffected   Carrier   Carrier   Affected

Risk factor for
each outcome: 25 percent   50 percent   25 percent

Dominant: ——————
Recessive: — — — —

Each parent carries one unaffected dominant
gene and one faulty recessive gene (bold).

FIGURE 7.4 Autosomal recessive inheritance

are called **recessive.** If a person carries a dominant gene for a disabling condition, then he will invariably experience that condition; if he passes that dominant gene to a child, the child will also be affected.

Autosomal Recessive Inheritance

As illustrated in Figure 7.4, for a disability to be transmitted through recessive inheritance, both parents must carry a recessive gene defect. Only those children who receive both recessive genes will manifest the phenotypical characteristics of the disability. If the child inherits both dominant genes, she will be unaffected entirely, and if she inherits only one recessive gene, she will be a carrier. This means that she will carry the gene but not be phenotypically affected.

X-Linked (Sex-Linked) Recessive Inheritance

When faulty recessive genes are carried on the X chromosome, the inheritance pattern for girls occurs just as in autosomal recessive inheritance. For boys, how-

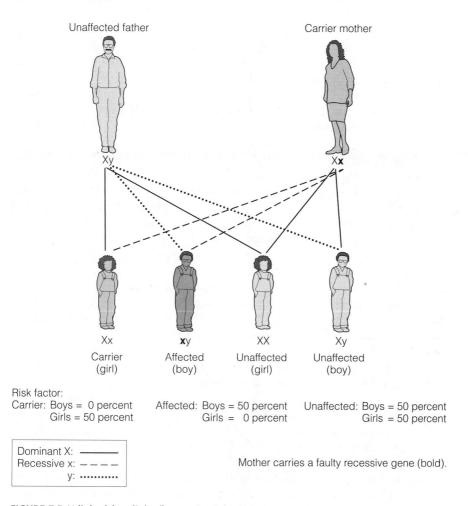

Risk factor:
Carrier: Boys = 0 percent   Affected: Boys = 50 percent   Unaffected: Boys = 50 percent
              Girls = 50 percent   Girls = 0 percent   Girls = 50 percent

Dominant X:	————
Recessive x:	– – – –
y:	··········

Mother carries a faulty recessive gene (bold).

FIGURE 7.5 X-linked (sex-linked) recessive inheritance

ever, X-linked inheritance is more complicated because they carry only a single X chromosome—by definition, the other chromosome is a Y. With only one X, a boy cannot possibly inherit a corresponding dominant gene to protect him from the effects of the faulty recessive gene. As a result, if a boy inherits a faulty recessive X-linked gene, the associated disability will show up even though he has only one. Figure 7.5 illustrates X-linked recessive transmission.

Penetrance, Variable Expressivity, and Polygenic Inheritance

Thus far, we have discussed only the most straightforward examples of inheritance, but further complexities exist even within these mechanisms. These further complications often indicate how much is yet to be learned about genetic transmission. One such example is **penetrance,** or the reliability of a faulty gene transmitting and producing a phenotypically recognizable abnormality. For some disabling conditions, penetrance is 100 percent: They always manifest themselves. Tay-Sachs, for example, is a fatal condition of the nervous system that is transmitted through autosomal recessive inheritance so that every child who receives the two faulty genes manifests the disease. Other conditions, however, have **high penetrance:** They usually show up, but not always. Still others have such **low penetrance** that they often do not appear phenotypically. One example occurs with the Fragile X chromosome: Approximately 20 percent of males with this chromosome condition show no apparent phenotypical abnormality (Reiss & Freund, 1990).

When the same genotype produces different symptoms or a different severity of symptoms in different individuals, it is called **variable expressivity.** Some, but not all, infants born with Down syndrome, for example, also have associated heart defects. The genotype for both of these groups *appears* to be identical.

Finally, some conditions result only from a particular combination of gene defects that may be transmitted separately and through different methods of inheritance. For an individual to manifest the condition, two or more of these gene defects must be present. This is called **polygenic inheritance.**

All of these complexities—penetrance, variable expressivity, and polygenic inheritance—involve several factors (some of which may be unknown) in hereditary transmission. Inheritance involving multiple factors is called **multifactorial inheritance.**

Genetic causality is even further complicated by the fact that some conditions can be caused by any one of several genetic abnormalities. In a way of speaking, there are sometimes many roads to the same place. For example, a rare genetic condition called *severe combined immune deficiency* (SCID) renders the immune system ineffective, because it functions much like AIDS. This was the much-publicized problem for David, who lived his life in an antiseptic plastic compartment designed to protect him from all bacteria and fungi. David's condition was caused by a defective gene on the X chromosome. SCID also can be caused by a gene defect on chromosome 20 (Thompson, 1994). As we will see, Down's syndrome can result from three different chromosomal abnormalities.

EXAMPLES OF GENETICALLY TRANSMITTED CONDITIONS

Tay-Sachs Disease

Like many other medically described conditions, Tay-Sachs disease is named after the physicians who first identified its characteristics. It is a catastrophic condition associated with deterioration in the central nervous system and is characterized by increasingly severe mental and physical retardation, blindness, and seizures. It is always fatal, often within the first 18 months but sometimes not until the third or fourth year of life.

Tay-Sachs is genetically transmitted through autosomal recessive inheritance. It is most frequently carried by people of Ashkenazic (Eastern European) Jewish backgrounds, although it can occur in the general population as well. The disease results from an enzymatic defect that destroys nerve cells.

Tay-Sachs is the more tragic in that the infant appears to develop normally for the first several months of life and then gradually deteriorates. Parents almost never know that the child has Tay-Sachs until after the deterioration begins and they have become secure in the expectation of normal development. Because there is no known therapy for the disease, families can only hopelessly and helplessly watch their child's inevitable decline and suffering. The responsible gene can be identified before conception in those who carry it, however, and prenatal testing can reveal the presence of Tay-Sachs in the fetus.

Lesch-Nyhan Disease

Lesch-Nyhan disease is another condition that results from an inherited enzymatic defect. Because of the severity of the condition, and the fact that it is transmitted through X-linked inheritance, it is found only in males.

> **FOR DISCUSSION** *Can you explain why a condition with a severe outcome, transmitted through X-linked inheritance, will be found only in males?*

Lesch-Nyhan is associated with cerebral palsy and usually with MR, although intellectual functioning can range from normal intelligence to severe mental retardation. Children with Lesch-Nyhan typically have slurred speech (because of motor damage associated with cerebral palsy), but they often develop good communication skills. Brain damage in Lesch-Nyhan is the result of a build up of excessive uric acid (Lesch & Nyhan, 1964). Children with Lesch-Nyhan used to die painfully from kidney disease associated with the formation of kidney stones, but these conditions can usually be managed somewhat, and life expectancy has been extended into the teens and beyond (Morales, 1999).

When children with Lesch-Nyhan first develop teeth, a severe and lasting form of **self-injurious behavior** (SIB) emerges. They bite their lips and fingers, and, even though pain sensation is normal, severely damage and frequently destroy tissue. They are also aggressive, biting and hitting others, and often spitting and cursing—all of which seem completely involuntary. In fact, when children with Lesch-Nyhan are in arm restraints, they are usually calm and often smiling and laughing—in marked contrast to their behavior when the restraints are removed. As they get older, they often actually ask for help in restraining their aggressive behavior.

Drug therapy to alter metabolism is sometimes useful in reducing the SIB, as is behavior modification. Rarely, however, is self-injury completely eliminated (Nyhan, 1994). As a result, sometimes the teeth must be extracted; there is a need for continual supervision, and almost all individuals who suffer from this condition spend some portion of the day in restraints. With difficulty in feeding and frequent vomiting, besides all of the above, caring for these children can be emotionally exhausting and physically demanding.

Table 7.1. Some Genetically Transmitted Conditions

Condition	Causal Description	Characteristics	Method of Inheritance	Incidence	Carrier Detection	Prenatal Detection
Cornelia de Lange syndrome	Unknown	Severe mental retardation	Unclear	1 in 10,000	No	Yes
Galactosemia	Metabolic disorder	Often fatal; MR in survivors; often can be prevented by diet	Autosomal recessive	1 in 40,000 births	No	Yes
Hydrocephalus	Obstruction causes fluid buildup in brain	Increasing mental retardation; usually fatal if untreated; surgery can often prevent damage	Multifactoral	1 in 1,000 infants	Yes, for hereditary type	Yes
Lesch-Nyhan syndrome	Enzyme deficiency	Mental retardation, cerebral palsy, and self-mutilation	X-linked recessive	1 in 380,000; probably underdiagnosed	No	Yes
Maple sugar or maple syrup urine disease	Metabolic disorder	Nervous system deterioration and early death, when untreated	Autosomal recessive	1 in 120,000; in Amish, 1 in 1,600	No	Yes
Neurofibromatosis	Neurocutaneous disorder (involves central nervous system and skin)	Varies considerably; sometimes mental retardation, often seizures	Autosomal dominant (or by mutation)	1 in 3,000	No	Probably available soon
Neural tube defects	Anencephaly: Parts of brain are missing; Spina bifida: Lower spine is not closed	Often early death; surgery may prolong life; Highly variable severity	Multifactorial; occurs in early pregnancy	Anencephaly: 1 in 1,000 birth; spina bifida: 3 in 1,000	No	Yes
Phenylketonuria (PKU)	Metabolic disorder	Mental retardation preventable by diet	Autosomal recessive	1 in 15,000; 1 in 80 whites is a carrier	No	Yes
Rett syndrome	Defective MECP2 gene on X chromosome	Normal development followed by mental and physical deterioration, seizures, SIB	Probably X-linked dominant; fatal to boys	1 in 10,000 to 1 in 15,000 girls	No	Not yet
Tay-Sachs disease	Enzyme disease	Usually fatal by 3 years; Progressive neuronal deterioration	Autosomal recessive	1 in 360,000; 1 in 2,500 Jewish couples	Yes	Yes
Tuberous sclerosis	Neurocutaneous	Varies; progressive; mental retardation, seizures, nonmalignant tumors	Autosomal dominant (or by mutation)	1 in 30,000	No	No
Wilson's disease	Metabolic disorder resulting in excessive copper in tissues	Progressive cerebral palsy and mental retardation; can be prevented with early detection	Autosomal recessive	1 in 1,000,000	No	No

Carrier detection of Lesch-Nyhan is not presently available, but prenatal testing can determine the condition's presence *in utero.* There is hope that Lesch-Nyhan and other severe metabolic disorders may eventually be eliminated through **gene therapy,** or the cloning of a new gene that will function in place of the defective gene. The implications of gene therapy are discussed in more detail later in the chapter.

Table 7.1 presents information about some of the better known genetically transmitted conditions that involve mental retardation.

COMMON CHROMOSOMAL CONDITIONS

Trisomy 21 and Other Trisomies

The term **trisomy** indicates that each cell has three **homologous** chromosomes rather than the typical paired two. Ordinarily, this condition develops because of errors in cell division during meiosis. The most common is **Trisomy 21,** which results in Down syndrome: Three homologous trisomy chromosomes appear on what would have been the 21st pair. Trisomy conditions also occur on other chromosome pairs. **Trisomy 18** and **Trisomy 13,** for example, are rarer than Trisomy 21, but they result in such severe congenital abnormalities that most infants do not survive their first year. A much milder example, **Trisomy 8,** is most common in males. The life span for those with Trisomy 8 appears to be normal, but mental retardation ranges from mild to severe (Pueschel & Thuline, 1991).

Down Syndrome

Down syndrome was first identified by J. Langdon Down, and it is now known to be the most common genetic condition to cause mental retardation (Epstein, 1999), even though 75 percent to 80 percent of conceptions that would result in babies with Down syndrome are spontaneously miscarried. Down described people with physical characteristics that (in his opinion) were typical of the races of Southeast Asia, people sometimes, but erroneously, called Mongolians (Down, 1866). For many years, Down syndrome was known as *mongolism,* and people who acquired it were called *mongols.* These outmoded terms are now recognized as pejorative and no longer used.

Recognizing the Presence of Down Syndrome The word **syndrome** implies that a condition is characterized by a group of typical signs and symptoms that can occur to greater or lesser extents. Symptoms of Down syndrome include low muscle tone (**hypotonia**), lack of the infant **Moro reflex** (in which the infant draws her arms in front of her chest when the surface on which she is lying is struck), and mental retardation. Congenital heart defects and **hypothyroidism** are also common. Typical physical characteristics include a depressed nasal bridge and small nose, small mouth, upward slant to the eyes, a single deep crease across

Three children with Down syndrome

© Earl & Nazima Kowall/Corbis; for illustrative purposes only

the center of the palm (**simian crease** or palmar crease) and small skin folds on the inner corner of the eyes (**epicanthal folds**). Infants with Down syndrome are especially susceptible to respiratory problems, and obstructed digestive tracts and childhood leukemia occur with greater than average frequency (National Down Syndrome Society, 1992). Down syndrome is equally common among all races and all social classes.

Three Causal Types   Down syndrome can occur because of any one of three chromosome problems: Trisomy 21, **mosaicism,** and **translocation.** The most common is Trisomy 21, which results from a failure in disjunction during meiosis; in other words, for some unknown reason, the chromosomes fail to divide properly (i.e., from 46 to 23 chromosomes). Scientists previously believed that the extra chromosome necessarily came from the ovum, but we now know that it can come from the sperm as well, perhaps in as many as 20 percent to 30 percent of all cases (Epstein, 1999). After age 35, women are progressively more likely to give birth to a child with Down syndrome, and there is some suggestion that because the ovum are carried in the female from conception—rather than produced throughout life as sperm are—the age of the ovum may be implicated in the likelihood of nondisjunction. This is clearly not the only reason for ovum disjunction failure, however, because 80 percent of all children with the condition are born to women younger than 35.

When problems with disjunction occur in mitosis (rather then meiosis), some cells have the trisomy pattern, while others do not. This occurrence is called **mosaicism,** which usually results in less severe symptoms.

Finally, Down syndrome also can result when part of a 21st chromosome breaks, often reattaching to another chromosome, usually the 13th, 14th, or 15th. This phenomenon is called *translocation,* and this type of transmission is often genetically inherited, whereas trisomy 21 and mosaicism are not.

Common Characteristics with Down Syndrome People with Down syndrome can have mental retardation from the minimal to the severe, while motor development and coordination are nearly always affected. Children walk, talk, and toilet train but at later than average ages. They attend school and often develop some reading and writing skills. As adults, they are frequently gainfully employed and live semiindependently in group homes or supervised apartments. Although such children are commonly believed to have perpetually sunny personalities, they are in reality subject to ordinary variations in mood.

Adolescents with Down syndrome experience the same changes at puberty as their peers, though puberty in boys may be somewhat delayed. Approximately half of all women are fertile and can bear children, but the risk of their offspring developing Trisomy 21 or some other developmental disability is approximately 35 percent to 50 percent. It had been assumed that men could not father children, but there has been at least one documented instance; with increased community integration, it is suspected that there will be more (Selikowitz, 1990).

Health and life span are highly dependent on whether heart defects, hypothyroidism, or leukemia develop and how they are managed. Although between 35 percent and 50 percent of children with Down syndrome have congenital heart defects, these defects often can be largely corrected by surgery, which reduces the likelihood of associated lung damage and increases longevity if successfully performed before 5 or 6 months of age (Kidd & Taussig, 1990). Today, there is also a high cure rate for the leukemia associated with Down syndrome, and hypothyroidism is readily discoverable with simple blood tests and easily treated. Timely

---

Down Syndrome in the News

Chris Burke, television celebrity from *Life Goes On,* is the editor of *News 'n Views,* a magazine published by the National Down Syndrome Society (NDSS). The magazine—written for young people with Down syndrome—features articles on job tips, movie reviews, and stories of highly achieving young people who have Down syndrome. According to Burke, the magazine also will be of interest to those without disabilities: "Everyone reading the magazine will better understand the hopes and goals of people with Down syndrome."

SOURCE: Adapted from "Rave reviews for *News 'n Views*" (1994), *National Down Syndrome Society* [NDSS] *Newsletter, 10*(2), 3.

detection is extremely important, however, because untreated hypothyroidism interferes with brain development and increases the severity of mental retardation (McCoy, 1990).

As a result of improved medical treatment, the average life span of someone with Down syndrome has risen from early adulthood to 55 years, while many individuals live into their 60s. By age 40, virtually all show Alzheimer's-type brain pathologies (according to brain scan technology), but many do not show clinical behavioral symptoms until age 50 or older, and a substantial proportion never do (Cody & Kamphaus, 1999).

Fragile X Syndrome

Fragile X is the most common known *inherited* form of mental retardation. Earlier called Martin-Bell syndrome, Fragile X is, as its name implies, a defect on the X chromosome, in the form of either a weak or a broken segment. Superficially, Fragile X appears to be transmitted through X-linked recessive inheritance, but there are deviations from the typical pattern. Sometimes women who are known to be carriers are symptom-free, as we would expect for recessive inheritance; in other instances, carrier females are affected (Freund, Abrams, & Reiss, 1991). Clarifying research indicates that first-generation carrier women are asymptomatic, but when the damaged chromosome is passed to their daughters, women in the second generation manifest symptoms of the syndrome (Freund, Reiss, & Abrams, 1993).

> **FOR DISCUSSION** *If women who carry the Fragile X chromosome can show symptoms, will the incidence of Fragile X likely be greater for males or for females?*

Recognizing the Presence of Fragile X Diagnosis of Fragile X depends on microscopic identification of the fragile site on the long arm of the X chromosome. Not all cells contain a damaged X, so the percentage of affected cells determines the percent of fragility. The percent of affected cells is related to the severity of symptoms in females, but apparently not in males (Reiss & Freund, 1990).

A person with Fragile X syndrome often has a long face, large ears, prominent jaw and forehead, **hypotonia,** and flat feet. In males after puberty, abnormally large testicles (**macro-orchidism**) develop. These features, however, vary among those with Fragile X while occurring frequently in other populations, so diagnosis cannot be made on the basis of physical phenotype alone.

Common Characteristics with Fragile X Mental retardation in males with Fragile X tends to be more severe than in females. In preschool boys, cognition is more consistent with their normal peers but not as they get older. Both males and females tend to have relatively strong scores on verbal tests, including vocabulary and early reading skills, but they are weaker on visual–spatial tasks and visual motor coordination. There is relatively greater difficulty with number and

This young man with Fragile X has the facial features typical of the syndrome.

Photo courtesy of Nancy Abrams and Simon Feather, FRAXA Research Foundation, www.fraxa.org

math concepts and often relatively good long-term memory but particular deficits in short-term *visual* memory.

Behavioral manifestations of Fragile X in children often include hyperactivity, attention deficits, and self-injury. Some characteristics are similar to those associated with autism (a condition described in Chapter 9), including **perseveration** of speech (repeating the same words over and over) and **echolalia** (repeating what others say word for word without comprehension). Other autistic-like behaviors often seen in children with Fragile X are social avoidance, gaze aversion, hypersensitivity to sound, repetitive smelling of nonfood objects, and motor behaviors such as rocking and twirling (called *stereotypical behaviors* or **stereotypies**) (Kerby & Dawson, 1994; Hagerman, 1996). However, severe autistic-like behaviors are most likely to occur in children from ages 2 to 7.

In spite of their problems, people with Fragile X can learn many things and have their own individual strengths and weaknesses. As with all children, their social development is of paramount importance. Because academic and adaptive success is so much greater when children (and adults) are socially appropriate, the development of skilled social behavior is an extraordinarily important issue of development for the child with Fragile X (Ghuman et al., 1998).

Table 7.2 Some Chromosomal Anomalies Associated with MR

Condition	Causal Description	Characteristics	Incidence
Cri du Chat	Deleted segment of chromosome 5	Mental retardation (often severe)	1 in 50,000
		Congenital heart disease	
		Shrill "cat-like" cry	
Down syndrome	Trisomy 21	Mental retardation	1 in 800 to 1 in 1,000
	Mosaicism	Typical facial features	By maternal age 36, 1 in 300
	Translocation	Congenital heart disease	By age 42, 1 in 70
			By age 48, 1 in 15
Fragile X syndrome	Damaged or broken segment of X chromosome	Mental retardation	1 in 1,000 males
		Hyperactivity	1 in 600 females
		Typical facial features	
Prader-Willi syndrome	Abnormality on chromosome 15	Mental retardation	1 in 5,000 to
		Poor muscle tone	1 in 100,000
		Insatiable appetite	
		Typical facial features	Often undiagnosed
		Aggression	
Williams syndrome	Microdeletion of chromosome 7	Mental retardation	1 in 10,000
		Heart and skeletal defects	
		Typical facial features	

Table 7.2 describes some of the chromosomal abnormalities that can be associated with mental retardation.

GENETIC COUNSELING
AND PRENATAL TESTING

Genetic counseling is sometimes available before a child is conceived, and it can determine whether the would-be parents are carrying identifiable genetic defects. Such testing is called *carrier detection,* but it is not available for every known condition. (See Table 7.1 for examples.) When faulty genes are detected, genetic counselors can describe the likelihood that a disability will occur, and the parents can use that information to help them decide whether to conceive a child, adopt a child, or decide against parenting altogether. Sometimes, couples opt to proceed with conception and then rely on prenatal testing to determine whether the faulty gene has actually been transmitted.

For many conditions, **prenatal testing** can determine whether a fetus is actually affected. The most commonly used prenatal test is **amniocentesis:** Fluid is extracted from the uterus by means of a hollow needle inserted through the abdominal wall; the fluid contains naturally discarded skin cells from the fetus. The fluid is analyzed chemically, and the cells within are cultured and examined microscopically to determine their chromosomal composition. Recently, DNA analytical methods have been developed that are capable of more finely detailed analysis of the genes themselves (Jorde, Carey, & White, 1997). Amniocentesis is routinely recommended for women ages 35 and older (primarily because of the increased risk of Down syndrome) or when a particular problem is suspected.

Amniocentesis has a quite small risk of inducing miscarriage: less than 0.5 percent. Cultures are sometimes unsuccessful and can therefore give no information, and the test can sometimes miss existing conditions. Most often, however, amniocentesis gives accurate information about the presence or absence of hundreds of genetic defects (Batshaw & Perret, 1992).

When a genetic problem is discovered, parents are faced with the choice of whether to continue or abort a pregnancy. For many people, the fact that amniocentesis cannot be carried out before the 14th week or so of pregnancy makes a hard decision even more difficult.

Another type of prenatal test, **chorionic villus sampling** (CVS), can be performed as early as six to eight weeks after conception. A needle is inserted through either the vagina or the abdominal wall to extract a small plug of tissue from the end of one of the hairlike projections (the chorionic villi) on the membrane that surrounds the embryo. This procedure entails a slightly higher risk of miscarriage, however, and a slight chance of causing limb deformities. In addition, the failure rates for CVS vary widely from hospital to hospital, and the genetic information received from the test does not always match that of the fetus (Wymelenberg, 1990).

An **ultrasound scanner** aims high-frequency sound waves at the uterus and translates their reflections onto a video monitor. Ultrasound is used with both chorionic villus sampling and amniocentesis to reduce the risk of injury. By itself, it can often determine the presence of hydrocephalus, as well as other structural malformations, and it is used to guide prenatal corrective interventions.

Two additional techniques are often used in prenatal diagnosis. In **fetoscopy,** a small tube with a light source on the end is inserted into the uterus to inspect the fetus for limb deformities. The tube also can obtain a fetal blood sample to test for the presence of hemophilia, sickle-cell anemia, and certain neural defects. When performed early in pregnancy, **maternal blood analysis** can reveal the presence of kidney disease, abnormal closure of the esophagus, **anencephaly** (absence of large portions of the brain), and **spina bifida** (abnormal opening in the spinal column).

Prenatal Intervention

Sometimes, conditions discovered through prenatal testing can be corrected or alleviated before the child is born; for example, **phenylketonuria** (PKU), a hereditary condition caused by a defective enzyme that prevents the body from metabolizing an essential amino acid. Early detection and prevention through change in the baby's diet protects the infant from brain damage and retardation (Waisbren, Brown, de Sonneville, & Levy, 1994). Although many states have mandatory screening requirements, these tests necessarily take place after the child is born, sometimes with a substantial wait for results, so that any necessary dietary changes are often delayed. Discovery in utero ensures that the newborn infant can receive immediate treatment at birth. Another metabolic disorder, **maple sugar urine disease** or maple syrup urine disease, can likewise be detected in utero. Tests for this disease are not routinely administered to new babies, and when undetected, infants typically die within a few weeks of birth (Batshaw & Perret, 1992).

Hydrocephalus Hydrocephalus is a condition that results from an obstruction in the brain that prevents the normal flow of cerebrospinal fluid from the brain through the spinal cord and to eventual discharge through the kidneys and urinary tract. This fluid is continually manufactured in the ventricles of the brain; when it cannot be normally discharged, there is inevitable brain damage and often death. Surgery can place a shunt at the base of the skull to allow the fluid to drain. It is usually successful in alleviating the most tragic results, but some damage still may already have occurred by the time the child is born. Recently, techniques have been developed that allow in utero surgery, but there are frequent complications and the practice is controversial.

Ethics and Implications

Prenatal testing involves important ethical issues that have caused serious debate: On the one hand, parents often worry about whether their expected infant is developing normally, and the technology is available to reassure them. What is more,

---

Plastic Surgery for People with Down Syndrome: A Useful Treatment or Example of Prejudice?

Plastic surgery has been performed on people with Down syndrome since 1977, although such operations have been more frequent in Europe than in the United States. The surgery primarily involves changing the look of facial features by removing a section of the tongue and inserting facial implants. Although proponents claim that surgery can result in improved speech, breathing, and better general health, reduced social stigma is cited as the major advantage (May & Turnbull, 1992). Critics respond that there is little evidence of any actual functional benefit, and that surgery is never completely successful in eliminating typical facial features (Arndt, Lefebvre, Travis, & Munro, 1986; Novoselsky, Katz, & Kravetz, 1988). Op-

ponents believe that the responsibility for social acceptance resides with society, and that children should not be subjected to a painful surgical procedure (and its associated risks of complication) simply to conform.

If surgery can be shown to improve health or speech clarity, then it might gain wider acceptance. But if the only advantage is changed appearance, then working to improve prejudicial attitudes could be more productive and involve less physical risk. In fact, the large numbers of prospective parents who hope to adopt children with Down syndrome and the eagerness of many college students to work with such children are heartening indications of increasing social interest and acceptance.

physicians can be alerted to the need for special procedures that can modify or lessen damage. On the other hand, there is concern about the widespread use of expensive procedures (including prenatal testing, fetal monitoring during delivery, and cosmetic surgery) that involve some risk and frequently provide no real benefit.

Adjusting to New Expectations

There has been much written about the extent to which parents of children with disabilities go through a period of denial—a time when they cannot bring themselves to admit the presence or the severity of a disability. Although recent evidence suggests that the role of denial in family adjustment has been overstated, it is natural for any of us to need time to adjust to severely changed expectations and requirements. When prenatal testing reveals the presence of a serious disability, parents are forced to face issues that involve their own abilities and resources before the child is even born.

Without question, prenatal testing can provide valuable information. Parenting is a serious responsibility, and a child with a disability presents an extended set of profound parenting challenges. Whether these challenges are more demanding than those offered by children without recognizable or nameable disabilities depends so much on the individual circumstances of the child and family that such a question is impossible to answer in advance—and may never be answerable. Still, the sooner we know the types of challenges we face, the sooner we can confront those challenges and begin to gather helpful and necessary resources.

Because medical science cannot yet correct or treat most genetic and chromosomal disorders, parents often face the question of whether to continue with a pregnancy or elect a therapeutic abortion when they receive an unfavorable prenatal report. In these times of harsh debate about abortion, this issue is obviously controversial. In regard to fetuses with disabilities, the debate involves matters beyond the right-to-life and prochoice positions. One of these involves the influence of attitudes and assumptions that people may have about the worth of those who have disabilities.

Cultural misunderstanding and prejudice against disabilities in general and mental retardation in particular (together with the need for haste) may influence some parents to terminate a pregnancy and later regret that decision. In addition, the question of abortion may no longer concern effects on the mother's life, health, or psychological well-being but rather focus on the desirability of the particular child so that an otherwise wanted pregnancy is terminated. Abortion of fetuses with known abnormalities has been supported at times as a form of prevention (Hansen, 1978) or eugenic control (McCormick, 1974). Parents' fears about their ability to handle a child with a disability also may be fueled by overly pessimistic predictions of the child's future.

Physicians find themselves vulnerable to lawsuits when they do not provide prenatal testing options and a child is later born with a condition related to mental retardation. In such cases, courts have awarded parents compensation and punitive damages for negligent prenatal counseling that resulted in what has been termed "wrongful birth" (Fleisher, 1987).

One Mother's Experience

Anna, whose first baby was born with Tay-Sachs, describes the importance of prenatal testing to her:

"After watching our baby slowly die over his first two years of life from

Tay-Sachs disease, we definitely decided we would have prenatal testing. That is the only way we dared to attempt another pregnancy."

SOURCE: From Isle, 1993.

FOR DISCUSSION   *What responsibility do physicians have for advising patients of existing technology? How should widespread testing be financed?*

The issues that surround therapeutic abortion are understandably complex. Much of the concern comes specifically in response to frequent abortions in cases of Down syndrome and other relatively less serious conditions. In these instances, the experiences of those who are actually and enjoyably rearing such children may encourage prospective parents. Further, there are waiting lists of people who want to adopt children with manageable disabilities. In the case of a fetus with Tay-Sachs or another tragic or fatal enzyme deficiency, the options and outcome are clearly different.

In any case, parents who face such serious challenges have varying emotional and financial resources, and there may be significant competing considerations. It is important that physicians have the experience to provide factual available information from community and service-oriented sources (in addition to medical ones) and that they provide alternative options and sensitive guidance that will help parents make their own independent, knowledgeable decisions (Pueschel, 1991).

THE FUTURE OF GENETIC RESEARCH

The Human Genome Project

The **Human Genome Project** (HGP) is the largest biological research project ever undertaken. Funded primarily by national governments, its goal is to identify and then decipher all of the genes inherited at conception, some 50,000 to 100,000. This means that scientists are beginning to understand the exact chemical structure of the DNA for every gene and exactly where each gene belongs on the 23 sets of chromosomes. This process is called **gene mapping** and is illustrated in Figure 7.6. As a result, the possibility is increasing that healthy genes will one day be artificially created and that faulty genes will be repaired.

The project is international in scope, with individual national projects coordinated by the **Human Genome Organization** (HUGO), which seeks to avoid the problems of international competition and secrecy (Goodman, 1998). The or-

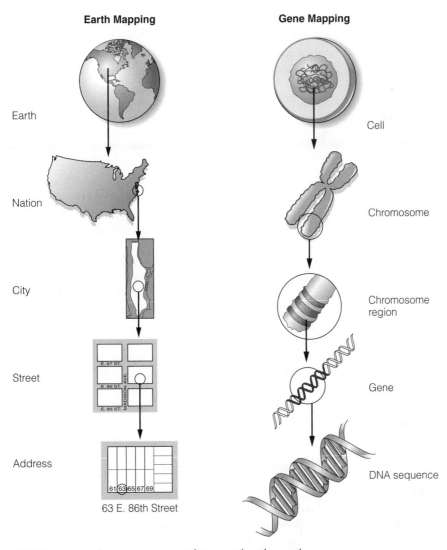

FIGURE 7.6 Mapping genes compared to mapping the earth

SOURCE: Adapted from L. Wingerson (1990), *Mapping our genes.* New York: Dutton.

ganization hopes to ensure that findings from the project are shared among all nations. Still, private companies took up their own projects and have progressed even more quickly than the U.S. government's initiative, so it remains to be seen what products will emerge and when.

Genetic Manipulations

Gene cloning and other genetic therapies are not simply wild science fiction stories that foreshadow far distant possibilities for future generations: They are realities in today's medical world. In 1990, the first gene transplant was successfully performed on Ashanthi DeSilva, a 4-year-old girl with SCID (see p. 152). A normal copy of the defective gene was inserted into her white blood cells, with the result that her own immune system could now protect her. Since then, gene transfers have been performed on hundreds of patients with a wide variety of illnesses (Thompson, 1994).

The potential for improved wellness from mapping the genetic code and developing corresponding gene therapies is enormous. New ways to treat or prevent cancer, heart disease, and more than 3,000 known genetic conditions are more and more likely. Chromosome 21 was the first to be fully mapped, and the sequencing of its 1,000 genes progresses, with findings rapidly being made (Patterson, 1995). With the hope of eventual intervention and cure, researchers are specifically looking for the genes that are related to the mental retardation and heart defects associated with Down syndrome. Similar work is taking place with more than 1,500 other genetically induced conditions, and this number dramatically increases each year (Goodman, 1998).

Information from gene mapping and sequencing will work in combination with other new technologies for use in genetic counseling. Already, tests that require only rinsing the mouth with water can sometimes reveal whether people carry genes for cystic fibrosis or sickle-cell anemia. Such innovations are making genetic testing less expensive and more accessible.

In spite of the fact that genes are constantly repairing themselves from the harmful effects of various forces in the environment, cumulative damage eventually occurs. It may also be possible, however, to estimate the environmental damage to a particular individual's genes from smoking, air pollution, and other toxins. Such testing would enable physicians to identify dangerous gene mutations long before clinical effects could emerge. Physicians might, for example, eliminate a cancer years before it would actually manifest itself (Wingerson, 1998).

Ethical Considerations

Certainly, people with MR are no less valuable as human beings than those without disabilities, and affected individuals and their families sometimes change and grow in positive ways that they believe result from the disability. Still, virtually all of them agree that they would not ask for and would prefer not to have such challenges. Recognizing this fact, the NDSS (an organization of family and professional advocates for people with Down syndrome) provides financial support to genetic researchers who are working to correct chromosome 21 defects. For families of a child with Lesch-Nyhan or for someone with multiple sclerosis, the possibility of gene therapy provides a long-awaited miracle, not only for them but also for others who may be spared the serious difficulties, tragedy, and heartbreak that genetic disorders cause.

Inherent in the technology, however, are many complex and potentially dangerous possibilities. The capacity to identify genetic problems easily and routinely by necessity precedes the means to eliminate or cure them. The gene and the DNA structure responsible for sickle-cell anemia, for example, have been understood for some time, yet no treatment has been thus far successful (Wingerson, 1990). As treatments for genetic disorders do become available, they are likely to be expen-

---

The Promises of Modern Genetics

Darren is a college student with a rare genetic disorder that makes him increasingly physically disabled. He describes his response to the possibility that researchers will find the responsible gene:

"I thought, Finally! There's someone out there who's doing some work, instead of just telling me, 'Go home and don't worry about it.' That started to make me change inside. I think as long as you know there's something out there, that there's a chance, there's someone working, that's what makes you feel good."

SOURCE: From L. Wingerson (1990), *Mapping our genes.* New York: Dutton.

---

sive, and it is probable that such expense will engender serious prejudices. How might insurance companies react to the news, for example, that someone is definitely going to develop a serious and expensive condition? Or how might an employer or potential employer respond (Bishop & Waldholz, 1990)? What is the probability that characteristics other than disease and disability will be altered or managed? Remembering the thousands of people who were involuntarily sterilized during this century (see Chapter 3), we might wonder whether prospective parents who *carry* the genes for disabling conditions could be denied the right to reproduce (Smith, 1994). Who will control this technology? How can it be controlled?

> **FOR DISCUSSION** *What are some possible means of regulation? Who, in your opinion, should have power over the use of genetic technology?*

The practical realities that result from genome research will be regulated, not only by science but also by law—and law is responsive to the moral and political positions of the day, as well as the attitudes and prejudices of the culture. How wisely and ethically do we deal with our current technologies? What part will education and religion ultimately play in such decisions?

With this brave new world of possibilities comes an extraordinarily sobering responsibility. As is common with our new technologies, individual scientists and researchers often have the intelligence and skill to develop innovations that promise revolutionary cultural improvement, yet society at large lacks the wisdom and foresight to manage them responsibly. There are also often dangerous and perhaps disastrous potentialities that scientists themselves do not admit or foresee. In fact, we might predict with each apparent advance in science, a kind of downside through abuse, misuse, or social ignorance. We can be sure that the moral and ethical decisions surrounding genetic technology will have truly profound and long-lasting effects.

> **FOR DISCUSSION** *Discuss other technologies that carry profound implications. What are they and how are they being managed?*

▌▌ LOOKING AHEAD ▶

From the overview of many of the genetic and chromosomal disorders presented in this chapter, and the discussion of the available methods of intervening to prevent or lesson the severity of the related intellectual disability, it is clear that cures for most of these conditions remain in the future. For the majority of people with mental retardation, however, the causal influences are not genetic but social and psychological factors and events that could be alleviated. Chapter 8 covers several of these contributing factors and discusses ideas and programs to eliminate them.

INFOTRAC COLLEGE EDITION

Cindy arrived yesterday with her mother for her first day in your classroom. From her mother, you learned that Cindy has been diagnosed with Fragile X syndrome. Because you want to learn as much as you can about Fragile X in order to help Cindy, you look up the disorder using *InfoTrac College Edition*. Please describe what you have learned from your research, and, specifically, how you will use that information to enhance Cindy's classroom experience.

REFERENCES

Arndt, E. M., Lefebvre, A., Travis, F., & Munro, I. R. (1986). Fact and fantasy: Psychosocial consequences of facial surgery in 24 Down syndrome children. *British Journal of Plastic Surgery, 39,* 498–504.

Batshaw, M. L., & Perret, Y. M. (1992). *Children with disabilities: A medical primer* (3rd ed.) Baltimore, MD: Paul H. Brookes.

Bishop, J., & Waldholz, M. (1990). *Genome.* New York: Simon & Schuster.

Cody, H., & Kamphaus, R. W. (1999). Down syndrome. In S. Goldstein & C. R. Reynolds (Eds.), *Handbook of neurodevelopmental and genetic disorder in children.* New York: Guilford.

Down, J. L. H. (1866). Observations on an ethnic classification of idiots. *London Hospital, Clinical Lectures and Reports, 3,* 259–262.

Epstein, C. J. (1999). The future of biological research on Down syndrome. In J. A. Rondal, J. Perera, & L. Nadel (Eds.), *Down's syndrome: A review of current knowledge* (pp. 210–222). London: Taylor & Francis.

Fleisher, L. S. (1987). Wrongful births. When is there liability for prenatal injury? *American Journal of Diseases of Children, 141,* 1260–1265.

Freund, L. S., Abrams, M. T., & Reiss, A. L. (1991). Brain and behavior correlates of the Fragile X syndrome. *Current Opinion in Psychiatry, 4,* 667–673.

Freund, L. S., Reiss, A. L., & Abrams, M. T. (1993). Psychiatric disorders associated with Fragile X in the young female. *Pediatrics, 91*(2), 321–329.

Ghuman, J. K., Freund, L., Reiss, A., Serisint, J., & Folstein, J. (1998). Early detection of social interaction problems: Development of a social interaction instrument in young children. *Journal of Developmental and Behavioral Pediatrics, 19*(6), 411–419.

Goodman, L. (1998). The Human Genome Project aims for 2003. *Genome Research, 8,* 997–999.

Hagerman, R. J. (1996). Fragile X syndrome. *Child and Adolescent Psychiatry Clinics of North America, 5,* 881–894.

Hansen, H. (1978). Decline of Down's syndrome after abortion reform in New York state. *American Journal of Mental Deficiency, 83*(2), 185–188.

Hodapp, R. M., & Fidler, D. J. (1999). Special education and genetics: Connections for the 21st century. *Journal of Special Education, 33*(3), 130–149.

Isle, S. (1993). *Precious lives painful choices: A prenatal decision-making guide.* Long Lake, MN: Wintergreen Press.

Jorde, L. B., Carey, J. C., & White, R. L. (1997). *Medical genetics.* St. Louis: Mosby.

Kerby, D. S., & Dawson, B. L. (1994). Autistic features, personality, and adaptive behavior in males with the Fragile X syndrome and no autism. *American Journal of Mental Retardation, 98*(4), 455–462.

Kidd, L., & Taussig, H. B. (1990). *The heart and Down syndrome.* New York: National Down Syndrome Society.

Lesch, M., & Nyhan, W. L. (1964). A familial disorder of uric acid metabolism and central nervous system function. *American Journal of Medicine, 36,* 561–570.

Matalainen, R., Airaksinen, E., Mononen, T., Launiala, K., & Kaariainen, R. (1995). A population-based study on the causes of severe and profound mental retardation. *Acta Paediatrica, 84,* 261–266.

May, D. C., & Turnbull, N. (1992). Plastic surgeons' opinions of facial surgery for individuals with Down syndrome. *Mental Retardation, 30*(1), 29–33.

McCormick, T. R. (1974). Ethical issues in amniocentesis and abortion. *Texas Reports on Biology and Medicine, 32,* 299–309.

McCoy, E. (1990). *Endocrine conditions in Down syndrome.* New York: National Down Syndrome Society.

Morales, P. C. (1999). Lesch-Nyhan syndrome. In S. Goldstein & C. R. Reynolds (Eds.), *Handbook of neurodevelopmental and genetic disorders in children* (pp. 478–498). New York: Guilford.

National Down Syndrome Society (1992). *Questions and answers about Down syndrome.* New York: NDSS.

Novoselsky, A., Katz, S., & Kravetz, S. (1988). Children with Down syndrome: Their evaluation by their peers before and after plastic surgery. *Issues in Special Education and Rehabilitation, 5,* 89–99.

Nyhan, W. L. (1994). The Lesch-Nyhan disease. In T. Thompson & D. B. Gray (Eds.), *Destructive behavior in developmental disabilities: Diagnosis and treatment* (pp. 181–197). Thousand Oaks, CA: Sage.

Patterson, D. (1995). The integrated map of human chromosome 21. In C. J. Epstein, T. Hassold, I. T. Lott, L. Nadel, & D. Patterson (Eds.), *Etiology and pathogenesis of Down syndrome* (pp. 43–55). New York: Wiley-Liss.

Pueschel, S. M. (1991). Ethical considerations relating to prenatal diagnosis of fetuses with Down syndrome. *Mental Retardation, 29*(4), 185–190.

Pueschel, S. M., & Thuline, H. C. (1991). Chromosome disorders. In J. L. Matson & J. A. Mulick (Eds.), *Handbook of mental retardation* (2nd ed., pp. 115–138). New York: Pergamon Press.

Reiss, A. L., & Freund, L. (1990). Fragile X syndrome. *Biological Psychiatry, 27,* 223–240.

Smith, J. D. (1994). Reflections on mental retardation and eugenics, old and new: Mensa and the human genome project. *Mental Retardation, 32*(3), 234–238.

Selikowitz, M. (1990). *Down syndrome: The facts.* New York: Oxford University Press.

Thompson, L. (1994). *Correcting the code: Inventing the genetic cure for the human body.* New York: Simon & Schuster.

Waisbren, S. E., Brown, M. J., de Sonneville, L. M. J., & Levy, H. L. (1994). Review of neuropsychological functioning in treated phenylketonuria. *Acta Paediatrica* (Supplement 407), 98–103.

Wingerson, L. (1990). *Mapping our genes: The genome project and the future of medicine.* New York: Dutton.

Wingerson, L. (1998). *Unnatural selection.* New York: Bantam.

Wymelenberg, S. (1990). *Science and babies: Private decisions, public dilemmas.* Washington, DC: National Academy Press.

8

Biological and Psychosocial Influences and Prevention

This chapter focuses on the interaction between biological and psychosocial influences, and it outlines several ways in which these influences can lead to mental retardation. It also discusses methods of intervention and prevention.

There is seldom a clear distinction between biological and environmental influences, even at the genetic level. Although genetic influences are clearly biological, the phenotypical outcome is often influenced by environmental events, as we have seen. In fact, environmental toxins and pollutants can actually cause genetic mutations. Nevertheless, the last chapter focused primarily on genetic causation that is transmitted through heredity or related to chromosomal disjunction and which can be meaningfully described without major reference to the environment.

Most biological causes of retardation, however, are so intertwined with environmental and psychosocial issues that it is impossible to gain a meaningful understanding outside that context. Likewise, it is the rare social circumstance that results in retardation separate from any biological influence. Therefore, it is often impossible even to place a particular cause in either the biological or environmental category. A brain infection that results in mental retardation, for example, is clearly a biological event, yet that infection may have been caused by a virus contracted from the environment. When mental retardation is the result of lead poisoning, clearly the environment is at fault. Yet lead poisoning is more likely to result in retardation when children are very young and when their bodies contain low levels of iron. These factors are obviously biological—except that iron deficiency results from poor nutrition, which is, in turn, a psychosocial issue.

You see, then, how these factors intertwine and why it is usually impossible to place causes exclusively in one category or another. As you proceed through this chapter, keep this essential complexity in mind. Environmental toxins, infant mortality, and prenatal care (the first three topics discussed in this chapter) clearly show the interaction between biological and psychosocial issues and how prevention depends upon cultural solutions.

SOME PSYCHOSOCIAL INFLUENCES

Environmental Toxins

People who live in poverty and, as a related circumstance, those from minority groups, are by far the most likely to be affected by environmental hazards that can result in mental retardation. Undesirable hazardous facilities such as waste dumps are usually located in low-income areas, as are air- and water-polluting industries. Both the homes and workplaces of low-income people are thus more apt to be toxically contaminated (Cvetkovich & Earle, 1992). Environmental pollution is an important social and biological issue that affects not only the quality of life, but also the incidence of mental retardation for the increasing numbers of people who are affected by poverty.

People from the middle and upper classes, however, are by no means untouched by toxic hazards: Entire communities have been served notice of abnormally high lead levels in their drinking water, while many lead-contaminant inks and dyes are still widely used. High levels of polychlorinated biphenyls (PCBs) found in Great Lakes fish also have been implicated in the incidence of certain developmental disabilities (Jacobson, 1998). These incidents are plain warnings that reckless management of air, water, and soil quality inevitably affects everyone.

FOR DISCUSSION *What environmental hazards exist in your community? What is being done to eliminate them?*

Infant Mortality and Morbidity Rates

A nation's *infant mortality rate* (the number of babies born alive who die before their first birthday) is closely related to the incidence of developmental disabilities. The United States has the highest rate among 21 industrialized countries (Picard, Del Dotto, & Breslau, 2000). This death rate—as high as 18 per 1,000 in many U.S. urban areas—is strongly associated with the large number of babies who are born prematurely or with **low birth weight** (LBW). Of those low–birth-weight babies who survive, many have disabilities. Although these complications are sometimes the result of congenital abnormalities or prenatal exposure to toxins, they occur most often in women who do not receive adequate prenatal care (Lewis, 1999).

Prenatal Care

Two factors—whether or not a prospective mother receives prenatal care and the quality of that care—are important not only to her baby's survival, but also to his health and future development. The incidence of disabilities associated with MR is high for low-birth-weight babies, and poor prenatal care is ordinarily associated with poverty.

Poor women frequently receive little or no prenatal care because they are unable to pay for it. Those who have low-paying jobs (or work part-time) neither have employer-provided insurance nor are eligible for Medicaid. These women must rely on public health clinics, which are not available in many areas and often have long waiting lists. When new patients are accepted, it is not unusual for them to wait several months for their first appointment. In addition, most clinics have daytime hours only, which means lost work time and pay for many women. Clinics that have expanded their hours have had marked increases in the numbers of patients seeking care (Stringer, 1998). Poor women also often have no available transportation to reach clinics. To complicate matters even further, some clinics only see patients on a first-come, first-served basis—which can mean an early morning arrival followed by a two- or three-hour wait to see a physician for only a few minutes. Women who must take young children with them may find these conditions overwhelmingly discouraging.

Many women who are eligible for Medicaid are not enrolled in the system, while others either do not know they are eligible or do not know how to apply. Application forms may be as long as 40 pages and have as many as 100 questions.

Merely *applying* often requires two or more trips to a Medicaid office, which always requires long waits. Even a single missing document such as a utility bill can preclude eligibility. Women whose lives are already chaotic and stressed or who do not have the skills to decipher complicated instructions and maintain well-organized and complete records are ill equipped to complete this process.

Prospective mothers who do have Medicaid often must rely on clinics anyway—with all of the described problems—because many physicians do not accept Medicaid patients because of its extensive paperwork, slow claims processing, uncertain payment, and reimbursement rates that are far lower than physicians' customary fees (Stringer, 1998). After a lifetime of poor nutrition, high stress, and unhealthy environmental conditions, many Medicaid recipients have high-risk pregnancies, and some physicians, already plagued by exorbitant malpractice-insurance rates, fear the increased risks of unfavorable outcomes accompanied by lawsuits. In reality, however, few low-income women sue for malpractice, because they have as little access to the legal system as to the medical. Malpractice lawsuits are often accepted based on a contingency fee for a percentage of the award, and because awards are based (in part) on lost earnings, attorneys have little incentive to take such cases.

Five principal federal programs provide prenatal care and nutritional supplements for low-income women:

1. Medicaid,
2. maternal and child health services block grants,
3. the Special Supplemental Food Program for Women, Infants, and Children (WIC),
4. community health centers, and
5. migrant and rural health centers.

Were these existing services better coordinated with one another at the community level, they probably could provide more effectively for the needs of most pregnant women. With similar administrative rules and regulations, including eligibility requirements and cooperative enrollment plans, more women and babies could be helped, and money would be saved (Widerstrom, 1999).

A Biological Constraint: Critical Period As we seek to understand psychosocial prenatal damage and judge the probable effectiveness of various interventions, we must consider the biological concept of **critical period.** A critical period is that time when harmful influences can permanently interfere with development, so if a particular structure or behavior does not develop then, it never will. Table 8.1 describes critical periods for some major physiological structures. Initial brain development, our most important consideration, begins in approximately the third week of gestation and continues during the first two years of life. During this entire time, development can be disrupted; but interventions to offset such harmful influences also are especially likely to be effective in this period. As you learn about additional causes of mental retardation, you will see that a healthy environment is essential for normal brain development throughout the critical prenatal period.

Table 8.1 Some Critical Periods for Prenatal Development

Structure	Most Critical Gestational Weeks
Brain	3 through 40
Heart	3 through 6
Eyes	4 through 8
Upper and lower limbs	4 through 7
Ears	4 through 9
Teeth	6 through 8

Maternal Health and Nutrition

Good maternal health and nutrition are prerequisites for optimal prenatal development. It is not surprising that poverty limits both. Poor maternal nutrition has serious consequences for the intellectual development of the fetus, particularly when the mother's diet is inadequate during the final trimester (Bendich, 1993). Babies from such pregnancies are more likely to be premature or especially small when full-term, have a small head circumference, and die during their first year. Many are unresponsive and have an abnormally high-pitched and irritating cry when aroused. When these babies do survive, learning problems are common as they get older.

Prematurity and Low Birth Weight

As we have seen, poverty and poor prenatal care are associated with increased risks of prematurity and low birth weight. Both conditions, however, also can be caused by other circumstances, including maternal infection or illness, genetic errors, the ingestion of toxic substances, and accidents.

Prematurity refers to births that occur before the 37th week of gestation (the normal period is 40 weeks). Premature babies are often tiny and have immature circulatory and pulmonary systems (hearts and lungs). They are more likely to suffer respiratory problems that can result in **anoxia** (damagingly low levels of oxygen). They are also subject to **cerebral hemorrhage** from ruptures of immature blood vessels in the brain. The resulting brain damage is often associated with mental retardation and cerebral palsy (Fletcher et al., 1997).

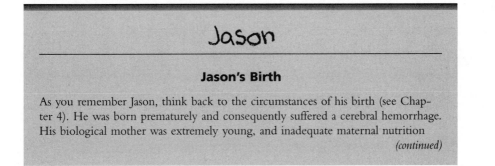

Jason

Jason's Birth

As you remember Jason, think back to the circumstances of his birth (see Chapter 4). He was born prematurely and consequently suffered a cerebral hemorrhage. His biological mother was extremely young, and inadequate maternal nutrition

(continued)

and late or nonexistent prenatal care probably contributed to the birth complications. Given all of these factors, Jason's developmental problems are not surprising. His bad start on the journey of life has stolen the physical and psychological advantages Jason would otherwise have had. Although he may yet overcome or adjust to the illness and developmental delay he is currently encountering, no one can give back to him the healthy infancy and associated developmental experience that he has missed.

Low-birth-weight (LBW) babies are born full-term but nevertheless weigh less than 2,500 grams (5 lbs., 8 oz.). These babies also are termed *small for gestational age* (SGA) and **small for date,** a condition that can occur in both premature and full-term babies. Low-birth-weight babies are more likely to die during their first year of life and more likely to have disabilities that often include mental retardation.

The last several decades have brought major improvements in postnatal care for premature infants, with the result that even the smallest babies often survive. Many of these infants, however, have severe developmental disabilities, and more have milder learning problems. Similarly, low-birth-weight babies are twice as likely as those of normal weight to later repeat a grade in school—three times as likely if they also grow up in poverty (Newman & Buka, 1991). Although intensive and extensive hospital care has improved dramatically (so that more premature babies survive) there has been no corresponding decrease in the number of premature births and low-birth-weight babies who are born. When premature

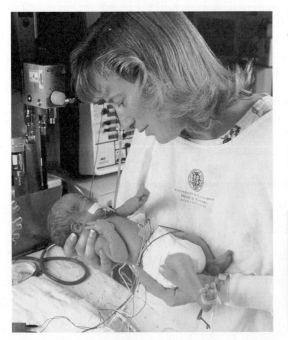

More premature infants survive than ever before.

© Jonathan Nourok/PhotoEdit

This infant is at greater risk for developmental disabilities because she was born with low birth weight.

© Laura Dwight/Corbis

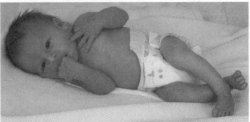

and low-birth-weight pregnancy outcomes are prevented, the savings in human and material costs are enormous.

> **FOR DISCUSSION**   *What factors discussed so far make premature birth less likely? As the chapter proceeds, keep track of additional methods to reduce this incidence.*

Adolescent Pregnancy

Infants from teen pregnancies are at high risk for developmental disabilities and even for death. In fact, the death rate for babies of mothers between ages 15 and 19 is 13 percent higher than for older mothers; for girls younger than 15, the rate increases by 60 percent. Both premature delivery and low-birth-weight babies are more common for young mothers. The likelihood that a 15-year-old girl will have a low-birth-weight baby is twice that of women ages 20 to 24 (McWhirter et al., 1993), and these risks are even greater for those who live in poverty.

Joyce

Joyce's Friend Kim

Let's return to Joyce, and see how things are going, because there have been changes in her life as a result of her last assessment (see Chapter 5). Once Joyce began spending time with Lisa (her peer tutor) at school, they got to know each other well and actually became friends. Together, they have attended several out-side school-related activities. At the same time, Joyce's grandmother has become more restrictive of Joyce's other outside activities, so that she is spending little time with her old crowd. At first, Joyce especially resented the loss of contact with her boyfriend, who was unwilling to visit Joyce at her home or join in school-related activities. But an event involving Joyce's good friend Kim has caused her to view this "loss" quite differently.

Kim (now 14) and Joyce have been close since early childhood. In fact, it was Kim who introduced Joyce to the "fast" crowd with which she had been spending time. Three weeks ago, Kim (who was 7½ months pregnant) gave birth to a two-pound, five-ounce baby girl. Last week, the infant (who had been on a respirator since birth), suffered a severe cerebral hemorrhage and died. Joyce was completely shocked. It had never entered her mind that such a thing would actually happen, though Olive (Joyce's adult friend) had warned her that babies of young mothers often have serious problems. To her family, Joyce has said little, but she has confided to Lisa that since the baby's death, she knows that she is not ready to risk a pregnancy.

The reasons for the high rate of mortality and developmental disabilities among babies of young mothers are many. Often young girls do not get proper nutrition, because they may not concern themselves with getting a complete diet, and they rarely take vitamin and mineral supplements. In addition, they may engage in high-risk behaviors involving drug use, especially nicotine and alcohol. By definition, their youthfulness means they may not have the physical maturity to support a healthy pregnancy and delivery, although recent studies have shown that with proper prenatal care, age alone does not usually determine an unfavorable outcome (Williams & Decoufle, 1999).

Seriously compounding these risk factors, 50 percent of adolescent mothers seek no prenatal care during the first months of pregnancy (80 percent for those younger than 15). Pregnant girls less than 15 develop anemia 92 percent more often than those older than 20 (McWhirter et al., 1993), a dangerous condition that requires medical checkups to detect and correct.

In ways other than the human cost of increased mental retardation, teen pregnancy is a major social and economic problem in the United States. Although the rate of teen pregnancy in the United States fortunately has decreased over the last decade, it continues to occur at the rate of 51.5 births per 1,000 (close to 1 million births per year), and it remains a serious problem for infant health (Smith, Martin & Ventura, 1999).

Of all adolescent pregnancies, 40 percent end in abortion, though this option is not readily available—and therefore occurs less often—among the economically poor (Alan Guttmacher Institute, 1998). More than 90 percent of all those who give birth keep their babies rather than offer them for adoption, even when they have inadequate resources to care for them. Both adolescent birth and abortion rates in the United States are the highest of any developed nation in the world, yet U.S. teens are no more sexually active (Berk, 2000).

Cross-cultural and international statistics are important not only because they indicate the relative extent of the U.S. problem, but also because they prove that high incidence is not inevitable. The conditions of poverty that help produce the high rate of adolescent pregnancy in the United States are less severe in these other countries, even though they (as nations) have no greater resources. Teen pregnancy is part of larger social and economic problems that include the availability of livable wages and employment opportunities, welfare regulations, health care, child care, and education.

The undeniable reason why teens get pregnant is that they are sexually active. There are numerous complexities, however, perhaps the most important of which is the contrastingly low rate of contraceptive use. Only 22 percent of sexually active teenage girls and 33 percent of boys use birth control.

Many young people know far more about the explicit "how-to" details of sexuality (which they can easily get from television, movies, and magazines) than they know about the actual physiological likelihood and corresponding risks of conception and childbearing. Young people's beliefs about what makes conception more or less likely are often riddled with inaccuracies—for example, that a girl cannot become pregnant the first time she has intercourse. Many girls also reported unwarranted fears and beliefs about side effects from birth control. Sex education is an important (though by itself not necessarily sufficient) part of pregnancy prevention, and such programs are well established in countries with lower adolescent pregnancy and abortion rates.

> **FOR DISCUSSION** *What rumors about getting pregnant have you heard circulated among teens that you know to be untrue?*

Many teenage girls, especially those from backgrounds of poverty, have low self-esteem and little vision of a future beyond parenting. It is true that girls who have babies are much less likely to finish high school and more likely to depend on public assistance (Hotz, McElroy & Sanders, 1997). Many find themselves in life-long struggles in which, despite employment, they strive to meet nearly impossible demands of child and health care. Many work and manage on extremely low incomes without health benefits, often living with family members. Only to compound the problem, their children—even when they do not have clear disabilities—are more likely to obtain poorer education and bear children earlier than those born to older mothers (Hardy et al., 1997).

Unfortunately, these arguments can have little influence on girls who see no opportunity for work and economic success in any case. In fact, for many girls who live in poverty, having a baby during the teen years may make little difference to their eventual career and economic status, because emerging successfully from an impoverished childhood is so difficult in itself. Still, there is little doubt that the additional responsibility for a child makes the trap of poverty even more intricate to unlock (Brien & Willis, 1997). These young girls need some other realistic and attainable vision of their future and of a means whereby they can meet their needs; otherwise, postponing parenthood will not make much sense to them.

Equally common, especially among girls from more "advantaged" circumstances, is an ambivalence about sex that precludes responsible contraceptive use. On the one hand, they believe that good girls do not engage in sexual intercourse, and since they are, of course, good girls they do not need birth control. On the other hand, they find themselves (often coerced by cultural and peer-related factors) in a situation where sexual activity does occur. They then attribute this to a "mistake" that they swear will not be repeated. Thus, they fail to come to terms with their own sexuality, and pregnancy is often the result. In fact, as many as 87 percent of all young girls who get pregnant report that they did not expect to have sex and that it "just happened" (Wymelenberg, 1990). In contrast, girls who discuss contraceptive use with their partner before becoming sexually active are more likely to use birth control throughout the relationship—and far less likely to experience an unplanned pregnancy.

Girls who have close, nurturing relationships with their mothers and can communicate about sexual feelings and behaviors are more likely to develop the insight that enables them to postpone sexual activity until they have the experience and maturity to choose their partners wisely and avoid unwanted pregnancy. Teens who have academic motivation and career goals are also more likely to behave responsibly. In addition, those few school-based health clinics in the United States that provide counseling about responsible behavior (and make contraceptives readily available) have been able to reduce first-time and repeat pregnancies substantially among their student populations. Such clinics are common in those nations with fewer pregnancy problems (Zabin & Hayward, 1993). When contraceptives are free and easily available, unwanted pregnancies are reduced.

Finally—and crucially—far more attention needs to be focused on boys. Some social programs concentrate on increasing the emotional and financial investment of fathers; even so, dads rarely contribute to the child's financial support and are often not in a position to do so because they are less likely to finish high school or get a GED than their peers. By the time their babies reach school age, more than three-fourths of fathers are completely uninvolved in their lives (Lerman, 1993). There are few cultural incentives for unwed fathers to take responsibility for their offspring. In fact, they are often encouraged to think of irresponsible sexual behavior primarily as proof of virility and even as proof of their "macho" status. Changes in such attitudes are necessary if the problems of adolescent pregnancy are to be effectively addressed.

Teratogens

Just as with adolescent pregnancy, cultural and social circumstances help determine the damage caused by **teratogens,** or environmental entities that cause the development of abnormal structures in an embryo or fetus. Examples include drugs and other toxic chemicals, as well as infections and diseases. When pregnant women are subjected to teratogens, fetal development is altered and disabilities often result.

Infectious Disease Neurological dysfunction and brain damage in children can occur because of maternal infection. For example, congenital **rubella** syndrome (which produces mental retardation, deafness, and other disabilities) usually results when pregnant women contract rubella (often called "three-day measles"), especially during the first three months of gestation. Childhood immunization programs designed to eliminate measles in adult women have been highly effective in reducing the incidence of this condition, but nearly one-quarter of childbearing-aged women have not been immunized and are therefore susceptible (Lee, Ewert, Frederick, & Mascola, 1992).

Sometimes, however, infections that show mild, few, and even no symptoms in the mother severely damage the fetus. **Toxoplasmosis** is one such infection; it is caused by a parasite commonly found in mammals and birds, and contracted by humans through infected meat or cat feces. Children born infected with the toxoplasma virus often have visual defects and seizures, as well as severe mental retardation.

Another example is **cytomegalovirus** (CMV) infection. Probably the most common viral disease causing mental retardation, CMV results in MR, blindness, deafness, cerebral palsy, seizures, and microcephaly (Phelps, 1998). While some children are born obviously affected, others appear normal at birth but mild or severe symptoms appear later. Some children with CMV who appear to be asymptomatic remain undiagnosed but have later learning problems and other mild disabilities. Although CMV affects people from all social classes, people from low-income families have a greater incidence of the condition.

Additional maternal infections that can cause MR include AIDS, chicken pox, genital herpes, syphilis, and tuberculosis (Berk, 2000). Some infections contracted

This young woman with fetal alcohol syndrome and her mother educate others about the consequences of FAS.

Matt Bernhardt/Associated Press

in infancy—rather than transmitted prenatally—can also cause mental retardation. For example, several types of viral encephalitis cause brain inflammation, which often results in permanent damage. Another condition, **neonatal meningitis,** causes inflammation of the brain-lining membranes. It is fatal in more than 50 percent of instances, and survivors often are affected by hydrocephalus, seizures, hearing defects, and mental retardation.

Fetal Alcohol Syndrome Women who drink alcohol during their pregnancies risk giving birth to babies with **fetal alcohol syndrome** (FAS), now a leading cause of mental retardation in the United States (Streissguth, Barr, Bookstein, Sampson, & Olson, 1999). Besides MR, a child with FAS often has poor attention, hyperactivity, seizures, and distinct facial features—including widely spaced eyes, short eyelid openings, a small upturned nose, and a thin upper lip. In addition, babies with FAS are often of low birth weight and have small heads, which suggests intrauterine growth retardation and incomplete brain development. The child with FAS may also suffer eye, nose, throat, heart, and immune-system defects.

The most conservative estimate of the incidence of FAS is 0.33 per 1,000 live births (in the Western world), but this figure misses many women who do not get prenatal care. In Seattle, Washington, for example, the prevalence rate is 1 in 700 live births, but on some Indian reservations the figure ranges from 1 in 8 to 1 in 750. In the United States, FAS costs anywhere from $74.6 million per year to

$321 million, two-thirds of which goes toward treatment for MR (Abel & Sokol, 1993). None of the above statistics include children with **fetal alcohol effect** (FAE) who show many of the symptoms of FAS (often including MR) or the cost of such children's long-term inability to join the workforce.

A developing fetus has less ability to eliminate and metabolize alcohol, so an amount that is virtually undetectable to the mother can adversely affect her developing baby. The more a woman drinks, the more likely are FAS or FAE. As little as two ounces of alcohol per day in early pregnancy has resulted in children with disabilities and FAS facial features, and as little as one drink a day has been associated with slower reaction time and attention problems in children of middle-class women, even though these women stopped drinking as soon as they discovered they were pregnant (Sampson et al., 1989). Drinking several drinks within a few hours (as someone might at a party) has also been associated with damage, even in those who do not ordinarily drink. While genetic, nutritional, age, and other health factors influence the probability of FAS or FAE, clearly there is no truly safe level of alcohol use during pregnancy.

Although in individual instances, the IQ associated with FAS may vary over time, as a rule the intellectual effects are stable and long-lasting (Streissguth, 1997). Although IQ deficits range from mild to quite severe, the most damaging long-term effects appear to result from behavioral and intellectual problems that are not reflected in the IQ score. Problems with concentration, attention, impulsivity, dependency, and problems with abstractions such as time and space, cause and effect, and in generalizing from one situation to another make independent adult functioning difficult (Streissguth et al., 1999). Because many people with FAS and FAE come from families that are themselves severely challenged and have few personal and social resources to help, they often do not receive the guidance and protection that would keep them out of trouble and enable them to function more effectively—a burden that then falls on society.

Long-term studies of people with FAS in the United States, Sweden, and Germany have so far shown that educational efforts and improved environmental circumstances do little to reverse the poor judgment, reduced common sense, and inability to make meaningful deductions from experience that are so typical of the behavior of people with FAS (Spohr, Willms, & Steinhausen, 1993). Remember, though, that most of those with FAS come from unstable and neglectful early environments. Studies show that few remain with their biological mothers after the early months, and a large percentage of these mothers die before their children reach adolescence. Certainly these circumstances could interfere with early development in addition to the biologic effects of FAS. If intervention is to have any hope of real success, then it apparently must begin immediately upon birth and will depend upon better knowledge of FAS among obstetricians and pediatricians (Streissguth & Kanter, 1997).

Because the effects of FAS may be especially difficult to ameliorate, and because they have such serious human and economic consequences, prevention is crucial. Some states are involved in general public awareness activities or individually focused intervention programs for women at high risk of giving birth to a child with FAS, but evidence indicates that public awareness efforts alone have not been effective in reducing the incidence of FAS. There have been at least two university and hospital-based programs, however, that have demonstrated significant reductions in prenatal drinking and therefore FAS, but these programs included both large public awareness efforts and individual counseling and education of women at high risk. Such efforts may provide models of effective prevention for much needed future efforts (Phelps, 1998).

Nicotine Cigarette smoking is related to prematurity, low birth weight, miscarriage, and infant death. Newborns of smoking mothers have decreased attention and muscle tension and increased risk of early and persistent asthma and cancer (Batshaw & Conlon, 1997). These effects occur regardless of social class, although they are compounded by poverty and other risk factors. Many children of smoking mothers have problems that do not show up until school age, including learning disabilities and poor attention.

Damage to infants occurs because smoking restricts blood flow to the fetus, increases levels of carbon monoxide in fetal blood, and causes abnormal placental growth, which results in decreased weight gain (Newman & Buka, 1991). Because these same risk factors exist from secondary smoke (Makin, Fried, & Watkinson, 1991), pregnant women should not be exposed to the cigarette smoking of other people either at home or at work. Damage is most pronounced from heavy smoking or smoke exposure early in the pregnancy, but stopping (or even cutting down) at any time during pregnancy results in better fetal weight gain and fewer long-term damaging effects (Li, Windsor, Perkins, Goldenberg, & Lowe, 1993; Stjernfeldt, Berglunds, Lindsten, & Ludvigsson, 1992).

Cocaine More women of childbearing age in the United States use **cocaine** than any other illicit drug, and hundreds of thousand of babies are born addicted in the United States every year (Landry & Whitney, 1996). Babies born to mothers who are addicted to cocaine experience withdrawal symptoms and seizures, as do babies of heroin-addicted mothers. They are low birth weight and sometimes have microcephaly and limb defects (Hoyme et al., 1990). Babies exposed to cocaine have long-term difficulty in handling unstructured tasks. Their play behavior is disorganized and erratic, and they score lower on developmental tasks (Beckwith & Howard, 1991). Although babies born to mothers who use "crack" (a highly concentrated smokable form of cocaine) show the most severe early damage to their central nervous systems, even fathers' cocaine use (the effects of which are passed at conception) can cause birth defects (Yazigi, Odem, & Polakoski, 1991). Research suggests that babies born addicted to cocaine can have long-term deficits in attention and may suffer from behavior problems, hearing defects, and seizures (Moroney & Allen, 1994). Although the long-term result of prenatal cocaine use on later adolescent and adult functioning remains to be seen, these early findings suggest that there may be problem-solving and real-world comprehension difficulties similar to those found with fetal alcohol syndrome.

Marijuana Although research has thus far shown few differences between unexposed infants and babies born to mothers who use marijuana during pregnancy, there is an association with low birth weight, increased irritability, and abnormal startle reflexes, signs that are often precursors of later learning disabilities (Dahl, Scher, Williamson, Robles, & Day, 1995). Particularly disturbing is an increased risk of **placenta abruptia** during the deliveries of these infants—a complication in which the placenta prematurely pulls away from the uterus and causes hemorrhaging. This condition endangers the lives of both mother and baby and can result in fetal anoxia.

Lead Poisoning Lead poisoning results in mental retardation, hearing impairment, and retarded physical growth (Phelps, 1999). Fortunately, the incidence of severe lead poisoning has decreased over the last several decades: Lead additives in gasoline have been phased out (for the most part), lead solder in food cans has been greatly reduced, and lead joints in new water pipes have been eliminated. Even though lead-based house paint has not been produced for two decades, however, old paint (especially in deteriorating housing or in housing renovation) still remains the major lead health hazard. Some estimates suggest that, in spite of improvement in lead cleanup, possibly 40 percent of U.S. children have blood lead levels in the range associated with measurable intellectual deficits (Bellinger, Leviton, Waternaux, Needleman, & Rabinowitz, 1987), a circumstance equally severe in other industrialized countries (Chang, 1999). Again, most of these children live in areas of poverty (as many as 60 percent), but lead contamination also exists in many middle- and upper middle-class communities. Lead is still found in numerous common products, including cable covering, brass and bronze, foil, ammunition, and artists' paints to name a few (Chadzynski, 1987). Many communities also have high lead levels in their water supplies and ground soil.

While both adults and children are vulnerable to damage from lead, children are particularly susceptible. Lead enters the body through ingestion or the inhalation of tiny particles. It circulates through the bloodstream and sequesters in bone and organs, including the kidneys, liver, and brain, where it destroys cell tissue. Because children are more prone than adults to putting their hands and other objects in their mouths and to chewing on wood surfaces, they usually ingest greater quantities of lead. More important, however, adults' bodies can excrete lead more easily, while children retain a larger percentage.

The severest lead poisoning manifests in irritability, vomiting, abdominal pain, seizures, coma, and sometimes death—symptoms that can result when a 2-year-old eats a dime-sized paint chip (Pesce & Pesce, 1991). But mental retardation can occur at levels much lower than those that produce obvious symptoms (Mendelsohn et al., 1999). For this reason, detecting the presence of dangerously high lead levels must rely on blood-screening procedures. Although the higher the exposure to lead, the more certain that mental retardation will result, research for more than two decades has shown that even relatively low levels of lead can result in reduced cognitive ability, including serious learning disabilities (Bellinger et al., 1987; Finkelstein, Markowitz, & Rosen, 1998; Mendelsohn et al., 1999). Also troubling is that the toxic effects of lead and other metals are also implicated in the learning problems of that extremely large number of people for whom the cause remains uncertain.

Safe Removal of Lead Paint

In some urban areas, regulations require that children who have dangerously high blood lead levels as a result of deteriorating lead-based paint must be removed from the home while the landlord makes the property safe for their return. However, the most widely used and inexpensive removal methods, sanding and burning, fill the house with toxic lead dust and subject workers to toxic poisoning, and children who return to this now "safe" environment suffer increased brain damage (Chisolm, 1987). Because the smallest particles are the most readily digested and absorbed, these methods only make lead more accessible and dangerous.

The safest removal procedures involve covering old wood floors (where cracks can contain lead-based dust) with polyurethane, vinyl linoleum, or deck paint; replacing old wood windows; treating walls by repainting small areas; and covering large peeling surfaces with paneling or drywall and tightly sealing edges. If paint must be removed from woodwork, a smokeless heat gun is far better than torching, and cleanup requires a high-efficiency particle accumulator (HEPA) vacuum rather than an ordinary home vacuum, just as in the removal of asbestos (Etre, Reynolds, Burmeister, Whitten, & Gergely, 1999).

Although recent research has documented intellectual deficits associated with lead in otherwise healthy middle-class children, the circumstances of poverty make damage even more likely. For one reason, lead is more readily absorbed on an empty stomach and in people who are low in iron or calcium. Also a high percentage of the housing in low-income areas has peeling and deteriorating lead paint, and low-income industrial areas often have heavy concentrations of lead toxins in ground soil and house dust. Furthermore, adult women who have accumulated lead in their bones release this lead into the placenta during gestation, unwittingly poisoning their children even before birth (Pesce & Pesce, 1991).

Because the amount of lead necessary to cause damage during fetal development is even lower than for young children, the probability that many low-income women are passing lead damage to an increasingly large percentage of the population is virtually certain (Fletcher, Gelberg, & Marshall, 1999). If that were not enough, men who work where there are high lead levels have lower sperm counts and misshapen and less mobile sperm—conditions that may point to an additional source of birth defects (Elkington, 1985).

If the presence of lead is detected early, nutritional supplements and medication can result in improved intellectual performance, but actual brain damage cannot be reversed. What is more, medication is not effective in eliminating lower levels of lead that may cause milder damage, and there is extremely troubling evidence that drug therapy may even speed redistribution of blood lead to the brain (Chisolm, 1987). Clearly, prevention is the only effective alternative.

Lead poisoning is yet another entirely preventable cause of retardation. Yet, as a society, we allow economic and technological considerations to outweigh our concern for children's developing brains, so that while cleanup slowly proceeds (with opposition from special-interest groups) large percentages of our children lose their best abilities for productive, creative, independent living. From this loss, conservative economic costs figure in the millions per year. But the human costs are incalculable.

Accidents

A substantial number of developmental disabilities are caused by accidents—probably tens of thousands per year (Cone, 1988). Often, severe head injuries result in mental retardation, and a substantial number of these are the result of auto accidents involving teenagers.

Efforts to prevent teen auto accidents have ordinarily focused on behavior change. It was previously thought, for example, that young people who took driver-training classes were less often involved in accidents, but research has shown no difference between formally trained and untrained young drivers (Vernick et al., 1999). In fact, such programs allow more of the youngest drivers on the road, so the final effect is to increase the number of teens who become seriously disabled. Because programs designed to change the driving behavior of teens have not been effective, many writers and researchers believe it will be necessary to increase the minimum driving age to reduce these accidents.

Although teens have the highest rate of serious auto accidents by age group, by far most auto accidents that result in death or serious injury involve alcohol, and those who drink and drive are primarily adults. More than 50 percent of people who are killed while driving are intoxicated as revealed by their blood alco-

---

Double Jeopardy for Drivers: Youth and Alcohol

Jerry is only recently a student in a separate school for people with severe developmental disabilities. One warm night last fall after a football game in which Jerry made the winning touchdown, he and two friends drove off a dark country road, hitting a tree and rolling the car in which they were riding. All three boys had been drinking. Both of Jerry's friends were killed, and Jerry received a severe head and spinal cord injury that paralyzed him from the neck down, destroyed his ability to speak, and severely reduced his intellectual abilities.

These days, Jerry's favorite activity is to float with the help of special equipment in the pool provided by his school. He needs help for every element of self-care, and his social contacts have

been reduced to family members and those who work with him at school. Seeing Jerry now, it is hard to imagine that a little more than a year ago, he was an outgoing and popular athlete heading for a possible college scholarship. Jerry's life has obviously changed catastrophically: His physical and mental challenges have increased enormously, while his personal resources to meet those challenges have been seriously reduced. Because of Jerry (and hundreds of thousands of other young people who have experienced similar tragedies), youth groups such as Students Against Drinking and Driving (SADD) are becoming more common and peer pressure against drinking and driving among youth is mounting.

hol levels, and many nonintoxicated and innocent people are killed or disabled in accidents caused by drunk drivers. Because of these statistics and the human loss and suffering they represent, there has been increased pressure on legislators and law enforcement agencies to apprehend drunk drivers and impose serious penalties for this behavior.

Child Abuse and Neglect

Official statistics report that nearly 1 million children in the United States were abused or neglected by their parents in 1998 (U.S. Department of Health and Human Services, 2000). This is clearly an underestimate, however, because many cases are never reported. The documented rate of child maltreatment has escalated dramatically since the 1980s, although recent statistics show declines. As a direct result of abusive attacks, however, many children suffer developmental disabilities (Cone, 1988) and emotional damage.

Although abuse occurs in families from all educational and socioeconomic levels, stressful living conditions are often involved, including poverty, unemployment, overcrowded quarters, and frequent moves (Garbarino, 1997). Remember, however, that most parents who live with stressful conditions do not abuse their children, and even though a disproportionately high percentage of abusive parents were themselves abused in childhood (from 30 percent to 60 percent), the remainder did not repeat the cycle (Buchanan, 1996).

Research has identified characteristic features of abusers. Abusing parents usually perceive stressful situations as unmanageable (Wolfe, 1985), are often immature, have demanding and unrealistic expectations of their children, and spend less time playfully touching and talking to them (Starr, 1982). Notably, they often condone violent behaviors toward both children and spouses (Straus, 1980). Finally, parents who abuse have few support systems among family and friends.

In such families, children who already have developmental disabilities may be especially in danger of abuse and neglect (Belsky, 1993). As babies, they are likely to either demand no attention or be difficult to soothe, and they may have irritatingly high-pitched cries. They often require increased care; and if they learn slowly, they may further enrage an already overly demanding parent. Disabling conditions and the familial stress they produce are usually ongoing, so children with disabilities may remain at risk even after their peers have grown less likely to be abused.

> **FOR DISCUSSION** *Describe how children from some families may be at multiple risk for developmental disabilities. What factors and circumstances may work together to create this risk?*

A picture emerges, then, of the abusive parent: He lacks good parenting and stress-management skills, is immature, may have a difficult child, and gets little support in managing his problems. However, none of these associated characteristics are decisive enough to enable prediction of individual abusers. Most prevention strategies have relied, therefore, on educational campaigns to change social attitudes toward violent child rearing, thus discouraging punitive parenting while encouraging the report of abuse. Some communities also have initiated programs of "respite" care and parent and stress management training for people who find themselves lashing out. In cultures where violence is less acceptable in general, where physical punishment toward children is discouraged, and where effective nonviolent parenting techniques are favored—Sweden, for example—fewer child-abuse problems exist (Zigler & Hall, 1989). For cultures such as the United States, where violence is glorified and the physical punishment of children is frequently considered normal, the problem of child abuse is likely to remain widespread.

CULTURAL IMPLICATIONS
AND PUBLIC POLICY

Now that we have covered many of the social and biological influences on retardation, which are often associated with poverty but occur at all socioeconomic levels, we can return with new insight to the subject of what is termed "cultural-familial retardation" (see Chapter 4). Remember that the cultural-familial category makes up the overwhelming majority of the cases of the mildest retardation, which in turn involves by far the greatest number of diagnosed people. It is found in people who live in poverty and have a close relative with retardation; the actual cause is unknown.

One theory of the cause of familial mild retardation is that it occurs by nature, representing the naturally occurring low end of the normal curve of intelligence—and for some people this may indeed be the case. But we have seen that for a high percentage of these people, technology and industry (lead and other environmental toxins), social habits (alcohol and other drugs, abuse, and neglect), and the circumstances of poverty itself (poor nutrition and inadequate medical care) contribute to or explain intellectual deficits. These causes do not occur naturally and are by no means inevitable. In fact, in Sweden, where the incidence of poverty has been greatly reduced over the last half century, the incidence of MR attributable to unknown causes has also declined dramatically (Hagberg, Hagberg, Lewerth, & Lindberg, 1981).

That all of these causes have self-perpetuating elements is of grave concern for society. Women poisoned by lead pass its toxicity to their offspring, who may be even more affected and then pass this environmental legacy to their own children. Alcohol and drugs in pregnancy produce children who grow into adults with poor judgment and a likelihood of engaging in high-risk and personally damaging behaviors. Furthermore, such people may actually be physiologically prone to produce children who are vulnerable to drug damage.

Culturally, we are faced then with severely increasing economic demands and educational challenges, while more and more children are born into devastating social conditions and with fewer and fewer personal resources to help them rise above those conditions. Many of these children (like Joyce Elger from our case studies) do not have the official diagnosis of MR, and they may have problems that differ in important ways from people with more severe retardation. Still, they have genuine intellectual limitations, but because they are undiagnosed fewer social

Law Enforcement Against Prenatal Child Abuse

The damage to children from prenatal drug use and the devastating social consequences of ignoring the problem have led to suggestions of extreme measures to treat the problem. Some people have proposed that women who continue to drink alcohol or take cocaine during pregnancy (especially if they have previously given birth to a cocaine-addicted child or one with FAS) should be arrested for child abuse and locked away from those drugs until after their children are born. In fact, in a few instances, localities have done just this.

It is not surprising that this idea is controversial. First, the feasibility of such a mammoth undertaking is questionable, if only because of the short-age of prison space. Second, such laws are likely to discourage many women from bringing themselves to the attention of authority figures by seeking prenatal care. Third, there is medical concern about the effects on the fetus of sudden drug withdrawal. Finally, in many areas of the country, there are already more pregnant women seeking safe drug treatment than there are available services. In fact, many inpatient residential programs (which have the highest and safest success rate) deny admission to pregnant women (Hawley & Disney, 1992). It may itself be an injustice to imprison a woman for an addiction for which no safe help is available.

services are available to meet their needs. Stemming this disastrous tide will clearly require both individual and social behavioral changes.

Denial is often the individual reaction to information about increased risk of mental retardation, especially as a result of behaviors presumably under personal control—such as smoking and alcohol use. People may cite examples of others whom they know who apparently escaped damage ("John's mother smoked, and he's fine") or give an instance of someone with mental retardation who was not exposed to such risks ("Susie has mental retardation, and her mother didn't drink a drop"). True, there are few high-risk behaviors for which the outcome is absolutely certain. Even dogs who chase cars occasionally survive to old age. As a society, however, when we know that certain behaviors are probably going to result in brain damage, the human and economic costs for ignoring that knowledge are extremely high.

FOR DISCUSSION *If women are involuntarily incarcerated while pregnant, should they be returned home with their babies after delivery? Why or why not? If not, how should we care for these babies?*

The extent to which individual citizens become involved with and take responsibility for social issues, however, is affected by their ability to imagine constructive action and by their sense of power and control over the circumstances involved. The failure to act is often motivated more by a sense of futility than by apathy (Cvetkovich & Earle, 1992). When a danger is immediate, identifiable, and directly threatening, outrage often leads to action, especially when the people involved perceive the possibility of effecting change. On the other hand, when people feel they do not have any real control over a dangerous or threatening situation, they will often engage in emotional coping mechanisms, including wishful thinking and minimizing the threat: "Maybe it won't actually hurt us (me)," or "It's probably no big deal." Or they may simply avoid thinking about the situation at all (Hallman & Wandersman, 1992).

LOOKING AHEAD

This chapter has presented many social and environmental influences that contribute to the incidence of mental retardation, and it has discussed some of the methods for eliminating or decreasing the widespread nature of these destructive social conditions. It is all too clear, however, that social influences continue to produce the preventable conditions that result in mental retardation for many hundreds of thousands of babies each year. What will it take to mobilize society to real prevention? Obviously, awareness of a dangerous situation must precede action, and there must then be some clear idea of the action to take. It is true that problems can seem overwhelming at a national or worldwide level, but social programs have been effective both in reducing the effects of poverty and the incidence of mental retardation. Examples of successful programs include the prenatal care and WIC programs discussed early in this chapter. In Chapter 10, we will take up the topic of early intervention, discuss programs that have been especially effective, and learn about common stumbling blocks to success.

First, however, Chapter 9 discusses some developmental disabilities experienced by many people with mental retardation. These disabilities are not causes but rather conditions that may accompany MR and that have implications for the appropriate educational and community services required for successful community living. With most of these conditions, mental retardation is likely, if not virtually certain, and children diagnosed with these would be appropriate for further assessment and early intervention.

INFOTRAC COLLEGE EDITION

As Chapter 8 shows, poverty sometimes plays a role in the development of mental retardation. In *InfoTrac College Edition,* enter the keyword *socioeconomic status.* Choose one article that discusses a health topic and socioeconomic status. What is the author's strongest argument? What is the weakest argument? Provide evidence for your choices.

REFERENCES

Abel, E. S., & Sokol, R. J. (1993). A revised conservative estimate of the incidence of FAS and its economic impact. *Alcoholism: Clinical and Experimental Research, 15*(3), 514–524.

Alan Guttmacher Institute. (1998). *Facts in brief—Teen sex and pregnancy.* New York: Author.

Batshaw, M. L., & Conlon, C. J. (1997). Substance abuse: A preventable threat to development. In M. L. Batshaw et al. (Eds.), *Children with disabilities* (4th ed., pp. 143–162). Baltimore, MD: Paul H. Brookes.

Beckwith, L., & Howard, J. (1991, April). *Development of toddlers exposed prenatally to PCP and cocaine.* Paper presented at biennial meetings of the Society for Research in Child Development, Seattle, WA.

Bellinger, D., Leviton, A., Waternaux, C., Needleman, D., & Rabinowitz, M. (1987). Longitudinal analyses of prenatal and postnatal lead exposure and early cognitive development. *New England Journal of Medicine, 316,* 1037–1042.

Belsky, J. (1993). Etiology of child maltreatment: A developmental ecological analysis. *Psychological Bulletin, 114,* 413–434.

Bendich, A. (1993). Lifestyle and environmental factors that can adversely affect maternal nutritional status and pregnancy outcomes. In C. L. Keen, A. Bendich, & C. C. Willhite (Eds.), *Maternal nutrition and pregnancy outcome* (pp. 255–265). New York: New York Academy of Sciences.

Brien, M. J., & Willis, R. J. (1997). Costs and consequences for the fathers. In R. A. Maynard (Ed.), *Kids having kids* (pp. 95–144). Washington, DC: Urban Institute.

Buchanan, A. (1996). *Cycles of child maltreatment.* Chichester, UK: Wiley.

Chadzynski, L. (1987). Environmental issues. In *Proceedings of the National Conference, Childhood Lead Poisoning: Current Perspectives* (pp. 92–102). Indianapolis, IN.

Chang, V. (1999). Lead abatement and prevention of developmental disabilities. *Journal of Intellectual & Developmental Disability, 24*(2), 161–168.

Chisolm, J. J., Jr. (1987). Changing sources of lead poisoning. In *Proceedings of the National Conference, Childhood Lead Poisoning: Current Perspectives* (pp. 7–17). Indianapolis, IN.

Cone, J. D. (1988). Prevention. In V. VanHasselt, P. Strain, & M. Hersen (Eds.), *Handbook of developmental and physical disabilities* (pp. 61–78). New York: Pergamon.

Cvetkovich, G., & Earle, T. C. (1992). Environmental hazards and the public. *Journal of Social Issues, 48*(4), 1–20.

Dahl, R. E., Scher, M. S., Williamson, D. E., Robles, N., & Day, N. (1995). A longitudinal study of prenatal marijuana use. Effects on sleep and arousal at age 3 years. *Archives of Pediatric and Adolescent Medicine, 149*(2), 145–150.

Elkington, J. (1985). *The poisoned womb: Human reproduction in a polluted world.* New York: Penguin.

Etre, L. A., Reynolds, S. J., Burmeister, L. F., Whitten, P. S., & Gergely, R. (1999). An evaluation of the effectiveness of lead paint hazard reduction when conducted by homeowners and landlords. *Applied Occupational Environmental Hygiene, 14*(8), 522–529.

Fletcher, A. M., Gelberg, K. H., & Marshall, E. G. (1999). Reasons for testing and exposure sources among women of childbearing age with moderate blood lead levels. *Journal of Community Health, 24*(3), 215–227.

Fletcher, J. M., Landrey, S. H., Bohan, T. P., Davison, K. C., Brookshire, B. L., Lachar, D., Dramer, L. A., & Francis, D. J. (1997). Effects of intraventricular hemorrhage and hydrochepalus on the long-term neurobehavioral development of preterm very-low-birthweight infants. *Developmental Medicine & Child Neurology, 39,* 596–606.

Finkelstein, Y., Markowitz, M. E., & Rosen, J. F. (1998). Low-level lead-induced neurotoxicity in children: An update on central nervous system effects. *Brain Research Reviews, 27*(2), 168–176.

Garbarino, J. (1997). The role of economic deprivation in the social context of child maltreatment. In M. E. Helfer, R. S. Kempe, & R. D. Krugman (Eds.), *The battered child* (5th ed., 49–60). Chicago: University of Chicago Press.

Hagberg, B., Hagberg, G., Lewerth, A., & Lindberg, U. (1981). Mild mental retardation in Swedish school children. *Acta Paediatra Scand, 70,* 445–452.

Hallman, W. K., & Wandersman, A. (1992). Attribution of responsibility and individual and collective coping with environmental threats. *Journal of Social Issues, 48*(4), 101–118.

Hardy, J. B., Shaprio, S., Astone, N. M., Miller, T. L., Brooks-Gunn, J., & Hilton, S. C. (1997). Adolescent childbearing revisited: The age of inner-city mothers at delivery is a determinant of their children's self-sufficiency at age 27 to 33. *Pediatrics, 100*(5), 802–810.

Hawley, T. L., & Disney, E. R. (1992). Crack's children: The consequences of maternal cocaine abuse. *Social Policy Report. Society for Research in Child Development, 6*(4), 1–23.

Hotz, B. J., McElroy, S. W., & Sanders, S. G. (1997). The costs and consequences of teenage childbearing for mothers. In R. A. Maynard (Ed.), *Kids having kids* (pp. 55–94). Washington, DC: Urban Institute.

Hoyme, H. E., Jones, K. L., Dixon, S., Jewett, T., Hanson, J. W., Robinson, L. K., Msall, M. E., & Allanson, J. E. (1990). Prenatal cocaine exposure and fetal vascular disruption. *Pediatrics, 85,* 743–747.

Jacobson, S. W. (1998). Specificity of neurobehavioral outcomes associated with prenatal alcohol exposure. *Alcoholism: Clinical & Experimental Research, 22*(2), 313–320.

Landry, S. H., & Whitney, J. A. (1996). The impact of prenatal cocaine exposure: Studies of the developing infant. *Seminars in Perinatology, 20,* 99–106.

Lee, S. H., Ewert, D. P., Frederick, P. D., & Mascola, L. (1992). Resurgence of congenital rubella syndrome in the 1990s. *Journal of the American Medical Association, 267,* 2616–2620.

Lerman, R. I. (1993). A national profile of young unwed fathers. In R. I. Lerman & T. J. Ooms (Eds.), *Young unwed fathers* (pp. 27–51). Philadelphia: Temple University Press.

Lewis, M. (1999). A path analysis of the effect of welfare on infant mortality. *Journal of Sociology & Social Welfare, 26*(3), 125–136.

Li, C. Q., Windsor, R. A., Perkins, L., Goldenberg, R. L., & Lowe, J. B. (1993). The impact on infant birth weight and gestational age of nicotine-validated smoking reduction during pregnancy. *Journal of the American Medical Association, 269*(12), 1519–1524.

Makin, J. W., Fried, P. A., & Watkinson, B. (1991). A comparison of active and passive smoking during pregnancy: Long-term effects. *Neurotoxicology and Teratology, 13,* 5–12.

McWhirter, J. J., McWhirter, B. T., McWhirter, A. M., & McWhirter, E. H. (1993). *At-risk youth: A comprehensive response.* Pacific Grove, CA: Brooks/Cole.

Mendelsohn, S. L., Dreyer, R. P., Fierman, A. H., Rosen, C. M., Legan, L. A., Kruger, H. A., Lim, S. W., Barasch, S., Au, L., & Courtlandt, C. D. (1999). Low-level lead exposure and cognitive development in early childhood. *Journal of Developmental & Behavioral Pediatrics, 20*(6), 425–431.

Moroney, J. T., & Allen, M. H. (1994). Cocaine and alcohol use in pregnancy. In O. Devinsky, F. Feldmann, & B. Hainline (Eds.), *Neurological complications of pregnancy* (pp. 231–242). New York: Raven Press.

National Center for Health Statistics. (1999). *Health United States 1997–1998 and injury chartbook.* Hyattsville, MD: Department of Health & Human Services.

Newman, L. F., & Buka, S. L. (1991). Clipped wings. *American Educator,* Spring, 27–42.

Pesce, J., & Pesce, A. J. (1991). *The lead paint primer: Questions and answers on lead paint poisoning.* Melrose, MA: Star Industries.

Phelps, L. (Ed.) (1998). *Health-related disorders in children and adolescents: A guidebook for understanding and educating.* Washington, DC: American Psychological Association.

Phelps, L. (1999). Low-level lead exposure: Implications for research and practice. *School Psychology Review, 28*(3), 477–492.

Picard, E. M., Del Dotto, J. E., & Breslau, N. (2000). Prematurity and low birthweight. In K. O. Yeates, M. D. Ris, & H. G. Taylor (Eds.), *Pediatric neuropsychology: Research, theory, and practice* (pp. 237–251). New York: Guilford.

Sampson, P. D., Streissguth, A. P., Barr, H. M., & Bookstein, F. L. (1989). Neurobehavioral effects of prenatal alcohol: Part II. Partial least squares analysis. *Neurotoxicology and Teratology, 11,* 477–491.

Smith, B. L., Martin, J. A., & Ventura, S. J. (1999). Births and deaths: Preliminary data for July 1997–June 1998. *National Vital Statistics Reports, 47*(22), 1–32.

Spohr, H. L., Willms, J., & Steinhausen, H. C. (1993). Prenatal alcohol exposure and long-term developmental consequences. *Lancet, 341,* 907–910.

Starr, R. H., Jr. (1982). A research-based approach to the prediction of child abuse. In R. H. Starr, Jr. (Ed.), *Child abuse prediction: Policy implications* (pp. 105–134). Cambridge, MA: Ballinger.

Stjernfeldt, J., Berglunds, L., Lindsten, J., & Ludvigsson, J. (1992). Maternal smoking and irradiation during pregnancy as risk factors for child leukemia. *Cancer Detection and Prevention, 16,* 129–135.

Straus, M. A. (1980). Stress and physical child abuse. *Child Abuse and Neglect, 4,* 75–88.

Streissguth, A. P. (1997). *Fetal alcohol syndrome: A guide for families and communities.* Baltimore, MD: Paul H. Brookes.

Streissguth, A. P., Barr, H. M., Bookstein, F. L., Sampson, P. D., Olson, H. C. (1999). The long-term neurocognitive consequences of prenatal alcohol exposure: A 14-year study. *Psychological Science, 10*(3), 186–190.

Streissguth, A. P., & Kanter, J. (Eds.). (1997). *The challenge of Fetal Alcohol Syndrome: Overcoming secondary disabilities.* Seattle, WA: University of Washington Press.

Stringer, M. (1998). Personal costs associated with high-risk prenatal care attendance. *Journal of Health Care for the Poor and Underserved, 9*(3), 222–235.

U.S. Department of Health and Human Services. (2000). HHS Web page: www.hhs.gov/news/press/2000pres/20000410.html.

Vernick, J. S., Li, G., Ogaitro, S., MacKenzie, E. J., Baker, S. P., & Gielen, A. C. (1999). Effects of high school driver education on motor vehicle crashes, violations, and licensure. *American Journal of Preventive Medicine, 16,* 40–46.

Widerstrom, A. H. (1999). Identification and treatment of risk factors in newborns and infants in the United States. *Enfance, 51*(1), 79–91.

Williams, L. O., & Decoufle, P. (1999). Is maternal age a risk factor for mental retardation among children. *American Journal of Epidemiology, 149*(9), 814–824.

Wolfe, D. A. (1985). Child-abusive parents: An empirical review and analysis. *Psychological Review, 97,* 462–482.

Wymelenberg, S. (1990). *Science and babies: Private decisions, public dilemmas.* Washington, DC: National Academy Press.

Yazigi, R. A., Odem, R. R., & Polakoski, K. L. (1991). Demonstration of specific binding of cocaine to human spermatozoa. *Journal of the American Medical Association, 266,* 956–1959.

Zabin, L. S., & Hayward, S. C. (1993). *Adolescent sexual behavior and childbearing.* Newbury Park, CA: Sage.

Zigler, E., & Hall, N. (1989). Physical child abuse in America: Past, present, and future. In D. Cicchetti & V. Carlson (Eds.), *Child maltreatment* (pp. 203–253). New York: Cambridge University Press.

9

Related Developmental Disabilities

eople with MR are subject to the same illnesses and other disabilities as any-one else. There are, however, some conditions that are especially common in people with mental retardation, because the brain insult that results in MR often extends to other areas and functions of the brain. These related disabilities include **autism, cerebral palsy, seizure disorders,** and **attention deficit hyperactivity disorder,** and all are found in people with typical intellectual functioning as well as those with retardation. This chapter describes these disabilities and discusses **etiology** and treatment approaches.

AUTISM

Autism is a syndrome with serious consequences for social development and independent life functioning. It occurs in approximately 1 in 500 individuals (Centers for Disease Control and Prevention, 2001) among all racial and ethnic groups throughout the world, and it is approximately four times more common in boys than in girls. Although research consistently shows that some 70 percent to 90 percent of people with autism are also mentally retarded (Autism Society of America, 1999; Ratey et al., 2000), individual diagnosis of MR is difficult. There is no available means to test IQ in people who lack communicative oral or gesture language, so the diagnosis of MR must rely on functional assessment.

Symptoms of autism ordinarily emerge before 30 months, and development is often unusual from earliest infancy, especially in the *uneven* progress that takes place in children with autism. For example, these children usually experience motor milestones (sitting, crawling, and walking) at typical ages but fail to develop normal language. Sometimes talking begins as expected and then disappears; other times language never develops or only quite slowly. Even when people with autism develop a wide vocabulary, they cannot engage in quick, interactive conversation, especially about abstract ideas or emotions. This uneven development is crucial in distinguishing autism from other mental disorders, and it can help differentiate someone with autism from someone with severe mental retardation alone (Romanczyk, Lockshin, & Navalta, 1994).

Other characteristics of the syndrome involve an array of unusual responses to people, objects, and sensation, many of which are shown in Table 9.1.

In addition to those symptoms listed, children with autism will often demand an identical routine every day, even to the point of insisting that a caregiver use the exact same words in conversation (Klin & Volkmar, 1999). For example, the child's mother may say one morning, "Now it's time for breakfast. Sit down and eat your cereal." Her child will thereafter require her to repeat the same phrases every morning, and he may engage in prolonged and intense temper tantrums if these expectations are not met. It is also common that children with autism are bothered if household objects are moved so much as an inch, and will replace them to their original position.

Table 9.1 Some Characteristics Associated with Autism

Stimulus	Unusual Response
Objects	Repeatedly lines up objects in a particular order.
	Spends long periods spinning or twirling objects.
	Becomes unusually attached to objects rather than to people.
People	Relates to people as if they were objects. Does not seem aware of self and others as separate living entities.
	Makes unusual eye contact.
	Avoids being touched.
Sensation	Routinely smells objects and people.
	Abnormally fearful of some routine noises while seemingly oblivious to noises ordinarily perceived as loud or startling.
	Extremely sensitive to touch in some instances while often oblivious to pain or injury.
	Unusually attracted to particular colors or lights.

SOURCE: Adapted from L. Wing (1993), *Children apart: Children with autism and their families.* Bethesda, MD: Autism Society of America.

Whereas these children usually have extremely limited interests, they may obsess on those, and typically spend time in stereotypical behaviors such as body rocking and hand flapping as well as exhibit motor peculiarities such as walking on their toes (Ratey et al., 2000). A few may engage in extreme self-injurious behavior and aggression. Autism is also associated with high rates of seizure disorders, attention deficit hyperactivity disorder, and tic disorders (Tsai, 1993).

Autism was first identified in 1943, when Leo Kanner published descriptions of 11 children who had what he considered a unique form of "psychotic illness." These young patients were characterized by an inability to relate to people and situations in a normal manner from the beginning of life. They all exhibited extremely unusual language development. Almost all of the mothers reported that, as babies, their children had failed to assume an anticipatory posture to being picked up (Kanner, 1943). Kanner named this disorder **early infantile autism.**

Whereas some early researchers believed that autism was a type of schizophrenia (Bettelheim, 1967; Creak, 1961; Mahler, 1965), Kanner insisted that infantile autism could be differentiated from other disorders by the early onset of extreme self-isolation and the child's marked resistance to change. Autism is now professionally recognized as a distinct developmental disability, and is classified in DSM-IV among the **pervasive developmental disorders** (PDD). Figure 9.1 describes the DSM-IV criteria for autism.

These symptoms of abnormal functioning in social interaction, meaningful language, and symbolic and imaginative play must begin before age 3. When children have several pronounced autistic characteristics but do not fit the strict criteria for autism, they are often given a diagnosis of **unspecified pervasive developmental disorder.** However, one or two symptoms of autism (rocking or

A. A total of six (or more) items from (1), (2), and (3), with at least two from (1), and one each from (2) and (3):

(1) qualitative impairment in social interaction, as manifested by at least two of the following:

   (a) marked impairment in the use of multiple nonverbal behaviors such as eye-to-eye gaze, facial expression, body postures, and gestures to regulate social interaction

   (b) failure to develop peer relationships appropriate to developmental level

   (c) a lack of spontaneous seeking to share enjoyment, interests, or achievements with other people (e.g., by a lack of showing, bringing, or pointing out objects of interest)

   (d) lack of social or emotional reciprocity

(2) qualitative impairments in communication as manifested by at least one of the following:

   (a) delay in, or total lack of, the development of spoken language (not accompanied by an attempt to compensate through alternative modes of communication such as gesture or mime)

   (b) in individuals with adequate speech, marked impairment in the ability to sustain a conversation with others

   (c) stereotyped and repetitive use of language or idiosyncratic language.

   (d) lack of varied, spontaneous make-believe play or social imitative play appropriate to developmental level

(3) restricted repetitive and stereotyped patterns of behavior, interests, and activities, as manifested by at least one of the following:

   (a) encompassing preoccupation with one or more stereotyped and restricted patterns of interest that is abnormal either in intensity or focus

   (b) apparently inflexible adherence to specific, nonfunctional routines or rituals

   (c) stereotyped and repetitive motor mannerisms (e.g., hand or finger flapping or twisting, or complex whole-body movements)

   (d) persistent preoccupation with parts of objects

FIGURE 9.1 DSM-IV criteria for autism

SOURCE: Taken from American Psychiatric Association (1994), *Diagnostic and Statistical Manual of Mental Disorders* (4th ed.). Washington, DC: Author. Copyright 1994 American Psychiatric Association. Reprinted with permission.

poor attention, for example) are commonly found in children with mental retardation and do not indicate PDD.

Characteristics central to autism—especially impairments in social interaction and the presence of repetitive and stereotyped patterns of behavior—also occur in **Asperger syndrome.** Because people with Asperger syndrome do not show impairments in language or cognitive functioning but otherwise show the characteristics of autistic disorder, many researchers believe it is simply a mild form of autism (Pennington, 1991). However, this assumption remains controversial for the time

What Is It Like to Have Autism?

For Donna Williams, autism has meant a sensory life of endless fascination and frustration, and her experiences have culminated in two highly successful books. For Temple Grandin, autism has caused an agonizing search to calm her nervous system, leading first to an obsession with cattle chutes and then to a respected academic career in animal husbandry. In her descriptions of autistic experience, Grandin speaks of sensory abnormalities in the perception of sound, vision, and touch and of problems of selective attention, but she does not report problems with verbal comprehension. Williams, on the other hand, describes living in what was often a completely unpredictable and incomprehensible world in which her own and others' speech was often meaningless. Both describe intense anxiety and the experience of being overwhelmed by sensory input. As children, they shared the tendency to withdraw completely from and "tune out" the unpleasant and unmanageable stimuli and environmental demands that others usually take for granted.

Thankfully, they have broken sufficiently from the social isolation of autism to provide fascinating insights into a world that most of us can merely glimpse from outside. In doing so, they give valuable advice to families and professionals who want to help those with autism understand the perceptions of the "normal" world.

SOURCE: Adapted from T. Grandin (1984), My experiences as an autistic child and review of selected literature, *Journal of Orthomolecular Psychiatry, 13*(3), 144–174; and D. Williams (1992), *Nobody nowhere: The extraordinary autobiography of an autistic* (New York: Times Books).

being at least (Romanczyk, Lockshin, & Navalta, 1994; Schopler, Messibov, & Kunce, 1998).

Etiology

Prior Theories Early theories implicated the family, especially the mother, in the onset of autism. Bruno Bettelheim, the author of widely read and well-accepted books including *Truants from Life* and *The Empty Fortress,* insisted that autism is psychogenic in origin and that the mother's personality characteristics actually cause the disorder (Bettelheim, 1955; 1967). Among other things, Bettelheim called these women "rejecting," "narcissistic," "impersonal," "indifferent," and "detached." Bettelheim believed that these characteristics prevented the child with autism "from interacting with others and hence from forming a personality through which to deal with the environment." He also claimed that "the experience that [the autistic child's] own actions make no difference is what stops him from becoming a human being" (Bettelheim, 1967, p. 25). For Bettelheim, the social isolation of autism was a *psychological* response to rejection such that the child "keeps his feelings from being felt, from coming to consciousness, and thus prevents himself from acting in line with his feelings" (p. 318).

This theory has caused untold additional misery and undeserved guilt for women who already had to deal with the pain of a seriously disabled child. In the meantime, research has found absolutely no evidence that parents of children with autism have negative personality characteristics associated with the disorder. To the contrary, some early studies found that mothers of children with autism spend more time reading to them and fathers more time playing with them (Cantwell, Baker, & Rutter, 1979). In addition, other researchers found a lower than typical incidence of divorce and psychosis in families of children with autism (Gittelman & Birch, 1967; Lowe, 1966). In reality, these families can be distinguished only by their normality.

Many people working in the field of autism consider this "mistake" an important lesson for those who develop and disseminate psychological theories. Although there is every reason to believe that families who must deal with autism adjust to their challenges and go on with satisfying and productive lives, theories of parental causation—now thankfully discredited—certainly did not make that adjustment easier. Rimland (1964) states this idea well: "To add a heavy burden of shame and guilt to the distress of people whose hopes, social life, finances, well-being and feelings of worth have been all but destroyed seems heartless and inconsiderate in the extreme" (p. 65).

In fact, it was Rimland (1964) who took an important role in discrediting the maternal theory of causation among the professional community of clinicians and researchers. He argued persuasively that there was no evidence that parents reject their children with autism, let alone that such rejection could cause autism. Instead, research findings show that autism is related to brain dysfunction. Emotional difficulties in autism, according to this view, result from information-processing problems rather than cause them. Rimland's initial interest in autism was motivated by the fact that his own son was born with the disorder—yet another example of the important contributions made by family members to the field of developmental disabilities (Rimland, 1994).

Current Theories Today, virtually all professionals agree that autism is a neurologically based disruption in sensory and cognitive processes, but neither the exact neurological abnormalities nor their corresponding processing disruptions can yet be precisely described. It also remains unknown for certain what causes the neurological abnormalities in the first place.

Remember that autism is a **syndrome** rather than a specific disease. Just as with mental retardation, autistic symptoms and characteristics undoubtedly result from more than one cause. As medical and psychological knowledge progresses, it will be possible to differentiate clear subtypes (Rapin, 1991).

There is evidence that autism is sometimes genetic in origin, although the precise method of inheritance is not known, and it may be that some environmental event must occur in addition to a genetic predisposition (Rutter et al., 1990). Such an event could be a birth injury or a virus, but the exact conditions remain to be determined. In addition, autistic-like symptoms are often seen in other genetic conditions, including Fragile X syndrome, untreated phenylketonuria, and neurofibromatosis (see Chapter 7) (Santangelo & Folstein, 1999).

Some but not all people with autism show signs of brain atrophy, a condition also found in people with some other disabilities such as schizophrenia. And in

---

Hints for Working with People with Autism

Discovering what items and activities are attractive to someone with autism is more important than simply focusing on what she "should" like. Because some forms of self-stimulation (rocking, teeth grinding, singsong humming) may be an individual's attempt to block out unmanageable stimuli and reduce anxiety, providing that particular stimulation for her may free her to pursue other tasks. Sitting close and humming an uncomplicated and repetitious tune, for example, may satisfy this function. Likewise, swinging *gently* on a swing may enhance concentration and verbal expression for some— although swinging should never be vigorous or forced because it could induce seizures in some individuals. Some children may find comfort in wrapping themselves or being wrapped tightly in a blanket, or they may enjoy being brushed or rubbed with fabric.

When someone has a strong or obsessive interest in something that may seem trivial or bizarre, then that interest can sometimes be turned to educational and professional advantage—as in the example of Temple Grandin's obsession with cattle chutes. In a further example, Grandin gives these hints for making educational use of a fixation with automatic doors: "At the elementary level, tasks could be simple, such as requesting the door company to send its catalog. Adults might think such a catalog boring, but the child with autism who has a door fixation would find it fascinating. Math and geography could be involved by asking the child to find the door company on a map and measure the miles to it from the school" (Grandin, 1988, p. 6).

---

many cases there are irregularities in the limbic and cerebellar areas of the brain (Abell et al., 1999).

Treatment

Although drugs can help alleviate some of the symptoms of autism (hyperactivity and aggression in particular), no drug treatment can yet cure or modify the central problems of the disorder itself. Vitamin therapy (usually Vitamin B_6 in combination with magnesium) has been found to improve the speech and behavior of as much as 50 percent of people with autism, but it is certainly not a cure (Rimland, 1994).

The most effective treatment, thus far, is behavioral training. Studies have shown that behavioral treatment can result in improvements in both language and social skills while decreasing disruptive behaviors, especially aggression (Lovaas & Buch, 1997).

Behavior therapy has been particularly effective when started by age 3 and when parents are taught to provide additional training at home. For example, nineteen 7-year-old children who had previously received 40 hours of therapy per week gained as many as 20 IQ points, and they subsequently received more integrated school placements (Lovaas, 1987). Behavioral training for these youngsters focused on the development of speech and language, on toy play, self-care, and

Hoax or Miracle?

Facilitated communication (FC) has been called a "miracle" because it seems to allow children who have been completely socially isolated to express their deepest emotions. In FC, a child uses a spelling board or machine to communicate with others. The facilitator provides emotional support and steadies the child's hand or wrist to compensate for motor problems. Children who have never said a word or shown any sign of language comprehension have (in their first FC session) written such things as "I am not retarded," "I can read," and "My mother feels I'm stupid, because I can't use my voice properly" (Biklen, 1990).

Critics claim that it is the facilitator—not the child—who is actually communicating in a kind of "Ouija board" effect in which even the facilitator is not aware of his influence. Virtually every research study to date has found that children are able to communicate only when the facilitator also sees or hears the question asked, but never when the child alone knows the question (Jacobson et al., 1994; Szempruch & Jacobson, 1992; Wheeler, Jacobson, Paglieri, & Schwartz, 1993).

It's true that mechanical methods of communication have proved invaluable for many people who would otherwise remain isolated. Susan— the child from our case studies with cerebral palsy—is an important example. In addition, nonverbal children with autism have sometimes been taught to sign or to use other symbol systems (Nishimura, Watamaki, Hara, Sato, & Wakabayashi, 1998). When children demonstrate the ability to manage a communication system on their own, or when facilitation involves only a touch on the shoulder or standing in proximity, there is no ambiguity and no debate. Controversy arises only when the sole means of communication requires that the child's hand or arm is held so that every movement is made by both child and facilitator.

If a facilitator, knowingly or not, is the true source of communication, then parents are deluded as to a child's progress and may therefore fail to provide alternative behavioral treatment that is known to be effective even though slower

and more time-consuming (Jacobson et al., 1994). Also, there have been cases where families were subjected to serious harm because sexual abuse was reported via FC, and no such thing apparently had happened (Hostler, Allaire, & Christoph, 1993).

On the other hand, many parents and teachers do believe that their children have been helped through FC. For one thing, they report that their own attitudes toward the child change: They expect more and provide more opportunities. Some children communicate with several facilitators (including teacher and parent), and these relationships are strengthened. Most children seem to love FC, and their behavior often improves. Understandably, people find it difficult (and perhaps unreasonable) to deny their own experience, even in the face of contrary research reports.

Some studies, however, have demonstrated valid communication of information about which the facilitator was unaware (Weiss, Wagner, & Bauman, 1996; Cardinal, Hanson, & Wakeham, 1996; Sheehan & Matuouzzi, 1996), and perhaps for some children a little bit of extra help and encouragement can provide the confidence that enables them to demonstrate new communication abilities. In addition, children should be given *every* available opportunity to demonstrate their skills. Still, the evidence is overwhelming that even scrupulously honest and well-intentioned people can unknowingly influence the outcome of FC. As a result, when someone demonstrates sudden, dramatic, and previously altogether unsuspected communication abilities, objective verification is especially important.

Central to the debate about facilitated communication is the nature of the processing problems in autism itself. Do people with autism comprehend the language of those around them and simply have trouble expressing their understanding, or are language comprehension problems inherent to the disorder? If (and so long as) someone is unable to comprehend meaningful language, then in-depth communication is impossible, even through facilitated means.

social and recreational skills. Follow-up six years later showed that all but one had maintained their gains, and eight children (based on testing and observation) could not be distinguished from their normal peers. No child in the control group had achieved normal functioning (McEachin, Smith, & Lovaas, 1993).

Notice that all of the children in the Lovaas study benefited from training, but only eight achieved the functioning level of their typical peers. It is not known whether earlier intervention would have increased that number, or whether the children who made more modest gains were actually different in some unknown but important way. The intensive behavioral approaches used in the Lovaas studies are currently used in UCLA intervention programs with preschoolers, many of whom show impressive gains. These interventions include techniques similar to those that provide the basis for most educational and behavioral interventions used in populations with and without retardation. Chapter 11 will explore some of these procedures.

CEREBRAL PALSY

Cerebral palsy (CP) is a disorder of movement and posture that results from injury to the motor control areas of the brain. Approximately 60 percent to 70 percent of those with CP also have mental retardation, and approximately 10 percent of those with MR also have CP (Ratey et al., 2000). Many people with CP, then, have normal intelligence, and some are even intellectually gifted.

The severity of the motor problems that result from CP varies from very mild (slight clumsiness) to extremely severe (complete inability to control the muscles of any part of the body). The areas of the body affected by CP depend upon the location of the brain damage.

CP can be classified according to severity, by location of brain damage, or by the parts of the body that are affected as described in Table 9.2. Regardless of the area affected, motor problems take three primary forms: (1) **spasticity,** or when muscle jerking and rigidity take over any voluntary attempts at movement; (2) **athetosis,** or involuntary writhing muscular movements that are unrelated to but interfere with voluntary control; and (3) mixed, which is a combination of the first two. There are several other far less common types, including **ataxia** (poor motor coordination and balance), **rigidity** (disabling muscle tension as limbs are extended), and **tremor** (involuntary shaking movements). The location of the brain damage determines both the type of CP (for example, spasticity) and the affected body region (see Table 9.2).

Etiology

The brain damage that causes cerebral palsy can result from many of the same conditions that cause MR (discussed in Chapter 7 and 8), especially prematurity, low birth weight, and other birth complications such as breech birth, which can result in anoxia. CP can also occur because of childhood injury or infectious diseases such as toxoplasmosis and cytomegalovirus (see Chapter 6). Although usually the more

Table 9.2 Classification by Affected Area of the Body

Classification	Affected Area
Monoplegia (rare)	One arm or leg
Hemiplegia	Arm and leg on same side
Double hemiplegia	Arms and legs on both sides, but arms and one side more involved
Diplegia	Legs more involved than arms
Triplegia	Three limbs (usually both legs and one arm) and trunk
Paraplegia	Both legs and lower body
Quadriplegia	Arms and legs on both sides, and the trunk

extensive the brain damage, the more severe are both conditions, there is no necessary relationship between the severity of cerebral palsy and the degree of mental retardation. As we can see with Susan, the mobility problems that result from cerebral palsy may be extensive, while learning problems are mild or even nonexistent.

Treatment

The necessity of interdisciplinary treatment is particularly obvious with cerebral palsy. First, people with CP may have associated speech problems that require the attention of a speech pathologist. CP also may present threats to general health that require close attention by a physician. In addition, a physical therapist can provide or prescribe muscle exercise, and an occupational therapist can recommend assistive technology and instruct in its use. Infant **cognitive stimulation** programs are important because they can actually enhance motor development in babies with CP (Palmer et al., 1988). There may also be later difficulties with peer relationships and social issues, because of the necessity to adjust to limitations in functioning, but counseling can be helpful in addressing these problems. Coordination of these services—in addition to educational instruction—is essential for the effective treatment of people with CP.

Although CP is not a degenerative disorder—that is, the causal brain damage does not get worse with time—muscle control and function can worsen because of disuse or poor posture. With spasticity, for example, insufficient exercise can lead to *muscle contractors,* in which tendons shorten and pull so that joints become immovable (Eichstaedt & Lavay, 1992). For all forms of CP, therefore, strengthening both affected and unaffected muscle groups is important. For these reasons, proper exercise and adaptive equipment that promotes good posture are essential treatments.

The design and manufacture of adaptive equipment and assistive technology for people with physical disabilities have become an impressively creative and expanding industry. Functional aids include inexpensive but invaluable devices, as well as highly complex and costly innovations, such as motorized wheelchairs that can be operated by hand, foot, or head. Rehabilitation engineers customize inserts to stabilize bodies in the position that are the most comfortable and functional for the individual. They also design equipment to help people feed them-

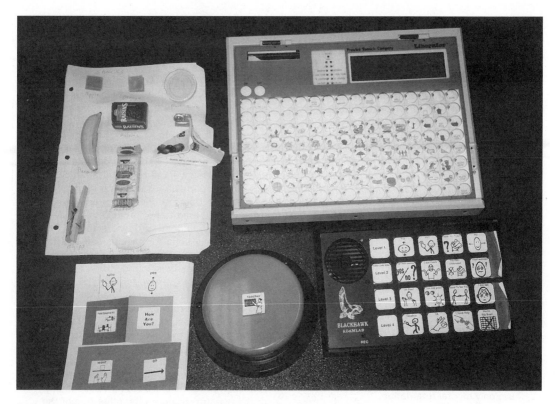

Examples of nonelectronic and electronic communication devices

Courtesy of Katherine Heller

selves and reach and retrieve objects. Battery-operated controls can be carried on a wheelchair tray and are so sensitive that they can respond to a smile or a breath to operate lights, televisions, microwave ovens, and electric windows.

Communication boards range from a few simple concrete object choices to pictures, thousands of words, and alphabet spelling. Computer-driven voice synthesizers allow a student to answer questions in class or speak to an audience. And an amazing array of software helps people with disabilities learn at their own pace about subjects as diverse as math, cooking, making friends, and traveling the world. With multimedia computers and CD-ROMs, these lessons are interactive and include sound and video. For someone who is planning a career in the field of developmental disabilities, technological help now comes in an ever-expanding wave of options.

> **FOR DISCUSSION** *How can these and other innovations that you have seen or can imagine be used to help people become more independent and involved in the community? Think especially about adaptations in school, work, and recreational settings.*

Challenges for a Speech Pathologist

Penny Cesco is a speech pathologist in a school funded for children with mental retardation and other developmental disabilities, in Cincinnati, Ohio. The school where she teaches has "reverse mainstreaming"—that is, students without disabilities also attend school there. In this interview, Penny described her professional responsibilities, as well as some of the challenges and satisfactions she experiences in her work. She also gives advice to students who are thinking about going into the field of speech pathology.

Speech pathology is a very wide field: Some pathologists work in school settings, others in clinics or hospitals. In college, we learned how to identify, diagnose, and remediate a wide range of speech problems. But that was just the tip of the iceberg. When you get out and start working, that's when you really specialize and become an expert in one field. For me, that specialization has become language and mental retardation. But I do work with children who have other related disabilities. There are children here who have vision impairments, hearing impairments, cerebral palsy, and autism—not just children who have only mental retardation.

I work with preschoolers, as well as older children, and I see each one twice a week. I do all classroom collaboration therapy. I don't do any pull-out therapy, so I see the children right in their classroom. This means that I have to use a wide range of methods to help them communicate as independently as possible with the tasks they are doing in the classroom. In the past, children would go to the speech therapy room and then go back to the classroom. But they wouldn't communicate about the same things or have the same communication needs in my therapy room that they do all day. Now we're looking at the whole child, and all of us are working as a team to understand what kids can do, to build on their strengths and to identify their needs.

We even manage our assessments differently than we used to. Now the teacher and I look at the child together. We play with him and see what kind of communication skills he has, and what his fine motor and gross motor skills are like. With the older kids, we do a lot of learner inventories where we also talk to the parents

and make them part of the assessment team. We ask what they think their child could be doing in five years, and what their goals are for their child. There aren't too many standardized tests out there for individuals with mental retardation. We have to do a lot of observations and interviews to build our individualized plans.

Technology has helped a lot, because now kids have so many more communication devices. One of my personal satisfactions is seeing these devices open doors for kids. There are some students who used to be considered "behavior problems," and now that they are able to communicate, their behavior has changed. Just today at lunch, one of my older students (he's 16), came into the teachers' lounge to pop some popcorn in the microwave for himself and his class. He was able to program the time himself and wait for the corn to pop, but when it came time to get the bag out, it was too hot. He was able to use his communication device to say "I need help getting this bag of popcorn out, please." So, instead of just not doing the task, or having a temper tantrum, he could communicate and ask for help. I wasn't involved in any of it. I was just sitting on the other side of the table watching, and knowing that a year ago he couldn't have done that. He used to hit the walls with his fist and stomp his feet. He would reach over and pinch other kids. He doesn't do any of that anymore.

My advice to students is to get out of the classroom and get as much hands-on experience in as many settings as you can. Once you get some experience you can go back to the textbook and read about a new syndrome or a new technique and say, "Oh, yes, I could try that with a certain kid," whereas before it was just dry. It didn't relate to a person. There was no glue to stick it to your brain. If you get a mental picture of a kid, or of the real situation, then you can learn.

Some people say "I don't know how you work with your students. I just couldn't do it." Well, I don't see my kids as "those poor students." I don't pity them. I see their small gains, and I get very exited about all the things they can do.

Susan

Susan and Her Computer

We return now to Susan to learn more about both her disability and her ability to manage it. Susan's CP is classified as *triplegia* of the mixed type, a classification that doesn't fit perfectly, because both of her arms are involved to some extent (although she has better control of her right arm and hand than her left). Susan does not have enough control to use a standard computer keyboard, but she manages well with the addition of a keyguard.

Susan's computer has a calculator, a dictionary, and a student organizer (including a calendar that has daily scheduling features and sound reminders). It has both sound and motion graphics. Susan is also learning to use an expensive voice-capability synthesizer, which means that she will no longer need the one-on-one attention of someone looking at her computer monitor in order for her remarks to be "heard." Soon she may actually be able to speak out of turn in class—a moment of real accomplishment for Susan!

In response to a goal in her recent IEP, Susan uses her organizing program to prompt herself about her morning routine, which she now manages far more independently. When she gets to school, the teacher spends several minutes with Susan entering that day's curriculum schedule, which (for some activities) Susan can follow on her own. In the evening, Susan spends a few more minutes with her mother or her home aide, Jolene, planning any new home tasks or extra activities for the next day.

Because her computer is loaded with games and activities, it is highly entertaining and might keep Susan from being social with her classmates—except, fortunately, they think it is the "coolest thing," and they are eager to join in for games and jungle safaris. It also means, however, that Susan must learn to discipline herself about the appropriate times to explore on her own and the right times to listen and concentrate on scheduled studies.

Susan's equipment is extremely expensive, and she is, therefore, fortunate to come from a wealthy family. Private insurance does not usually cover such equipment, nor does Medicaid. As a result, many children in her situation suffer reduced functioning and even impaired development.

SEIZURE DISORDERS

Epilepsy is the diagnostic term for people who have *recurring* (chronic) seizures (Trimble, Ring, & Schmitz, 2000). A seizure is the condition of abnormal electrical discharge in the brain that results in various predictable motor behaviors, depending upon the type of seizure. Someone who experiences only one or two occurrences or has seizures associated with an acute condition (such as low blood sugar, adverse drug reactions, and high fevers) does not have epilepsy (Coulter, 1993).

Table 9.3 International Classification System for Seizures

Seizure Classification	Area of Abnormal Brain Activity
Partial seizures	Begin in a small localized area
Generalized seizures	Extend to both sides of brain
Unilateral seizures	Extensive area but limited to one side of brain
Unclassified	Location cannot be determined

SOURCE: Adapted from M. R. Trimble, H. A. Ring, & B. Schmitz (2000), Epilepsy. In B. S. Fogel et al. (Eds.), *Synopsis of neuropsychiatry* (pp. 469–489). Philadelphia: Lippincott-Williams & Wilkins.

Seizure disorders are more common in people with autism, cerebral palsy, and mental retardation than in the general population. Of people with MR but without CP, 21 percent have epilepsy. In people with both MR and CP, 50 percent have epilepsy (Hauser & Hesdorffer, 1990). Although epilepsy is most common in people with severe mental retardation, achieving seizure control is no less likely with severe intellectual impairment than for those with milder MR (Marcus, 1993). Seizures are classified according to the area of the brain in which the abnormal neuronal activity occurs (see Table 9.3).

Most **generalized seizures** are of the **tonic–clonic** type (formerly called *grand mal*) during which there is first a *tonic* phase: The body becomes rigid, breathing stops, and the person loses consciousness and may turn blue. This is followed by a *clonic* phase in which the body is seized by repeated and alternating muscle contractions and relaxations. These seizures can last from less than one minute to 20 minutes or more—but usually no more than five minutes. Impending seizures may be forewarned by **auras**—unique sounds, odors, or physical feelings particular to the person's own experience. After the seizure, there is often drowsiness, nausea, headache, and fatigue.

Absence seizures (sometimes called *petit mal*) are another type of generalized seizure. Here contractions are usually not consciously experienced; the individual simply loses consciousness for a few moments. When this happens, she is almost always unaware of the event, and because she does not lose motor control, others may be unaware also. To someone looking at a person having an absence seizure, it may seem that she has simply "tuned out" for a moment. Absence seizures are most common in children and are often outgrown (Perry-Varner, 1996).

Partial seizures are sometimes also called *focal seizures*. One example is a psychomotor (temporal lobe) seizure, which often involves simple motor movements such as lip smacking or head turning. Consciousness may be lost or impaired, and the event is rarely remembered. It is common for seizures to begin with partial brain activity and then become generalized.

FOR DISCUSSION *If you have read* Silas Marner, *you may recognize descriptions of Marner's behavior; they sound strikingly similar to partial seizures. Can you think of other examples from literature of people with epilepsy? How have they been portrayed?*

When someone has a seizure (depending upon the type):

1. Remove hazardous objects from the vicinity.
2. Place cushioning material under the head.
3. Do *not* try to put anything in the person's mouth.
4. Stay until the seizure is over and consciousness is regained—after the seizure, turning the individual on his side can sometimes facilitate breathing.
5. Carefully record events and report any signs of injury.

Get medical help if:

1. Breathing does not resume.
2. One seizure follows another.
3. A significant injury occurs.
4. The seizure lasts more than 5 minutes (or more than is typical for the individual).
5. The person has no history of seizures.
6. The seizure is clearly different from previous ones.

FIGURE 9.2 Emergency treatments for seizure victims

SOURCE: Adapted from F. P. Orelove & D. Sobsey (1987), Seizure disorders and medications. In F. P. Orelove & D. Sobsey (Eds.), *Educating children with multiple disabilities: A transdisciplinary approach* (pp. 129–156). Baltimore, MD: Paul H. Brookes.

Etiology

People can be born with a seizure disorder, or they may develop it after a brain injury. In some cases, it is genetically predisposed, but more often it is related to brain damage that occurs because of birth trauma, prematurity and low birth weight, an Rh blood factor, environmental toxins, brain infections, or childhood diseases such as measles (Newmark, 1983; Trimble, Ring, & Schmitz, 2000). Whereas seizures are always related to abnormal electrochemical activity in the brain, in many cases no brain damage can be detected, and electrical brain activity appears normal as measured by EEG. This illustrates once again how much of our brain activity and function is yet unavailable even to measurement, let alone professional understanding.

Treatment

The primary treatment for epilepsy is antiseizure medication. Physicians rely on the reports of those who witness seizures so they can prescribe the correct drug type and dosage. Keeping a careful record of exactly what transpires is thus crucial to treatment. Important details include how long the seizure lasted, what the person looked and acted like, the events that preceded the seizure, and those that followed after (Orelove & Sobsey, 1987). Figure 9.2 provides guidance for helping someone who is having a seizure.

Information drawn from careful observation of seizure activity can also help prevent future incidents. In some people, for example, seizures can be provoked by environmental events such as missed meals, excessive fluid or salt intake, fatigue, or stress. Occasionally, they are brought on by visual stimuli such as flashing lights. Sometimes an individual may behave in a particular way each time he is about to have a seizure, and the occurrence can be prevented if this pattern is interrupted.

Some children also have learned to induce seizures voluntarily, and recognizing patterns can be important in stopping this behavior (Orelove & Sobsey, 1987). Because medication can have serious side effects such as decreased alertness, fatigue, nausea, and dizziness, it is especially important to take advantage of available behavioral methods to prevent seizures.

Although people with epilepsy can sometimes be injured during a seizure, they are more likely to be harmed by overprotection. People with seizure disorders (even those who also have extremely severe MR) can be safely included in school and community activities, and the apparent necessity of any potential restriction must be weighed carefully against the associated loss of life experience.

> **FOR DISCUSSION**   *Based on what you have learned about behavior during seizures and about preventing seizures, what accommodations can be made to help people enter into community, residential, work, and recreational settings?*

In the past, social stigma has been the major impediment for people with seizure disorders, but as the public becomes more educated, attitudes are improving. Hopefully, as more and more people with MR, CP, and seizure disorders are included as rightful members of the community, public understanding will continue to increase (Dreifuss, 1995).

BEHAVIOR DISORDERS

Behavior disorders including disruptiveness, poor self-esteem, problems of attention and hyperactivity, and self-injurious behavior (SIB) are common in people with mental retardation. SIB, however, is most common among people with severe intellectual limitations (Tu & Smith, 1983).

Self-Injurious Behavior

Self-injury in people with mental retardation can range from mild pinches or occasional head bangs during temper tantrums to the mutilation that occurs in Lesch-Nyhan (see Chapter 7), unconsciousness, and death (King, 1993). The most common methods of self-injury for people with MR include head banging and hitting, eye gouging, scratching, and biting their fingers and arms.

Like other forms of behavior, SIB has multiple causes, and it is not always possible to pinpoint the exact cause for individual cases. Still, in some specific conditions (especially Lesch-Nyhan) it is highly likely that SIB is the result of the same organic brain damage that causes the syndrome's other symptoms. In other instances, SIB may be caused by a physiological need for stimulation or a chemical imbalance, or it may be a learned response to boredom, a method to gain attention or avoid tasks, or a means of communication (Hillery, 1999; Singh, Singh, & Ellis, 1992).

Table 9.4 Examples of Nonverbal Communicative Behavior

Behavior	Possible Meaning
Smile	Yes or I like that.
Taps fingers	I want something.
Stands up	I want to leave.
Yells or hoots	Pay attention to me.
Bangs head or screeches	Stop that or leave me alone.

It is extremely important to note that the initial cause for SIB may be different from the reason or reasons that it continues. This is because a behavior can first occur as a result of organic or physiological abnormalities but then be taken up by the child who has discovered that it provokes attention or provides escape from unpleasant tasks. Still, there may also be people for whom SIB is entirely involuntary, and for whom it serves no behavioral function whatsoever (King, 1993).

> **FOR DISCUSSION** *Can you describe other more common behaviors that probably begin for one reason and then continue for different ones?*

Behavior modification is the primary treatment for SIB, although medications are often useful as well (Hillery, 1999). Be aware, though, that behavioral therapy is often effective in improving conditions that are known to be biologically based (such as autism), so its success does not imply a behavioral cause. It is, in fact, possible to gain some behavioral control over many physiological processes, including heart rate and the induction of seizures.

In the many instances where SIB is serving some current function, identifying that function is crucial to developing an effective behavioral treatment. Chapter 11 describes methods for identifying the function of behavior. As with the design of any effective treatment, careful and insightful observation provides the key, and Table 9.4 gives examples of behaviors (in addition to SIB) that may, in fact, be methods of communication. Although a particular behavior's meaning is individual and may indicate different things in different people, some likely meanings of specific behaviors are shown.

Attention Deficit Hyperactivity Disorder (ADHD)

Although officially termed **attention deficit hyperactivity disorder** (ADHD), the central characteristic of ADHD is not hyperactivity but a severe difficulty in focusing and concentrating on mental tasks. Those children who are also

An individual must have at least six symptoms to a degree that is maladaptive and inconsistent with his or her developmental level.

1. Often fails to give close attention to details or makes careless mistakes in schoolwork, work, or other activities.
2. Often has difficulty sustaining attention in tasks or play activities.
3. Often does not seem to listen when spoken to directly.
4. Often does not follow through on instructions and fails to finish schoolwork, chores, or duties in the workplace (not due to oppositional behavior or failure to understand instruction).
5. Often has difficulties organizing tasks and activities.
6. Often avoids or dislikes tasks or is reluctant to engage in tasks that require sustained mental effort (such as schoolwork or homework).
7. Often loses things necessary for tasks or activities (e.g., toys, school assignments, pencils, books, or tools).
8. Is often easily distracted by extraneous stimuli.
9. Often forgetful in daily activities.

FIGURE 9.3 Criteria for ADHD—predominantly inattentive

SOURCE: Taken from American Psychiatric Association (1994), *Diagnostic and Statistical Manual of Mental Disorders* (4th ed.). Washington, DC: Author. Copyright 1994 American Psychiatric Association. Reprinted with permission.

hyperactive may have particular difficulty in remaining seated in school, and they often show increased motor activity even during sleep (Stormont, Stebbins, & McIntosh, 1999).

Whereas many children with ADHD are hyperactive, a substantial minority are not—to the contrary, they are quiet and even withdrawn. These children are especially likely to be overlooked in school, where teachers may simply believe they are "dreamers" or "slow." ADHD has been thought to be four times more common in boys, but recent studies indicate that this ratio is probably lower: Boys may simply be more likely to have associated hyperactivity, while girls are disproportionately undiagnosed because they are more often quiet and withdrawn (Gaub & Carlson, 1997). In spite of these general trends, hyperactivity *or* withdrawal can be found in both girls and boys.

In addition to problems with concentration (and perhaps hyperactivity), children with ADHD also may be impulsive and aggressive, characteristics that often lead to social inadequacies and poor self-esteem. ADHD is commonly associated with mental retardation, although the majority of children with ADHD have normal intelligence and may even be gifted.

The DSM-IV describes the three subtypes of ADHD: predominantly inattentive, predominantly hyperactive-impulsive, and combined. The criteria for the predominantly inattentive type are listed in Figure 9.3, and the criteria for the hyperactive-impulsive type are in Figure 9.4. To receive the ADHD diagnosis for the combined subtype, a child must have at least six symptoms from each list (a total of 12) that have lasted a minimum of six months.

The above impairments must first occur in two or more settings (such as home or school) by no later than 7 years of age. Further, they cannot be accounted for

Six or more of the following symptoms have persisted for at least six months to a degree that is maladaptive and inconsistent with developmental level:

Hyperactivity

1. Often fidgets with hands or feet or squirms in seat.
2. Often leaves seat in classroom or in other situations in which remaining seated is expected.
3. Often runs about or climbs excessively in situations where it is inappropriate (in adolescents or adults, may be limited to subjective feelings of restlessness).
4. Often has difficulty playing or engaging in leisure activities quietly.
5. Is often "on the go" or often acts as if "driven by a motor."
6. Often talks excessively.

Impulsivity

1. Often blurts out answers to questions before the questions have been completed.
2. Often has difficulty awaiting turn.
3. Often interrupts or intrudes on others (e.g., butts into conversations or games).

FIGURE 9.4 Criteria for ADHD—predominantly hyperactive-impulsive

SOURCE: Taken from American Psychiatric Association (1994), *Diagnostic and Statistical Manual of Mental Disorders* (4th ed.). Washington, DC: Author. Copyright 1994 American Psychiatric Association. Reprinted with permission.

by pervasive developmental disorder, schizophrenia, or other psychotic or mental disorders. Finally, the symptoms must have been present for the past six months (American Psychiatric Association, 1994).

Pediatricians, psychiatrists, and psychologists are usually the professionals who make an official diagnosis of ADHD, but they rarely have the opportunity to observe the child for more than a short time, and they rely heavily on reports from parents, teachers, occupational therapists, and others who spend considerably more time with the child. Usually the judgment of these observers is rated on any one of several scales used to aid in diagnosis—for example, the Connors Teacher or Parent Rating Scales (Connors, 1990). For this reason, families and professionals must be familiar with the criteria for attention deficit and be able to recognize the symptoms.

FOR DISCUSSION   *When observing a child with ADHD, what specific information would you record?*

Behavioral observations and ratings alone may often not be sufficient to determine whether a child is actually experiencing problems with concentration and focus, and they cannot provide the specific information about possible differences in children's visual and auditory attention that is so important for educational planning. To fill this need, hundreds of assessment instruments are available (some of them computerized) to help determine the nature of a child's attentional problems. Because most of these tests have limited reliability and validity data to back

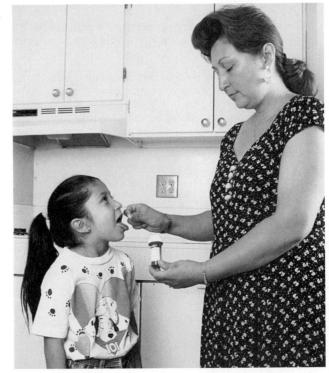

Most children with ADD have improved concentration with medication—especially when used in combination with behavioral interventions.

© Michael Newman/PhotoEdit

them up, they cannot be relied upon for a clear diagnosis, but they can focus and clarify more casual observation.

Etiology Although there is no firm conclusion on what causes ADHD, evidence suggests that it is a chemical or neuroanatomical disruption in the area of the brain that controls attention and concentration (Lerner, Lowenthal, & Lerner, 1995). As with other disorders that we have studied, there are undoubtedly several influences on the development of this disruption in the first place. Two of the most common are genetics and maternal exposure to toxins—including alcohol, cigarettes, and lead (Milberger, Biederman, Faraone, Guite, & Tsuang, 1997).

Innovations in technology to study brain functioning are making contributions to understanding brain alterations in people with ADHD and hyperactivity. **Magnetic resonance imaging** (MRI)—which converts magnetic signals into video images of individual brain sections—and **positron emission tomography** (PET) have demonstrated clear differences in both brain structure and metabolism (Hynd, 1992; Zametkin et al., 1990). Brain electrical activity mapping (BEAM) is an especially exciting advance over the electroencephalogram (EEG) in measuring electrical activity in the brain.

Treatment The primary treatments for ADHD are drug therapy and behavior modification. Whereas research indicates that drug therapy can be especially effec-

---

1. Poor appetite (especially if it persists and there is weight loss)
2. Insomnia (especially if it is severe and persists)
3. Rebound effect (symptoms get worse when drug wears off—dosage times may need to be readjusted)
4. Abdominal pain (physician may recommend that medication be taken with meals or may discontinue or change to another type if severe)
5. Mood changes: tearfulness, irritability (especially when pronounced and persist beyond the first week or two)
6. Headaches (especially if severe and persistent)
7. Elevated pulse and blood pressure (beyond mild and expected changes)
8. Signs of hallucinations*
9. Tics*

*These are extremely rare and usually indicate another preexisting condition, but they are especially serious and require immediate action.

FIGURE 9.5 Some possible side effects of stimulant medication

SOURCE: Adapted from K. Ideus & P. Cooper (1995), Chemical cosh or therapeutic tool? Towards a balanced view of the use of stimulant medication with children diagnosed with attention deficit/hyperactivity disorder. *Therapeutic Care & Education, 4*(3), 52–63.

tive, sometimes behavioral training can be even more so (Frazier & Merrell, 1997), although the best results come from the two in combination (Barkley, 1997). Because the symptoms of ADHD are usually long-lasting, it is especially important that children learn to cope with and manage the associated difficulties (Whalen & Henker, 1991). Control over attention problems often can be most effectively gained when the intensity of the symptoms are modified with medication, while the child simultaneously learns strategies to focus attention and inhibit impulsivity.

The medications most often used in the treatment of ADHD are psychostimulants (usually Ritalin, Dexedrine, or Cylert) and less often antidepressants (including Prozac, Norpramin, and Elavil). Antidepressants are most often used when children with ADHD are also severely anxious or depressed (Lerner, Lowenthal, & Lerner, 1995). Occasionally, antihypertension medication may be used. For just a few children, special diets and vitamin therapy have been effective, but not for most.

Sometimes, parents are reluctant to place their child on medication, because they are worried about side effects. However, most children show improvements in attention, hyperactivity, impulsivity, behavior, and academic productivity when medically treated, and they experience only mild and short-term drug-related symptoms (Ideus & Cooper, 1995; Swanson et al., 1993). The most common side effects are a temporary decrease in appetite and an initial difficulty in sleeping. The occasional child who appears withdrawn, sad, or "zombie-like" is almost certainly overmedicated.

Most side effects are related to dosage, so the child's physician should be consulted for possible changes in medication level if the symptoms in Figure 9.5 are observed. The responsibility falls primarily to teachers and parents for determining whether a child is responding well to medication and for noting the presence of

Chronic forgetfulness

Problems with time management

Tendency to take on far too many projects

Generally disorganized lifestyle: frequently late and rushed

Difficulty managing checkbook and finances

Frequent moves or job changes

Tendency to speak without considering others' reactions

Tendency to interrupt

Difficulty controlling temper

Difficulty managing paperwork on the job

Chronic pattern of underachievement

Pattern of periodic depression

Difficulty in maintaining long-term relationships

Pattern of interests that are taken up and then dropped

Difficulty concentrating when reading

FIGURE 9.6 Signs of ADD in adulthood

SOURCE: Adapted from CHADD (Children and Adults with Attention Deficit Disorders) Web page: www.chadd.org/.

side effects. It is crucial, therefore, that they be knowledgeable about the side effects of medication and alert to measures of improved performance. The correct dosage is individual, and children must be observed carefully to be sure that their medication is appropriate to enhance academic success, without creating additional difficulties (Barkley, 1997). Because there is evidence that the dosage at which a child is most well behaved and compliant is sometimes too high for optimum learning, drug effectiveness must be judged by academic performance rather than by docility (Swanson, 1985).

ADD Residual While it used to be believed that children outgrew ADHD, it is now known that a majority of people continue to experience symptoms in adulthood (Wilens et al., 1999). Even though hyperactivity does improve, attentional difficulties continue to manifest in problems with organization and consistent attention to detail. Figure 9.6 lists some common characteristics of adults with ADD.

The outcome for children with ADHD as adults is better when the disorder does not involve aggressiveness, no additional learning disabilities (or only mild ones) are involved, and families are organized and supportive (Schwean, 1999). The treatment for ADD in adults is similar to that for children: medication and behavioral and cognitive training.

▌▌ LOOKING AHEAD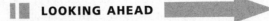

Although coordination and cooperation among disciplines are essential to best practice for the treatment of anyone with retardation, the presence of related dis-

Autism

   Autism Society of America, Inc. (ASA)

   7910 Woodmont Ave., Suite 300

   Bethesda, MD 20814-3015

   Phone: 1-800-3AUTISM Ext. 150

   E-mail: info@autism-society.org

   Web site: http://www.autism-society.org

Cerebral Palsy

   American Academy for Cerebral Palsy and
   Developmental Medicine

   6300 North River Rd., Suite 727

   Rosemont, IL 60018-4226

   Phone: (847) 698-1635

   E-mail: woppenhe@ucla.edu

   Web site: http://149.142.183.10/new/home.html

Epilepsy

   Epilepsy Foundation of America (EFA)

   4351 Garden City Dr.

   Landover, MD 20785

   Phone: (800) EFA-1000

   E-mail: webmaster@efa.org

   Web site: http://www.efa.org

Attention Deficit–Hyperactivity Disorder

   Children and Adults with Attention Deficit
   Disorders (CHADD)

   8181 Professional Pl., Suite 201

   Landover, MD 20785

   (800) 233-4050

   Web site: http://www.chadd.org/

*Attention Deficit–Hyperactivity Disorder
(continued)*

   National Attention Deficit Disorder
   Association

   1788 Second St., Suite 200

   Highland Park, IL 60035

   Phone: (847) 432-ADDA

   E-mail: mail@add.org

   Web site: http://www.add.org/

Assistive Technology

   Tools for Life Demonstration Center

   College of Health and Professional Studies

   Georgia Southern University

   P.O. Box 8098

   Statesboro, GA 30460-8098

   http://www2.gasou.edu/tools/tools.htm

   ABLEDATA

   8630 Fenton St., Suite 930

   Silver Spring, MD 20910

   http://www.abledata.com

Other Related Disabilities

   Special Education Resources Page

   http://www.special ed.miningco.com/
   education/specialed/

   National Information Center for Children
   and Youth

   U.S. Office of Special Education Programs

   http://www.nichcy.org

FIGURE 9.7 Sources of information on disabilities related to MR

orders only accentuates this need. In this chapter we have studied some of the interdisciplinary treatments important for those who have disorders related to MR. In Chapter 10, we will study specific examples of current systems that have been designed to facilitate and enhance interdisciplinary and transdisciplinary effectiveness in early intervention.

You may be wondering how you can find out more about the related disorders presented here. Figure 9.7 lists organizations to which you can write for information. Many of these groups will send materials, including regular newsletters, either free or for a small fee.

INFOTRAC COLLEGE EDITION

Recently there has been much talk about a possible link between autism and the routinely administered Measles-Mumps-Rubella (MMR) vaccine. Enter *autism* as the keyword in *InfoTrac College Edition,* and review the articles related to this topic. Report what you find, and give specific evidence for your answer.

REFERENCES

Abell, F., Krams, M. Ashburner, J., Passingham, R., Friston, K., Frockowiak, R. Happe, F. Frith, C., & Frith, U. (1999). Neuroanatomy of autism: A voxel-based whole brain analysis of structural scans. *Neuroreport: For Rapid Communication of Neuroscience Research, 10*(8), 1647–1651.

American Psychiatric Association. (1994). *Diagnostic and Statistical Manual of Mental Disorders* (4th ed.). Washington, DC: Author.

Autism Society of America. (1999). *What is autism?* Bethesda, MD: Author.

Barkley, R. A. (1997). *ADHD and the nature of self-control.* New York: Guilford.

Bettelheim, B. (1955). *Truants from life.* Glencoe, IL: The Free Press.

———. (1967). *The empty fortress: Infantile autism and the birth of the self.* New York: The Free Press.

Biklen, D. (1990). Communication unbound: Autism and praxis. *Harvard Educational Review, 60*(3), 291–314.

Cantwell, D. P., Baker, L., & Rutter, M. (1979). Families of autistic and dysphasic children. *Archives of General Psychiatry, 36,* 682–687.

Cardinal, D. N., Hanson, D., & Wakeham, J. (1996). Investigation of authorship in facilitated communication. *Mental Retardation, 34*(4), 231–242.

Centers for Disease Control and Prevention. (2001). Web site: http://www.cdc.gov/.

Connors, C. K. (1990). *Connor's rating scales.* Los Angeles: Western Psychological Services.

Coulter, D. L. (1993). Epilepsy and mental retardation: An overview. *American Journal on Mental Retardation, 98,* 1–11.

Creak, M. (1961). Schizophrenia syndrome in childhood: Progress report of a working party. *Cerebral Palsy Bulletin, 3,* 501–504.

Dreifuss, F. E. (1995). Prevention as it pertains to epilepsy. *Archives of Neurology, 52*(4), 363–366.

Eichstaedt, C., & Lavay, B. (1992). *Physical activity for individuals with mental retardation.* Champaign, IL: Human Kinetics Books.

Frazier, M. R., & Merrell, K. W. (1997). Issues in behavioral treatment of attention-deficit/hyperactivity disorder. *Education & Treatment of Children, 20*(4), 441–461.

Gaub, M., & Carlson, C. L. (1997). Gender differences in ADHD: A meta-analysis and critical review. *Journal of the American Academy of Child and Adolescent Psychiatry, 36,* 1036–1045.

Gittelman, M., & Birch, H. G. (1967). Childhood schizophrenia: Intellect, neurologic status, perinatal risk, prognosis, and family pathology. *Archives of General Psychiatry, 17,* 16–25.

Grandin, T. (1984). My experiences as an autistic child and review of selected literature. *Journal of Orthomolecular Psychiatry, 13*(3), 144–174.

———. (1988). Teaching tips from a recovered autistic. *Focus on Autistic Behavior, 3*(1), 1–8.

Hauser, W. A., & Hesdorffer, D. C. (1990). *Epilepsy: Frequency, causes and consequences.* New York: Demos.

Hillery, J. (1999). Self-injurious behavior and people with developmental disabilities. In N. Bouras (Ed.), *Psychiatric and behavioural disorders in developmental disabilities and mental retardation* (pp. 109–120). New York: Cambridge University Press.

Hostler, S. L., Allaire, J. H., & Christoph, R. A. (1993). Childhood sexual abuse reported by facilitated communication. *Pediatrics, 91*(6), 1190–1192.

Hynd, G. W. (1992). Neurological aspects of dyslexia: Comments on the balance model. *Journal of Learning Disabilities, 25,* 110–113.

Ideus, K., & Cooper, P. (1995). Chemical cosh or therapeutic tool? Towards a balanced view of the use of stimulant medication with children diagnosed with attention deficit/hyperactivity disorder. *Therapeutic Care & Education, 4*(3), 52–63.

Jacobson, J. W., Eberlin, M., Mulick, J. A., Schwartz, A. A., Szempruch, J., & Wheeler, D. L. (1994). Autism, facilitated communication, and future directions. In J. L. Matson (Ed.), *Autism in children and adults: Etiology, assessment, and intervention.* Pacific Grove, CA: Brooks/Cole.

Kanner, L. (1943). Autistic disturbances of affective contact. *Nervous Child, 2,* 217–250.

King, B. H. (1993). Self-injury by people with mental retardation: A compulsive behavior hypothesis. *American Journal on Mental Retardation, 98*(1), 93–112.

Klin, A., & Volkmar, F. R. (1999). Autism and other pervasive developmental disorders. In S. Goldstein & C. R. Reynolds (Eds.), *Handbook of neurodevelopmental and genetic disorders in children* (pp. 247–274). New York: Guilford.

Lerner, J. W., Lowenthal, B., & Lerner, S. R. (1995). *Attention deficit disorders: Assessment and teaching.* Pacific Grove, CA: Brooks/Cole.

Lovaas, O. I. (1987). Behavioral treatment and normal educational and intellectual functioning in young autistic children. *Journal of Consulting and Clinical Psychology, 55,* 3–9.

Lovaas, O. I., & Buch, G. (1997). Intensive behavioral intervention with young children with autism. In N. N. Singh et al. (Eds.), *Prevention and treatment of severe behavior problems: Models and methods in developmental disabilities* (pp. 61–86). Pacific Grove, CA: Brooks/Cole.

Lowe, L. H. (1966). Families of children with early childhood schizophrenia: Selected demographic information. *Archives of General Psychiatry, 14,* 26–30.

Mahler, M. S. (1965). On early infantile psychosis: The symbiotic and autistic syndromes. *Journal of the American Academy of Child Psychiatry, 4,* 554–568.

Marcus, J. C. (1993). Control of epilepsy in a mentally retarded population: Lack of correlation with IQ, neurological status, and electroencephalogram. *American Journal on Mental Retardation, 98,* 47–51.

McEachin, J. J., Smith, T., & Lovaas, O. I. (1993). Long-term outcome for children with autism who received early intensive behavioral treatment. *American Journal on Mental Retardation, 97*(4), 359–372.

Milberger, S., Biederman, J., Faraone, S. V., Guite, J., & Tsuang, M. T. (1997). Pregnancy, delivery, and infancy complications and attention deficit hyperactivity disorder: Issues of gene–environment interaction. *Biological Psychiatry, 41*(1), 65–75.

Newmark, M. E. (1983). Genetics of epilepsies. In F. E. Dreifuss (Ed.), *Pediatric epileptology* (pp. 89–116). Boston: John Wright–PSG.

Nishimura, B., Watamaki, T., Hara, K., Sato, M., & Wakabayashi, S. (1998). Long term communication training of totally mute autistic children using manual signs and written language. *Japanese Journal of Child & Adolescent Psychiatry, 39*(4), 352–363.

Orelove, F. P., & Sobsey, D. (1987). Seizure disorders and medications. In F. P. Orelove & D. Sobsey (Eds.), *Educating children with multiple disabilities: A transdisciplinary approach* (2nd ed., pp. 129–156). Baltimore, MD: Paul H. Brookes.

Palmer, F. B., Shapiro, B. K., Wachtel, R. C., Allen, M. C., Hiller, J. E., Harryman, S. E., Mosher, B. S., Meinert, C. L., & Capute, A. J. (1988). The effects of physical therapy on cerebral palsy: A controlled trial in infants with spastic diplegia. *New England Journal of Medicine, 318,* 803–808.

Pennington, B. F. (1991). *Diagnosing learning disorders: A neuropsychological framework.* New York: Guilford.

Perry-Varner, E. (1996). Seizure disorders. In P. J. McLaughlin & P. Wehman (Eds.), *Mental retardation and developmental disabilities* (2nd ed., pp. 173–185). Austin, TX: Pro-Ed.

Rapin, I. (1991). Autistic children: Diagnosis and clinical features. *Pediatrics, 87,* 751–760.

Ratey, J. J., Dymek, M. P., Fein, D., Joy, S., Green, L. A., & Waterhouse, L. (2000). Neuro-developmental disorders. In B. S. Fogel, R. B. Schiffer, & S. M. Rao (Eds.), *Synopsis of neuropsychiatry* (pp. 245–271). Philadelphia: Lippincott-Williams & Wilkins.

Rimland, B. (1964). *Infantile autism.* New York: Meredith.

———. (1994). The modern history of autism: A personal perspective. In J. L. Matson (Ed.), *Autism in children and adults: Etiology, Assessment, and Intervention* (pp. 1–12). Pacific Grove, CA: Brooks/Cole.

Romanczyk, R. G., Lockshin, S. B., & Navalta, C. (1994). Autism: Differential diagnosis. In J. L. Matson (Ed.), *Autism in children and adults: Etiology, Assessment, and intervention* (pp. 99–126). Pacific Grove, CA: Brooks/Cole.

Rutter, M., Macdonald, H., LeCouteur, A., Harrington, R., Bolton, P., & Bailey, A. (1990). Genetic factors in child psychiatric disorders—empirical findings. *Journal of Child Psychology and psychiatry, 31,* 39–83.

Santangelo, S. L., & Folstein, S. E. (1999). Autism: A genetic perspective. In H. Tager-Flusberg et al. (Eds.), *Neurodevelopmental disorders* (pp. 431–447). Cambridge: MIT Press.

Schopler, E., Messibov, G. B., & Kunce, L. J. (Eds.). (1998). *Asperger syndrome or high-functioning autism?* New York: Plenum.

Schwean, V. L. (1999). Looking ahead: The adjustment of adults with disabilities. In V. L. Schwean et al. (Eds.), *Handbook of psychosocial characteristics of exceptional children* (pp. 587–610). New York: Kluwer Academic/Plenum.

Sheehan, C. M., & Matuozzi, R. T. (1996). Investigation of the validity of facilitated communication through the disclosure of unknown information. *Mental Retardation, 34*(2), 94–107.

Singh, N. N., Singh, Y. N., & Ellis, C. R. (1992). Psychopharmacology of self-injury. In J. K. Luiselli, J. L. Matson, & N. N. Singh (Eds.), *Self-injurious behavior: Analysis, assessment and treatment* (pp. 307–351). New York: Springer-Verlag.

Stormont, M., Stebbins, M. S., & McIntosh, D. E. (1999). Characteristics and types of services received by children with two types of attention deficits. *School Psychology International, 20*(4), 365–375.

Swanson, J. M. (1985). Measures of cognitive functioning appropriate for use in pediatric psychopharmacological research studies. *Psychopharmacological Bulletin, 21,* 887–890.

Swanson, M., McBurnett, K., Wigal, T., Pfiffner, L., Lerner, M., Williams, L., Christian, D., Tamm, L., Willcutt, E., Crowley, K., Clevenger, W., Khouzam, N., Woo, C., Crinella, G., & Fisher, T. (1993). Effect of stimulant medication of children with attention deficit disorder: A review of reviews. *Exceptional Children, 60*(2), 154–162.

Szempruch, J., & Jacobson, J. W. (1992). *Evaluating facilitated communications of people with developmental disabilities.* Rome, NY: Rome Developmental Disabilities Services Office.

Trimble, M. R., Ring, H. A., & Schmitz, B. (2000). *Epilepsy.* In B. S. Fogel et al., *Synopsis of neuropsychiatry* (pp. 469–489). Philadelphia: Lippincott-Williams & Wilkins.

Tsai, L. Y. (1993). *Medications for treatment of autism and associated disorders.* (Available from Luke Y. Tsai, MD, Professor and Director of Developmental Disorders Clinic, University of Michigan Medical Center, Ann Arbor, MI.)

Tu, J. B., & Smith, J. T. (1983). The Eastern Ontario survey: A study of drug-treated psychiatric problems in the mentally handicapped. *Canadian Journal of Psychiatry, 28,* 270–276.

Weiss, M. J. S., Wagner, S. H., & Bauman, M. L. (1996). A validated case study of facilitated communication. *Mental Retardation, 34*(4), 220–230.

Whalen, C. K., & Henker, B. (1991). Therapies for hyperactive children: Comparisons, combinations, and compromises. *Journal of Consulting and Clinical Psychology, 59,* 126–137.

Wheeler, D. L., Jacobson, J. W., Paglieri, R. A., & Schwartz, A. A. (1993). An experimental assessment of facilitated communication. *Mental Retardation, 31*(1), 49–60.

Wilens, T. E., McDermott, S. P., Biederman, J., Abrantes, A., Hahesy, A., & Spencer, T. J. (1999). Cognitive therapy in the treatment of adults with ADHD: A systematic chart review of 26 cases. *Journal of Cognitive Psychotherapy, 13*(3), 215–226.

Williams, D. (1992). *Nobody nowhere: The extraordinary autobiography of an autistic.* New York: Times Books.

Wing, L. (1993). *Children apart: Children with autism and their families.* Bethesda, MD: Autism Society of America.

Zametkin, A. J., Nordahl, T. E., Gross, M., King, A. C., Semple, W. E., Rumsey, J., Hamburger, S., & Cohen, R. M. (1990). Cerebral glucose metabolism of adults with hyperactivity of childhood onset. *New England Journal of Medicine, 323,* 1361–1364.

Part III

Learning Within the Community: Developing Skills and Abilities

10

Early Intervention

Chapter 8 considered the importance of prevention and showed that knowledge is available now to prevent a majority of the causes of mental retardation before children are even born. These include those cases resulting from alcohol and other toxins, poor nutrition, and the absence of prenatal care. In Chapter 9, we saw several conditions that often involve mental retardation, some of which stem from social circumstances that are potentially preventable. This chapter describes several early intervention programs that have been shown to reduce the incidence of mental retardation.

Although prevention programs seek to preempt mental retardation in the first place, early intervention usually refers to techniques used to reverse or improve retarded development. It is often impossible, however, to clearly distinguish between prevention and early intervention. For example, programs that provide prenatal care and proper nutrition to pregnant women are clearly aimed at prevention, while preschool programs for children with existing disabilities are aimed at early intervention. But that same preschool program may also be designed to prevent retardation in children **at-risk** or to prevent behavioral problems in children with disabilities (Specht, 1989). Likewise, nutritional supplements may prevent disabilities for some children and correct problems for others (Keogh, Wilcoxen, & Bernheimer, 1986).

RATIONALE FOR EARLY INTERVENTION

Even when children are born with brain damage, MR may not be inevitable. Many researchers believe that the infant brain (especially when younger than 1 year old) is highly **plastic** and can be literally shaped (for better or worse) far more easily than later in life (Stiles, Bates, Talk, Trauner, & Reilly, 1999). Although destroyed brain cells cannot regenerate at any stage of development, the brains of young children are better able to compensate for injury. Certain parts of the brain are primarily responsible for language, for example, and when these areas are damaged in adults, the ability to speak or understand language is adversely affected. In children, however, another area of the brain may be able to take over the language functions (Stiles, 1998).

Brain plasticity is only partial, because some areas of the brain are already specialized for just one single function at birth (Grattan, DeVos, Levy, & McClintock, 1992). Even so, because of the brain's *tendency* to plasticity, retardation in children with damage may be less severe when intervention is started early. Likewise, in children who are at-risk for developing retardation, MR may be prevented if measures are taken when the child is extremely young (Ramey & Ramey, 1998). The importance of early intervention cannot be overstated.

FOR DISCUSSION *Because of brain plasticity, is it true that any condition resulting in MR can be corrected if intervention is early and intensive? Why or why not?*

Early intervention is also important, because initial learning provides the basis for later learning. A child's development is dependent upon both genetically driven biological maturation *and* environment, so a lack of stimulation and experience in early development can result in intellectual delay (Luster & Dubow, 1992). For this reason, early intervention is crucial for children who are severely deprived or neglected. Adoption studies show that children reared in more advantaged homes show substantial intellectual advantages over otherwise similar youngsters reared in low SES environments—evidence that emphasizes the importance of environmental interventions (DeBerry, Scarr, & Weinberg, 1996).

FUNCTIONS OF EARLY INTERVENTION

Early intervention is designed to meet several functions, depending upon the circumstances of the child and family. It is designed first to help children gain the basic skills and abilities necessary for later learning—learning that can prevent increased delay. Important among these skills are language and communication. Second, it may provide supports for the family and the child that can stop the development of secondary disabilities such as behavior problems or increased physical disabilities (Hamilton, Goodway, & Haubenstricker, 1999). For example, a child with MR may use self-injurious behavior to avoid difficult tasks—a problem for which parent training is often critical (see Chapter 9). Or, because of inadequate adaptive equipment, a child with cerebral palsy may develop strictures that can further inhibit physical mobility. Third, the family of a child with a disability may experience stress that can adversely affect the child's development. Intervention can help alleviate this stress by providing the family with needed supports and coordinating crucial services (Dunst, Trivette & Deal, 1994).

ELIGIBILITY FOR EARLY INTERVENTION

Early intervention is relevant for at least three groups of children, each with different characteristics. In the first group are children whose environmental or biological circumstances place them at-risk for MR, but who currently show no signs of developmental delay. Among these children are some who were premature or of exceptionally low birth weight, as well as children who live in poverty and have one or more immediate family members with retardation.

In the second group are children who apparently function within the retarded range but can "catch up" with normal development, usually through intervention. These children often fall within the group known as cultural-familial or have otherwise experienced severely damaging environmental conditions such as abuse and neglect.

Third and finally, there are those who have clearly identifiable conditions associated with MR. These children—who include those with the genetic conditions described in Chapter 7 such as Down syndrome and Fragile X—are likely to have lifelong developmental problems, but they can function far more effectively with appropriate intervention and supports.

These three groups should be distinguished, because there are often unique expectations and goals for the outcome of intervention that require different program approaches (Bricker, 1986). For one example, children with severe disabilities may have physical health needs and may require adaptive assistance, neither of which is relevant for those at-risk. On the other hand, those low-income families with children at-risk may have specific economic and job-training needs not shared by higher-income families.

FOR DISCUSSION   *Describe some of the goals and expectations you would imagine appropriate for a child with Down syndrome who comes from a middle-class family, and compare those with what you might expect for a child "at-risk" for MR because of poverty and parental retardation. In what ways are they different? In what ways are they the same?*

SOME TYPES OF EARLY
INTERVENTION PROGRAMS

Early intervention programs are sometimes **home-based** so that interventionists either provide treatment in the family home or train caregivers to work with children there. Other programs are **center-based,** with children and families receiving services in a central location away from home. Many programs include both settings.

Among the services provided by early intervention programs are intellectual and physical stimulation for infants, toddlers, and preschoolers; occupational and physical therapy; speech and language services; day care; respite care; financial counseling; social and recreational opportunities; parent support groups; legal services; transportation; counseling for children and families; and parent training (Crocker, 1992; Noonan & McCormick, 1993). Not all programs provide all of these services, and some provide services that are not listed here. Increasingly, programs are individually tailored for families' specific needs.

Home-based and center-based programs both have advantages and disadvantages. Evidence shows that when parenting skills are taught in the home, for instance, they are more likely to be implemented in everyday life (Bakken, Miltenberger, & Schauss, 1993). Home-based programs have the further advantage for infants of avoiding travel and exposure to outside contagions. Such programs are expensive, however, because highly paid personnel must spend time traveling to and from client homes. Furthermore, parents get no respite from their own children and have no opportunity to talk with other caregivers. To offer families the advantages of both program types, both center- and home-based elements are included when appropriate and where possible.

EFFECTIVENESS OF EARLY INTERVENTION

One of the earliest and most often cited studies demonstrating the success of early intervention was initiated in the 1930s by Harold Skeels, and because of the work's interesting nature and its historical importance, we present it here in some depth. Skeels found alternative placements for two toddlers then living in an orphanage. Probably as a result of environmental deprivation, these little girls were functioning within the retarded range—at the 6- and 7-month developmental levels, though they were actually 13 and 16 months of age, respectively. At that time, it was believed that children with such severe developmental delays were incurably retarded and unsuitable (by state law) for adoption, so Skeels's counterdemonstration was of real importance (Kirk, 1977).

Orphanages in the 1930s were overcrowded, and there was generally no time for staff members to talk to or play with babies. The prevailing medical model placed little or no importance on emotional attachment or intellectual stimulation, and babies were kept in hospital cribs until they were 6 months old, often with protective sheeting on the sides that kept them from seeing out. They were diapered and bathed quickly, fed with propped bottles, and provided with neither toys nor mobiles (Skeels, 1966).

Conditions improved somewhat for babies ages 6 to 24 months, because they were then housed in small dormitories that contained two to five larger individual cribs that allowed them to move around a bit and see each other. They were placed on the floor for brief play periods, and a few toys were available, but there was still little interaction with caregivers (Skeels, 1966). Such were the circumstances for the two little girls found by Skeels.

Some relief from overcrowding was often provided when children were transferred from orphanages to institutions for the retarded. For these two girls, such arrangements seemed appropriate, and they were placed in a women's ward in a state institution. Six months passed before Skeels saw the girls again, by which time they had changed so dramatically that he no longer recognized them. Far from the "emaciated, undersized . . . pitiful little creatures" who "lacked muscle tone or responsiveness" and "spent their days rocking and whining," they were instead active, happy children who seemed entirely "normal" (Skeels, 1966, pp. 5, 6). Upon repeat testing, the toddlers were functioning at age level, and as a result were transferred back to the orphanage and subsequently adopted.

What could have happened in the institution to result in so pronounced a change in such a short time? As it turned out, the girls had been the object of much interest and attention by the residents, attendants, and nurses. Staff members often included them in outings on their days off and frequently purchased toys and books for them. Because these experiences had apparently been so successful in enhancing the development of the two children, it was thought that others who were experiencing pronounced delays and would eventually be transferred to institutions for the retarded anyway might also benefit from early placement.

Over a year's time, Skeels succeeded in transferring a new group of 11 children to two Iowa institutions as "houseguests." Again, these children were placed on wards with older women, where they typically received one-to-one attention. There was, in fact, considerable competition among wards to see which one would have its "baby walking or talking first" (Skeels, 1966, p. 17).

FOR DISCUSSION   *If placements varied in terms of the attention and stimulation the babies received, would you expect that they would show differences in rates of development? Do you think any such differences would persist when the children became adults? Why or why not?*

Each child remained in the MR institution until "the decision was made that he had attained the maximum benefit from his 'house-guest' experience" (Skeels, 1966, p. 21), at which time he was either made available for adoption or became an official resident of the institution. The average length of stay was approximately 19 months, and a final follow-up test occurred approximately 2½ years later.

After the "experimental" period, Skeels discovered that 12 children with characteristics similar to the experimental group had remained in the orphanage, so these orphanage children formed a contrast group. Table 10.1 shows initial and follow-up IQ measures for both groups. Because the institutional children had improved so much, nearly all were adopted, while IQ decline for many of the orphanage children ensured that they would remain wards of the state.

Another follow-up study was conducted when the participants ranged from 25 to 35 years of age. The outcome for the two groups was impressively different in both educational level attained and professional achievement. On the average, people who had experienced the MR institution eventually completed almost 12 years of school, and eight actually graduated from high school. In contrast, people who had stayed in the orphanage averaged fourth-grade levels, and only one graduated from high school. The median income for the experimental group (no doubt related to educational achievement) matched that for the participants' home state, while those from the contrast group made only one-fourth as much money.

The Skeels study has been criticized for its methodology and statistical analysis (Goodenough & Maurer, 1961), and it is virtually certain that the good outcome of the "experimental" group was related to its members' lifelong experiences and not simply to early intervention (Clarke & Clarke, 1976; Ramey & Baker-Ward, 1982). Since the 1939 Skeels and Dye studies, however, many other studies have shown that increased growth and development does result from early intervention efforts. And even if an early intervention program cannot be expected to protect a child from a lifetime of damaging experiences, studies have demonstrated some surprisingly long-term effects, even in spite of subsequent environments (Lazar &

Table 10.1 Individual Scores from the Skeels Orphanage Study

	Experimental Group							
	Before Transfer		After Transfer					
	Initial Test		Last Test			Follow-up		
Case	Age (mos.)	IQ	Age (mos.)	IQ	IQ Change	Age (mos.)	IQ	Total Change
1	7.0	89	12.8	113	+24	56	118	+29
2	12.7	57	36.8	77	+20	65	68	+11
3	12.7	85	25.2	107	+22	55	116	+31
4	14.7	73	23.1	100	+27	55	116	+43
5	13.4	46	40.0	95	+49	93	90	+44
6	15.5	77	30.1	100	+23	65	102	+25
7	16.6	65	27.5	104	+39	68	109	+44
8	16.6	35	43.0	93	+58	77	96	+61
9	21.8	61	34.3	80	+19	63	63	+2
10	23.3	72	45.4	79	+7	74	92	+20
11	25.7	75	51.0	82	+7	72	92	+17
12	27.9	65	40.4	82	+17	67	90	+25
13	30.0	36	89.0	81	+45	118.0	94	+58
Mean	18.3	64.3	38.4	91.8	+27.5	71.4	95.9	+31.6
S.D.	6.6	16.4	17.6	11.5	15.0	16.7	16.3	17.0
Median	16.6	65.0	36.8	93.0	+28.0	67.0	94.0	+29.0
	Contrast Group							
14	11.9	91	55.0	62	−29	81	64	−27
15	13.0	92	38.3	56	−36	81	52	−40
16	13.6	71	40.9	56	−15	75	80	+9
17	13.8	96	53.2	54	−42	82	51	−45
18	14.5	99	41.9	54	−45	62	35	−64
19	15.2	87	44.5	67	−20	101	89	+2
20	17.3	81	52.9	83	+2	77	91	+10
21	17.5	103	50.3	60	−43	73	49	−54
22	18.3	98	39.7	61	−37	74	78	−20
23	20.2	89	48.4	71	−18	106	75	−14
24	21.5	50	51.6	42	−8	91	68	+18
25	21.8	83	50.1	60	−23	96	61	−22
Mean	16.6	86.7	47.2	60.5	−26.2	83.3	66.1	−20.6
S.D.	3.2	13.9	5.6	9.7	14.1	12.3	16.5	25.6
Median	16.3	90.0	49.3	60.0	−30.0	81.0	66.0	−24.0

SOURCE: Adapted from H. M. Skeels (1966), Adult status of children with contrasting early life experiences: A follow-up study. *Monographs of the Society for Research in Child Development, 31*(3).

Darlington, 1982; Schweinhart, Berrueta-Clement, Barnett, Epstein, & Weikart, 1985; Polit, Quint, & Riccio, 1988; Ramey & Ramey, 1998).

More Early Examples

Another early example (Kirk, 1958) showed that not only children who are free from organic damage benefit from early intervention, but also that physical handicaps in themselves could result in cognitive delay because of reduced intellectual experience; such delay could be avoided, however, if children were provided with appropriate intervention. In addition to the Kirk study, scores of others have demonstrated the effectiveness of early intervention for children with organic problems (Bricker & Sheehan, 1981; Hanson, 1981).

One other program—the Portage Project—served both at-risk children and those with existing disabilities (mild to severe) in a home-based multidisciplinary program. Children in the program (birth to 6 years) received stimulation, practice, and instruction in self-help, cognitive, motor, and social skills, as well as in language development. Portage Project children gained an average of 15 months on developmental indices over an 8-month period (Bricker & Kaminski, 1986; Shearer & Shearer, 1976).

Carolina Abecedarian Project

An ongoing example of effective early intervention is provided by the Carolina Abecedarian Project, which was initiated in 1972 to study whether intervention could prevent the intellectual declines so often experienced by children born at-risk because of extreme poverty. One hundred and eleven families were randomly assigned to either an educational experience or a control group. For the educational group, children attended a center-based preschool program, beginning by 3 months of age. Instruction in the preschool program focused on motor, social, and cognitive development with a particular emphasis on the development of communication skills (Campbell, Helms, Sparling, & Ramey, 1998). The center was operated five days a week, 50 weeks a year, and free transportation was provided for anyone who needed it. Free nutritional, health, and social work services were provided for both the educational and control groups—but only the education group attended the preschool.

Follow-up results through 12 years of age have shown that although both groups experienced IQ declines with increasing age, children in the educational group lost far fewer points (Ramey & Ramey, 1998). It is important to note that children in the control group were six times more likely than those in the preschool group to have scores that fell within the retarded range (Campbell et al., 1998).

In Project Care, an extension of the Carolina Abecedarian Project, one experimental group received both an educational, center-based, day care program and home-based family education, while another experimental group received home-based treatment only (Ramey & Ramey, 1998). The day care experience was the Abecedarian program, while family education consisted of an educator visit to the home every 10 days for one hour each day to help parents develop problem-solving skills that could be applied to daily life. Children were tested on the Bayley Scales at 6, 12, 18, and 24 months and on the Stanford-Binet test at 36 months. Results indicated that the day care and education group scored significantly better at all ages than either the control or family-education–only groups (and there was no difference between the last two groups). Thus, home visits alone were not enough to prevent severe declines in children's scores, while the center-based day care program was more successful (Wasik, Ramey, Bryant & Sparling, 1990)

Research has overwhelmingly found that early intervention is effective. The issue is no longer whether it is worthwhile to intervene with children who have disabilities or are at-risk, but rather what form that intervention should take.

PROGRAM EVALUATION

Program evaluation is a crucial part of successful intervention, and the studies cited in the first part of this chapter provide examples of evaluation research. Because of such studies, we can be sure that the skills and abilities of people with mental retardation can improve, and we know that because a child functions within the retarded range when she is young does not always mean she will experience delayed or retarded functioning later in life.

Many intervention studies, however, have methodological and statistical problems that keep them from providing answers to more specific questions (Bricker, 1986). Particularly with early studies, it was often not possible even to determine that it was the early intervention program that was responsible for children's improved functioning rather than some other factor in their lives (Dunst, 1986). More recent studies that randomly assign participants and use other controls for competing variables provide much better evidence of the effect of early intervention; and because of the great number of studies that replicate early intervention findings, the effect of early intervention cannot be doubted.

The challenge for evaluation researchers today, though, goes beyond simply proving the effectiveness of intervention efforts to asking specifically which aspects of intervention programs promote improvement and which do not. For example, with educational interventions, are there particular materials or methods that are especially effective? Are certain personality characteristics or interventionist skills crucial (Bailey & Simeonsson, 1986)? Are some settings (i.e., home- or center-based programs) more effective, and does this vary for different families or as the result of other circumstances? *Intervention* covers an incredibly complex and varying array of activities, ranging from a home visit once a month to intensive, coordinated programs that involve physical health, education, and social services. Although we know that intervention can be effective, it is critical to understand which programs and techniques are *most* successful.

1. Does the program meets its explicit goals?
2. Does it create additional problems for children or families?
3. Are families positive about it?
4. Does it promote integration?
5. Does it facilitate family support?

FIGURE 10.1 Outcome measures for an early intervention program

Furthermore, whereas many early studies limited the criterion for success merely to IQ, there are several other (and perhaps more important) indications of the effectiveness of early intervention (Bailey & Simeonsson, 1986). Among these categories are better social skills and increased friendships, improved family functioning, more efficient daily living skills, more appropriate behavior, higher self-esteem, greater independent functioning, and eventual employment success. Figure 10.1 lists some additional possible success measures for evaluating aspects of a program apart from the functioning of participants.

Much of early intervention research suffers from a lack of theoretical clarity, while goals for intervention (and related variables) have likewise been unclear (Bailey & Simeonsson, 1986). What is more, such goals may extend beyond direct outcomes for the individual child and family to those that seek to benefit the community and larger society. For example, early intervention may be successful when it results in more children who can be maintained in less-restrictive school settings and who can remain in the home or community as opposed to an isolated residential setting. Furthermore, success may be measured in terms of reduced costs when children develop greater independence and require fewer services. Likewise, societal benefits can occur in the form of increased human productivity. Well-articulated theory can identify the particular intervention procedures that are expected to result in specific changes for the child and family, and on that basis, it shapes the research design to evaluate outcomes effectively.

FOR DISCUSSION *What other benefits might communities gain from successful early intervention? Can you identify examples from your own community?*

THE ROLE OF VALUES IN
DESIGNING INTERVENTIONS

Intervention programs must be based not only on explicit theory, but also on clearly defined values. The very act of determining what makes a successful outcome implies the necessity of value judgments, so evaluation research should be— *must* be—a value-laden process (Dokecki, 1986).

Does the Intervention:

1. strengthen families?
2. enhance community?
3. protect the family from unwarranted intrusion?
4. minimize stress by making essential resources available?
5. promote shared responsibility among parents and service providers?
6. protect individual family members from abuse and severe neglect?

FIGURE 10.2 Values in family-centered intervention

SOURCE: Adapted from P. R. Dokecki (1986), The impact of evaluation research on policymaking. In L. Bickman & D. L. Weatherford (Eds.), *Evaluating early intervention programs for severely handicapped children and their families* (pp. 311–334). Austin, TX: Pro-Ed.

Evaluation research is designed quite differently depending upon the type of program being evaluated: for example, (1) a single, specific center-based preschool program; (2) a system of preschool programs (e.g., Head Start); or (3) a system of highly individualized planning efforts for the coordination of multiple services such as under Part C of PL 105-17 (discussed later in this chapter). Even though evaluation for these varied programs will require diverse methods, evaluation should be viewed always as an ongoing and dynamic process that involves both evaluation of the extent to which a program meets its goals and the desirability of those goals themselves. If research is to be effective, then it must not only be explicit for particular outcome measures, but also study the connection *between* those outcomes and program goals and values.

Examples of values often relevant for intervention programs are shown in Figure 10.2.

RESEARCH AND POLICY COLLABORATION

If research is to affect program development and public policy, then collaboration is essential among researchers, practitioners, and policy makers. Because policy makers are seldom involved in either the research or practitioner roles (and vice versa), there is typically a gap and sometimes even conflict among these respective points of view. Still, differences must be confronted while at the same time common goals are acknowledged. One such common aim might be the increased ability of communities to contribute to the development of people with retardation.

Differences may sometimes be apparent in terms of problem-solving styles. Researchers tend to value restraint, for example, as well as a conservative approach to change that waits upon evidence before forming opinions and beliefs. On the other hand, policy makers often value a bold, persistent, and opportunistic approach that seeks to sustain support in the face of challenges and looks for the opportunity to assert particular preconceived ideals (Rein & White, 1977). In part because of these differences, policy makers have been unwilling to wait for research

Elementary school children who attend Head Start are less likely to need special education or repeat a grade.

© Paul Conklin/PhotoEdit

on effectiveness before launching widespread programs, and researchers have too infrequently designed studies really useful to policy makers. More and more, however, public policy and professional practice drive research planning, and researchers are evaluating existing programs and policy efforts (Dokecki, 1986). Evaluation researchers, policy makers, and practitioners must work together in designing and carrying out cost-feasible and cost-effective programs for intervention.

Head Start: An Example of Collaboration Among Research, Practice, and Policy

Head Start is a nationwide, federally funded program that provides preschool experience for economically disadvantaged children. It serves as early intervention for some children who are at risk, as well as for others who have identified disabilities.

Research has shown that children who attend Head Start are better prepared (at school entry) than their comparable peers who do not attend a preschool program; they are also less likely to attend special education classes or repeat a grade (McKey et al., 1985). Furthermore, those children who have below-average cognitive skills show the largest gains; this is especially true when those children are African-American (Lee, Brooks-Gunn, & Schnur, 1988). Programs vary widely, though, and some are more successful than others. It is especially important, therefore, to identify those program attributes that are responsible for the greatest success, not only to ensure the highest benefit for all Head Start youngsters but also to make the best use of the more than $3 billion spent annually on Head Start programs and to justify program expansions to serve even more children (U.S. Department of Health and Human Services, 1999).

Unfortunately, it is difficult for research consumers to draw fair conclusions about early intervention programs from research reports, because judgments about the worth of a particular study and the fairness of the author's stated conclusions require time-consuming study of research design and statistical analysis. In other words, to make truly valid judgments about a study, readers must have the knowledge and expertise to have carried it out in the first place, and they must take the considerable time and effort required to apply these skills to the report. For most consumers this is impractical; they must rely on getting a sense of "what most studies find" by reading the conclusions of large numbers of studies.

Recently a statistical technique called *meta-analysis* has been used to help readers synthesize results from numerous studies. One such study, the Head Start Synthesis Project (McKey et al., 1985), reports the results of 210 research reports on Head Start programs. From these findings, it is clear that Head Start programs have reliable short-term effects. Because meta-analysis is a kind of averaging technique, however, it still cannot reveal which individual programs are most effective.

Some studies agree in pointing to crucial variables, however. An important factor in the success of preschool intervention programs, for example, is whether teachers have had early childhood training. In fact, the presence of such training is more important than the number of years of schooling or of degrees (Ruopp, Travers, Glantz & Coelen, 1979). For this reason, the federal government has mandated that all Head Start classrooms have at least one teacher with a child development associate credential or equivalent (Collins, 1993). Figure 10.3 lists specific curriculum content essential to the training of early intervention teachers. In addition, preschool programs need validated curriculum models and frequent teacher team meetings to plan and evaluate daily activities (Schweinhart & Weikart, 1986).

---

1. Knowledge of developmental processes
2. Behavior management and instructional skills
3. Ability to synthesize input from a variety of sources
4. Skills and information to evaluate program effectiveness

FIGURE 10.3 Skills and knowledge important for effective intervention

SOURCE: Adapted from D. Bricker & R. Kaminski (1986), Intervention programs for severely handicapped infants and children. In L. Bickman & D. L. Weatherford (Eds.), *Evaluating early intervention programs for severely handicapped children and their families* (pp. 51–78). Austin, TX: Pro-Ed.

Although children who attend Head Start programs show gains in IQ scores, improvements typically decline over time (Lee, Brooks-Gunn, Schnur, & Liaw, 1990). If the cognitive gains made by these severely disadvantaged children are to be maintained, then changes probably must occur in the lives of their parents or caretakers (White, Taylor, & Moss, 1992). Recent **two-generation program strategies** are designed to address the effects of unemployment, illiteracy, and drug and alcohol abuse in the families of many Head Start children (McLloyd, 1998).

Even though Head Start programs themselves are financially unable to provide the job training, employment counseling, adult education, and drug treatment these problems so urgently require, these issues can be addressed through collaboration with other agencies. One such effort is now being tried in a few communities, combining the federally funded JOBS program and Head Start. Because most Head Start programs typically provide only part-day or selected day experiences, one goal of this venture is to extend day care for children whose families are engaged in education, job training, or employment through the JOBS program. Another goal is to provide case management for wider family needs (Smith, Blank, & Collins, 1992).

Even Start is another model program designed and piloted through Head Start, combining family literacy with a child development program. Even Start services include adult basic education, parent–child interaction training, and early childhood education programs. Research indicates that parents and children who are enrolled in Even Start programs do make gains in literacy and cognitive skills as compared with control groups (U.S. Department of Education, 1998). Head Start programs have collaborated in other projects with state and local health, education, and treatment agencies to provide families with opportunities for self-sufficiency. Research evaluating these efforts will be crucial in discovering their most successful elements and in guiding federal, state, local, and private expenditures.

> **FOR DISCUSSION**   *In your opinion, how crucial are changes in families' self-sufficiency to later educational and economic success for their children? Please explain your thinking.*

PL 105-17 and IDEA—Part C

In the United States, the federal government has played a significant (and probably indispensable) role in promoting early education for children with disabilities. With the 1986 passage of PL 99-457 (an amendment to PL 94-142), funding was offered that encouraged states to provide free public preschool education for children from ages 3 to 5. Family services and transition planning for these eligible preschoolers were also provided. States could receive federal money for preschoolers only if they also contributed funds and provided the required services, and all states were soon in compliance.

It is Part C of PL 105-17, though, that offers the outstanding model for early intervention service delivery. Part C provides states with financial assistance for developing and implementing a "statewide, comprehensive, coordinated, multidisciplinary, interagency program of early intervention services" (Garwood, Fewell, & Neisworth, 1988, p. 4) for eligible infants and toddlers (ages birth to 3) and their families. Although Part C is voluntary, every state in the United States (plus the District of Columbia, Puerto Rico, and the territories) is either now providing services or developing plans to do so (Noonan & McCormick, 1993).

The federal plan provides guidelines for intervention programs nationwide, while leaving the responsibility for determining how these plans can best be carried out to individual states. States appoint a lead agency that develops a "child find" system (more on this below), implements public awareness, and coordinates interagency agreements that are designed to use existing resources as much as possible (Ad Hoc Part H Work Group, 1995). More and more, it is up to individual localities to identify their unique needs and coordinate resources to meet those needs.

Infants and toddlers are eligible under Part C if they experience developmental delays (as defined under state guidelines), or if they have a diagnosed physical or mental condition that is strongly related to a developmental delay—such as Down syndrome or cerebral palsy. Services must be provided for physical, cognitive, language and speech, and psychosocial and self-help needs as individually required by the child. Figure 10.4 lists some of the services that can be provided.

Each child and his family must receive an individualized multidisciplinary assessment that provides the basis for identification of appropriate services. A detailed and written service plan—the **individualized family service plan** (IFSP)—is developed by a multidisciplinary team. The family is always a member of the team, and the IFSP is evaluated and updated yearly and reviewed every six months. Figure 10.5 presents the essential aspects of an IFSP; Figure 10.6 provides an example of steps included in the Part C early intervention process, from the initial inquiry through the appointment of a family service coordinator to the transition plan that eases the move from Part C to preschool services.

assistive technology devices and services	physical therapy
audiology	psychological services
family training, counseling, and home visits	service coordination
health services	social work services
medical services for diagnosis or evaluation	special instruction
nursing services	speech and language pathology
nutrition services	transportation and related costs
occupational therapy	vision services

FIGURE 10.4 Some services provided by Part C

SOURCE: Adapted from 34 *Code of Federal Register* (CFR) 303.12(d), as presented in Ad Hoc Part H Work Group (1995).

Every individual family service plan must include the following:

1. A written multidisciplinary assessment of the child's current level of functioning in cognitive, communicative, social, emotional, physical, and adaptive development.
2. A statement of the family's resources, priorities, and concerns.
3. A description of the services that the child and family need, including method, frequency, and intensity.
4. A statement of expected intervention outcomes, including criteria, procedures, and time lines.
5. A statement of the natural environments in which early intervention services will be provided.
6. Projected dates for initiation of services and expected duration.
7. The name of the service coordinator who will be responsible for implementing and coordinating the plan with other agencies and people.
8. The procedures to ensure successful transition from infant services to preschool programs.

The IFSP must be reviewed every six months and evaluated and updated yearly.

FIGURE 10.5 Individual family service plans

SOURCE: Adapted from Noonan & McCormick (1993).

Services specified in the IFSP can include parent training; counseling, speech, occupational, or physical therapy; and some health services related to the child's disability. These may be offered in the home, clinic, or other care center. All services must be approved by the parents before they are carried out.

The heavy emphasis on interagency and interdisciplinary cooperation in the Part C legislation is important, not only because it acknowledges the necessity of collaboration among service providers in early intervention, but also because it sets a precedent for service delivery throughout the child's life span. And because it recognizes the interrelationships among child, family, and community, it encourages a systems perspective among professional disciplines.

Coordination of Services

Coordination of services is a crucial element for early intervention plans. Figure 10.7 illustrates the overwhelming array of early intervention options that families may need to enhance the development of their children. Those services listed are by no means comprehensive, and there are myriad additional agencies and service providers who offer educational and residential training and other service options for intervention. Some of the providers shown in Figure 10.7 exist in some areas, but not in others.

Locating the appropriate services and service providers (and even learning what services are available) is a formidable task, one that requires familiarity and experience with agencies in a particular community. With rare exceptions, families cannot initially be expected to have the specialized knowledge to negotiate

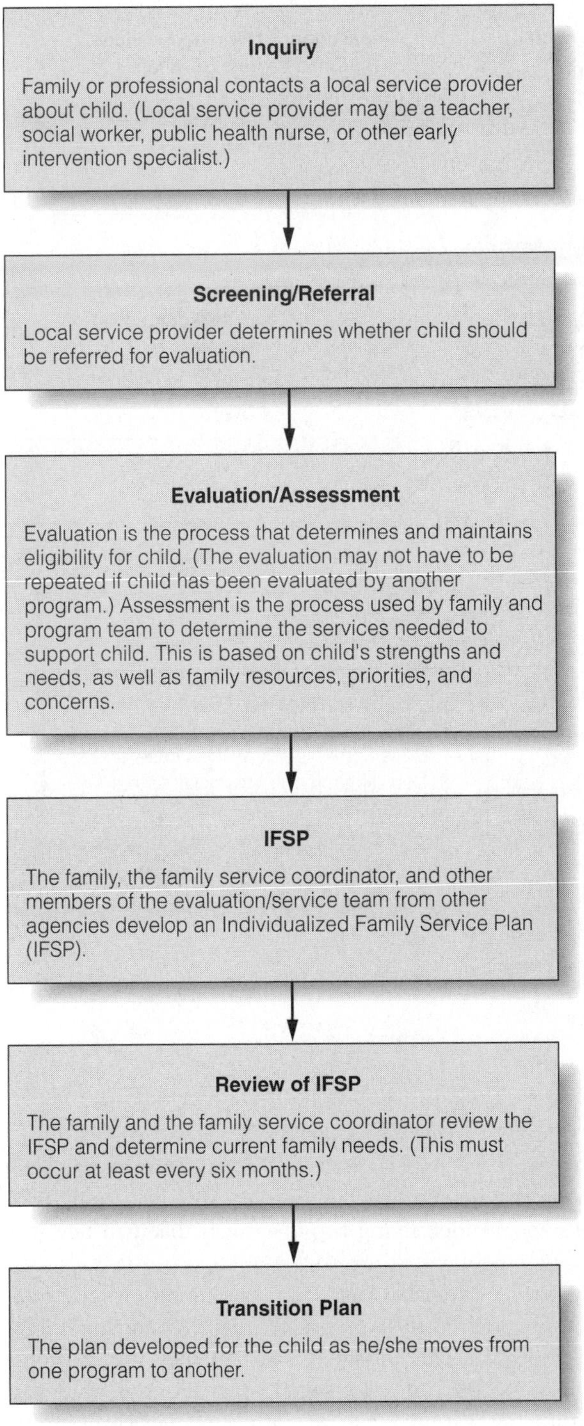

Inquiry

Family or professional contacts a local service provider about child. (Local service provider may be a teacher, social worker, public health nurse, or other early intervention specialist.)

↓

Screening/Referral

Local service provider determines whether child should be referred for evaluation.

↓

Evaluation/Assessment

Evaluation is the process that determines and maintains eligibility for child. (The evaluation may not have to be repeated if child has been evaluated by another program.) Assessment is the process used by family and program team to determine the services needed to support child. This is based on child's strengths and needs, as well as family resources, priorities, and concerns.

↓

IFSP

The family, the family service coordinator, and other members of the evaluation/service team from other agencies develop an Individualized Family Service Plan (IFSP).

↓

Review of IFSP

The family and the family service coordinator review the IFSP and determine current family needs. (This must occur at least every six months.)

↓

Transition Plan

The plan developed for the child as he/she moves from one program to another.

FIGURE 10.6 A typical sequence of events as a child moves through the early intervention process mandated by Part C

Adapted from *Early On: Michigan's Family Guidebook to Early Intervention Services.* May, 1993.

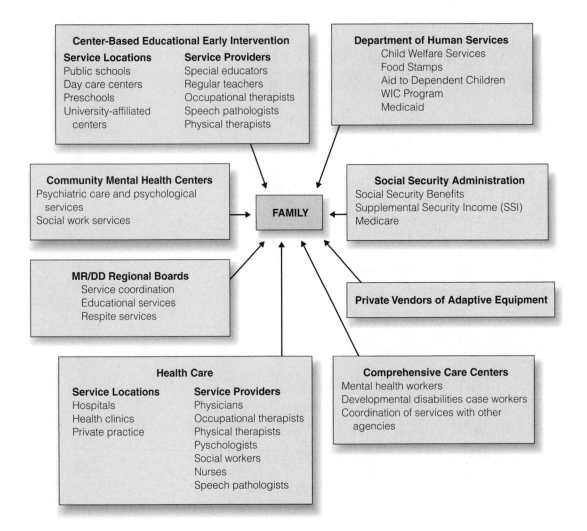

FIGURE 10.7 Community services for families

this maze (although, after a few years' experience, they often become true experts). The family service coordinator therefore has a crucial role in helping parents understand their options and in identifying those services that will be most helpful and effective.

The number and kind of services available vary from community to community. As a rule, there are far more options in large urban areas than in rural communities. Inner-city families, however, can be isolated in that they may have no transportation to reach services and few informal social supports; thus, they can easily be "lost" and cut off from any real involvement with the larger community.

The Importance of Agency and Family Collaboration: A Real-World Example

Sister Barbara Cline (recall her from her farm at the beginning of Chapter 1) is Early On coordinator for 15 counties in southwestern Michigan. Early On is a multiagency program that coordinates services for children birth to 3 years (under Part C) and relies upon collaboration among agencies, including public health departments, departments of social services, community mental health agencies, and schools. Here she discusses the importance of agency coordination and cooperation with families:

When the subject of coordination of services for families first became a real issue here some people would say, "Well, here we coordinate all of our services very well." I had the suspicion that they were coordinated well at the agency administration level, but I wasn't really sure how well they were coordinated at the level of actual family services. So we did a research project on that issue. At the time, I happened to be working with a family that had eleven agencies involved with them, and it took six months to get all of those agencies to share information about the family. When they finally did, it was discovered that different agencies had different goals for and expectations of the parents, and

in some instances these goals and expectations were conflicting. This family was at-risk for losing their children because of neglect (and in the end the children were put up for adoption); but when we looked back over what happened, we thought this was probably a family that—with the right support—could have kept their children. One day I went to see this family, at about three in the afternoon, and the mom met me at the door and said, "Well, you're number six today." And I said, "How much time can you spend with your children when you are entertaining six professionals who are supposedly trying to make life better for you." As we looked back at the family later, we realized that of those 11 agencies (or services) they really only needed three. If those three had worked together, the family might still be together, and the seven other agencies could have been helping other families.

When we first started talking about coordination, people kept saying, "Okay, how much money are you going to give us to do this?" And I said, "I'm not going to give you any money to do it. You're going to save money by doing it."

It may be more difficult for families in rural areas to become "invisible" to the mainstream culture.

Furthermore, where many service options exist, families can be overwhelmed by agency demands. For families already living stressful and chaotic lives, agency intervention may only add to that stress and confusion. It is the service coordinator's job to listen to families and connect them with the resources that can help reduce stress and strain and maximize healthy, optimal functioning. The family, of course, has the ultimate say in this process.

In instances where abuse and serious neglect put a child in danger, community agencies do have the responsibility to intervene, regardless of family cooperation.

Even then, however, it is critical that families have input and that intervention plans be tailored to meet the special needs of each family.

CHALLENGES IN IMPLEMENTATION

Parental Involvement

One basic assumption of many early intervention programs has been that parent involvement (in practice, usually the mother) is related to success for the child (Casto & Mastropieri, 1986; Powers & Bruey, 1988). *Involvement* in this sense does not refer to family participation in developing an intervention plan, but the actual delivery of intervention training. Sometimes this assumption is based on the idea that the child's disability is primarily the result of inadequate parenting (as with theories of environmental deprivation) or that uninformed parenting practices inhibit what progress the child could be making.

For example, it is now well shown that mutually rewarding interactions between a child and caregiver are important to normal development (Gindis, 1995). With infants, positive interactions often depend on the caregiver's ability to "read" the child's communicative signals. Usually a responsive caregiver can tell whether an infant is tired, hungry, bored, or ill, as well as whether she is in the mood to play, wants to cuddle, and so on. Nonnurturing or conflicting interactions can occur, because the behavior of infants with disabilities is sometimes difficult to interpret or because the caregiver may not know what to look for—or even that she should be looking. In such situations, coaching parents in effective respond-

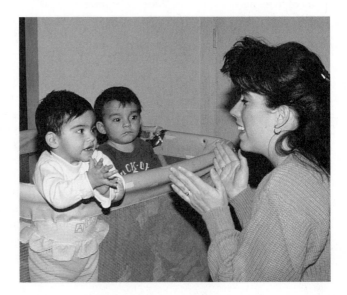

Developmentally appropriate interaction with adults is integral to normal development.

© Tony Freeman/PhotoEdit

ing techniques can facilitate the child's development (Sameroff, Bartko, Baldwin, Baldwin, & Seifer, 1998).

In other instances, focus on parent involvement may simply reflect the same belief that is integral to transdisciplinary practice: The child will benefit from training experiences that are repeated often and in many settings. For children with MR, this can be especially important, because they typically have problems with **generalization** (Powers & Bruey, 1988).

According to Bricker (1986), however, the term *parent involvement* has referred to the actual delivery of services, parents' participation within the classroom (Kroth, 1989), mother–child interaction (Nye, 1989), and parent assessment of child behaviors (Field, Dempsey, Hallock & Shuman, 1978) in addition to other meanings. Given the wide use of the term, it is not surprising that the research literature is mixed in finding superior outcomes with family involvement (Casto & Mastropieri, 1986; Ramey, Bryant, Sparling, & Wasik, 1985; Ramey & Ramey, 1998). In fact, whether parent involvement increases program effectiveness no doubt depends upon the type of intervention in question, as well as the individual circumstances of the family (Strain & Smith, 1986; Baker, Landen, & Kashima, 1991).

Families themselves have sometimes taken exception to professional assumptions about involvement and have offered their own point of view (Turnbull & Summers, 1987). Some believe that they are asked to take on service provision roles that are incompatible with their view of parenting. These families are not so interested in "fixing" the child or in sending him the message that he needs to be "fixed," as they are in providing unconditional love. They want simply to accept him as he is. For both parents and professionals, however, there exists an ever-present dilemma between the extent to which one "should" adopt an attitude of acceptance toward a child's difference and diversity and the desire to intervene in favor of positive change. Finding a healthy balance here is especially important, because intolerance toward children's differences can result in their lowered self-esteem, while too much tolerance can result in failure to provide the high expectations and supports that promote growth and development (Specht, 1989).

Some parents also feel that professionals do not take overall family functioning into account, and that they sometimes disregard the effect that a particular intervention will have on the family's quality of life. As an example, Featherstone (1980) has described her reaction to the request that she spend an extra five minutes three times a day brushing son Jody's teeth with an electric toothbrush—a procedure suggested to keep Jody's gums from growing over his teeth (a result of the seizure medicine drug Dilantin.) Although this seemed a minimal and reasonable request to the occupational therapist who made it, Helen Featherstone had another point of view:

> Jody . . . is blind, cerebral-palsied, and retarded. We do his physical therapy daily and work with him on sounds and communication. We feed him each meal on our laps, bottle him, change him, bathe him, dry him, put him in a body cast to sleep, launder his bed linens daily . . . [all] designed to minimize his miseries and enhance his joys and his development. . . . Now you tell me that I should spend fifteen minutes every day on something that

Jody will hate, an activity that will not help him to walk or even defecate, but one that is directed at the health of his gums. This activity is not for a finite time, but forever. It is not guaranteed to help, but "it can't hurt." And it won't make the overgrowth go away but may retard it. Well, it's too much. Where is that fifteen minutes going to come from? What am I supposed to give up? Taking the kids to the park? Reading the bedtime story to my eldest? Washing the breakfast dishes? Sorting the laundry? Grading students' papers? Sleeping? Because there is no time in my life that hasn't been spoken for, and for every fifteen-minute activity that is added, one has to be taken away. (Featherstone, 1980, pp. 77–78)

Featherstone's comments point once again to the importance of working *with* families to meet their needs, as well as understanding the intricate and competing system of those needs (Seligman, 1999). Whether parent involvement is crucial (or even important) depends upon the type of involvement and the goal of intervention so that the notion of "involvement" is now giving way to the concept of family support (Turnbull & Summers, 1987).

Family-Centered Focus

Family support implies a family-centered focus. According to Turnbull & Summers (1987), a major difference with a family-centered focus is that the service delivery system is no longer seen as the center of the universe; instead, families become central. This means that service agencies neither are assumed to have all the correct answers about what is best for the family nor are given the authority to set priorities. Families are asked instead what assistance they need most, and service providers work with the family to meet these needs. Sometimes needs are tangible, involving economics, skill development, or vocational training; at other times, they may have more to do with emotional issues, such as respite, socialization, intimacy, and self-esteem (Seligman, 1999).

From a family-centered point of view, the needs and strengths of all family members are necessarily viewed as important, and the notion of family often includes extended members and key friends of the family, as well as parents and siblings. Families must be viewed individually, because those members who are most likely to work effectively with a child vary from one situation to the next, just as does the individual who needs the most support. Although the primary interest of the service provider may be the welfare of the child, the needs of that child cannot be separated from the needs of the family as a whole. Improvement in problem behaviors exhibited by the child, for example, are likely to lessen the overall stress of the family; likewise, when families experience decreased stress in areas not directly related to the child (such as other relationships or economic burdens), the child usually benefits (Powers & Bruey, 1988). Because of such naturally occurring interactions, family needs must be the focus of intervention.

This concept of "families first" is strengthened by the belief that families should stay together, if at all possible. In contrast to a time just decades ago, when it was thought that children with mental retardation should be reared by professionals in institutional settings, there is now a commitment to keeping families together and to facilitating the participation of children with disabilities within their communities. There has been a concomitant and growing recognition of the disruption to children's lives caused by removing them from their families, so that even when there is doubt about the ability of a family to provide a safe and healthy environment, children are placed out of the home only as a last resort. Emphasis is placed instead on identifying strengths within the family system and on working with the family to increase those strengths—to the benefit of the child.

Although early intervention programs can result in important developmental gains for children with disabilities, any outside intervention represents a degree of intrusion into the family system and creates a disruption in the balance of relationships that also affects the child. Whereas some parents are eager to work with professionals, others feel at a disadvantage and may believe that professionals "look down" on them with little understanding of the realities of the parents' lives (Specht, 1989). Still others view intervention as interference by strangers, and they may carry strong values in favor of dealing with family problems within the family. Professionals must be sensitive to the reality of intrusion and work with families in designing the most effective intervention plan.

Intervention strategies to teach parents verbal stimulation techniques offer an example of the need for sensitivity to family values and priorities. Verbal stimulation can be provided by talking to babies while they are being diapered, fed, and dressed. Such interventions can be easily incorporated into an existing routine, but they often require a change in viewpoint by parents. In addition, they obviously depend upon cooperation and may require newly acquired values. Other interventions (such as time-consuming behavioral training programs) may be welcomed by some families; for others, though, such increased demands could contribute to the breakup of the family.

While family participation in the planning process is always crucial, it is not essential that every family become training providers for its children (White, Taylor, & Moss, 1992). Center-based preschool programs have been successful on their own, and family training does not always provide additional benefits (Baker, Landen, & Kashima, 1991; Ramey et al. 1985; Ramey & Ramey, 1998). As more is known about the types of interventions that are most successful and the characteristics that influence success, individual programs can be designed to be more effective.

Studies usually indicate that early intervention programs are more effective when highly structured (Casto & White, 1985). Programs that have a defined theoretical base, clear goals, and well-ordered methods to meet those goals tend to be more successful. In addition, it is generally found that children make greater gains the earlier intervention is begun. There have been studies, however, that have found outcomes as good or better when children were as old as 3 or 4 before intervention began (Casto & Mastropieri, 1986). As with parental involvement, the most effective structure and the best age for initiating intervention may vary, depending upon whether the child has an existing handicap or is at risk, as well as other child and family characteristics (Strain & Smith, 1986).

Identifying Infants with Disabilities

For children with disabilities to receive appropriate early intervention services, they must first be located and identified as eligible. When infants are born with a recognizable condition associated with mental retardation, the attending physician or hospital often makes a referral to service agencies. In other instances, family members may suspect developmental problems and seek help for the child. Many times, unfortunately, developmental problems are not discovered until the child enters a preschool or elementary school program.

To identify eligible children as early as possible (and in compliance with Part C), all states now have a *child find* or similar service that provides information and referrals. In addition, child find organizations actively attempt to locate children with possible disabilities by working in cooperation with other community agencies and by advertising their existence to the community at large. When children are identified as potentially eligible, they are provided with assessment services for infants and young children as described in Chapter 5.

Identifying Infants at Risk

Intervening with children who are at risk would probably achieve the greatest reduction in the number of people with mental retardation. Remember that the overwhelming percentage of people with MR demonstrate milder forms without any detectable organic impairment. For those people, disability typically is not apparent until after 10 months of age (Ramey, MacPhee, & Yeates, 1982), and several studies show that early intervention can actually prevent or reduce cognitive deficits for them (Ramey et al., 1992; Ramey, Mulvihill, & Ramey, 1996; Ward, 1999).

For early intervention to be feasible from cost and implementation standpoints, however, it is essential to identify which children will actually benefit from early intervention—that is to ask, Which children are truly at risk?

As we have seen, studies show that child abuse, prematurity, low birth weight, perinatal anoxia, poverty, and many other such factors are related to deficits in children's intellectual functioning. Fortunately, only a minority of those who are affected by these conditions actually develop cognitive problems. (Rojahn et al., 1993). If prevention efforts are to be effective, then they must be implemented for the entire at-risk population,* but early intervention could be provided only for those who would actually develop disabilities if they could be accurately identified. However, because the development of retardation is complex and involves interacting influences, it is not possible to predict future MR on the basis of single factors alone.

Poverty provides a concrete example. Although children from low SES backgrounds are at increased risk for MR, the vast majority do not develop retarda-

---

*Designing prevention efforts for the entire at-risk population makes sense, because hundreds of thousands of people would be spared the challenges of mental retardation, and because prevention efforts are typically less expensive than early intervention.

Cultural and Ethnic Concerns

The need for sensitivity to cultural and ethnic differences among families is well accepted, but less often considered are differences in risk prediction. For example, one study found that later problems in intellectual development for African-American children were best predicted (in order of importance) by mother's education, birth order, and the month in which prenatal care began. For white children, however, the three best predictors (also in order of importance) were siblings previously deceased, mother's education, and ma-

ternal age (Ramey et al., 1982). Similarly, those variables that appear to best predict good IQ performance for children from both African-American and white families do not appear important for Hispanic-American families (Bradley et al., 1989).

Such differences are not well understood. Research that clarifies the relationship between culturally and ethnically related factors and development will be essential for both identifying children truly at-risk and developing effective intervention.

---

tion. It is not simply low SES status that predicts MR, but particular individual conditions and circumstances closely associated with poverty. Often the circumstances of poverty—that is, the constant demands of problems for which there are inadequate resources—create stress that interferes with healthy development. Further, the very social and political creation of a lower class engenders conditions that inherently require different coping strategies and encourage the development of different skills than exist for middle- or upper-class people (Ogbu, 1997). To a large extent, lower scores on IQ tests reflect these differences (see Chapter 5). In addition, low SES parents may have little education themselves or little time (or inclination) to play with or teach their children, although this certainly is not always the case. To complicate matters further, MR in low SES families is influenced by the presence of toxins and other health hazards that exist disproportionately in their environment (see Chapter 8) and are beyond the reach of families' individual skills and coping capacities.

Generally speaking, the more risk factors that exist for a given child, the more likely that intellectual deficits will result (Rojahn et al., 1993). If a child is born prematurely, grows up in poverty with abusive parents, has little experience with cognitive tasks, suffers from poor nutrition, and lives in a house contaminated with lead-based paint, then her chances of developing MR are extremely high.

Yet even where multiple risk factors exist, some children escape damage (Rojahn et al., 1993). Understanding the key components of this **resilience** has been of particular interest to those who are interested in helping youngsters fight the effects of potentially damaging events. One important attribute of resilience is the ability to cope successfully with challenges, so service supports that help young children learn adaptive strategies are essential (Greenbaum & Auerbach, 1998; Lewis, 1999). Individual characteristics of the child—such as adaptability, extroversion, responsiveness, and alertness—also play a part in his resilience to stressful conditions, so supports that enhance these characteristics are also important. Ultimately, it is the combination of both environmental and biological factors that poses the greatest risk of retardation.

> **FOR DISCUSSION**   *To date, there is little research evidence about the kinds of experiences that can promote resilience. Can you imagine certain kinds of experiences that might help children develop some of the resilience-associated characteristics? Describe why you think these experiences would be effective.*

Understanding the complexities of risk from a systems perspective helps researchers and service professionals recognize and identify the important factors in healthy development. A child's culture, social class, neighborhood, educational and early intervention opportunities, caregiver characteristics, and individual personality all interact in a multidirectional system. When the child is viewed as part of a system that involves intricate balances, it becomes clear that sufficient stress (from interacting biological and environmental causes) can overburden that system. This conceptualization can help professionals identify the intervention supports that will help restore balance for the child and family and promote optimum development (Bronfenbrenner, 1995). Early intervention programs that are designed from a systems perspective include elements that seek to improve stressful and damaging conditions beyond the individual child herself. One such example, the Yale Project, demonstrated significant long-term improvements in the economic and educational status, housing conditions, and self-sufficiency of participating families, as well as in cognitive skill gains for their children (Rescorla & Zigler, 1981; Zigler, 1994).

Identifying children at risk will depend upon the development of formulas that accurately reflect complex interacting influences, and reliable identification methods are crucial in providing intervention services to those who need them most. In current practice, however, definitions of risk and methods of determining risk vary enormously. In some states, for example, children are considered at risk only if they already demonstrate a potentially disabling condition. Other states allow services for children at psychosocial risk but often disagree on the factors that determine eligibility (Brown, Thurman, & Pearl, 1993). Continued research in identifying those conditions that predict risk will be essential in establishing valid criteria for early intervention eligibility.

PROGRAM CONTENT

It is impossible to describe a "typical" intervention program, because the content varies so greatly and programs are often specifically designed for particular individuals. Even within the components of an intervention program, such as preschool services, there is great variety.

Table 10.2 Approaches to Program Content Development

Approach	Function
Developmental	Milestones: Focuses on teaching behaviors that would typically be expected at the child's age.
Piagetian stages	Provides experiences with materials and concepts that represent cognitive attainments in Piaget's stages.
Functional and ecological	Teaches functional life skills in relevant applied settings.
Applied behavioral	Applies behavioral techniques to teach behaviors and skills and to measure outcomes.

SOURCE: Adapted from D. Bricker & R. Kaminski (1986), Intervention programs for severely handicapped infants and children. In L. Bickman & D. L. Weatherford (Eds.), *Evaluating early intervention programs for severely handicapped children and their families* (pp. 51–78). Austin, TX: Pro-Ed.

Early intervention programs may take an applied behavior analysis, or ecological and functional, or developmental approach; any of these can occur in either a home-based or center-based setting. Center-based programs also may sometimes include children without disabilities or serve children with disabilities exclusively (Klein & Sheehan, 1987). Program content may be different, too, for youngsters who are at risk than for those with existing disabilities. Nevertheless, we can still describe the main approaches to programming and give content examples for each. Table 10.2 presents brief descriptions of each approach.

More and more programs are attempting an eclectic array of approaches that offer education and training in many areas and through several instructional methods. Many programs, for example, work on motor and cognitive development, social and behavioral skills, and self-help life skills through a combination of direct teaching, behavioral management, and discovery methods. Table 10.3 describes age-appropriate activities that are designed to stimulate exploration and discovery.

EARLY INTERVENTION:
JASON'S EXPERIENCE

When 6-month-old Jason was adopted, Cathy already knew that he had brain damage as a result of a cerebral hemorrhage shortly after his premature birth. Because the brain damage was medically documented and because brain damage is so often related to developmental disabilities, Cathy knew that Jason was likely to be eligible for early intervention services. Because she already had two other children with disabilities and operates a day care facility that includes children with disabilities, Cathy was already unusually well informed about existing services and requirements for eligibility—even before she adopted Jason.

Soon after she brought Jason home, Cathy contacted a local Part C agency, shared what she knew of Jason's developmental problems—and told her contact

Table 10.3 Directions for Some Developmentally Appropriate
Activities Used in the Carolina Abecedarian Project

Age (months)	Activity	Description
0–6	Building trust	Respond quickly to baby's crying. Cuddle, rock, and talk to baby while diapering, feeding, and bathing, as well as just for fun.
	Propping baby to see	Prop baby with pillows and provide toys for baby to look at or manipulate. Talk to baby about what she sees and touches.
	Beginning "conversations"	Hold baby about seven or eight inches from your face. Talk in a lively, animated voice, with lots of facial expression, and then wait for baby to "respond" by making a sound of his own. When he does, vocalize in return. Continue taking turns.
6–12	Naming with a mirror	Place a mirror where the child can easily see herself. Touch her mouth and say, "Mouth." Help her touch her mouth, eyes, and nose as you name each. Smile and have fun.
	Imitating	Bang on a pan with a spoon, kiss a doll, clap hands, or spread arms wide or take any of many other actions. Ask baby to do what you did. Express pleasure and praise when he responds.
	Problem solving	Give the child a box with a small hole in the top and a larger one in the side. Let her drop a toy in the box. Encourage and help her find the toy "both ways"—that is, through both holes. Help less as she gains skill. Say, "Can you see it?" "Can you get it?" or "You got it all by yourself!"
	Hiding a picture	Cover one end of a box with a big image of something the child knows. Show it to the child, then turn the box to another side. Encourage him to find the image, using the object name: "Find the kitty" or "Find Susie."
12–18	Helping pick up	Provide a large container for toys. Encourage the child to drop toys in the container. Take turns and let her choose which toy to drop. Have fun, and don't insist that she pick up every one.
	Making lines	Find places (sand, mud, steamy windows, dusty tables) where you and the child can make lines with your fingers or a stick.
	Starting to undress	Unfasten the child's shoes and pull them off over each heel so that he need only pull them off from each toe. Do the same with socks. Unfasten shirts and remove one sleeve. Praise his achievements and independence.
	Saying and doing words	Show and tell the child to spread arms wide, stand on toes, and stand on head or any one of several other actions. Encourage him to imitate words and actions.

SOURCE: Adapted from J. Sparling & I. Lewis (1979), *Learning games for the first three years.* New York: Walker & Co.

there that she wanted early intervention services for Jason. At that first phone call, the agency set up an appointment for an early intervention specialist to visit Jason at home. Cathy, Jason, and the specialist were present at that home visit, where Cathy shared information about Jason's brain injury. The interventionist completed a screening evaluation and determined that Jason should be referred for assessment. (See Figure 10.7 for the steps in the Part C process.) Cathy requested the same service coordinator from Rick and Justin's teams for Jason's program.

Three days later, Cathy and Jason began the evaluation and assessment process. Eligibility was determined on the basis of the physical report of brain damage and

Table 10.3 *(continued)*

Age (months)	Activity	Description
18–24	More word learning	Be specific in labeling a child's actions and the objects she sees and touches. Also, repeat her words often by using them in a sentence. For example, if she points to and says "Flower," respond with "Yes, that is a very pretty flower."
	Sorting shapes	Use small balls and blocks and plastic containers with either round or square holes in the lid. Help the child explore and find out which objects will drop into which container. Shaking the containers and pouring the objects out is part of the fun.
	Paint with water	Use a sponge and some water in a sand pail to let the child "paint" on porch steps, sidewalks, tree trunks, or rocks.
	Matching and grouping colors	Get three of the same object (e.g., toothbrushes or socks) with two of them the same color and one different. Help and encourage the child to choose which objects are the same color and which one is different.
24–30	Dress up	Provide scarves, hats, adult clothes, and jewelry. Let the child choose what he wants to wear and let him dress up. Laugh and have fun *with* him, but be careful not to laugh *at* him.
	Seeing in new ways	Provide a magnifying glass with which child can look at familiar objects. Share her wonder.
	Showing one and two	Arrange objects in groups of one, two, and "many." Help child to identify the groups and gradually encourage him to do so on his own.
	Learning cooperation	Give each of two or more toddlers one end of a small blanket or large towel. Let them shake and bounce a light ball on the blanket.
30–36	In, out, and around	With toys or other objects (e.g., small shoes and a doll bed), show the child the meaning of *in, on, under,* and *around.* Then let him show you.
	Using words for time	Help child understand the concept of time by relating words and phrases such as *after,* "in a few minutes," and "about lunch time" to events. For example, "After lunch, we will read a story." "Daddy will be here after nap time."
	What's gone	Select two toys and have the child hide her eyes. Hide one toy behind your back and then ask child to look and tell you which one is gone.

from the psychological and speech determination of developmental delay. Jason was assessed by a psychologist, an occupational therapist, an audiologist, and a speech pathologist. Information was also obtained from his most recent pediatric visit. All of these professionals met with Cathy to discuss their results, and together they decided upon the team to work on Jason's behalf. A week later, Cathy received a written report that identified Jason's strengths and needs, and it reflected her own priorities and concerns.

At this first evaluation, Cathy had no idea about what problems she would eventually face with Jason; he had been with her only a few weeks, and although

Grand Public School System
Family, Infant, and Preschool Program

Individualized Family Support Plan

Background Information	Family Member's Name	Relationship to Child
Child's name: Jason Dwayne Family name: Cunningham Date of birth: 8-27-98 Age: 6 months County: Kenton	Catharine Justin Richard (Ricky)	Mother Brother Brother

Family Support Team

Name	Title	Agency	Date
	Parent		2/23/99
	Grandmother		2/23/99
	Service coordinator	Part-C Family, infant and preschool program	2/23/99
	Occupational therapist	County health services	2/23/99
	Psychologist	County mental health services	2/23/99
	Preschool teacher	Employee of Cathy's day care facility	2/23/99
	Respiratory physician	Private practice	8/25/99

Team Review Dates

6-mo. review: 8/25/1999   (Age 12 months—not shown)
12-mo review: 2/25/2000   (Age 18 months)
18-mo. review: 8/20/2000   (Age 24 months—not shown)
24-mo. review: _____

Assessment of Child's Level of Functioning
at Initial Assessment and at Age 18 Months

Cognitive domain	Communicative domain	Social and emotional domain	Physical domain	Adaptive domain
Bayley Scales of Infant Development	Speech and hearing evaluation	Home visit checklist	Physical exam Learner inventory	Home visit checklist
CA: 6 months DQ: 2 months	Normal hearing Language: Birth to 2 months	Responsiveness: 4 months	2 months	2 months
CA: 18 months DQ: 8 months	Expressive: 6 months Receptive and gesture: 12 months	12 months	Asthma Motor skills: 6 months	10 months

(continued)

Child's Strengths (CA: 18 months)	Family's Strengths
Happy and social when physically well Strong receptive and gesture language Alert to surroundings Responsive to cuddling and comforting	Strong affectionate bonds among family members Commitment to Jason's treatment programs Knowledgeable about community resources Mom is a strong advocate for her children Support from extended family

Family Concerns and Priorities

2/23/99 CA: 6 months
1. Evaluation and prediction of Jason's expected rate of development.
2. Get set up and started in early intervention program.
3. Obtain information about how to handle Jason's motor-related feeding problem.

2/25/2000 CA: 18 months
1. Gain better control over Jason's asthma.
2. Find increased respite help.
3. Reduce the number of necessary professional appointments.

Need and Outcome Statement	Support and Resource	Course of Action	Family Evaluation

FIGURE 10.8 Jason's IFSP

she was concerned about managing his motor-related feeding problem, she expected to get along with Jason much as she had with Justin and Ricky. Her only priorities were to start Jason in the intervention process and obtain an evaluation and assessment that would confirm or correct her own estimate of Jason's developmental level. She was also hoping for predictions about his expected rate of progress. The IFSP reflected these concerns and priorities. Jason's IFSP for both the initial assessment and age-18-months follow-up combined are presented in Figure 10.8.

By the 6-month review, Cathy was experiencing considerable stress because of Jason's poor feeding and weight gain. Even more disturbing, Jason had recently been hospitalized with his first asthmatic attack (after which time the pulmonary physician joined the early intervention team). These events are reflected in the IFSP for that period. At the earlier evaluation, Cathy had felt confident and in control, but by that first review she was searching for techniques and supports that would offer relief from mounting worry and frustration.

By the 12-month evaluation, Cathy was feeling truly overwhelmed. Fortunately, several decisions (concerning changes in medication and increased respite for Cathy) were made at that team meeting that eventually resulted in a far better health and family situation for Jason. These improvements were reflected in the next review (8/20/2000), at which time Jason appeared to be making developmental gains. (Children with respiratory problems are frequently too tired to take an active part in educational and social activities, so improvement in their physical condition often results in increased ability to profit from other forms of intervention [Keogh, Wilcoxen, & Bernheimer, 1986]).

The team decisions (and the assessment process leading to them) are described in some detail in Chapter 5. The primary issues were Cathy's priorities for control of the asthma, increased respite, and decreased appointment demands.

▌▌ LOOKING AHEAD

Chapter 10 has provided a detailed overview of current programs and trends in early intervention, and it has described some of the early program efforts and related research that led to the current federal and state support of early intervention. This chapter also explored some of the most important issues for further program development and evaluation. Finally, we followed Jason and Cathy as they went through many of the steps in the early intervention process.

Chapter 11 will discuss principles and techniques that are often used in behavioral and cognitive interventions for people with mental retardation during their early years (as well as later in their lives).

INFOTRAC COLLEGE EDITION

Perhaps the most widely known early intervention program is Head Start. Enter *Head Start* as the *InfoTrac College Edition* keyword, and find an article on outcomes for Head Start children. What did you learn from this article?

REFERENCES

Ad Hoc Part H Work Group (1995). *Helping our nation's infants and toddlers with disabilities and their families: A briefing paper on Part H of the Individuals with Disabilities Education Act (IDEA), 1986–1995.* Preliminary report submitted to the Federal Interagency Coordinating Council.

Bailey, D. B., Jr., & Simeonsson, R. J. (1986). In L. Bickman & D. L. Weatherford (Eds.), *Evaluating early intervention programs for severely handicapped children and their families* (pp. 109–232). Austin, TX: Pro-Ed.

Baker, B., Landen, S., & Kashima, K. (1991). Effects of parent training on families of children with mental retardation: Increased burden or generalized benefit? *American Journal on Mental Retardation, 96*(2), 127–136.

Bakken, J., Miltenberger, R. G., & Schauss, S. (1993). Teaching parents with mental retardation: Knowledge versus skills. *American Journal on Mental Retardation, 97*(4), 405–417.

Bradley, R. H., Caldwell, B. M., Rock, S. L., Barnard, K. E., Gray, C., Hammond, M. A., Mitchell, S., Seigel, L., Ramey, C. T., Gottfried, A. W., & Johnson, D. L. (1989). Home environment and cognitive development in the first 3 years of life: A collaborative study involving six sites and three ethnic groups in North America. *Developmental Psychology, 25*(2), 217–235.

Bricker, D. D. (1986). An analysis of early intervention programs: Attendant issues and future directions. In R. J. Morris & B. Blatt (Eds.), *Special education: Research and trends* (pp. 28–65). New York: Pergamon.

Bricker, D., & Kaminski, R. (1986). Intervention programs for severely handicapped infants and children. In L. Bickman & D. L. Weatherford (Eds.), *Evaluating early intervention programs for severely handicapped children and their families* (pp. 51–78). Austin, TX: Pro-Ed.

Bricker, D., & Sheehan, R. (1981). Effectiveness of an early childhood intervention program as indexed by measures of child change. *Journal of the Division for Early Childhood, 4,* 11–27.

Bronfenbrenner, U. (1995). The bioecological model from a life course perspective: Reflections of a participant observer. In P. Moen, G. H. Edler, Jr., & K. Luscher (Eds.), *Examining lives in context: Perspectives on the ecology of human development* (1st ed., pp 599–618). Washington, DC: American Psychological Association.

Brown, W., Thurman, S. K., & Pearl, L. F. (Eds.). (1993). *Family-centered early intervention with infants and toddlers: Innovative cross-disciplinary approaches.* Baltimore, MD: Paul H. Brookes.

Campbell, F. A., Helms, R., Sparling, J. J., & Ramey, C. T. (1998). Early-childhood programs and success in school: The Abecedarian study. In W. S. Barnett & S. S. Boocock (Eds.), *Early care and education for children in poverty: Promises, programs, and long-term results.* Albany: State University of New York Press.

Casto, G., & Mastropieri, M. A. (1986). The efficacy of early intervention programs: A meta-analysis. *Exceptional Child, 52*(5), 417–424.

Casto, G., & White, K. R. (1985). The efficacy of early intervention programs with environmentally at-risk infants. *Journal of Children in Contemporary Society, 17*(1), 37–50.

Clarke, A., & Clarke, A. (1976). *Early experience: Myth and evidence.* New York: The Free Press.

Collins, R. C. (1993). Head Start: Steps toward a two-generation program strategy. *Young Children, 48*(2), 25–73.

Crocker, A. C. (1992). Data collection for the evaluation of mental retardation prevention activities: The fateful forty-three. *Mental Retardation, 30*(6), 303–317.

DeBerry, K. M., Scarr, S., & Weinberg, R. (1996). Family racial socialization and ecological competence: Longitudinal assessments of African-American transracial adoptees. *Child Development, 9,* 133–150.

Dokecki, P. R. (1986). The impact of evaluation research on policymaking. In L. Bickman & D. L. Weatherford (Eds.), *Evaluating early intervention programs for severely handicapped children and their families* (pp. 311–334). Austin, TX: Pro-Ed.

Dunst, C. J. (1986). Overview of the efficacy of early intervention programs. In L. Bickman & D. L. Weatherford (Eds.), *Evaluating early intervention programs for severely handicapped children and their families* (pp. 79–148). Austin, TX: Pro-Ed.

Dunst, C. J., Trivette, C. M., & Deal, A. (Eds.). (1994). *Supporting and strengthening families. Vol. 1: Methods, strategies and practices* (pp. 152–160). Cambridge, MA: Brookline Books.

Featherstone, H. (1980). *A difference in the family: Life with a disabled child.* New York: Basic Books.

Field, T., Dempsey, J., Hallock, N., & Shuman, H. (1978). The mother's assessment of the behavior of her infant. *Infant Behavior and Development, 1,* 156–167.

Garwood, S. G., Fewell, R. R., & Neisworth, J. T. (1988). Public law 94-142: You can get there from here! *Topics in Early Childhood Special Education, 8*(1), 1–11.

Gindis, B. (1995). The social/cultural implication of disability: Vygotsky's paradigm for special education. *Educational Psychologist, 30,* 77–81.

Goodenough, F., & Maurer, K. (1961). The relative potency of the nursery school and the statistical laboratory in boosting the IQ. In J. Jenkins & D. Paterson (Eds.), *Studies in individual differences.* New York: Appleton-Century-Crofts. (Originally published in 1940.)

Grattan, M. P., DeVos, E., Levy, J., & McClintock, M. K. (1992). Asymmetric action in the human newborn: Sex differences in patterns of organization. *Child Development, 63,* 273–289.

Greenbaum, C. W., & Auerbach, J. G. (1998). The environment of the child with mental retardation: Risk, vulnerability, and resilience. In J. A. Burack & R. M. Hodapp (Eds.), *Handbook of mental retardation and development* (pp. 583–695). New York: Cambridge University Press.

Hamilton, M., Goodway, J., & Haubenstricker, J. (1999). Parent-assisted instruction in a motor skill program for at-risk preschool children. *Adapted Physical Activity Quarterly, 16*(4), 415–426.

Hanson, M. (1981). Down's Syndrome children: Characteristics and intervention research. In M. Lewis & L. Rosenblum (Eds.), *The uncommon child.* New York: Plenum.

Keogh, B. K., Wilcoxen, A. G., & Bernheimer, L. (1986). Prevention services for at-risk children: Evidence for policy and practice. In D. C. Farran & J. D. McKinney (Eds.), *Risk in intellectual and psychosocial development* (pp. 287–311). Orlando, FL: Academic Press.

Kirk, S. A. (1958). *Early education of the mentally retarded: An experimental study.* Urbana, IL: University of Illinois Press.

Kirk, S. (1977). General and historical rationale for early education of the handicapped. In N. Ellis & L. Cross (Eds.), *Planning programs for early education of the handicapped.* New York: Walker & Co.

Klein, N., & Sheehan, R. (1987). Staff development: A key issue in meeting the needs of young handicapped children in day care settings. *Topics in Early Childhood Special Education, 7*(1), 13–27.

Kroth, R. (1989). School-based parent involvement programs. In M. J. Fine (Ed.), *The second handbook on parent education* (pp. 119–143). San Diego: Academic Press.

Lazar, I., & Darlington, R. B. (1982). *Monographs of the Society for Research in Child Development, 47* (2-Sup-3), 1–151.

Lee, V. E., Brooks-Gunn, J., & Schnur, E. (1988). Does Head Start work? A 1-year follow-up comparison of disadvantaged children attending Head Start, no preschool, and other preschool programs. *Developmental Psychology, 24*(2), 210–222.

Lee, V. E., Brooks-Gunn, J., Schnur, E., & Liaw, F. R. (1990). Are Head Start effects sustained? A longitudinal follow-up comparison of disadvantaged children attending Head Start, no preschool, and other preschool programs. *Child Development, 61*(2), 495–507.

Lewis, J. (1999). Research into the concept of resilience as a basis for the curriculum for children with EBD. *Emotional & Behavioral Difficulties, 4*(2), 11–22.

Luster, T., & Dubow, E. (1992). Home environment and maternal intelligence as predictors of verbal intelligence: A comparison of preschool and school-age children. *Merrill-Palmer Quarterly, 38,* 151–175.

McKey, R. H., Condelli, L., Ganson, H., Barrett, B., McConkey, C., & Plantz, M. (1985, June). *The impact of Head Start on children, families, and communities.* (Final Report of the Head Start Evaluation, Synthesis, and Utilization Project). Washington, DC: CSR, Inc.

McLoyd, V. C. (1998). Children in poverty: Development, public policy, and practice. In I. Sigel & A. Renninger (Eds.), *Handbook of child psychology. Vol. 4: Child psychology in practice* (5th ed., pp. 135–208). New York: Wiley.

Noonan, M. J., & McCormick, L. (1993). *Early intervention in natural environment: Methods and procedures.* Pacific Grove, CA: Brooks/Cole.

Nye, B. A. (1989). Effective parent education and involvement models and programs: Contemporary strategies for school implementation. In M. J. Fine (Ed.), *The second handbook on parent education* (pp. 325–345). San Diego: Academic Press.

Ogbu, J. U. (1997). Understanding the school performance of urban blacks: Some essential background knowledge. In H. J. Walbert & O. Reyes (Eds.), *Children and youth: Interdisciplinary perspectives* (pp. 190–222). Thousand Oaks, CA: Sage.

Polit, D. F., Quint, J. C., & Riccio, J. A. (1988). *The challenge of service to teenage mothers: Lessons from Project Redirection.* New York: Manpower Demonstration Research Corp.

Powers, M. D., & Bruey, C. T. (1988). Treating the family system. In M. D. Powers (Ed.), *Expanding systems of service delivery for persons with developmental disabilities* (pp. 17–41). Baltimore, MD: Paul H. Brookes.

Ramey, C., & Baker-Ward, L. (1982). Psychosocial retardation and the early experience paradigm. In D. Bricker (Ed.), *Intervention with at-risk and handicapped infants.* Baltimore, MD: University Park Press.

Ramey, C. T., Bryant, D. M., Sparling, J. J., & Wasik, B. H. (1985). Project CARE: A comparison of two early intervention strategies to prevent retarded development. *Topics in Early Childhood Special Education, 5*(2), 12–25.

Ramey, C. T., Bryant, D. M., Wasik, B. H., Sparling, J. J., Fendt, K. H., & LaVange, L. M. (1992). Infant health and development program for low birth weight, premature infants: Program elements, family participation, and child intelligence. *Pediatrics, 3,* 454–465.

Ramey, C. T., MacPhee, D., & Yeates, K. O. (1982). Preventing developmental retardation: A general systems model. In L. A. Bond & J. M. Joffee (Eds.), *Facilitating infant and early childhood development.* Hanover, NH: University Press of New England.

Ramey, C. T. , Mulvihill, B. A., & Ramey, S. L. (1996). Prevention: Social and educational factors and early intervention. In J. W. Jacobson & J. A. Mulick (Eds.), *Manual of diagnosis and professional practice in mental retardation* (pp. 215–227). Washington, DC: American Psychological Association.

Ramey, C. T., & Ramey, S. L. (1998). Prevention of intellectual disabilities: Early interventions to improve cognitive development. *Preventive Medicine: An International Devoted to Practice & Theory, 27*(2), 224–232.

Rein, M., & White, S. H. (1977). Can policy research help policy? *Public Interest, 49,* 119–136.

Rescorla, L. A., & Zigler, E. (1981). The Yale Child Welfare Research Program: Implications for social policy. *Educational Evaluation and Policy Analysis, 3,* 5–14.

Rojahn, J., Aman, M. G., Marshburn, E., Moeschberger, M. L., King, E. H., Logsdon, D. A., & Schroeder, S. R. (1993). Biological and environmental risk for poor developmental outcome of young children. *American Journal on Mental Retardation, 97*(6), 702–708.

Ruopp, R., Travers, J., Glantz, G., & Coelen, C. (1979). *Children at the center: Summary findings and policy implications of the National Day Care study.* Cambridge, MA: Abt Associates.

Sameroff, A. J., Bartko, W. T., Baldwin, A., Baldwin, C., & Seifer, R. (1998). Family and social influences on the development of child competence. In. M. Lewis & C. Feiring (Eds.), *Families, risk, and competence* (pp. 161–185). Mahwah, NJ: Lawrence Erlbaum.

Schweinhart, L. J., Berrueta-Clement, J. R., Barnett, W. S., Epstein, A. S., & Weikart, D. P. (1985). The effects of the Perry Preschool Program on youths through age 19: A summary. *Topics in Early Childhood Special Education, 5*(2), 26–35.

Schweinhart, L. J., & Weikart, D. P. (1986). What do we know so far? A review of the Head Start synthesis project. *Young Children, 41*(2), 49–55.

Seligman, M. (1999). Childhood disability and the family. In V. L. Schwean & D. H. Saklofske (Eds.), *Handbook of psychosocial characteristics of exceptional children* (pp. 111–131). New York: Kluwer Academic/Plenum.

Shearer, D., & Shearer, M. (1976). The Portage Project: A model for early childhood intervention. In T. Tjossem (Ed.), *Intervention strategies for high-risk infants and young children.* Baltimore, MD: University Park Press.

Skeels, H. M. (1966). Adult status of children with contrasting early life experiences: A follow-up study. *Monographs of the Society for Research in Child Development, 31*(3), 1–56.

Skeels, H. M., & Dye, H. B. (1939). A study of the effects of differential stimulation on mentally retarded children. *Convention Proceedings of the American Association on Mental Deficiency, 44,* 114–136.

Smith, S., Blank, S., & Collins, R. (1992). *Pathways to self-sufficiency for two generations: Designing welfare-to-work programs that strengthen families and benefit children.* New York: Foundation for Child Development.

Sparling, J., & Lewis, I. (1979). *Learning games for the first three years: A guide to parent/child play.* New York: Walker & Co.

Specht, F. (1989). Prevention and intervention from the perspective of child psychiatry. In M. Brambring, F. Losel, & H. Skowronek (Eds.), *Children at risk: Assessment, longitudinal research, and intervention* (pp. 405–415). New York: Berlin.

Stiles, J. (1998). The effects of early focal brain injury on lateralization of cognitive function. *Current Directions in Psychological Science, 7,* 21–26.

Stiles, J., Bates, E. A., Talk, D., Trauner, D., & Reilly, J. (1999). Linguistic, cognitive and affective development in children with pre- and perinatal focal brain injury: A ten-year overview from the San Diego Longitudinal Project. In C. Rovee-Collier (Ed.), *Advances in infancy research* (Vol. 13). Norwood, NJ: Ablex.

Strain, P. S., & Smith, B. J. (1986). A counter-interpretation of early intervention effects: A response to Casto and Mastropieri. *Exceptional Children, 53*(3), 260–265.

Turnbull, A. P., & Summers, J. A. (1987). From parent involvement to family support: Evolution to revolution. In S. M. Peuschel (Ed.), *New perspectives on Down syndrome.* Baltimore, MD: Paul H. Brookes.

U.S. Department of Education. (1998). *National evaluation of the Even Start Family Literacy Program.* Washington, DC: Author.

U.S. Department of Health and Human Services. (1999). *Head Start fact sheet.* Washington, DC: Author.

Ward, S. (1999). An investigation into the effectiveness of an early intervention method for delayed language development in young children. *International Journal of Language & Communication Disorders, 34*(3), 243–264.

Wasik, B. H., Ramey, C. T., Bryant, D. M., & Sparling, J. J. (1990) A longitudinal study of two early intervention strategies: Project CARE. *Child Development, 61*(6), 1682–1696.

White, K. R., Taylor, M. J., & Moss, V. D. (1992). Does research support claims about the benefits of involving parents in early intervention programs? *Review of Educational Research, 62*(1), 91–125.

Zigler, E. (1994). Reshaping early childhood intervention to be a more effective weapon against poverty. *American Journal of Community Psychology, 22*(1), 37–47.

11

Behavioral and Cognitive Intervention

Chapter 10 covered early intervention programs and their success. This chapter goes into detail about the behavioral techniques used in early intervention programs and most other teaching programs for children and adults. Behavioral and cognitive techniques have been successful in teaching social skills, communication, daily living skills, work skills, responsibility, and self-control, and thousands of published studies demonstrate this effectiveness. Behavioral techniques have also been used to reduce such problem behaviors as tantrums, self-injury, and noncompliance. Behavioral and cognitive principles are integral, of course, to learning, thinking, *and* outward behavior, and therefore they are essential in intervention with learning and behavioral problems of all kinds. Knowledge of behavioral techniques is essential to anyone who works with individuals with mental retardation, and this chapter provides enough information for the reader to begin to understand how these techniques can be applied.

The skills that most individuals learn on their own usually must be explicitly taught to people with mental retardation. In addition, young people with MR are sometimes more aggressive and have a greater incidence of attention and anxiety- and immaturity-related problems than people with typical development (Dudley, Ahlgrim-Delzell, & Calhoun, 1999). Unfortunately, these behaviors often extend into adulthood. In addition, stereotypical behaviors—such as rocking, twirling, and other repetitive motor behaviors—occur in up to 60 percent of people with severe disabilities (Rojahn, 1986), and self-injurious behaviors are common, often requiring heavy medication or restraints. Fortunately, behavioral and cognitive principles can be successfully applied to all of these problems.

Broadly speaking, all learning occurs in the context of reinforcement, imitation, or, more typically, both; that is to say, any learned behavior or acquired information results from having seen an example or because the individual derives from it some emotional pleasure or some other form of (**intrinsic**) satisfaction, or a tangible (**extrinsic**) reward (such as money), or desired items. Because these ideas underlie all learning, it is essential for professionals working with people with MR to understand the specific principles of reinforcement and modeling (see Chapter 2) and be able to apply them. Toward that goal, this chapter focuses on the application of behavioral and cognitive principles to use in working with people who have mental retardation.

> **FOR DISCUSSION**   *Can you think of any examples of learning that happens in ways other than through reinforcement, punishment, or imitation? For such examples, are the elements of reinforcement or modeling subtly involved or completely absent?*

BASIC PRINCIPLES OF
APPLIED BEHAVIOR ANALYSIS

When behavioral principles are used either to help an individual learn new behaviors or to change problem behaviors, it is necessary to design a specific behavioral plan. The system of methods used in such practical situations is called **applied behavior analysis.**

The first step in developing a behavioral program is to outline a broad conceptual plan that describes the general purpose and goals. For example, a plan may be designed to help a child (John) improve his daily living skills so that he can become more independent and free his caregivers from the necessity of personal care tasks—just as would be expected in normal development.

Once a conceptual plan is in place, specific goals may then be identified. To continue with the daily living example, toothbrushing may be among the learning goals identified for John, where the exact desired behavior must be stated in measurable terms. This means that specific measurable criteria will be defined for what John will do and where and how he will do it.

COLLECTING OBSERVATIONAL DATA

Success in teaching John new skills will certainly require familiarity with his existing abilities and typical responses, and, for that purpose, collecting observational information is invaluable. In fact, all aspects of applied behavioral analysis (from the development of a program, through implementation and follow-up) depend upon data collection. (Such data collection also forms the basis for functional assessment as discussed in Chapter 5). A behavioral analysis typically begins with the collection of **anecdotal** data that, to be most useful, should be highly structured and include details about the exact time of a behavior, as well as where it took place, who was present, what seemed to prompt its occurrence, and what happened afterward. There should also be descriptions of what the behavior looks like and its intensity—strength, loudness, and so on (Alberto & Troutman, 1995). Anecdotal information is often used to identify the likely antecedents, consequences, and setting events (setting events are described later in this chapter) that are associated with a behavior.

Figure 11.1 offers an example of an anecdotal report for a young woman (Paula) who frequently pinches herself, staff members, and other residents in the group home where she lives. Similar anecdotal reports for each incident (maintained over a specified time period) would suggest possible circumstances that prompt Paula's pinching (antecedents), as well as information about what reinforcements keep the behavior going.

> **FOR DISCUSSION** *Based on the anecdotal report in Figure 11.1, what are some tentative guesses about the situations in which Paula may pinch, as well as about how she is reinforced for pinching?*

Gathering anecdotal evidence is simply the first step in understanding the antecedents and reinforcers that relate to a particular behavior. Once relevant variables have been identified, more formal data can be recorded about the frequency of those variables to confirm whether hypotheses are well founded.

To determine the frequency of behavior before intervention begins, baseline data are also collected. It is equally essential to gather information about the

8/17/2000

2:20 P.M.   Paula and I were standing in the grocery line waiting to be checked out with our groceries. I was looking ahead at the cashier, when Paula grabbed my arm and began pinching. I turned and said very sharply, "Stop that." Paula grinned and turned away. I was very angry, but I did not speak to Paula again until we were walking to the car. Then I said, "You know I'm really mad at you for pinching me like that don't you?" Paula said "yes" and hung her head. When we got home Paula went in and watched T.V., while I put the groceries away. I left her alone until dinner time, and by then I had calmed down, so that I wasn't mad at her anymore, and I felt like I could talk to her again. I went in and got her to promise that she wouldn't pinch again.

FIGURE 11.1 Anecdotal report for Paula by group home staff person

Because this task is designed for a 5-year-old with some fine motor problems, the toothbrush and toothpaste should be laid out on the counter of the basin with the tube's cap removed. A cup of water should be available by the basin.

1. Pick up paste in right hand.
2. Pick up toothbrush with left hand.
3. Squeeze small amount of paste onto brush.
4. Place tube back on counter.
5. Transfer brush to right hand.
6. Brush top teeth first, beginning at the right and proceeding all the way to the left with an up-and-down motion.
7. Remove brush from mouth and spit excess liquid into basin.
8. Brush bottom teeth (up-and-down motion), starting from the right and working toward the left.
9. Remove brush and spit.
10. Place brush on basin counter.
11. Pick up cup in right hand.
12. Take some water into mouth from cup.
13. Rinse and spit.

FIGURE 11.2 Task analysis for toothbrushing

occurrence of a behavior during treatment, and then compare it to the baseline to determine the effectiveness of intervention.

Behaviors may be recorded according to **rate** (number of occurrences in a specified time period), **duration** (length of time a behavior lasts), or **latency** (length of time before behavior starts).

Information can also be gathered from self-report inventories, interviews, and behavior checklists. A detailed discussion of these methods was presented in Chapter 5.

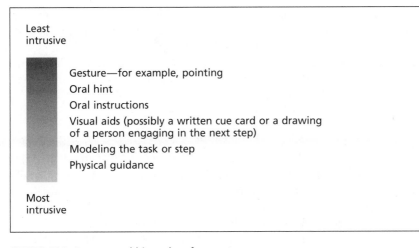

Least
intrusive

Gesture—for example, pointing
Oral hint
Oral instructions
Visual aids (possibly a written cue card or a drawing
of a person engaging in the next step)
Modeling the task or step
Physical guidance

Most
intrusive

FIGURE 11.3 A suggested hierarchy of prompts

FINDING THE RIGHT REINFORCER

Recall that a reinforcer is *any consequence of a behavior that increases the likelihood that the behavior will reoccur.* Obviously, the successful application of principles of reinforcement depends upon finding a consequence that is rewarding for the *particular* individual, especially because a response that is reinforcing for one person may be punishing for another. Some children with autism, for example, may experience attention and praise as punishing, even though for most children these would be reinforcing (Schreibman, 1988). It is *always* necessary to discover what the individual likes well enough to entice him to work or change. Although there are some reinforcers that almost all individuals will find rewarding, some of the most effective ones are unique, so individual assessment is essential.

Here, again, data collection and analysis are important tools for identifying potent reinforcers. Such data can be collected through interviews with the individual or her caretakers or by carefully observing the person's behavior. Usually, when someone engages in a behavior often, it is a sign that she finds that behavior reinforcing, and frequently occurring behaviors can often be used to reinforce less frequent or less likely ones. For example, a child who spends much free time listening to music will probably be reinforced by gaining the opportunity to do so at unaccustomed times. On the other hand, desirable events that are only rarely available may be especially effective reinforcers, as when someone who has not had a vacation from work for several years suddenly has the opportunity to take an all-expenses-paid trip (Kazdin, 1994).

REINFORCING MULTISTEP TASKS

Task Analysis

If new behaviors are especially complex or have several steps, a **task analysis** can provide the basic step-by-step information for establishing a system of reinforcement.

A task analysis breaks down complex behavior into discrete and simple units that each can be reinforced on the way to mastery of the entire task. Figure 11.2 illustrates a task analysis for a daily living skill.

Task analyses are used as the basis for teaching academic skills, including math, as well as behaviors important for community living, such as employment-related tasks or leisure skills.

Prompting

After a task analysis is established, prompts can help ensure that the desired behavior actually occurs. Prompts can be physical (as when the learner is physically guided through a task), oral (as with rules, instructions, or hints), or visual (such as pictures, written words, or visual gestures). In addition, a task (or a step in a task) can be modeled to demonstrate the desired behavior.

Several principles are important to the most effective use of prompting. First, prompts should be implemented sparingly so that they are used only when the learner could not perform the step without them. Second, the type of prompt chosen should be the least intrusive that will enable the behavior. For example, if an individual is learning to make a tuna sandwich but stops in confusion at the step of opening the can, pointing to the can opener may be a sufficient reminder. If it is, then the spoken hints or directions are not necessary. Because physical prompting is at the most intrusive level, it should be used only if no other prompt is effective. Figure 11.3 suggests a hierarchy for organizing prompts from least to most intrusive.

Fading, or the gradual removal of prompts, encourages performance of the desired behavior without reliance on outside help. One technique is to gradually remove prompts one at a time, beginning with the most intrusive and ending with the least. In the case of physical guidance, this same principle can be applied so that less and less physical pressure is used, leaving the learner actually responsible for more and more of his own movement. Finally, the facilitator may simply move through the motions with hands above (but not actually touching) the learners' so that the learner is actually performing the task without physical help. Used this way, the procedure is called **graduated guidance.**

Yet another method is to delay prompts for longer and longer periods of time (typically a matter of seconds) to give the learner a greater chance to respond on her own. Finally, after a learner appears to be doing well with an initial system of prompts, the least intrusive prompt can be tried to see if it is then sufficient.

Shaping

The principles of operant conditioning are based on reinforcing preexisting behavior. This is the notion of "catch them being good," whereby caregivers watch for children engaging in appropriate behavior and then provide generous reinforcement. For people with mental retardation, though, many important behaviors may not occur spontaneously, so direct teaching is often required. Shaping provides a means for teaching behaviors that are too complex to be acquired through ex-

Appropriate behavior smoothes the way for successful community integration.

© Robert Finken/Jeroboam

planation and for which there is neither adequate motivation nor ability for learning through imitation alone.

With shaping, the individual is reinforced in behaviors that are increasingly closer to the target behavior. For example, if the target behavior were setting the table, then the learner might be first reinforced for simply carrying the required plates and utensils to the table, then for arranging them in place settings, then for placing each setting group at a place, and so on until the desired task had been thus achieved.

Although shaping is a straightforward concept, in practice it requires several important decisions for which there are no absolute answers. First, it is essential that the final goal behavior is clearly defined and that a reasonable starting place is chosen. Second, steps to the goal must be outlined and described based on task analysis; if those steps are too far apart, then the learner is likely to fail (and there will be no opportunity for reinforcement). If the steps are too close together, then time will be wasted, boredom may set in, and the learner may be insulted. Finally, it is important not to linger too long at each step or move ahead too quickly. Because some of these decisions cannot be made before the shaping procedure begins, considerable fine-tuning may be required once it is seen how someone responds (Alberto & Troutman, 1995).

Chaining

Completion of a task analysis provides steps in the behavioral chain that can then be mastered by the learner in manageable units. Initially, each step can be performed and reinforced individually. With time, the first two steps can be completed before reinforcement occurs, then the first three, and so on until the entire task is completed at once. Beginning with the first step and adding steps to the last is called **forward chaining.**

With backward chaining, the direction of the procedure is reversed: The chain begins with the last step, and steps are added in reverse order to the beginning. Figure 11.4 illustrates backward chaining.

Although the distinction between shaping and chaining may seem subtle at first, there are clear differences, and Figure 11.5 contrasts these distinctions.

For teaching toothbrushing with backward chaining, the task analysis in Figure 11.2 is reversed as follows:

1. Steps 1 through 12 are either performed for the individual or he receives the maximum help, and only number 13 (rinse and spit) is performed on his own.
2. Next, he is reinforced for performing both steps 12 and 13 on his own.
3. As learning proceeds, the learner is required to perform the next step in the backward chain before receiving reinforcement until the first step is added and he is carrying out the entire task on his own.

FIGURE 11.4 Backward chaining for tooth brushing

Shaping: *Each* increasingly closer stop toward the goal behavior is reinforced. Early reinforced behaviors lead up to the goal behavior but are not the goal themselves.

Chaining: Every step is part of the goal task. Steps are chained together so that an increasing number of steps must be carried out before reinforcement is received.

FIGURE 11.5 Differences between shaping and chaining procedures

Token Economies

Token economies are systems of reinforcement that are designed to teach desirable and appropriate behaviors. They are ordinarily used with groups but are sometimes developed for individuals, and they have been remarkably successful in a variety of settings (Glynn, 1990; Van Hasselt, Hersen, Egan, McKelvey, & Sisson, 1989). As with any system of reinforcement, the individual, his preferences in reinforcers, and his individual behavioral patterns must guide the plan's development.

In a token economy, people earn tokens (secondary reinforcers) that can later be exchanged for tangible (backup) reinforcements such as food, other commodities, activities, or privileges. Tables 11.1 and 11.2 present some of the details from a token economy carried out in the group home in which Paula (from the above examples) and two other young women live.

There are both advantages and disadvantages to token systems. Because tokens work well as reinforcers (depending, of course, on the desirability of the backup reinforcers), significant changes in behavior are typically seen (Alberto & Troutman, 1995). One reason why tokens are effective is that they can be awarded immediately upon performance, whereas the activity or object that backs up the token usually requires a wait. This is especially the case when the object is expensive, in which case tokens can keep desired behavior going long enough for a "big" reinforcement to be earned. Also, tokens are easily administered on the spot and do

Table 11.1 Token Economy in Paula's Group Home

Points Can be Earned for	Number Earned	Points Are Lost for	Number Lost per Incident
Picking up own room	300 per day	Yelling at housemates or staff	50
Daily jobs	500 per day	Loud belching	25
Dressing appropriately for weather	250 per day	Pinching self or others	300
Vigorous exercise for 25 minutes	300 per day	Throwing objects	150 to 1,000
Washing hands before eating	50 per meal	Refusing to get out of bed in the morning	300

Table 11.2 Backup Reinforcers

Reinforcements to Be Earned	Cost in Points
Low-fat ice cream	100
Other low-fat snacks	25 to 300
Dinner out	2,000
Bowling	2,000
Renting a movie	500

There is a daily limit for the ice cream and snacks and a weekly limit for eating out and bowling.

not require the same interruption of ongoing activity that often comes with re-ceiving the backup—that is to say, a token is more likely to be simply put aside, whereas receiving the actual reward is more distracting. This is especially mean-ingful in work and school environments in which on-task behavior is valued. Be-cause tokens are backed up by a great variety of reinforcers, it is important to note that the system can be engineered to appeal to individual differences.

Although theft and counterfeiting of tokens is sometimes a concern, tokens can be made unique for individuals, and they can be items not easily reproduced or obtained elsewhere (Kazdin, 1994). Hoarding may sometimes take place, too, because gathering large numbers of tokens "buys" the opportunity to misbehave for long periods, and all the while, saved tokens continue to be exchanged for backup rewards. To discourage this, systems can require the exchange of tokens at stated intervals or insist that items be purchased as each quota of tokens is earned.

The main drawback to token systems is the same one that exists for all tangi-ble reinforcement: People may be taught to perform the target behaviors only when they are going to receive tokens. In some situations (such as group homes), the token economy may be carried out indefinitely—just as with the money ex-change in the larger culture. Often, though, the real goal is to help someone per-form appropriately—on their own—without need for tokens.

Remember, though, that token systems are only needed when the natural en-vironment does not adequately reinforce appropriate behavior. If behavior is to become self-sustaining, therefore, people must learn to respond to reinforcements that take place in the course of natural living, and it is equally important that the natural environment encourage appropriate behaviors.

Oftentimes, individuals do learn to respond to praise, expressions of positive emotion from others (smiling, clapping, "high fives"), and other affectionate dis-plays such as hugs or handshakes when these are paired with tokens. When this happens, tokens can be gradually faded. Needless to say, if the natural environ-ment does not then provide these reinforcers, problem behavior almost certainly will reemerge. As a consequence of the uncertainty of reinforcement, then, it is especially important for individuals to learn to feel good about themselves for en-gaging in appropriate behavior so that long-term maintenance is more likely. For that reason, cognitive-behavioral techniques of self-management (described below) can be especially effective.

Contracts

When an individual cooperatively and willingly enters into a behavioral plan with an understanding of the goals, effectiveness is apt to be enhanced (Salend & Ehrlich, 1983). One way to ensure that goals and contingencies are understood is to draw up a contract to which all involved parties agree. For some people with mental retardation, drawings and pictures are an interesting way to clarify proce-dures, and they can even make the contractual documents fun to design.

The contract should clearly describe the desired behaviors, and the reinforce-ments for engaging in them, along with other pertinent information about the settings and situations in which behaviors are expected. Be sure, however, that the learner is easily able to perform the target behaviors before they are specified by contract.

MORE TECHNIQUES
FOR PROBLEM BEHAVIORS

Dealing well with problem behaviors requires knowing about and applying the methods described thus far, and it may also call for additional ones. Changing problem behaviors is a special case of learning, because the individual must drop a learned behavior in addition to acquiring a new one to replace it. Dealing with both of these at once will increase the complexity of the assessment and treatment phases.

Remember, though, that it is indispensable to gain an understanding of why someone does what she does before a behavioral plan can be designed, and this means finding one or more existing antecedents and consequences of the problem behavior. In other words, we must identify when an individual misbehaves and what she is getting from it. Once we have answers to those questions, the fundamental task of behavioral change is to eliminate the reinforcing consequence for the problem behavior and offer that same consequence (or one equally reinforcing) for some other appropriate behavior.

EXTINCTION

Extinction is the guiding principle in eliminating problem behavior. As you learned in Chapter 2, when the reinforcing consequence is withheld, the particular behavior eventually is extinguished. If a child is misbehaving in order to get his parent's attention, for instance, and the parent refuses to pay attention to those behaviors, then the child will eventually give them up. The old behavior will be extinguished.

The extinction process has three important drawbacks, however. First, the behavior will almost certainly increase before it drops away. With our attention example, the child will undoubtedly misbehave more intensely and even desperately as he sees that his usual strategy is no longer working. As misbehavior escalates and becomes dangerous or destructive (such as severe self-injury), it obviously cannot be ignored.

Second, although the original problem behavior may be abandoned, the individual will usually try to find another way to get what he wants. Left to chance, the new strategy may be at least as problematic as the old one. This is especially true when the reinforcing consequence is something for which the person has an intense or even innate need—such as for attention. For these reasons, extinction is almost always accompanied by a method that replaces the old behavior with a new one that is at least equally successful in obtaining reinforcement.

FOR DISCUSSION   *Can you think of examples where problem behavior was ignored and behavior worsened? Explain.*

Third, it can be a long time before a behavior extinguishes, during all of which time it is crucial that there is absolutely no reinforcement for the problem behavior. For our example, this means that the child's attention-seeking misbehavior must be *completely* ignored for as long as it continues—days, weeks, or months. The time to extinction will take even longer if the child is intermittently reinforced, so even one tiny "slip"—sometimes just a nuance in body tension or facial expression—can set the process back. In many living or teaching situations, it may be nearly impossible to ignore bad behavior consistently for so long, especially because a child will invariably misbehave in his most irritating manner when the parent or teacher can least manage it—say, on a morning when she has just received a traffic ticket, *and* has a splitting headache, *and* has her arms full of slipping grocery bags or books.

STRATEGIES OF DIFFERENTIAL
REINFORCEMENT

Because of the problems inherent in using extinction alone, it is almost always necessary to simultaneously reinforce new behaviors as old ones are eliminated or reduced. In the next section, differential reinforcement techniques will be seen to supply an additional means for eliminating problem behaviors.

Differential Reinforcement
of Other Behaviors

With **differential reinforcement of other behaviors** (DRO), a reinforcing stimulus is offered whenever the problem behavior does not occur for a specific period of time. If John typically has high rates of self-injury, for example, he might be reinforced whenever he does not injure himself for five minutes. As he learns that he will no longer get the outcome he desires as a result of self-injury, but only when he does not, then the time required for reinforcement can gradually be increased. The eventual goal, of course, is the complete elimination of self-injury.

There are, however, some things to watch out for with DRO. For one, people with mental retardation may not have many available behaviors. When a self-injury or other problem behavior is eliminated, he may have nothing else to do—which may lead him to resume self-injury out of boredom and as he tires of the reinforcer. It is often necessary, therefore, to teach new behaviors in addition to simply reinforcing the absence of a problem behavior. And the chosen reinforcer must be "worth" giving up the accustomed behavior.

Differential Reinforcement of Alternative or Incompatible Behaviors

With **differential reinforcement of alternative** (DRA) or **incompatible** (DRI) **behaviors,** the individual not only gets the desired consequence for giving up the problem behavior, but also is taught new behaviors as substitutes. With DRA, this new behavior serves the same function as the old, so if John previously injured himself to get attention, he is now given attention *only* for new behaviors—perhaps singing songs or engaging in cooperative tasks. When these new behaviors are impossible to carry out at the same time as (or are incompatible with) the old problem behavior, the reinforcement strategy is called DRI. When John's hands are engaged with a task, for example, he is not able to hit his head, so reinforcement of tasks that involve his hands is DRI.

Differential Reinforcement of Lower Rates of Behavior

Sometimes people engage in behaviors that are problems only because they happen too frequently or too quickly. Teachers may want their students to speak in class, for example, but also to allow others the chance to speak. Learners often may be performing the correct behaviors in the correct sequence (as in dressing, for example) but at a speed that inhibits success. **Differential reinforcement of lower rates of behavior** (DRL) uses a specific schedule of reinforcement to teach individuals to act less often or more slowly.

With DRL, learners are asked either to increase the time that passes between behaviors or to reduce the behaviors that occur within a specified time (Alberto & Troutman, 1995). If the stated frequency goal is met, then there is a reinforcing consequence. For example, children like to be "silly," laughing at nothing and falling all over themselves and others. Sometimes adults are willing to accept these behaviors, but not if they last too long or occur too frequently. Many times parents or teachers may want to encourage children to reduce their silliness without necessarily insisting that they give it up altogether. In such cases, the child might be told that she would receive a special "treat" if she were silly only a certain number of times during a specified period. If one reinforcing consequence of her silliness is attention, then the child could pick out a game or activity involving adult attention as a reward for meeting the goal and thereby receive attention for appropriate behavior.

DRL schedules are often designed to reduce the frequency of a behavior gradually rather than impose a drastic reduction all at once. For our silliness example, if baseline analysis showed that 20 episodes occurred in an average two-hour period, then our final goal might be to reduce them to two for that same period. An initial goal, however, could be to reduce them to 10 per period, then to 5,

Helping Ricky Reduce His Temper Tantrums

Ricky is Jason's 4-year-old older brother (recall our case studies). When Ricky was 3, he began to have temper tantrums, the first of which was in response to his apparent frustration at being unable to pull out a toy from under the couch. As Ricky's tantrums evolved, they often occurred when Jason required immediate attention (most typically when Jason was having a seizure) or when Ricky was faced with a task demand. These tantrums usually involved some combination of screaming, beating his head against the floor, and holding his breath. On two occasions, Ricky passed out in the throes of a tantrum.

Understandably, Cathy did not want to let things go that far, so that at the onset of a tantrum she rushed to pick Ricky up and comfort him. This attention—sometimes coupled with the fact that he then got out of whatever task he was faced with—served only to reinforce the tantrums. Because the tantrums were becoming more frequent, Cathy asked the psychologist on Ricky's team to assist her in developing a plan to help him control his temper.

Cathy and the psychologist decided to use DRI in combination with extinction to accomplish their goal. For the seizure situations, Ricky was told in advance that when Jason had a seizure, Ricky's help would be needed to bring a blanket and pillow, for which he would receive a special treat. When Ricky complied by helping and once Jason was positioned comfortably, Cathy turned her attention to Ricky. Any crying or fussing on Ricky's part was ignored. After helping, Ricky received a special activity with Cathy.

In task situations, Ricky's attempts to escape through tantrums were also ignored, and guided compliance was used in completing the task. Then Ricky was reinforced for finishing, typically with a favorite food or drink accompanied by praise.

In both situations, Ricky's tantrums decreased dramatically. He has not had a tantrum during a seizure for several months, and tantrums in response to tasks have been reduced to one mild episode every other week.

and finally to 2, always keeping in mind that the reinforcement for reducing the time spent in silliness must be something the child enjoys at least as much.

Differential reinforcement strategies may be easily confused, because at first they seem to involve subtle distinctions. To help minimize confusion and distinguish their characteristics, Table 11.3 lists the defining features of DRO, DRA, DRI, and DRL.

Table 11.3 Comparisons Among Differential Reinforcement Strategies

Strategy	Reinforces
DRO	Absence of the target behavior for a specified time
DRA	Behaviors other than the target
DRI	Behaviors incompatible with the target
DRL	Only when the target occurs at a specified frequency

VARIABLES THAT INFLUENCE THE
EFFECTIVENESS OF REINFORCEMENT

Our discussion of behavioral treatment has concentrated so far on a straightforward notion of stimulus and response events that takes this form:

Antecedent ⟶ Behavior ⟶ Consequence

In reality, however, behavior often occurs in a much more complicated context, and variables other than the immediate antecedent influence both the behavior and the effectiveness of a particular reinforcement.

In an illustration of this, Haring and Kennedy (1990) discovered that the context of behavior alters the effectiveness of reinforcement and punishment. Their participants (who had severe disabilities) had reduced problem behavior with DRO reinforcement where time-outs were ineffective. In a leisure context, however, DRO did not change behavior, but time-outs did. Apparently, when these participants were faced with a task, DRO encouraged persistence, while time-outs simply reinforced problem behavior by permitting escape. In the leisure context, however, the activity itself was apparently more rewarding than the DRO, while leaving the activity through time-out was an effective punishment. Such findings highlight the importance of taking surrounding circumstances into consideration when designing a behavioral program; and because a particular behavioral plan may be effective in some situations and not in others, analyzing the context can point the way to discovering the flaws in a treatment program.

As another example, sometimes a behavior can be influenced by the characteristics of a task itself. Dunlap and Plienis (1991) discovered that young people with developmental disabilities were better able to complete unsupervised tasks when those tasks involved lesser demands. When children were to pick up items and put them away on their own, they were more successful when there were 20 items to pick up rather than 70 or 100. Changes in task demands, then, can help ensure success. An easy start, together with gradual increases in task demands, may promote better final performance than beginning with high expectations. Analyzing task characteristics is therefore vital, and manipulating task demands may be as important as choosing an effective reinforcer.

Setting Events

Other variables, often called **setting events,** may have similar influences on behavior and can explain why a reinforcement may seem adequate sometimes and not at others. By definition, setting events alter the effectiveness of a reinforcement and thus influence changes in behavior (Horner, Vaughn, Day, & Ard, 1996). Setting events can be physiological conditions—such as hunger, illness, and fatigue—or circumstances of the environment—including the presence or absence of favorite people, disturbing noises, or extreme fluctuations in temperature (Kantor, 1959). Research has shown that such physiological states and

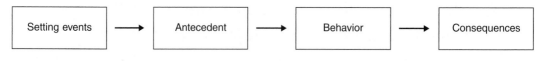

FIGURE 11.6 Relationship of setting events to behavioral components

environmental variables can influence both the alertness and the ability to learn for people with developmental disabilities (Guess et al., 1993).

Setting events can also include a prior stimulus–response episode itself (Bijou & Baer, 1961). Figure 11.6 shows the relationship of any of these setting events to other behavioral components.

To illustrate setting events more fully, let us look at a classroom situation in which Dianne, a child with severe disabilities, has learned to feed herself at lunch. Typically, when her bowl and special spoon are placed in front of her (antecedent), Dianne begins to feed herself and continues until she is finished (behavior). At the end of the meal, she is given attention and praise and permitted to spend 15 minutes in a favored activity (consequence reinforcement).

Occasionally, however, when her bowl and spoon are placed in front of her, Dianne begins to scream and cry. Through a process of careful data collection, it was discovered that her crying usually occurred on days when she either had a cold or had slept little the night before. The illness and lack of sleep were both setting events, because they diminished the effectiveness of the accustomed reinforcement (praise and attention) for feeding herself.

Unwanted changes in behavior can sometimes be avoided by eliminating setting events entirely or by making fewer demands when setting events are present. In any case, recognizing the existence of setting events is essential for understanding the stimulus control of behavior.

Many problem behaviors are influenced and maintained by multiple influences. **Pica** (compulsive eating of nonfood items) and **rumination** (repeated regurgitation and swallowing of food), for example, are often maintained by environmental and physiological influences beyond immediate antecedents and consequences (Gardner & Graeber, 1993). Because of the complexity of behavioral influences, a multidisciplinary approach is often required so that medical professionals, behavioral specialists, teachers, and other involved people work together to establish successful behavioral plans.

Context and setting events illustrate both (1) the complexity of behavior and (2) the necessary strategies for teaching new behaviors and managing problem ones. In addition, they provide yet another illustration of the usefulness of a systems viewpoint. When behavior is viewed not only at the level of a simple stimulus–response event, but also with an understanding of the multiple and interacting influences within which it occurs, then successful intervention is far more likely.

1. Have more positive procedures, such as differential reinforcement strategies, been considered?
2. Does the student currently have or have access to a pool of reinforcers?
3. Have the rules of appropriate behavior and the results (fines) for infractions been clearly explained and understood?
4. Has the ratio of the size of the fine to each instance of misbehavior been thought out?
5. Can the reinforcers be retrieved?
6. Will appropriate behavior be reinforced in conjunction with the use of response-cost?

FIGURE 11.7 Points to consider when setting up response-cost contingencies

Adapted from P. A. Alberto & A. C. Troutman (1995), *Applied behavior analysis for teachers.* Englewood Cliffs, NJ: Merrill.

PUNISHMENT

Recall that punishment is *any consequence of behavior that makes that behavior less likely to reoccur.* The use of punishment is controversial, yet there is considerable agreement that people do learn to respond more appropriately when they experience punishing consequences from problem behavior—especially if more desirable behaviors are reinforced at the same time (Kazdin, 1994). This section describes several common techniques of punishment and discusses some of the details of their successful application.

Response-cost measures work on the principle that removal of a reinforcer following inappropriate behavior acts as a punisher in decreasing that behavior. An example is the withdrawal of tokens for misbehavior as described previously in the section on token economy.

Although response-cost systems have been used successfully without incurring many of the undesirable side effects typically associated with punishment (see the following section on overcorrection), there are cautions. Note that motivation to do well can be undermined when the reinforcement for appropriate behavior is overshadowed or outweighed by the consequences of problem behavior. For example, the fear of the hurt or embarrassment caused by losing a token may discourage a child from trying a task that could gain a reinforcement. For this reason, among others, it is better to rely on reinforcement when at all possible and resort to methods of punishment (no matter how mild) only when reinforcement alone is not effective. It is also important to make the cost of poor behavior reasonable and just. When using response-cost, always be sure that people understand and can perform the appropriate behavior and can clearly see the connection between inappropriate behavior and reinforcement withdrawal. Figure 11.7 offers a checklist for deciding upon a response-cost procedure.

Time-out is another technique frequently used to stem problem behavior. This response-cost measure assumes that the environment is reinforcing and that removal from it will act as a punisher. Time-outs are often used in schools, group homes, and work settings for people with retardation. A time-out typically means segregating the individual for a brief period. There may be a designated time-out chair or at home the individual may simply go to his room.

A time-out can be effective if the environment from which the individual is removed is indeed reinforcing; it typically fails when it serves to free someone from demands and situations that they actually find punishing. Just as with reinforcers, punishers such as time out are individually specific, because what is punishing to one person may be reinforcing to another.

Time-out also can be offered as a self-management strategy rather than as a punishment. With this variation, individuals can go to a time-out area on their own when they are experiencing emotional stress in lieu of acting out in spoken or physical aggression.

Overcorrection is a method of punishment that may be effective in a variety of settings and simultaneously have educational value (Foxx & Bechtel, 1983). With overcorrection, problem behavior is followed by the repeated practice of an appropriate act. For example, an individual who slams doors may be required to open and close the door quietly several times following one incident of door slamming. If possible, the overcorrection is performed in response to spoken prompts, but sometimes physically guided compliance is required.

The act of overcorrection should always have a sensible relationship with the inappropriate behavior (Foxx & Bechtel, 1982). This can take the form of **restitution** for the problem behavior so that someone who threw items in a fit of temper, for example, would be required to straighten the whole room and not simply pick up the thrown items. Overcorrection can also take the form of **positive practice** as in the door-slamming example above. Both restitutional and positive practice procedures are regarded as educational, because they provide training in an appropriate action.

Overcorrection should always be used in combination with reinforcement. Typically, overcorrection is followed by praise or a more tangible reinforcement. The procedure is used most effectively when the restitutional or practice behavior takes only a short period of time (Carey & Bucher, 1986).

Some of the negative side effects of overcorrection are fairly obvious. The individual may refuse to perform the overcorrection or may become aggressive in response to forced compliance, which results in even greater unpleasantness for all involved. This is less likely, however, if overcorrection is approached with a positive and friendly attitude, is associated with an adequate reinforcer, and is of relatively short duration. As with other forms of behavioral treatment, the process is eased when the learner understands and cooperates with the purpose of the procedure. In spite of the drawbacks, overcorrection procedures have frequently been effective even with those who have severe retardation (Linscheid, Iwata, & Foxx, 1996).

Rarely, far more aversive forms of punishment have been used by professionals in an attempt to discourage the most serious problem behaviors. These include restraint, spraying the offending individual with water or lemon juice, and electric shock. The use of any punishment has negative side effects that must be thoughtfully considered, and these become of greater concern as the level of aversion increases. Such side effects and their ethical considerations are discussed later in the chapter.

When behavior is analyzed in detail with regard to complexity, and behavioral programs are designed with a clear understanding of the influences maintaining a behavior, then punishment is not usually necessary. Although punishment is often effective, several important side effects discourage its use. To begin with, it may elicit aggression and resentment—especially physical punishment, which actually models, and therefore teaches, the use of aggressive solutions to problems (Strassberg, Dodge, Pettit, & Bates, 1994). It is important to note that it does not by itself teach appropriate alternative behaviors, and it can cause the punished individual to become fearful and withdrawn and to avoid the punisher. Although the danger of these side effects increases with the severity and frequency of punishment, they are serious enough in any instance; thus, whenever possible, behavior programs should rely exclusively on reinforcement or on manipulating task requirements and setting events, and they should avoid using punishment.

OBJECTIONS AND ALTERNATIVES
TO AVERSIVE STIMULI

Probably no more controversial topic exists in behavioral treatment than techniques of aversive consequences (Repp & Singh, 1990). In addition to the objections to punishment in general, there are specific ethical objections to the use of consequences that inflict pain or are especially noxious.

To begin with, the use of aversive stimuli contradicts our ideas of humane treatment. There are, for example, laws in our society that protect ordinary citizens from painful assault—laws that remain in effect despite possible arguments that the assault was for the "person's own good." In the case of children, child-abuse laws prohibit the use of extraordinary force, and other legislation prohibits the use of electric shock with prisoners. Because of these precedents, the infliction of aversive treatments (such as shock) seem all the more inappropriate for people who may not understand the reasons for it and who are unable to complain to any authority.

Aversive treatments, however, are most commonly used only in extreme instances—for example, with individuals who are the victims of severe self-abuse. Such people often injure themselves to the point of endangering their own lives, so either necessary restraint or medication must inhibit them. In these instances, both parents and professionals may believe that short-term aversive therapy—if it allows someone to gain meaningful life participation—is preferable to a lifetime of self-abuse and restraint. This is even more true when the aversive therapy is less physically damaging than the abuse itself (Konarski, 1990).

Foxx, Zukotynski, and Williams (1994) recorded the incident of Joe, whose self-biting, scratching, and head banging produced lacerations severe enough to require medical treatment. Joe was also dangerously aggressive and inflicted attacks on others that resulted in permanent injuries (including scarring and the loss of a finger). In spite of blindness and mental retardation, Joe's physical strength, his ability to locate caregivers, and his aggressiveness placed anyone who worked with him at serious risk.

All medical and behavioral treatments had failed with Joe, whether in institutional or group settings, and baseline analyses showed that (in environments of low demands) Joe would attack himself, others, or the environment more than 18 times a day. After a program of one-second electric shocks in response to aggression, Joe's dangerous behavior was reduced to fewer than a single incident per day, and the severity of that aggression was far milder. It is important to note that treatment included teaching Joe new behaviors that would serve the same function as the aggression, as well as new social and independent living skills that offered reinforcement for learning. Perhaps most compelling of all, because of Joe's reduced aggression, he was subsequently able to participate in community activities, including workshop, swimming, gym class, horseback riding, hiking, and speech and music therapy (Foxx, Zukotynski, & Williams, 1994).

Still, some professionals insist that individuals can learn to give up self-abuse by means of such nonaversive techniques as differential reinforcement strategies (described earlier), and they often can (Meyer & Evans, 1989; Smith, 1990). Certainly, aversive treatments should be used only as a last resort, and considerable effort must be put into nonaversive treatments first. Only if these fail—*and* aversive treatment is less damaging than the existing self-abuse—should such methods be used (Butterfield, 1990). Effectiveness of treatment can never be the sole argument for the use of aversive procedures; rather the potential side effects of any treatment must always be considered, and the least intrusive effective method should be finally chosen (Horner, 1990; Konarski, 1990).

Sadly, for some people with severe SIB, electric shock *is* the last resort, because alternative programs, no matter how well-designed and implemented, fail to work. And worse, even electric shock is not always effective, because some individuals appear to habituate to shock, and SIB returns after an initial decline. For others, shock may reduce but not completely eliminate the hurtful behavior. In such cases, punishment with shock may continue over a period of years, although the daily frequency may be low.

As with so many other ethical issues surrounding mental retardation, there are no easy answers to the matter of aversive therapy. Decisions about the use of punishments must consider effectiveness, alternative treatments, duration of treatment, and intensity of treatment (at the very least)—and evidence on these variables is often less than clear-cut.

GENTLE TEACHING

Whereas most objections to behavioral procedures are directed toward those that involve punishment, some authors argue against the behavioral viewpoint itself.

The fun of working together can often take the place of problem behavior.

© Martin Chaffer/Stone

Gentle teaching is an approach that stresses the importance of building a relationship rather than modifying behavior (McGee, 1993; McGee & Menolascino, 1991). Gentle teaching seeks to create interdependence and companionship through the practice of unconditional acceptance, tolerance, and valuing the individual.

The concept of gentle teaching is based on the idea that all people desire companionship and belonging so that, as relationships are built, people learn to value closeness and warmth. As a result, they also learn to value and care for others. With gentle teaching, the use of either reward or punishment is avoided, as are restraint and physical immobilization. The intention is not to gain compliance (especially in the beginning) but to simply experience "being with" the person, expressing warmth and acceptance, and as such the method requires a fund of patience and understanding.

Gentle teaching is a philosophical approach, and there is as yet little research to provide evidence of its effectiveness. Its thesis is that it is dehumanizing to base interactions on the premise that all human behavior and motivation are responses to reward and punishment (McGee, 1993). Instead, the goal is to get along with others (clients and students included) by creating a relationship in which mutual valuing occurs.

At first glance, the success of behavioral principles might seem to be widely documented, while demonstration of the effectiveness of gentle teaching methods depends upon anecdotal evidence. These two methods, however, are not mutually exclusive. When behavioral treatments are carried out with stern coldness and distance rather than warmth and good feeling, they are not as likely to succeed. The method of approach for behavioral intervention is important especially because there is long-standing research evidence that liking and identification strongly influence the rate of imitation (Bandura, 1977). Because the relationship between an individual and caretaker or teacher is a determining factor on the amount of possible influence, behavioral change techniques cannot be viewed separately from the relationship in which they take place. As a result, the development of a friendly and positive relationship with client and students should be the first priority of a therapist, teacher, or other service provider.

Joyce

Positive Results from Gentle Teaching

An important goal for Joyce's IEP team was to help her find a vision of herself and her future (see Chapter 5). All agreed that it was important that she imagine what she might like to do and be, and that she begin to try out in some of these areas. Because Joyce was so easily influenced by her peers, there was even more reason to get her involved with people who could both set a good example for her and help her build self-esteem.

In ninth grade, Joyce left the self-contained environment and was mainstreamed into regular high school classes—although she still got help from resource teachers. Joyce tried out for the marching band's dance group through the prompting of Lisa (the regular education student who was working with Joyce in peer tutoring sessions in eighth grade), and she was accepted into that group. As a result, she also gained the acceptance of new friends, which—along with a highly visible and official part to play in the athletic program—contributed to Joyce's enhanced self-image.

As for a transition to a career, Joyce's home economics teacher, Mrs. Clary, took a particular interest in Joyce and noticed her flair for sewing. Joyce was initially self-conscious and even resistant to Mrs. Clary's attention, however—a pattern that was consistent with her responses to other adults outside of her family circle.

Mrs. Clary had read about gentle teaching and believed that if she could build a good relationship with Joyce, she could guide her toward activities that could lead to eventual career opportunities. To avoid embarrassing her or pushing her further away, Mrs. Clary began by working with groups of students in which Joyce was included.

At first, Mrs. Clary encouraged these students in a warm and accepting manner, joked with them, and generally got to know them better. Eventually, Joyce began to warm up and spoke more freely and openly with Mrs. Clary.

As time went on, Joyce and her teacher built a warm and trusting relationship, and Mrs. Clary was able to encourage Joyce to apply her sewing skills to intricate patterns, which turned out to be highly successful. From this success, Joyce gained additional confidence and, because her work was displayed in the school, she gained more respect and positive approval from other students.

Ultimately, Mrs. Clary introduced Joyce to an acquaintance who operated a fabric store, where Joyce began part-time work. After some time, her employer included Joyce in some of the classes given by the store for the public. Joyce did have some difficulty orally explaining sewing steps, but this was not important because she was able to demonstrate techniques in a way that proved helpful for customers.

COGNITIVE TECHNIQUES

For someone to live on her own, take care of her own physical needs, and gather the financial resources for essentials, she must be able to make accurate judgments about all kinds of workday situations she may encounter. It is also necessary to make decisions that lead to success. Effective judgment and decision making require the possession and application of useful cognitive strategies.

These cognitive strategies may provide the greatest challenge for people with retardation. Behavioral techniques are often successful in teaching complicated skills even to those with severe intellectual disabilities. Usually, however, these skills are specific to the problem and the context in which they are taught. But people with mental retardation often have a great deal of trouble transferring (**generalizing**) what they learn to different situations, even when those situations are similar to the one in which the skill was taught (Langone, 1990).

Recent cognitive research, however, suggests that problem solving and critical thinking can be situation-specific for anyone, and that the application of cognitive skills and strategies can depend strongly upon relevant experience in the context in question (Alibali, 1999). Furthermore, experience leads to the development of knowledge and strategies for those with MR, in much the same way as for others. To the extent that the experiences of people with retardation are limited and constrained, generalization is likely to be all the more difficult. Conversely, a crucial element of the education and training of people with MR is the opportunity to engage in numerous and varied experiences in the community in which their skills will eventually be employed.

A special challenge for those who intervene in the lives of people with disabilities, therefore, is to help them learn the skills that will allow them to control their own lives as much as possible. This ability has been called **self-determination** (Wehmeyer, Palmer, Agran, Mithaug, & Martin, 2000) or **self-regulation** (Whitman, 1990).

Making Choices

An important element in gaining self-regulation is the chance to experience making choices and decisions (Whitman, 1990). People with mental retardation often are not allowed the opportunity to make choices, yet evidence shows that people with even the severest intellectual disabilities can determine at least some aspects of their lives if situations are structured in ways that allow them to do so. Non-verbal people with severe intellectual impairment, for example, can often learn to pick a preferred item from an assortment. The opportunity to make choices can help promote a sense of control over one's life—an element that research with widely diverse populations has shown to be crucial to the absence of stress and the promotion of physical health (Krause, Jay, & Liang, 1991). In addition, experience in choice and decision making can help decrease the dependency found with many people with retardation (Bybee & Zigler, 1999).

Self-Management

Self-management is a technique used to teach individuals greater control over themselves and their lives. In self-management, the individual himself learns to use the behavioral techniques of reinforcement, punishment, and prompts to manage his own behavior. Figure 11.8 lists important elements in teaching self-management.

In self-management, one learns to identify and label instances of both appropriate and inappropriate behavior by watching someone else model the behavior and then by responding with the correct label. If Roy were learning to eat quietly with his mouth closed, for example, the teacher would model both behaviors (chewing noisily and chewing quietly), and Roy would label the behavior in each instance as "eating quietly" or "eating loudly." After Roy was able to make that discrimination accurately, he would go on to identify and label those behaviors in himself.

Next, Roy would be taught to monitor his own eating behavior, and he would help himself to a food treat after eating his meal quietly. If he ate loudly, he would take no food treat. At the beginning, Roy would receive prompts for whether or not he should give himself the reinforcement, but as he progressed the prompts would be faded. During the training phase, the teacher would emphasize how good it feels to receive the treat and be in control, as well as how sad it feels to miss the treat and be out of control. Pairing the tangible reward with an expression of good feeling in this way helps Roy internalize appropriate emotional responses to his own behavior and thus lessens the need for a tangible reinforcer.

Typically, monitoring lasts for a specified period of time, and there is a timing device to indicate when the monitoring period is over. Usually there is also a system for recording what behavior occurred during the period. For Roy, the prompts and tangible reinforcers were gradually faded, but in some systems (especially work systems) where tangible reinforcement (money) is always expected, extrinsic reinforcement would remain part of the self-management program. Figure 11.9 describes procedures for designing a self-monitoring system.

Imagery Procedures

Guided imagery is another technique to help people learn to manage their own behavior. One method is to have an individual imagine her own appropriate behavior and then imagine a pleasant and reinforcing outcome. In training, the

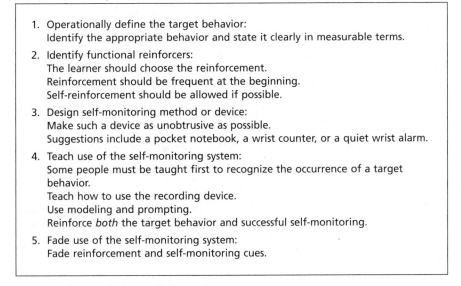

1. The individual learns to identify and label appropriate and inappropriate instances of the target behavior.
2. The individual learns to identify and label when she herself is engaging in appropriate and inappropriate instances of the target behavior.
3. The individual learns to monitor her own behavior for appropriate and inappropriate instances.
4. The individual administers her own reinforcement or punishment for her own instances of the target behavior.
5. Praise that involves feelings of self-satisfaction for self-control are paired with a tangible reinforcer.
6. Teaching prompts and tangible reinforcers, if used, are gradually faded.

FIGURE 11.8 Elements of self-management training

1. Operationally define the target behavior:
   Identify the appropriate behavior and state it clearly in measurable terms.

2. Identify functional reinforcers:
   The learner should choose the reinforcement.
   Reinforcement should be frequent at the beginning.
   Self-reinforcement should be allowed if possible.

3. Design self-monitoring method or device:
   Make such a device as unobtrusive as possible.
   Suggestions include a pocket notebook, a wrist counter, or a quiet wrist alarm.

4. Teach use of the self-monitoring system:
   Some people must be taught first to recognize the occurrence of a target behavior.
   Teach how to use the recording device.
   Use modeling and prompting.
   Reinforce *both* the target behavior and successful self-monitoring.

5. Fade use of the self-monitoring system:
   Fade reinforcement and self-monitoring cues.

FIGURE 11.9 Self-Monitoring Procedures

Adapted from Dunlap, L. K., Dunlap, G. & Koegel, L. K. (1991), Using self-monitoring to increase independence. *Teaching Exceptional Children, 24*(3), 17–22.

professional describes an imagined scene for the individual, who then retells the scene back to the professional. With someone who has limited oral abilities, supplemental pictures can be used in addition to or instead of verbal descriptions (Cautela & Kearney, 1993).

Guided imagery is always carried out when the learner is relaxed and receptive. As with self-management, the good feelings that are associated both with the reinforcer and with a sense of self-control are accented. The pairing of the idea of a tangible reinforcement with good feelings (and of good feelings with the idea of self-control) is critically important because the association helps the individual internalize reinforcement for appropriate behavior. To the extent that someone feels good about himself for behaving appropriately, it is more likely that he will be able to manage his own behavior without outside intervention.

Susan

Using Imagery and Self-Verbalizations to Manage Feelings

Although Susan usually got along well with her classmates, and they were typically kind to her, she was extremely sensitive to teasing. Her feelings were easily hurt, often in circumstances where no one intended to tease or to offend. When hurt, Susan would become withdrawn, refusing to speak or even to look at others, and she would often maintain such behavior for an hour or more.

In consultation with Susan's teacher, Dr. Schaffer, her psychologist, developed an imagery plan to help Susan manage her feelings better. Because these techniques allowed Susan to receive therapy away from school—while mentally practicing her behavior in the school setting—there was no requirement for classwork time or involvement of school personnel. Susan even learned to provide her own reinforcement!

In the imagery sessions, Dr. Schaffer asked Susan to take a deep breath, relax as completely as possible, close her eyes and imagine the following scene:

> Susan, imagine that you are sitting in your chair at school, playing with your favorite computer game—*TicTactics*. Your friend Bryan is playing with you. When you can imagine this, will you please raise your hand? (Susan raises her hand.)
>
> You are having a lot of fun and you feel very happy. Suddenly, Bryan says something that really hurts your feelings. You feel very upset and angry with Bryan, and you don't want to play with him, or talk to him, or even look at him. But you really want to take care of your feelings and get back to your game and all the fun you were having. So you say to Bryan, "My feelings are hurt. I need a few minutes." Then, you take some deep, slow breaths, and imagine giving yourself a big hug. And you say to yourself, "No matter what anyone says or does, I am a very worthwhile person. I am a lot of fun. I have a lot to offer." Now imagine eating your very favorite treat, a double chocolate sundae. Soon you are feeling much better, and you are ready to go back to your game. So you say to Bryan, "I'm ready to go back and play now." You feel so good, because you took care of your feelings, and you are ready to play. Now, can you tell me that story?

Susan repeats the story back to Dr. Schaffer. Because repetition of the imagery and self-verbalization technique is so important, Dr. Schaffer gave the written script to Jolene (Susan's home aide) and taught her to go through it with Susan. Susan and Jolene practiced the script for 20 minutes every day for six months. Susan now uses this technique when her feelings are hurt, and she is able to return to work or play much more quickly.

SOURCE: Adapted J. Groden & J. R. Cautela (1984), Use of imagery procedures with students labeled "trainable retarded." *Psychological Reports, 54*, 595–605.

THE IMPORTANCE OF
MOTIVATIONAL CHARACTERISTICS

When someone is eager and persistent in their efforts toward a task, we can say that she is motivated. For children without retardation, motivation predicts grades as accurately as IQ (Neisser et al., 1996); the same is true for those with retardation, for whom motivation—perhaps not surprisingly—is an important aspect of success (Haywood & Switzky, 1986). Often those with MR are predominantly motivated by extrinsic factors; that is, they are reinforced by factors outside themselves. But everyone who is intrinsically rather than extrinsically motivated—with MR or not—is able to learn more effectively (Switzky, 1994).

Because those with an extrinsic motivational style respond better to external reinforcements, successful teaching should begin with tangible rewards. At the same time, if those external rewards are paired with good feelings about the self (for example, "It feels so good to be _____ or do _____"), individuals can develop far greater intrinsic motivation.

▌▌ LOOKING AHEAD ━━━▶

This chapter has described some of the techniques that can be used to help children learn new behaviors and change old ones. Even though these techniques are presented here in a separate chapter on behavior, the basic principles described are relevant to and integrally involved with all areas of human relationships and learning. In addition, the systems within which we live all operate by the same principles, and analyses of the setting events, antecedents, and consequences of system variables may be at least as important as similar functional analyses for the individual client (McClannahan & Krantz, 1993).

It is similarly crucial to understand that the topics presented here are interrelated with one another. In practice they must be viewed not as discrete topics, but as interacting aspects of a larger approach to conscious and effective intervention—one that involves both people with MR and those with whom they have contact. Finally, it is important to recognize the integral role that the application of these techniques play in successful community integration for both children and adults.

As you turn to Chapter 12 and consider the formal educational environment for those with mental retardation, consider too how the cognitive–behavioral techniques learned here will figure essentially in the development and implementation of instructional planning. And, as this text proceeds, the obvious application of behavioral techniques for helping children with MR adjust to and fit in with the school community will become increasingly clear.

INFOTRAC COLLEGE EDITION

Positive reinforcement should be central to most behavioral intervention strategies. Enter *positive reinforcement* as the keyword in *InfoTrac College Edition,* and choose an article that describes a specific use of positive reinforcement. What was the intervention? What was the outcome of the intervention? How was the outcome evaluated?

REFERENCES

Alberto, P. A., & Troutman, A. C. (1995). *Applied behavior analysis for teachers* (4th ed.). Columbus, OH: Merrill.

Alibali, M. W. (1999). How children change their minds: Strategy change can be gradual or abrupt. *Development Psychology, 35,* 127–145.

Bandura, A. (1977). *Social learning theory.* Englewood Cliffs, NJ: Prentice-Hall.

Bijou, S. W., & Baer, D. M. (1961). *Child development I: A systematic and empirical theory.* Englewood Cliffs, NJ: Prentice-Hall.

Butterfield, E. C. (1990). The compassion of distinguishing punishing behavioral treatment from aversive treatment. *American Journal on Mental Retardation, 95*(2), 137–141.

Bybee, J., & Zigler, E. (1999). Outerdirectedness in individuals with and without mental retardation: A review. In E. Zigler & D. Bennett-Gates (Eds.), *Personality development in individuals with mental retardation* (pp. 165–205). New York: Cambridge University Press.

Carey, R., & Bucher, B. (1986). Positive practice overcorrection: Effects of reinforcing correct performance. *Behavior Modification, 10,* 73–92.

Cautela, J. R., & Kearney, A. J. (Eds.). (1993). *Covert conditioning casebook.* Pacific Grove, CA: Brooks/Cole.

Dudley, J. R., Ahlgrim-Delzell, L., & Calhoun, M. L. (1999). Diverse diagnostic and behavioral patterns amongst people with a dual diagnosis. *Journal of Intellectual Disability Research, 43*(2), 70–79.

Dunlap, G., & Plienis, A. J. (1991). The influence of task size on the unsupervised task performance of students with developmental disabilities. *Education and Treatment of Children, 14*(2), 85–95.

Dunlap, L. K., Dunlap, G., & Koegel, L. K. (1991). Using self-monitoring to increase independence. *Teaching Exceptional Children, 24*(3), 17–22.

Foxx, R. M., & Bechtel, D. (1982). Overcorrection. In M. Hersen, R. Eisler, & P. Miller (Eds.), *Progress in behavior modification* (Vol. 13, pp. 227–288). New York: Academic Press.

———. (1983). Overcorrection: A review and analysis. In S. Axelrod & J. Apsche (Eds.), *The effects of punishment on human behavior* (pp. 133–220). New York: Academic Press.

Foxx, R. M., Zukotynski, G., & Williams, D. E. (1994). Measurement and evaluation of treatment outcomes with extremely dangerous behavior. In T. Thompson & D. B. Gray (Eds.), *Destructive behavior in developmental disabilities* (pp. 261–273). Thousand Oaks, CA: Sage.

Gardner, W. I., & Graeber, J. L. (1993). Severe behavioral disorders in persons with mental retardation: A multimodal behavioral diagnostic model. In R. N. Fletcher & A. Dosen (Eds.), *Mental health aspects of mental retardation: Progress in assessment and treatment* (pp. 45–69). New York: Lexington Books/Macmillan.

Glynn, S. M. (1990). Token economy approaches for psychiatric patients. *Behavior Modification, 14,* 383–407.

Groden, J., & Cautela, J. R. (1984). Use of imagery procedures with students labeled "trainable retarded." *Psychological Reports, 54,* 595–605.

Guess, D., Roberts, S., Siegel-Causey, E., Ault, M., Guy, B., & Thompson, B. (1993). Analysis of behavior state conditions and associated environmental variables among students with profound handicaps. *American Journal on Mental Retardation, 97*(6), 634–653.

Haring, T. G., & Kennedy, C. H. (1990). Contextual control of problem behavior in students with severe disabilities. *Journal of Applied Behavior Analysis, 23*(2), 235–243.

Haywood, H. C., & Switzky, H. N. (1986). Intrinsic motivation and behavioral effectiveness in retarded persons. In N. Ellis & N. Bray (Eds.), *International review of research in mental retardation* (Vol. 14, pp. 1–46). New York: Academic Press.

Horner, R. (1990). Ideology, technology, and typical community settings: Use of severe aversive stimuli. *American Journal on Mental Retardation, 95,* 166–168.

Horner, R. N., Vaughn, B. J., Day, H. M., & Ard, W. R., Jr. (1996). The relationship between setting events and problem behavior: Expanding our understanding of behavioral support. In L. K. Koegel, R. L. Koegel, & G. Dunlap (Eds.), *Positive behavioral support: Including people with difficult behavior in the community* (pp. 381–402). Baltimore, MD: Paul H. Brookes.

Kantor, J. R. (1959). *Interbehavioral psychology.* Granville, OH: Principia Press.

Kazdin, A. E. (1994). *Behavior modification.* Pacific Grove, CA: Brooks/Cole.

Konarski, E. A., Jr. (1990). Science as an ineffective white knight. *American Journal on Mental Retardation, 95,* 169–171.

Krause, N., Jay, G., & Liang, J. (1991). Financial strain and psychological well-being among the American and Japanese elderly. *Psychology and Aging, 6,* 170–181.

Langone, J. (1990). *Teaching students with mild and moderate learning problems.* Boston: Allyn & Bacon.

Linscheid, T. R., Iwata, B. A., & Foxx, R. M. (1996). Behavioral assessment. In J. W. Jacobson & J. A. Mulick (Eds.), *Manual of diagnosis and professional practice in mental retardation* (pp. 191–198). Washington, DC: American Psychological Association.

McClannahan, L. E., & Krantz, P. J. (1993). On systems analysis in autism intervention programs. *Journal of Applied Behavior Analysis, 26*(4), 589–596.

McGee, J. (1993). Gentle teaching for persons with mental retardation: The expression of a psychology of interdependence. In R. J. Fletcher & A. Dosen (Eds.), *Mental health aspects of mental retardation: Progress in assessment and treatment.* New York: Lexington Books.

McGee, J. J., & Menolascino, F. J. (1991). *Beyond gentle teaching: A nonaversive approach to helping those in need.* New York: Plenum.

Meyer, L. H., & Evans, I. M. (1989). *Nonaversive interventions for behavior problems: A manual for home and community.* Baltimore, MD: Paul H. Brookes.

Neisser, U., Boodoo, G., Bouchard, T. J., Jr., Boykin, A. W., Brody, N., Ceci, S. J., Halpern, D. F., Loehlin, J. C., Perloff, R., Sternberg, R. J., & Urbina, S. (1996). Intelligence: Knowns and unknowns. *American Psychologist, 51,* 77–101.

Repp, A. C., & Singh, N. N. (1990). *Perspectives on the use of nonaversive and aversive interventions for persons with developmental disabilities.* Sycamore, IL: Sycamore.

Rojahn, J. (1986). Self-injurious and stereotypical behavior of noninstitutionalized mentally retarded people: Prevalence and classification. *American Journal of Mental Deficiency, 91,* 268–276.

Salend, S. J., & Ehrlich, E. (1983). Involving students in behavior modification programs. *Mental Retardation, 21*(3), 95–100.

Schreibman, L. (1988). *Autism.* Newbury Park, CA: Sage.

Smith, M. D. (1990). *Autism and life in the community: Successful interventions for behavioral challenges.* Baltimore, MD: Paul H. Brookes.

Strassberg, Z., Dodge, K., Pettit, G. S., & Bates, J. E. (1994). Spanking in the home and children's subsequent aggression toward kindergarten peers. *Development and Psychopathology, 6,* 445–461.

Switzky, H. N. (1994). *Motivation and mental retardation: A reprise and future directions for research.* Presented at the Fourth International Conference on Mental Retardation, Arlington Heights, IL.

Van Hasselt, V., Hersen, M., Egan, B., McKelvey, J., & Sisson, L. (1989). Increasing social interaction in deaf-blind severely handicapped young adults. *Behavior Modification, 13,* 257–272.

Wehmeyer, M. L., Palmer, S. B., Agran, M., Mithaug, D. E., & Martin, J. E. (2000). Promoting causal agency: The self-determined learning model of instruction. *Exceptional Children, 66*(4), 439–453.

Whitman, T. L. (1990). Self-regulation and mental retardation. *American Journal on Mental Retardation, 94*(4), 347–362.

12

Educational Issues

In Chapter 11, you learned many of the behavioral and cognitive techniques that are used for instruction with people who are mentally retarded. In this chapter, you will see how these techniques can be used to enable students with disabilities to join in learning and extracurricular activities with their peers. In addition, Chapter 12 presents many of the innovations and methods that present-day educators use to meet the goals of educating *all* children. In particular, it describes the educational placement options available for children with MR, as well as some of the instructional methods used in teaching them. In addition, it explains the importance of facilitating the passage between formal schooling and entry into the adult world, especially for children with disabilities, while it also describes current methods for ensuring the success of that important transition.

Our schools now face serious challenges imposed by the culture of which they are a part. Modern children suffer increasing poverty, homelessness, drug addiction, and alienation—serious social and cultural problems that inevitably affect the extent to which schools are able to educate and ultimately graduate students who are ready not only to live productive lives themselves but also to combat and reduce those very problems with which they themselves have been reared. Even while faced with such demands, however, many schools are managing to provide effective educational experiences for children who have a wider range of abilities than ever before.

Because modern schools strive to educate children from increasingly diverse backgrounds and are committed both legally and idealistically to providing an effective education for all children—regardless of intellectual ability—more than ever the cooperation of the larger society is absolutely required. In addition to the support of state and local governments, the coordinated efforts of families, businesses, and community leaders are essential. Effective educational practice depends upon interdisciplinary collaboration that emerges from a recognition of the multiplicity of influences on today's children—and from one that values and respects the efforts of all involved. Educational issues are not only of interest to those who expect to be special educators or general education teachers, but also of central importance to anyone interested in people with mental retardation.

> **FOR DISCUSSION**   *How might students who plan careers in nursing, social work, or therapeutic recreation apply their knowledge about educational services and instructional methods to benefit children with special needs?*

SCHOOL PLACEMENT OPTIONS

The Individuals with Disabilities Education Act (PL 105-17/IDEA) entitles all children with mental retardation (regardless of severity) to a free public education in the least restrictive environment (LRE). As a result, all public schools provide educational opportunities for children with MR. Many parochial schools have special education programs too, and many other private schools (both day and residential) offer an education for individuals with special needs. Though these other

Full inclusion in the regular classroom
Partial inclusion in the regular classroom
Separate special education classroom in regular school
Separate school
    Day program
    Residential

FIGURE 12.1 Alternative placement options

options do exist, the vast majority of children with mental retardation attend public schools.

Within the public school system, there are also many alternatives, although these differ among school districts. In addition to special education programs within the regular schools, some districts have separate schools exclusively for children with disabilities, and others have separate schools primarily but not exclusively for those with disabilities, and include some regular students in their classrooms.

Within the general education system itself, children with disabilities are sometimes educated entirely within separate classrooms, though more commonly even special education students with severe disabilities are included (at least part of the day) in some classes (or activities) with typical children (Arnold & Serpas, 1993). Increasingly, too, children with mental retardation receive *all* of their educational services in the same classroom and extracurricular settings as their nondisabled peers. Figure 12.1 lists alternatives for educating children with MR.

Inclusion: The Philosophical Ideal

Inclusion is both a practice and an ideology. In practice, it means that children with disabilities are included in the regular classroom rather than receive their education in separate special education classes. As an ideal, this is the natural outgrowth of normalization.

Recall that normalization is a principle that insists upon the right of people with disabilities to take full part in ordinary life. In keeping with this principle, inclusion is based on the belief that all children are entitled to membership in a regular classroom with same-age peers, disabilities notwithstanding. It is this philosophy that drives the **Regular Education Initiative** (REI), a movement that seeks to unite regular and special education to serve the needs of all children. REI developed in response to a proposal by Madeleine Will, former assistant secretary of the Office of Special Education in the federal Department of Education (Will, 1986). She suggested that general education and special education systems join forces to meet the needs of all children within the regular classroom. According to this plan, special educators would team teach with, be consultants for, or provide support services for regular educators. The goals of the REI go beyond inclusion, because they specifically aim for radical change in the structure of service delivery within the schools (Lipsky & Gartner, 1990). Still, inclusion provides the primary mechanism for that change.

Proponents of the REI have several reasons for believing that children with mental retardation are better served in a regular class. One important factor is the influence that nondisabled peers can have as role models of age-appropriate behavior. As we learned in Chapter 2, modeling is a basic mechanism for learning, so school hours spent with same-age peers offer a profound learning opportunity.

For children with retardation, the strongest predictors of successful integration in both work and home settings are (1) the absence of maladaptive behaviors and (2) the presence of good social skills. These variables are more important than either IQ or academic skills (Haney, 1988). If children are to be welcomed in ordinary community work and leisure environments, then they must be able to get along well with others—a skill that requires ample practice. For these reasons, children with mental retardation must be included in as many community activities with nondisabled people as possible; in that important effort, schools play a major role. After all, the ultimate goal of education is for children to eventually function successfully in the adult world.

> **FOR DISCUSSION**   *In what other community settings besides schools can children with disabilities take part?*

The inclusion of children with mental retardation can also offer an advantage to typical children. If we, as a community, are committed to the idea that people with MR have a right to remain with their families, neighbors, and peers, then it is important to rear our children with that reality. It is natural for young people (and, perhaps, for anyone) to be afraid of those who look or behave in a way that seems unusual. When children share everyday activities with others who have disabilities, they learn that variations in physical and mental functioning are to be expected, and they develop a more accepting attitude. If, in the process, children also learn that it is appropriate and desirable to both provide and receive help and assistance from one another, it is an added benefit.

Dissatisfaction with Special Education

Before the turn of this century, most children with mental retardation were either taught in separate residential institutions or, for those with milder conditions, regular classrooms with same-age peers. Those within the regular schools were sometimes helped along at their own level, although many dropped out as they saw that they could not keep up. After 1900, a few separate classes for "slower learners" began to appear within some public schools—although schools were in no way required to provide special services. By the 1940s and 1950s, parents and advocates of special children had developed a large number of separate day schools (Brown et al., 1994). As special classes (and special separate schools) became more common, a debate also emerged about "the best place" for educating youngsters with special needs.

Those who believed that separate special education was ineffective cited research showing that children with MR taught in special classes were no better either academically or in their adjustment to school than those taught in the regular classroom (Dunn, 1968). Extraordinarily high dropout rates (56 percent) for students in special education were cited. There also have been allegations that the special education system is untenably expensive, exists mostly to perpetuate itself, and has become intractable (Stainback & Stainback, 1984).

> **FOR DISCUSSION**   *Studies that compare achievement and adjustment of students with retardation in regular and special education classes compare average scores. What would be found if approximately the same number of those in both settings scored above and below the average? If this were the case, then what could such studies predict about the "best placement" for an individual student? Please explain.*

Critics cite the many existing problems with accurate assessment and labeling (see Chapter 4) and charge that placement in special classes has largely been the result of teacher and peer rejection (Lipsky & Gartner, 1987). Thus, special education has been sometimes seen as housing students who are unable to get along with others, do not fit the regular system, or are excluded for reasons of misunderstanding or prejudice. Statistics showing that special education classes are filled disproportionately with minority students (see Chapter 4) fuel this criticism.

REI advocates believe that the emphasis on identifying deficits (and placement based on those deficits) must change to emphasize the identification of strengths and educational strategies based on those strengths. Such notions are consistent with the ideas of Gardner and his perspective of multiple intelligences (see Chapter 2).

Advocates of *separate* special education, on the other hand, point out that some children—particularly those with severe learning problems—may actually be better served in a self-contained environment, where all of the activities are relevant to their needs and where they can get more one-on-one attention from the staff. Furthermore, students with severe behavioral problems are by definition highly disruptive and can seriously interfere with the learning environment of other students (Walker & Bullis, 1990). Also, children with extensive medical needs require services that are often unavailable in regular schools (Russell & Forness, 1985).

A compromise between these positions occurs with the practice of **mainstreaming,** an early response to PL 94-142, whereby students with disabilities are integrated with nondisabled peers for a portion of the day, often for activities that do not involve academics. Typical mainstream settings include recess, lunch, physical education, and art. In addition, special students (usually with milder disabilities) have been mainstreamed in certain subjects where, with minimal help, they can keep up on their own.

The IDEA mandate for least restrictive environment was intended to promote integration and normalization, and it has encouraged placement in public rather than separate schools, and in regular rather than special classes. It does not

Mainstreaming: Education for a child with disabilities with same-age peers in settings where the child can keep up.

Least restrictive environment: Provision in IDEA that requires students with disabilities to be educated to the maximum extent appropriate alongside their peers without disabilities.

Regular Education Initiative (REI): Movement to combine the resources of special education and general education to serve all students.

Inclusion: Education of students with disabilities in general education classrooms.

Educational integration: The term for inclusion most often used outside the United States.

FIGURE 12.2 Comparison of terms

specifically state, however, that the regular class setting is the least restrictive environment for every child.

Inclusion differs philosophically from mainstreaming primarily in its conviction (promoted most radically by REI) that *all* children are entitled to an education with their same-age peers. The philosophy of inclusion, then, is to place children in the general education setting for all subjects and to bring special education services to the child rather than take the child out of the class to the services.

Distinctions among the terms *mainstreaming, inclusion, least restrictive environment,* and *Regular Education Initiative* are subtle and far from absolute. Many authors think of *inclusion,* for example, simply as a term more modern than *mainstreaming.* Moreover, all of the above terms are most often heard in the United States, while **educational integration** is the term more commonly used in Canada, Australia, Great Britain, and other European countries (Hardman, Drew, & Egan, 1996). The various terms used to describe the practice of educating children with disabilities with their same-age nondisabled peers are summarized in Figure 12.2.

Inclusion in Actual Practice

Virtually no one would argue with the ideals that underlie inclusion, but in actual practice there is controversy and there are problems. For one thing, many teachers in regular education have had little or no preparation for teaching children with disabilities (Freiberg, 1994), and many did not expect to do so when they entered teaching. When confronted with special needs children, some teachers have felt "at a loss" and have been frustrated and resentful with a challenge that they felt unprepared to meet.

At least as important, children have sometimes been included—"dumped," some say—in general education settings without accompanying resources to meet their special needs. An example is when several children with severe learning and behavior problems are included in a regular classroom without help from special educators or aides. Such practices have been severely criticized as attempts to save

A Special Education Teacher Discusses One Separate School

Steve Goodman is a special education teacher at the Ottawa Area Center in western Michigan and a doctoral candidate in applied behavior management. Here he talks about some of the advantages of a separate center-based school for children with severe disabilities.

One of the advantages of a center-based program is that all of the disciplines are located in the same building. We have the occupational therapist, physical therapist, nursing staff, and speech therapist who are all right here. Instead of spending so much time traveling from program to program, they have a chance to get to know the students well, and the staff all know each other well, too. I think that's a benefit, and that it contributes to good communication.

Another nice thing is that they had our students in mind when the facility was built. The rooms are designed so that everything is wheelchair-accessible, including the countertops and the size of the doorways and corridors. When the bus pulls up, there is a wheelchair ramp, and even the playground items are all accessible.

We have some students who are medically fragile and others who have severe behavior problems. Some of those kids went to regular schools, and they weren't making it at all. I know some people would argue against this, but I believe that we provide a service for those students. If regular schools are going to serve these kids, then they will have to provide nursing staff and behavior specialists to take care of their needs—and they certainly are not doing that now.

We can also be a stepping stone for some who have come here right from residential institutions. We can provide a transition between the institution and the larger community.

But there are disadvantages, too. One is that the staff are the ones modeling social skills for our students, and they really need peer modeling, too. Also, we are out in the country, and it's hard to teach community-based skills in a community setting when we are surrounded by cornfields. We do take field trips and go on the bus to the bowling alley and roller skating. But it's a problem to be so far away. So there are both advantages and disadvantages.

money at the expense of children with disabilities. As changes within the special and regular education alternatives evolve, it will be essential that funds intended to provide services for children with special needs are not diverted from those children and that children with disabilities are not left to flounder in the general education system under the guise of promised "normalcy" (Kauffman, 1990).

Finally, for the few children with extremely severe intellectual or behavioral disabilities (and who also may be medically fragile), the regular class not only may provide no advantage, but also may actually pose a disadvantage. It will be crucial that more segregated options remain available for such children as these.

FOR DISCUSSION   *How might schools be designed to provide the advantages of both center-based separate schools and regular general education schools?*

There are persuasive research findings insisting that both academic and social skills are improved in regular class settings, *if effective programming is in place* (even for children with severe disabilities, including autism) (Cafiero, 1998; Staub, 1998). In the absence of appropriate programming, however, these improvements do not occur—and in such instances regular class inclusion can actually be detrimental (Gottlieb, Alter, & Gottlieb, 1990).

STEPS TOWARD SUCCESSFUL INCLUSION

For the vast majority of children with disabilities, inclusion can be a viable option, *if* the regular education setting is designed to accommodate them. Classes in which teachers lecture at the front of the room, where students are merely passive note takers, or where the sheer number of students enrolled is already too large are not conducive to learning for any student—least of all those with special needs (Hocutt, Martin, & McKinney, 1990).

The MRDD Division of the Council for Exceptional Children has submitted a position statement on the need for adequate preparation and training for inclusion. In part, it states:

> It is the position of the Board that preparation and training are essential to insure the creation of schools that effectively include students with developmental disabilities. Such preparation and training must focus not just on students with developmental disabilities in the area of academic study and social skills but on all members of the educational community. This preparation and training must include other students, parents, secretarial and custodial staff, bus drivers, professional support staff, teachers and administrators . . . and . . . must include knowledge of disabilities, encouragement of appropriate attitudes, legal and ethical issues, collaboration and methods of friendship development. Specific preparation and training is also necessary for teachers and administrators in assessment, advanced collaboration skills, effective practices for direct instruction and service delivery, transition, and the evaluation of educational outcomes. (Smith & Hilton, 1997)

With inclusion—as with any other venture—problems will inevitably occur, and it is not possible to overstate the importance of a positive attitude. That is not to say that every problem can be solved simply by believing that it can—because solutions often involve gaining new information, learning new skills, or obtaining new services or materials. Nevertheless, a positive attitude is the one essential variable; and although that alone may not be sufficient, without it only failure is assured (Hanrahan, Goodman, & Rapagna, 1990). This willingness to find answers might best be termed a "problem-solving approach" to whatever difficulties arise. In addition to a willing attitude, successful inclusion depends upon teacher and student preparation, particular knowledge and skills, material support, and adequate monitoring and evaluation of the transition from separate to general education (Walker & Bullis, 1990).

Teacher and Student Attitudes

One major factor in preparing regular education teachers involves learning the concept of normalization and the advantages of inclusion to both regular and special education students. Whenever regular teachers develop a genuine interest in helping students with disabilities learn, success is far more likely; without that willingness, failure is almost certain. To help teachers understand the importance of inclusion for special students, therefore, many schools offer in-service workshops and other training opportunities.

It is equally important that regular class students understand the goals of inclusion and actively welcome and encourage the participation of students with special needs. To promote understanding and acceptance, schools often schedule special assemblies in which adults with disabilities describe their challenges and successes and provide role models for young people. There also may be empathy-training sessions in which regular students get a chance to participate in activities (often with the opportunity to try out adaptive equipment) that help them understand the challenges of individuals with learning impairments or physical disabilities.

A crucial element in getting students to welcome those with diverse needs is to seek their help in achieving that goal. Once children understand the importance of respect and acceptance for special students, they should be asked, "How do you think we can accomplish these goals? What are your ideas?" Involving students in planning for inclusion will make the goals mutually theirs and help avoid a situation in which mandates are "imposed" by adults. When students adopt inclusion goals as their own, they are far more likely to follow the venture and participate in its success.

Books that Reflect Diversity

Children are influenced in important ways by the books they read. Books explain the world, and they influence children's attitudes and beliefs about the way the world both is and should be. The illustration of children with disabilities (including mental retardation) in books and school posters is significant to their acceptance in both school and the larger community; yet probably no other group has been so underrepresented and misrepresented in children's and adult's literature, the popular press, and films.

In a review of hundreds of children's books, Blaska and Lynch (1998) found only 2 percent had any reference to people with disabilities, and only a fraction of those involved people with mental retardation. Such low numbers provide a distorted reflection of the actual frequency of people with disabilities in the population and mirror instead the past prevailing attitude of "out of sight, out of mind." More recently, though, books that portray children with disabilities in an accurate and respectful manner have become available (Blaska & Lynch, 1998). Teachers must insist that children's books offer stories about all children (with and without disabilities), and teachers must seek out those books that provide accurate and empathic portrayals of the lives and abilities of children with mental retardation.

Circle of Friends: One Way to Encourage Understanding

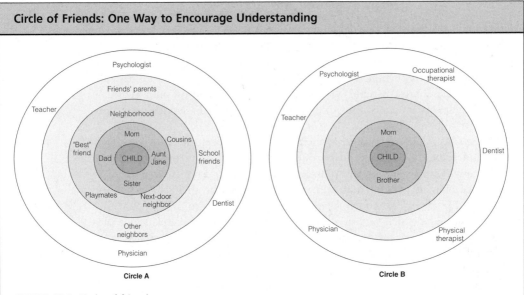

FIGURE 12.3 Circle of friends

The circle of friends is a technique for explaining the social goals of inclusion. Students are shown circles that illustrate typical patterns of relationship such as the ones above. In Figure 12.3, Circle A shows the relationship pattern for most people without disabilities.

The individual himself is in the middle circle; the next circle indicates those people to whom he is closest (and who are always on his side). The third circle represents those people who are important in his life but not quite as close as those in the second. The fourth is for people who are friendly acquaintances, neighbors, or peers. In the outermost circle are people who are paid to be in his life, such as teachers and physicians.

Circle B illustrates that for many who have disabilities, the only people in their lives are family members and a large number of paid people. These drawings provide a means for students to understand the importance of filling the empty circles.

Once students have generated ideas for meeting this goal, two or three peers can be chosen as a welcoming group to see that the new included student feels comfortable and learns the ropes. Initially, it is best to choose class leaders for this role, because then other class members will be more eager to get involved. With such a circle of friends, the initial transition from a separate class can be eased, and the chance of a successful adjustment is greatly enhanced.

Knowledge and Skills

Although understanding and acceptance are the essential first components in teacher preparation, the process cannot stop there. Teachers also need knowledge of the instructional and organizational methods that are most likely to be effective with special students. They also need to be proficient with the behavioral and cognitive techniques (see Chapter 11) that will help them create a disciplined and respectful classroom in which all students can learn. Such training is, of course, an advantage for any teacher, whether or not students have formally identified disabilities.

Teachers also benefit from a knowledge of disabilities. As he becomes more familiar with the characteristics and capabilities of students with disabilities, the teacher will be better able to apply his skills to good advantage and probably become more accepting as well.

Although special education teachers also are usually certified to teach regular education, teacher education for regular educators unfortunately does little to prepare them for working with children with special needs. Such undergraduate preparation is but one essential aspect, however, of the creation of communities that acknowledge disabilities as a frequent and therefore normal part of human existence and one that promotes the recognition of people with disabilities as legitimate participants in community life. As people with disabilities take their rightful place in community living, not only teachers, but also all professionals (whether physicians, dentists, psychologists, social workers, or others) will need to be prepared to serve a diverse and integrated—rather than select and segregated—population.

> **FOR DISCUSSION**   *With the goal of community integration in mind, why is education about disabilities important for all professionals? Describe possible circumstances in which professionals will be likely to use this information even though they are not working in a field typically thought of as related to disabilities.*

Emotional and Material Support

To help students with diverse needs meet their educational goals, teachers need both emotional and material support. This means they require encouragement when they meet challenges, as well as actual physical and intellectual assistance.

In that context, the school principal plays an essential role in successful inclusion. To begin with, she is in a position to create an atmosphere of encouragement and cooperation that influences teachers and students alike, so when teachers experience problems and setbacks, they have support for working out those difficulties. Equally important, the principal can set priorities that provide teachers with essential material supports.

For successful inclusion, the expertise of special educators is crucial. It is to them that regular educators must turn for help in devising instructional methods, for information about disabilities, and as a wellspring of actual experience from which they can draw (Stump & Wilson, 1996). Furthermore, as inclusion efforts develop and expand, both special and regular teachers will need to team with other disciplines in providing the services that effective education requires (Bauer & Shea, 1999).

Educators should also have access to the effective behavioral technology that is available to help most students adjust to community living in and out of the classroom (Kratochwill & Sheridan, 1990). Unfortunately, teachers seldom have adequate support in this crucial area. Because behavioral problems threaten successful inclusion—perhaps more than any other single challenge—support in developing effective interventions (together with help in implementing those plans) represents an essential piece of the successful inclusion picture.

Advantages of Behavioral Consultation

Because appropriate behavior is so important for successful community integration (including educational inclusion), some professionals believe that behavioral management should be a more integral part of school programming than is currently the case. Even for many students who are not officially labeled, self-discipline and self-determination are major problems. Although many teachers are skilled in behavioral management techniques, they can often benefit from collaboration with behavior specialists in instances in which students exhibit extreme or unusually intractable problem behaviors (Kratochwill & Sheridan, 1990).

Behavioral consultants provide indirect services to a client, usually through a teacher or parent who then works directly with the child. Consultants assist in identifying and analyzing problem behaviors, as well as in guiding the consultee through treatment, implementation, and evaluation. Ongoing collaboration between consultant and consultee is crucial to ensure success, because program revisions are commonly required during the course of an intervention.

Because students exist within a much larger community of family and school, programs may involve changes in this wider environment and cannot simply focus on a student's personal behavior. Furthermore, goals may often aim to prevent difficulties such as inappropriate placements or escalating behavioral problems.

To increase the availability of behavioral consultation, some professionals have suggested that school psychological services should change their emphases from assessment and eligibility to consultation for classroom problems and issues of student adjustment. The opportunity to develop such collaborative relationships may be enhanced by the current trend toward team assessment and eligibility determination, thus freeing school psychologists to spend increased time in behavioral consulting and collaboration for all students.

Finally, evaluation research will play an invaluable role in determining the characteristics and settings associated with the greatest academic improvement, and in identifying the most effective methods for creating a school atmosphere that is best suited to the success of all students. Although children with disabilities have a right to remain with their peers—and such inclusion can benefit children both with and without disabilities—we must ensure that the emotional and educational welfare of children is not sacrificed for the ideal (Smith & Bassett, 1990; Hocutt, Martin, & McKinney, 1990). Evaluation research must be an integral piece of system modifications and changes, even as it continues to play an increasing role in the existing educational environment.

INSTRUCTIONAL METHODS FOR MEETING THE NEEDS OF DIVERSE POPULATIONS

Students in *all* settings (not just in special education) vary in intellectual, social, behavioral, and emotional characteristics (Stainback, Stainback, & Forest, 1989), and many of the failures for regular students are created by inadequate consideration of individual differences. Like Joyce Elger in our case stories, there are countless students who are not officially labeled but who have real needs for individual help. When such needs are ignored, these students usually fail or drop out (Schumaker & Deshler, 1988). Effective education for each child means finding a way to meet the needs of at-risk but unlabeled students, as well as those who are officially acknowledged.

The following section discusses effective instructional methods for teaching students who have diverse needs and abilities. Although these methods have been found to be effective for children with disabilities in the regular classroom, they are just as applicable to separate special education settings.

Teaching Children with Fetal Alcohol Problems (FAS and FAE)

Children with fetal alcohol syndrome (FAS) and fetal alcohol effect (FAE) (see Chapter 8) face serious challenges to their growth and development as independently functioning people. Although those with FAE show less severe intellectual and physical disabilities, their problems may be "even more frustrating than those of youngsters with FAS. Children often appear normal, more is expected of them, and they are less likely to qualify for special services" (Kleinfeld & Wescott, 1993, p. 27.)

Incorporating drawing and singing into lesson plans are two ways to help children with FAS (and FAE). Perhaps because many of these children have good visual skills, their memory recall is often enhanced when they draw a picture (or watch someone else draw one) of facts and concepts. It is important to note that these good results seem to occur only when children view or participate in the actual process of drawing, not when they are passive viewers of pictures from books or magazines. Putting ideas to music also can help children remember, and it can aid in refocusing their attention; soft background music can help them stay calm.

Lack of visual clutter is important. Rooms should be arranged so that children can readily see which activity goes on in which areas. For the same reasons, worksheets and handouts should be visually simple and make liberal use of white space. Children with FAS should be assigned short tasks that are simply and clearly defined; tests should be short and should not be timed.

Visual cues can help with the problems that children with FAS often experience when changing activities and attempting to adjust to new ones. Pictures can be used as reminders of class routine, and handpuppets can act to signal activity changes. One should always explain new situations several times in advance, making sure to use eye contact, touch, or the child's name to get his attention. Instructions and lessons can be recorded on audiotape, too, so that the students can listen to them over and again. The use of headphones can protect other children from disturbance and provide a noise screen for the child with FAS.

Because children with FAS can easily become overwhelmed by stimuli, it is important to provide a quiet or safe place to which they can withdraw and calm down. Often they can learn to control impulsive behavior through modeling, role-playing, and practice. As with any child, it is best to redirect their unruly behavior, reward good behavior, and avoid punishment.

Adapted from J. Kleinfeld & S. Wescott (1993), *Fantastic Antone succeeds.* Anchorage: University of Alaska Press.

Peer Tutoring

Peer tutoring is a technique in which same- or different-age pairs of students work together on a common goal. Ordinarily this occurs within a single classroom, though some schools have programs that assign students from different classes (and sometimes different grades) to work together. Peer tutoring has several advantages for both tutors and tutees. First, because tutors themselves have more recently mastered content material, they may be better able to identify confusing aspects and thus better explain ideas so that the learner can understand. Besides, the learner may enjoy the attention of the tutor and gain both an advocate and a new friend from the relationship. As a result, the learner may be especially motivated to work at the lessons. Peer tutoring also provides a means for students to receive extra one-on-one instruction. Finally, as many practicing teachers have observed, a concept is never understood so well as when one attempts to teach it, so peer tutors gain expertise themselves from the rich experience of teaching.

Cooperative Learning

In **cooperative learning,** groups of students work together toward a common goal. To achieve their goal, cooperation and mutual responsibility are required of the entire group (Meese, 1994). When groups are composed of students of mixed abilities, cooperative learning offers the advantages of peer tutoring as well as a situation in which children with lower abilities have legitimate, valued, and crucial functions within the group. Because cooperation is required, conflicts inevitably arise, which creates the opportunity for students to learn important social skills such as conflict management and leadership. The ability to achieve goals through teamwork is a highly valued necessity in employment settings from fast food restaurants to corporate management, and to become an effective collaborator is of enormous benefit for all students—just as it is for all professionals.

Research indicates that students with intellectual disabilities are often better accepted by their peers both in the classroom and outside when they are taught by cooperative methods in contrast to control groups taught by lecture and individual assignment (Madden & Slavin, 1983). Highly persuasive evidence also demonstrates that cooperative learning results in enhanced achievement scores for students with and without mental retardation (Stevens, Madden, Slavin, & Farnish, 1987).

The specific collaborative methods used in these studies varied in several ways, but the two essential elements are: (1) a team goal that requires the cooperation and achievement of all members, and (2) individual assessment of achievement. Individual assessment means that, in addition to the successful completion of the goal, each student receives individual testing of his knowledge and performance to ensure that each group member is learning and contributing. Often these scores are based on improvements from previous performance or in some other way take into account the varying abilities of group members.

Finally, there are many curricular systems for devising effective lessons based on cooperative learning, including Student Teams Achievement Divisions (STAD) (Slavin, 1990), Team Assisted Individualization (TAI) (Slavin, Leavey, & Madden, 1986), and Cooperative Integrated Reading and Composition (CIRC) (Madden,

Computers can add excitement to learning and even provide opportunities for social interaction.

© Elizabeth Crews

Slavin, & Stevens, 1986). All of these programs can be used in a classroom of students with diverse needs (Slavin, 1984; Slavin, Stevens, & Madden, 1988).

Computer-Aided Instruction

The recent emergence of computer instruction in the classroom corresponds with the widespread use of computers in business, industry, and higher education. Young people who now enter the workforce must be familiar with computer operation, regardless of the setting in which they plan to work. Computers, however, provide additional advantages for those with disabilities—that is, they actually provide a means for communication and an opportunity for learning that could exist through no other means (Susan's story in Chapter 9 is an example).

Computers can be a fun and exciting way for children to learn new concepts and improve their skills. They allow children to progress at their own rate of learning, while also offering a mechanism for group activities. Children with attention problems may be better able to focus on computer activities, in part because such activities are often fast-paced and multisensory. Computers also provide a kind of one-on-one responsiveness that frees teachers to work individually with other children. Hundreds of choices for educational software offer visually appealing, multisensory instruction for all ages, ability levels, and subjects.

Susan

Susan's Team: Peer Tutoring, Cooperative Learning, and Computer Instruction

When we last saw Susan, she was learning to manage her reactions to teasing and her tendency to have her feelings hurt so easily. Susan now has built-in opportunities to practice her new skills, because her teacher, Ms. Anderson, includes many cooperative learning assignments in her lesson planning.

Most recently, Susan took part in a team assigned to develop a computer presentation to demonstrate equivalent fractions. The other members of her group—April, Dan, and Joe—were chosen so that there would be an equal number of boys and girls in the group, and because those students represented a mixture of math abilities. April and Dan have a good grasp of fifth-grade math and are working beyond that level. Joe is currently mastering fifth-grade work, and Susan is working on concepts typical of those first presented in second grade.

The team's initial task was to choose a name for the group and to assign each person to project roles. Although some team members had worked together before, these particular students had not previously formed a team, so these beginning tasks gave them the opportunity to get to know each other and begin to develop a team spirit.

Susan's team earned group points for (1) the effectiveness with which they demonstrated equivalent fractions with their program; (2) for the clarity with which each member could explain and demonstrate the workings of the program; (3) for staying on task, and checking each other's understanding of the task; and (4) for encouraging each other's participation and managing disagreements in a friendly and constructive manner. In addition, each team member earned points for the group on individual assessment of material related to the group task. April and Dan were tested on their ability to apply calculation of equivalent fractions to real-world applications. Joe took a test on procedural calculations of equivalent fractions, and Susan was tested on her ability to show her understanding of $\frac{1}{2}$ and $\frac{3}{4}$ with concrete objects.

Susan's team took one week to finish its computer program. The group members had two computers available to them (including Susan's), and Susan was assigned the role of entering information into her computer (with the team's guidance). The other three team members took turns working with Susan and working on the other computer. At the end of each session, they reviewed their progress with Ms. Anderson, smoothing out any problems they were having and deciding on strategies for the next session.

When a disagreement arose about the stimulus materials to use for the task, the team had an opportunity to practice its conflict-management skills. Susan wanted to use fashions, and Joe wanted to use race cars to demonstrate fractional concepts, while April and Dan believed the materials should be something that could be more easily and obviously divided into equal parts. It was eventually decided to use circles and squares for the main demonstration of the concept and then to show how simple equivalent fractions could be used in measuring material for fashions and in manufacturing car parts.

Through this exercise, Susan and her teammates gained hands-on experience with equivalent fractions, gained new computer skills, experienced success in conflict management, enhanced their friendly relationships with each other, and last, but not least, had a very good time.

Interdisciplinary Practice

Whether children with mental retardation are educated in a separate special education classroom or in a regular class, transdisciplinary cooperation for speech, occupational therapy, and psychological and other services provides real advantages and is considered current best practice. As discussed in Chapter 1, special services can often be best administered in a child's educational setting, where the benefits gained are more likely to be generalized to activities throughout the day. Service provision within the classroom also provides an opportunity for interaction and discussion among professionals on a child's team that results in clarification of goals, and it also acts to prevent overlap and conflict. Figure 12.4 shows some of the objectives for therapists and teachers in providing such collaborative services.

Direct Instruction Techniques

Techniques of direct instruction—including reinforcement, modeling, task analysis, chaining, prompts, graduated guidance, and visual aids (see Chapter 11)—are at the heart of most instructional methods. Notice, for example, how peer tutoring, collaborative learning, and computer-aided instruction all involve the use of some of these teaching skills.

Unlike other youngsters, students with intellectual disabilities typically do not make spontaneous use of rehearsal, and they need direct instruction in strategy and memory skills (Torgesen, 1982). They also require more explicit and repetitive instruction in problem-solving strategies such as setting their own goals, monitoring their own performance, and identifying their mistakes.

Picture sequencing (such as that used in guided imagery techniques; see Chapter 11) can help students organize their time and activities. A similar method, **picture task analysis,** can be used to aid children with both severe and mild disabilities (Roberson, Gravel, Valcante, & Maurer, 1992) in comprehending instructions and concepts, and in enhancing memory storage and recall. In picture task analysis, photographs, line drawings, or other characters and symbols are used to represent each step in a task analysis. The teacher reviews each step with the student by pointing to the representation and reading an accompanying sentence. The teacher then models the task step-by-step while the student follows along with each picture. For her turn, the student reverses roles and uses the picture task analysis to prompt the teacher in each step. Then, finally, the student begins performing steps herself until the teacher's presence is eventually faded.

In these procedures—as indeed with most teaching techniques—immediate feedback is crucial for success. When children respond accurately, a nod and a smile, repetition of the correct answer (e.g., "Yes, that's right, next you get the

Therapist Objectives

1. Consult with teachers about the needs of all students in the classroom.
2. Demonstrate suggestions until the teachers become proficient in teaching the skills to their students.
3. Engage in at least some direct assessment and instruction where appropriate (possibly team teaching).
4. Discuss student progress within the program and program changes as a result of student performance.

Teacher Objectives

1. Provide the therapist with a description of the instructional objectives for each student (social skills, self-care, academic skills, etc.).
2. Seek information for incorporating the therapist's objectives into other curriculum domains.
3. Implement suggestions.
4. Record student performance.
5. Use recorded information in discussing student progress and in making program revisions.

FIGURE 12.4 Objectives for therapists and teachers

SOURCE: Adapted from J. Nietupski, G. Scheutz, & L. Ockwood (1980), The delivery of communication therapy services to severely handicapped students: A plan for change. *Journal of the Association for the Severely Handicapped (JASH)*, 5(1), 13–23.

scissors"), or a word of praise can let them know that they have succeeded. When inaccuracies occur, students should be guided gently and immediately toward success. This can be accomplished through rephrasing the question or through prompts and verbal encouragement (Meese, 1994.) Successful teaching techniques and skills of reinforcement and feedback should be shared between parents and teachers and used to enhance the success of the working partnership between them as members of a student's team.

Education Through the Arts

Music, dance, painting, and drawing provide a medium for students to demonstrate not only their emotions, but also their ideas. For students with MR, these can offer a powerful means of communication and sharing that may not be otherwise available, and for the teacher of students with intellectual disabilities, the arts provide a treasury of instructional resources. Some children can understand ideas much better when they are illustrated in pictures and drawings than when they are verbally explained (for example, children with FAS; see Chapter 8). Through the arts, students also can practice and experience self-determination (Harris, 1993). Children of all intellectual abilities can participate, too, and some students with academic limitations may find their own special opportunity to shine through an art form.

Drama is yet another art form that offers a strong occasion for children with severe disabilities to interact with their nondisabled peers. Miller, Rynders, and

Schleien (1993) found that students with mental retardation were capable of carrying out imaginary roles, and that drama eliminated the risk involved in taking part in group activities. By means of make-believe, the children in their study were able to put aside self-consciousness and the fear of making a mistake and were able to "throw themselves into" their imaginary roles. Especially encouraging was the bond of camaraderie that was created in the dramatic sessions between regular and special students, a closeness that carried over afterward into the outside world.

Remember that role-playing is a technique frequently used to demonstrate new concepts and allow students with MR the chance to try out and perfect new skills. The same student abilities that allow for successful role-playing can be applied to other dramatic and imaginary situations in which all students can learn and laugh together and build relationships that provide the basis for integrated community life.

Incorporating Multiple Approaches

Teaching is a demanding profession that requires knowledge of and skillful management of cognitive, emotional, developmental, and behavioral principles within the context of highly developed pedagogical methods. One of the most challenging elements is knowing what to do when, and which technique will work and for whom. That knowledge and expertise can only really come from the experiences of watching effective teachers and trying many strategies on one's own.

No one best method or technique is suitable for every situation or student. Most research shows, for example, that both sight word and phonics methods for teaching reading are successful. Some children benefit more from one of those than the other, and many benefit the most with both, so students should have the advantage of being exposed to more than one method (Conners, 1992). The best teachers use multiple approaches, remain open to new ideas, and constantly evaluate the results of their own efforts in terms of their students' achievement.

TRANSITION

The move from the life of a high school student to that of an adult is nearly always challenging, and most young people require considerable assistance at that juncture. For some, adults give help in applying to and choosing a college, while assistance for others is required in leasing a first apartment or finding a job. For students with disabilities, such help is essential.

Statistics reveal the poor employment outcomes for the more than 50,000 young adults with disabilities who graduate from high school each year (Rusch, Szymanski, & Chadsey-Rusch, 1992). When we consider the even greater number who drop out before graduation, the necessity for helping these young people in their adjustment to adult responsibilities becomes unmistakably clear. Fortunately, there is evidence that transition services can result in substantially brighter futures for many of these youth (Rusch & Phelps, 1987).

Step 1. Gather and share relevant information with the team.

Step 2. Include parent and student input.

Step 3. Study the current environments and activities of the student and decide upon needed changes.

Step 4. Specify future opportunities where the student can develop new skills, abilities, and experiences.

Step 5. Design plans to realize the team's vision for the student.

FIGURE 12.5 Steps in transition planning

Transition services are now mandated for every student served under PL 105-17 (IDEA). The portion of the individualized education plan (IEP) that covers transition plans is called the **individualized transition plan** (ITP). Many of the skills necessary for success in the adult world, however, require much practice and experience and are best learned throughout the developing years (social skills would be a prime example). It is not adequate, therefore, to wait until high school to begin thinking about a child's future. Educational experiences should be planned *now* for the adult skills that children will inevitably require. Figure 12.5 will show the steps in transition planning.

Interagency Collaboration

Transition provides yet another example of the need for interdisciplinary collaboration in service delivery. Within the school system, several professionals may be involved, including teachers, counselors, and special therapists. The student herself and her parents are, of course, indispensable members of the team. In addition, though transition plans are usually coordinated by the school system, the expertise and involvement of other agencies are also required by the ITP team. Besides schools, agencies often involved in transition planning include rehabilitation agencies, parent and advocate organizations, Big Brother and Big Sister programs, community colleges and universities, vocational and job-training agencies, and residential living providers.

Sharing information is a primary function of interagency collaboration. Schools must provide agencies with the number of students who will be seeking employment and the types of services that these students will need, whereas job-training agencies should supply information about the numbers and kinds of jobs that are available in the community. In addition, good communication between schools and potential employers or job agencies will enhance the available opportunities for graduating students. Finally, school and community agencies can often form arrangements in which they share staff members and other resources that are mutually beneficial (McDonnell, Ferguson, & Mathot-Buckner, 1992), and they also can cooperatively arrange for data collection and evaluation of the success of transition programs (Bates, Bronkema, Ames, & Hess, 1992).

The Dilemma of At-Risk and Unlabeled Youth

Unlike young people with labeled disabilities such as MR and LD, many students have problems in school but are not entitled to an IEP or ITP. Under previous definitions, many of these students would have been diagnosed with mental retardation. Some of these students have been subsumed under the learning disabilities category, but many have not because they do not fit the typical LD profile (wide discrepancies in skills). Still, they have genuine intellectual—and often social adjustment—problems. These students receive neither the life skills nor the occupational training that could make a positive difference in their successes in adult life.

In addition, some students who are labeled with mild retardation or learning disabilities (and who are often included in regular classrooms) likewise fail to receive the life skills training they need. These students have high dropout rates and low rates of successful employment after leaving high school. For many of these students, there is convincing evidence that transition plans that include a career education curriculum would make the difference between later success and failure (Rusch & Phelps, 1987).

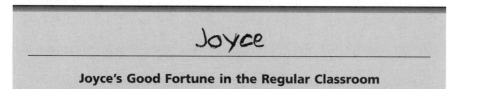

Joyce's Good Fortune in the Regular Classroom

Joyce is a good example of the type of student who is quite likely to fall through the cracks and not get the extra help she needs to become a successful adult because her intellectual and adaptive abilities do not make her eligible for mandated services. She is also the type of student who would often be called a slow learner. In her elementary and middle-school years, Joyce was educated in a classroom for children with learning disabilities, although she did not meet the typical profile of a student with LD—and in many districts she would not have received that label. For Joyce, the LD placement had both advantages and disadvantages, but one emphatic advantage was that she received an IEP.

Now in high school, Joyce is included in regular classes, even though she still needs extra support and guidance toward specific life experiences to help her gain the skill and the practice she needs to succeed. Joyce is receiving that guidance because she has an IEP and because her teachers have taken an interest in her. But these are aspects of fortune that many young people in Joyce's situation do not enjoy. Support and guidance from her teachers and her peer tutor have helped Joyce fit in with her classmates and enjoy extracurricular high school activities, and they also have provided her with occupational experiences that will likely lead to future employment. Surely all young people deserve these advantages.

SELF-DETERMINATION

Self-determination involves learning to take responsibility for one's own behavior and for decisions about life choices—from the everyday matters of choosing what to eat and what to wear to major decisions about where to live and work. Yet no one is completely self-determined; we all live within the constraints of law, family, public opinion, and socioeconomic opportunity. The sense of being in control of one's life, however, is an integral aspect of adulthood and affects both mental and physical health. Often professionals (or others) will decide that people with mental retardation are incapable of making their own decisions, because they do so illogically or irrationally—while a great many so-called normal people commonly make decisions on criteria other than logic or reason. Individuals sometimes toss a coin, draw straws, or decide based on what "feels right" or on what will please others (Racino, 1992). Most of us are entitled to make decisions on whatever basis we choose. Therefore, although it is important for people with MR to learn to make considered and wise choices, it sometimes helps to remember that the very fact that someone has a disability can make the standards by which they must live *more* stringent than they are for others.

Many people with MR display **outerdirectedness** in that they rely too much on external cues (see Chapter 6). This means that they depend upon clues from the environment even when these clues are not relevant or when they are capable of solving the problem on their own. This tendency on the part of those with MR can combine with overprotectiveness or lack of confidence on the part of parents and service providers and preclude students from making their own decisions and learning from their own mistakes. It is of the utmost importance that people with mental retardation are encouraged to rely on their own cognitive skills and opportunities through trial and error to both succeed and fail (Bybee & Zigler, 1999).

Opportunities for decision making and self-determination should be infused throughout the curriculum from the preschool years. By high school, transition plans must be based on student's individual abilities and interests, and to the maximum extent possible, students should make their own decisions about their future goals.

CAREER EDUCATION

Career education is a concept that constitutes a curriculum plan that covers the three major domains identified as essential for children with exceptionalities: (1) occupational guidance and preparation, (2) personal and social skills, and (3) daily living skills (Brolin, 1991). Because it is necessary to teach the skills that will actually be needed in community life, the selection of these skills is **community-referenced.** This means that school personnel work in cooperation with home and community services to design goals that are customized to the individual. There is much overlap among skills that make up the three categories, and they

Daily Living Skills

Managing personal finances
    Count money and make correct change.
    Use banking services.

Selecting and managing a household
    Choose adequate housing.
    Set up household.

Caring for personal needs
    Dress appropriately.
    Practice personal safety.

Raising children and meeting marriage responsibilities

Buying, preparing, and consuming food
    Purchase food.
    Prepare meals.

Buying and caring for clothing
    Purchase clothing.
    Wash or clean clothing.

Exhibiting responsible citizenship

Using recreational facilities and engaging in leisure

Getting around the community
    Know traffic and safety rules.
    Find way around community.

Personal and Social Skills

Achieving self-awareness
    Identify interests and abilities.
    Identify emotions.

Acquiring self-confidence
    Express feelings of self-worth.
    Accept and give praise.

Achieving socially responsible behavior
    Respect the rights and property of others.
    Behave appropriately in public places.

Maintaining good interpersonal skills

Making adequate decisions

Communicating with others

Occupational Guidance and Preparation

Knowing and exploring occupational possibilities

Selecting and planning occupational choices

Exhibiting appropriate work habits and behaviors
    Follow directions and observe regulations.
    Work at a satisfactory rate.

Seeking, securing, and maintaining employment

Exhibiting sufficient physical and manual skills

FIGURE 12.6 Examples of life skills included in career education curriculum

SOURCE: Adapted from D. E. Brolin (Ed.) (1991), *Life-centered career education: A competency based approach* (3rd ed.) Reston, VA: Council of Exceptional Children.

often all fall under the broader category of **life skills.** Many of these are listed in Figure 12.6.

Occupational Guidance and Preparation

Because there is much more to working in the community than simply learning the vocational skills necessary to do the job itself, students need training in such related areas as transportation, interviewing, and work habits. The abilities involved in work–related training are so broad that they more accurately fall under career education than vocational training.

    The selection of a particular curriculum for occupational training must be based upon the student's interests and capabilities. When young people have had no job experience, they cannot be expected to know the type of work for which they are best suited. The first step in such training, then, is to give students a sampling of various jobs so that they can experience options and identify preferences (McDonnell, Hardman, & Hightower, 1989). After students have had a chance to try out several job settings, it becomes more feasible to focus on specific job

Young people with mental retardation can do many things on their own.

© Elizabeth Crews

training. Students eligible for services under IDEA are entitled to a free public education through 21 years of age, so they can sample jobs and learn job-related skills in the early years of transition (approximately 14 to 18) and then spend the last two or three years in specific job training.

During these training periods, students often receive on-the-job help from a job coach. This coach can provide on-site job training and supervision and help keep things on an even keel by assisting the student with behavioral and social skills. Such specialized help eases the adjustment from a school to a work setting. Because there is evidence that the continued presence of a job coach can interfere with student integration with co-workers, however, (Udvari-Solner, Jorgensen, & Courchane, 1992), the assistance of the job coach should be gradually withdrawn over the transition period so that the student is taught to rely on herself as much as possible.

Social Skills

The importance of good social skills to successful community adjustment could hardly be overstated, whether in a regular classroom or in a work, residential, or leisure setting. In fact, retention in the job market for adults with MR depends upon adequate social skills. Yet, paradoxically, it is virtually impossible for a child with mental retardation to learn good social skills unless they are included in community activities. Therefore, the child who is included early and often and who receives social skills training from the time she is very young enjoys a considerable advantage.

Many of the same social skills especially valued by employers are also important in school and home life: asking for assistance, following directions, respond-

1. Beginning or entering an activity.
2. Keeping an activity or an event going.
3. Following rules and regulations.
4. Reinforcing and rewarding others.
5. Influencing others to stop a behavior.
6. Sharing information and feelings.
7. Indicating preferences.
8. Coping with negative situations.
9. Dealing with anger.
10. Solving problems.

FIGURE 12.7 Important social skills for all students

SOURCE: Adapted from R. S. Neal (1984), Teaching social routines to behaviorally disordered youth. In J. K. Grosenick, E. McGinnis, S. L. Huntze, and C. R. Smith (Eds.), *Social/affective interventions in behavioral disorders.* Des Moines: Iowa Department of Public Instruction.

ing well to criticism, getting needed information before a job begins, and offering assistance to others (Chadsey-Rusch & O'Reilly, 1992). In addition to these, it is essential that each of us learns to cope appropriately with interpersonal challenges and not respond with physical or verbal aggression. The fact that people with mental retardation must learn to handle insults, aggression by others, and injustice only serves to place them in situations we all face.

As with any other instruction, the selection of which skills to teach should naturally be based on the individual's needs. Once the relevant skills are selected, modeling and role-playing are then used to teach and reinforce them. It is important to help students identify both appropriate and inappropriate examples of a particular skill. If Bob is learning an acceptable means of getting the attention of peers, for example, he must begin by understanding which behaviors are appropriate and which are not—first through teacher modeling and then through his own role-playing. After he understands what he should do, he will need to apply his new skill in both practice and spontaneous situations. Needless to say, reinforcement for his efforts will be crucial for his success.

Several social skills curriculum packages on the market help teachers design instructional programs to meet individual students' needs. One example is *Skillstreaming* (McGinnis & Goldstein, 1997), which focuses on interpersonal skills in school and recreational settings.

Social skills instruction provides yet another opportunity for students with mixed abilities to work together, because all students need practice in getting along with others. Social skills training can be combined with cooperative learning techniques to help all students learn to manage interpersonal challenges such as those in Figure 12.7.

Independent Living Skills

For people with more severe disabilities, explicit instruction in the skills of daily living is an essential part of the school curriculum. Where individuals are included full-time in a regular classroom, many daily living skills can be practiced as a matter of course such as eating lunch and taking outerwear on and off. Even so, additional training must usually take place elsewhere. Even for people with milder retardation (or for individuals with intellectual problems that remain unlabeled), instruction in daily living skills can spell the difference between success and failure in an independent adult lifestyle.

Instruction in daily living frequently begins at the level of early intervention—often through occupational therapy services—and may continue through the elementary school years. At the high school level, independent living skills are ideally addressed within the career education curriculum.

Community-Based Instruction

Life skills must be learned by doing in an actual on-site setting if possible. Because students with mental retardation have problems generalizing skills learned in one context to situations in another, direct instruction ought to take place in settings where a student will be expected to perform. With job training, the importance of instruction in the employment setting is obvious. Likewise, it is difficult to imagine how someone can learn her way around the community without actually traveling the route. It may be less clear, though, that many other life skills are also best learned in the actual settings where they will be needed. Daily living skills such as washing clothes and cooking may require quite different procedures in settings where the layouts and equipment are different. In like manner, shopping requires practice in stores, and counting change and budgeting money are best learned through actual experience.

Community-based instruction is a crucial instructional component in effectively generalizing life skills to real-world settings. What is more, students who take part in community-based instruction show improvements in adaptive behavior (McDonnell, Hardman, & Hightower, 1993). These gains are especially apparent in socialization, communication, personal living, and community living. Furthermore, these gains have been experienced by students with severe disabilities (and who have extensive educational needs), as well as by those with milder conditions.

Because actual experience is so essential to the education of people with MR, community-based instruction is an integral part of an effective transition plan. Community instruction can be supplemented by experiences involving role-playing, videotaping, or other creative simulations (Cuvo & Klatt, 1992), but there is no true substitute for practice in community settings.

> **FOR DISCUSSION**   *What are some ways that community businesses and industries can participate in community-based instruction?*

■■ LOOKING AHEAD

Based on the discussions in this chapter, it is clear that any restructuring of the existing educational system must consider several important factors. The success of any new school system will depend upon a cooperative, accepting, and non-competitive atmosphere in which respect and encouragement among students and staff are a major priority. In such an environment, diversity is seen as an advantage from which students can learn the problem-solving skills for living in a multicultural world. Students can learn from and draw upon the problem-solving strengths of several cultures and are no longer restricted by the limitations of one viewpoint.

This learning can only take place, of course, when students have plenty of opportunities to interact with each other, so segregated learning should be minimized. At the same time, all students must have options for learning the home, career, and community skills that will allow them to live as independently and productively as possible. Every student needs both the social experiences and life skills training that will enable him to succeed in the often difficult and challenging adult world.

Prerequisites for such school environments are adequate faculty and staff support and manageable class sizes. Special education expertise must be readily available through team teaching or consultation, and all teachers must have continuous access to behavioral expertise, including consultation and in-class support services.

Families are integral to the collaborative and cooperative approach that will facilitate student acceptance and involvement in schools. Many families of those with MR have been at the forefront of changes that have promoted acceptance and services for their children. But for other families, many of the same social and cultural problems faced by school systems threaten or preclude the caring and skilled interaction that make families effective advocates for each other. Chapter 13 takes up these issues of family life, adjustment, and healthy functioning and examines ways that professionals can facilitate good working relationships with families.

INFOTRAC COLLEGE EDITION

Consistent with the goals of community integration, children with mental retardation should be included in school-related activities with their peers whenever possible. In *InfoTrac College Edition,* enter the keyword *inclusion,* and read three articles that discuss inclusion of special-needs children in school activities. What points of agreement did you find among the three authors? About what did they disagree?

REFERENCES

Arnold, M., & Serpas, D. (1993). Training teachers to address the needs of students with severe mental retardation. *Education, 111*(4), 549–552.

Bates, P. E., Bronkema, J., Ames, T., & Hess, C. (1992). State-level interagency planning models. In F. R. Rusch, L. DeStefano, J. Chadsey-Rusch, L. A. Phelps, & E. Szymanski (Eds.), *Transition from school to adult life: Models, linkages, and policy* (pp. 115–130). Sycamore, IL: Sycamore Publishing.

Bauer, A. M., & Shea, T. M. (1999). *Inclusion 101: How to teach all learners.* Baltimore, MD: Paul H. Brookes.

Blaska, J. K., & Lynch, E. C. (1998). Is everyone included? Using children's literature to facilitate the understanding of disabilities. *Young Children, 53*(2), 36–38.

Brolin, D. E. (Ed.). (1991). *Life-centered career education: A competency based approach* (3rd ed.). Reston, VA: Council of Exceptional Children.

Brown, L., Nisbet, J., Ford, A., Sweet, M., Shiraga, B., York, J., & Freiberg, K. L. (Eds.). (1994). *Educating exceptional children* (7th ed.). Guilford, CT: Dushkin.

Bybee, J., & Zigler, E. (1999). Outerdirectedness in individuals with and without mental retardation: A review. In E. Zigler & D. Bennett-Gates (Eds.), *Personality development in individuals with mental retardation* (pp. 165–205). New York: Cambridge University Press.

Cafiero, J. (1998). Communication power for individuals with autism. *Focus on Autism and Other Developmental Disorders, 13*(2), 113–121.

Chadsey-Rusch, J., & O'Reilly, M. (1992). Social integration in employment and postsecondary educational settings: Outcomes and process variables. In F. R. Rusch, L. DeStefano, J. Chadsey-Rusch, L. A. Phelps, & E. Szymanski (Eds.), *Transition from school to adult life: Models, linkages, and policy* (pp. 245–263). Sycamore, IL: Sycamore Publishing.

Conners, F. A. (1992). Reading instruction for students with moderate mental retardation: Review and analysis of research. *American Journal on Mental Retardation, 96*(6), 577–597.

Cuvo, A. J., & Klatt, K. P. (1992). Effects of community-based, videotape, and flash card instruction of community-referenced sight words on students with mental retardation. *Journal of Applied Behavior Analysis, 25*(2), 499–512.

Dunn, L. M. (1968). Special education for the mildly retarded. Is much of it justifiable? *Exceptional Children, 35*(1), 5–22.

Freiberg, K. L. (Ed.). (1994). *Educating exceptional children.* Guilford, CT: Dushkin.

Gottlieb, J., Alter, M., & Gottlieb, B. W. (1990). Mainstreaming academically handicapped children in urban schools. In J. Lloyd, N. Singh, & A. Repp (Eds.), *The Regular Education Initiative: Alternative perspectives on concepts, issues, and models* (pp. 95–112). Sycamore, IL: Sycamore Publishing.

Haney, J. I. (1988). Toward successful community residential placements for individuals with mental retardation. In L. W. Heal, J. I. Haney, & A. R. Novak Amado (Eds.), *Integration of developmentally disabled individuals into the community* (2nd ed., pp. 125–168). Baltimore, MD: Paul H. Brookes.

Hanrahan, J., Goodman, W., & Rapagna, S. (1990). Preparing mentally retarded students for mainstreaming: Priorities of regular class and special school teachers. *American Journal on Mental Retardation, 94*(5), 470–474.

Hardman, M. L., Drew, C. J., & Egan, M. W. (1996). *Human exceptionality: Society, school, and family.* Boston: Allyn & Bacon.

Harris, C. D. (1993). *Project PARTnership: A Model program for encouraging self-determination through access to the arts.* Washington, DC: VSA Educational Services.

Hocutt, A., Martin, E., & McKinney, J. D. (1990). Historical and legal context of mainstreaming. In J. Lloyd, N. Singh, & A. Repp (Eds.), *The Regular Education Initiative: Alternative perspectives on concepts, issues, and models* (pp. 17–28). Sycamore, IL: Sycamore Publishing.

Kauffman, J. M. (1990). Restructuring in sociopolitical context: Reservations about the effects of current reform proposals on students with disabilities. In J. Lloyd, N. Singh, & A. Repp (Eds.), *The Regular Education Initiative: Alternative perspectives on concepts, issues, and models* (pp. 57–66). Sycamore, IL: Sycamore Publishing.

Kleinfeld, J., & Wescott, S. (1993). *Fantastic Antone succeeds.* Anchorage: University of Alaska Press.

Kratochwill, T. R., & Sheridan, S. M. (1990). Advances in behavioral assessment. In T. B. Gutkin & C. R. Reynolds (Eds.), *The handbook of school psychology* (2nd ed., pp. 328–364). New York: John Wiley.

Lipsky, D. K., & Gartner, A. (1987). Capable of achievement and worthy of respect: Education for handicapped students as if they were full-fledged human beings. *Exceptional Children, 54*(1), 69–74.

————. (1990). Restructuring for quality. In J. Lloyd, N. Singh, & A. Repp (Eds.), *The Regular Education Initiative: Alternative perspectives on concepts, issues, and models* (pp. 43–56). Sycamore, IL: Sycamore Publishing.

Madden, N. A., & Slavin, R. E. (1983). Effects of cooperative learning on the social acceptance of mainstreamed academically handicapped students. *Journal of Special Education, 17,* 171–182.

Madden, N. A. , Slavin, R. E., & Stevens, R. J. (1986). *Cooperative integrated reading and composition: Teacher's manual.* Baltimore, MD: Johns Hopkins University, Center for Research on Elementary and Middle Schools.

McDonnell, J., Ferguson, B., & Mathot-Buckner, C. (1992). Utah community employment placement project. In F. R. Rusch, L. DeStefano, J. Chadsey-Rusch, L. A. Phelps, & E. Szymanski (Eds.), *Transition from school to adult life: Models, linkages, and policy* (pp. 33–50). Sycamore, IL: Sycamore Publishing.

McDonnell, J., Hardman, M., & Hightower, J. (1989). Employment preparation for high school students with severe handicaps. *Mental Retardation, 27,* 396–404.

————. Impact of community-based instruction on the development of adaptive behavior of secondary-level students with mental retardation. *American Journal of Mental Retardation, 97,* 575–584.

McGinnis, E., & Goldstein, A. P. (1997). *Skillstreaming the elementary school child: New strategies and perspectives for teaching prosocial skills.* Champaign, IL: Research Press.

Meese, R. L. (1994). *Teaching learners with mild disabilities: Integrating research & practice.* Belmont, CA: Wadsworth.

Miller, H., Rynders, J. E., & Schleien, S. J. (1993). Drama: A medium to enhance social interaction between students with and without mental retardation. *Mental Retardation, 31*(4), 228–233.

Neal, R. S. (1984). Teaching social routines to behaviorally disordered youth. In J. K. Grosenick, E. McGinnis, S. L. Huntze, and C. R. Smith (Eds.), *Social/affective interventions in behavioral disorders.* Des Moines: Iowa Department of Public Instruction.

Nietupski, J., Scheutz, G., & Ockwood, L. (1980). The delivery of communication therapy services to severely handicapped students: A plan for change. *Journal of the Association for the Severely Handicapped (JASH), 5*(1), 13–23.

Racino, J. A. (1992). Living in the community: Independence, support, and transition. In F. R. Rusch, L. DeStefano, J. Chadsey-Rusch, L. A. Phelps, & E. Szymanski (Eds.), *Transition from school to adult life: Models, linkages, and policy* (pp. 131–152). Sycamore, IL: Sycamore Publishing

Roberson, W. H., Gravel, J. S., Valcante, G. C., & Maurer, R. G. (1992). Using a picture task analysis to teach students with multiple disabilities. *Teaching Exceptional Children, 24*(4), 12–15.

Rusch, F. R., & Phelps, L. A. (1987). Secondary special education and transition from school to work: A national priority. *Exceptional Children, 53,* 487–492.

Rusch, F. R., Szymanski, E., & Chadsey-Rusch, J. (1992). The emerging field of transition services. In F. R. Rusch, L. Destefano, J. Chadsey-Rusch, L. A. Phelps, & E. Szymanski (Eds.), *Transition from School to adult life: Models, linkages, and policy* (pp. 5–16). Sycamore, IL: Sycamore Publishing.

Russell, A. T., & Forness, S. R. (1985). Behavioral disturbance in mentally retarded children in TMR and EMR classrooms. *American Journal of Mental Deficiency, 89*(4), 338–344.

Schumaker, J. B., & Deshler, D. D. (1988). Implementing the Regular Education Initiative in secondary schools: A different ball game. *Journal of Learning Disabilities, 21*(1), 36–42.

Slavin, R. E. (1984). Team assisted individualization: Cooperative learning and individualized instruction in the mainstreamed classroom. *Remedial and Special Education, 5*(6), 33–42.

Slavin, R. E. (1990). *Cooperative learning; Theory, research and practice.* Englewood Cliffs, NJ: Prentice-Hall.

Slavin, R. E., Leavey, M. B., & Madden, N. A. (1986). *Team accelerated instruction—Mathematics.* Watertown, MA: Mastery Education Corp.

Slavin, R. E., Stevens, R. J., & Madden, N. A. (1988). Accommodating student diversity in reading and writing instruction: A cooperative learning approach. *Remedial and Special Education, 9*(1), 60–66.

Smith, D. D., & Bassett, D. S. (1990). The REI debate: A time for systematic research agendas. In J. Lloyd, N. Singh, & A. Repp (Eds.), *The Regular Education Initiative: Alternative perspectives on concepts, issues, and models* (pp. 149–160). Sycamore, IL: Sycamore Publishing.

Smith, J. D., & Hilton, A. (1997). The preparation and training of the educational community for the inclusion of students with developmental disabilities: The MRDD position. *Education and Training in Mental Retardation and Developmental Disabilities, 32*(1), 3–10.

Stainback, W., & Stainback, S. (1984). A rationale for the merger of special and regular education. *Exceptional Children, 51*(2), 101–111.

Stainback, S., Stainback, W., & Forest, M. (1989). *Educating all students in the mainstream of regular education.* Baltimore, MD: Paul H. Brookes.

Staub, D. (1998). *Delicate threads: Friendships between children with and without special needs in inclusive settings.* Bethesda, MD: Woodbine House.

Stevens, R. J., Madden, N. A., Slavin, R. E. & Farnish, A. M. (1987). Cooperative integrated reading and composition: Two field experiments. *Reading Research Quarterly, 22,* 433–454.

Stump, C. S., & Wilson, C. (1996). Collaboration: Making it happen. *Intervention in School and Clinic, 31*(5), 310–312.

Torgeson, J. K. (1982). The learning disabled child as an inactive learner: Educational implications. *Topics in Learning and Learning Disabilities, 2*(1), 45–52.

Udvari-Solner, A., Jorgensen, J., & Courchane, G. (1992). Longitudinal vocational curriculum. In F. R. Rusch, L. Destefano, J. Chadsey-Rusch, L. A. Phelps, & E. Szymanski (Eds.), *Transition from School to adult life: Models, linkages, and policy* (pp. 285–320). Sycamore, IL: Sycamore Publishing.

Walker, H. M., & Bullis, M. (1990). Behavior disorders and the social context of regular class integration: A conceptual dilemma? In J. Lloyd, N. Singh, & A. Repp (Eds.), *The Regular Education Initiative: Alternative perspectives on concepts, issues, and models* (pp. 75–94). Sycamore, IL: Sycamore Publishing.

Will, M. C. (1986). Educating children with learning problems: A shared responsibility. *Exceptional Children, 52,* 411–416.

Part IV

Community Life: Roles, Rights, and Responsibilities

13

Family

F rom the educational challenges presented in Chapter 12, it is clear that co-operation between families and schools is important for promoting effective learning and integration. This chapter focuses on family adjustment to a child's disability and to the family's relationship with professionals in education and other service provision. It also discusses family characteristics, composition, and diversity, and it describes findings from the professional literature about families of children with disabilities. It highlights the individuality of families and the complexity of family life. Chapter 13 also underlines the systems perspective of this text by showing that effective service provision for children with disabilities must—by necessity—be informed about and responsive to the goals and needs of the entire family. Thus, the chapter highlights techniques that can facilitate successful collaboration between families and professionals.

WHO ARE FAMILIES?

Besides the once typical family composed of Dad, Mom, and children, families today are enormously diverse, and many are now headed by a single parent (U.S. Bureau of the Census, 1998). In family units in which the parents are divorced, sometimes the ex-partners both seek to play an important role in rearing their children, even while living in separate households. At other times, the custodial parent may assume primary responsibility, with the other taking little active part. Stepfamilies are becoming increasingly common, too, and have their own unique role adjustments and relationships.

In addition to families with divorce, increasing numbers of mothers have never been married, and the majority of these women rear their children with little paternal input (Coley, 1998). Other families may include extended family members—often grandparents or aunts and uncles—who are decisive figures in the children's lives. And, more and more, single parents (such as Cathy in our case stories) and same-sex parents are adopting children—sometimes children with special needs. In addition to the variety in composition, families differ ethnically and racially as well, and they bring varying cultural, traditional, religious, and philosophical attitudes, beliefs, and experiences to the context of family life.

Because families are so diverse, we cannot describe a single set of reactions, problems, and needs that adequately reflects all or even most families. Families—like children with disabilities themselves—must be understood as individuals. Even so, professionals can learn to be sensitive to experiences that are common to many families and to problems that frequently occur. Research findings on families are helpful when they alert professionals to important possibilities in working with families, but it is essential that such knowledge does not become stereotyped and that the behavior and responses of family members are not reinterpreted to fit what professionals already "know." Professionals must be able to see families for who they are and not be blinded by presumptions or project a ready-made bias.

Most families of a child with mental retardation enjoy many happy and satisfying times together.

© Elizabeth Crews

ADJUSTMENT

For the family of a child with mental retardation, the moment of discovering that the child has a problem or special need is often experienced as traumatic, even earth-shaking. No doubt, the emotional impact of that moment is inevitable, but there is nevertheless considerable evidence that the manner in which parents learn of their child's disability has an important effect on the ease or difficulty of the family's initial adjustment.

Initial Reactions

With newborns, mental retardation can only be assumed based on the presence of a related disability. The responsibility for bringing a disability to the parent's attention usually falls to physicians, nurses, or other early intervention professionals. Parents' initial reactions are importantly influenced by the manner in which they are told and the information that is received at that time. In addition, parental social class, education, and extent of social isolation, as well as the type and degree of the disability itself, are meaningful factors (Challela, 1981). It is essential that professionals understand the depth of emotion and the extent of initial disappointment that such news almost certainly engenders. Figure 13.1 offers examples of the emotional responses that parents have reported.

"I have never before or since felt so helpless, so crushed, just as if the future of my life had been destroyed."

"I'd been given a life sentence."

"My worst fear of pregnancy had been realized."

"It was as if we knew two different little precious individuals—the one who brought with it our dreams, and the other with a life so different, so painful from the one we had envisioned for all three of us. What had an innocent child who had never touched the world done to deserve this? I couldn't and didn't go to work for a week. I just lay in bed and held my baby."

FIGURE 13.1 Parents' feelings and reactions to the news of their child's disability

SOURCE: From J. Finnegan (1993), *Shattered dreams—Lonely choices.* Westport, CT: Bergin & Garvey.

As early as the mid-1960s, research indicated that families want clear information about their child's disability as early and as honestly as possible (Carr, 1970; Drillien & Wilkinson, 1964; Raech, 1966). It is equally important, of course, that such information be imparted with kindness, thoughtfulness, and empathy. Parents should be told of their child's disability when they are together if at all possible, and they should receive this news in private rather than in a hospital room where other parents are present or in hallways or waiting rooms. Furthermore, they need a private place afterward to talk and to plan. Although the need for privacy seems obvious, many parents have not been given these basic considerations, and, as a result, they sometimes carry deep and lasting resentment (Tingey, 1988).

Parents can be helped in the initial adjustment by being told of their child's disability with the child present. The child should be called by name, and information about children with similar disabilities should be given using the expression "children *with* [a particular condition]," rather than speaking of the child as synonymous with the disability (see Chapter 4) (Tingey, 1988). One should *not* say, for example, "Jo is a Down syndrome child" or "Fragile X kids almost always. . . ."

> **FOR DISCUSSION**   *Why and in what ways might the presence of the child and using the child's name help some parents at this difficult time?*

Parents respond to being told of their child's disability in individual ways: Some may cry, others may not express themselves openly, and still others may respond with disbelief. While all parents experience a sense of loss and grief, these feelings may be expressed in markedly different ways. Professionals must be sensitive to parents' unique response styles and allow them to handle their feelings in their own way (Chisholm, Pappas, & Sharp, 1997).

One common reaction is shock. Initially, parents may be bewildered, confused, and unable to take in large amounts of information. Their primary needs

Parents may need help to see the child as a unique person and to remove the label of the diagnosis from the child.

Parents experience a series of peaks and valleys. They do not accept the situation "once and for all" but continually deal with old problems and newly emerging concerns.

Parents may need help to realize that family needs must supersede the child's needs and that no one person can be the single focal point of the family.

Although parents need information, they do not need predictions as to the adult or life skills that the child will eventually attain. Because any attainment is at least partly determined by life experiences and training, it cannot be accurately forecast even for nonhandicapped infants.

More than anything, parents want understanding—they do not want pity for themselves or for their child.

FIGURE 13.2 Important issues in counseling parents

SOURCE: Adapted from C. Tingey (1988), *Down syndrome: A resource handbook.* Boston: Little, Brown.

may be to learn the basics of the condition and to have an opportunity to talk about their feelings if they so choose. For this reason, when parents are first informed, it is better to give them resources for finding information and to reassure them that help is available than provide lengthy or technical explanations.

Often, other parents with children who have similar disabilities can be helpful. Professionals can put parents in contact with support groups, which in turn provide information, the opportunity to talk with someone who has "been there," and a chance to share strategies for coping and making progress.

During the first weeks and months, many parents find professional counseling helpful. Counselors can provide the occasion for parents to work through some of their feelings of grief and loss, and they can help parents understand that it is natural for that process to take many months. In addition, counselors can help parents focus on the child's strengths and teach them coping strategies to manage stress. Figure 13.2 lists important issues regarding parental counseling needs.

DECISIONS FOR ADOPTION
OR OUT-OF-HOME PLACEMENT

Sometimes parents of children with mental retardation decide that they are not able to rear their child themselves. Because there are would-be parents who are eager to adopt children with particular special needs, adoption can provide a child with a home and family while permitting birth parents to know that they have done their best to place their child in a nurturing environment.

Parents may choose adoption for many reasons. They may believe they are too old to rear a child to adulthood, or they may already be overextended with other

Reading current literature on the disability

Talking with families of children who have a similar disability

Observing children with similar disabilities

Talking with parents who considered an adoption plan

Talking with parents who have adopted

Talking with professionals

FIGURE 13.3 Sources of information for making a decision about adoption

children or obligations. Perhaps they are honest with themselves about their inability to accept a child with disabilities, or perhaps they suffer from illness or chronic depression themselves. Finally, they may simply know they are "unable to cope" (Finnegan, 1993).

Ironically, not so long ago, the only option offered parents was institutionalization, while now the only option typically offered is to rear the child at home. Parents who do not believe they can manage that task in the child's best interests often experience rejection and disapproval from family members and professionals. These parents may be subtly or explicitly pressured to keep their children in the same way that parents were once pressured to institutionalize them, yet these parents are themselves the only ones who can really judge whether they can manage a child with disabilities.

When parents discover through prenatal testing that their child will have an MR-related disability, adoption can offer an alternative to abortion. When parents discover their child's disability postnatally, the decision to rear the child at home or to choose adoption is typically made during the first few weeks, while the parents are still reeling from the discovery. It is especially important that parents are encouraged to obtain the information that can help them make the decision that will be best for them—and therefore best for their baby. Suggestions for gathering this kind of information are offered in Figure 13.3.

Few decisions are so heart-wrenching as deciding to place one's child for adoption, although counseling may help parents clarify their decision and deal with their feelings of loss and grief, regardless of what they decide. The majority of families who choose an adoption plan ultimately do so because they are convinced that the adoptive family can offer their child a better life than they themselves could provide. Although professionals cannot make such a choice for families, they can offer support in a way that enables families to make the best decision.

Out-of-Home Placement

Though certainly less common than 30 years ago, some families still decide to place their child in an outside residential setting. Several options for residential living are available and will be discussed in more detail in Chapter 14. Like adoption, the decision for the child to reside outside the home is a difficult one, with many factors typically involved. For one thing, there is a somewhat greater tendency for individuals with more severe conditions to be residentially placed—including those with more severe behavioral problems—especially as they get older (Bromley & Blacher, 1991; Rousey, Blacher, & Hanneman, 1990; Tausig, 1985). The strongest predictor of whether a child will be placed outside of the home, however, is the presence of other stresses on caregivers. External burdens may include financial problems, poor health, and other child care responsibilities, among a host of other personal problems (Black, Molaison, & Small, 1990). Furthermore, lack of support services may contribute to caregiver stress, just as appropriate services can alleviate it. Effective support systems, therefore, can lessen the need for out-of-home placement (Kobe, Rojahn, & Schroeder, 1991).

There are cultural differences in the likelihood of outside placement, with white parents more likely to do so than either African-American or Latino families (Blacher, Hanneman, & Rousey, 1992). To some extent, at least among African-American mothers, this difference is related to different perceptions about the severity of the stress caused by their children and the mothers' better use of coping strategies. These findings emphasize again the importance of individual family characteristics in eventual adjustment. If professionals are to provide effective services for those with mental retardation, then they must understand family dynamics and plan treatment programs accordingly.

Adaptation: Dealing with Stress

Ultimately, most parents do decide to rear their child at home, and—as for any child—this is usually an advantage. Research has demonstrated, in fact, that there are typically numerous social, adaptational, and intellectual benefits to family life rather than institutional living (Lakin & Bruininks, 1985).

Once parents become acclimated to the fact of their child's disability and determine to rear their child themselves, stress usually shifts to the day-to-day realities of caregiving. Although children with mental retardation provide much satisfaction and joy for their parents, stress is inevitable, though the major stressors are often related to health and behavior problems rather than the mental retardation itself. In the words of one parent whose daughter has Rett syndrome, "We're not fair to ourselves, . . . if we don't let others know about the thorns between the roses, about the burden. Stacie is the light of my life and the depth of my despair" (Hunter, 1987, p. 537).

Family stress—needless to say—is limited by no means to those who have children with mental retardation, for assuredly all families experience a significant degree of stress. Research findings are consistent, however, in showing that families who have children with mental retardation typically experience additional stresses that other families do not have (Dyson, 1993; Browne & Bramston, 1998). There is much variability, however, in the way families accommodate to such stress and the extent to which they may be badly affected by it. Some families adapt well, develop an effective routine, and experience a high level of family functioning, whereas others are devastated or destroyed. This difference is to some extent explained by certain child characteristics, including responsiveness, temperament, repetitive behavior patterns, and requirements for greater care that increase stress for parents (Beckman, 1983). In addition, the severity of child behavior problems and the number of handicapping conditions are also important contributors to emotional and physical wear and tear (Cameron & Orr, 1989). There is evidence that family stress increases as children with mental retardation grow older (Bristol & Schopler, 1984), though some research indicates that middle childhood may be a more stressful period than infancy, early childhood, or adolescence (Orr, Cameron, Dobson, & Day, 1993).

One factor that strongly affects the extent to which families are able to manage is the mediating influence of quality family relationships (Dyson, 1993; Sarimski, 1997). Families are also better able to adjust when they have adequate economic and social resources. When they have the financial means to obtain needed equipment and services (along with an informal support system on which they can count for help), families are better able to manage high levels of stress.

Although child characteristics, good family relationships, and economic status influence the extent to which families are able to adapt to stress, family perceptions also play a key role. Events that are stressful for one family may not be so for another because of differences in the way those families interpret the same events (Dyson, 1991; Orr, Cameron, & Day, 1991). Families with strong religious faith, for example, may perceive the disability in terms that help to make their struggles more meaningful (Weisner, Beizer, & Stolze, 1991). The subjective nature of family response also has important implications for service delivery because it underscores, once again, the extent to which services must be individually designed. Although it may *appear* that families are experiencing a high degree of stress, interventions remain inappropriate, unless the family itself perceives a need for outside help. Professionals must listen to families, therefore, and must identify and explore with them their perceptions of the need for intervention and services (Orr, Cameron, & Day, 1991).

For some parents, unfortunately, disappointment over their child's disability does not dissipate and resolve with time. In these instances, parents may experience **chronic sorrow**—a long-lasting sadness and depression that is frequently accompanied by low self-esteem (Mallow & Bechtel, 1999). More often, however, families adapt well and carry on their lives in ways similar to those without the challenge of mental retardation, yet sadness may recur periodically, especially at times that are typically developmental milestones such as entry into school, graduation, or the time when other young people are entering college or getting married (Bristol, 1987; Eakes, Burke, & Hainsworth, 1998).

Still, even the most difficult situations are usually easier to manage and less stressful when they are predictable. For example, although a child may have severe behavior problems, families can learn to anticipate the circumstances that incite tantrums or upsets, and they can develop skills that make problem behavior less likely and less severe. Situations that are highly unpredictable, however, are more difficult to manage—as when children have multiple health problems with constantly changing crises and challenges.

Even at that, families usually accommodate to increased caregiving demands and behavioral challenges and ultimately enjoy a level of family functioning that is little different from other families. Figure 13.4 shows examples of such accommodation.

In fact, many families who have children with MR do more than simply adapt or adjust. They enjoy their children and family life, experiencing happy and sat-

Mother stays home from work to care for children.

Mother goes to work to be able to afford equipment or services.

Parents alternate time off from work for medical appointments.

Family moves to a larger home to accommodate the needs of a wheelchair or other special equipment.

Family childproofs the home.

Parents put a lower priority on housework and a higher priority on child care activities.

Parents enlist the aid of relatives and extended family to help with child care.

Parents adjust certain aspects of their marriage relationship to accommodate a child's special needs.

Parents act on advice from families and friends about where to find professional help.

FIGURE 13.4 Possible family accommodations

SOURCE: Adapted from R. Gallimore, R. S. Weisner, L. P. Bernheimer, D. Guthrie, & K. Nihira (1993), Family responses to young children with developmental delays: Accommodation activity in ecological and cultural context. *American Journal on Mental Retardation, 98*(2), 185–206.

isfying times with one another just as much as and sometimes even more than do other families.

UNIQUE REACTIONS OF FATHERS

Although we must keep in mind that not everyone fits the "typical" pattern, fathers and mothers often react differently to their children with mental retardation. Many studies report a higher level of stress for mothers than for fathers (Beckman, 1991), though some studies indicate similar levels for both (Krauss, 1993; Rousey, Best, & Blacher, 1992).

Mothers and fathers may experience stress, however, as a result of different aspects of their child's MR. Fathers, for example, may feel higher levels of anxiety related to their child's temperament and her difference from social norms (Mallow & Bechtel, 1999). Mothers, however, experience more stress that is related to the personal consequences of parenting—variables related to her own health, restrictions in roles, and effects on her relationship with her spouse (Krauss, 1993). Furthermore, a father may experience greater difficulty in emotionally attaching to his child (Beckman, 1991). The important implications of this finding will bear heavily on early intervention programs because they are ordinarily focused on the mother–child relationship when they should no doubt include fathers as well.

In addition, a father's stress level may be more strongly affected by his immediate family environment. When fathers perceive their families to be adaptable and cohesive, they experience less stress, whereas these factors seem less important for mothers. On the other hand, mothers seem more influenced by the effects of **social support** and have less stress when they have strong support networks (Krauss,

1993). Both parents, however, experience less stress when they have more *informal* supports—for example, friendships and supportive extended family (Beckman, 1991).

Sometimes fathers who have children with mental retardation withdraw from the family into work–related or other activities. When this happens, mothers inevitably assume additional caregiving responsibilities, and because they are already experiencing heavier role restriction, these added responsibilities can contribute to conflict or estrangement between parents (Lamb & Meyer, 1991). Nevertheless, many fathers who have children with mental retardation take considerable part in child care responsibilities, and in such situations, mothers report greater satisfaction and less stress themselves (Rousey, Best, & Blacher, 1992).

SIBLINGS

Siblings of children with mental retardation, like all siblings, experience both joy and distress in living with their brother or sister. Thus, many young people report satisfaction in playing with and learning to cope with a sibling with retardation. They often take great pleasure, too, in the accomplishments of their brother or sister, and they develop feelings of warmth and empathy for all people with special needs, as well as a tolerance for differences in general and an increased altruism (Powell & Ogle, 1985). These positive findings have been consistent for more than two decades (Boer & Dunn, 1992; Grossman, 1972).

At the same time, children may feel resentment about the extra attention their sibling with MR requires and feel anxious about how to treat and get along with him or her. Not unlike many parents, they may even feel guilty because their brother or sister has special problems and limitations that they do not have (Powell & Ogle, 1985).

Early research on siblings suggested that they were negatively affected by the necessity to take on greater caregiving responsibilities for their sibling. It was assumed that they had to "grow up too soon" and were given more household chores than other children their age. It was further suggested that their own opportunities for socialization were inhibited as a result (Farber, 1959). But more recent research indicates that although siblings of children with mental retardation do have more child care responsibilities, they do not have as many other household duties as their peers. In fact, it seems that parents may be reluctant to give their typical children household chores simply because they are aware of the extra time these youngsters spend in caring for siblings. As it turns out, these additional child care tasks do not negatively affect the quality of children's relationships with their brother or sister and do not deprive them of other socialization experiences (Stoneman et al., 1991). Siblings of children with MR invite friends over and go out to play as often as do other children.

Siblings' perceptions of their parents' attitudes about the child with a disability powerfully influence their own behavior and adjustment. When parents are

Siblings usually enjoy and take pride in their brothers and sisters with mental retardation.

© Suzanne Arms/Jeroboam

open and honest about the child's disability and provide information for siblings, adjustment and understanding are enhanced; but when parents do not talk with their children about the disability, siblings often do not ask questions. In such situations, siblings may be afraid to ask for information about the retardation because they are afraid of displeasing their parents or don't want to cause their parents pain. Given that kind of potential empathy, it is important that siblings understand that they are not responsible for protecting their parents, but that their parents can be relied upon to take care of them.

Siblings may need general information about the nature of the disability, the causes of it, and reassurance that it is not contagious. They may also have questions about whether their brother or sister is likely to get any better. Table 13.1 presents a set of the concerns siblings may have that require guiding information.

Siblings also have concerns about their parents' expectations of them. They wonder about how to ask questions, their parents' feelings, and what they can do to help their parents. In addition, they need to talk about their own feelings and about their brother or sister's relationship with and acceptance by peers, extended

Table 13.1 Issues of Concern for Siblings of Children with Mental Retardation

Concern	Questions
Cause of the disability	Why does my sister have mental retardation?
	Will future brothers and sisters also have it?
	Whose fault is it?
Feelings of the child with MR	Is my brother in pain?
	Does he have the same feelings I do?
	What does he think about?
	Does he know me?
	Does he love me and my parents?
	Why does he behave so strangely?
Prognosis	Can my sister be cured?
	Will she improve?
	Can she grow out of this?
	Can treatment really help?
Needed services	What special help will he need?
	Who are these professionals who work with him?
	What do they do with him?
How to help	What am I supposed to do with my sister?
	What can I expect from her?
	Can I help teach her?
	Should I protect her?
Where the child lives	Why does my brother live at home?
	Why doesn't he live at home?
	Wouldn't another place be better for him?
The future	What will happen to my sister in the future?
	Will she always be with us?
	Will she go to school?
	Will she get married and have a family?
	Will she ever live on her own?
	Will I be responsible for her?

SOURCE: From T. H. Powell & P. A. Ogle (1985), *Brothers and sisters: A special part of exceptional families.* Baltimore, MD: Paul H. Brookes. Adapted with permission.

family, and neighbors, both at school and within the community. Guidelines for communicating effectively with siblings are offered in Figure 13.5.

From a systems perspective, professionals must certainly be concerned not only with the child with MR and her parents, but also with the other children in the family. It is important that professionals understand and anticipate siblings' probable concerns and be prepared to help them develop and adjust. Formal training sessions that teach siblings to work with their brother or sister can promote more positive interaction in both formal and informal settings, in addition to more pos-

Actively listen.

Take your time.

Serve as a model for asking questions and seeking information.

Be knowledgeable.

Be sincere and honest.

Provide understandable answers that are consistent with the child's developmental level.

FIGURE 13.5 Suggestions for effective communication

SOURCE: Adapted with permission from T. H. Powell & P. A. Ogle (1993), *Brothers and sisters: A special part of exceptional families.* Baltimore, MD: Paul H. Brookes.

itive interactions between the siblings. Siblings can be taught skills of reinforcement, prompting, identification of behaviors, task analysis, chaining, and various strategies to handle problem behaviors—all of which encourage effective interaction. When siblings are engaged in formal training, however, it is important to follow four simple guidelines:

1. Neither the child with MR nor her sibling should be forced to participate.
2. The task and the environment need to be arranged to ensure success.
3. Both children should be rewarded for their interaction.
4. Such training is usually most appropriate when the teaching sibling is chronologically older than the child with MR (Powell & Ogle, 1985).

Whether interaction between siblings involves formal teaching sessions or typical sibling play, satisfying sibling relationships enhance the development of all involved. We have seen that the brother or sister develops responsibility and a sense of genuine altruism. For the child with MR, too, social interaction is enhanced and learning opportunities are increased. Thus, in working together, parents and professionals can play an important role in facilitating positive relationships between siblings with and without disabilities.

FAMILIES SPEAK FOR THEMSELVES

The preceding sections illustrate the effect that a child with mental retardation has on the entire family for better and for worse. Families, like children with disabilities, come in all shapes and sizes. They have their own personalities and temperaments, their own talents and limitations. They share some common challenges, and yet they are individuals with their own unique experiences and views of the world. In the following excerpts, parents talk about their exceptional children and about their struggles and victories as parents—sharing both the intense stress and the deep joy of family life. The first excerpts are from *A Child Called Noah,* by Josh Greenfeld, a book composed of journal entries about life with his son, who has autism. These entries clearly express both the frustration and anger this father is experiencing.

> Noah . . . is static. "Love is feedback," as Skinner says. And we don't get any from Noah. In fact, sometimes his singsong vacuousness gets on my nerves, the what-to-do-with-Noah problem overwhelms me, and suddenly I just want to strike out at him. Can I help it if I don't always love him as much as I want to?
>
> Noah was up at 3:00 A.M. and chewed his shirt to a thread during the long night. And this morning he's been pinching everyone. I guess he's trying to tell us something. But what? What? I never knew that the most agonizing word in the English language could be *what*. (Greenfeld, 1972)

Most parents do feel some resentment toward their children at times, regardless of whether their child has a disability. And although this may be natural, anger against one's offspring also causes feelings of guilt. Professionals can help by listening to parents' feelings with empathy and without judgment. In the following excerpt, Kathy Hunter speaks openly about the pain and difficulty that comes with parenting her daughter who has Rett syndrome, an ultimately fatal condition that includes mental retardation and increasing disability.

> We're not fair to ourselves . . . if we don't let others know about the thorns between the roses, about the burden. Stacie is the light of my life and the depth of my despair. I feel the pain of putting away my wishful dreams for her and my heart aches as she moves further away from me. I am torn between providing enough for her and not too much at the expense of my other children. There is a silent sadness deep within my heart that can't even be shared in words, for it is too painful. As she grows older, my love multiplies tenfold, but so does the work. These are the thorns between the roses. If we are to truly help one another we need to acknowledge the burden and the pain as well as the unconditional love. (Hunter, 1987)

Rearing a child with a condition involving MR often is extremely challenging. In her book about her son with brain damage, Ingrid Rimland is honest both about the stress-producing symptoms of her son's condition and the frustration and loneliness of living in a world where others seldom understand.

> How many times was I admonished:
>
> ". . . not a trace of discipline . . . !
>
> . . . can't you try to calm him down . . . ?
>
> . . . is there no way to make him mind . . . ?"
>
> Can the chaotic world of one's dreams be controlled? Have you tried to run and fight when you are bolted to the floor? Erwin bit and kicked and screamed and spun in circles at my feet—for years! He chewed up my newspaper and ripped apart my tablecloth and devoured my plants—leaves, roots,

and all. He would chew on his fingers and lips until they were bloody, or gnaw on his nails until they were gone. (Rimland, 1984)

Perhaps most important to understand and the most difficult for parents, however, are the complexity and ambivalence of their feelings—as well as the uncertainty surrounding the decisions and the choices they must make. Jean, whose son Jeremy has multiple physical and mental disabilities, responded this way to being asked how Jeremy has altered her life:

> In a way, it has altered it positively. Years ago, I wouldn't even know how to talk to a child like Jeremy. I would have wondered what you say to them and if they understand. So, I think that growth is very positive. And now I am working with Early On [an agency that provides advocacy and services]. If Jeremy were a regular child, I still wouldn't be actively involved this way, and for me that's very positive. I get to do some policy-making things in Lansing, and these activities validate my self-worth. But, the flip side is that sometimes I'm too active. I tend to focus so very much time on Jeremy's needs. Now, for example, I'm putting so much time and effort into working out Jeremy's school transition that I'm missing Justin's field trips. I say, "Well, Justin, you can speak for yourself. I have to go with Jeremy, because he can't speak for himself." I try to explain that to him, but I don't know if he understands it or not. If I don't fight for Jeremy, though, nobody else will. That's one thing that I have heard professionals say repeatedly, "If you want to make change, you parents, you need to get out there and make change." And I'm so sick of hearing that. I want to say, "Well, why don't you change it! Why don't you help move the process along?" (Wassenaar, 1994)

As Jean suggests, the birth of a child with mental retardation brings with it the opportunity for tremendous growth and learning. Susan Goodship, another mother of a child with Rett syndrome, makes an important observation about the approach that parents take, one that is equally important for professionals: "If they try to see the world through her [the child's] eyes, not only will they be able to help with some of her difficulties, but they will have a new slant on life that other families miss" (Goodship, 1987).

In the preface to his son Nigel's book, Douglas Hunt has additional advice for parents of children with mental retardation—and in particular for those who have children like Nigel who have Down syndrome:

> I feel that we, his parents, owe a few more words of encouragement to those who face the same problem we have had.
>
> Problem is the word; not tragedy.
>
> Nigel has brought us untold joy. He has been loving, considerate, generous, and immensely rewarding. In many ways we have faced far fewer problems than do most parents of modern teenagers. In many ways he is far more capable of looking after himself. And he has started his first book at the age of seventeen. (Hunt, 1967)

Finally, Robert Perske gives several suggestions to parents of a child with retardation. Although he, too, speaks from the point of view of a parent whose child has Down syndrome, his advice can be helpful to all parents and professionals:

> Accept the fact that the "child of your dreams" never was and never would have been. All parents must acknowledge this sooner or later. Your problem: you must do it sooner.
>
> Love your child exactly as he or she is. Real love does not demand that persons change into what we want them to become before we can start loving them.
>
> Take advantage of the early discovery of your child's handicap. The sooner you find professionals and advocates willing to help you and your youngster, the better. *Early intervention is crucial.*
>
> Take comfort in knowing it is better that your child's birth came now, rather than thirty years ago. Today supportive persons are available who have experienced what you are going through. . . . Thirty years ago, you would have been torn between two terrible choices—keeping your child at home with no help from anyone . . . or sending your youngster away. (Perske & Perske, 1986)

We can see that the circumstances faced by families of a child with retardation vary enormously. Mental retardation is associated with such a wide range of conditions that often almost the only factor in common *is* the mental retardation—and the MR itself is usually not the primary challenge. Instead, the greatest problems often come from associated physical and behavioral characteristics.

Some parents have been philosophically stoic, optimistic, and even bright about these challenges. Others have been angry and deeply grieved. Some have been all of these and more. Often it has been the very refusal of parents gracefully to accept their child's limitations—in fact, their very anger (even fury) and grief—that has driven them to fight with such extraordinary energy and persistence for educational and community opportunities for their children. And yet, when parents have first found and then expressed acceptance of their children, it has helped both professionals and the public to find greater acceptance as well. And aren't we all faced with this same essential struggle: between accepting ourselves—and our own inherent worth—on the one hand, and striving to change and improve (often against seemingly insurmountable odds) on the other? And isn't it often this struggle itself that stimulates our own development?

FORMAL AND INFORMAL SUPPORTS

The support that families receive can often spell the difference between their ability to cope or the experience of ongoing crisis. As we have seen, that support can come in formal ways, such as through professionals working in schools and other agencies, or informally from the help of family and friends.

Grandparents, Other Relatives, and Neighbors

Grandparents and other extended family members can provide a significant source of informal social support for the child with MR and her family. Changes in family composition have affected the traditional grandparenting role so that grandparent support ranges from occasional baby-sitting to full-time caregiving. Research has indicated that maternal grandmothers may be especially helpful in mitigating family stress.

Extended family members can be particularly effective helpers when they understand and accept the child's disability (Lian & Aloia, 1994). On the other hand, when extended family members struggle with their own grief and upset or deny or minimize the effects of the child on the family, they may only serve to create an additional source of family stress. For this reason, some family service provision agencies have included educational and support services for extended family members (Sonnek, 1986).

Often grandparents and others are included in treatment plans using a family services approach, and grandparents sometimes engage in outreach efforts to provide support and information for other grandparents with newly diagnosed grandchildren. As with the role of parents, the presence of a child with mental retardation does not dictate the roles of grandparents or other family members, but it is only one in an array of circumstances that determines how active and supportive extended family members are.

Respite Care

Respite care is an important source of social support for families who have a child with mental retardation. These services provide needed relief from caregiving responsibilities and offer families the chance to take otherwise impossible vacations or spend time with other family members.

Respite can be support that is either formal (provided by professionals) or informal (provided by friends or relatives). Approximately one-half of formal respite services are carried out in families' homes (Slater, 1986). Originators of respite programs include group homes, public or private institutions, volunteer and advocacy agencies, parent cooperatives, and foster care homes.

We have already seen how families who have a child with retardation undergo particular stress and how respite can help alleviate it (Botuck & Winsberg, 1991). Furthermore, families most often indicate that respite care is their most needed service priority (Abelson, 1999). Evidence shows, however, that some families who could benefit from respite do not avail themselves of the service (Marc & McDonald, 1988). Some families may not want to leave their loved ones with individuals outside of the family for fear that they will not be looked after properly. For parents who have experienced their child's lifetime of rejection and who have been greeted with a litany of complaints about their child's behavior and performance, the belief that their child will be lovingly cared for by outside professionals may be understandably foreign. Some families also may feel guilty for not being able to always manage on their own. In addition, many respite programs

- Parents experience difficulty finding people who are competent in responding to the needs of their child.
- Many people are unwilling to assume the responsibility of respite care.
- Parents place great value on developing trust and confidence in the care provider.
- Leaving a child with a care provider can create anxiety for parents.
- Families need assistance in balancing the needs of family members.

FIGURE 13.6 Problems in finding adequate respite care

SOURCE: Adapted from C. L. Salisbury & J. Intagliata (1986), *Respite care: Support for persons with developmental disabilities and their families.* Baltimore, MD: Paul H. Brookes.

have frequent staff turnover or problems attracting enough respite providers. These providers also are too often inadequately trained to manage severe behavioral or medical problems. Figure 13.6 lists some difficulties that families experience in locating and using respite care.

Before parents will use respite services, they must first feel they are entitled to respite and that it will be a positive experience for their child as well as for themselves. Furthermore, they must be aware of their own levels of fatigue and stress (Curran & Bongiorno, 1986). Typically, parents are more comfortable receiving respite care in their own home, but in some situations having someone come into the home may only increase existing stress. When children have severe behavior problems, for example, families may most need to have some quiet, crisis-free time together in their own home. Families also may not always have the resources or the opportunity to leave their homes and go someplace else (Cutler, 1986).

Sometimes cash subsidy programs allow families to seek their own respite providers rather than require them to use a particular community service. Families often prefer this type of assistance because it allows them to find the most comfortable respite situation that best suits their needs.

Respite services are most often sought by parents of younger children rather than parents of adults, perhaps because older parents reared their children at a time when few services were available and when stigmatization may have been greater. Many of these parents have long assumed the solitary role of protector for their child. Good respite experiences, however, can be particularly important in such instances because they can reassure aging parents that responsible, caring individuals are available in the community to provide services for their family member. Such parents may be dealing with worries of what will happen to their adult child when they are gone, and respite care can be a bridge to more permanent arrangements (Cutler, 1986).

Respite care can sometimes be the deciding factor in whether individuals with mental retardation can remain with their families. Individual parents may band together (with the help of professionals) and develop their own parent cooperatives, seek outside community services, or rely on in-home providers. And if such services can enable families to stay together and avoid out-of-home placements, then they are cost-effective and perhaps invaluable.

Collaboration Among Families and Professionals

The importance of collaboration has been emphasized throughout this text, and nowhere is collaboration more critical than between professionals and families. The child with mental retardation is best served when parents and professionals form a partnership in the child's true interests. In the past, professionals have too often viewed themselves as experts and authorities whose job it is to make plans for children and families, to give them information about what they should do, and to solve problems for them—but these previous roles are in direct opposition to working *with* parents in partnership.

When professionals make service delivery plans *for* families rather than *with* them, it can actually harm rather than help. Imposing services can create more family stress, and programs that are inadequate and inappropriate can intrude upon parents' ability to make good decisions in solving their own family problems.

Because of the sometimes authoritarian stance of professionals, the relationship between parents and professionals has often been uneasy. In the worst instances, parents have felt intimidated, unheard and disregarded. In reality they are under no obligation to professionals. Rather, they have the right and responsibility to identify their own needs, choose when they will work with professionals, help set policy, design service programs, and take part in modifying those programs so that families are themselves best served (Gartner, Lipsky, & Turnbull, 1991).

It is essential that professionals do not automatically assume that parents are inadequate to their challenges or that the family system is unhealthy. Just as with the child herself, negative expectations about families can become a self-fulfilling prophecy that actually interferes with family functioning; on the other hand, appropriately high expectations can act to support families in finding solutions to their problems. Collaboration first requires a positive attitude on the part of the professional, who sees parents as potential partners with the capacity to adapt to their situation. Second, the partnership between parents and professionals must be viewed as a process that becomes increasingly better as all involved improve their understanding and skills (Fine, 1991).

Good collaboration depends upon understanding the family system with its individual roles and balances. To that end, it can be helpful to think about one's own family system: values, attitudes, traditions, and customs, roles assumed within the family, existing rules, how and by whom decisions are made, how affection is expressed, how connections are made with extended family, and the part played by spirituality and religion (Fine, 1991).

Although the feelings and perceptions of everyone involved need to be heard and validated, the focus of collaboration is on setting goals, evaluating resources, identifying steps to be taken, establishing a time line for accomplishing goals, and providing opportunities for evaluation and feedback (Fine, 1991). Figure 13.7 presents steps that professionals and families can follow in ordering and structuring such a collaborative process (Simeonsson, Bailey, Huntington, & Comfort, 1986).

1. Problem definition
2. Goal selection
3. Strategy selection
4. Implementation
5. Evaluation

FIGURE 13.7 Steps in effective problem solving

SOURCE: Adapted from R. Krehbiel & R. L. Kroth (1991), Communicating with families of children with disabilities or chronic illness. In *Collaboration with parents of exceptional children,* Brandon, VT: Clinical Psychology Publishing.

COMMUNICATION

Because families and professionals learn from each other, effective collaboration depends upon good communication, central to which is *listening*. Poor listening has two distinct characteristics. The first is to talk excessively, and the second is to hear what is said but fail to understand the *speaker's* meaning (Krehbiel & Kroth, 1991). One way to improve good listening is to restate in one's own words the ideas and feelings the speaker has expressed.

The primary responsibility for establishing rapport and setting the tone for collaborative partnership falls to the professional. Such rapport requires—in addition to effective communication—a high degree of mutual trust. The development that allows an honest and effective working relationship takes time, patience, and commitment.

For the parents' part, it is particularly important that they be aware of the professional's agenda, goals, and methods. At the same time, families need to be encouraged that their own contribution of information and involvement is crucial to the partnership. Although professionals may believe it is their job to give information, families know how much information they need and how much they can take in at a particular time. Listening to families' needs is crucial.

FAMILY EMPOWERMENT

Effective collaboration leads to family empowerment (Dunst, 1997). Sometimes professionals believe they must have all the right answers about the services families need and the strategies that should be used to solve problems related to their child. But when service providers successfully convince parents of their professional authority, the results can be counterproductive and even detrimental as families become dependent upon others and fail to look to their own resources to solve problems. In contrast, family and professional partnerships imply that each member has an important contribution to make and that each voluntarily enters the partnership (Clifford & Warner, 1987). The roles of each must be determined by the partnership, and successful collaboration relies upon the honesty to share real views and the willingness to work through inevitable differences of opinion.

Table 13.2 Characteristics of Empowering Collaborative Relationships

Attitudes and Beliefs	Helping Behaviors	Responses and Consequences
Emphasis on family responsibility for meeting needs and solving problems.	Listen actively and reflectively.	Accept and support family decisions.
High expectations regarding family competency.	Help families clarify concerns and needs.	Minimize the sense of family indebtedness.
Emphasis on building upon family strengths.	Offer help that is congruent with the family's appraisal of needs.	Maintain confidentiality at all times, and share information only with permission.
	Promote acquisition of competencies to meet needs, solve problems, and achieve aspirations.	
	Emphasize collaboration as the mechanism for meeting needs.	
	Allow final decision making to rest with the family.	

Empowerment implies that families have the rights, responsibilities, and skills to contribute to a good working relationship.

When families are empowered, they have the skills they need to work effectively with others and make decisions and solve problems. They also have access to and control of the resources they need (Dunst & Paget, 1991). The idea of empowerment of families is much like that of self-determination discussed in previous chapters in that professionals must assume that families already have or are able to gain the competency required to manage their own lives effectively. For families—just as for individuals with MR themselves—positive and successful experiences bring forth needed competencies so that the expectations and opportunities inherent in true partnerships can enhance the families' sense of control over their own lives. To this end, collaborative partnerships with families must be based on identification and recognition of family strengths. Table 13.2 offers several characteristics of a successful and empowering collaborative relationship.

Multicultural Family Diversity

That people with mental retardation should enjoy full integration within their communities is the major premise of this book. Children, however, live within multiple communities. First, they are citizens of the world community to which we all belong. Next, they reside within a national community, their town or city, their neighborhood communities, and, finally their particular families. These community relationships coexist with one another, so although a child may live within a particular city, at the same time her membership in the Hispanic community, African-American community, or Polish community is an active feature of her family's heritage.

To illustrate the extent of cultural diversity currently in communities, the foreign-born population residing within the United States exceeds 30 million. During the 1990s, more than 250,000 Hispanic individuals entered the country each year (U.S. Bureau of the Census, 1998). With populations so diverse, professionals must be able to work effectively with multiple cultural groups.

Families who come from diverse ethnic and racial backgrounds have varying cultural values, attitudes, and traditions, all of which influence their responses toward people with disabilities, as well as their attitudes toward and responses to professional service providers (teachers, health service providers, social workers, psychologists, and so on). Differences among families include the composition of the family itself—where grandparents and friends may be included as part of a nuclear family—as well as the expected roles and obligations of their members. In addition, individuals from different cultural backgrounds may have markedly different ideas about the causes of disability—ideas directly related to their religious and spiritual beliefs.

> **FOR DISCUSSION** *How would you (as a professional) approach parents who believed their preschooler's mental retardation was the result of evil spirits? The parents believe it is pointless to provide special education or other early intervention services and instead take their child to spiritual sessions with a folk healer.*

As a result of such ethnic differences, individuals from different cultural backgrounds often have somewhat unique responses to the birth of a child with disabilities and have different ideas about what should be done for a child with mental retardation. These cultural differences can have important implications for the ways in which families provide support for members with disabilities; and such traits may bear heavily on their acknowledgment and acceptance of disability and the way they perceive and respond to educational and mental health agencies and professionals.

When attitudes, beliefs, and expectations are markedly different for parents than for the professionals who are working with them, serious misunderstandings can occur. As one example, teachers who approach families in an informal manner may intend to demonstrate friendliness, but the family may interpret that behavior as a lack of professional ability (Correa & Weismantel, 1991). To avoid such misunderstandings, it is the responsibility of professionals to familiarize themselves as much as possible with the cultural influences on the families with whom they work.

For families and professionals to work together effectively as a team, it is necessary that each party have a good understanding of the goals and priorities of other team members. These can be quite different, as has been seen, and importantly influenced by cultural membership. The ultimate goal for professionals should be to enlist the participation of family members in the interdisciplinary team and provide effective services within the wider family cultural system. Service providers not only need to understand the culture from which families come, but also must be able to mobilize and use the resources from these multicultural communities (Cockrell, Placier, Cockrell, & Middleton, 1999).

Cultural, ethnic, and racial differences are sometimes complicated by the social circumstances of poverty and, in the case of immigration, the necessity to adjust to an alien culture. What is more, many individuals who come from different cultural backgrounds are struggling with learning a new language in addition to other issues that arise from their recent immigration.

Understanding diverse cultures is further complicated by the fact that a particular cultural heading or label can conceal important family and intracultural differences. Individuals who fall under the heading *Hispanic,* for example, may have immigrated to the United States for diverse reasons—from seeking improved economic situations to fleeing from war. The reason for immigration brings with it many emotional and practical implications that involve a family's expectations of life in the new country, and it affects the problems such a family tries to manage.

Besides all this, culture itself is a living and changing entity, and professionals must catch a sense of this dynamic culture—in motion though it is—and they cannot rely on stereotypical notions or knowledge of cultural traditions. Service providers must understand the individual's culture as the individual lives and experiences it, and providers need to know the meaning and force of particular cultural roots for the specific individual.

Understanding cultural trends can give professionals clues about the areas and issues to watch out for, but the key to working effectively with families is *listening to* and *observing* the reality of those individual and unique families themselves. Knowing that godparents within Hispanic families (or elders within Asian) are often looked to as decision makers having key influences on the attitudes and behavior of other family members can alert professionals to these dynamics within particular families. But such general knowledge should not drive the assumption that similar dynamics are in place in every culturally similar family (Correa & Weismantel, 1991).

FOR DISCUSSION   *Because you recognize the importance of understanding your students' or clients' cultural heritage, you want to learn as much as you can about that heritage and how it affects your particular student or client. How do you proceed?*

Other important cultural differences can include nonverbal forms of communication in which members of some cultural groups stand closer or touch others more often than is typical in Western cultures. One cultural group may avoid making eye contact as a sign of respect, while other groups would view this same behavior as a sign of disinterest or insincerity. In spite of such nonverbal differences, the key to good communication remains active listening. Through careful observation, listening to what parents have to say, and openness to families' backgrounds and goals, effective communication can be achieved. Table 13.3 provides examples of cultural beliefs that may effect intervention in culturally diverse situations.

If professionals are to involve parents successfully in team intervention, then they must find common ground upon which to base their partnership. Professionals should get to know the child's family through home visits, attendance at cultural events and festivals, and dining in neighborhood restaurants, as well as by finding out about the family's spiritual beliefs. As with any collaborative effort, the success of multicultural teams depends upon the attitudes of the professionals

Table 13.3 Some Diverse Cultural Beliefs with Implications for Effective Team Functioning

Ethnic Group	Cultural Belief or Quality	Implications
Mexican-American	Spiritual healing	Understand that health-related, special education, or mental health services may be secondary to the family's hope of a cure.
		Healers may be a support system for the family.
Puerto Rican	Compadres	Extended family system may include godparents, close friends, and neighbors.
		Respect the involvement of nonfamily members in the decision-making process.
		Use extrafamilial subsystems to provide support for parents.
Japanese	Avoidance of confrontation	Parents are not likely to challenge a professional in a meeting, even if they are unhappy with the recommendations.
Native American	Acceptance of fate	Acceptance of the child and focus on the child's strengths by professionals.

SOURCE: From V. I. Correa & J. Weismantel (1991), Multicultural issues related to families with an exceptional child. In M. J. Fine (Ed.), *Collaboration with parents of exceptional children.* Brandon, VT: Clinical Psychology Publishing.

involved. Service providers must take a problem-solving approach to identifying barriers and then mobilize existing resources to overcome those barriers. Such resources are often found within the cultural community of the family itself.

Unfortunately, parents from culturally diverse backgrounds are sometimes seen as threats to effective child intervention and are actively discouraged from participation. This is most likely when the goals of the service provider are perceived to be in conflict with those of the family. Individuals who seek to understand the cultural influences on those with whom they work must first be clear about their own values, beliefs, and ideas about effective parenting and then approach teamwork with sincere respect for everyone involved. Figure 13.8 shows several linguistic and cultural characteristics that are important to understanding individual families.

If effective intervention for all children with mental retardation is to take place within the community, then school systems and other service agencies must make themselves a part of the communities they serve. As with all interventions, evaluation plays a primary role in continued and improved effectiveness. Evaluation should determine whether the program actually meets the family's needs and if parent involvement has, in fact, increased as a result of outreach efforts. An essential ingredient is asking individuals from the community, as well as families themselves, to review the program and its evaluation.

Aging Parents

For families of a child with MR, family life and the importance of family influence does not end when the child reaches adulthood. Large numbers of aging parents have at least partial responsibility for such a child and, as with younger children, family life for people with MR who reach adulthood involves both positive and negative experiences, gratification, and frustration.

Linguistic and Cultural Characteristics

1. How much of the new country's language is spoken in the home?
2. What is the parents' literacy level?
3. What are the family's religious practices?
4. How long have the group and family been in their new country?
5. If the culture group migrated, why?
6. Does the family return to its native country for visits?
7. If the family members were refugees, did they flee war?
8. What reasons did they have for settling in the particular school area?
9. What roles are assigned to family members?
10. Did the children previously go to school?
11. What was school like in the country of origin?
12. What aspirations does the family have for its children?
13. What special customs and beliefs of the group may affect the behavior of the children in school?

Perceptions of the Child

1. How does the family react to the child?
2. How do members of the cultural group view children with disabilities and mental retardation in particular?
3. What are the medical practices in the culture (e.g., folk medicine)?
4. What are the family's beliefs about the cause of the disability?

FIGURE13.8 Key family characteristics

SOURCE: Adapted from V. I. Correa & J. Weismantel (1991), Multicultural issues related to families with an exceptional child. In M. J. Fine (Ed.), *Collaboration with parents of exceptional children.* Brandon, VT: Clinical Psychology Publishing.

As parents themselves age, caring for their adult children at home can become more difficult. For older parents, support services such as day programs or employment opportunities for their adult child often become pivotal in whether the family can manage. Needed professional services—including counseling, support groups, respite, and especially out-of-home day programs and employment—have considerable influence on reducing frustrations. The gratification of family life, however, is closely tied to the relationship between parents and adult children, and this relationship is strongly influenced by the presence or absence of behavior problems (Greenberg, Seltzer, & Greenley, 1993).

With advancing age, parents also become increasingly concerned about what will happen to their adult children after they are gone. Even so, large numbers of parents put off placement planning until there is a crisis—often the death or serious illness of the caregiving parent (Janicki, Otis, Puccio, Rettig, & Jacobson, 1985). Many families report, however, that they need more information about residential programs, guardianships, and financial planning, as well as better access to family counseling (Heller & Factor, 1993). Such information could help families make these important long-term decisions.

For those families who do make advance plans, most prefer that another family member (often a sibling, and most often a sister) take over the care. For those who prefer a residential option, maladaptive behaviors are the most often mentioned reason (Heller & Factor, 1993).

▌▌ LOOKING AHEAD ▶

The extent to which one can adjust to living with a child who has retardation depends, as Bronfenbrenner reminds us (see Chapter 2), on characteristics of the family, the child, and the larger culture. For the mother, it may depend upon her patience, her ability to deal with children in general, and the extent to which her own needs can be met through nurturing and caring for others—or must be met through some other creative endeavor. Just as children are individuals with individual personalities and talents, so parents are with all of their own strengths and weaknesses. Not everyone can manage a child with severe disabilities and provide the support and experience that will best help that child grow. Perhaps not everyone should try.

This chapter has focused primarily on children with mental retardation, their families, and their family relationships with professionals. Given the complexity of families today, we have seen the importance of planning service delivery within a family systems perspective. The next chapter will take up issues of adult living, and it will include decisions about where to live, changing family relationships (as the individual with MR takes on adult roles), and the problems and satisfactions that come with finding paid employment and other means of contributing to society. As we will see, effective collaboration among professionals and between professionals and families remains crucial in facilitating these important transitions.

INFOTRAC COLLEGE EDITION

The social support of extended families can be important to the adjustment of families with children who have mental retardation, yet extended families play different roles among cultures. Enter *extended family* as the keyword in *InfoTrac College Edition*. What did you find about the relationship between extended families and cultures? Please give several examples.

REFERENCES

Abelson, A. G. (1999). Respite care needs of parents of children with developmental disabilities. *Focus on Autism and Other Developmental Disabilities, 14*(2), 96–100.

Beckman, P. (1983). Influence of selected child characteristics on stress in families of handicapped infants. *American Journal of Mental Deficiency, 88*(2), 150–156.

———. (1991). Comparison of mothers' and fathers' perceptions of the effect of young children with and without disabilities. *American Journal on Mental Retardation, 95*(5), 585–595.

Blacher, J. B., Hanneman, R. A., & Rousey, A. B. (1992). Out-of-home placement of children with severe handicaps: A comparison of approaches. *American Journal on Mental Retardation, 96*(6), 607–616.

Black, M. M., Molaison, V. A., & Small, M. W. (1990). Families caring for a young adult with mental retardation: Service needs and urgency of community living requests. *American Journal on Mental Retardation, 95*(1), 32–39.

Boer, F., & Dunn, J. (Eds.). (1992). *Children's sibling relationships: Developmental and clinical issues.* Hillsdale, NJ: Erlbaum.

Botuck, S., & Winsberg, B. G. (1991). Effects of respite on mothers of school-age and adult children with severe disabilities. *Mental Retardation, 29*(1), 43–47.

Bristol, M. (1987). The home care of children with developmental disabilities: Empirical support for a model of successful family coping with stress. In S. Landesman, P. M. Vietze, & M. J. Begab (Eds.), *Living environments and mental retardation.* Washington, DC: American Association on Mental Deficiency.

Bristol, M., & Schopler, E. (1984). A developmental perspective on stress and coping in families of autistic children. In J. Blacher (Ed.), *Families of severely handicapped children.* New York: Academic Press.

Bromley, B. E., & Blacher, J. (1991). Parental reasons for out-of-home placement of children with severe handicaps. *Mental Retardation, 29*(5), 275–280.

Browne, G., & Bramston, P. (1998). Parental stress in families of young people with an intellectual disability: The nurse's role. *Australian Journal of Advanced Nursing, 15*(3), 31–37.

Cameron, S. J., & Orr, R. R. (1989). Stress in families of school-aged children with delayed mental development. *Canadian Journal of Rehabilitation, 2,* 137–144.

Carr, J. (1970). Mongolism: Telling the parents. *Developmental Medical Child Neurology, 12,* 213–221.

Challela, M. S. (1981). Coping with a mentally retarded child. In A. Milunsky (Ed.), *Coping with crisis and handicap.* New York: Plenum Press.

Chisholm, C. A., Pappas, D. J., & Sharp, M. C. (1997). Communicating bad news. *Obstetrics and Gynecology, 90*(4), 637–639.

Clifford, D., & Warner, R. (1987). *The partnership book* (3rd ed.). Berkeley, CA: Nolo Press.

Cockrell, K. S., Placier, P. L., Cockrell, D. H., & Middleton, J. N. (1999). Coming to terms with "diversity" and "multiculturalism" in teacher education: Learning about our students, changing our practice. *Teaching and Teacher Education, 15*(4), 351–366.

Coley, R. L. (1998). Children's socialization experiences and functioning in single-mother households: The importance of fathers and other men. *Child Development, 69*(1), 219–230.

Correa, V. I., & Weismantel, J. (1991). Multicultural issues related to families with an exceptional child. In M. J. Fine (Ed.), *Collaboration with parents of exceptional children* (pp. 83–102). Brandon, VT: Clinical Psychology Publishing.

Curran, N. Q., & Bongiorno, H. H. (1986). Parents' perspectives: Focus on need. In C. L. Salisbury & J. Intagliata (Ed.), *Respite Care: support for persons with developmental disabilities and their families* (pp. 89–98). Baltimore, MD: Paul H. Brookes

Cutler, B. C. (1986). The community-based respite residence: Finding a place in the system. In C. L. Salisbury & J. Intagliata (Ed.), *Respite care: Support for persons with developmental disabilities and their families* (pp. 167–194). Baltimore, MD: Paul H. Brookes

Drillien, C. M., & Wilkenson, E. M. (1964). Mongolism: When should parents be told? *British Medical Journal, 2,* 1306–1307.

Dunst, C. J. (1997). Conceptual and empirical foundations of family-centered practice. In R. J. Illback & C. T. Cobb (Eds.), *Integrated services for children and families: Opportunities for psychological practice* (pp. 75–91). Washington, DC: American Psychological Association.

Dunst, C. J., & Paget, K. D. (1991). Parent-professional partnerships and family empowerment. In M. J. Fine (Ed.), *Collaboration with parents of exceptional children* (pp. 25–44). Brandon, VT: Clinical Psychology Publishing.

Dyson, L. L. (1991). Families of young children with handicaps: Parental stress and family functioning. *American Journal on Mental Retardation, 95*(6), 623–629.

Dyson, L. L. (1993). Response to the presence of a child with disabilities: Parental stress and family functioning over time. *American Journal on Mental Retardation, 98*(2), 207–218.

Eakes, G. G., Burke, M. L., & Hainsworth, M. A. (1998). Middle-range theory of chronic sorrow. *Image—The Journal of Nursing Scholarship, 30*(2), 179–184.

Farber, B. (1959). Effects of a severely mentally retarded child on family integration. *Monographs of the Society for Research in Child Development, 24*(2): 1–112.

Fine, M. J. (1991). The handicapped child and the family: Implications for professionals. In M. J. Fine (Ed.), *Collaboration with parents of exceptional children.* Brandon, VT: Clinical Psychology Publishing.

Finnegan, J. (1993). *Shattered dreams—lonely choices: Birthparents of babies with disabilities talk about adoption.* Westport, CT: Greenwood.

Gallimore, R., Weisner, R. S., Bernheimer, L. P., Guthrie, D., & Nihira, K. (1993). Family responses to young children with developmental delays: Accommodation activity in ecological and cultural context. *American Journal on Mental Retardation, 98*(2), 185–206.

Gartner, A., Lipsky, D. K., & Turnbull, A. P. (1991). *Supporting families with a child with a disability: An international outlook.* Baltimore, MD: Paul H. Brookes.

Goodship, S. (1987). Stress in the family of the Rett's child. *Brain Development, 9,* 539–542.

Greenberg, J. S., Seltzer, M. M., & Greenley, J. R. (1993). Aging parents of adults with disabilities: The gratifications and frustrations of later-life caregiving. *The Gerontologist, 33*(4), 542–550.

Greenfeld, J. (1972). *A child called Noah: A family journey.* New York: Holt, Rinehart, & Winston.

Grossman, F. K. (1972). *Brothers and sisters of retarded children.* Syracuse, NY: Syracuse University Press.

Heller, T., & Factor, A. (1993). Aging family caregivers: Support resources and changes in burden and placement desire. *American Journal on Mental Retardation, 98*(3), 417–426.

Hunt, N. (1967). *The world of Nigel Hunt: The diary of a Mongoloid youth.* New York: Garret Publications.

Hunter, K. (1987). Rett syndrome: Parents' view about specific symptoms. *Brain & Development, 9*(5), 535–537.

Janicki, M. P., Otis, M. R., Puccio, P. S., Rettig, J. S., & Jacobson, J. W. (1985). Service needs among older developmentally disabled persons. In M. P. Janicki & H. M. Wisniewski (Eds.), *Aging and developmental disabilities: Issues and approaches* (pp. 289–304). Baltimore, MD: Paul H. Brookes.

Kobe, F. H., Rojahn, J., & Schroeder, S. R. (1991). Predictors of urgency of out-of-home placement needs. *Mental Retardation, 29*(6), 323–328.

Krauss, M. W. (1993). Child-related and parenting stress: Similarities and differences between mothers and fathers of children with disabilities. *American Journal on Mental Retardation, 97*(4), 393–404.

Krehbiel, R., & Kroth, R. L. (1991). Communicating with families of children with disabilities or chronic illness. In M. J. Fine (Ed.), *Collaboration with parents of exceptional children* (pp. 103–128). Brandon, VT: Clinical Psychology Publishing.

Lakin, K. C., & Bruininks, R. J. (1985). Contemporary services for handicapped children and youth. In R. H. Bruininks & K. C. Lakin (Eds.), *Living and learning in the least restrictive environment* (pp. 3–22). Baltimore, MD: Paul H. Brookes.

Lamb, M. E., & Meyer, D. J. (1991). Fathers of children with special needs. In M. Seligman (Ed.), *The family with a handicapped child* (2nd ed., pp. 151–180). Boston: Allyn & Bacon.

Lian, M. J., & Aloia, G. (1994). Parental responses, roles, and responsibilities. In S. K. Alper, P. J. Schloss, & C. N. Schloss (Eds.), *Families of students with disabilities* (pp. 51–94). Boston: Allyn & Bacon.

Mallow, G. E., & Bechtel, G. A. (1999). Chronic sorrow: The experience of parents with children who are developmentally disabled. *Journal of Psychosocial Nursing and Mental Health Services, 37*(7), 31–35.

Marc, D., & MacDonald, J. (1988). Respite care—Who uses it? *Mental Retardation, 26,* 93–96.

Orr, R. R., Cameron, S. J., & Day, D. M. (1991). Coping with stress in families with children who have mental retardation: An evaluation of the double ABCX model. *American Journal on Mental Retardation, 95*(4), 444–450.

Orr, R. R., Cameron, S. J., Dobson, L. A., & Day, D. M. (1993). Age-related changes in stress experienced by families with a child who has developmental delays. *Mental Retardation, 31*(3), 171–176.

Perske, R., & Perske, M. (1986). *Hope for the families* (3rd ed.) Nashville: Abingdon Press.

Powell, T. H., & Ogle, P. A. (1985). *Brothers and sisters: A special part of exceptional families.* Baltimore, MD: Paul H. Brookes.

Raech, H. (1966). A parent discusses initial counseling. *Mental Retardation* (March–April), 25–26.

Rimland, I. (1984). *The furies and the flame.* Novato, CA: Arena Press.

Rousey, A., Best, S., & Blacher, J. (1992). Mothers' and fathers' perceptions of stress and coping with children who have severe disabilities. *American Journal on Mental Retardation, 97*(1), 99–109.

Rousey, A., Blacher, J. B., & Hanneman, R. A. (1990). Predictors of out-of-home placement of children with severe handicaps: A cross-sectional analysis. *American Journal on Mental Retardation, 94*(5), 522–531.

Salisbury, C. L., & Intagliata, J. (1986). *Respite care: Support for persons with developmental disabilities and their families.* Baltimore, MD: Paul H. Brookes.

Sarimski, K. (1997). Behavioural phenotypes and family stress in three mental retardation syndromes. *European Child and Adolescent Psychiatry, 6*(1), 26–31.

Simeonsson, R. J., Bailey, D. B., Huntington, G. S., & Comfort, M. (1986). Testing the concept of goodness of fit in early intervention. *Infant Mental Health Journal, 7*(1), 81–94.

Slater, M. (1986). Respite care: A national perspective. In C. L. Salisbury & J. Intagliata (Ed.), *Respite Care: support for persons with developmental disabilities and their families* (pp. 69–88). Baltimore, MD: Paul H. Brookes.

Sonnek, I. M. (1986). Grandparents and the extended family of handicapped children. In R. R. Fewell & P. F. Vadsey (Eds.), *Families of handicapped children: Needs and supports across the life span* (pp. 99–120). Austin, TX: Pro-ED.

Stoneman, Z., Brody, G. H., Davis, C. H., & Crapps, J. M. (1991). Ascribed role relations between children with mental retardation and their younger siblings. *American Journal on Mental Retardation, 95*(5), 537–550.

Tausig, M. (1985). Factors in family decision-making about placement for developmentally disabled individuals. *American Journal of Mental Deficiency, 89,* 352–361.

Tingey, C. (1988). *Down syndrome: A resource handbook.* Boston: Little, Brown.

U.S. Bureau of the Census. (1998). *Population estimates program.* Washington, DC: U.S. Government Printing Office.

Wassenaar, J. (1994). Personal communication.

Weisner, T., Beizer, L., & Stolze, L. (1991). Religion and families of children with developmental delays. *American Journal on Mental Retardation, 95*(6), 647–662.

14

Adult Living and Work

Whereas Chapter 13 focused on the families of those with mental retardation, this chapter takes an in-depth look at the residential living options beyond family for people with MR and the factors that make adjustment to community living most likely. It also focuses on career development and the supports that may be needed to make the work life of those with MR most productive and satisfying.

RESIDENTIAL OPTIONS

For the greater part of this century, most people with mental retardation have lived in large, publicly financed institutions. With the deinstitutionalization movement (see Chapter 3), this situation changed, so now literally hundreds of licensing categories exist for facilities that provide residential services for those with MR (Hill & Lakin, 1986). Generally speaking, available residential options have moved from larger to smaller facilities, from publicly to privately operated, from geographically distant to local communities, and from depending upon in-house services to depending upon community service providers. Some of the many possibilities for residential living are shown in Figure 14.1.

COMMUNITY INTEGRATION
AND DEINSTITUTIONALIZATION

As we saw in Chapter 13, most people with mental retardation currently live with their families. Of the approximately 78 million people with MR in the United States, only a little more than 300,000 receive outside residential services (Lakin, Braddock, & Smith, 1996). The trend in residential living is clearly turning from large, state-run institutions toward smaller community placements. From 1980 to 1993, the number of people in large state institutions (that is, with 16 or more residents) declined by 45.5 percent (The Arc, 1995). Even so, as of June 1996, more than 62,000 people remained in such state institutions. These individuals usually have more severe retardation and are more likely to have additional disabilities—although many people with equally severe conditions live successfully in small community placements (Cunningham & Mueller, 1991).

The movement away from large residential facilities has been in direct response to ideological changes concerning the potential of those with MR, and about the rights of those with disabilities in general to live and work with others in their communities. Exposed abuses within institutions also have encouraged the shift toward normalization as a guiding principle (see Chapter 3), and vocal parent advocates have been important influences in this accomplishment.

The move toward community living has not been without challenge, however. In fact, most parents who had sons or daughters living within such facilities were satisfied with the services they received and opposed both the concept of normal-

Independent living	Small intensive care home
Supported independent living	Intermediate care facility (ICF/MR)
Family	Nursing home
Residential training school	Large private institution
Adult foster care	Large public institution
Group home	

FIGURE 14.1 Some examples of residential living options

ization and community placement planning (Spreat, Telles, Conroy, Feinstein, & Colombatto, 1987). Parental objections to deinstitutionalization fell mainly into five categories:

1. disagreement with the normalization concept,

2. difficulty accepting the notion of deinstitutionalization after they had already made the difficult decision to institutionalize (usually based on strong professional recommendations),

3. skepticism about the quality of the community service system,

4. resentment of the "heavy-handed" process of deinstitutionalization, and

5. concern over the stability of funding for new programs (Latib, Conroy, & Hess, 1990).

To begin with, based on their years of sometimes bitter experience, parents often found it difficult to believe that their children were ever going to significantly change. Such parents had come to terms with the idea that their children were not "normal" and feared that normalization efforts would be a setup for still more disappointment. The very fact that professionals had, in the first place, maintained that institutionalization was the only correct and rational decision and now were reversing that position only added to parents' skepticism and even resentment.

Furthermore, parents rightly perceived, especially in the case of closing institutions, that they were to have little influence on the decision regarding new placements. They were concerned that their daughters and sons would now be faced with the trauma of continual change and adjustment—in place of the stability that the institution had provided. Many parents also had children with medical complications, which they feared could not be adequately managed by community services. In many cases, parents had imagined that their child's future care was settled, and now at the very time of their own advancing age, they were faced with new worry of an unknown future for their child. And, finally, parents were not convinced that the money for community placements could be counted upon for any significant length of time (Latib, Conroy, & Hess, 1990).

Parents' negative attitudes toward deinstitutionalization, however, usually changed after clients had been living in community placements for a time; and

Colorful, light, and bright; perceptually warm and diverse	Windows of the size, type, and placement ordinarily found in homes
Small and self-contained	Space for individual possessions
Bedrooms for one or two residents	Doors between rooms
Family dining facilities	Baths and showers designed for privacy
Toilet, faucets, showers, and other fixtures that are typical of homes	Access to light switches and thermostats
Variety in design and furnishings	Access to "risky" features such as stairs, electrical outlets, and hot water

FIGURE 14.2 Characteristics typical of homelike environments

SOURCE: Adapted from W. Wolfensberger (1975), *The origin and nature of our institutional models.* Syracuse, NY: Human Policy Press.

the parents were initially less negative when they had actually visited community group homes (Grimes & Vitello, 1990; Spreat et al., 1987). Follow-up studies three to five years after community placements showed that parents were only somewhat more accepting of normalization, although they did believe that their son or daughter was happier, reported greater happiness themselves, and believed that the services received and the quality of the environment were superior to the institution (Larson & Lakin, 1991; Kraushaar & Elliott, 1995). Families are still concerned, however, about the stability of services and funding, issues that present very real problems as we shall see.

Today, most large institutions have changed substantially in response to normalization. Many have developed small cottage systems, in which they separate individuals into smaller, more manageable groups. They make far greater efforts now to involve their residents in community activities, and they offer their own facilities and personnel as resources to the community. Some institutions offer respite care for community families, for example, and provide behavioral consulting for community group homes.

Even so, large residential facilities obviously require a great deal of structure, even regimentation, to operate effectively. This is so whether they are institutions for people with MR, military barracks, or private preparatory schools for adolescents from wealthy families. Certainly none of these, however, are places that most of us would consider appropriate to live out our entire lives, largely because we do not consider them homelike (Robinson & Thompson, 1999). (Figure 14.2 lists features of a homelike environment.) Almost all institutions today acknowledge the limitations of large permanent residential placements and are working to help find community placements for their residents—even for those with the most severe disabilities.

FOR DISCUSSION   *Access to "risky" architectural features is listed as a characteristic of a homelike environment. Do you think people with mental retardation should be protected from such risks? If so, in what manner? If not, why not?*

The box below introduces Donald, who has severe disabilities and resides in a state institution. (He is also the author's cousin.) The box provides excerpts from an interview with Don's social worker about the problems of finding community placements for clients such as Don.

Realities of Community Placement

Don is 36-years-old and lives at the Warren G. Murray Center in Centralia, Illinois. In spite of his profound retardation, deafness, autism, and behavior problems, he enjoys and profits from the trips he occasionally takes into the community. If the proper supports were available for him, he probably could live in a less-restrictive environment. To live successfully in a community setting, Don would need a placement in which he could receive constant supervision, occasional medical treatment for his ears, and be on a strict behavioral plan. In the following excerpt, Bill Hayes, director of social work at Murray, talks about the difficulties of finding the services needed for more severely involved people within the community:

Many of our clients here have serious behavioral problems, problems that the community facilities don't feel prepared to manage. Successful integration of these clients will require structured, well-developed behavioral programs—and personnel with the expertise to carry them out.

Other clients have serious medical problems, such as very bad heart problems, or very bad bone problems [osteoporosis], so that if someone doesn't lift them just right, they can snap a bone. Or, some have severe diabetes. Here we have our own physicians, nurses, and a dentist. A lot of the physicians in the community are reluctant to serve people in group homes or in family homes. We sometimes bring people from the community here to have dental evaluations, because they can't find someone in the community to do it. Physicians and dentists in the community too often say that they don't have the ex-

pertise or their schedules are too busy. If community integration is to be successful, professionals in the community— physicians, psychologists, psychiatrists, and others—will need to be prepared to work with individuals who have developmental disabilities. I've been here 17 years, and the whole time I've been here the facility directors that I've been under have always wanted to cooperate with the community to get folks out there, but there needs to be more people trained in the community to care for the needs of this population. So we end up with clients who are ready to go into the community, and we are looking for placements for them, but they are still here because the services aren't out there.

While students are in college, I think it's a good opportunity for them to have some kind of experience with people with mental retardation. Then, when somebody comes into their office or their business, and that person is a little different than what the professional is used to, the professional knows how to deal with it. They're not afraid of it.

One of the things I'd like to say to your students is that if they are professionals working for an organization that does not typically provide services to people who have developmental disabilities, then they are going to have to face a choice as to whether they want to deal with that population or not. If they decide to avoid doing so, and they still feel that state institutions aren't the best place for residential services for those with developmental disabilities, then they are part of the problem, rather than part of the solution.

Private Residential Treatment Schools

Usually, when we think of institutions we might assume them to be large state-run facilities, but many private boarding schools offer educational programs for children and adolescents. These programs are usually expensive—as much as $76,000 a year or more—although some do accept Medicaid or Medicare payments. Typically, they offer a full range of habitation services, including adaptive equipment, recreational opportunities, and physical, occupational, and speech therapy. Some of these programs also offer community group home placement for youngsters enrolled in their schools.

The typical advantage of such programs is that significant individualized attention is offered from a variety of professionals, including behavior specialists and medical practitioners, who are specifically geared toward helping their clients develop skills that will enable them to live and work in the community as adults. Today, public institutions strive toward these same goals, but small private institutions have the resources to offer better salaries and benefits, hire personnel who have more training and education, and provide lower staff-to-client ratios, and they also have the incentive to please parents and guardians who pay expensive tuition for the services they receive. Furthermore, these facilities serve only children and adolescents; they do not act as lifelong caretakers.

COMMUNITY LIVING

As seen in Figure 14.1, numerous residential settings exist within the community for people with MR, yet all of them share the goal of including residents in the typical activities of the population. For children, these include family life, school, and peer friendships. For adults, they involve home life, work, and leisure and recreational pursuits. Although the extent to which an individual can participate in these activities depends upon the nature and severity of his disabilities, it is usually medical problems and behavior problems rather than IQ that preclude participation.

The majority of people with mental retardation and developmental disabilities who live within the community now reside in homes with six or fewer people (Lakin, Braddock, & Smith, 1996). Most adult residents in community placements spend their days in a work-type setting. Many have paid employment either in community jobs or sheltered workshops. Others are in day programs that provide vocational training or occupational therapy. Residents take part as much as possible in housekeeping duties and meal preparation, and they engage in recreational activities both in the home and outside in the community.

Indeed, the typical day for a group home resident is much like that of any other adult: She gets up in time for work, dresses, and prepares and eats breakfast. She may use public transportation to get to work, or transportation may be provided. After work, she returns home, prepares the evening meal, then watches television or goes out to a planned activity. The major difference in her life is likely to involve the number of her friendships, the extent to which she actually interacts with citizens in the community, and the amount of personal control that she exerts over her life. Although residents in community placements do exercise more choice over matters in their lives than their counterparts in large institutions, the opportunities for choice—even in community residences—are too few (Stancliffe, 1997; Stancliffe & Abery, 1997).

Studies of behavior change for those moved from institutions to smaller community living placements generally show increases in adaptive behavior (Larson & Lakin, 1989; Lynch, Kellow, & Willson, 1997), though the behavioral areas of change vary: Some residents may experience language gains, while others may show improved social skills, daily living skills, or vocational abilities. Sometimes these gains have not been maintained over time, because improvements may initially result primarily from increased opportunity to engage in behaviors that were impossible in the old setting, such as the opportunity to help prepare meals or perform housekeeping duties. But similar changes have also been found in institutional control groups where the programmatic focus changed from custodial to therapeutic care. Although there is no question that many community placement options afford opportunities for taking part in recreational, social, and work-related activities that institutional living precludes, skill maintenance and continued improvement seem dependent upon ongoing and effective training to help make the most of these new possibilities (Phillips, 1998).

Community Acceptance

Perhaps the ultimate measure of the success of community integration is the extent to which an individual is accepted as a legitimate part of the community and to which that individual feels she "belongs." For most of us, such acceptance means that we have friends upon whom we can rely for companionship and support, and neighbors who at the least wave a friendly greeting. The reception to community group homes by members of the community, however, has been mixed. Statistics on the percentage of group homes that encounter opposition vary, but in some instances objection has been strong enough to block the opening of a home (Lubin, Schwartz, Zigman, & Janicki, 1982).

Two main reasons community members oppose residential programs are (1) the supposed effects on property values and (2) fears about risks to health and safety. But research has shown that property values do not decline with the introduction of group homes, and people with MR pose no greater threat to neighborhood safety than do other citizens. Because neighbors' fears are in reality unfounded, some planners have advocated an educational approach to establishing community residences in which neighbors are invited to open houses and home providers meet with community groups. There is some evidence, however, that educational efforts are associated with *greater* rather than less opposition (Seltzer, 1984).

FOR DISCUSSION   *When supporters contact area citizens and businesses in an educational effort before establishing a neighborhood group home, opposition is sometimes greater than when no such effort is made. What explanation can you provide for this finding?*

Once a residence is established, opposition typically declines. It is an interesting fact that those people who are most favorable toward community residences are those who actually have such a residence in their neighborhood (Kauffman & Krebs, 1993). It appears, therefore, that education does not always take the place of actual experience and that proximity does increase acceptance.

Even as community acceptance rises with the presence of group homes, there are still far too few placements, and a major impediment to community living is the simple shortage of available housing. In some urban areas of the United States, hundreds of people are waiting for housing—sometimes as many as are actually placed. And a substantial number of families still do not know that residential services exist or where or how to apply.

Community "Institutionalization"

Although community living has provided many more experiences and opportunities for people with MR—including the important advantages of living in a homelike setting and involvement in the activities of the world—many writers have increasingly warned of the institutional characteristics retained within community placements. Even more disturbing, some homes that originally provided high-quality care in an innovative and enthusiastic atmosphere have deteriorated into routinized and impersonal service provision (Landesman, 1988).

The ironic institutionalization of community residences can occur for several reasons. For one thing, simply living in a small residence within an established neighborhood does not itself guarantee that residents will actually form outside relationships. For most clients who live in group homes, their only real relationships are with staff and family (Lord & Pedlar, 1991), and staff members too often become the residents' main link to the outside world, the source of structure for "normal" home life, and primary companionship. This bond is stronger because the majority of group home residents do not form friendships with their housemates. To the contrary, relationships among residents are often continuous sources of friction and tension.

Because clients in small community settings depend so heavily on staff for physical, environmental, and emotional support, frequent staff turnover is especially problematic. Unfortunately, turnover rates are highest among small nonpublic settings that house from one to six residents (Mitchell & Braddock, 1994; Larson, 1997), mostly because of low pay and poor benefits, but also because of inadequate staff training and preparation. This problem actually worsened as the difference in wages between public and private residential facilities doubled from 1982 to 1992 (Mitchell & Braddock, 1993; Larson, 1997).

Even more basic to clients' everyday lifestyle, however, is the reported tendency of community placement settings to become overly rigid in routine and governed by inflexible rules. One key element of daily life for most of us, for example, is the freedom and responsibility to make choices. We decide when to get up and when to go to bed, what to eat and when to have meals; we choose the clothes that most appeal to us; and we decide which leisure activities we prefer, as well as determine those in which we will not participate. In some placements, however, these basic choices are sacrificed to efficiency and ease of management.

Even those people with more severe retardation are usually capable of making some fundamental choices (see Chapter 11), but too often they are given no opportunity to do so (McConkey, Morris, & Purcell, 1999).

This tendency toward rigidity and inflexibility is fostered and reinforced by standards for licensing and certification. Certain licensing requirements are certainly necessary, but some authors charge that too much emphasis is often placed on paperwork and documentation while client outcomes are ignored or underplayed (Holburn, 1992). Critics also cite the debilitating and counterproductive effects of too many rules that have too little direct relation with outcome goals. These effects include impersonalized staff–resident relations, minimal spontaneity, and prohibited innovation (Holburn, 1990). Furthermore, when service providers and direct-care staff are severely penalized for failing to comply with regulations, dishonest reporting of compliance is encouraged and even reinforced (Cullari, 1984).

These authors stress the importance of research and evaluation methods that determine the effect of regulations on issues of genuine client benefit, while citing instances of rules that appear to have no good effect. For example, is a requirement that there must be an alphabetical list of clients names on file likely to benefit clients in a home with only six people (Shea, 1992)? When such regulations become numerous and time-consuming, client welfare is compromised.

In line with the recommendations of those who seek changes in regulatory practices and methods of evaluation, commercial organizations that are particularly successful in meeting their customers' needs place their focus on customer outcomes rather than on carrying out specified procedures (Blunden, 1988). Such organizations stay in close contact with their customers at all levels of the organization and are committed to action and innovation. They provide opportunities for staff to communicate, identify problems, and formulate possible solutions. Such a system relies upon forming a group of *key stakeholders* who work together to plan improvements and assess outcomes. In the case of community residential services, these stakeholders might include clients, families, staff members, and associated professionals.

FOR DISCUSSION *Recent authors stress the importance of holding residential providers responsible for client outcomes rather than for particular procedures. Can you give examples of both outcomes and procedures, and explain why outcomes are preferred?*

Intermediate Care Facilities (ICF/MR) and the Home and Community-Based Services (HCB) Waiver Program

The extent to which licensure and certification promote the problems of community institutionalization is the more critical, because the majority of those who receive residential services rely for payment on Medicaid, which pays only for placements that carry particular types of certification. One important source of such placements are termed intermediate care facilities–MR (or ICF/MR).

Facilities licensed ICF/MR vary greatly: They can be small three- or four-person group homes or large operations of 16 or more people; some offer services to clients who require little in the way of supervision and training, whereas others provide services for people with severe and multiple disabilities. They all have in common the advantage of Medicaid eligibility, however, and the associated regulations thus carry a substantial incentive for compliance.

Partly in response to concerns about overregulation and client quality of life, in 1981 Congress enacted the Home and Community-Based Services (HCBS) waiver program for individuals with Medicaid. Since 1992 especially, the trend has been toward more HCBS placements so that many ICF/MR openings have been transferred to this new system. The HCBS program has provided the opportunity for more people with MR to live in smaller, less-regulated community homes (Anderson, Sandlin, Prouty, & Lakin, 1996; Smith, Prouty, & Lakin, 1996).

In this same spirit, those individuals who develop certification and licensure requirements have worked to correct bureaucratic inflexibilities. Some states, for example, now request a self-evaluation as part of the documentation for approval. This, at least, gives the provider an opportunity to state his own goals and bring forward some of the accomplishments he values most highly. Other states have more dramatically changed their systems (Newton, Ard, Horner, & Towes, 1996). The Office of Developmental Disability Services in Oregon, for example, has developed a program that focuses on outcomes, not regulations; it also relies on measures based on interviews of personnel, clients, and families, as well as on direct observation of clients' lifestyles to assess the degree of independence, productivity, and integration in their lives. These new regulations encourage personnel to engage in continuous improvement toward these value-based goals. More such changes are needed, however, because research suggests that less-regulated and more flexible residential systems actually result in better outcomes for clients at the same or even lower cost (Conroy, 1996).

FACTORS IN SUCCESSFUL
COMMUNITY ADJUSTMENT

Definition of Adjustment

Once individuals are placed in community settings, it becomes crucial to evaluate whether they have adjusted successfully. But what evidence would point to such success? Early studies of adjustment focused on whether individuals remained in the new setting or were returned to institutional living (Haney, 1988). And, although this measure does reveal some minimal level of success, it neither adequately describes actual changes in the residents' lifestyle nor takes into account the adjustment of many residents who enter community placements from family settings.

As we have learned, most people with MR live with their families, but as these individuals grow older, their peers are making the important move away from their families of origin into more independent living situations. For individuals with MR, it is similarly important to achieve greater levels of independence and begin to do things on their own as much as possible. For all community residents, then, one notable sign of success is the extent of self-sufficiency they achieve.

One measure of increasing independence derives from studies of improved adaptive behavior scores on scales such as the Adaptive Behavior Scale (ABS) (see Chapter 5). Recently, such indices include more open-ended interviews with the client and family and rely more heavily on direct observations of behavior.

Currently, most studies of adjustment focus on the person's quality of life. Research on adjustment to community and quality of life indicates that at least four primary elements are involved: physical, material, social, and cognitive well-being (Blunden, 1988). Physical and material well-being are self-explanatory; social well-being involves such aspects as access to other community members and settings; relationships with family, friends, and colleagues; basic adaptive abilities; and respect from others. Cognitive well-being involves one's own subjective assessment of good quality of life. More recent analyses confirm the relevance of similar factors for understanding adjustment (McGraw, Bruininks, Thurlow, & Lewis, 1992).

Adjustment Outcomes

Early studies of adjustment focused on individual client characteristics and indicated that the presence of maladaptive behavior was a major factor in poor adjustment and failure in community placement (Intagliata & Willer, 1982). The type of community placement, however, can make substantial differences in adjustment outcome and quality of life for residents. For example, it has been found that people in foster homes are more likely to be accepted by neighbors, whereas those in group homes tend to have better daily living skills and more contact with family members (Chen, Bruininks, Lakin, & Hayden, 1993). Furthermore, community residences of similar size differ substantially in the way they function, and these functional differences also affect outcomes for clients (Meador, Osborn, Owens, Smith, & Taylor, 1991). In fact, environmental variables (type of programming, amount of independence encouraged, training, education, and attitudes of staff) predict adjustment outcome better than do individual characteristics such as IQ (Hull & Thompson, 1980).

A current progress report on the state of community integration would show that most people with MR do live within the community and participate frequently in community activities. Some of these people have also formed friendships with those in the community—and, in the case of group home residents, with other residents. More often, though, the difficulty of forming relationships remains a barrier to full inclusion. Furthermore, residence life often involves too much regimentation and too little opportunity to make choices or control one's own life.

Clearly, the goals of **habilitation** cannot be sacrificed to total freedom for clients to "do their own thing." Many residents obviously need supervision, training, and guidance, particularly in matters that involve health, medicine, and potential stigmatization. But service providers still need to find ways to teach and encourage decision making within each habilitation plan (Bannerman, Sheldon,

- Emphasize teaching independent living skills and other new behaviors that clients prefer.
- Encourage clients' comments about what they will learn.
- Teach clients how to choose.
- Find opportunities for choice during both scheduled activities and leisure times.

FIGURE 14.3 Ways to offer choice *and* habitation

Adapted from D. J. Bannerman, J. B. Sheldon, J. A. Sherman, & A. E. Harchick (1990), Balancing the right to habilitation with the right to personal liberies: The rights of people with developmental disabilities to eat too many doughnuts and take a nap. *Journal of Applied Behavior Analysis, 23*(1), 79–89.

Sherman, & Harchik, 1990; Wehmeyer, 1992). Figure 14.3 offers suggestions for choice in training programs.

Many clients have shown that they are capable of making informed decisions about important matters, such as where they will live or work. Although they may ultimately be able to ask the questions and gather the information they need to make these decisions, usually they must be explicitly taught to identify alternatives, judge consequences, and seek out necessary resources before they spontaneously begin to use these skills. Considerable practice is necessary, too, before they can generalize to new contexts (Foxx, Faw, Taylor, Davis, & Fulia, 1993). Methods for teaching choice skills include modeling and role-playing, group discussion and practice, and self-management and self-control procedures (see Chapter 11).

In addition to more involvement with decision-making, many with MR in community residences need increased opportunity to make friends, and they need training in the skills required to do so. One important source of relationships, however, is one's own family, and family involvement is very high with individuals living in community placements. (By some estimates, approximately 81 percent have families who visit at least once a month.) The extent to which families are involved with client's lives, however, is related primarily to the characteristics of and opportunities offered by the community residence (Baker & Blacher, 1993). Some community residences do not encourage family involvement, perhaps because they see parents as likely to "interfere" with adult children's lives. Sibling visits, though, were found actually to reduce stress for home providers, and besides, if clients are to maintain close family ties, community residence providers must find ways for families to assume a comfortable and legitimate part in residents lives (Blacher & Baker, 1992; Stoneman & Crapps, 1990).

Independent (Supported) Living

As for any of us, the ultimate goal for people with MR is to live independently and make their own decisions—which many with MR can certainly do. To help even more individuals reach this goal, training programs in independent living have been established. Studies have shown that such training is related to long-term adjustment in independent living. But it is important to note that it may not

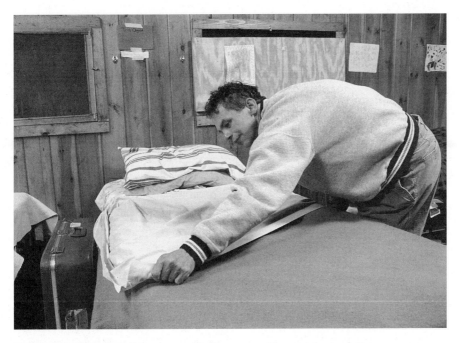

Relatively independent living is a reality for many with mental retardation.

© S. D. Young-Wolfe/PhotoEdit

be the skill instruction that is most relevant to success (Lozano, 1993) but rather the friendships developed and the ongoing support received that results in clients' increased ability to remain on their own. Staff members often become primary advocates and benefactors and guide clients in establishing relationships with neighbors and other community members.

There is encouraging evidence that many with MR who live independently become increasingly competent with age, and that this growth comes primarily as a consequence of actual situations that call on their attempts to succeed and that offer genuine opportunities for trial and error, success and failure. In other words, people with MR—like those without—learn best from real-life challenges presented when independent living is actually given a try. For this reason, programs that presume individuals must first prove their competence and earn the right to live on their own may actually preclude the very experiences that would facilitate the development of that competence (Lozano, 1993).

Certainly, the more severe one's disability, the more help and support one needs in living; but, the central principle—that one must first make an attempt with the inherent risk of failure and likelihood of success—remains true in any learning situation. Possibly for that reason, there are increasingly those who advocate the provision of support in one's *own* home for all who have mental retardation—no matter the severity.

It is important to recognize that the word *independent* is a relative term. Few people—with or without disabilities—truly live or would even want to live independently. Instead, we all rely on friends and family for every kind of support, whether financial or material, moral or spiritual for friendship, companionship, and advice. Likewise, who has not experienced failure? Everyone fails—at one thing or another—more or less constantly, and most of our successes are preceded by at least one and often several failed attempts. It is because failure is common and inevitable that developing persistence is so important: The most successful people are usually also the most persistent. Yet, for those who have retardation, failure in independent or community living is often seen as evidence that the individual is not ready to try and thus returns them to a more restrictive setting (Edgerton, 1988). If those with MR are to succeed, then they must have the chance to try new things (even if this only starts with getting dressed or making a sandwich), and they, their families, and their service providers must be willing to risk failure and be ready to use disappointments to develop self-confidence and the essential will to try again.

WORK

By definition, *work* is physical or mental effort or activity directed toward producing or accomplishing something. This purposeful accomplishment is central to adult life; it is the means by which we become useful and maintain our dignity. Freud emphasized this centrality when he said that the culmination of healthy development is the ability to love and work. Although *work* in this larger sense does not always involve wage earning, to earn one's own keep (or at least a part of it) is a critical element of human endeavor.

Work provides the same benefits for those with mental retardation as it does for others. It can increase self-esteem, furnish opportunities for socialization, provide a legitimate place within the community, and offer wages from which one can gain a measure of autonomy and independence. Research indicates, in fact, that the experience of working for wages results in increased scores on measures of perceived competence, social responsibility, and independence—even for those with more severe MR (Gersten, Crowell, & Bellamy, 1986).

Sheltered Workshops

Before the 1960s, it was generally assumed that mental retardation precluded an individual's ability to work. During the '60s, however, sheltered workshops and day programs were initiated so that those with MR could learn and carry out job skills. Although sheltered workshops do provide opportunities for employment, there are serious drawbacks to the sheltered setting. Workers are segregated and do not have the opportunity to take part in the community, few people actually move on to community work from workshops, and wages are typically extremely low. The skills required in workshop jobs tend to be repetitive manual assembly tasks and not easily generalized to other work (Rusch, 1986). Although sheltered workshops remain in operation and now employ approximately 1 million people in the United States, emphasis is increasingly shifting to prepare clients for community jobs.

Community Employment

For people with mental retardation, opportunities for work are increasing. There is new emphasis on providing community-based employment options, both in the United States and internationally (Parmenter, 1993). Research that began in the early 1970s has consistently demonstrated that even people with severe mental disabilities are capable of learning and carrying out complex work-related tasks—*if* they receive the appropriate training and support. Furthermore, both state and federal programs that provide financial assistance are moving toward work incentives and away from penalties for earned wages (Mayer, Laird, & Trach, 1992). Some of the advantages of community employment are competitive salaries, social integration and socialization, reduced stigmatization, and variety and choice in job options.

Disincentives to employment are increasingly fewer within government programs, but many remain to potentially discourage competitive employment. Certain incentives and disincentives, however, actually contradict each other. When work incentives are raised—for example, when it is possible to work without losing essential health benefits—then working becomes more attractive to those with marginal incomes. In another example, some programs require that an individual be determined incapable of working before they are eligible for benefits. Obviously, here the notion of incapable by definition rules out working. If eligibility were based instead on the job supports needed to work, then more individuals could be productive, while still receiving additional benefits (Walls, Dowler, & Fullmer, 1990).

This is especially important because many individuals with mental retardation are capable of working part-time but could not manage the long hours or the high-wage job necessary for self-support. The jobs they can obtain, furthermore, seldom offer health insurance. If such people could work part-time without losing essential health benefits, then it would enable them to make a contribution to society at the same time that they decrease their dependence on public money.

In fact, community employment has several economic advantages. To begin with, most studies have found that workers earn more in integrated than in sheltered settings (Schuster, 1990). When they earn more, they are able to support themselves (at least partially) rather than have to depend upon public funds for support—which represents a significant savings to taxpayers. And, of course, workers in competitive employment become taxpayers themselves. Finally, the costs of running competitive businesses are borne by the business owners, whereas sheltered workshop facilities are primarily publicly funded.

There are advantages to employers, too, in hiring people with mental retardation. For one, they can receive a tax subsidy for the first two years of employment for eligible people (Conley & Noble, 1990), and there are programs available that subsidize an employee's wage during an extended training period. During this time, training is provided by a **job coach** who is paid by a service provider and not by the business itself. In addition, people with MR often make dependable workers who take their responsibilities seriously and change jobs infrequently.

Finally, community employment provides visibility for people who have mental retardation within the community, allows others to see that people with MR can lead useful and productive lives, and shows that they do possess skills and abilities. The higher the visibility, the higher the public expectations about the potential of citizens with retardation. There is also the hope that visibility within the public will help others become accustomed to the reality of intellectual differences and encourage greater acceptance and reduced stigmatization.

Measures of success in community employment include job retention, increased earnings, a favorable benefit–cost ratio, and satisfaction with the job by the employee. Many with mental retardation are successful in competitive employment settings, and when they are not, the reason most often cited is inappropriate social behavior. Other reasons for job loss have included slow working rate, seemingly low initiative, poor communication skills, unacceptable personal appearance, and health problems resulting in frequent absences (Lagomarcino & Rusch, 1988).

Two good predictors of employment success in community settings are personal autonomy and adaptability. Employers want workers who can carry out tasks on their own and who are flexible enough to adapt to the changes in routine that are so common in business (Rusch, Martin, & White, 1985).

TRAINING AND SUPPORT

People with mental retardation—even more than others—need training and support to develop the skills and abilities necessary for successful employment, and numerous programs now exist to make this possible. Many of these programs divide the training process into steps that allow a gradual transition to community employment. Figure 14.4 illustrates one model for such a step program.

Though programs usually model themselves after the five steps in Figure 14.4, recent thinking suggests that the process cannot end there. Changing jobs plays an integral part in career development for the general population. People gain experience, learn more about their own abilities and interests, and move ahead in their careers by accepting new opportunities. In the field of mental retardation, however, it is frequently assumed that an individual will stay where she has been placed unless she fails in that work environment (Pumpian, Fischer, Certo, & Smalley, 1997). Models of supported employment need to recognize the natural role of job change in lifelong careers and provide for that eventuality.

Employers have listed several qualities especially valued in any employee:

1. The ability to ask for help when needed and to follow directions,
2. the capacity to respond well to criticism,
3. a helping spirit that results in offering assistance to co-workers, and
4. the conversational skill to greet and converse with others (Chadsey-Rusch, 1990).

Many of the techniques presented in Chapter 11—such as prompting, self-management, and imagery—are integral to helping clients learn the social and behavioral skills needed for success. As an example, self-management training tech-

Step 1. Identify possible job placements and those related skills necessary for success in those jobs.

Step 2. Establish community-based training sites to teach necessary skills.

Step 3. Provide short-term training within the community setting.

Step 4. Place clients into targeted jobs within six months.

Step 5. Long-term follow-up with training and supports of decreasing intensity.

FIGURE 14.4 Possible transitional steps to successful community employment

SOURCE: Adapted from J. L. Gifford, F. R. Rusch, J. E. Martin, & D. M. White (1984), Autonomy and adaptability in work behavior of retarded clients. In N. R. Ellis & N. W. Bray (Eds.), *International review of research in mental retardation.* New York: Academic Press.

1. Explaining the importance of particular social skills.
2. The opportunity to observe many examples of appropriate behavior.
3. Practice sessions in which to role-play appropriate behavior.
4. Accurate and constructive feedback concerning the performance.

FIGURE 14.5 The four components of social skills training

Adapted from F. R. Rusch (Ed.). (1990) *Supported employment: Models, methods, and issues.* Sycamore, IL: Sycamore.

niques may use both external and self-produced cues to facilitate training (Rusch, Martin, & White, 1985). In such a case, a trainee might learn that when other employees go to the break area, it is time for his break as well (an external cue). Or he might learn to use an unobtrusive wrist beeper (self-produced cue) to prompt break times.

FOR DISCUSSION *What other stimuli, naturally occurring within the work environment, could act as prompts and cues?*

People with MR may not know how to manage problems encountered on the job. For example, if an employer asks to have equipment moved, but the piece is heavy, the employee may not know how to ask for help in an effective manner, and temper tantrums and other inappropriate behavior may be the result. Behavioral management techniques are often used in these social skill situations to teach strategies to solve such common problems. Role-playing techniques can also be successful in teaching appropriate social skills (Shafer, Brooke, & Wehman, 1985). But employees succeed best when they have the opportunity to practice many examples of likely problem situations before they arise in the workplace. Figure 14.5 lists the important elements of programs designed to teach social skills.

The Point

*In 1972, three northern Kentucky parent associations came together to form what was the Northern Kentucky Association for the Retarded (NKAR) and is now the **Point**. Judi Gerding, who has a son with mental retardation, is the president of the Point. This private, nonprofit organization provides educational, vocational, and community residential services for hundreds of area individuals. The Point's vocational opportunities include a restaurant, laundry service, and maintenance company where people with MR receive on-the-job training preparing them to find gainful employment in the community. The two women pictured at the right are trainees at the Point Restaurant, in Covington, Kentucky. After their training, they will be prepared for employment in the food industry. In the following excerpt from my interview with president Judi Gerding, this dedicated parent and community leader discusses some of the accomplishments of the Point's vocational training programs, as well as some of their challenges:*

These young women are gaining valuable work experience.

Lynda Crane

We opened Point Restaurant in August of '82 as our first training program for people in food service. It's been a wonderful program. We have placed over 175 people in area businesses, and since we can only train three or four people at a time, we feel like those are good numbers. Unfortunately, food service does not get most of our people off the tax rolls, because employers usually don't want to offer more than 22 hours of work. Otherwise they have to pay benefits. So, in order to get off the tax rolls, some of our people have to work two jobs. On the other hand, though, 22 hours is a nice amount for some based on their stamina and what they are able to do. So, it's had its pluses and minuses.

After the restaurant was off the ground, we received a grant in 1984 through the Arc to start the Point Maintenance Company, where we do commercial cleaning. Our crew meets here at 3 P.M. and works till about 11 P.M. or midnight. We have some very good contracts. For three of

the companies, we clean every night—one we've been working for twelve years. There are a number of companies we clean twice a week, and many we do just once a week.

Unlike the restaurant, in the maintenance company some of our trainees get good 40-hour-a-week jobs. This is good for those who are capable of working that much. Recently, we brought in a second van and crew; the work is definitely there. Five years ago we also opened the Point Laundry Company, where our people are trained to work at various laundries, small hotels, and small nursing homes. This has been wonderfully successful. We do 1.7 million pounds of laundry a year, in an integrated work setting. Besides our regular workers, we provide opportunities for high school students to get work experience. The Point Laundry has become a respected community presence and we now do all the laundry for the Cincinnati Omni and Crowne Plaza hotels.

Although simulated situations can be used to teach social and practical skills (Shafer, Inge, & Hill, 1985), training in actual community settings is more likely to result in good on–the-job adjustment because it does not require generalization of skills to new settings. Supported employment programs work to provide on-the-job training to help ensure success for people who have not been considered traditionally eligible for competitive employment.

Supported Employment

Supportive employment services may be provided by rehabilitation facilities, state or county mental retardation or mental health agencies, residential facilities, or other agencies. In addition, transitional supportive services between school and work are often provided by special education programs. No matter which agencies provide supportive services, good practice assumes that the needs of individuals should drive the development of the technology in career training, rather than the available technology dictating who is eligible for services.

There are several approaches to supported community employment, including individual placement, clustered placement, the **mobile crew model,** and the **entrepreneurial model** (Rusch & Hughes, 1990). The individual placement model locates and places an individual in an integrated community job and provides support for the individual while training; the support gradually decreases afterwards. The other three models all focus on *groups,* with the clustered model locating jobs for several people who work closely together in one location, whereas the mobile crew model moves a group of several individuals to diverse locations to work. An example of a mobile crew is described in the interview on the facing page.

In the entrepreneurial model, a community business (typically manufacturing) hires groups of people with retardation to do assembly work. The business provides the marketing of the product and the work environment for the assembly of the product, while the MR service agency provides a portion of the labor force. In these cases, employees with mental retardation work alongside people without disabilities in an integrated community work setting. For most clients, the entrepreneurial model is considered transitional (Baumeister & Morris, 1992).

Most of the current interest in supported employment focuses on the individual model because it is the one that provides the greatest community integration and the most normalizing experience. All of these models, however, aim to place people with MR in real community jobs, to use applied behavioral techniques to train individuals for success, and to take a systems approach to service provision by considering the needs of the individual, those of the employer, and the capabilities of the service organization in developing job-placement plans (Trach, 1990). Figure 14.6 presents the goals for supported employment.

Once employers are located, the focus must move to obtaining good matches between an employer and employee. Unfortunately, this is an area where too little attention is paid to employee preferences for job tasks and settings, in spite of the increase in motivation and success that results from a good fit. We take it for granted that job choices for most of us should be guided by our abilities and preferences, but it is often assumed that people with mental retardation are incapable of making such choices. To the contrary, supported employment efforts *should* be consumer-directed (i.e., directed by the prospective employee) to the greatest possible extent.

Appropriate training and support promote work success for those with MR.

Michael Newman/PhotoEdit

- Locate opportunities for paid work.
- Ensure that work is performed to employers' satisfaction.
- Integrate employees into the social and physical environment of the workplace.
- Provide ongoing support for the employee.
- Maintain the supported employment organization's capacity to continue to provide services.

FIGURE 14.6 Program characteristics essential for supported employment organizations

SOURCE: Adapted from J. S. Trach (1990), Supported employment program characteristics. In F. R. Rusch (Ed.), *Supported employment: Models, methods, and issues.* Sycamore: IL: Sycamore Publishing.

If those with MR are to direct their job careers, then they must first become familiar with—and learn to express—their own job likes and dislikes. Once preferences have been identified, trial experiences in the community can help employees check whether those jobs they expect to prefer are actually the ones they like best.

Supported employment, then, is a multistep process ranging from identifying prospective jobs in the first place through the provision of long-term support and assistance to the employee. The steps in this process are illustrated in Table 14.1.

Table 14.1 Steps in Supportive Employment Service Provision

Step	Example
1. Clarify financial details of public support.	Determine ways to minimize losses from disability payments *in advance* of job placement.
2. Determine job possibilities.	Make a list of the top six entry-level jobs in the area.
3. Contact potential employers and identify those who are willing to participate in the supported employment program.	Initial contact can be made by mail, with telephone follow-up.
4. Establish community job-assessment sites.	Individual tries out an entry-level job, on a limited part-time basis, with support, and without pay, in order to assess existing skills.
5. Match clients with jobs.	Use job preferences and client skills and abilities to provide a good match.
6. Begin job tryout.	Client works a few hours a day for several weeks at the first and second job choices.
7. Conduct self-managed performance evaluation.	Employee determines whether her evaluation of her own work matches that of her employer.
8. Redesign the job.	Work environment may be changed to eliminate barriers.

SOURCE: Adapted from J. E. Martin & D. E. Mithaug (1990), Consumer-directed placement. In F. R. Rusch (Ed.), *Supported employment: Models, methods, and issues.* Sycamore, IL: Sycamore.

Notice from Table 14.1 that employers and prospective employers may need to design and modify the work setting so that their employees with MR have the greatest chance of success. This can mean eliminating parts of jobs, sharing jobs with other employees, changing the method of performing a task, or changing the time limits in which a task can be performed. This is also the time to design color-coded equipment or visual prompts for task performance. For the person with mental retardation, often relatively simple and minor job modifications can mean the difference between success and failure.

Indirect Services

Besides providing direct services to employees and employers, supported employment also offers indirect and external services that enhance the environment so that success for the client is more likely. These indirect services include advocate training and counseling and discrete discussions with co-workers as to what they can expect from the new employee and ways that they can be helpful and supportive (Buckley, Mank, & Sandow, 1990). For those with retardation who are working in the competitive marketplace, co-workers can be important allies. And by providing support for employees with MR, co-workers learn vital new skills that benefit the company as a whole. Although co-workers may sometimes offer support, training, and advocacy on their own—simply as a gesture of friendliness and concern—studies show that formal instruction can help them be more effective in their efforts because they may not know how to model tasks and provide feedback in ways that are most likely to help new employees learn.

Whether or not they engage in instruction, however, co-workers' attitudes and responses to employees with mental retardation can make the critical difference between success and failure. Because attitudes are so important, it is essential that support people identify and measure existing attitudes in assessing the workplace atmosphere. Because of this, subjective responses to the work performance of an employee are sometimes sought from co-workers in addition to employers and employees themselves (Hughes, Rusch, & Curl, 1990). Such information can help support people identify and correct problem areas in the workplace.

FOR DISCUSSION *Suppose workers in a fast food restaurant were feeling increasingly resentful because they did not believe that their co-worker with MR was doing his job and noticed especially that he did not sweep up scraps of food from under tables when he cleaned them. Among other things, they were saying to each other that he "did not belong in their restaurant." How would you help improve the situation?*

Supportive programs not only must focus on the needs of employees, employers, and co-workers, but also must consider the importance of those individuals from other disciplines who have an influence on the client and can affect the success of the work experience. Besides rehabilitation counselors (or employment specialists), there may be special education teachers, psychologists, physicians, nursing staff, residential staff, or occupational therapists who appear in the client's life. Too often, professionals in each discipline know little about the others, while it is essential that each take all of these roles, functions, and goals into account when designing individualized plans. This is the answer, then, to the question that students sometimes ask: "Why do I have to know about supported employment [for example], when I am really going to be in special education?" Each of us carries out our profession in the context of the other, and we can no longer afford to focus narrowly only on our own. Our education—and our practice—must take an interdisciplinary perspective (Szymanski, Hanley-Maxwell, & Parker, 1990).

The field of supported employment is growing, and the current shortage of personnel suggests an increasing need in the coming years because many supported employment programs are currently hindered by the need for qualified personnel. Figure 14.7 provides information about the educational background and training appropriate for individuals who seek positions as supported employment personnel.

A specialist in supportive employment must develop the skills to gain the support of families, employers, and other agency personnel, such as residential or sheltered workshop staff members. Figure 14.8 introduces some of the competencies that are important for employment specialists.

Most professionals in supported employment have a Bachelor's or a Master's degree in education, psychology, social work, sociology, or rehabilitation counseling. People who enter the field should have knowledge and skills in the following areas:

- Applied behavior analysis and management
- Systematic instruction
- Educational assessment and data-based programming
- Curriculum development for people with disabilities
- Emergency medical procedures
- Physical aspects of people with multiple disabilities
- Interagency coordination: working with other professionals and families
- Vocational education and transition for people with disabilities
- Legal issues and advocacy

FIGURE 14.7 Elements of education and training for supported employment professionals

Adapted from J. M. Everson (1991), Supported employment personnel: An assessment of their self-reported training needs, educational backgrounds, and previous employment experiences. *Journal of the Association for Persons with Severe Handicaps, 16,* 140–145.

1. Knowledge of potential jobs
2. Familiarity with tax credit and Social Security procedures
3. Skill in techniques of systematic instruction
4. Skill in strategies of behavioral management
5. Knowledge of principles of business operations
6. Excellent interpersonal communication skills
7. Familiarity with environmental modifications and adaptive equipment
8. Knowledge of other agency roles and function

FIGURE 14.8 Employment specialist competencies

Adapted from P. Wehman, P. Sale, & W. S. Parent (1992), *Supported employment: Strategies for integration of workers with disabilities.* Boston: Andover Medical Publishers.

Community Attitudes

Community members usually have positive views of employment for those with mental retardation, even when the disabilities are severe (Black & Meyer, 1992). Within the workplace, too, interactions between employees with MR and those without are frequent and friendly (Rusch, Hughes, Johnson, & Minch, 1991). In fact, co-workers of those with MR often spontaneously take on training and advocacy roles and offer an important natural resource for support. Yet interactions between co-workers without disabilities differ in several ways from those between co-workers and employees with retardation. Less joking and teasing takes place, for example, and interactions are initiated primarily by workers without MR (Ferguson, McDonnel, & Drew, 1993). This means that for many employees with retardation, the friendly interaction that makes work more fun and enjoyable is

---

College Life

For many who are reading this text, graduating from high school meant moving on to college instead of going straight into working life. College provides a place to gain and perfect skills that will be the basis for a later career, and it is often the first step to independence and self-reliance. Many colleges are now providing opportunities for students with mental retardation, and most colleges believe they have a legitimate role in the education of students with MR (McAfee & Sheeler, 1987). Some offer training sites for job skills that are competitively marketable, so that students may learn restaurant skills (through working in the cafeteria) or maintenance skills (through housekeeping duties in dorms and classrooms.) Others provide space in which the public school system can provide training in a college setting, where students can be exposed to the vocational and social activities of their peers. And a few are now offering integrated classroom experiences that bring students directly into academic life rather than leave them looking on from the outside. Some colleges have a staff member designated to coordinate services for students with disabilities (including MR), and some provide counseling and faculty training.

Although some colleges are expanding on-campus opportunities for those with MR, most are concerned about limited financial resources and do not see programs for students with retardation as a high priority. Few, therefore, include services for students with MR in their long-range institutional plans. Yet grants are available that will fund program development for the MR population, and continued advocacy could make application for such grants increasingly likely.

---

absent; unfortunately, in those instances where sociable friendships do develop, they seldom extend beyond the workplace.

These various findings are important to supportive training and instructional programs. By its nature, supportive employment supposes that employees will need to learn many new skills. Of these, actual task-related skills may be the least problematic. Remember that most job losses occur not because employees do not carry out the mechanics of their job appropriately, but because they have problems with appropriate social behavior. Social skills and friendly co-worker relationships are obviously key issues for supportive employment training. It is interesting to note, however, that more interactions take place between employees with MR and their co-workers when job coaches are not present (Ferguson, McDonnell, & Drew, 1993). Job coaches, therefore, need to help their clients learn the job and the necessary associated skills as quickly as possible and phase out of the picture, thereby allowing clients to begin to build their own relationships and encouraging co-workers to fill the supportive roles.

Transitional Training

Although supported employment programs focus on training, placing, and supporting adults in community jobs, other programs provide similar services for adolescents making the transition from school to work life. Transitional programs accept the responsibility for preparing students for adult work and recognize that success in employment is much more likely when students learn the necessary skills while still in school—rather than when they confront the realities of the work world for the first time as adults. There is also an increasing acknowledgment of the important role of actual community employment in that learning so that the emphasis in work-preparation programs has shifted from prevocational training to on-the-job experience. More and more, then, community training is offered to students with severe disabilities, as well as those with milder conditions.

If such transitional preparation is to be successful, then an interdisciplinary systems approach to community job training is crucial. The cooperation of school districts, vocational rehabilitation offices, transportation purveyors, adult service provision agencies, medical and social services, family, and students are all necessary in planning and implementing community transitional programs (White & Bond, 1992). Involved agencies may coordinate efforts by applying for joint funding and participating together in student IEP planning sessions.

The elements of transitional programs are similar to those of supported employment for adults and include

- vocational assessment of the student's skills and preferences,
- work skills preparation,
- job coaching (task training at the work site and mediation of problems), and
- a follow-up evaluation of the success of the experience using comments from students, co-workers, and supervisors.

In addition, the transitional experience includes relevant class work in job-related and community-living skills, and students earn credit for both the school-based and community-based aspects of the program. Programs sometimes include the opportunity for **job sampling** so students can try out several job options to determine the best fit.

Because success on the job is determined (as we have seen) as much or more by personality and behavioral characteristics as by task-related skills and abilities, transitional programs focus on personal development. Figure 14.9 lists behaviors that are often emphasized.

All education—from the early years on—aims to prepare young people for adulthood, and self-determination is among the most important behaviors for that later success (Wehmeyer, 1992). Although in the transitional high school years, learning to make decisions becomes central, it is too late to begin teaching choice skills at that time. Children should exercise and develop their abilities to make choices and decisions from the earliest ages, yet there is evidence that special educators and parents do not focus on these skills. In fact, efforts to express preferences on the part of children with MR are too often viewed simply as avoidance maneuvers rather than efforts at independence, and they have typically been ignored (Brown, Gothelf, & Guess, 1998). Yet lack of control in anyone's life is related to learned helplessness, low self-esteem, and loss of motivation, while both high self-esteem and motivation are elements essential in later success. As a consequence, all educational programming should focus explicitly on finding ways to

Punctuality and on-task behaviors
Politeness and common courtesy
Following instructions
Appropriate interaction with co-
workers and supervisors

Task completion
Ability to work independently
Appropriate use of break time
Observation of safety rules

FIGURE 14.9 Attributes and abilities stressed in transitional education

SOURCE: Adapted from S. White & M. R. Bond (1992), *Transition services in large school districts: Practical solutions to complex problems.*

encourage choice and self-determination and to help students practice these skills through role-playing, modeling, instruction and rehearsal. This text frequently highlights and stresses the matter of choice because it is so critically important—and so often overlooked.

ISSUES IN AGING

The population of elderly people with developmental disabilities is substantial—with more than 173,000 older than 60 living in the United States (in 1995), a figure expected to double by 2025. To some extent, the service needs of elderly people differ from those who are younger; however, as for people in general, age changes for those with retardation are highly variable and individual (Slomka & Berkey, 1997). Even so, it is important to be aware of the changes that occur with age and the alterations in service provision that these new circumstances may require.

To begin with, those who work with older people must be knowledgeable about typical aging processes and should receive training in care management for the elderly. They must be sensitive to ordinary aging concerns, including changes in vision and the importance of frequent dental checkups and well-fitting dentures. They must be alert to increases in blood pressure or changing dietary needs. They must understand the role of appropriate exercise in maintaining one's health in later years, and they should know how to develop effective and individual exercise programs or how to locate someone who can teach them those skills.

A satisfying social life is a key factor not only to happiness and life satisfaction in later years, but also to preserving good health. If anything, there is an increased need for community social support as individuals with MR get older. In general, older people who reside in smaller residential facilities (such as foster homes or group homes with fewer than 16 residents) are more likely to enjoy social inclusion than are those in larger institutions (Anderson, 1993). Unfortunately, many individuals remain in large state institutions and nursing homes even though there are indications that a significant number have adequate health and functional abilities to live in less-restrictive settings. More community residential placements and increased flexibility in existing ones would go a long way toward correcting this problem.

As we have learned, many people with MR enjoy the benefits of employment. Important work advantages include social opportunities with co-workers and the sense of belonging that one gains from contributing to an organized enterprise. Eventually, elderly people with MR (like others) face the necessity of retirement and the associated loss of these social and personal roles. Many in the general population look forward to retirement for the leisure to pursue other goals or spend more time with friends and family. For people with MR, however, retirement can mean isolation and loss of purpose—though negative outcomes from retirement are not inevitable. A substantial number of retirees with MR remain active within their homes and communities. Furthermore, options for phasing out employment, continuing work beyond retirement age, or moving to part-time status are even more available to those with retardation than to the typical worker (Sutton, Sterns, & Park, 1993). The key to successful retirement for those with MR (as in other areas of life) is planning based on the individual's needs, desires, and abilities.

Sadly, health conditions that result in dementia become more common in later years, and some of these conditions such as Alzheimer's disease are found more frequently among people with MR. This increased occurrence of **dementia** is primarily found in people with Down syndrome. Most of those older than 40 with Down syndrome show neuropathological signs of an Alzheimer's-like condition, and a significant number develop clinical signs as well. Eventually, virtually all people with Down syndrome show neuropathological indicators of the condition, but even at the oldest ages not all of them actually develop the disease (Zigman, Schupf, Haveman, & Silverman, 1995).

Dementia involves declines in memory that may range from forgetting the whereabouts of a recently placed object or where a caregiver has gone, to losing the ability to remember the sequence of a well-learned task. Dementia is typically progressive, beginning with mild losses and then becoming more severe. People with Alzheimer's—and other conditions that involve dementia—ultimately become unable to care for any of their needs.

Most of the elderly with MR, however, remain active and interested in their lives and the world around them: They express unique likes and dislikes, and they have the desire to be useful and happy just as when they were younger. Although the elder years may require changes and modifications in activities and responsibilities, they do not automatically mean more restrictive living placements or an end to productive existence.

▮▮ LOOKING AHEAD ▶

In this chapter, you have become familiar with the many options for living and working that are now available to people with mental retardation. Predictors of successful adjustment in living and working situations have been discussed, and recent ideas for improving upon life for those with MR were presented, especially in the areas of residential living and work. As we all know, however, there is far more to life than where one lives and works. The importance of friendships, active social life beyond home and work, and the development of worthwhile and satisfying leisure activities cannot be overstated. Chapter 15 covers recreation and leisure pursuits, as well as friendships and other committed relationships and the roles of these crucial areas of life for people with mental retardation.

INFOTRAC COLLEGE EDITION

Work environments can provide natural supports for those with mental retardation. You have been invited to present a workshop at a professional conference on the topic of natural supports. Enter *natural supports* (be sure to use the plural term) as the keyword in *InfoTrac College Edition,* and report on the topics and examples you find that you will include in your workshop presentation.

REFERENCES

Anderson, D. J. (1993). Social inclusion of older adults with mental retardation. In E. Sutton, A. R. Factor, B. A. Hawkins, T. Heller, & G. B. Seltzer (Eds.), *Older Adults with Developmental Disabilities* (pp. 79–93). Baltimore, MD: Paul H. Brookes.

Anderson, L., Sandlin, J., Prouty, B., & Lakin, K. C. (1996). Trends and milestones: States converting community ICFs/MR to HCBS waiver. *Mental Retardation, 34*(6), 402.

Arc, The. (1995). Personal communication.

Baker, B. L., & Blacher, J. B. (1993). Out-of-home placement for children with mental retardation: Dimensions of family involvement. *American Journal on Mental Retardation, 98*(3), 368–377.

Bannerman, D. J., Sheldon, J. B., Sherman, J. A., & Harchik, A. E. (1990). Balancing the right to habilitation with the right to personal liberties: The rights of people with developmental disabilities to eat too many doughnuts and take a nap. *Journal of Applied Behavior Analysis, 23*(1), 79–89.

Baumeister, M., & Morris, R. K. (1992). Rural delivery model for vocational education. *Teaching Exceptional Children,* Summer, 40–43.

Blacher, J., & Baker, B. L. (1992). Toward meaningful family involvement in out-of-home placement settings. *Mental Retardation, 30*(1), 35–43.

Black, J. W., & Meyer, L. H. (1992). But . . . is it really work? Social validity of employment training for persons with very severe disabilities. *American Journal on Mental Retardation, 96*(5), 463–474.

Blunden, R. (1988). Programmatic features of quality services. In M. P. Janicki, M. W. Krauss, & M. M. Seltzer (Eds.), *Community residences for persons with developmental disabilities: Here to stay* (pp. 117–122). Baltimore, MD: Paul H. Brookes.

Brown, F., Gothelf, C. R., & Guess, D. (1998). Self-determination for individuals with the most severe disabilities: Moving beyond chimera. *Journal of the Association for Persons with Severe Handicaps, 23*(1), 17–26.

Buckley, J., Mank, D., & Sandow, D. (1990). Developing and implementing support strategies. In F. R. Rusch, (Ed.), *Supported employment: Models, methods, and issues* (pp. 131–144). Sycamore, IL: Sycamore.

Chadsey-Rusch, J. (1990). Teaching social skills on the job. In F. R. Rusch (Ed.), *Supported employment: Models, methods, and issues* (pp. 161–180). Sycamore, IL: Sycamore.

Chen, T., Bruininks, K., Lakin, C., & Hayden, M. (1993). Personal competencies and community participation in small community residential programs: A multiple discriminant analysis. *American Journal on Mental Retardation, 98*(3), 390–399.

Conley, R. W. & Noble, J. H. (1990). Benefit–cost analysis of supported employment. In F. R. Rusch (Ed.), *Supported employment: Models, methods, and issues* (pp. 271–288). Sycamore, IL: Sycamore.

Conroy, J. W. (1996). The small ICF/MR program: Dimensions of quality and cost. *Mental Retardation, 34*(1), 13–26.

Cullari, S. (1984). Everybody is talking about the new institution. *Mental Retardation, 22*(1), 28–29.

Cunningham, P. J., & Mueller, C. D. (1991). Individuals with mental retardation in residential facilities: Findings from the 1987 National medical expenditure survey. *Mental Retardation, 96*(2), 109–117.

Edgerton, R. B. (1988). Perspectives on the prevention of mild mental retardation. In F. J. Menolascino & J. A. Stark (Eds.), *Preventive and curative intervention in mental retardation.* Baltimore, MD: Paul H. Brookes.

Everson, J. M. (1991). Supported employment personnel: An assessment of their self-reported training needs, educational backgrounds, and previous employment experiences. *Journal of the Association for Persons with Severe Handicaps, 16,* 140–145.

Ferguson, B., McDonnell, J., & Drew, C. (1993). Type and frequency of social interaction among workers with and without mental retardation. *American Journal on Mental Retardation, 97*(5), 530–540.

Foxx, R. M., Faw, G. D., Taylor, S., Davis, P. K., & Fulia, R. (1993). "Would I be able to . . . ?" Teaching clients to assess the availability of their community living life style preferences. *American Journal on Mental Retardation, 98*(2), 235–248.

Gersten, R., Crowell, F., & Bellamy, T. (1986). Spillover effects: Impact of vocational training on the lives of severely mentally retarded clients. *American Journal of Mental Deficiency, 90*(5), 501–506.

Grimes, S. K., & Vitello, S. J. (1990). Follow-up study of family attitudes toward deinstitutionalization: Three to seven years later. *Mental Retardation, 28*(4), 219–225.

Haney, J. I. (1988). Toward successful community residential placements for individuals with mental retardation. In L. W. Heal, J. I. Haney, & A. R. N. Amado (Eds.), *Integration of developmentally disabled individuals into the community* (2nd ed., pp. 125–168). Baltimore, MD: Paul H. Brookes.

Hill, B. K., & Lakin, K. C. (1986). Classification of residential facilities for individuals with mental retardation. *Mental Retardation, 24*(2), 107–115.

Holburn, C. S. (1990). Rules: The new institutions. *Mental Retardation, 28*(2), 89–94.

———. (1992). Rhetoric and realities in today's ICF/MR: Control out of control. *Mental Retardation, 30*(3), 133–141.

Hughes, C., Rusch, F. R., & Curl, R. (1990). Extending individual competence, developing natural support, and promoting social acceptance. In F. R. Rusch (Ed.), *Supported employment: Models, methods, and issues* (pp. 181–198). Sycamore, IL: Sycamore.

Hull, J. T., & Thompson, J. C. (1980). Predicting adaptive functioning of mentally retarded persons in community settings. *American Journal of Mental Deficiency, 85*(3), 253–261.

Intagliata, J., & Willer, B. (1982). Reinstitutionalization of mentally retarded persons successfully placed in family-care and group homes. *American Journal of Mental Deficiency, 87*(1), 34–39.

Kauffman, D. W., & Krebs, S. J. (1993). *Assessing neighborhood attitudes toward group homes for the mentally handicapped as a function of proximity.* Paper presented at annual meeting of the Midwest Psychological Association, Chicago, IL.

Kraushaar, K., & Elliott, D. (1995). *State school closure: Fort Worth and Travis Employee Surveys 1993 and 1994, Parent/Family Surveys, 1993 and 1994 Results.* Abilene, TX: Southwest Institution for Developmental Disabilities.

Lagomarcino, T. R., & Rusch, F. R. (1988). Competitive employment: Overview and analysis of research focus. In V. VanHasselt, P. Strain, & M. Hersen (Eds.), *Handbook of developmental and physical disabilities.* New York: Pergamon Press.

Lakin, K. C., Braddock, D., & Smith, G. (1996). Trends and milestones: Majority of MR/DD residential service recipients now in homes of 6 or fewer residents. *Mental Retardation, 34*(3), 198.

Landesman, S. (1988). Preventing "institutionalization" in the community. In M. P. Janicki, M. W. Krauss, & M. M. Selzer (Eds.), *Community residences for persons with developmental disabilities: Here to stay* (pp. 105–116). Baltimore, MD: Paul H. Brookes.

Larson, S. A. (1997). A longitudinal study of turnover among newly hired residential direct support workers in small community homes serving people with developmental disabilities. *Dissertation Abstracts International Section A: Humanities & Social Science, 58*(6-A), 2086.

Larson, S. A., & Lakin, C. K. (1989). Deinstitutionalization of persons with mental retardation: Behavioral outcomes. *Journal of the Association for Persons with Severe Handicaps, 14,* 324–332.

———. (1991). Parent attitudes about residential placement before and after deinstitutionalization: A research synthesis. *Journal of the Association for Persons with Severe Handicaps, 16,* 25–38.

Latib, A., Conroy, J., & Hess, C. M. (1990). Family attitudes toward deinstitutionalization. In N. W. Bray (Ed.), *International review of research in mental retardation* (Vol. 16, pp. 67–93). New York: Academic Press.

Lord, J., & Pedlar, A. (1991). Life in the community: Four years after the closure of an institution. *Mental Retardation, 29*(4), 213–221.

Lozano, B. (1993). Independent living: Relation among training, skills, and success. *American Journal on Mental Retardation, 98*(2), 249–262.

Lubin, R. A., Schwartz, A. A., Zigman, W. B., & Janicki, M. P. (1982). Community acceptance of residential programs for developmentally disabled persons. *Applied Research in Mental Retardation, 3,* 191–200.

Lynch, P., Kellow, J. T. & Willson, V. L. (1997). The impact of deinstitutionalization on the adaptive behavior of adults with mental retardation: A meta-analysis. *Education and Training in Mental Retardation and Developmental Disabilities, 32*(3), 255–261.

Martin, J. E., & Mithaug, D. E. (1990). Consumer-directed placement. In F. R. Rusch (Ed.), *Supported employment: Models, methods, and issues* (pp. 87–110). Sycamore, IL: Sycamore.

Mayer, J. A., Laird, W. H., & Trach, J. S. (1992). Income allowance policies of state Medicaid agencies as work incentives or disincentives for ICF/MR residents. *Mental Retardation, 30* (4), 215–219.

McAfee, J. K., & Sheeler, M. X. (1987). Accommodation of adults who are mental retarded in community colleges: A national study. *Education and Training in Mental Retardation,* December, 262–267.

McConkey, R., Morris, I., & Purcell, M. (1999). Communications between staff and adults with intellectual disabilities in naturally occurring settings. *Journal of Intellectual Disability Research, 43*(3), 194–205.

McGraw, K. S., Bruininks, R. H., Thurlow, M. L., & Lewis, D. R. (1992). Empirical analysis of multidimensional measures of community adjustment for young adults with mental retardation. *American Journal on Mental Retardation, 96*(5), 475–487.

Meador, D. M., Osborn, R. G., Owens, M. H., Smith, E. C., & Taylor, T. L. (1991). Evaluation of environmental support in group homes for persons with mental retardation. *Mental Retardation, 29*(3), 159–164.

Mitchell, D., & Braddock, D. (1993). Compensation and turnover of direct-care staff in developmental disabilities residential facilities in the United States: Wages and benefits. *Mental Retardation, 31*(6), 429–437.

———. (1994). Compensation and turnover of direct-care staff in developmental disabilities residential facilities in the United States: II Turnover. *Mental Retardation, 32*(1), 34–42.

Newton, J. S., Ard, W. R. Jr., Horner, R. H., & Towes, J. D. (1996). Focusing on values and lifestyle outcomes in an effort to improve the quality of residential services in Oregon. *Mental Retardation, 34*(1), 1–12.

Parmenter, R. R. (1993). International perspective of vocational options for people with mental retardation: The promise and the reality. *Mental Retardation, 31*(6), 359–367.

Phillips, J. F. (1998). Applications and contributions of organizational behavior management in schools and day treatment settings. *Journal of Organizational Behavior Management, 18*(2–3), 103–129.

Pumpian, I., Fischer, D., Certo, N. J., & Smalley, K. A. (1997). Changing jobs: An essential part of career development. *Mental Retardation, 35*(1), 39–48.

Robinson, J. W., & Thompson, T. (1999). Stigma and architecture. In. E. Steinfeld & G. S. Danford (Eds.), *Enabling environments: Measuring the impact of environment on disability and rehabilitation* (pp. 251–270). New York: Kluwer Academic/Plenum.

Rusch, F. R. (1986). Introduction to competitive employment programs. In F. R. Rusch (Ed.), *Competitive employment issues and strategies* (pp. 3–6). Baltimore, MD: Paul H. Brookes.

Rusch, F. R., & Hughes, C. (1990). Historical overview of supported employment. In F. R. Rusch (Ed.), *Supported employment: Models, methods, and issues* (pp. 5–14). Sycamore, IL: Sycamore.

Rusch, F. R., Hughes, C., Johnson, J. R., & Minch, K. E. (1991). Descriptive analysis of interactions between co-workers and supported employees. *Mental Retardation, 29*(4), 207–212.

Rusch, F. R., Martin, J. E., & White, D. M. (1985). Competitive employment: Teaching mentally retarded employees to maintain their work behavior. *Education and Training of the Mentally Retarded* (Sept.), 182–189.

Schuster, J. W. (1990). Sheltered workshops: Financial and philosophical liabilities. *Mental Retardation, 28*(4), 233–239.

Seltzer, M. M. (1984). Correlates of community opposition to community residences for mental retarded persons. *American Journal of Mental Deficiency, 84*(1), 1–8.

Shafer, M. S., Brooke, V., & Wehman, P. (1985). Developing appropriate social-interpersonal skills in a mentally retarded worker. In P. Wehman & J. W. Hill (Eds.), *Competitive employment for persons with mental retardation from research to practice* (Vol. 1, pp. 358–375). Richmond: Virginia Commonwealth University Press.

Shafer, M. S., Inge, K., & Hill, J. W. (1985). The development of automated banking services for mentally retarded persons: A pilot study. *Competitive employment for persons with mental retardation from research to practice* (Vol. 1, pp. 376–397). Richmond: Virginia Commonwealth University Press.

Shea, J. R. (1992). From standards to compliance, to good services, to quality lives: Is this how it works? *Mental Retardation, 30*(3), 143–149.

Slomka, G. T., & Berkey, J. (1997). Aging and mental retardation. In P. D. Nussbaum (Ed.), *Handbook of neuropsychology and aging* (pp. 331–347). New York: Plenum.

Smith, G., Prouty, R., & Lakin, K. C. (1996). Trends and milestone: The HCB Waiver Program: The fading of Medicaid's "institutional bias." *Mental Retardation, 34*(4), 262.

Spreat, S., Telles, J. L., Conroy, J. W., Feinstein, C., & Colombatto, J. J. (1987). Attitudes toward deinstitutionalization: National survey of families of institutionalized persons with mental retardation. *Mental Retardation, 25*(5), 267–274.

Stancliffe, R. J. (1997). Community living-unit size, staff presence, and residents' choice-making. *Mental Retardation, 35*(1), 1–9.

———, & Abery, B. H. (1997). Longitudinal study of deinstitutionalization and the exercise of choice. *Mental Retardation, 35*(3), 159–169.

Stoneman, Z., & Crapps, J. M. (1990). Mentally retarded individuals in family care homes: Relationships with the family-of-origin. *American Journal on Mental Retardation, 94*(4), 420–430.

Sutton, E., Sterns, H. L., & Park, L. S. (1993). Realities of retirement and pre-retirement planning. In E. Sutton, A. R. Factor, B. A. Hawkins, T. Heller, & G. B. Seltzer (Eds.), *Older Adults with Developmental Disabilities* (pp. 95–106). Baltimore, MD: Paul H. Brookes.

Szymanski, E., Hanley-Maxwell, C., & Parker, R. M. (1990). Transdisciplinary service delivery. In F. R. Rusch (Ed.), *Supported employment: Models, methods, and issues* (pp. 199–214). Sycamore, IL: Sycamore.

Trach, J. (1990). Supported employment program characteristics. In F. R. Rusch (Ed.), *Supported employment: Models, methods, and issues* (pp. 65–82). Sycamore, IL: Sycamore.

Walls, R. T., Dowler, D. L., & Fullmer, S. L. (1990). Incentives and disincentives to supported employment. In F. R. Rusch (Ed.), *Supported employment: Models, methods, and issues* (pp. 251–270). Sycamore, IL: Sycamore.

Wehmeyer, M. L. (1992). Self-determination and the education of students with mental retardation. *Education and Training in Mental Retardation, 27*(4), 302–313.

White, S., & Bond, M. R. (1992) Transition services in large school districts: Practical solutions to complex problems. *Teaching Exceptional Children, 24*(4), 44–47.

Wolfensberger, W. (1975). *The origin and nature of our institutional models.* Syracuse, NY: Human Policy Press.

Zigman, W., Schupf, N., Haveman, M., & Silverman, W. (1995). *Epidemiology of Alzheimer Disease in mental retardation: Results and recommendations from an International conference.* Washington, DC: American Association on Mental Retardation.

15

Social Life and Recreation

A s we have seen, social isolation can be a real and ongoing problem for those with mental retardation—one that can be difficult to overcome. This chapter examines the challenges of and opportunities for social life for people with MR and discusses ways in which those opportunities can be enhanced. Several variables influence whether or not individuals with MR enjoy social support—including where they live, the intelligence level of the other people with whom they live, their own level of retardation, and their gender (Krauss, Seltzer, & Goodman, 1992; Williams & Asher, 1992). For example, those who live in small residences tend to have more friends but less contact with family members than do those who live at home. Those people with MR who live in large residences tend to have less outside social support than either of the other groups. Males and those with more severe retardation are more isolated regardless of the setting—though this does not mean that they are completely without the social support of friends and family.

All people with MR need social activities and a network of friends. They need to feel accepted and valued by others beyond those who must accept them because of work and living arrangements. Although both of those settings can provide the opportunity for deepening friendships, the available evidence suggests how seldom this is the case. Everyone wants to feel a sense of belonging that can be attributed to who they are as a person—a feeling of belonging that can come only through friends.

How does someone with mental retardation go about meeting people who will accept her, include her, and relate to her as a true friend? One possibility is by volunteering to help others through both formal and informal activities (Firth & Rapley, 1990). As one example, the author's mother lived in a building predominantly inhabited by senior citizens. Among the tenants, however, was a young woman with Down syndrome. As a result of this young woman's friendly and outgoing (though not intrusive) approach to the other residents, she soon became recognized by them and developed many acquaintances with whom friendly encounters were frequent. She also made cards for holidays and gave them to her neighbors as gifts, and she was available to help in other small ways: opening doors and carrying packages. Soon, she was an accepted and valued part of the community and included in outings and parties with her friends.

Often, however, people with mental retardation neither automatically develop the behavioral and social skills necessary to achieve friendships on their own nor are they usually in a living situation where they have frequent contact with community members. In these instances, it becomes the responsibility of professionals and staff to help them succeed socially.

DEVELOPING FRIENDSHIPS

Certainly friendships develop from acquaintances, but how do we know when a relationship has crossed the line from one to the other? In other words, how can we define *friendship*? One useful definition might be that a friendship involves the

Increasingly people with retardation join in established community activities.

© S. D. Young-Wolfe/PhotoEdit

"elements of choice, reciprocity, commitment, and permanence in time" (Firth & Rapley, 1990, p. 58). From this definition, we can clearly see that even those with profoundly serious intellectual disabilities can develop friendships. In fact, evidence suggests that there is no relationship between level of IQ and the number of friendships that one enjoys. No doubt there are differences in the nature of the interdependence, the interactional elements of a particular friendship, or in the complexity of verbal contribution, but variations in these characteristics do not preclude reciprocal, enjoyable, committed relationships that deepen with time.

Successfully developing and maintaining a network of friendships within the community involves two components. One is the personal development of necessary behaviors, attitudes, and skills, and the other is finding the opportunities and activities necessary for friendships to develop. Developing friendships, then, involves much more than simply getting out into the community to engage in leisure activities. Rather it depends upon the nature and quality of the interaction that takes place, whether at work, home, or recreation. Effectively promoting successful relationships between students or clients with MR and others therefore must become a primary goal for those who work with mental retardation—one that pervades planning in all areas of life.

Attitudes, Behaviors, and Skills

Within the general population, people who are lonely have more negative attitudes toward others and are less responsive to them; they also experience lower self-esteem and are less likely to disclose information about themselves and their feelings to others than are people who have satisfying friendships (Ernst & Cacioppo, 1999). Research indicates that individuals with mental retardation who do not have friendships demonstrate similar characteristics, although they are less likely to express negative attitudes towards others (Clegg & Standen, 1991). On the other hand, those who have at least one close friend, express more positive feelings about themselves. Self-esteem, then, appears to be importantly related to whether individuals have friends.

In general, people with mental retardation appear to have more negative self-concepts than those who do not have MR (Widaman, MacMillan, Hemsley, Little, & Balow, 1992). In addition, those with MR commonly list personal relationships as one of their most problematic areas, and a substantial proportion report that they are socially unfulfilled (Halpern, Close, & Nelson, 1986). If problems with self-concept and esteem are related to less satisfying social relations, then can programs to improve self-concept result in more successful relationships? The answer is somewhat unclear. For one thing, most of the research on self-concept in those with MR focuses on adolescence, a time when problems with identity and self-concept are frequent for all groups. In fact, most adolescents with MR struggle with the same issues of independence, sexuality, personal uniqueness, and concerns about the future that are the preoccupations of most youths (Zetlin & Turner, 1985). In fact, given the difficulties with comprehension and communication that these young people experience—coupled with fewer opportunities for successful transitional experiences, their own awareness of the likelihood of increased dependence, and frequent stigmatization—it is not surprising that they demonstrate differences in their identity development when compared with other teens. The wonder is that these differences are actually small and quite similar to the differences that exist between typical boys and girls. In other words, girls tend to show identity problems in some areas of their lives—in how meaningful their life seems, for example, or its stability—that are greater than those shown by boys and comparable to adolescents with developmental disabilities (Levy-Shiff, Kedem, & Sevillia, 1990).

The one exception is in the area of physical attributes. Young people with MR are especially likely to report low confidence and satisfaction with their appearance and other physical abilities. It is also true, however, that the range of responses in this area has been especially large (that is, some people report substantial concerns, while others report virtually none). It is likely, therefore, that those young people who have clear differences in their appearance or who experience motor and coordination problems simply perceive that these realities are responsible for many of their life difficulties. In summary, then, it is true that individuals with MR have (on the average) lower self-esteem than those without—especially at adolescence—but these differences are not especially large and appear to be intimately related to the more obvious features of their disabilities.

A second problem involves identifying the nature of the intervention that might help these young people feel better about themselves. One idea is that people with mental retardation may be able to "come to terms" with their disability—and therefore feel better about themselves—if they accept themselves as people who *do* have retardation and are therefore different. This thinking is in line with methods of consciousness raising used by women and ethnic groups to understand the social and political nature of the stigmatization against them and to develop a sense of pride in their own group membership. In regard to mental retardation, Szivos and Griffiths (1990), for example, report on a group of young adults who—in the process of group therapy—moved through several phases of thinking to a greater acceptance of themselves. These phases began with denial of their disability and then moved through impersonal statements about their association with others who have retardation, followed by an exploration of some of the social issues of stigmatization associated with retardation, and then finally to some measure of acceptance of their disability. Szivos and Griffiths admitted, however, that these young people (even at the self-acceptance stage) were more likely to admit that their disability had its compensations than they were to see it as a benefit—as might women or African-Americans, for example. In fact, for one young woman, it was clear that her refusal to believe she had a disability served a self-protective function—one that she was not emotionally ready to manage without.

It is clear that coming to terms with and accepting one's own limitations are often difficult processes for many people. Protective defenses ultimately limit our ability to solve our problems and deal effectively with others, yet they also protect us when we are too emotionally vulnerable or lack the skills to function otherwise. In fact, there is evidence that some diagnosed people who do not believe they have mental retardation have more friendships than those who accept their diagnoses (Clegg & Standon, 1991). If this is the case, then interventions might better concentrate on strategies that promote friendships and train the necessary skills to maintain friendships rather than focus on therapies that aim for "acceptance." Currently, the complexities among acceptance of limitations, self-esteem, and the development of successful friendly relationships are not completely understood; and neither are their implications for effective intervention.

Problems with personal relationships and the development of friendships appear to exist for those with retardation across the life span, beginning with toddlers and preschoolers and continuing through the elder years, and programs to help promote increased and more satisfying friendships are in place for all ages (Anderson, Lakin, Hill, & Chen, 1992). As preschoolers, children with mental retardation are more likely to play by themselves or simply play next to other children than they are to actually interact with them. These play styles are common for all very young children, but youngsters with developmental disabilities continue these patterns well beyond the time when other children begin to coordinate their play with others. This might at first seem simply a manifestation of developmental delay, except that their play styles typically lag behind their cognitive development in other areas (Guralnick, 1986). In other words, even as judged by their own rate of development, children with mental retardation experience particular problems in social relations.

Children with MR may be vulnerable to peer-related problems for three main reasons. First, children with mental retardation often have expressive language problems, and their inability to carry on age-expected "conversation" makes cooperative social play more difficult (Knopp, Baker, & Brown, 1992). Second, children who experience intellectual delays are often involved in preschool and other play situations primarily with other children who have delays. Attempts at interaction with other such children may be less likely to result in positive responses, and in segregated settings there are no models of age-appropriate play for them to imitate. Third, there is evidence that parents and teachers of children with delayed development are more directive and provide less reinforcement for autonomous behavior, even when it is cooperative (Guralnick, 1986).

> **FOR DISCUSSION** *If you know of a situation in which a young child with disabilities has been able to interact with a typical peer, can you describe ways that each child has benefited?*

EDUCATION IN SOCIAL SKILLS

Unless children with mental retardation have help, they may fail to develop the social and cognitive skills necessary to make friends (Adams & Markham, 1991). Typically, children who are well liked demonstrate several characteristics that promote friendships: They share play materials, organize and structure play, assist others with tasks, bestow appropriate affection, and respond positively to the overtures of their peers (Newcombe, Bukowski, & Pattee, 1993). These behaviors not only elicit positive responses from others, but also serve to extend play and therefore promote increased social interaction. There have been many studies in which children with mental retardation have been trained to behave in these socially desirable ways, and their positive interactions with others increased (Meyer & Putnam, 1988). Similarly, training in cognitive problem solving that includes practice in generating solutions to social problems can help children make friends (Healey & Masterpasqua, 1992). For example, a child might role-play how best to convince another child to share or how to wait for a turn. Consistent with training and teaching studies in other skills, however, these new social and cognitive behaviors do not automatically generalize to the actual settings or situations. People with MR (whether children or adults) may know what to do in a given situation and still not demonstrate the appropriate behavior in an actual event

(Soodak, 1990). Before they can do so, extended practice in everyday circumstances is usually required.

To begin training in the actual setting, however, may be counterproductive. When transacting business with clerks in stores or when responding to a stranger may not be the best time to launch into a training session. Sometimes it works better to begin training at school or at home, develop "scripts" for particular situations through role-playing, and then engage in extensive practice in community situations (Schloss & Wood, 1990).

Because extensive training and practice are often necessary to help children with mental retardation develop social skills, these skills should be taught from the youngest ages. Many of the skills that help maintain friendships are probably learned best from other children (Brinker, 1985). Inclusion into settings with normally developing peers can provide young children with MR the advantage of experience with age-appropriate forms of play *if* teachers and staff members effectively use the opportunity. Initially, adults need to provide structured opportunities and guidance, and then it is important that they stand back and let the children themselves manage as much as possible (Meyer & Putnam, 1988).

Children without disabilities are often eager to interact with youngsters who have MR. It may be that they enjoy the helping role, and that this compensates for some loss of equality or mutuality. Regardless, children do voluntarily and enthusiastically enter into inclusive relationships. It is not just children, either, who are willing to befriend people with MR. Over time, the author's students have entered into projects in which they sought out people with mental retardation with whom they then spent friendship time. Even in those instances when particular students had little previous experience with the difference of mental retardation and were initially fearful or self-conscious, they almost invariably reported feeling comfortable within a couple of visits. The new friends experienced many mutually enjoyable times together, and many of those friendships have endured for years.

Research has demonstrated that peers without disabilities can be integral in increasing the frequency and quality of social interactions on the part of others with even quite severe mental retardation. Haring and Breen (1992), for example, recruited junior high school peers to promote inclusion of students with mental retardation into groups of their friends. The efforts of the peers resulted not only in the students with MR making friends with others, but also in improved attitudes and ratings of friendship by the regular students. These new friendships extended to activities *outside* of school both after school and on weekends—activities that were not specifically promoted by adults. It is essential to note, however, that the recruited peers were formally prepared for their roles through initial discussion and ongoing meetings. They were trained to institute particular techniques and to collect ongoing data on the progress that students with MR made. Figure 15.1 lists the discussion outline for the first meeting attended by the recruits. It indicates the kind of information that peers received about the purpose of inclusion and gives a sense of the careful planning that went into the peer intervention.

Peer-mediated support and intervention has been successful not only with nondisabled peers, but also with peers who have disabilities themselves. As an

A. What?
1. Have a group of students who are already friends include a new person in their social clique.
B. Why?
1. Quality of life
2. Teach skills through modeling
3. School inclusion
4. Disability awareness
5. Value of a new member in the clique
C. Why us?
1. Common interests
2. Common classes
D. Who?
1. Student .
2. Four or five nondisabled peers
3. Adult facilitator
4. Classroom teacher
E. How?
1. Map students' and peers' schedules.
2. Assign times to hang out together.
3. Include student in normal routine.
4. Group decides what and how to teach.
5. Take data.

F. When?
1. During assigned time per day
2. Whenever you feel like it
3. During group meeting one lunch period per week
G. Commitment
1. From peers:
   a. This is a good thing for each peer.
   b. This is a good thing for the group.
   c. Include student as a friend.
   d. Attend weekly group meetings.
   e. Be open and honest.
   f. Take data.
2. From adults:
   a. Maintain peer routines.
   b. Develop interaction schedules.
   c. Provide all written information.
   d. Be sensitive to peer feedback.
   e. Teach skills as needed.
   f. Use peer suggestions.
   g. Be responsive to peer comments.

FIGURE 15.1. Outline of information provided to members of peer support group

SOURCE: Adapted from T. G. Haring & C. G. Breen (1992), A peer-mediated social network intervention to enhance the social integration of persons with moderate and severe disabilities. *Journal of Applied Behavior Analysis, 25*(2), 319–333.

example, Stewart, Van Houten, and Van Houten (1992) found that interventions that trained peers with MR in a residential setting to help other adults with MR improved social interaction for everyone involved—and that improvement extended to other interactions with other residents not specifically targeted for intervention.

One major stumbling block in the way of developing friendships is the absence of communication skills. Many people with low intellectual development do not develop spoken language that is sufficient for conversation—and in some instances, spoken language may not be present at all. For some people with low language skills, though, functional use of language can be trained. Through the use of some of the applied behavioral techniques discussed in Chapter 11 (including functional analysis and appropriate use of contingencies), individuals with severely low social skills can learn to use spoken language well enough to gain appropriate attention, meet some basic needs, make some choices, and reduce problem behavior that can stand in the way of friendly relationships (Durand & Carr, 1991). Training functional communication skills can also promote maintenance of good social skills even after the training period is over and can aid in generalization of the skills to new circumstances (Durand & Carr, 1992). Effective generalization of social skills can also be facilitated through self-monitoring (Schloss & Wood, 1990), and although maintenance and generalization of social skills training have historically presented problems, it has been demonstrated that people do maintain their new social skills and can apply them in diverse settings when appropriate training and follow-up are instituted (Foxx & Faw, 1992).

For those who are unable to use functional language, augmentative communication may substantially increase the ability and motivation to interact. Motivation, in fact, is one essential element for those who develop friendships. When the effort to communicate is difficult, tedious, or typically results in misunderstanding, then the motivation to interact is understandably low. Many people with poor language skills may be accustomed to communicating only with head shakes or other gestures and therefore take on the role of responder, rather than initiator, almost exclusively. When people with mental retardation find that they can use augmentative systems successfully (including picture boards and other symbol devices), they initiate conversational exchanges more frequently and are more likely to extend conversation—especially when they are trained to use the new system to meet social needs (Dattilo & Camarata, 1991). Peer mediators can be helpful in both teaching and implementing the social use of augmentative communication systems (Romski, Sevcik, & Wilkinson, 1994).

We have seen that appropriate social skills and behaviors are integral to the development of friendships, and that improvements in these areas can be gained by those with mental retardation. Some social situations are more difficult to manage than others, however, and there is evidence that circumstances that involve confrontation and social criticism are especially difficult for people with MR (Lali, Pinter-Lali, Mace, & Murphy, 1991). This does not seem surprising, though, in light of the difficulty that these situations present for most of us. Even in these especially challenging areas, children and adults with mental retardation can grow, learn and improve.

Recreational and Leisure
Opportunities for Friendship

Even with high self-esteem and excellent social skills, people need opportunities to meet others and the stability and continuity to develop a relationship. In the past, people with mental retardation were isolated, and development of friendships outside of the residential setting was impossible. Needed improvements remain to help those with MR become established socially within their neighborhoods and larger communities, but the situation has improved dramatically from previous times. Whether individuals are able to avail themselves of these opportunities

The Board of Directors of the Mental Retardation/Developmental Disabilities Division of the Council for Exceptional Children recognizes that many individuals with mental retardation and other developmental disabilities have the potential to participate in community activities, live independently, function successfully in the work environment and be truly included in society. The Board further recognizes that among these same individuals there is a high prevalence of obesity, below average fitness levels, a greater risk of developing coronary heart disease and that many are often not adequately trained for and/or lack the requisite physical ability to perform many vocational tasks over long periods of time.

It is the position of the Board that adequate educational opportunities and experiences that address health, fitness, and wellness concepts must be provided for children and adults with mental retardation and other developmental disabilities. Specifically, all such individuals should be afforded opportunities to participate in educational programs that address:

- Proper nutritional practices
- Personal hygiene
- Healthy lifestyle choices
- Physical fitness and other recreational activities
- Hazards associated with the use of alcohol, tobacco, and illicit substances
- Stress reduction
- Sexual responsibility and safety

FIGURE 15.2 MRDD board position statement

depends primarily on the support they receive from their families, teachers, and service staff. Figure 15.2 presents part of the position statement unanimously adopted in 1997 by the Council on Exceptional Children's MRDD Board regarding health and wellness of those with mental retardation.

Important to meeting the goals of the MRDD Board position are the skills and abilities to make good use of leisure time and the opportunity to engage in recreational pursuits. Where once leisure was seen primarily as a diversion with little real therapeutic value, the appropriate use of leisure time is now recognized as integral to health and wellness (Carter, Nezey, Wenzel, & Foret, 1999; Larson & Suman, 1999). Leisure skill education should be generalizable and result in greater independence in leisure and recreation, and many recreational services that offer training, educational, and recreational opportunities are widely available for both children and adults with MR through schools and other community agencies. Figure 15.3 shows some reasons why leisure education is important.

Programs that succeed in meeting the goals in Figure 15.3 must be well planned and carried out by experienced professionals. Typically, a program for recreation and leisure development begins with an assessment of the physical fitness, nutrition, stress level and emotional adjustment, interests, preferences, skills, and expectations of the individual to be served. At its best, this is an interdisciplinary effort that involves a physician, dietitian, psychologist, educator, recreation therapist, occupational therapist, physical therapist, and other professionals (York & Rainforth, 1995). An individualized program can then be set up that is age-

- Play participation and increased leisure skills are related to increases in skill level in a variety of other curriculum areas.
- Increases in play skills are related to decreases in negative and inappropriate excess behaviors.
- Constructive use of leisure time is related to the success of people with significant disabilities who live in community environments.
- Having a repertoire of enjoyable and preferred leisure and recreation activities is essential for quality of life and the development and maintenance of positive relationships with family and friends.

FIGURE 15.3 Reasons for pursuing leisure education

SOURCE: Adapted from S. J. Schleien, L. H. Meyer, L. A. Heyne, & B. B. Brandt (1995), *Lifelong leisure skills and lifestyles for persons with developmental disabilities* (pp. 4–5). Baltimore, MD: Paul H. Brookes.

The Recreational Therapist

Recreational therapists (RTs) are professionals who function as members of an interdisciplinary team that delivers treatment and recreational services to people with physical or mental disabilities and to those who are elderly. RT professionals use a variety of techniques such as art, music, drama, dance, animal-assisted therapy, sports, games, and outings to build clients' self-confidence, mental and physical health, motor skills, coordination, independence, and social skills.

Approximately 80 percent of recreational therapists function in acute health care settings such as hospitals, rehabilitation centers, and long-term care facilities. Most of the other RT professionals may be found in community-based programs, or day care programs for the elderly and those with disabilities and residential facilities.

The U.S. Department of Labor reports that recreational therapy will be one of the 30 fastest-growing professions within the next few years, with a projected growth rate near 40 percent. The major reasons for this growth are increased demands for long-term care of those who are elderly, adult day care, physical and psychiatric rehabilitation services, and community-based inclusion programs for those with disabilities, including mental retardation.

SOURCE: Adapted from M. K. Fleming (1998), *Recreational therapy.* Cincinnati: College of Mount St. Joseph.

appropriate and fits well with existing interests and abilities. It is important that such a program also fit well within the person's lifestyle, other life goals, and educational objectives, and also addresses the need for free and unprogrammed time during the day.

Leisure and recreational activities that promote health and wellness should begin in childhood and continue throughout the life span. Furthermore, they should take place in all of the environments that make up the life of the individual (and the lives of those without disabilities). These include school, home, community recreation activities, and social events that take place in the community

Table 15.1 Six Areas for Leisure and Recreation

Activity	Example
School and extracurricular	Looking at books, participating in sports, taking elective classes
Activities with family and friends at home and in the neighborhood	Board and yard games, bike riding, gardening
Physical fitness	Aerobics and other exercise routines, regular sports, lifting weights
Activities with family and friends in the community	Going to restaurants, shopping malls, concerts, movies
Activities to do alone in the community	Going to the public library, taking walks

SOURCE: Adapted from S. Schleien, L. Meyer, L. Heyne, & B. Brandt (1995), *Lifelong leisure skills and lifestyles for persons with developmental disabilities.*

such as bowling, movies, restaurants, swimming pools, and community centers. Table 15.1 lists six major areas in which leisure and recreation activities normally occur.

Ideally, people with mental retardation should take part in preexisting community activities, although their full participation may require modifications in access to facilities, necessary equipment, and the processes of the activity itself—which may require professional assistance and advocacy. Figure 15.4 illustrates possible modifications.

For those with conditions that involve serious physical disabilities, adaptive equipment may make participation possible. Microswitches, in particular, can enable individuals to operate appliances (e.g., radios and CD players), computers, and other leisure-related equipment. Evaluation and reassessment of leisure programs are essential to long-term success, particularly where adaptive equipment is involved. Equipment can become inoperative, and abilities change so that some modifications may no longer be necessary, while new ones may become needed (Schleien, Meyer, Heyne, & Brandt, 1995). Furthermore, microswitches or other adaptive equipment should not be used when direct operation of equipment can be taught.

The definition of what constitutes participation must change with the individual. For those with significant conditions, participation may involve pointing to pictures or objects, or expressing pleasure through expression or vocalization. They may take part by rolling or scooting across the floor to gain proximity to an activity or by remaining relaxed while carried by someone else. Some example assessment concerns for developing a program for the movement component of activities are described in Figure 15.5. These include mobility to the activity, positioning during the activity, and physical participation.

Although much progress has been made in educating the general population, community participants may still need preparation if the inclusion of those with MR is to be successful for all involved (Rynders & Schleien, 1991). When all participants understand any adaptations required and are given information about how they can behave to best ensure fun and success in the activity, then they are

1. Design the environment to fit individual needs.
   a. Lower the net in a volleyball game.
   b. Reduce the size of the playing field.
   c. Make boundaries more tangible (e.g., use cones or flags).
2. Modify and adapt equipment.
   a. Use large, brightly colored foam balls.
   b. Use a batting tee rather than a pitcher.
   c. Use lighter and larger equipment.
3. Reduce the time limit of play.
   a. Use frequent rest periods.
   b. Reduce the number of minutes played in a period.
4. Develop feedback and reinforcement techniques.
   a. Insert buzzers or bells on goals to reinforce the concept of scoring.
   b. Reinforce displays of teamwork sharing.
5. Modify degrees of moving objects and mobility.
   a. Have objects (e.g., balls) move slowly.
   b. Increase the number of players participating on a team.
6. Ensure some form of success.
   a. Avoid elimination games.
   b. Stress self-competition or cooperative play rather than team competition.

FIGURE 15.4 Some strategies for modifying activities

SOURCE: Adapted from C. B. Eichstaedt & B. W. Lavay (1993), *Physical activity for individuals with mental retardation: Infancy through adulthood*. Champagne, IL: Human Kinetics Books.

1. Does the person's current movement repertoire allow independent performance of the task?
2. Can the person learn required movements not now in her current repertoire?
3. Does the task provide an opportunity to teach or reinforce movements needed to perform other priority activities?
4. Does the person use substitute movements that achieve the desired outcome without producing undesirable or detrimental movement patterns that can ultimately result in decreased function?
5. What handling techniques are effective to facilitate required movements?
6. Would using a splint improve performance of this and other tasks without limiting other aspects of participation?
7. Would other adaptations improve participation?

FIGURE 15.5 Considerations in assessment of movement abilities

SOURCE: J. York & B. Rainforth (1995), Enhancing leisure participation by individuals with significant intellectual and physical disabilities. In S. J. Schleien, L. H. Meyer, L. A. Heyne, & B. B. Brandt (Eds.), *Lifelong leisure skills and lifestyles for persons with developmental disabilities* (pp. 113–132). Baltimore, MD: Paul H. Brookes.

more likely to be comfortable and accepting. Fortunately, there are many examples of programs in which children or adults with MR have successfully participated with others from the community. Often these experiences result in enjoyment and enhanced skills for those with MR while promoting more accepting attitudes on the part of others. After a two-week integrated camping experience for children ages 8 to 13, for example, children without disabilities were more likely to initiate activities with children who had severe disabilities, their friendship ratings increased, and camp operators' attitudes toward providing integrated camping experiences improved (Rynders, Schleien, & Mustonen, 1990).

As we have seen throughout this text, the behavior of the individual with MR seems to have the greatest influence on acceptance—more so than skill level, IQ, or the mental retardation label itself. In fact, there is evidence that adult community members may be more likely to initiate overtures of friendliness toward newcomers whom they know have MR than they would be toward a stranger without that label (Sparrow, Shinkfield, & Karnilowicz, 1993). The inhibiting influence of disruptive behavior on acceptance, however, once again points to the importance of effective behavioral training and management to community-integration efforts.

Networking is central to the success of including individuals with mental retardation in existing recreational programs and services (Rynders & Staur, 1995). Concerned professionals across disciplines must make connections with community organizations, citizens, parents, and people with MR and collaborate to create recreational opportunities in which all community members can participate.

Perhaps even more than in other areas of life, however, individual preferences should play a guiding role in leisure and recreation planning. Preferences should be considered when deciding upon activities, and opportunities for choice should be plentiful within the activity itself (Dattilo, 1991). As examples, people can demonstrate choice by selecting materials for art projects, choosing partners, or choosing preferred seats. For those with the severest disabilities, choices may be indicated by eye movements, facial expressions, or sounds of eagerness or dismay.

Preference may also be directed toward community inclusion itself. There is evidence that people with MR may not always want to participate with others in the community, and they may sometimes also prefer to engage in activities with those who have mental retardation. In one study, adults with Down syndrome stated a preference for bowling with others who also had Down syndrome (Neumayer, Smith, & Lundegren, 1993). It is possible, of course, that such a choice is the result of unhappy experiences in integrated settings, and professionals need to do all they can to promote friendly acceptance within the wider community, but outlawing segregated activities may rob people with MR of the opportunity of control in leisure life where choice and preference are integral to enjoyment.

> **FOR DISCUSSION**   *Tom, who is 20 years old, works part-time busing tables at a local restaurant, lives in a group home, and has few leisure activities, although he is physically able. His only social activities are outings with others from his residence, and he makes it clear that he does not want to participate in additional activities. You feel sure that it would be better for him if he were to get involved in the community and engage in more physical exercise. How do you proceed?*

As the MRDD board position statement indicates, many of those with MR—like many people in the general population—could improve their health, fitness, and

Special Olympics International

Special Olympics International (SOI) is probably the most widely known recreational program especially for those with mental retardation. Founded in 1968 by Eunice Kennedy Shriver, SOI has programs in more than 100 countries and chapters in all 50 U.S. states. National and local competitions are held annually both winter and summer, and world games take place every two years, alternating between winter and summer games (Special Olympics International [SOI], 1993).

Although Special Olympic games have succeeded in providing healthy activities for hundreds of thousands of people with MR and have brought the subject of retardation out of seclusion and into world view and worthy of attention and concern, SOI also has been the subject of recent controversy. Critics have charged that SOI typifies the segregated approach to recreation, and that it portrays athletes' accomplishments as the subject of heart-rending appeals for charity that lack dignity and legitimacy (Biklen & Knoll, 1987).

In response, SOI has developed new opportunities for integrated participation through three programs:

1. Unified Sports, in which athletes with and without MR (matched by age and skill level) compete together;
2. Partners Clubs, in which high school and college-age volunteers act as assistant coaches and spend additional time with Special Olympians in recreational and leisure pursuits; and
3. Sport Partnerships, in which Special Olympians participate with high school athletes through school programs (Eichstaedt & Lavay, 1993). In addition, SOI has developed the Motor Activity Training Program (MATP) for people with severe physical disabilities and MR (SOI, 1992).

Athletes in SOI train for at least eight weeks before participating, and coaches attend a training school followed by a final exam. The training that athletes receive, however, appears to vary according to the experience and skill of coaches, and there is an attempt to maximize the physical benefit that athletes receive by improving the quality of their training.

Evaluative research on outcomes of SOI competition for athletes and on public attitudes is sparse and provides methodological challenges, but some evidence indicates that athletes experience enhanced self-esteem and confidence through participation. In addition, one study of attitudes toward Special Olympics showed that both parents and professionals have highly positive views of the program, especially in regard to its self-esteem benefits for athletes. Professionals were more likely than parents to be concerned with issues of segregation, whereas parents were more concerned about administrative problems (Klein, Gilman, & Zigler, 1993). With more than 1 million participants every year, this clearly popular program continues to grow both in appeal and in the variety of programs it offers.

longevity if they were to become more physically active. Studies show that physical exercise programs have resulted in increased liking for and participation in sports for children, as well as improved cardiovascular functioning, work performance, and weight control for adults (Fernhall, 1993; Chanias, Reid, & Hoover, 1998). Although such programs may require activity modifications and skill training for some people, they often require only encouragement, modeling, and reinforcement, even for those who have significantly disabling conditions (King & Mace, 1990).

Those with MR have the same needs for intimacy as others have.

© Robert Foothorap/Jeroboam

SEXUALITY AND SEX EDUCATION

Although certain physical differences can affect the sexual development of some people with mental retardation, by far the most determining factors are social and cultural. Among the physical influences are a delay in secondary sex characteristics that sometimes occur and a higher incidence of impotence and sterility in some specific conditions that are related to MR, particularly when these conditions are markedly severe (Rowe & Savage, 1987). Both men and women with Prader-Willi syndrome, for example, have underdeveloped secondary sex characteristics and sterility. In addition, men with Down syndrome are typically unable to produce pregnancy, although they are capable of sexual intercourse; women with Down syndrome, on the other hand, sometimes conceive and bear children. Most people with mental retardation, however, develop customary physical sex characteristics and have typical sexual feelings and desires. Many also experience satisfying sexual relationships.

Attitudes Toward Sexuality in People with MR

For the most part, the prevailing attitude toward sexuality in those with mental retardation has been fear, disgust, or both (Rowe & Savage, 1987) based primarily on bigotry and stereotypes. In general, people with mental retardation have been viewed as devoid of the normal feelings experienced by others. Frequently, they

Parents of children with mental retardation are concerned with the following sexual issues:

1. How to talk about sexuality with their children—when to begin, what to say, and how to say it so that it can be understood.
2. How to help their children deal with and understand their sexual feelings.
3. Protecting their children from being abused and teaching them not to exploit others.
4. Determining whether their children should use birth control, what method should be used, when sterilization would be appropriate, and who should make these decisions.
5. Dealing with homosexual and masturbatory activities.
6. Determining their children's ability to make judgments and the ability to be independent and socially responsible.
7. Determining if their children will marry or reproduce. Talking to their children about other options.
8. Understanding how their children's disabilities may affect their physical development and sexuality.
9. Helping their children develop positive self-esteem, confident body image, and comfort with their sexuality. Helping to give children a feeling that they have a right to be sexual but assisting them in making wise choices in how they express their sexuality.
10. Determining how to encourage and provide social opportunities for their children.

FIGURE 15.6 Sexual issues of concern to parents

SOURCE: Adapted from P. J. Wallis (1991), Issues in social-sexuality for handicapped persons, their families, and professionals. In M. J. Fine (Ed.), *Collaboration with parents of exceptional children*. Brandon, VT: Clinical Psychology Publishing.

have been viewed as either asexual or dangerously unable to control themselves. People with MR, it is true, do sometimes engage in sexual exhibitionism or other inappropriate sexual behaviors, but this is not typical, and when it does occur it is often due to the lack of proper training and the absence of acceptable sexual outlets. The more damaging attitude, perhaps, is the assumption that people with MR have neither the capacity nor the need to express love and affection in the same way as others (Hingsburger, 1991).

The social climate surrounding sexuality in those with MR is further complicated by the fact that families are often understandably worried about the possibility of exploitation. As a result, parents may become defensive about their young or adult child's sexuality or deny it entirely. Many parents, of course, are eager to approach sexuality issues positively and constructively, but few parents are really comfortable talking about their children's sex lives. When professionals approach parents on this topic, therefore, it should be with sensitivity and should focus on issues of love, affection, and social adjustment and not focus solely on physical details (Hingsburger, 1991; Huntley & Benner, 1993). Figure 15.6 shows several of the concerns and responsibilities parents have in regard to their children's (including their adult children's) sexual development.

Although residential staff members are usually eager to encourage their clients to live "normal" satisfying lives in the area of sexuality, they are many times concerned

Table 15.2 Myths and Facts Regarding Sexuality in People with Mental Retardation

Myths	Facts
There are always delays in sexual development.	Delays depend on the source and severity of the disability: Most individuals with nongenetically based syndromes, for example, mature at the same rate as their peers.
Those with MR display a higher (or lower) fertility rate.	The fertility rate depends upon the severity and cause of the disability and is influenced by age, degree or frequency of sexual activity, marital status, and socioeconomic status.
Those with MR do not experience the same sexual needs as the "normal" population.	The sexual needs and desires are usually the same.
People with mental retardation cannot assume responsibility for their sexuality.	Many are sexually active and highly responsible; determining factors for such responsibility include training, severity of intellectual deficit, and emotional and psychological factors.
Frequent masturbation can cause mental or physical harm.	Depending on socialization, guilt is sometimes present; depending on technique, skin irritation can occur. No serious problems exist.
Those with MR are oversexed and out of control.	The frequency of sexual activity is lower than their peer groups. Sometimes social skills and understanding are lacking, often because of poor training.
People with mental retardation remain childish and innocent forever.	Maturity occurs within several matrices: intellectual, physical, sexual, social, emotional, psychological, and so on. Clients will continue to mature even when apparently delayed in one or two areas.
Those with MR are not able to marry.	Higher functioning people can sustain a marriage. Marital failure results from problems similar to those found in the general population.
Children of parents with MR will be affected themselves.	By and large, this is not true. The greatest percentage of children born to people with MR have IQs within the normal range.
People with mental retardation cannot raise children.	With community supports, many prove to be capable parents.
Effective use of temporary measures of birth control is not possible.	With training and supervision, higher functioning clients can effectively use the pill.
Sex education will result in overstimulation and sexual activity will occur when it otherwise would not.	Sex education does not stimulate sexual activity; rather, it promotes appropriate expression and social responsibility.

SOURCE: W. S. Rowe & S. Savage (1987), *Sexuality and the developmentally handicapped: A guidebook for health care professionals.* Lewiston, NY: Edwin Mellen Press.

with public opinion and their own liability in the event of pregnancy or abuse. They also may not know how to react to or advise about sexual issues. Even among those who work in the field of mental retardation, myths and misunderstandings abound concerning the facts of sexuality in the population with MR. Table 15.2 reveals several of these most common myths and contrasts them with reality.

The idea that people with mental retardation remain essentially children has had an unfortunate influence on the response of families and professionals toward sexuality in that population. As is shown in Table 15.2, development is not usu-

- Ignorance and lack of knowledge
- Overcompliance
- Unrealistic view that everyone is a friend
- Limited and restricted social opportunities
- Low self-esteem
- Limited assertiveness and ability to refuse

FIGURE 15.7 By-products of living in an extremely protected environment that does not address sexuality

ally consistent in all areas. Because someone is functioning at a much earlier level of development intellectually does not mean they are also physically underdeveloped or that their physical needs and emotions remain immature. To the contrary, the view of those with MR as sexually childlike often functions to help families and professionals avoid a troublesome topic more than it reflects the reality of life.

Unfortunately, such a view can actually promote the problems it seeks to avoid. For one thing, it can make sex education seem irrelevant or undesirable. Why should an "innocent child" need to know about sex? And if such things are discussed, won't they naturally want to explore and experiment? Ignorance about appropriate sexuality, however, only makes any existing vulnerability more pronounced. It is true that the deficits in reasoning and problem solving experienced by many people with MR can make them vulnerable to exploitation. Statistical estimates suggest, in fact, that people with MR are considerably more likely to be sexually abused than those in the general population—and the incidence in the general population is appallingly high (Muccigrosso, 1991). If only for that reason, it is essential to their safety that individuals with mental retardation know which behaviors are and are not appropriate in specific circumstances. Sex education teaches this crucial information and it provides the training through role-playing and practice that offers individuals the means to extricate themselves from problematic situations (Hazeltine & Miltenberger, 1990).

FOR DISCUSSION *You know your adult client Becky is engaging in sexual intercourse with her boyfriend, and you are convinced that she needs information and guidance to help her manage her relationship safely. Becky's parents are furious at the suggestion of sex education and demand that she be kept away from "that jerk." What do you do?*

Too often, the view of innocence leads also to the belief that the innocent person must be watched and "protected" at all times. Figure 15.7 lists several reasons why overprotection can render people with MR more vulnerable to sexual abuse.

Education and counseling in the prevention of sexual abuse are seldom available for people with mental retardation, although good programs are becoming more frequent (Whitehouse & McCabe, 1997). Excellent curricula, including audiovisual materials, are available to teach young students, adult learners, and families to avoid situations of sexual abuse, as well as help deal with the aftereffects in victims (Muccigrosso, 1991).

In addition to making people more vulnerable to exploitation, overprotection seriously infringes on that individual's rights and on the opportunities to experience a normal life. Sex education plays an important part in the training necessary for those with MR to take their place in the community, and it opens the way for them to develop friendships and relationships more safely, whether or not those relationships are sexual.

Furthermore, the assumption that sexual feelings, desires, and exploration will not take place in the absence of discussions about sexuality is not correct. Most infants or young children—whether or not they have mental retardation—discover that touching their genitals is pleasurable. They explore their bodies and experience sexual feelings, regardless of any discussion of what is happening. Most of the inappropriate behavior displayed by people with MR happens as a result of ignorance rather than lack of self-control. Many people with mental retardation are unable to find answers to their questions on their own. It may even be difficult to formulate questions, and they may be easily discouraged by negative responses to their attempts. When they are given explicit information and training, however, they can develop appropriate behaviors. People with mental retardation can learn the importance of privacy when masturbating, for example, and they can learn when it is appropriate to touch others and the kinds of touching that are allowed in varying circumstances.

FOR DISCUSSION *Imagine that you have adult clients Sue and Bob, who are in love with one another. They want to spend all of their time alone together in Sue's room. You know they are physically intimate (or soon will be), and you are worried about pregnancy. Furthermore, they frequently talk about getting married, and you feel sure this is unrealistic. How do you proceed?*

Professional staff members frequently find themselves in a difficult situation in regard to the sexual rights and expression of their clients. After all, the staff goal is to be responsive to the needs of clients and to help them take on the responsibilities for their own lives as much as possible—in fact, unnecessarily taking over the clients' life and taking on responsibility for it is unethical. At the same time, the professional finds herself in a position in which she may be held responsible if things do not go well. If a client becomes pregnant or contracts a disease, for example, the staff person may well be asked to answer for it. Figure 15.8 addresses some of the issues that professionals must manage.

The risk inherent in issues of sexuality, though, is not so different from those in other areas. Risks are inherent in many physical activities (swimming and horseback riding, for example) and cannot be perfectly avoided. Risks also exist if clients are permitted to go out in the world (to work or to the store) on their own, yet use of public transportation is a common goal in rehabilitation plans. In the area of sexuality, as well as in other areas of life, appropriate and effective training reduces the risks of engaging in the normal activities of life. Table 15.3

- How do we respond in a professional manner and provide appropriate professional recommendations, support, and feedback when the topic may be directly opposed to our personal value systems and thus cause a great deal of discomfort?
- How do we assess a client's or student's knowledge before we begin an educational or counseling program?
- How do we determine a client's or student's ability to understand his own or someone else's actions and make responsible decisions—that is, use informed consent?
- How do we facilitate the provision of information without overstepping parental

boundaries or being in conflict with parental values?
- How do we work with parents so that they are more accepting and more positive about their child's sexuality?
- How do we determine when a student's or client's behavior is a result of sexual abuse and not her disability?
- How do we deal with clients who exhibit aggressive behaviors, perhaps as a result of sexual frustration?
- How do we proceed with educating or counseling students and clients without clear policies in place?

FIGURE 15.8 Issues for professionals in regard to clients' sexuality

SOURCE: Adapted from P. J. Wallis (1991), Issues in social-sexuality for handicapped persons, their families, and professionals. In M. J. Fine (Ed.), *Collaboration with parents of exceptional children*. Brandon, VT: Clinical Psychology Publishing.

Table 15.3 Suggestions for Teaching about Privacy and Sexuality

Concept	Activity
Create and model privacy.	Knock before you enter when a client or student is in a bedroom or bathroom. Avert your eyes when a client is naked or shows a private sexual part, and explain that you are embarrassed rather than angry. Suggest he cover up or adjust his clothing before you turn back around. If the client needs personal, private assistance, make sure you take him to a private place to give that help.
Engage in concrete instruction.	Go over a client's or student's life with him and explore what private places are for him. Make sure to distinguish between private "to do" and private "to talk." Teach him to use whispering and proximity to create a private moment.
Teach about appropriate touch.	Show that you feel uncomfortable with certain *kinds* of touch, *not* just touch to "private parts." Teach the difference between casual, informal touch and "feel good" touch.
Show that privacy is not dirty.	Often people with retardation equate privacy or personal parts of the body with something that is "dirty" or "bad." Clients need to know that all body shapes and sizes are good and that all body parts contribute to whole and healthy functioning.
Demonstrate that privacy is not punishment.	Because confinement to their room or other time-out procedures are often used for punishment, clients may respond to private time alone with aversion. It is often necessary to spend time associating private times with pleasurable activities.

SOURCE: D. Hingsburger (1991), *I contact: Sexuality and people with developmental disabilities*. Mountville, PA: VIDA Publishing.

offers suggestions for helping those with MR learn about privacy and appropriate behavior.

ELEMENTS OF EFFECTIVE SEX EDUCATION

For sex education to be successful, everyone involved must be comfortable: clients, parents, and professionals (Wallis, 1991). And to be really effective in helping people with MR make appropriate decisions about their sexual behavior, sex education programs must address more than the physical aspects of sexuality. Such programs should focus on developing interpersonal relationships more generally, finding opportunities to socialize, the responsibility that one has for one's own body, the right and the ability to say "No," and information about AIDS and other sexually transmitted diseases (Huntley & Benner, 1993). In addition, programs need to address the specific needs of the individual rather than simply present a generic curriculum. Such programs must be practical and based upon individual assessment. Relevant issues to consider are whether the individual already has a sexual partner, whether she is experiencing sexually related behavior problems, the level of social skills she possesses, the individual's cognitive reasoning skills, and her own goals and preferences.

MARRIAGE AND PARENTING

In spite of the advances outlined previously in this text, it is still illegal in many states for people with mental retardation to marry. Legal prohibition against marriage for those with MR was in part designed with the intent to protect the longevity of union—although there is no evidence of correlation between IQ and the incidence of divorce. Further, such laws hope to afford protection to marriage partners. However, with statistics showing that violence occurs at some point in two-thirds of all marriages, IQ within the typical range does not seem to offer greater safety to spouses. Finally, laws against marriage in the population with MR were designed to prevent procreation and the propagation of mental retardation itself. But prohibiting marriage does not preclude pregnancy, and most mothers with mental retardation have children with normal IQs (see Chapter 7).

Outlawing marriage, however, does make it more difficult for those with intellectual impairment to form unions that are sanctified by society and perpetuates the idea that marriage is not a suitable option for them. Nevertheless, many people with mental retardation do marry. Although such couples frequently need assistance in some areas of life, it is probably no more than they would if they were single.

Successfully dealing with the issues of marriage is one thing, however, and parenting is quite another. To begin with, one can reasonably hope that spouses will offer help and support to each other; in contrast, infants and young children depend entirely upon their parents for their very lives and therefore bring with them vital demands. Even though children pose serious challenges, however, those with MR (at least in the United States) have the same human and legal right to bear and rear children as anyone else. The issue of parenthood, therefore, poses serious ethical conflicts and dilemmas.

While advocates for those with MR (notably The Arc) declare that individuals with mental retardation are capable of rearing children either on their own or with some assistance, others who work in parent training and intervention describe a situation in which many children are at significant risk (Feldman, 1998). As a society, then, how do we maintain our advocacy for people with intellectual disabilities while simultaneously maintaining our responsibility for the health and well-being of children?

One factor that appears to play a critically important part in whether or not parents with MR can parent adequately is socioeconomic status (SES). Needless to say, parenting is a highly demanding job—and the demands become so much greater when one also must deal with financial problems, inadequate housing, and lack of transportation. For parents who often cannot read or tell time, it is virtually impossible to meet the paperwork and interview requirements necessary to obtain public assistance without help.

Many parents with MR are able to learn the skills to parent young children, but as their children grow older, parents can be faced with increasing challenges in discipline and control. Most parents with mental retardation do require help from their families or society to meet all the role demands of independent living and parenting. Unfortunately, many parents with MR do not have help and come to the attention of the social service system only when they are reported to the state's human services department for some failure. The service system has already failed many of these (usually) single mothers: They may not have received special education, and often their children are removed from them without their having the opportunity to learn the skills or obtain the resources they need to prevent it. In some instances, children have even been removed from the parental home without any evidence of abuse or neglect but simply on the basis of parental retardation alone (Marafino, 1990).

In the United States, the social service supports required by this low SES population are not adequate to meet their needs, and the foster care system is not providing an effective alternative. And when parents escape the notice of the social service system entirely, their children may suffer from inadequate nutrition, the lack of appropriate developmental stimulation, and the absence of medical treatment. Clearly, these are serious problems and in such instances the rights of neither parents nor children are effectively protected.

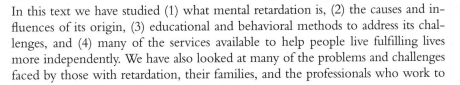

LOOKING AHEAD

In this text we have studied (1) what mental retardation is, (2) the causes and influences of its origin, (3) educational and behavioral methods to address its challenges, and (4) many of the services available to help people live fulfilling lives more independently. We have also looked at many of the problems and challenges faced by those with retardation, their families, and the professionals who work to help them. In the final chapter, we will further discuss the role of advocacy, discover some of the future directions in the field, and consider a vision of what might be accomplished.

INFOTRAC COLLEGE EDITION

The effects of social isolation on people with mental retardation are similar to those found in other populations. Enter *social isolation* as the keyword in *InfoTrac College Edition*. From these articles, which other groups are affected by social isolation, and what are the effects?

REFERENCES

Adams K., & Markham, R. (1991). Recognition of affective facial expressions by children and adolescents with and without mental retardation. *American Journal on Mental Retardation, 96*(1), 21–28.

Anderson, D. J., Lakin, K. C., Hill, B. K., & Chen, T. (1992). Social integration of older persons with mental retardation in residential facilities. *American Journal on Mental Retardation, 96*(5), 488–501.

Biklen, D., & Knoll, J. (1987). The disabled minority. In S. Taylor, D. Biklen, & J. Knoll (Eds.), *Community integration for people with severe disabilities* (pp. 3–24). New York: Teachers College Press.

Brinker, R. P. (1985). Interactions between severely mentally retarded students and other students in integrated and segregated public school settings. *American Journal of Mental Deficiency, 89,* 587–594.

Carter, M. J., Nezey, I. O., Wenzel, K., & Foret, C. M. (1999). Leisure education with caregiver support groups. *Activities, Adaptation & Aging, 24*(2), 67–81.

Chanias, A. K., Reid, G., & Hoover, M. L. (1998). Exercise effects on health-related physical fitness of individuals with an intellectual disability: A meta-analysis. *Adapted Physical Activity Quarterly, 15*(2), 119–140.

Clegg, J. A., & Standen, P. J. (1991). Friendship among adults who have developmental disabilities. *American Journal on Mental Retardation, 95*(6), 663–671.

Dattilo, J. (1991). Recreation and leisure: A review of the literature and recommendations for future directions. In L. S. Meyer, C. A. Peck, & L. Brown (Eds.), *Critical issues in the lives of people with severe disabilities* (pp. 171–193). Baltimore, MD: Paul H. Brookes.

Dattilo, J., & Camarata, S. (1991). Facilitating conversation through self-initiated augmentative communication treatment. *Journal of Applied Behavior Analysis, 24*(2), 369–378.

Durand, V. M., & Carr, E. G. (1991). Functional communication training to reduce challenging behavior: Maintenance and application in new settings. *Journal of Applied Behavior Analysis, 24*(2), 251–264.

———. (1992). An analysis of maintenance following functional communication training. *Journal of Applied Behavior Analysis, 25*(4), 777–794.

Eichstaedt, C. B., & Lavay, B. W. (1993). *Physical activity for individuals with mental retardation: Infancy through adulthood.* Champagne, IL: Human Kinetics Books.

Ernst, J. M., & Cacioppo, J. T. (1999). Lonely hearts: Psychological perspectives on loneliness. *Applied & Preventive Psychology, 8*(1), 1–22.

Feldman, M. A. (1998). Parents with intellectual disabilities: Implications and interventions. In J. R. Lutzker (Ed.), *Handbook of child abuse research and treatment* (pp. 401–420). New York: Plenum Press.

Fernhall, B. (1993). Physical fitness and exercise training of individuals with mental retardation. *Medicine & Science in Sports & Exercise, 25*(4), 442–450.

Firth, H., & Rapley, M. (1990). *From acquaintance to friendship: Issues for people with learning disabilities.* Worchester, UK: BIMH Publications.

Fleming, M. K. (1998), *Recreational therapy.* Cincinnati: College of Mount St. Joseph.

Foxx, R. M., & Faw, G. D. (1992). An eight-year follow-up of three social skills training studies. *Mental Retardation, 30*(2), 63–66.

Guralnick, M. J. (1986). The peer relations of young handicapped and nonhandicapped children. In P. S. Strain, M. J. Guralnick, & H. M. Walker (Eds.), *Children's social behavior: Development, assessment, and modification.* Orlando, FL: Academic Press.

Halpern, A. S., Close, W. D., & Nelson, D. J. (1986). *On my own: The impact of semi-independent living programs for adults with mental retardation.* Baltimore, MD: Paul H. Brookes.

Haring, T. G., & Breen, C. G. (1992). A peer-mediated social network intervention to enhance the social integration of persons with moderate and severe disabilities. *Journal of Applied Behavior Analysis, 25*(2), 319–333.

Hazeltine, B., & Miltenberger, R. G. (1990). Teaching self-protection skills to persons with mental retardation. *American Journal on Mental Retardation, 95*(2), 188–197.

Healey, K. N., & Masterpasqua, F. (1992). Interpersonal cognitive problem-solving among children with mild mental retardation. *American Journal on Mental Retardation, 96*(4), 367–372.

Hingsburger, D. (1991). *I contact: Sexuality and people with developmental disabilities.* Mountville, PA: VIDA Publishing.

Huntley, C. F., & Benner, S. M. (1993). Reducing barriers to sex education for adults with mental retardation. *Mental Retardation, 31*(4), 215–220.

King, D., & Mace, F. C. (1990) Acquisition and maintenance of exercise skills under normalized conditions by adults with moderate and severe mental retardation. *Mental Retardation, 28*(5), 311–317.

Klein, T., Gilman, E., & Zigler E. (1993). Special Olympics: An evaluation by professionals and parents. *Mental Retardation, 31*(1), 15–23.

Knopp, C., Baker, B., & Brown, K. (1992). Social skills and their correlates: Preschoolers with developmental delays. *American Journal on Mental Retardation, 96,* 357–366.

Krauss, M. W., Seltzer, M. M., & Goodman, S. J. (1992). Social support networks of adults with mental retardation who live at home. *American Journal on Mental Retardation, 96*(4), 432–441.

Lali, J. S., Pinter-Lali, E., Mace, F. C., & Murphy, D. (1991). Training interactional behaviors of adults with developmental disabilities: A systematic replication and extension. *Journal of Applied Behavior Analysis, 24*(1), 167–174.

Larson, R. W., & Suman, V. (1999). How children and adolescents spend time across the world: Work, play, and developmental opportunities. *Psychological Bulletin, 125*(6), 701–736.

Levy-Shiff, R., Kedem, P., & Sevillia, Z. (1990). Ego identity in mentally retarded adolescents. *American Journal on Mental Retardation, 94*(5), 541–549.

Marafino, K. (1990). Parental rights of persons with mental retardation. In B. Whitman & P. Accardo (Eds.), *When a parent is mentally retarded.* Baltimore, MD: Paul H. Brookes.

Meyer, L. H., & Putnam, J. (1988). Social integration. In V. Van Hasselt, P. Strain, & M. Hersen (Eds.), *Handbook of developmental and physical disabilities* (pp. 107–133). New York: Pergamon Press.

Muccigrosso, L. (1991). Sexual abuse prevention strategies and programs for persons with developmental disabilities. *Sexuality and Disability, 9*(3), 261–271.

Newcombe, A. F., Bukowski, W. M., & Pattee, L. (1993). Children's peer relations: A meta-analytic review of popular, rejected, neglected, controversial, and average sociometric status. *Psychological Bulletin, 113,* 99–128.

Neumayer, R., Smith, R. W., & Lundegren, H. M. (1993). Leisure-related peer preference choices of individuals with Down syndrome. *Mental Retardation, 31*(6), 396–402.

Romski, M. A., Sevcik, R. A., & Wilkinson, K. M. (1994). Peer-directed communicative interactions of augmented language learners with mental retardation. *American Journal on Mental Retardation, 98*(4), 527–538.

Rowe, W. S., & Savage, S. (1987). *Sexuality and the developmentally handicapped: A guidebook for health care professionals.* Lewiston, NY: Edwin Mellen Press.

Rynders, J., & Schleien, S. (1991). *Together successfully: Creating recreational and educational programs that integrate people with and without disabilities.* Arlington, TX: The Arc–United States; National 4-H; and the Institute on Community Integration, University of Minnesota.

Rynders, J. E., Schleien, S. J., & Mustonen, T. (1990). Integrating children with severe disabilities for intensified outdoor education: Focus on feasibility. *Mental Retardation, 28*(1), 7–14.

Rynders, J. E., & Staur, N. A. (1995). Inclusionary community leisure services. In S. J. Schleien, L. H. Meyer, L. A. Heyne, & B. B. Brandt (Eds.), *Lifelong leisure skills and life-styles for persons with developmental disabilities* (pp. 147–160). Baltimore, MD: Paul H. Brookes.

Schleien, S. J., Meyer, L. H., Heyne, L. A., & Brandt, B. B. (1995). *Lifelong leisure skills and lifestyles for persons with developmental disabilities.* Baltimore, MD: Paul H. Brookes.

Schloss, P. J., & Wood, C. E. (1990). Effect of self-monitoring on maintenance and generalization of conversational skills of persons with mental retardation. *Mental Retardation, 28*(2), 105–113.

Soodak, L. (1990). Social behavior and knowledge of social "scripts" among mentally retarded adults. *American Journal on Mental Retardation, 94*(5), 515–521.

Sparrow, W. A., Shinkfield, A. J., & Karnilowicz, W. (1993). Constraints on the participation of individuals with mental retardation in mainstream recreation. *Mental Retardation, 31*(6), 403–411.

Special Olympics International. (1992). *Motor activities training program fact sheet.* Washington, DC: Author.

———. (1993). *Fact sheet.* Washington, DC: Author.

Stewart, G., Van Houten, R., & Van Houten, J. (1992). Increasing generalized social interactions in psychotic and mentally retarded residents through peer-mediated therapy. *Journal of Applied Behavior Analysis, 25*(2), 335–339.

Szivos, S. E., & Griffiths, E. (1990). Group processes involved in coming to terms with a mentally retarded identity. *Mental Retardation, 28*(6), 333–341.

Wallis, P. J. (1991). Issues in social-sexuality for handicapped persons, their families, and professionals. M. J. Fine (Ed.), *Collaboration with parents of exceptional children.* Brandon, VT: Clinical Psychology Publishing.

Whitehouse, M. A., & McCabe, M. P. (1997). Sex education programs for people with intellectual disability: How effective are they? *Education and Training in Mental Retardation and Developmental Disabilities, 32*(3), 229–240.

Widaman, K. F., MacMillan, D. L., Hemsley, R. E., Little, T. D., & Balow, I. H. (1992). Differences in adolescents' self-concept as a function of academic level, ethnicity, and gender. *American Journal on Mental Retardation, 96*(4), 387–404.

Williams, G. A., & Asher, S. R. (1992). Assessment of loneliness at school among children with mild mental retardation. *American Journal on Mental Retardation, 96*(4), 373–385.

York, J., & Rainforth, B. (1995). Enhancing leisure participation by individuals with significant intellectual and physical disabilities. In S. J. Schleien, L. H. Meyer, L. A. Heyne, & B. B. Brandt (Eds.), *Lifelong leisure skills and lifestyles for persons with developmental disabilities* (pp. 113–132). Baltimore, MD: Paul H. Brookes

Zetlin, A. G., & Turner, J. L. (1985). Transition from adolescence to adulthood: perspective of mentally retarded individuals and their families. *American Journal of Mental Deficiency, 89,* 570–579.

16

Vision, Progress, and Advocacy

Voices in Discourse
Self-Advocacy

Progress and Remaining Challenges

Changes in Professional Preparation

Additional Considerations

Attitudes and Community Integration

InfoTrac College Edition

References

Community integration occurs within the larger context of our whole society's task to rebuild community ties and establish relationships beyond our immediate families and work environments. Success depends upon looking past our differences and focusing on our common values, building a basis for understanding, and then entering a discourse aimed at reaching mutual community goals.

The kind of discourse needed to build consensus requires a level of skill and personal maturity that we—as participants in that discourse—often lack. Necessary attitudes include a willingness to admit that our own way of viewing the world may not be complete or adequate to the task of effective change, acknowledging that we can benefit from a clearer understanding of another's point of view, and conceding that our work is impeded in the absence of attitude change (Edgar, 1994). The necessary skills include introspection and reflection on our own assumptions, the ability to listen accurately and without presumption, and the ability to communicate our ideas clearly and persuasively while remaining flexible and open to change. For our discourse to be productive, we must ensure the participation of family, professionals, other advocates, and, especially, consumers.

VOICES IN DISCOURSE

The voices of families raised in advocacy and support have provided the major impetus for change and progress in the field of mental retardation. Some of the myriad ways that families have engaged in effective advocacy are listed in Figure 16.1.

In response to their loved ones' unmet needs, some family advocates have actually moved into service provision. As we saw with Judi Gerding in Chapter 14, they have founded residential homes, schools, and vocational training programs. It is families that have provided the bulk of support for one another, and there are now parent support groups in almost every community in the United States and in many nations throughout the world.

However, much remains to be done to improve parent–professional relations and, especially, to increase the opportunities and reality of true collaboration. As professionals and parents enter into a true partnership, service provision will consequently become more responsive to consumer needs.

Just as parents often have felt unheard in seeking support for their children, direct-service personnel often have felt similarly disempowered. Teachers, residential service providers, and others frequently have too little flexibility to make individualized decisions and too little input into the development of procedures and regulations. The trend now, however, does seem to be toward greater community control so that localities have more say about the details of program development for which national and state money is spent. This could result in an opportunity for more influence from those who are on the front lines, although bureaucratic and political complexities are considerable even at the local level and are likely to stand in the way of true grassroots influence unless there are improvements in communication, selfless commitment, and willingness to compro-

Families often:

- serve as lobbyists
- monitor agency services
- testify at hearings
- participate in human rights seminars
- work to change public attitudes
- knock on doors in neighborhoods where group residences are proposed
- start citizen advocacy offices
- support self-advocacy organizations
- start innovative training programs
- develop "grapevine" lists of understanding physicians and dentists—and "grapevine" lists of professionals to avoid
- write books on developmental disabilities
- give speeches to community organizations
- come to one another's aid in crises

FIGURE 16.1 Family advocacy efforts

SOURCE: Adapted from R. Perske & M. Perske (1986), *Hope for the families* (3rd ed.), Nashville: Abingdon Press.

mise. Furthermore, some substantial gains have come from federal legislation and involvement, and sufficient oversight to ensure that these gains are not lost is essential. Achieving the appropriate balance between local and federal control remains a challenge.

Self-Advocacy

Conspicuously infrequent in this text (and in most of what has been written on mental retardation) are the voices and words of those we hope to understand. Even so, those with MR have much to say about their lives and the supports they receive. They do, in fact, have a vision for the profession.

To begin, they have something to say about the pain of being "different" and of the difficulty of functioning with intellectual challenges. In the following example, a young woman reveals self-consciousness about her difference, while stating her wish to return to a favorite place with her sister and her sister's boyfriend. These excerpts were recorded by her mother.

> "I'd like to go back with Melanie and her sweetie," Collette decided, referring to her younger sister and her current beau, "if they wouldn't be offended by us," she added cautiously. (Kaufman, 1986, p. 38)

She also reveals the frustration of needing help in a situation where some others would not and the effect of that need on her self-esteem:

> I wanted to buy a card—I tried to. I went into the store and bought one, but it was the wrong kind. I didn't want to go ask the man to read it to me. I wanted to do it myself." She said she made her purchase, rushed home to Edgar [her husband] and had him read to her only to discover that although the sentiments were appropriate, the card was written for a

man to give to a woman. "I can't even buy a stupid card!" she cried out in despair. (Kaufman, 1986, p. 39)

And again, indicating her desire to take care of herself and struggling to solve her own problems, she says to her mother:

> See, these are all the things we're trying to solve. I don't like telling you our business. I feel embarrassed. I feel it's not right nor nothing. We're going through a very difficult, hard stage. (Kaufman, 1986, p. 41)

Self-advocates also have much to say about the role they believe is theirs in professional organizations. Here, Nancy Ward, chair of a self-advocacy organization called Self-Advocates Becoming Empowered, offers suggestions for making professional conferences more accessible to self-advocates:

> [M]ake things so we can understand it. Conference sessions have all these research titles, so we don't understand what they are going to be about, and we don't even go to them. I can just imagine how hard it would be to understand a presenter in these sessions. I think both the titles and the presentations should be understandable.
>
> Another way to involve us is to lower the membership dues: $80 to $100 is a lot of money for us. We need supports like getting our money for meals ahead of time instead of afterwards. It shouldn't be assumed that we have up-front money like professionals do. Most of us live on very limited income.
>
> One other hope I have is that someday there will not be a need for self-advocacy or parent organizations because people with disabilities will just be a part of society and accepted. But I don't think that will happen in my lifetime. (Ward, 1996, pp. 121, 122)

Self-advocates also have a clear vision of the role they should play among individuals with disabilities. Harvey Pacht, director of public education and group support for the Self-Advocacy Association of New York State, says the following:

> First of all, the self-advocacy movement should try to help people with disabilities to become aware that they are citizens and have rights, like all other people do. . . . Also, we have to empower them to speak up on behalf of themselves. For those who don't have the ability to speak for themselves, other people, who know them very well and understand what they want, feel, and need will have to speak for them. Those who advocate on behalf of others need to be honest and trustworthy.

And, he adds this advice for professional organizations (and perhaps for textbook authors, too):

> Another thing is that agencies and organizations like AAMR should stop using the words "mental retardation." Too many people have misused the word, to the point where it has become a negative label. We should put our efforts toward changing the terminology because the current language offends so many people. (Pacht, 1996, p. 124)

- Share information about self-advocacy with students and clients.
- Encourage participation and help provide the supports needed to participate.
- Establish a local self-advocacy group.
- Encourage convention participation.
- Encourage staff involvement.
- Listen to the voices of individual students and clients.
- Listen to the voices of the movement.

FIGURE 16.2 Ways to seek a closer partnership with self-advocacy groups

SOURCE: Adapted from J. R. Dudley (1996).

Self-advocacy organizations formed by individuals with intellectual disabilities can now be found across the United States and the world. Self-advocates sit on the boards and committees of national and state organizations and present at conventions (The Arc, 1996). In addition, their advice and comments are solicited by state and national legislators. Just as with parent organizations, there is every reason to believe that self-advocates and self-advocacy groups will increase and become even more influential. Figure 16.2 presents advice to service providers in regard to self-advocacy organizations.

PROGRESS AND REMAINING CHALLENGES

The central concept of this text is community integration, and in that area much progress has been made—although much still remains to do. Just a few decades ago, children with MR were placed in institutions, where it was expected they would spend their lives. It was assumed that they were incapable of learning, and no effort was made to educate them. Now education for children with developmental disabilities (including those with the severest disabilities) is mandated by law, and many children with MR are educated alongside their peers in regular classrooms. Furthermore, there are even some postsecondary educational options (Meers, 1992). In addition, many more adults with mental retardation live in community homes, and it is commonplace for citizens with retardation to work at community jobs.

There have been significant advances in the biological understanding of MR and in medical prevention of many conditions associated with it. Improvements in technology are helping many with severe physical disabilities live fuller and more satisfying lives. In addition, the financial resources available for educational and social services has increased enormously, stimulating a comparable increase in the number of available programs and supports (Wolfensberger, 1991).

We have learned, however, that there is far more to community integration than deinstitutionalization. The mere presence of a child in a regular classroom does not imply that she is accepted by her teacher or peers or that she is receiving

If full community integration is to become a reality, advocacy is essential.

AP Photo/Terry Gilliam

the education that is most appropriate for her needs. And, although many adults with MR work in community jobs, many others are homeless, unemployed, or working in jobs that ignore their real strengths and abilities. Just as bad, many children who need special help are still missed by the educational system; they move so frequently that they are not assessed as eligible or are homeless and attend school infrequently. Furthermore, countless adults struggle daily with intellectual disabilities without the benefit of support services. These individuals are often vulnerable to exploitation, hunger, homelessness, and loneliness (Wolfensberger, 1992).

The challenges for those who provide education and other services to those with MR are in many ways more profound than they have ever been. The number who need services continues to soar in line with increased social stratification, the numbers of people who live in poverty, and the related conditions that can result in mental impairment. The complexity of the service system is staggering, turnover can be appallingly high, and, by some accounts, a shocking number of agencies actually create more problems for those with MR than they solve (Wolfensberger, 1992).

How are young professionals to correct such problems—and what is to prevent them from feeling so overwhelmed and hopeless that they fail to try? In truth, no one of us can solve problems that are so widespread and so severe. We can only speak out against the inequities we witness, make our own contributions to progress, and work together toward continuous improvement. We can remember the ideals that initially led us to our professions and remain guided in all circumstances by the well-being of those we serve. We can accept the limitations of our knowledge and our ability to know the "truth," and we can be open to new ideas and different points of view.

The fact is that there are often coexisting, if not multiple, truths, and it is essential to find some balance for these if we are to be effective. Some instances of coexisting truths involve theories of retardation—for example, that mental retardation is both a social construct *and* a biological entity. Others involve ideology: that special education is a civil right, a privilege, *and* a responsibility. Still others relate to practical matters: People with MR need to be protected, and they also need to be independent.

FOR DISCUSSION *How is it that seemingly contradictory ideas can often be simultaneously valid? Can you explain, for example, how special education can be a civil right, a privilege, and a responsibility—all at the same time?*

If we can develop the necessary intellectual skills and appropriate attitudes, then we will be better able to address the challenges that lie ahead. Below are some of these challenges.

1. How do we move to include children as full participants in the educational system while at the same time safeguarding their access to needed individual supports?

2. How do we help community residents form friendships with neighbors and other community members at a time when all such friendships are becoming more difficult to maintain?

3. How do we find better ways to assess skills and abilities not just to define eligibility, but also to effectively match needs and services?

4. How do we improve coordination of services and avoid their duplication?

5. How do we increase responsiveness to the needs of the service population so that individuals are clearly better off as recipients?

6. How do we make sure we do not simply reproduce countless community "mini-institutions"?

7. How do we move service provision more under the direction of local communities and therefore more within the control of consumers, families, and direct service professionals?

8. How do we provide better crisis intervention services for the eligible homeless and ensure that fewer people fall through the cracks of the service system?

9. How do we increase the number of community residential placements?

CHANGES IN PROFESSIONAL PREPARATION

As interdisciplinary practices become firmly entrenched in service provision, and as professionals are expected to provide services within a systems perspective, the university and college curriculum must reflect these changes. It will no longer be sufficient that students understand the content area of their own disciplines—instead, they will need to be familiar with other related disciplines and be able to see how their own theories, methods, techniques, and expectations fit within the larger network.

Furthermore, if community integration is to become a reality, then all citizens, businesspeople, and professionals must face the reality of intellectual differences and the need for community responsiveness and flexibility. Business owners, managers, physicians, dentists, and others must come to expect variation in the strengths and abilities of their customers and clients and they will be educated with that expectation in mind.

In that sense, mental retardation can no longer be seen as a specialty field but must be approached as a characteristic that occurs with common regularity among the human population—an anticipated element of diversity. As such, it belongs among the multicultural elements of every postsecondary curriculum.

ADDITIONAL CONSIDERATIONS

If we are to improve the quality of service delivery for people with MR, then we need to consider the histories of our schools, agencies, and the field itself. To progress in any endeavor, we must learn from our mistakes, and certainly this is no less true in the field of mental retardation. First, once a problem area is identified—for example, "children in special classes are not gaining the acceptance we would like" or "we are having trouble maintaining good attendance in a center-based early intervention program"—we need to find answers to specific questions, including:

1. Have we or others had such problems before, and if so, when?
2. What solutions have we tried and what have been the results?
3. Have there been examples of programs that are more successful in this regard?
4. If so, how can we identify the strategies they used?
5. To whom might we go for advice and suggestions?

Such a historical problem-solving approach is essential to the continuous improvement of our programs.

Second, our view of the past, present, and future aspects of a problem must take an international focus. We will be better able to take that view as we join in study and discussion with those from other countries. To that purpose, several

U.S. organizations—including the AAMR, the Association for Persons with Severe Handicaps (TASH), the ARC, and the President's Committee on Mental Retardation—have founded the United States International Council on Mental Retardation and Developmental Disabilities. The purposes of this organization include

- promoting the welfare of people with MRDD everywhere,
- seeking a cooperative resolution of universal issues of human and legal rights,
- promoting international activities relating to the rights and opportunities of people with MR,
- increasing U.S. support for relevant international activities, and
- ensuring U.S. participation within international organizations (The Arc, 1998).

Finally, most of the difficulties we face in service delivery can be understood in terms of problems in human relationships. Whether the challenges involve gaining additional financial support or frustrations with legislators, supervisors, students or clients, families, or citizen attitudes, increasing our skills in communicating and collaborating will help us become more responsive and successful in our efforts.

ATTITUDES AND
COMMUNITY INTEGRATION

Stigmatization and exclusion of those with mental retardation happen for many reasons. Chief among them are that many of us respond to the fact of *difference*—especially when it implies weakness, suffering, or dependency—with nervousness and fear. This tendency is accentuated when the perceived individual is viewed only from a distance. Usually, when we get to know someone personally, we begin to recognize their strengths and attributes or at least begin to view them as less threatening. For this reason, those who advocate inclusion believe that public familiarity with those who have retardation will decrease stigmatization—and evidence does support this view. It is also clear, however, that proximity alone does not ensure acceptance or respect.

When an individual is viewed as inferior, stigmatization is the result, even though it may be masked by sincere—and kindly motivated—efforts to provide help. As an example, some people with intellectual disabilities have resented and avoided special education services because of their belief that the very acceptance of special help proves and acknowledges inferiority and dependency (Kozma & Illjes, 1993).

In reality, however, none of us are independent; we all rely on each other in numerous ways. Our very survival depends upon the presence and cooperation of others and upon our respectful interaction with the natural world. To the extent that we recognize and admit our interdependence and acknowledge our mutual need, stigmatization will decrease.

Individual relationships are central to the vision of community integration.

© Will Hart/PhotoEdit

The success of community integration relies on a cultural atmosphere that permits giving and receiving without social penalty, and which approves and respects cooperation and mutual support among community members. The key to community integration is an attitude of acceptance and openness that allows individuals to see past obvious differences to the human capacities of those with disabilities. This attitude goes beyond tolerance—to respect and appreciation for diversity (Payne, Miller, Hazlett, & Mercer, 1984). In such an atmosphere, the need for support does not automatically produce lowered self-esteem and stigmatization, and people with disabilities are not only permitted social positions that allow legitimate contributions, but also are included in ways that inherently acknowledge a genuine role. Essential to such a culture is the deep understanding that acts, attitudes, and conditions that debase one member of our community debase us all.

INFOTRAC COLLEGE EDITION

Sometimes the most effective advocacy is self-advocacy. Enter *self-advocacy* as the keyword in *InfoTrac College Edition*. Based on the resulting articles, what should a course in self-advocacy include?

REFERENCES

Arc, The. (1996). Personal communication.

————. (1998). *The United States International Council on Mental Retardation and Developmental Disabilities.* Web page: http://www.thearc.org/council/council.html

Edgar, E. (1994). *A profession in denial: The consequences of ignoring the condition of mild mental retardation.* Paper presented at DMRDD-CEC conference, Evanston, IL.

Dudley, J. R. (1996). Seeking a closer partnership with the self-advocacy movement. *Mental Retardation, 34,* 255–256.

Kaufman, S. (1986). Life history in progress. In L. L. Langness & H. G. Levine (Eds.), *Culture and retardation: Life histories of mildly mentally retarded persons in American society.* Boston: D. Reidel.

Kozma, T., & Illjes, S. (1993). Education and disability in Hungary. In S. J. Peters (Ed.), *Education and disability in cross-cultural perspective.* New York: Garland.

Meers, G. D. (1992). Getting ready for the next century: vocational preparation of students with disabilities. *Teaching Exceptional Children,* Summer, 36–39.

Pacht, H. (1996). My thoughts: Self-advocacy, professional organizations, and the public. *Mental Retardation, 34*(2), 123–124.

Payne, J. S., Miller, A. K., Hazlett, R. L., & Mercer, C. D. (Eds.). (1984). *Rehabilitation techniques: Vocational adjustment for the handicapped.* New York: Human Sciences Press.

Perske, R., & Perske, M. (1986). *Hope for the families* (3rd ed.). Nashville: Abingdon Press.

Ward, N. (1996). Supporting in self-advocacy national organizations: Our role and yours. *Mental Retardation, 34,* 121–122.

Wolfensberger, W. (1991). Reflections on a lifetime in human services and mental retardation. *Mental Retardation, 29*(1), 1–15.

————. (1992). The growing threat to the lives of handicapped people in the context of modernistic values. *Disability & Society, 9*(3), 395–413.

Glossary

absence seizures. Brief temporary loss of consciousness, such as may occur in petit mal epilepsy.

accommodation. Process of adaptation that allows an individual to alter old schemes and create new ones to better adjust to the environment.

adaptive skills areas. Specific performance behaviors specified in the AAMR's 1992 definition of mental retardation.

Addams, Jane. American social reformer who established Hull House, one of the first settlement houses for welfare work in the United States.

allosomes. X and Y chromosomes in organisms that determine the sex of an individual.

American Association on Mental Retardation (AAMR). Advocacy organization whose mission is to "promote progressive policies, sound research, effective practices, and universal human rights for people with intellectual disabilities."

Americans with Disabilities Act. Legislation passed by the U.S. Congress in 1990 to prohibit discrimination against people with disabilities and to guarantee them equal access to employment, public services, public accommodations, and telecommunications.

amniocentesis. Prenatal test to detect a genetic disorder or maternal-fetal blood incompatibility by extracting fluid with a needle and syringe from the amniotic sac and then analyzing that fluid.

anecdotal. Made of anecdotes, or short entertaining accounts of usually personal or biographical incidents.

anencephaly. Congenital absence of the brain and spinal cord.

anoxia. Deficiency of oxygen; when severe, causes mental retardation or death.

applied behavior analysis. Procedures that use modeling and conditioning to eliminate inappropriate behaviors and increase appropriate behaviors.

articulation. Clear production of meaningful speech sounds.

Asperger syndrome. Disorder with many of the symptoms of autism but with normal language development and no mental retardation.

ataxia. Failure or irregularity of muscular coordination, especially when voluntary movement is attempted.

athetosis. Involuntary slow, twisting movements of the upper extremities, particularly the hands and fingers.

at-risk. Category of eligibility for early intervention services indicating the likelihood of developmental disabilities because of biological or environmental factors, if no intervention occurs.

attention deficit hyperactivity disorder. Condition occurring in children who have poor concentration and are overly active.

auras. Subjective olfactory, visual, auditory, taste or thought sensation that precedes a seizure.

autism. Syndrome first appearing in early childhood that involves symptoms of aloneness, inability to relate to others, highly repetitive play, and language disturbances.

autosomes. Chromosome other than sex chromosomes; not involved in the determination of gender.

Bandura, Albert. Social learning theorist who demonstrated that children learn from observing the behavior of others.

behavior modification. Psychological methods for changing observable behavior patterns using the principles of reinforcement.

best practice. Term used to indicate those techniques that are currently considered the most effective and desirable.

Binet, Alfred. Early advocate of special education and one developer of the first IQ test.

blank slate. Metaphor for the mental state of the newborn, meant to suggest that mental and behavioral development is entirely a product of environmental influences.

bodily-kinesthetic intelligence. One type of intelligence described by Howard Gardner; ability to think about moving oneself in space such as with the ability to dance or play sports.

Brofenbrenner, Urie. Developmental psychologist who emphasizes the importance of understanding the child within the context of the larger environment, including neighborhood, community, and culture.

Buck, Carrie. Young woman who became the test for sterilization laws in a case decided by the U.S. Supreme Court.

career education. More inclusive term than *vocational education;* meant to suggest the importance of preparing young people for lifelong work rather than simply jobs.

carrier. Person who carries a recessive gene and does not show the phenotype but can pass the gene on to offspring who could then manifest a resulting disabling condition.

center-based. Service programs carried out in a location other than the home of the recipient.

cerebral hemorrhage. Bleeding as a result of the rupture of a blood vessel in the brain.

cerebral palsy. Neuromuscular disability resulting from damage to the brain before the third year of life.

chromosome. One of the threadlike structures in the nucleus of a cell that contains the information of heredity; genes are arranged in linear order along the chromosomes.

chorionic villus sampling. Procedure used to test for presence of genetic disorders and performed during the first trimester of pregnancy; tissue can be obtained from the developing placenta by a needle passed through the woman's abdominal wall or cervix under ultrasound guidance.

chronic sorrow. Lifelong grief in response to a child's disability.

clone. Group of genetically identical cells descended from a common ancestor cell; all cells in a clone have precisely the same DNA; occur in nature and are also made by molecular geneticists.

cocaine. Widely abused illegal drug obtained from the leaves of the coca plant.

cognitive development. Development of mental abilities related to ideas and reasoning.

cognitive stimulation. Environmental input that influences the development of ideas and reasoning.

community integration. Inclusion within the community of people with mental disabilities as rightful participants.

community-referenced. Instructional methods directly related to events naturally experienced in the world.

computerized axial tomography (CAT). An imaging method that X rays the brain from many different angles, feeding the information into a computer to produce a series of cross-sectional images.

concrete operational stage. Mental abilities depending on logical reasoning; thought by Piaget to occur in the stage of concrete operations.

cooperative learning. Goal-directed learning that occurs through study and exploration with others.

craniostosis. Congenital hardening of the cranial sutures, making brain growth impossible without surgery.

critical period. Period of time during which an attribute must develop—or it never will.

cultural-familial. Mental retardation thought to be caused by family and cultural influences on the individual.

cytomegalovirus. Common virus that may produce mild effects in adults but have serious effects on fetal development, including brain damage, growth failure, and blindness.

Darwin, Charles. Naturalist who developed the theory of natural selection, which became the foundation for the theory of evolution.

dementia. Loss or impairment of mental powers; often first noticed in memory loss.

deoxyribonucleic acid (DNA). Double-stranded molecule that encodes hereditary information.

detailed recordings. Term used to describe method of data description in applied behavioral analysis.

Developmental Disabilities Act. Originally passed in 1963 and most recently reauthorized in 2000; act provides federal funds to support the development and operation of state councils, protection and advocacy systems, university centers (formerly known as university affiliated programs), and other projects of national significance for those with developmental disabilities.

developmental disability. Variety of disorders that can interfere with a person's ability to learn new skills and behaviors.

developmental norms. Set of behaviors and associated ages by which time those behaviors should normally occur.

developmental position. Describes learning in those with mental retardation as similar to but slower than normal.

Dewey, John. Influential educator in the early 20th century who emphasized hands-on learning and opposed authoritarian methods in teaching.

Diagnostic and Statistical Manual of Mental Disorders. Third and fourth editions (DSM-III and DSM-IV) of manual published by the American Psychiatric Association that provides the criteria for diagnosing mental disorders.

dialectical theories. Process of getting at the truth by exchanging logical arguments; L. S. Vygotsky believed that intellectual development occurs through dialectical social interaction.

difference position. Describes learning in those with mental retardation as qualitatively different from that which typically occurs.

differential reinforcement of alternative behaviors. Reinforcement of behavior(s) other than the target; often abbreviated DRA.

differential reinforcement of incompatible behaviors. Reinforcement of behavior that is incompatible with the target; often abbreviated DRI.

differential reinforcement of lower rates of behavior. Reinforcement only when the target occurs at a specified frequency; often abbreviated DRL.

differential reinforcement of other behaviors. Reinforcement when target behavior is absent for a specified time; often abbreviated DRO.

disability. Physical or mental impairment that prevents or restricts normal achievement.

disequilibrium. Uncomfortable condition of being out of balance; in Piaget's theory, when a child sees that his former ideas are incorrect, the discomfort of losing mental balance accompanies his push to the next stage of intellectual development.

Dix, Dorothea. Well-known 19th-century social reformer who worked on behalf of prison inmates, the destitute, and those with mental illness.

dominant inheritance. Mechanism through which a gene manifests itself when present in a single copy.

Down syndrome. Chromosomal disorder that usually results in mental retardation; caused by the improper disjunction of the 21st pair of chromosomes.

duration. Term used in applied behavior analysis to describe length of time a target behavior lasts.

early infantile autism. Diagnostic term first used by Leo Kanner to describe the syndrome now called autism.

echolalia. Imitation of someone's speech without understanding its meaning.

ecological systems. Perspective of development and behavior causation that recognizes the mutual interacting influences and dependencies of an individual's various social and cultural environments.

educational integration. Term for inclusion most often used in Canada, Australia, Great Britain, and other European countries

electroencephalogram (EEG). Record of the summed activity of cortical cells picked up by wires placed on the skull.

emotional development. Process by which children develop feeling sensations and responses.

entrepreneurial model. Employment model in which a community business (typically manufacturing) hires groups of people with retardation, usually to do assembly work.

enzyme. Protein acting as a biochemical catalyst, speeding the rate of a biochemical reaction without altering the nature of the reaction or being altered itself.

epicanthal folds. Prolonged fold of skin of the upper eyelid over the inner angle or both angles of the eye; also called *Mongolian folds.*

epistomologist. Individual who studies the nature and theory of knowledge.

Erikson, Erik. American psychoanalyst who enlarged Freud's theory of psychosexual stages to include a much wider social context.

etiology. Cause or causes of a given condition.

eugenics. Attempt to improve a population through selective breeding.

exosystem. In ecological systems theory, social settings that do not contain children but that affect their experiences in immediate settings.

expressive language. Aspect of language that describes what children can actually articulate.

extinction. In classical conditioning, decline of the conditioned response (CR) as a result of presenting the conditioned stimulus (CS) enough repetitions without the unconditioned stimulus (UCS).

extrinsic. From or coming from without; often refers to outside reinforcement for a task or behavior.

facilitated communication. Controversial technique designed to help people with autism express their ideas; a facilitator provides physical support for an individual's hand over an alphanumeric keypad.

fading. Technique to gradually eliminate overt help and rewards for a task.

familial. Refers here to mental retardation that originates from family and cultural circumstances.

Farrell, Elizabeth. Founded the Council for Exceptional Children in 1918.

fetal alcohol effect. Condition of children who display some but not all of the effects of fetal alcohol syndrome.

fetal alcohol syndrome. Set of defects that results when pregnant women consume large amounts of alcohol during pregnancy.

fetoscopy. Insertion into the uterus of a small tube with a light source on the end to inspect the fetus for limb deformities; method also can obtain a fetal blood sample to check for the presence of hemophilia, sickle cell anemia, and certain neural defects.

fixed teams. Type of assessment team in which the same members work together to assess the performance of every individual.

flexible. Type of assessment team in which different members form the team depending upon the individual's specific assessment needs.

formal labels. Names with professional sanction that are applied to conditions or syndromes.

formal operational stage. Piaget's final stage in which adolescents develop the capacity for abstract, scientific thinking; begins approximately at age 11.

forward chaining. Method for teaching a task that breaks the task into steps beginning with the first and proceeding to the last.

Fragile X syndrome. Most common inherited form of mental retardation, involving a weak spot on the X chromosome; more common in males than females.

Freud, Sigmund. Austrian psychoanalyst who developed the theory of psychosexual stages in development and the psychoanalytic concepts of the id, ego, and superego.

functional literacy. Ability to read that is limited to words often seen in public, such as *Exit, Stop,* and *Restrooms.*

Galton, Sir Francis. British anthropologist who is considered to be the founder of the "science" of *eugenics.*

Gardner, Howard. American psychologist who developed the theory of *multiple intelligences.*

gene. Fundamental unit of heredity; a sequence of DNA that codes for the creation of a specific protein or which carries out a specific function.

gene mapping. Determining the ordered relationships and distances between different genes or DNA segments on a chromosome.

gene therapy. Process of cloning a gene to perform the appropriate metabolic task.

generalization. Ability to apply an idea or skill to a wide variety of situations other than the one in which it was first learned.

generalized seizures. Seizures in which the whole brain is involved with a loss of consciousness and the entire body gripped by involuntary muscle contractions.

generalizing. Practice of generalization.

genome. All of the genetic material contained in the chromosomes of a particular individual.

genotype. Genetic makeup of an individual.

Gesell, Arnold. American psychologist and pediatrician who defined norms for developmental ages.

gestalt. An integrated whole that cannot be derived from the sum of its parts.

Goddard, Henry Herbert. American psychologist best known for a study of *Deborah Kallikak* and her family, through which he offered a hereditary interpretation of crime and degeneracy.

graduated guidance. Technique in which a teacher moves through the motions of a task with hands above (but not actually touching) the learner's hands, thus providing help without actual physical touch.

guided imagery. Teaching technique in which individuals are asked to imagine certain circumstances, tasks, or events in detail as they are described by a facilitator.

habilitation. Acquisition and use of skills to allow for successful functioning in independent living and employment.

habituation. Gradual reduction in the strength of a response because of repetitive stimulation.

Hall, G. Stanley. American psychologist and educator; instrumental in the development of educational psychology.

handicap. Mental or physical impairment that prevents or interferes with normal mental or physical activities and achievement.

high penetrance. Usually causes a genotype to show up phenotypically.

home-based services. Services carried out in the individual's home for children at risk of developmental disabilities and people with mental retardation.

homologous. Similar in fundamental structure and origin but not necessarily function.

Howe, Samuel Gridley. One of the first people to open a day treatment center and residential facility for people with mental retardation.

Human Genome Organization. Organization (often abbreviated as HUGO) developed to coordinate the individual national projects that make up the Human Genome Project.

Human Genome Project. International scientific collaboration to gain basic understanding of the entire genetic blueprint of a human being.

hypothyroidism. Condition caused by deficiency in thyroid secretion; results in lowered basal metabolism.

hypotonia. Reduced tension; relaxation of arteries. Loss of tonicity of the muscles.

imitation. Something derived or copied from an original. The ability to imitate an important developmental accomplishment.

incidence. Frequency or occurrence of any event or condition over a period of time and in relation to the population in which it occurs such as the incidence of a disease.

inclusion. Term most often used to describe the presence of children with mental retardation and other disabilities in the regular classroom.

individualized education plan (IEP). Document required by federal law that details the year's plan for every child who is disabled.

individualized family service plan (IFSP). Document prepared as part of the voluntary component of PL 99-457; developed by a multidisciplinary team with the assistance of parents and detailing the year's plan for children with disabilities from birth to age 2 and their families.

individualized transition plan (ITP). Document prepared as part of PL 105-17 (the most recent revision of IDEA); provides a plan to facilitate the move from school to work environments.

Individuals with Disabilities Education Act (IDEA). The 1990 amendment to PL 94-142, which modified PL 94-142 and changed the name of the law to reflect a sensitivity to preferred terminology.

infanticide. Killing of an infant.

informal labels. Terms commonly used for human conditions that have no official sanction.

intellectual development. Growth of the knowledge base, as well as cognitive processes such as ideas and strategies.

interactionists. Theorists who attribute development to an interaction between heredity and environment.

interdisciplinary collaboration. System in which members of different disciplines work together toward a common goal.

interpersonal intelligence. Ability to relate well to other people, motivate them, and negotiate solutions to others' problems.

intersubjectivity. L. S. Vygotsky's idea that learning partners must agree upon labels, terms, and methods of a task so that learning can take place.

intrapersonal intelligence. Self-knowledge and the ability to motivate one's self and manage one's emotions.

intrinsic. Belonging to the essential nature of a thing; often refers to the inherent reinforcement in a task or behavior.

Itard, Jean-Marc-Gaspard. French physician who took on the task of educating Victor, the wild boy of Aveyron.

James, William. American philosopher and psychological theorist; often called the father of psychology.

job coach. Person who provides on-the-job training to individuals with disabilities.

job sampling. Procedure for trying out jobs to find the one best suited for the client with mental retardation.

Kallikak, Deborah. Resident of Vineland Training School, a residential facility for people with mental retardation; her family was the subject of Henry Goddard's *The Kallikak Family: A Study in the Heredity of Feeblemindedness.*

latency. State of being concealed, hidden, or inactive.

learned helplessness. Pattern of submissiveness that develops in individuals when they believe their actions are of no consequence and outcomes are beyond their control.

learning disability. Specific learning disorder that results in poor school achievement despite an average or above-average IQ.

learning theories. Theories of intellectual development that attribute the overwhelming influence to experience.

Lesch–Nyhan disease. Inherited metabolic disease that only affects males.

life skills. Abilities needed to function as an independent individual within the community.

linguistic intelligence. Kind of intelligence exhibited by people who communicate well either orally or in writing.

Locke, John. English philosopher who advanced the theory that development is entirely the effect of experience; popularized the metaphor of the newborn infant as a *blank slate.*

logical-mathematical intelligence. Ability to reason with and apply an understanding of numbers.

long-term memory. Ability to retrieve information from storage after a few days or several years.

low birth weight. Term applied to babies who are carried to term but weigh less than 25 grams (5 lbs., 8 oz.) at birth.

low penetrance. Genotype that seldom shows up phenotypically.

macro-orchidism. Abnormally large testicles.

macrosystem. In ecological systems theory, the values, laws, customs, and resources of a culture that influence experiences and interactions at inner levels of the environment.

magnetic resonance imaging (MRI). Use of nuclear magnetic resonance to produce images of biological structures, especially human tissues and organs.

mainstreaming. Placement of pupils with learning difficulties in regular classrooms for part of the school day.

maple sugar urine disease. Inherited metabolic disease named for its characteristic odor of urine and sweat; also known as maple syrup urine disease.

maternal blood analysis. Procedure performed early in pregnancy to reveal the presence of kidney disease, abnormal closure of the esophagus, anencephaly, and spina bifida.

meiosis. Process of cell division through which gametes are formed and the number of chromosomes in each cell is halved.

Mendel, Gregor. Austrian monk known as the father of genetics and the developer of the principles of heredity.

mesosystem. In ecological systems theory, connections between children's immediate settings.

metacognitive. Awareness and understanding of various aspects of thought.

microcephaly. Abnormal and congenital small head often seen in mental retardation.

microsystem. In ecological systems theory, the activities and interaction patterns in the child's immediate surroundings.

mitosis. Process of cell duplication in which each new cell receives an exact copy of the original chromosomes.

mobile crew model. Moves a group of several individuals to diverse locations to work.

Montessori, Maria. Italian physician and pioneer educator who acted as an advocate for children with mental retardation.

Moro reflex. Defensive reflex in which the infant draws her arm across her chest in an embracing manner when the surface on which she rests is struck.

mosaicism. For the purposes of this text, a type of Down syndrome in which only some but not all cells have the added partial 21st chromosome.

motor development. Infant and childhood development of the muscular and coordinative abilities for movement.

multifactorial inheritance. Genetic inheritance that involves many factors.

musical intelligence. Abilities that underlie the skills of musicians, singers, and composers.

mutation. Any change that alters the sequence of *nucleotide* bases on a DNA strand.

naturalist intelligence. Ability of those who readily learn and use plant and animal classifications.

neonatal meningitis. Condition that causes inflammation of the brain-lining membranes; fatal in more than 50 percent of instances; survivors often are affected by hydrocephalus, seizures, hearing defects, and mental retardation.

noble savages. Metaphoric term used by Jean-Jacques Rousseau to describe the inherent goodness essential to the nature of the newborn child.

normalization. Bringing the circumstances and behavior of persons with mental retardation in line with those of the general population.

nucleotide. DNA subunit consisting of a nitrogen-containing bases—adenine, cytosine, guanine, or thymine—that are chemically linked to a phosphate molecule and a sugar molecule; thousands of nucleotides link to form a DNA molecule; sequence in which they occur determines a gene's function.

nucleus. Control center of a cell; contains the chromosomes.

occupational therapist (OT). One who evaluates the self-care, work, play, and leisure time task performance skills of well and disabled clients of all ages; plans and implements programs and social and interpersonal activities that are designed to restore, develop, and maintain the client's ability to accomplish satisfactorily daily tasks required of his specific age and necessary to his particular role adjustment.

operant learning. Type of learning that results from the reinforcing properties of stimuli.

outerdirectedness. Looking to others for guidance or cues in developing appropriate responses in demanding situations.

overcorrection. Technique that requires a learner to compensate for an incorrect behavior or for misbehaving by redoing the task many times or by enlarging upon the original demand.

partial seizures. Type of seizure that involves only one area of the brain.

pedigree. Chart showing inheritance in a particular family.

peer tutoring. Teaching technique that involves instruction from a learner's classmate or another same-age individual.

penetrance. Frequency of individuals within a particular population who manifest a hereditary condition caused by a dominant or double recessive gene.

perseveration. Continued repetition of a meaningless word or phrase, or repetition of answers that are not related to successive questions asked.

pervasive developmental disorder. Diagnostic category that describes a severe disorder of social and relational development and the presence of compulsive behavior but which does not meet the criteria for autism.

phenotype. Observable properties of an organism manifested from its genotype.

phenylketonuria. Inherited metabolic disease resulting from the absence of an enzyme for digestion; causes an accumulation of toxic substances in the blood and urine; if undiagnosed and untreated at birth, causes mental retardation.

Piaget, Jean. Swiss psychologist best known for his theory of stages of intellectual development; was a major influence on the fields of psychology and education.

pica. Perversion of appetite and ingestion of nonfood materials such as starch, clay, ashes, and plaster.

picture task analysis. Step-by-step instruction for a task presented in pictures.

Pinel, Philipe. Superintendent of an asylum for people with mental illness and mental retardation in Paris and one of the first reformers to initiate humanitarian treatment.

PL 94-142. Education for All Handicapped Children Act of 1975 (now known as Individuals with Disabilities Education Act, or IDEA); law provides free appropriate public education in the least restrictive environment to all children and youth ages 3 to 21 who are disabled.

PL 99-457. Law extending the rights and privileges afforded to children who are disabled under PL 94-142 to children from birth to 5 years of age.

placenta abruptia. Premature separation of the placenta, usually during childbirth.

plastic. The flexibility of function in the developing neurons of infants and young children.

polygenic. Condition arising as a result of an interaction between two or more genes.

positive practice. Type of overcorrection in which the individual practices a behavior again and again.

positron emission tomography. Nuclear medicine technique for imaging internal body tissue; abbreviated as PET.

pragmatics. Pertaining to or concerned with the practical and social conventions of language.

prematurity. State of an infant born anytime before completion of the 37th week of gestation.

prenatal testing. Medical testing performed during pregnancy to reveal potential medical or disabling conditions in the fetus.

preoperational stage. One of Piaget's stages of intellectual development in which the child first uses symbols and engages in imaginative play.

prevalence. Number of cases of a disease present in a specified population at a given time.

psychoanalytic theory. Systematic description of mental functioning based on the interaction of conscious and unconscious psychological processes.

psychosexual developmental stages. Stages of infant and childhood emotional development postulated by Sigmund Freud to explain adult emotional problems.

psychosocial developmental. Theoretical enlargement of psychosexual stages to encompass wider social and emotional issues; Erik Erikson is best known for this work.

punishment. Any behavioral consequence that results in decreasing or eliminating the initiating behavior.

qualitative impressions. Impressions important in behavioral assessment that are based on a behavior's quality rather than quantity.

rate. Frequency of a behavior within a specified time limit.

rating scales. Assessment instruments used to quantify behaviors according to a standardized description.

receptive language. Ability to comprehend (as opposed to produce) language.

recessive inheritance. Condition that is apparent only when an individual inherits the same gene form from both parents.

reflex. Involuntary response to a stimulus.

Regular Education Initiative (REI). Movement within the educational community to include children with disabilities in the same educational settings as their peers.

reify. To treat an abstract idea as if it were a concrete entity.

reinforcement. Any behavioral consequence that results in maintaining or increasing the rate of the initiating behavior.

resilience. Ability to withstand potentially damaging events.

respite care. Service that provides care for individuals with disabilities while their usual caregivers take a break.

response-cost measures. Behavior modification technique based on the punishing effects of removing a reinforcer.

restitution. Providing meaningful compensation for harm done—for example, paying back money that was stolen with interest.

retrieval. Cognitive process that brings back to consciousness facts and events previously stored in long-term memory.

rigidity. Stiff and inflexible muscle tone found in specific subtypes of cerebral palsy.

Rousseau, Jean Jacques. French philosopher known for his view that children were born good and would naturally and optimally develop if not for the damaging effects of environment.

rubella. Acute infectious disease resembling both scarlet fever and measles but differing in its short course, slight fever, and absence of long term effects.

rumination. Repeated bringing up, rechewing, and swallowing of previously eaten food.

Seguin, Edouard. French-born American psychiatrist who pioneered modern educational methods for teaching people with severe forms of mental retardation.

seizure disorders. Physical conditions (formerly known as epilepsy) that involve involuntary convulsive motor movements and, in some types, temporary loss of consciousness.

selective attention. Focusing attention on one particular stimulus to the exclusion of others.

self-determination. Act of making choices for oneself; important for everyone but often denied those with mental retardation; also called *self-regulation*.

self-fulfilling prophecy. Behavioral expectations for an individual that influence him to behave in the expected way when he would not otherwise have done so.

self-injurious behavior (SIB). Behaviors causing harm or serious physical injury to oneself; sometimes occurs with individuals who have mental retardation.

self-management. Behavioral intervention in which the individual learns to use the behavioral techniques of reinforcement, punishment, and prompts to manage his own behavior.

self-regulation. Synonym for *self-determination*.

semantics. Aspect of language that involves meaning.

sensorimotor stage. Involves the coordination of sense information and motor behavior; the first of Piaget's developmental stages.

sensory development. Prenatal and postnatal development of sensory perception.

sensory register. Describes the component of the memory system that involves perception of sensory stimuli.

sequential reasoning. Reasoning that follows a step-by-step progression from one point to another.

SES. See *socioeconomic status*.

setting events. Events surrounding a stimulus–response–consequence sequence that influence the effects of the stimulus and consequence and the nature of the response.

sex chromosome. X and Y chromosomes that determine an individual's gender; two X chromosomes create a female, and an XY combination results in a male.

simian crease. Crease on the palm of the hand (also known as a *palmar crease*), so named because of its similarity to the transverse flexion crease found in some monkeys.

simultaneous reasoning. Ability to process several pieces of information at one time.

six-hour retardation. Child who is considered mentally retarded at school but appears to function normally with family and peers outside school.

Skinner, B. F. American psychologist who was well known for applying behavioral principles to the modification of human behavior.

small for date. Babies who are born at term but weigh less than would be expected for full-term babies.

social role valorization. More recent term for *normalization*; emphasizes the legitimate role of people with mental retardation in society.

Social Security Act. Original legislation that established the Social Security Administration and provided benefits to the elderly and those with disabilities.

social support. Physical and emotional support provided by family and friends.

socioeconomic status (SES). Definitional aspect of the class system within the United States based on income and property.

spasticity. Muscular condition involving prolonged contractions and increased reflexes of the tendons; a subtype of cerebral palsy.

spatial intelligence. Ability to solve problems involving the manipulation of real objects in space.

spina bifida. Physical condition involving the protrusion of the spinal membranes because of a fissure in the lower part of the spine.

stage theories. Theories that describe development as a series of qualitative changes that occur in a specified order, each stage involving a unique and predictable accomplishment.

standard deviation. Measure of the variability of statistical data.

state. Refers to a personality characteristic displayed by an individual only in certain situations.

subaverage. Below a normal or expected value.

sustained attention. Ability to focus attention and concentration on a particular matter for a prolonged period of time.

syndrome. Number of symptoms occurring together that make up a particular physical condition.

systems perspective. Point of view that considers multiple interacting influences.

task analysis. Breaking a task into its smallest basic components and arranging them in order from first to last.

Tay Sachs disease. Inherited disease transmitted by an autosomal recessive gene and resulting in neurological deterioration; symptoms include mental and physical retardation, blindness, and seizures, with death occurring usually before 18 months of age.

teratogens. Environmental elements that damage a fetus.

time-out. Disciplinary technique that removes a child from social interaction for a brief period of time.

tonic–clonic. Type of seizure that involves rapid alternating contractions and loss of muscle tone throughout the body.

toxoplasmosis. Disease of the nervous system resulting from the ingestion of a parasite; can cause mental retardation in the fetus of a pregnant woman.

trait. Personal characteristic that is stable (demonstrated in most situations) and relatively permanent.

transdisciplinary. Practice of sharing techniques, procedures, and goals across disciplines.

transitional IEP (ITP). Planning required by IDEA for children who move from early intervention to school and for young people who move from high school to the work world.

translocation. Subtype of Down syndrome in which a piece of the 21st chromosome breaks off and reattaches to another pair of chromosomes.

tremor. Involuntary shaking of the body or limbs.

trisomy. In genetics, having three homologous chromosomes per cell instead of two; on chromosome 8 (*Trisomy 8*), causes mild to severe mental retardation but children typically have normal life spans; on chromosomes 13 and 18 (*Trisomy 13* and *Trisomy 18*), causes severe congenital deformation and mental retardation, and children seldom survive their first year; on chromosome 21 (*Trisomy 21*), causes mental retardation, epicanthal folds, flat nose, and short stature.

two-generation program strategies. Intervention strategies aimed at both parents and children.

ultrasound scanner. Equipment that emits an inaudible sound in the frequency range of approximately 20,000 to 10,000,000,000 cycles per second; different velocities define tissues by density and elasticity, thus outlining the shapes of tissues and organs.

unspecified pervasive developmental disorder. Diagnostic category used when there is a severe and pervasive impairment in the development of reciprocal social interaction or verbal and nonverbal communication skills, or when stereotyped behavior, interests, and activities are present but the criteria are not met for a specific pervasive developmental disorder, schizophrenia, schizotypal personality disorder, or avoidant personality disorder.

variable expressivity. Extent to which a genotype is manifest in the phenotype of the individual.

Victor. French boy found alone in the woods of Aveyron; spent his early years without human contact.

Vocational Rehabilitation Act. Legislation now called the Rehabilitation Act that authorizes grants to the states for the provision of work-related rehabilitation services for people with disabilities.

Vygotsky, L. S. Soviet psychologist known for his theory that intelligence develops from social interaction.

Wilbur, Hervey B. American who opened the first private residence in the United States for people with mental retardation.

working memory. Conscious aspect of memory in which strategies can be applied for later retrieval of information; sometimes called *short-term memory.*

X-linked inheritance. Genetic material inherited through the mother's X chromosome; when X transmission involves a genetic error, boys and girls will be affected differently.

zone of proximal development. Concept offered by L. S. Vygotsky to describe various degrees of developmental readiness to understand and apply new ideas.

Index